Edmund Spenser

THE FAERIE QUEENE

Books Three and Four

D1118189

Edmund Spenser

THE FAERIE QUEENE

Books Three and Four

Edited, with Introduction, by
Dorothy Stephens

Hackett Publishing Company, Inc.
Indianapolis/Cambridge

09 08 07 06   1 2 3 4 5 6 7

For further information, please address
Hackett Publishing Company, Inc.
P.O. Box 44937
Indianapolis, IN 46244-0937

www.hackettpublishing.com

Cover art: Walter Crane illustration and ornament for Book Three, *The Faerie Queene*, ca. 1890.

Cover design by Abigail Coyle
Interior design by Elizabeth Wilson
Composition by Professional Book Compositors
Printed at Edwards Brothers, Inc.

Library of Congress Cataloging-in-Publication Data

Spenser, Edmund, 1552?–1599.
    The faerie queene / Edmund Spenser.
        p. cm.
    Series general editor, Abraham Stoll; volume editors: bk. 1, Carol Kaske; bk. 5, Abraham Stoll.
    Includes bibliographical references and indexes.
    ISBN 0-87220-808-7 (bk. 1) — ISBN 0-87220-807-9 (pbk. : bk. 1) —
    ISBN 0-87220-802-8 (bk. 5) — ISBN 0-87220-801-X (pbk. : bk. 5)
    1. Knights and knighthood—Poetry. 2. Epic poetry, English. 3. Virtues
—Poetry. I. Stoll, Abraham Dylan, 1969– . II. Kaske, Carol V., 1933– .
III. Title.
PR2358.A3K37 2006
821'.3—dc22

                                  2005026668

ISBN-13: 978-0-87220-856-8 (cloth, bks. 3 & 4)
        978-0-87220-855-1 (pbk., bks. 3 & 4)
ISBN-10: 0-87220-856-7 (cloth, bks. 3 & 4)
        0-87220-855-9 (pbk., bks. 3 & 4)

CONTENTS

For Wesley and Annette Stephens,
who know the pleasure of a good detour.

Introduction

1. Domesticity and Strangeness

In her private journals, written between 1798 and 1803, Dorothy Wordsworth frequently mentions sitting at the fireside in Dove Cottage with her brother to read Spenser's poetry aloud. Some mornings they walked in the orchard reading cantos of *The Faerie Queene*. For them, Spenser was a domestic practice, and the sound of his poetry was that of their own voices, even though the poetry that William Wordsworth wrote hardly resembled Spenser's.

Edmund Spenser lived more than two hundred years before the Wordsworths, during the English Renaissance, and he participated in a reflowering of English literature that included Marlowe, Shakespeare, Donne, Wroth, Jonson, Marvell, and Milton. Spenser's poetry strongly influenced his contemporaries and many writers who came afterward; Shakespeare borrowed from him, and Milton considered him a great moral teacher. (Milton admired him for his understanding that the willful ignorance of sin does not enable an intelligent embrace of goodness.) Two centuries later, the musicality of Spenser's verse exerted a powerful pull, not only on the Wordsworths, but also on other Romantic poets: Keats, Shelley, and Byron. But the Romantics had a passion for Shakespeare, as well, and it is with the latter passion that modern readers are more likely to feel a kinship. Because modern readers grow up hearing Shakespeare's plays quoted and then begin to read them in high school, we have at least the illusion that Shakespeare belongs to us. It is easy to imagine Dorothy and William Wordsworth reading Shakespeare by firelight; he is familiar, and he tells us who we are. The fact that this domestic Shakespeare is, to a great degree, a figment of our own imaginations—that the more carefully one looks at him, the stranger he becomes—does not impair our gut-level sense that he speaks our anxieties, desires, and hopes. In contrast, few modern readers grow up with Spenser. His strangeness—the distance between his thought processes and ours—is obvious, and it takes longer to fall in love with him than with Shakespeare. Once one begins to love Spenser, however, the process is irreversible, and his incontrovertible strangeness turns out to be one of his greatest assets.

The Faerie Queene is far from what most readers of the past two hundred years have expected of narration. Spenser's romance epic is not realistic: only a few of its characters have any psychological depth, and the most extensively developed character silently disappears three-fourths of the way through the poem. The six virtues illustrated by the six books are defined in ways that seem odd to modern minds. The poem's plots have several beginnings but no endings; there is no central crisis or *dénouement;* and, indeed, plot progression is secondary to almost everything else. Spenser's narrator positively glories in repetition at every level: not only do characters re-enact each other's stories, but they re-enact their own discoveries as though having forgotten the previous pages. Even the sentence structure and diction are repetitive, unabashedly indulging in double or triple negatives, redundant adjectives, and self-quotation.

To put a cap on it, when the author expresses his political opinions, they are as likely as not to be hotly contested by modern readers. His notions about the benefits of military suppression in Ireland make us cringe, and the poem declares more than once that the ideal woman is one who keeps her eyes fastened modestly on the ground.

Yet we read and learn from this poem precisely for all of the above reasons, intrigued by the knowledge that through poetry we can encounter a culture that had expectations, assumptions, and needs oddly different from our own. While acknowledging that we will never be able to understand Spenser or the Elizabethans fully, we can take steps in that direction. In the process, we may have the beneficial experience of looking back at our own culture only to find that it, too, has become strange and wonderful to us, no longer seeming purely inevitable and natural. So, for instance, we may become attuned to the fact that when we call a modern film, novel, or sculpture "realistic," we are heavily influenced by our own culture as to what makes a piece of art deserve that adjective. We are quite likely to consider a film realistic even though each of the rooms being filmed has only three sides, large blocks of time are skipped in the course of the story, and no actress in the film has pores. We are trained to overlook these anomalies.

But if various cultures achieve artistic realism along various routes, it is even more important to realize that realism has not been the goal of most artists throughout history. Indeed, although a modern reader might criticize Elizabethan literature for being unrealistic, our own culture's art aims for realism only fitfully. At some level, we know that flagrantly artificial musical lyrics or science-fiction stories may uncover deep truths about the pain of erotic rejection, desire, ambition, or prejudice, conveying these in ways that realism cannot.

Elizabethans admired artificially and intricately patterned surfaces. This does not mean they were more psychologically superficial than we are today; their interest in emblematization and allegory demonstrates their recognition that surfaces inevitably carry meaning. Instead of believing that surfaces merely conceal inner truth, they believed that we construct ourselves through our manipulation of surfaces. For example, if I dress in a certain way, I am making myself into the sort of person who dresses that way. Elizabethan artists and audiences were astutely aware that the human mind addresses the problems in our lives by means of emblems, metaphors, analogies, transferences, hypothetical thought experiments, and evasions that are anything but simple representations of what goes on in the world outside the mind. In fact, one could say that the average human mind produces an almost constant stream of allegory; that is, it weaves incoming bits of data into large and highly symbolic patterns. Neuroscientists and psychologists tell us that without this ability to allegorize and to construct patterns out of chaotic data, we human beings would be unable to perform many of the simplest intellectual operations and would have little sense of ourselves.

One type of artifice that may cause trouble for the modern reader of Elizabethan literature is repetition. Although the high rate of repetition in Elizabethan poetry is foreign to us, much of our music today is actually more repetitious than any music produced during Elizabeth's reign. We can learn a great deal about both Spenser's contemporaries and ourselves by noticing that what we might find tiresomely iterative, they found invigorating, and vice versa. Their appetite for repetition centered upon the written and spoken word, as they developed hundreds of ways to vary each literary theme and sound. When we read Spenser's entire canto devoted to the names and descriptions of rivers, we should ask ourselves seriously, rather than scathingly, what made this canto so admirably alive for its first audiences. We might remind ourselves that nature itself, at the most basic cellular and atomic levels, is highly invested in repetition. It is no wonder that every society that has ever existed on this planet has developed artistic forms in which to mimic, interpret, and ornament this natural investment.

At the same time, like many other remarkable works of literature, Spenser's romance epic is wonderfully inconsistent—which is another way of saying that it looks at every problem from multiple perspectives and gives voice to counter-arguments. So, for example, Spenser's frequently invoked image of the perfect woman as being modest and retiring finds a counter-argument in Britomart, the heroine of Book Three, who dons armor and goes on a quest to find her beloved, a man whom she has seen only in a crystal ball. Britomart is the Knight of Chastity, yet she does not fit the common sixteenth-century ideal of a chaste woman as someone who does not feel erotic desire before marriage. These inconsistencies cannot easily be smoothed over by saying that Spenser "really" wants women to be like Britomart, rather than like the shy and blushing paragons described elsewhere. Book Four introduces new inconsistencies, not the least of which is that its tenth canto retroactively changes the happily erotic union of Scudamour and Amoret at the end of Book Three into the result of an unwilling abduction. The poem's many faces represent its grappling seriously with difficult issues, and we will sell our reading experience short if we try to find one face that represents Spenser's point of view—or, on the other hand, if we settle for the lazy interpretation that the author is equally comfortable with all possibilities. A richer reading experience will result from the recognition that the poem often generates its own criticism, asking us to explore our political discomforts (as, for example, our discomfort with violence against politically disenfranchised groups). Like the rest of us, Spenser lived and moved in multiple contexts, each with its own discourse, its own mode of organizing ideas into speech. These contexts include those of the family, local and national governments, church, academia, and so on. Even the least literary of us must continually debate with ourselves how we can pass from one context to another while maintaining the illusion of internal consistency, and how we can reconcile the ideals of each context with those of the others—despite the fact that each of these contexts itself undergoes constant change.

We read Spenser, then, because his political and social questioning is genuinely complex and because he allows his text to make room, at least momentarily, for opinions that the poem as a whole does not openly espouse. In our less idealistic age, we can appreciate Spenser's recognition—whether it was conscious or not—that the most productive questions are those that can never be definitively answered, only approached from various angles. We read this epic because of its straight-faced sense of humor, often cast as self-irony—as when its narrator apologizes to one of his characters for continuing to invent an agonizing plot for her (IV.i.1). We read Spenser because of his superb ear, which transforms potentially awkward anachronisms into some of the most richly gorgeous verse ever written in English. We read him for his creation of a vast new mythological system that helped to reclaim the Arthurian genre for Arthur's self-proclaimed descendants, after France and Italy had appropriated the Briton hero in the Middle Ages. And we read him because, once we have become accustomed to the fact that his narrative does not have the same aims or methods that novels have, we find that he tells very good stories indeed.

2. Faerie Land

The Faerie Queene is set in the early Medieval period, roughly around the time of the fifth century, when the legendary King Arthur is still a prince. In other words, Spenser writes about a dim and distant past, although he envisions some of the characters in that past as ancestors of Elizabeth Tudor and often uses his "antique" characters to comment upon current events in the sixteenth century.

Spenser does not envision his fairies as diminutive creatures with gossamer wings; rather, they are creatures who look precisely like humans but who have limited supernatural powers. They move freely between Britain and Faerie Land, and they interact freely with the human characters. Like the humans, too, they are quite likely to wear chain mail of a design obsolete in Spenser's own time.

As outlined in "The Letter to Raleigh," Spenser originally intended to link the individual plots of twelve books with an overarching plot device centered upon Gloriana, the Faerie Queen herself, who would represent glory and, more specifically, Queen Elizabeth. Spenser would barely have been able to remember any monarch other than Queen Elizabeth, given that she ascended the throne in 1558 when he was about six years old and was still ruling when he died in 1599. By the time Spenser wrote *The Faerie Queene,* Elizabeth had become an icon of English national identity and colonial ambition, topics that Spenser addresses throughout his epic. In "The Letter to Raleigh," however, Spenser explains that he will also allegorize Elizabeth's more personal side in the character of Belphoebe. He sets forth the poem's intended structure: the Faerie Queen will send twelve of her worthy knights, representing twelve moral virtues, on twelve quests, each of which will occupy a separate book of the poem. Prince Arthur, who is not a member of Gloriana's court but who falls in love with her image when he sees her in a ravishing dream, will appear in every book. He will represent magnificence, a perfect combination of all twelve virtues. Implicitly, but powerfully, "The Letter to Raleigh" reveals that the poem will investigate the talents and virtues that are conducive to personal ambition—a subject that will bring national and personal interests warily together.

Spenser completed only six of the projected twelve books, though many modern scholars believe that, by the end of Book Six, he had said what he wanted to say. Some aspects of the plot that he outlines in "The Letter to Raleigh" never materialize. Most important, the Faerie Queen herself never appears, and although she is mentioned now and then by the characters, the poem's various adventures neither center upon her rhetorically nor seem dependent upon her rule within the plot. Richard Helgerson observes, "*The Faerie Queene,* unlike *Gerusalemme Liberata* [Tasso's epic], allows no place for the representation of a powerfully centralized and absolutist governmental order. It acknowledges and celebrates a sovereign lady, but it grants a high degree of autonomy to

individual knights and their separate pursuits, represents power as rela-
tively isolated and dispersed" (48). This decentralizing is foreshadowed in
"The Letter to Raleigh" when Spenser writes, "The generall end there-
fore of all the booke is to fashion a gentleman or noble person in vertu-
ous and gentle discipline." Whereas Machiavelli, Castiglione, and Elyot
write manuals for the fashioning of princes and courtiers, Spenser privi-
leges the "gentleman," whose rank includes those like himself, with no
claim to aristocracy. Despite his longing for a place at court, he is also in-
vested in strengthening power and prestige at the margins of Elizabethan
government.

3. How to Read the Poem

a. *Making Sense of the Grammar*

As foreign as it is to the English that we speak and write today, Spenser's
language is mostly modern. Modern English begins in the late Medieval
and early Renaissance periods, rather than in the historical period known
as Modern (i.e., the twentieth century to the present). The transition
from Medieval to Modern English, during which the pronunciation of
long vowels radically changed and verb forms continued to simplify, oc-
curred primarily in the fifteenth century, after Chaucer and before
Spenser or Shakespeare. Yet because Spenser admired Chaucer, and be-
cause Spenser joined other Elizabethan writers in believing that specific
word forms carried inherent meaning, he consciously made the experi-
ment of including in his epic many Medieval words and phrases. These
make his poetry sound deceptively older than Shakespeare's in some
ways, even though both writers participated in the late-sixteenth-century
proliferation of genres and redefinition of an artist as someone with a
personal claim to individual fame.

Nonetheless, Spenser's sentence structure is actually simpler and more
straightforward than that of Shakespeare, Donne, or Milton, and it is not
difficult to figure out his basic meaning. When in doubt about a specific
word, the reader can usually simply pronounce it aloud, trying out sev-
eral vowel sounds: when heard, "reskew" resolves itself into "rescue,"
"gard" becomes "guard," and "ribbands" are easily identifiable as "rib-
bons." Mentally substituting *i* for *y* when a word does not at first make
sense can also solve the problem: "yrke" turns out to mean "irk."

Elizabethans did not identify possessives with apostrophes, so some
words that appear plural are actually possessive, as in the phrase "my
Soveraines brest" (III.Proem.1). Although Elizabethans did not use quo-
tation marks, they have been added to this volume. It is helpful to

remember that a Renaissance writer could occasionally set up a useful ambiguity by making readers momentarily unaware that third-person narration had switched to first-person dialogue. Milton uses the technique brilliantly when his speaker's complaint changes imperceptibly into God's comforting words in the sonnet "When I consider how my light is spent." The editors of this series have judged, however, that the readers of this volume of Spenser's poetry will be aided more than they will be misled by the addition of quotation marks.

In Elizabethan English, transitive verbs may follow objective nouns. Thus, "that formost matrone me did blame" indicates that the matron blamed "me" (IV.x.54). An adverb may sound like an adjective: "A bevie of fayre damzels close did lye" means "A bevy of fair damsels did lie closely" (IV.x.48). Spenser's double negatives act as intensifiers rather than canceling each other out: "never none" means "really and truly never any," and triple negatives simply up the ante.

If one proceeds slowly at first, relishing the texture of Spenser's language and reading the poetry aloud, it soon becomes less foreign. This statement comes from the editor's years of observing even the most skeptical and daunted students become adept at reading Spenser.

b.   Making Use of Footnotes and Other Editorial Materials

"The Life of Edmund Spenser" and "The Letter to Raleigh," given as appendices to this volume, may serve as further introductions to the poem, or it may work best to read them after having progressed through a canto or two. The Index of Characters, which indicates where a particular character appears in the poem, will be especially useful to the reader who is looking back over previously read cantos in the process of writing an interpretation. The Textual Notes show important variants in early printings of the epic (given that we do not have a manuscript in Spenser's handwriting), and the Works Cited will give some idea of where to begin in reading Spenserian literary criticism.

Those who are new to Spenser will want to read as many of the footnotes as possible for the first few cantos, given that many apparently modern words have unexpected Elizabethan meanings. The Elizabethan word "merely," for example, means "completely," and the word "approve" means "test." When possible, this edition gives notes that make etymologies useful; for example, in addition to defining "poynant speare" as "piercing spear," the note indicates that the adjective "poynant" is actually a spelling of the modern word "poignant." The reader may then decide whether, in context, the poem is asking us to associate the spear's sharpness with a psychological pang of some sort.

Once a particular word has been defined in the notes several times, it no longer rates a note, but the reader may consult the Glossary at the end of the volume.

The editor has attempted to provide footnotes that will enable, rather than substitute for, the reader's own pleasures of interpretation. All commentary is to some degree interpretive, but the notes in this volume are designed chiefly to explain historical and social contexts that can aid the reader's understanding, in addition to mentioning literary influences upon Spenser's work. Now and then, bits of interpretation are intentionally included by way of leavening, to give the reader who is unfamiliar with Spenser some idea of approaches that may be taken, but the editor has intentionally avoided giving an overview of the current state of Spenserian scholarship. At the end of this Introduction, there is a sample list of some issues addressed by current Spenserian studies, but this list excludes the arguments that scholars have made with reference to those issues.

The notes for Book Four give slightly more interpretive material than do those for Book Three, under the assumption that by then, the reader will have less need for notes defining words or explaining grammar. Nonetheless, these brief mentions of critical arguments are designed not to cover the territory, but to spark the reader's interest in developing his or her own argumentative responses to the text.

After having read through this edition, the reader may well wish for more extensive commentary in some areas. An excellent edition for Spenserian scholars is the Longman text edited by A. C. Hamilton, whose notes, along with those in Thomas Roche's edition and the *Variorum,* were immensely useful in the preparation of the present volume. Another superb resource is the Wordhoard software by Martin Mueller et al., which is distributed for free from http://wordhoard.northwestern.edu and which allows for powerful searches within *The Faerie Queene.* The user may search, say, for all words that are used by Spenser but not by Shakespeare, or for all of the nouns that Spenser modifies with the adjective "civil."

The reader interested in further forays into Spenserian literary criticism may consult the Works Cited, with the caveat that it represents only works cited in this volume, rather than an overview of the state of the field. One can find a great deal of additional useful material by searching the MLA Bibliography Online and Early English Books Online, available through most university library Web sites.

c.   Relaxing as You Read

The extraordinary complexity of *The Faerie Queene* does not mean that your reading experience must be full of anxiety. Rest assured that even scholars who write books about this poem find it difficult to put all of the sections of each character's story into one coherent whole or to keep track of the relationships among cantos, and trying to figure out every tiny piece of the poem on a first reading could drive one mad. Dig into the poem's ambiguities and complexities only when they reach out to grab you and refuse to let go; this will happen often enough.

Do not try to make the entire poem say or represent one set of questions, much less one set of teachings. Canto by canto, the same character may serve varied allegorical purposes, depending upon the context. If a previously heroic character appears in the role of a buffoon, trust your instinct about the tone of each passage and, instead of deciding that the serious passage must "really" be comic or the comic passage must "really" be serious, figure out what each is doing on its own. When a character enters the poem anonymously, do not skip ahead in the text or notes to learn the character's name; instead, understand that the poem is asking us to examine the character before we have a convenient label for him or her. At times, the initial lack of a name helps us participate in the confusion or doubt experienced by other characters who are meeting the new character for the first time. Paul Alpers emphasizes the importance of the poem's happening *in the time it takes us to read,* rather than in the fictional time during which characters complete certain actions: "An episode in *The Faerie Queene,* then, is best described as a developing psychological experience within the reader, rather than as an action to be observed by [that reader]" (14). When Spenser's narrator encourages us to take one point of view and then causes us to revise our earlier perception, the sum total of this experience is neither that the second experience cancels out the first nor that the two are equally balanced. Rather, it is important that we have experienced the change from one perception to another while still having a memory of the first.

Similarly, whenever you figure out the grammar and diction of a particular passage and yet remain confused, trust that the poem is inducing confusion for some reason. Several times, for example, the narrator describes a heroic character and his or her foe in a stanza in which the pronouns for the two characters become vertiginously entangled. Ask yourself what the poem is saying to us by making us wonder, even temporarily, which character is which.

At the same time, realize that by calling attention to its own confusions and ambiguities, the poem is asking us *to attempt,* however imperfectly, to disentangle the strands. Part of the meaning of the poem is precisely this urge it induces in the reader: the flurried leafing back to earlier cantos in an attempt to find continuity, the teasing sense that an orderly pattern floats in our peripheral vision but disappears when we look directly at it.

In this sense, Spenser's epic is true to our everyday lives, in which we are unlikely to find one solution or theory that will cover all contingencies.

d. The Romance Epic Genre

Romance is a genre primarily of the Middle Ages, rather than of the nineteenth-century Romantic period, and the romance of the genre comes not only from erotic love plots but also from the exotic adventures of knights on horseback. Adventure of some sort is the one element that all romances have in common. *Sir Gawain and the Green Knight* is a romance *par excellence*—though few English examples of the genre before Spenser are as sophisticated and witty as *Sir Gawain,* which explores how difficult it is for a knight to reconcile the competing codes of chivalry, courtly love, and Christianity. It is important to understand that in the West, chivalry was largely a literary phenomenon, developed from the Medieval European crusaders' observations of Arab military etiquette. Even while massacring entire Arab towns or being taken prisoner themselves, the Europeans admired the Arab commanders' equestrian skills, courtly manners, artistic sensitivity, and policy of showing mercy toward their conquered opponents. (For more about Europeans' views of the Middle East, see IV.viii.44.3.n.) From the first, then, the romance genre was associated with locales and customs considered both foreign and alluring: French authors wrote about Arthurian Britain and ancient Rome, as well as about the Middle East. This geographical exoticism was paired with supernatural elements that were equally far from the authors' everyday lives. The heroes of romances were often aided in their quests by magic spells that helped them defeat superhuman monsters. Eventually, English authors began to use Arthurian legends of Britain, but like the French authors, they transformed the fairly crude early Medieval society in which an historical Arthur would have existed into a sophisticated, sparkling, and intellectually subtle series of fictions. Among other things, the emphasis upon courtly love, according to which knights swore to serve and honor highborn ladies, provided a counterpoint to the overt misogyny of the Medieval church theologians.

In the Renaissance, Italians such as Ariosto and Tasso combined the romance genre with the more ancient epic genre, and Spenser followed suit. Greek and Roman epics such as the *Odyssey, Illiad,* and *Aeneid* are long poetic narratives characterized by national or regional history (however mythologized), interest in the origins of a people, heroic deeds of characters who are human but larger than life, and highly technical descriptions of important battles. Through their imitations of ancient epic writers and of each other, Renaissance writers from various countries developed an interest in the ways that the history of one people might resemble that of another, and Renaissance romance epics often construct parallel histories. In *The Faerie Queene,* a fictional history of Faerie Land runs along beside a quasi-historical history of Britain, with the former providing commentary upon—and alternatives to—the latter.

An important difference between epic and romance is that whereas epic narrative—at least that of Western European epic—has a goal and a direction, the romance quest may deliberately wander, opening up new perspectives with every turn. Spenser plays the two narrative modes off each other, so the reader should not assume, without deliberation, that any given canto or book formulates an orderly, philosophical progression. Whereas some critics have seen Britomart as moving through her story from sexual naïveté to a more complex understanding of chastity, for example, John Watkins argues that her development from intellectual naïveté to sophistication is not accompanied by a similar development in her embodiment of the virtue of chastity (173). Romance and epic are uneasy companions, but that very uneasiness is conducive to a probing conversation.

e.   *Allegory and Word Play*

An allegory is essentially an extended allusion, a work of fiction in which the narrative events point toward another series of events or system of ideas. Thus, an account of knights in Faerie Land fighting one another may refer simultaneously to England's defeat of the Spanish Armada in Spenser's own lifetime—or to conceptual conflicts between Protestant and Catholic views of grace—or to struggles within the human psyche. Because Spenser's allegory usually signifies on several levels at once, it is tempting to decide that almost any allegorical key will work, but such is not the case. Always consider the surface first; if the tone and details of a particular passage ask the reader to sympathize with Squire Timias despite his failings, it would be wise to think twice before deciding that on another level, he is an allegorical symbol for the Antichrist.

An allegorical narrative is not a novel. When the decidedly nasty Duessa uses magic to make herself appear young, beautiful, and modest, other characters are consistently fooled into believing her disguise. In a novel, we might be asked to excuse the characters who are so fooled, given the strength of Duessa's magic, but in an allegory, being unable to see through a disguise often indicates that one lacks the moral perception to see truly. When Florimell continually runs away from lechers who persist in chasing her, the point is not simply that she is unfortunate, but that her chastity, though pure, differs in some important way from that of Britomart, who successfully fends off lascivious attackers.

Spenser's allegory is all the more satisfying because its major characters are never purely good or purely bad—nor, indeed, purely exemplars of holiness, temperance, chastity, friendship, justice, or courtesy. The hero of the Book of Temperance concludes his quest with an episode of violent intemperance, and the heroine of the Book of Chastity spends a great deal of time being uncertain as to what chastity means. *The Faerie Queene* is, as Jon Quitslund points out, about "individual psyches, female as well as male, and their construction by the institutions of society" (191). This means that the poem defines the six virtues through time— that is, the time in which the poem occurs, rather than the time represented by the plot. Additionally, the poem defines the virtues through the interactions among characters, and these interactions are just as likely to exist in the readers' minds as in the social contact among characters. In the plot of the poem, Adonis never meets Timias, yet because Adonis loves a woman who controls and satisfies him (III.vi.46–49) while Timias loves a woman who controls and shuns him (III.v.26–50, IV.vii.35–37), we might well hypothesize that the poem is asking us to develop ideas about the relationship between love and control by considering these characters together. Additionally, Spenser sometimes uses several minor characters to represent discrete aspects of one major character, as when Britomart's complicated chastity is diffracted among the simpler but diverse chastities of Amoret, Belphoebe, Florimell, and Æmylia. Whereas most novels prioritize the psychological development of individual characters, Spenser's allegory is more likely to generate psychological, political, and moral complexity through combinations of characters.

The allegory also asks us to see—or to construct, in the process of reading—exchanges of significance between characters and inanimate objects. Spenser is a master of the transferred epithet, in which an adjective grammatically modifies one noun but logically must describe another. When Malecasta rises in the middle of the night from "her wearie bed" and her servants find her "lying on the sencelesse grownd" (III.i.59, 63), it is clearly she who is weary and then senseless. Nevertheless, as Andrew Zurcher observes, the epithets' transference from person to thing "distributes will and activity into [inanimate objects] in a way peculiarly suited to allegory, and creates metonymic associations between agents and instruments. . . . Beds come to stand as emblems of weariness external to weary human subjects, and the ground becomes a symbol of senselessness. . . . [T]o fall to the ground in Spenser is to remember that you are dust, by enacting it" (e-mail to the editor).

Spenser uses many additional poetic devices to produce multiple layers of meaning. Like most of his contemporaries, he is fond of puns, enabled by the erratic spelling of Renaissance English. Because the *Oxford English Dictionary* (OED) lists words under every known spelling variant and gives dated examples of each sense of the word, it is particularly useful in helping modern readers decide when and how a pun operates. Sometimes a word may act as a pun on itself, when one definition of that word is on its way out and a significantly different definition is on its way in; for example, the sample sentences given in the OED for the word "villainous" demonstrate that in the sixteenth century, the word was changing from a synonym for "low-born and unmannerly" to a synonym for "wicked." This transition gave authors the opportunity to use the word ambiguously. The Glossary and notes to this edition often point out such instances.

Another layering device is the repetition of a word, phrase, or image in several contexts, with a slightly different meaning in each context. Such repetitions ask the reader to evaluate the contexts in light of each other.

An important layering device that Spenser takes from Ariosto is *interlacement,* the weaving of various plots in and out of each other. After following Timias' story for a couple of cantos, the narrator may mention that Timias has been having too full a life to think of his master, who has all this time been in another part of the forest—and suddenly the narrative switches to the master's story. The narrative may or may not revert to Timias later, and we may or may not learn what has happened to him in the meantime. The constant juxtaposition of plots, which is far more intense in Books Three and Four than in the previous books, again invites us to allow infusions of meaning from one plot to another.

f. Meter and Stanzaic Form

By rearranging and extending some existing stanza forms, Spenser invented a new and extraordinarily flexible stanza, which we now call the Spenserian Stanza: eight lines of iambic pentameter (with five stressed syllables) followed by one of iambic hexameter (with six stressed syllables), rhyming *ababbcbcc*. Italian could handle such a rhyme scheme easily, but the relative dearth of rhyming words in English makes the scheme more challenging. At the same time, because the fifth line ends with the same rhyme as the second and fourth, while the final two lines form an uneven couplet, the rhyme scheme allows the stanza to arrange itself simultaneously into several groupings:

> *abab bcbc c*
> *abab bcb cc*
> *ababb cbcc*
> *aba bb cbc c*

In addition, all of the *b*-rhymes form a group in our heads, as do all of the *c*-rhymes. Spenser uses these overlapping groupings to draw our attention to various relationships in the content of the lines.

The interlocking rhyme scheme impels the stanza forward, aided by Spenser's extraordinarily fluid use of iambs—even in long and grammatically complex sentences. Pushing against this onrushing rhythm is the hexameter line—also known as an Alexandrine—at the close of each stanza. The additional length of the Alexandrine, in conjunction with the couplet rhyme (*cc*), contributes to a sense of closure. Indeed, the final two lines of many stanzas have the sound of two-line proverbs, as though we were being given parting advice. The aural resemblance is, more often than not, illusory, as one stanza tumbles into the next without offering anything so neat as a concluding moral. Patricia Parker writes that the poem "seems to be exploring the implications of [lyric versus epic narrative] in its very form—narrative in its forward, linear quest and yet composed out of lyric stanzas that, like the enchantresses within it, potentially suspend or retard" (66).

4. Summaries of Books One and Two

Although the plot of *The Faerie Queene* is hardly its most important unifying feature, it will help the reader who begins with Book Three to know the general shape of Books One and Two. The Redcrosse Knight—who appears in Books Two and Three, as well—is the hero of Book One, the Legend of Holiness. Accompanied and coached by Una, who represents the True Church, he travels on a quest to free her parents from a dragon. In the course of this quest, he meets various enemies to holiness, including the wicked enchanter Archimago and the witch Duessa, who represent the falseness and deception of the Catholic faith. Although Redcrosse temporarily defeats Duessa, she will continue to assume various disguises in future books. At the end of Book One, after spiritual setbacks that almost result in despair, Redcrosse slays the dragon and marries Una. Her own father "the holy knotts did knitt, / That none but death for ever can divide" (I.xii.37), but if their marital union cannot be divided, their bodies can: after the wedding, Redcrosse fulfills his promise to return to the Faerie court to serve the Faerie Queen for six years. Una remains with her parents, mourning his absence. Her position is thus a preparation for that of Britomart, who in Book Three agonizes over the physical absence of a beloved whom she has met only in a vision.

Sir Guyon is the hero of Book Two, the Legend of Temperance, though he will also play an important role in Book Three. The Aristotelian virtue of temperance applies to all areas of life: the temperate person shuns excess or self-indulgence in any direction. (Two important interpretive questions are why Spenser puts this virtue before that of chastity and how he uses the characters to comment upon the relationship between these two virtues.) Accompanied by the Palmer, a pilgrim who gives him moral and spiritual guidance, Guyon travels on a quest to defeat the witch Acrasia, whose Bower of Bliss is a paradise of sensual pleasures. On the way, Guyon meets various intemperate characters, of whom some must be defeated or avoided, while others serve primarily as object lessons. The reader who begins with Book Three will need to know that in Book Two, Guyon coolly resists temptations and rides a famously calm horse. (His role in Book Three is less magisterial.) Two-thirds of the way through Book Two, Guyon finds a book titled *Antiquitee of Faery Lond,* reproduced in the succeeding canto as a chronicle of Briton kings from Brute to Gloriana (II.ix–x); this history will be considerably augmented in Book Three (III.iii.26–50 and ix.33–51). In the final canto of Book Two, Spenser uses Odyssean references to describe Guyon and the Palmer's journey to the wandering islands on which the seductive witch Acrasia lives in her Bower of Bliss. After the narrator has described the gorgeous birds, plants, and art of the Bower, Guyon intemperately smashes all of it.

5. Preparation for Book Three

a. Amazons

Although Britomart is not, strictly speaking, an Amazon, Spenser's conception of her is indebted to previous authors' accounts of the Amazons. These were a semi-legendary race of female warriors who consorted with men only in order to give birth to female babies. Male offspring were murdered, maimed, or banished soon after birth. Each woman cut off one of her breasts, so as to be able to draw a bowstring unimpeded, and Amazonian troops were famously brave in battle against the male armies of other societies. Like the ancient Greeks and Romans, Europeans used stories about Amazons both to praise their strength and to vilify their flouting of supposedly natural laws about women's subjection to men. Louis Montrose explains that the double face of the Amazonian image usually kept Elizabethans from using it to praise their queen, though Raleigh employed both faces of the image shrewdly in order to put political pressure on Elizabeth to demonstrate that she was not out to impair or banish the system of masculine rule (Montrose, 78).

b. Queen Elizabeth and Her Poet

In addition to making Britomart a female warrior, Spenser makes her the ancestor of Elizabeth, and the poem's technique of paralleling ancient and contemporary history allows Britomart simultaneously to mirror Elizabeth herself—with crucial differences. Like Elizabeth, Britomart is an emblem of chastity, but her chastity is only temporarily virginal, given that she is destined to marry. Elizabeth and her promoters used the idea of the Virgin Queen to link her with the cult of the Virgin Mary, a medium of prayer, grace, and comfort that was denied to Protestant worshippers in England after Elizabeth's father, Henry VIII, severed ties with the Catholic Church in Rome. Although the Virgin Queen was not divine, she was now represented as the earthly medium of all grace and comfort. Her mystically impenetrable body was held to insure that her island realm would remain similarly impenetrable (Stallybrass, 130). Yet whereas Catholicism considered virginity the highest state of chastity (that is, of sexually pure thinking and living) and praised the monastic life, Protestantism privileged marriage, considering the relationship of husband and wife a divinely sanctioned microcosm of that between monarch and subjects—which, in turn, was a divinely sanctioned microcosm of that between God and humanity. In other words, Protestantism emphasized the chastity of physical, emotional, and spiritual faithfulness within a marriage.

Each reader of Britomart's story must wrestle with the question of how the poem is asking us to view the Virgin Queen. The proems—groups of four to eleven stanzas that precede the first canto of each book—address Queen Elizabeth directly, in her capacity as the poem's primary inspiration, supporter, reader, pupil, and subject matter.

For all of her encouragement of such adulation, Elizabeth was far from feminist. Whereas she exploited her femininity by encouraging the powerful men around her to treat her—at least superficially—as though she were a desirable yet chaste, bountiful yet severe Petrarchan mistress (a role discussed in more detail below), she was astute enough to know that her political power lay in being an exception to the rule of women's submission. Her aim was not to change women's roles or opportunities—which actually may have deteriorated during her reign—but to demonstrate that she did not threaten her country's patriarchal tradition. To that end, she declared that although her physical body was that of a feeble woman, her mystical body was that of kingship. The latter body stretched beyond her personal self to include all of her subjects, and its time on earth stretched before and after her personal life to include all English monarchs.

Critics debate the extent to which Spenser actually believed the glowing mythology that was built around Elizabeth. In general, we postmodern readers tend to be cynical, assuming that no one could actually have failed to see through Elizabeth's rhetoric, but in making this assumption, we ignore the powerful and meaningful mythologies to which we ourselves subscribe. Despite their fictions, myths are not falsehoods; they articulate our deepest beliefs, desires, and needs. The reader of *The Faerie Queene* will do well, then, to treat the question of Spenser's perceptions of Elizabeth as a genuine issue, rather than as one with a foregone conclusion.

At the least, Spenser seems to have been attracted by Elizabeth's power and, on the other hand, to have felt competitive with respect to that power. Like other men of his time who were born into working-class families but rose to governmental positions by means of a humanist education, he was spurred by the humanist dictum that individual people had individual talents not restricted purely by ancestry. His talents were exercised by his two vocations: that of a secretary to the great, and that of a poet. The two were not nearly so distinct as they might be today: among many other things, his poetry was self-promotion. As Richard Rambuss argues, Elizabethans regarded secretaries not only as personal assistants to noblemen and women, but as the keepers of secrets. Spenser's choice to write in the mode of allegory, which veils and withholds information from all except the few who are worthy interpreters, demonstrated that he was worthy of high secretarial positions at the same time that it demonstrated the distance between himself and the aristocracy (Rambuss 1993, 4).

c. Petrarchism and Neoplatonism

The relationship between the narrator of *The Faerie Queene* and his "dearest dread," as he calls his sovereign (I.Pr.4), draws upon the standard relationship of the Petrarchan speaker to his lady. Even though previous Petrarchan poets had mostly been aristocrats writing in their spare time, rather than career poets like Spenser, he and they resembled one another in their use of poetry to worship an abstract femininity even as they appropriated it, mingling praise with self-promotion. From its inception with Petrarch in the fourteenth century, the Petrarchan sonnet sequence was a highly self-conscious genre, whose male speaker described his wooing of an inaccessible lady in terms that seriously analyzed his every mood swing, while at the same time ironizing his self-absorption.

Petrarchism was infused with Neoplatonism, a Medieval and Renaissance set of philosophies that rewrote Plato according to Christian and heterosexual ideals. Neoplatonically speaking, a woman's beauty was allied with moral purity and could lead the male wooer's soul to a higher philosophical plane, on which his soul would come to understand its ideal form and its source in God (Quitslund, 238). The fact that Petrarchan sonnets call the beautiful lady a "mistress" can be misleading; the term does not imply a physical union, and indeed, the mistress's social position, married state, or personal reluctance keeps her emotionally aloof from her suitor. Given that he desires her physically as well as spiritually, and yet admires her chastity, he veers incessantly from adoration to anger to guilt. Her absence and his longing cause great pain, but they also give him the gift of poetry. She controls him, but is created by his words.

When Britomart makes a formal complaint to the sea (III.iv.7–11), she joins the few other female poets in Spenser's era who struggled with what it meant to take on the Petrarchan speaker's role. The fiction of Queen Elizabeth's Petrarchan relationship with her courtiers was that she was in the role of the mistress, but for a woman to assume the *speaker's* position was more complicated. The few female poets needed to assert their own chastity and modesty at the same time that they fashioned speakers who articulated desire and even pursued the objects of that desire. Despite the Elizabethans' fondness for strong, talkative women onstage, living women who published could be accused of being public women—whores—in that they shared their inner secrets with male readers whom they did not even know. In other ways, as well, phrases attributed to a female Petrarchan speaker meant something different than did those same phrases attributed to a male speaker: so, for example, a female speaker who berated and humbled herself in the face of her beloved's perfections was simply doing what a woman was supposed to do, rather than emphasizing the power of her love or the artistic complexity of her emotional states.

This last point is especially important, given that love in Book Three entails great pain. Britomart declares memorably that love cannot be compelled by mastery (III.i.25), and readers have tended to take this declaration as a lesson directly from the author; however, as Jonathan Sircy observes, love in Book Three does nothing *except* compel by mastery (6). Whether the master is the beloved, Cupid, or a cruel enchanter, the only difference between the episodes in which the poem asks us to wish for the lover's freedom and those in which the poem asks us to celebrate the lover's bondage is that in the former sort of episode, the lover interprets his or her subjection as torture, whereas in the latter, the lover interprets that subjection as masochistic pleasure and succumbs to it willingly (Sircy, 6–9). Britomart's self-fashioning is inextricable from a certain loss of self, and we must decide where Spenser's emphases lie. We must also decide where he finds himself in this narrative.

d.   Female Physiology: Constancy and Inconstancy

According to sixteenth-century physiological theory, which was influenced by Pythagoras, Aristotle, and Galen, women's bodies were in flux and their minds were, as a result, unstable. Even though some philosophers opined that women were as perfect in their own way as men were, and some humanists believed that women could respond brilliantly to education, the prevailing notion was that even the most intellectually gifted woman was held back by her natural tendency toward instability. This was a serious matter, given that sexual constancy was the highest earthly virtue to which a woman should aspire. Precisely because women were inherently prone to err, they were held responsible for keeping themselves firmly in check—and for submitting to men's rule over them.

Critics have debated the extent to which the male Petrarchan speaker, with his violently unstable emotions, is constructed as partly feminine. The reader will want to keep such questions in mind while considering Book Three. It may also be useful to know that in Book Two, just before Guyon finds the chronicle of Briton kings in the turret-brain of an anthropomorphized castle belonging to a female character named Alma, he and Arthur find another turret chamber inhabited by a male figure named Phantastes. This chamber is filled with "Infinite shapes . . . / Such as in idle fantasies doe flit: / Infernall Hags, *Centaurs,* feendes, *Hippodames,* / Apes, Lyons, Aegles, Owles, fooles, lovers, children, Dames" (II.ix.50). Fools, lovers, and women keep company with mythological creatures—which are themselves the material of poetry written by men.

Britomart is beset with fancies (i.e., fantasies and fanciful desires), and when we interpret how the poem is using her character, it is useful to keep in mind that the poem sets up analogies between the predicted fruitfulness of her love and the productiveness—or lack thereof—of the poet's craft. If Britomart's chaste womb is destined to be the repository of Elizabeth's ancestor, her body and mind are nonetheless unstable in other ways, and her responses to unfamiliar situations often remind us that she is, after all, very young and very much in process.

e.   Homoeroticism in the Renaissance

Because homoeroticism is integral to a number of passages in Books Three and Four (that is, because these passages invite the reader to take pleasure in imagining a sexual charge between two characters of the same sex, whether or not the narrative actually depicts a sexual act), it is important to understand how homoeroticism was defined and regarded in sixteenth-century England. As scholars such as Alan Bray have shown, the horror with which many Elizabethans regarded homosexual acts and the fact that such acts were technically punishable by death did not mean that Elizabethan culture had a well-developed concept of homosexuality as a defining characteristic: "In principle it was a crime which anyone was capable of, like murder or blasphemy" (Bray, 40). People who engaged in homosexual acts were assumed, like everyone else, also to want to marry and have children. Indeed, the laws against sodomy were almost never enforced, and men were seldom accused of sodomy, except when two men of unequal social status caused fears that the inferior was gaining political control over the superior (Bray, passim). Women's same-sex relationships, in contrast, were seldom mentioned by ministers or in legal contexts, given that such relationships were less unlikely to cause imbalances of social power (Traub, 63–5). So long as women married and had children, their desire for other women was nonthreatening (Traub, 79). In literary contexts, however, both male and female homoerotic moments were freely represented. Just as we of the twenty-first century do not assume that the writer of a murder mystery is likely to be a murderer, sixteenth-century audiences did not assume that authors of homoerotic scenes or passages were thereby labeling themselves as members of a distinct class. Similarly, authors assumed—correctly, if their popularity during their lifetimes is any guide—that audience members of almost all sorts would be titillated by homoerotic scenes and passages. The exceptions were people who distrusted all amorous delights, but "To such," declares Spenser's narrator, "I do not sing at all" (IV.Pr.4).

f. Ireland

Books Three and Four are less obviously concerned about Anglo-Irish politics than is Book Five, but Spenser's experiences in Ireland (for which, see "The Life of Edmund Spenser" in this volume) permeate the entire poem. As secretary to Lord Grey de Wilton, Elizabeth's Lord Deputy in colonial Ireland, Spenser purchased an estate in that country and continued to live there, holding various minor governmental posts, long after Elizabeth had relieved Lord Grey of his position. Spenser wrote most of *The Faerie Queene* in Ireland, loving its landscape and admiring its poetry while nonetheless advocating brutal suppression of its people. According to Andrew Hadfield, Spenser was in the paradoxical position of believing that colonial expansion was necessary in order to maintain national identity, yet worrying that the English were diluting their identity by mixing their culture and bloodlines with those of the Irish (Hadfield 2004, 126). As Elizabeth grew too old to bear children and her cousin, James VI of Scotland, was discussed as a possible heir, it was clear that a merger of England and Scotland could pose a larger version of the same conundrum (ibid.).

This political paradox is reflected in Spenser's poetry. Richard McCabe observes that Spenser's epic fuses two modes of allegory: the moral and the colonial. Whereas moral allegory is comfortable with locating the potential for evil in characters who represent "us," colonial allegory projects the otherness of evil outward, uncomfortable with the idea that there is any overlap between self and other (18). Yet, as David Baker puts it, "Whatever Spenser was at the end of his life, he was no longer (if he ever had been) purely 'English'" (78). To what extent Spenser himself realized this is open for debate. In *The Faerie Queene,* the great knights' internal failings are continually revolved outward, onto "other" characters and onto the landscape, remaking the foreign every time a hero or heroine subdues a monster.

g. Endings

The truest observation one can make about Spenser's endings is that to the degree that they exist in the first place, they evaporate soon afterward. Marriages are followed by separation; imprisoned monsters escape; happy reunions are described in uncomfortable ways; and the narrator regularly abandons plots that he has promised to continue. Jonathan Goldberg urges Spenserian scholars to recognize that "failed endings are a part of the design of the poem" and to address the pleasures of this narrative frustration (1–2). We may also decide that some of the supposedly happy endings are actually better avoided, especially if one is thinking from the position of the female characters (Stephens, 27). But current Spenserian scholars largely agree that it is both more interesting and more honest to accept the endings in their inconstancy and incompletion than it is to imagine an ideal text in which they would all be "corrected." This editor does not want to spoil the reader's pleasure by describing in advance the two endings of Book Three, but it is to be hoped that the reader is now forewarned to be on the alert.

6. Preparation for Book Four

This edition puts Books Three and Four into one volume because Book Four is nearly impossible to understand without having first read its predecessor. (By the same token, this section on Book Four presumes that the reader will also have perused the much longer section above on Book Three.) Spenser published Books One, Two, and Three together in 1590, followed six years later by a second volume that included all six

books. There was thus a considerable gap between the original readers'
first encounter with Book Three and their encounter with Book Four.
Nonetheless, most of the main characters of Book Four come straight
from the previous book, and the two books share major plot lines. The
title page for Book Four announces "The Legend of Cambel and Telam-
ond, or of Friendship," but the fact that neither of these characters has
appeared in the previous book is immaterial, since they turn out chiefly
to be excuses for further commentary on Britomart, Amoret, Scud-
amour, Arthur, Artegall, and other familiar characters. The newly intro-
duced Telamond cannot even keep his own name straight; he appears
later as Triamond.

This sharing of major characters between the two books does not
mean that Book Four is simply a continuation of Book Three. Most ob-
viously, many of the events of Book Four occur before those of Book
Three in fictional time; that is, Book Four describes what events led up
to those that conclude Book Three. But more importantly, as Alpers
points out, it is a mistake to believe that the fictionally prior events de-
scribed in Book Four somehow explain those of the previous book
(109). Whereas Book Four depends upon Book Three, the reverse is not
precisely the case. Despite the fictional chronology, the rhetorical se-
quence places Book Four after Book Three, and we need to take seri-
ously our reading of Book Three on its own before we retroactively
analyze it from the position of Book Four.

McCabe argues that the final three books of *The Faerie Queene* enact a
process of self-examination as they quote and revise the first three books
(209). Hadfield sees Book Four as developing themes of Book Three
more deeply, "opening out and qualifying the discussions of love and
chastity into the more social and public arenas of friendship and wider
bonds of familial union" (2001, 128). Craig Berry writes, "[I]t seems that
Spenser, having borrowed avidly and often from the reputedly frivolous
Ariosto in the first three books, now turns to the serious resonances of
Chaucer's reputation to correct his image. . . ." (121); evoking these seri-
ous resonances even while choosing one of Chaucer's least didactic and
most romantic tales to revise is, for Spenser, "a way to embrace the con-
tradictions of his own career" (122). Whether we subscribe to one of
these three theories or to some other interpretation, we need to recog-
nize that the Books of Chastity and of Friendship have different aims.

Friendship was the subject of treatises in ancient Rome as well as in
Renaissance England, because it was seen not as merely a private virtue,
but as the basis for the larger patterns of cooperation that form a civil so-
ciety. Graham Hough notes that, despite the lack of one central plot,
"gradually it becomes apparent that we are observing a series of exempla

of true and false friendship" (183). In Hough's formulation, Books Three and Four belong together because the highest form of the "cosmic principle" of friendship is love, which Book Four delineates in its wider social context, after the more private context of Book Three (182–3). Yet erotic love repeatedly fails in the Book of Friendship, and even when it perseveres, it is often ugly and uncomfortable. Andrew Hadfield goes so far as to argue that Book Four implies "that women may be better off without the pains of male attention. . . . What seemed to have been endorsed at the end of the first edition of *The Faerie Queene*, heterosexual union, actually appears either to threaten stability or fail to satisfy human needs in the second" (2001, 125). Whether this revision of its earlier endorsement makes Book Four merely pessimistic or intriguingly exploratory is a matter of interpretation, but on a stanza-by-stanza basis, the book certainly has its share of beauty, pathos, insight, and astonishment.

7. Sources and Influences

Spenser was strongly influenced by the epic and pastorals of the ancient Roman writer Virgil, and by Ovid's interlocking stories of gods and humans who change into other forms. Additional Greek and Roman mythology came from Hesiod and from Homer's *Iliad* and *Odyssey*. Arthurian legend came primarily from Malory, while the emblems of Natalis Comes provided Spenser with a banquet of allegorical symbols. Spenser revered Chaucer as a model of vernacular English verse. More recent models for political and philosophical poetry combined with adventure were the Italian epics written by Dante, Petrarch, Ariosto, and Tasso. Spenser's contemporaries Raleigh and Harvey, who wrote lyric poetry, and Sidney, who wrote both lyric poetry and a prose romance, gave to Spenser's verse as much as they learned from it. Spenser drew his history and historical legend chiefly from Geoffrey of Monmouth, Holinshed, Hardyng, and Stow. His love-hate relationship with Neoplatonism was informed by Ficino, Bruno, Bembo, Pico della Mirandola, Ebreo, and, of course, Plato. For cosmology and natural philosophy, he drew from Boethius, Cicero, Lucretius, Plutarch, and Apuleius. His theories of what constituted a "gentleman" were considerably influenced by Castiglione.

8. Issues Addressed by Recent Spenserian Literary Criticism

The following list of sample issues pertains chiefly to *The Faerie Queene,* and especially to Books Three and Four. The hope is that they may kindle interest and help generate new questions.

a. When, if ever, does the poem allow "other" voices to speak through the text—e.g., voices from foreign or politically suspect points of view?

b. How does an awareness of race speak through this text? When, for example, does the narrator construct Muslims and the Irish as religious others, and when as racial others?

c. To what extent do any of the characters participate in animal being, and how does the poem distinguish animal being from that of humans?

d. What can we say about the poem's images of miscegenation between species? Think of species such as humans, fairies, animals, and gods.

e. How does the body write itself into this text? What does it mean, for example, when blood from a monstrous body turns into a gushing river or when love's pains are written into festering wounds?

f. According to Spenser, what is the status of suffering in relationship to friendship?

g. When disease speaks through this text, what is it saying?

h. How can the differences between Ovidian and Spenserian metamorphosis help us understand what Spenser is saying when his characters change their physical forms?

i. To what extent is the poem's narrator masculine or feminine, according to the poem's definitions of these terms? (It is extraordinarily difficult to answer this sort of question without imposing modern notions of gender or stereotypes of how people in the Renaissance would have defined gender.)

j. How do Books Three and Four use same-sex friendships to comment upon the virtues of Chastity and Friendship?

k. Are there aspects of the work that at first do not seem tied to gender, but on second glance are (e.g., modes of speech, methods of travel, or types of hospitality)?

l. What are the different sorts of power in this poem? Is there any way in which apparently powerless characters actually exert some sort of influence, either upon other characters or upon us as we read?

m. What does Book Three suggest about leadership and continence?

n. What is Spenser's conception of the interactions among history (that is, human accounts of events), memory, and desire?

o. In what ways do *The Faerie Queene* and Spenser's *View of the Present State of Ireland* complement or contradict each other as analyses of England's colonial prospects in Ireland?

p. According to Spenser, are justice and nature antithetical, co-operative, identical, unable to communicate with each other, both dependent on some third thing, or what?

q. How does this poem define types of fraud, and what are their sources?

r. What is the relationship between civility and pity in Book Four?

s. In what literary communities does this poem participate, and how?

t. In what ways do Spenser's minor poems (e.g., the *Epithalamion,* the *Amoretti,* and *The Shepheardes Calender*) complement or reinterpret particular passages of *The Faerie Queene?*

u. What *patterns* of metaphor does Spenser use, and where? What mileage does he get out of these patterns?

v. To which details does the poem ask us to pay attention, and which does it encourage us to overlook?

w. What relationship does this poem construct between the reader and the narrator? What sort of reader does this poem assume or induce?

THE FAERIE
QVEENE.

Difpofed into twelue books,

Fashioning

XII. Morall vertues.

LONDON
Printed for William Ponfonbie.
1590.

Title page to the 1590 edition of *The Faerie Queene* (STC 23081).

TO THE MOST MIGH-
TIE AND MAGNIFI-
CENT EMPRESSE ELI-
ZABETH, BY THE
GRACE OF GOD QVEENE
OF ENGLAND, FRANCE
AND IRELAND DE-
FENDER OF THE FAITH
&c.

Her most humble

Seruant:

Ed. Spenser

The thirde Booke
of the Faerie Queene.
Contayning
The Legend of Britomartis.
OR
Of Chastity.

1   It falls me[1] here to write of Chastity,
        The fayrest vertue, far above the rest;
        For which what needes me[2] fetch from *Faery*
        Forreine ensamples,[3] it to have exprest?
        Sith it is shrined in my Soveraines brest,[4]
        And formd so lively in each perfect part,
        That to all Ladies, which have it profest,
        Neede but behold the pourtraict[5] of her hart,
    If pourtrayd it might bee by any living art.

2   But living art may not least part expresse,
        Nor life-resembling pencill it can paynt,
        All were it *Zeuxis* or *Praxiteles.*[6]
        His dædale[7] hand would faile, and greatly faynt,
        And her perfections with his error taynt:
        Ne[8] Poets witt, that passeth Painter farre
        In picturing the parts of beauty daynt,[9]
        So hard a workemanship adventure darre,
    For fear through want[10] of words her excellence to marre.

---

[1] **falls me:** falls to me; is up to me.

[2] **what needes me:** why would I need.

[3] **ensamples:** examples.

[4] **Sith:** since; **in my Soveraines brest:** see Introduction, 5b.

[5] **pourtraict:** portrait.

[6] *Zeuxis* **or** *Praxiteles:* artists famed in ancient Greece for their skill in depicting women.

[7] **dædale:** referring to Daedalus, who made wings for himself and his son, Icarus, out of wax and feathers. Icarus flew too near the sun, which melted the wax and caused him to fall to his death. Daedalus is thus a symbol both of consummate artistry and of overly confident ambition.

[8] **Ne:** nor. No one really knows how this word—which Spenser uses frequently—would have been pronounced. The OED gives a long *e;* Monty Python gives a short *i* (in "The Knights Who Say 'Ni'"); some scholars read the word aloud with a long *a;* and others use the schwa (an unstressed vowel sound, as in the *a* of "about," the *e* of "item," or the *i* of "edible").

[9] **daynt:** dainty; delightful; precious; choice.

[10] **want:** lack.

3

3   How then shall I, Apprentice of the skill,
     That whilome[1] in divinest wits did rayne,
     Presume so high to stretch mine humble quill?[2]
     Yet now my luckelesse lott doth me constrayne
     Hereto perforce. But O dredd[3] Soverayne
     Thus far forth pardon, sith that choicest witt
     Cannot your glorious pourtraict figure playne,
     That I in colourd showes may shadow itt,[4]
And antique[5] praises unto present persons fitt.

4   But if in living colours, and right hew,[6]
     Thy selfe thou covet to see pictured,[7]
     Who can it doe more lively, or more trew,
     Then that sweete verse, with *Nectar* sprinckeled,
     In which a gracious servaunt pictured
     His *Cynthia*, his heavens fayrest light?[8]
     That with his melting sweetnes ravished,
     And with the wonder of her beames bright,
My sences lulled are in slomber of delight.

5   But let that same delitious Poet lend
     A little leave unto a rusticke Muse
     To sing his mistresse prayse, and let him mend,
     If ought amis her liking may abuse:[9]

---

[1] **whilome:** formerly.

[2] The fact that it was standard practice for an author to claim his own inadequacy does not mean we should take Spenser's self-deprecation lightly. He had no assurance that the Queen would approve of his poem, which allegorized her failings as well as her virtues, and he knew he was undertaking a project that could seem presumptuous: to write England's first national epic.

[3] I.e., yet my duty is to do precisely this (to dare to write about Elizabeth); **dredd:** dreaded. Monarchs were praised for inspiring a combination of fear, admiration, and love in their subjects.

[4] I.e., that I may hint at your glory through the beauties of allegory. See "The Letter to Raleigh" (p. 451) for Spenser's discussion of his conception of allegory.

[5] **antique:** pun on "antic," meaning "absurdly fantastic." Spenser's admiration for the medieval Chaucer prompted him to adopt some of Chaucer's antiquated English vocabulary and phrasing, which caused some ribbing from fellow authors.

[6] **hew:** form; condition.

[7] **pictured:** three syllables. Reading Spenser aloud with attention to the meter will give a feel for the times when he expects normally silent endings to be pronounced.

[8] Spenser's friend Sir Walter Raleigh had composed "Cynthia, the Lady of the Sea," an elegy to Elizabeth.

[9] I.e., let him correct my poem if she dislikes any of it.

Ne let his fayrest *Cynthia* refuse,
In mirrours more then one her selfe to see,
But either *Gloriana* let her chuse,
Or in *Belphœbe* fashioned to bee:
In th'one her rule, in th'other her rare chastitee.[1]

---

[1] Spenser invites Elizabeth to see herself allegorized in two of the characters in his epic: the queen Gloriana (who never actually appears, though she is often mentioned) and Belphoebe (modeled on the Greek Diana, virgin goddess of the hunt and the moon). "Belle" means "beautiful" in Italian; "phoebe" means "pure" or "radiant" in Greek and is a name for Diana in her role as moon goddess. Belphoebe will enter in Canto Five.

Canto One

Guyon encountreth Britomart,
Faire Florimell is chaced:[1]
Duessaes traines[2] *and Malecastaes*
champions are defaced.[3]

1 The famous Briton Prince and Faery knight,[4]
   After long wayes and perilous paines endur'd,
   Having their weary limbes to perfect plight[5]
   Restord, and sory wounds right well recur'd,[6]
   Of the faire *Alma* greatly were procur'd,[7]
   To make there lenger sojourne and abode;
   But when thereto they might not be allur'd,
   From seeking praise, and deeds of armes abrode,[8]
   They courteous conge tooke, and forth together yode.[9]

2 But the captiv'd *Acrasia* he[10] sent,
   Because of traveill long, a nigher[11] way,
   With a strong gard, all reskew to prevent,
   And her to Faery court safe to convay,
   That her for witnes of his hard assay,[12]
   Unto his *Faery* Queene he might present:
   But he him selfe betooke another way,
   To make more triall of his hardiment,[13]
   And seeke adventures, as he with Prince Arthure went.

---

[1] **chaced:** pun on "chaste" and "chased."

[2] **traines:** entrapments.

[3] The italicized four lines of alternating tetrameter and trimeter at the first of each canto are called an Argument; they briefly summarize the canto's plot.

[4] I.e., Prince Arthur and Sir Guyon. See Introduction, 4.

[5] **plight:** condition.

[6] **recur'd:** cured.

[7] **procur'd:** urged.

[8] **abrode:** abroad, far and wide. In the early medieval world about which Spenser writes, a knight was supposed to seek glory, fame, and praise. It is useful to compare attitudes toward ambition in this poem with those in *Beowulf,* in *Sir Gawain and the Green Knight,* and in *Utopia.*

[9] **conge:** farewell; **yode:** went.

[10] *Acrasia:* the seductress (see Introduction, 4); **he:** Sir Guyon.

[11] **nigher:** nearer.

[12] **assay:** effort.

[13] **hardiment:** courage and hardihood.

3   Long so they traveiled through wastefull[1] wayes,
        Where daungers dwelt, and perils most did wonne,[2]
        To hunt for glory and renowmed prayse;
        Full many Countreyes they did overronne,
        From the uprising to the setting Sunne,
        And many hard adventures did atchieve;
        Of all the which they honour ever wonne,
        Seeking the weake oppressed to relieve,
    And to recover right for such, as wrong did grieve.

4   At last as through an open plaine they yode,[3]
        They spide a knight, that towards pricked[4] fayre,
        And him beside an aged Squire there rode,
        That seemd to couch[5] under his shield three-square,
        As if that age badd[6] him that burden spare,
        And yield it those,[7] that stouter could it wield:
        He them espying, gan him selfe prepare,
        And on his arme addresse[8] his goodly shield
    That bore a Lion passant in a golden field.[9]

5   Which seeing good Sir *Guyon*, deare besought
        The Prince of grace, to let him ronne that turne.[10]
        He graunted: then the Faery quickly raught[11]
        His poynant speare, and sharply gan to spurne[12]
        His fomy steed, whose fiery feete did burne
        The verdant gras, as he thereon did tread;
        Ne[13] did the other backe his foot returne,
        But fiercely forward came withouten dread,
    And bent[14] his dreadful speare against the others head.

---

[1] **wastefull:** deserted.

[2] **wonne:** abide.

[3] **yode:** went.

[4] **pricked:** spurred his horse toward them.

[5] **couch:** crouch.

[6] **badd:** bade.

[7] **yield it those:** yield it to those.

[8] **addresse:** prepare.

[9] **passant in a golden field:** a description of a coat of arms depicting a lion walking, with its right forepaw raised, against a golden background.

[10] I.e., when good Sir Guyon saw this, he fervently asked Prince Arthur, as a favor, to let him take the challenge. Prince Arthur often brings, or mediates, grace of one sort or another in the poem.

[11] **Faery:** Guyon; **raught:** reached for.

[12] **poynant:** piercing (lit. poignant); **to spurne:** to spur.

[13] **Ne:** nor.

[14] **bent:** turned, aimed.

6   They beene ymett, and both theyr points arriv'd,
             But *Guyon* drove so furious and fell,[1]
             That seemd both shield and plate it would have riv'd;
             Nathelesse it bore his foe not from his sell,[2]
             But made him stagger, as[3] he were not well:
             But *Guyon* selfe, ere well he was aware,
             Nigh a speares length behind his crouper[4] fell,
             Yet in his fall so well him selfe he bare,[5]
        That mischievous mischaunce his life and limbs did spare.

7   Great shame and sorrow of that fall he tooke;
             For never yet, sith warlike armes he bore,
             And shivering[6] speare in bloody field first shooke,
             He fownd him selfe dishonored so sore.
             Ah gentlest[7] knight, that ever armor bore,
             Let not thee grieve dismounted to have beene,
             And brought to grownd, that never wast before;
             For not thy fault, but secret powre unseene,
        That speare enchaunted was, which layd thee on the greene.[8]

8   But weenedst thou,[9] what wight thee overthrew,
             Much greater griefe and shamefuller regrett
             For thy hard fortune then thou wouldst renew,
             That of a single damzell thou wert mett
             On equall plaine, and there so hard besett;
             Even the famous *Britomart*[10] it was,
             Whom straunge adventure did from *Britayne* fett,[11]
             To seeke her lover (love far sought alas,)
        Whose image shee had seene in *Venus* looking glas.[12]

---

[1] **fell:** cruel, dire (cf. "felon").

[2] **sell:** saddle.

[3] **as:** as if.

[4] **crouper:** crupper.

[5] **bare:** bore.

[6] **shivering:** prone to shattering other spears; quivering with energy.

[7] **gentlest:** most noble. The poem's speaker addresses Guyon directly.

[8] In Ariosto's *Orlando Furioso,* the virgin warrior Bradamante uses an enchanted spear that can defeat all knights (23.15).

[9] **weenedst thou:** if you knew.

[10] *Britomart:* her name allies British pride with martial prowess. Compare her fierce brand of chastity with other sorts of chastity and unchastity in the book.

[11] **adventure:** chance; quest; **fett:** fetch.

[12] We can think of meetings such as the one between Guyon and Britomart as allegorically representing relationships among the political, moral, or other concepts embodied in the two characters. In psychological terms, two characters meet because they need to meet each other, in order to work

9 Full of disdainefull wrath, he fierce uprose,
    For to revenge that fowle reprochefull shame,
    And snatching his bright sword began to close
    With her on foot, and stoutly forward came;
    Dye rather would he, then endure that same.
    Which when his Palmer[1] saw, he gan to feare
    His[2] toward perill and untoward blame,
    Which by that new rencounter he should reare:[3]
  For death sate on the point of that enchaunted speare.

10 And hasting towards him gan fayre perswade,
    Not to provoke misfortune, nor to weene[4]
    His speares default[5] to mend with cruell blade;
    For by his mightie Science he had seene
    The secrete vertue of that weapon keene,
    That mortall puissaunce mote not withstond:
    Nothing on earth mote[6] alwaies happy beene.
    Great hazard were it, and adventure fond,[7]
  To loose long gotten honour with one evill hond.

11 By such good meanes he him discounselled,
    From prosecuting his revenging rage;
    And eke the Prince like treaty handeled,[8]
    His[9] wrathfull will with reason to asswage,
    And laid the blame, not to his carriage,[10]
    But to his starting steed, that swarv'd asyde,

---

out something about their self-image or way of living in the world. Here, one could say that Chastity triumphs over mere Temperance, but that the two virtues work best together. Such an interpretation is oversimplified, however, given that Britomart is learning how to be chaste rather than flatly representing a static notion of chastity. We must also consider the tone of this episode, which is humorous not only at Guyon's expense, but also at Britomart's: she comes into view spoiling for a fight with someone, anyone; *Venus* **looking glas:** see ii.18.8.n.

[1] **Palmer:** a pilgrim, especially one who has been to Jerusalem. Through all of his travels, Guyon is accompanied by the Palmer, who gives him moral guidance.

[2] **His:** Guyon's.

[3] **reare:** cause.

[4] **weene:** believe.

[5] **default:** fault.

[6] **mote:** might.

[7] **fond:** foolish.

[8] I.e., and also the Prince made use of a similar entreaty.

[9] **His:** Guyon's.

[10] **his carriage:** the way Guyon had carried himself.

And to the ill purveyance of his page,
That had his furnitures[1] not firmely tyde:
So is his angry corage[2] fayrely pacifyde.

12   Thus reconcilement was betweene them knitt,
Through goodly temperaunce, and affection chaste,
And either[3] vowd with all their power and witt,
To let not others honour be defaste,
Of friend or foe, who ever it embaste,[4]
Ne armes to beare against the others syde:
In which accord the Prince was also plaste,
And with that golden chaine of concord tyde.
So goodly all agreed, they forth yfere[5] did ryde.

13   O goodly usage of those antique tymes,[6]
In which the sword was servant unto right;
When not for malice and contentious crymes,
But all for prayse, and proofe of manly[7] might,
The martiall brood accustomed to fight:
Then honour was the meed[8] of victory,
And yet the vanquished had no despight:[9]
Let later age that noble use envy,[10]
Vyle rancor to avoid, and cruel surquedry.[11]

14   Long they thus traveiled[12] in friendly wise,
Through countreyes waste, and eke well edifyde,[13]
Seeking adventures hard, to exercise
Their puissance, whylome full dernly[14] tryde:
At length they came into a forrest wyde,
Whose hideous horror and sad trembling sownd

---

[1] **furnitures:** saddlery and armor.

[2] **corage:** heart as the seat of emotion and thought.

[3] **either:** each.

[4] **embaste:** declared base.

[5] **yfere:** companionably.

[6] The fact that Spenser so often praises the past raises the question of what he is saying about Elizabeth's reign in the present.

[7] Note the layers of praise and irony for the female, yet manly, Britomart.

[8] **meed:** reward.

[9] **despight:** resentment.

[10] **envy:** admire, with overtones of being mortified at being less admirable oneself.

[11] **surquedry:** arrogance.

[12] Note the pun on "travail."

[13] I.e., through wastelands and also through built-up areas.

[14] **whylome:** while; **dernly:** dismally.

Full griesly seemd: therein they long did ryde,
Yet tract[1] of living creature none they fownd,
Save Beares, Lyons, and Buls, which romed them arownd.

15   All suddenly out of the thickest brush,
      Upon a milkwhite Palfrey all alone,
      A goodly Lady did foreby[2] them rush,
      Whose face did seeme as cleare as Christall stone,
      And eke through feare as white as whales bone:
      Her garments all were wrought of beaten gold,
      And all her steed with tinsell trappings shone,
      Which fledd so fast, that nothing mote him hold,
And scarse them leasure gave, her passing to behold.

16   Still as she fledd, her eye she backward threw,
      As fearing evill, that poursewd her fast;
      And her faire yellow locks behind her flew,
      Loosely disperst with puff of every blast:
      All as a blazing starre doth farre outcast
      His hearie beames, and flaming lockes dispredd,[3]
      At sight whereof the people stand aghast:
      But the sage wisard telles, as he has redd,[4]
That it importunes death and dolefull dreryhedd.[5]

17   So as they gazed after her a whyle,
      Lo where a griesly Foster[6] forth did rush,
      Breathing out beastly lust her to defyle:
      His tyreling Jade[7] he fiersly forth did push,
      Through thicke and thin, both over banck and bush
      In hope her to attaine by hooke or crooke,
      That from his[8] gory sydes the blood did gush:
      Large were his limbes, and terrible his looke,
And in his clownish hand a sharp bore speare[9] he shooke.

---

[1] **tract:** trace, track.

[2] **foreby:** nearby.

[3] **dispredd:** spread widely.

[4] **redd:** discerned, interpreted, predicted. The Lady's streaming hair makes her look like a comet, and her horrified gaze in the direction of whatever pursues her expands the simile to that of a wizard who interprets the comet as an omen of future disaster.

[5] **dreryhedd:** dreariness.

[6] **griesly Foster:** grisly forester.

[7] **tyreling Jade:** tired nag.

[8] **his:** the nag's.

[9] **clownish:** rustic; **bore speare:** cf. the stories of Adonis and the boar in stanza 38 and in vi.48. The boar spear may either fight lust or act as its tool.

18   Which outrage when those gentle[1] knights did see,
    Full of great envy and fell gealosy,[2]
    They stayd not to avise,[3] who first should bee,
    But all spurd after fast, as they mote fly,
    To reskew her from shamefull villany.
    The Prince and *Guyon* equally bylive[4]
    Her selfe pursewd, in hope to win thereby
    Most goodly meede, the fairest Dame alive:
But after the foule foster *Timias*[5] did strive.

19   The whiles faire *Britomart,* whose constant[6] mind,
    Would not so lightly follow beauties chace,
    Ne reckt of Ladies Love, did stay behynd,
    And them awayted there a certaine space,
    To weet[7] if they would turne backe to that place:
    But when she saw them gone, she forward went,
    As lay her journey, through that perlous Pace,[8]
    With stedfast corage and stout[9] hardiment;
Ne evil thing she feard, ne evill thing she ment.

20   At last as nigh out of the wood she came,
    A stately Castle far away she spyde,
    To which her steps directly she did frame.[10]
    That Castle was most goodly edifyde,[11]
    And plaste for pleasure nigh that forrest syde:
    But faire before the gate a spatious playne,
    Mantled with greene, it selfe did spredden wyde,
    On which she saw six knights, that did darrayne[12]
Fiers battaill against one, with cruel might and mayne.

---

[1] **gentle:** with the virtues of gentlemen and gentlewomen. See Glossary for a fuller explanation.

[2] **gealosy:** with righteous indignation, but the word also hints that they might like to be in the forester's place.

[3] **avise:** consult about.

[4] **bylive:** forthwith, quickly.

[5] *Timias:* Arthur's squire, whose name means "honored," from the Greek τιμήεις. Although Timias has appeared many times in Books One and Two, defending and aiding his master, this is the first time that he is named.

[6] See Introduction, 5d.

[7] **weet:** discover.

[8] **perlous Pace:** perilous path.

[9] **stout:** proud; brave; hardy.

[10] **frame:** direct.

[11] **edifyde:** erected.

[12] **darrayne:** wage.

21   Mainely[1] they all attonce upon him laid,
          And sore beset on every side arownd,
          That nigh he breathlesse grew, yet nought dismaid,[2]
          Ne ever to them yielded foot of grownd
          All had he lost much blood[3] through many a wownd,
          But stoutly dealt his blowes, and every way
          To which he turned in his wrathfull stownd,[4]
          Made them recoile, and fly from dredd decay,[5]
      That none of all the six before, him durst assay.[6]

22   Like dastard Curres, that having at a bay[7]
          The salvage beast embost[8] in wearie chace,
          Dare not adventure on the stubborne pray,
          Ne byte before,[9] but rome from place to place,
          To get a snatch, when turned is his face.
          In such distresse and doubtfull jeopardy,
          When *Britomart* him saw, she ran apace
          Unto his reskew, and with earnest cry,
      Badd[10] those same six forbeare that single enimy.

23   But to her cry they list[11] not lenden eare,
          Ne ought the more their mightie strokes surceasse,[12]
          But gathering him rownd about more neare,
          Their direfull rancour rather did encrease;
          Till that she rushing through the thickest preasse,[13]
          Perforce disparted their compacted gyre,[14]

---

[1] **Mainely:** mightily.

[2] **dismaid:** having lost all moral courage; defeated; appalled; discouraged. In addition, especially in this book about chastity, this word usually hints at a pun on "dismaid" (made no longer a maid; deflowered). Virgins of either sex could be referred to as maids.

[3] **All had he:** even though he had; **blood:** as Quitslund points out, it is worth noticing that throughout the poem, blood has associations with violence, vitality, love, desire, nourishment, fecundity, kinship, race, and holy communion (2006, online discussion).

[4] **stownd:** attack.

[5] **decay:** death.

[6] **assay:** put to the test, attack.

[7] **at a bay:** at bay.

[8] **embost:** exhausted and foaming at the mouth.

[9] **before:** to his face.

[10] **Badd:** bade.

[11] **list:** wished.

[12] **surceasse:** cease.

[13] **preasse:** press, crowd.

[14] **Perforce:** by force; **compacted gyre:** circling mass.

And soone compeld to hearken unto peace:
Tho gan she myldly of them to inquyre
The cause of their dissention and outrageous yre.

24   Whereto that single knight did answere frame;
        "These six would me enforce by oddes[1] of might,
        To chaunge my liefe,[2] and love another Dame,
        That death me liefer were, then such despight,[3]
        So unto wrong to yield my wrested right:
        For I love one, the truest one on grownd,[4]
        Ne list me chaunge; she th'*Errant damzell*[5] hight,
        For whose deare sake full many a bitter stownd,
        I have endurd, and tasted many a bloody wownd."

25   "Certes"[6] (said she) "then beene ye sixe to blame,
        To weene your wrong by force to justify:
        For knight to leave his Lady were great shame,
        That faithful is,[7] and better were to dy.
        All losse is lesse, and lesse the infamy,
        Then losse of love to him, that loves but one;
        Ne may love be compeld by maistery;[8]
        For soone as maistery comes, sweet love anone[9]
        Taketh his nimble winges, and soone away is gone."

26   Then spake one of those six, "There dwelleth here
        Within this castle wall a Lady fayre,
        Whose soveraine beautie hath no living pere,[10]
        Thereto so bounteous and so debonayre,[11]
        That never any mote with her compayre.
        She hath ordaind this law, which we approve,[12]

---

[1] **oddes:** statistical advantage.

[2] **liefe:** preference for a particular woman.

[3] **liefer:** preferable; **despight:** contempt.

[4] **on grownd:** in the world.

[5] Una, who has appeared in Book One, embodies religious truth. She errs literally rather than morally, wandering in search of her beloved. So does Britomart, of course.

[6] **Certes:** certainly.

[7] Refers to the Lady, but the meaning spills over to the knight.

[8] Despite her self-assured tone here, Britomart spends much of Book Three trying to figure out what the relationship between mastery and love is or should be.

[9] **anone:** anon, right away.

[10] **pere:** peer.

[11] **debonayre:** gracious.

[12] **approve:** enforce.

That every knight, which doth this way repayre,[1]
In case he have no Lady, nor no love,
Shall doe unto her service[2] never to remove.

27   "But if he have a Lady or a Love,
      Then must he her forgoe with fowle defame,
      Or else with us by dint of sword approve,[3]
      That she is fairer, then our fairest Dame,
      As did this knight, before ye hether came."
      "Perdy"[4] (said *Britomart*) "the choise is hard:
      But what reward had he, that overcame?"
      "He should advaunced bee to high regard,"
(Said they) "and have our Ladies love for his reward.[5]

28   "Therefore a read[6] Sir, if thou have a love."
      "Love have I sure," (quoth she) "but Lady none;
      Yet will I not fro mine owne love remove,
      Ne to your Lady will I service done,
      But wreake your wronges wrought to this knight alone,
      And prove his cause." With that her mortall speare
      She mightily aventred[7] towards one,
      And downe him smot, ere well aware he weare,
Then to the next she rode, and downe the next did beare.

29   Ne did she stay, till three on ground she layd,
      That none of them himselfe could reare againe;
      The fourth was by that other knight dismayd,
      All[8] were he wearie of his former paine,
      That now there do but two of six remaine;
      Which two did yield, before she did them smight.
      "Ah" (said she then) "now may ye all see plaine,
      That truth is strong, and trew love most of might,
That for his trusty servaunts doth so strongly fight."

---

[1] **repayre:** come.

[2] **her:** our lady; **service:** the service of a knight to his lady.

[3] **approve:** put to the test.

[4] **Perdy:** mild oath, literally "by God" (French *par dieu*).

[5] The delicious humor of multiple choices that all lead in the same direction is the mark of the Lady's single-minded lust, but the chaste Britomart will herself experience situations in which apparent choices turn out to mask forces that are nearly irresistible.

[6] **a read:** reveal.

[7] **aventred:** aimed.

[8] **All:** even though, even if.

30   "Too well we see," (saide they) "and prove too well
      Our faulty weakenes,[1] and your matchlesse might:
      For thy,[2] faire Sir, yours be the Damozell,
      Which by her owne law to your lot doth light,
      And we your liegemen faith unto you plight."[3]
      So underneath her feet their swords they mard,[4]
      And after her besought, well as they might,
      To enter in, and reape the dew reward:
   She graunted, and then in they all together far'd.

31   Long were it to describe the goodly frame,[5]
      And stately port[6] of *Castle Joyeous*,
      (For so that Castle hight[7] by commun name)
      Where they were entertaynd with courteous
      And comely glee[8] of many gratious
      Faire Ladies, and of many a gentle knight,
      Who through a Chamber long and spacious,
      Eftsoones[9] them brought unto their Ladies sight,
   That of them cleeped[10] was the *Lady of delight*.

32   But for to tell the sumptuous aray
      Of that great chamber, should be labour lost:
      For living wit, I weene, cannot display
      The roiall riches and exceeding cost,
      Of every pillour and of every post;
      Which all of purest bullion framed were,
      And with great perles and pretious stones embost,
      That the bright glister of their beames cleare
   Did sparckle forth great light, and glorious did appeare.

33   These stranger knights through passing, forth were led
      Into an inner rowme, whose royaltee
      And rich purveyance might uneath be red;[11]
      Mote Princes place be seeme so deckt to bee.

---

[1] Like his frequent double negatives, Spenser's "faulty" intensifies "weakenes" rather than compromising it.

[2] **For thy:** therefore.

[3] I.e., pledge ourselves to serve you.

[4] **mard:** marred; destroyed.

[5] **frame:** construction.

[6] **port:** appearance.

[7] **hight:** is called.

[8] **comely glee:** good cheer.

[9] **Eftsoones:** afterward; soon afterward.

[10] **cleeped:** called.

[11] **uneath:** scarcely; **red:** described.

Which stately manner when as they did see,
The image of superfluous riotize,
Exceeding much the state of meane degree,[1]
They greatly wondred, whence so sumpteous guize[2]
Might be maintaynd, and each gan diversely devize.

34 The wals were round about appareiled
   With costly clothes of *Arras* and of *Toure*,[3]
   In which with cunning hand was pourtrahed
   The love of *Venus* and her Paramoure,
   The fayre *Adonis,* turned to a flowre,[4]
   A worke of rare device,[5] and wondrous wit.
   First did it shew the bitter balefull stowre,[6]
   Which her assayd with many a fervent fit,
When first her tender hart was with his beautie smit.

35 Then with what sleights and sweet allurements she
   Entyst the Boy,[7] as well that art she knew,
   And wooed him her Paramoure to bee;
   Now making girlonds of each flowre that grew,
   To crowne his golden lockes with honour dew;
   Now leading him into a secret shade

---

[1] **meane degree:** inferior or low social status; middling social status.

[2] **guize:** appearance, manner of living—but with overtones of pretense and disguise.

[3] I.e., tapestries. Like Homer and Virgil, Spenser uses elaborately representational works of art to depict entire scenes that allegorize, or otherwise comment upon, major characters. Spenser also uses such works of art to comment upon the allegorical relationships among their makers, their owners, and their audiences. Cf. the different depictions of Venus in Cantos Six (in which the work of art is arguably the garden itself) and Eleven (in which the issues of ownership and authorship are particularly complex).

[4] In Ovid's *Metamorphoses,* Venus falls in love with a mortal youth, Adonis, and warns him not to risk his life by going hunting. He ignores her advice and dies after being gored in the groin by a wild boar. Heartsick, Venus changes his blood into an anemone flower, which is reborn every year for a brief period (10.524–739). In some Greek versions of the story, Zeus grants Aphrodite her wish that Adonis' spirit or resurrected self be able to spend half of each year with her.

[5] **device:** design and artistry.

[6] **stowre:** tumult.

[7] Cf. Venus' wooing of Adonis with Britomart's going on a quest to find her beloved, Artegall. The poem hints at the purpose of Britomart's quest in stanza 54, but reveals it fully only in the following canto.

From his Beauperes,[1] and from bright heavens vew,
    Where him to sleepe she gently would perswade,
Or bathe him in a fountaine by some covert glade.

36   And whilst he slept, she over him would spred
    Her mantle, colour'd like the starry skyes,
    And her soft arme lay underneath his hed,
    And with ambrosiall kisses bathe his eyes;
    And whilst he bath'd, with her two crafty spyes,[2]
    She secretly would search each daintie[3] lim,
    And throw into the well sweet Rosemaryes,
    And fragrant violets, and Paunces[4] trim,
And ever with sweet Nectar she did sprinkle him.

37   So did she steale his heedelesse hart away,
    And joyd[5] his love in secret unespyde.
    But for she saw him bent[6] to cruell play,
    To hunt the salvage[7] beast in forrest wyde,
    Dreadfull[8] of daunger, that mote him betyde,
    She oft and oft adviz'd him to refraine
    From chase of greater beastes, whose brutish pryde
    Mote breede him scath[9] unwares: but all in vaine;
For who can shun the chance, that dest'ny doth ordaine?[10]

38   Lo, where beyond he lyeth languishing,
    Deadly engored of a great wilde Bore,
    And by his side the Goddesse groveling
    Makes for him endlesse mone, and evermore
    With her soft garment wipes away the gore,
    Which staynes his snowy skin with hatefull hew:[11]
    But when she saw no helpe might him restore,
    Him to a dainty flowre she did transmew,
Which in that cloth was wrought, as if it lively grew.

---

[1] **Beauperes:** peers, friends.

[2] **crafty spyes:** spying eyes.

[3] **daintie:** delightful; precious; choice.

[4] **Paunces:** pansies.

[5] **joyd:** enjoyed; had intercourse with.

[6] **bent:** inclined.

[7] **salvage:** savage; wild.

[8] **Dreadfull:** feeling dread of.

[9] **scath:** harm.

[10] An apt question for Britomart, as well.

[11] **hew:** hue.

39   So was that chamber clad in goodly wize,
        And rownd about it many beds were dight,[1]
        As whylome was the antique worldes guize,
        Some for untimely[2] ease, some for delight,
        As pleased them to use, that use it might:
        And all was full of Damzels, and of Squyres,
        Dauncing and reveling both day and night,
        And swimming deepe in sensuall desyres,
    And *Cupid* still[3] emongest them kindled lustfull fyres.

40   And all the while sweet Musicke did divide[4]
        Her looser notes with *Lydian* harmony;[5]
        And all the while sweet birdes thereto applide
        Their daintie[6] layes and dulcet melody,
        Ay caroling of love and jollity,
        That wonder was to heare their trim consort.[7]
        Which when those knights beheld, with scornefull eye,
        They sdeigned[8] such lascivious disport,
    And loath'd the loose demeanure[9] of that wanton sort.

41   Thence[10] they were brought to that great Ladies vew,
        Whom they found sitting on a sumptuous bed,
        That glistred all with gold and glorious shew,
        As the proud *Persian*[11] Queenes accustomed:
        She seemd a woman of great bountihed,
        And of rare beautie, saving that askaunce

---

[1] **dight:** made ready.

[2] **untimely:** at inappropriate times.

[3] **still:** constantly, always.

[4] **divide:** descant.

[5] **Lydian harmony:** musical mode used in ancient Greece and associated with effeminate sensuality.

[6] **daintie:** delightful.

[7] **trim consort:** well-arranged harmony.

[8] **sdeigned:** disdained.

[9] **demeanure:** demeanor.

[10] **Thence:** from there.

[11] Western Europe associated eastern regions with effeminate luxury. (For their part, and with some justification, Asia and the Arabic world often regarded Western Europe as boorish and crude.)

Her wanton eyes, ill signes of womanhed,
Did roll too highly,[1] and too often glaunce,
Without regard of grace, or comely amenaunce.[2]

42   Long worke it were, and needlesse to devize[3]
        Their goodly entertainement and great glee:
        She caused them be led in courteous wize
        Into a bowre, disarmed for to be,[4]
        And cheared well with wine and spiceree:
        The *Redcrosse* Knight was soone disarmed there,
        But the brave Mayd[5] would not disarmed bee,
        But onely vented up her umbriere,[6]
    And so did let her goodly visage to appere.[7]

43   As when fayre *Cynthia*,[8] in darkesome night,
        Is in a noyous[9] cloud enveloped,
        Where she may finde the substance thin and light,
        Breakes forth her silver beames, and her bright hed
        Discovers to the world discomfited;[10]
        Of the poore traveiler, that went astray,
        With thousand blessings she is heried;[11]
        Such was the beautie and the shining ray,
    With which fayre *Britomart* gave light unto the day.

---

[1] Rather than rolling her eyes in circles, the Lady is rolling them to the side, a come-hither look. Ideally, women were supposed to keep their eyes demurely cast down; Spenser's speaker praises his bride for doing so in *Epithalamion,* stanza 9.

[2] **amenaunce:** noble bearing.

[3] **devize:** describe.

[4] Allegorically, to doff one's armor is to let down one's guard.

[5] **Mayd:** virgin; unmarried woman (presumed virginal).

[6] **umbriere:** the hinged visor of a helmet, which covers the face when lowered.

[7] In this canto, Spenser skillfully plays allegorical resonance against practical experience. In stanzas 42 through 51, the poem remains committed to the allegorical signif-icance of Britomart's virtuously keeping on her armor of chastity, while at the same time leading us to smile at the image of her sitting down to a banquet in full armor, helmet and all. The latter image does not undercut the former so much as it complicates it: Britomart must learn that chastity is anything but a straightforward, easily deployed virtue.

[8] Cynthia is another name for Artemis, goddess of the moon, which was associated both with chastity and with earthly inconstancy. Spenser and Raleigh had both used the name Cynthia to praise Elizabeth.

[9] **noyous:** annoying.

[10] **Discovers:** discloses; **the world discomfited:** the world that had been robbed of comfort (while she was covered).

[11] **heried:** glorified.

44   And eke those six, which lately with her fought,
        Now were disarmd, and did them selves present
        Unto her vew, and company unsought;
        For they all seemed courteous and gent,
        And all sixe brethen, borne of one parent,
        Which had them traynd in all civilitee,
        And goodly taught to tilt and turnament;
        Now were they liegmen to this Ladie free,[1]
And her knights service ought, to hold of her in fee.[2]

45   The first of them by name *Gardante*[3] hight,
        A jolly[4] person, and of comely vew;
        The second was *Parlante*, a bold knight,
        And next to him *Jocante* did ensew;
        Basciante did him selfe most courteous shew;
        But fierce *Bacchante* seemd too fell and keene;
        And yett in armes[5] *Noctante* greater grew:
        All were faire knights, and goodly well beseene,[6]
But to faire *Britomart* they all but shadowes[7] beene.

46   For shee was full of amiable grace,
        And manly terror mixed therewithall,
        That as the one stird up affections bace,
        So th'other did mens rash desires apall,
        And hold them backe, that would in error fall;
        As hee, that hath espide a vermeill Rose,
        To which sharpe thornes and breres the way forstall,[8]
        Dare not for dread his hardy hand expose,
But wishing it far off, his ydle wish doth lose.

---

[1] **free:** bountiful and, unlike her knights, beholden to no one.

[2] **in fee:** feudal term designating the service that a knight owed to his lord or lady.

[3] The knights are named for the six stages of lechery: gazing, conversing, dallying, kissing, carousing, and keeping late nights.

[4] **jolly:** sprightly; gallant; brave; splendid; handsome; pleasant; lustful.

[5] **in armes:** punning on arms as armour and a lover's arms.

[6] **beseene:** nice to look at.

[7] **shadowes:** the word can mean shadows, illusions, ghosts, or reflections in a mirror. In the next canto, we see that Britomart herself has fallen in love with an image in a mirror.

[8] **forstall:** impede.

47   Whom when the Lady saw so faire a wight,
         All ignorant of her contrary[1] sex,
         (For shee her weend a fresh and lusty[2] knight)
         Shee greatly gan enamoured to wex,[3]
         And with vaine[4] thoughts her falsed fancy vex:
         Her fickle hart conceived hasty fyre,
         Like sparkes of fire, that fall in sclender flex,[5]
         That shortly brent[6] into extreme desyre,
    And ransackt all her veines with passion entyre.

48   Eftsoones[7] shee grew to great impatience
         And into termes of open outrage brust,[8]
         That plaine discovered her incontinence,[9]
         Ne reckt shee, who her meaning did mistrust;[10]
         For she was given all to fleshly lust,
         And poured forth[11] in sensuall delight,
         That all regard of shame she had discust,[12]
         And meet[13] respect of honor putt to flight:
    So shamelesse beauty soone becomes a loathly sight.

49   Faire Ladies, that to love captived arre,
         And chaste desires doe nourish in your mind,
         Let not her fault your sweete affections marre,
         Ne blott the bounty of all womankind;
         'Mongst thousands good one wanton Dame to find:
         Emongst the Roses grow some wicked weeds;
         For this was not to love, but lust inclind;
         For love does alwaies bring forth bounteous deeds
    And in each gentle hart desire of honor breeds.

---

[1] Contrary, that is, to the Lady's assumptions and desires.

[2] **lusty:** vigorous, but perhaps also lustful.

[3] **wex:** grow.

[4] **vaine:** empty, in vain.

[5] **sclender flex:** slender flax—presumably a field of dessicated, combustible material.

[6] **brent:** burned.

[7] **Eftsoones:** afterward; soon afterward.

[8] **brust:** burst.

[9] **incontinence:** lack of sexual temperance; lack of temperance in general.

[10] **mistrust:** suspect.

[11] Spenser consistently associates pouring forth with sexual looseness.

[12] **discust:** shaken off.

[13] **meet:** appropriate.

50   Nought so of love this looser Dame did skill,[1]
            But as a cole to kindle fleshly flame,
            Giving the bridle to her wanton will,
            And treading under foote her honest name:
            Such love is hate, and such desire is shame.
            Still did she rove at her[2] with crafty glaunce
            Of her false eies, that at her hart did ayme,
            And told her meaning in her countenaunce;
        But *Britomart* dissembled it with ignoraunce.[3]

51   Supper was shortly dight[4] and downe they satt,
            Where they were served with all sumptuous fare,
            Whiles fruitfull *Ceres,* and *Lyæus*[5] fatt
            Pourd out their plenty, without spight[6] or spare:
            Nought wanted there, that dainty[7] was and rare;
            And aye[8] the cups their bancks did overflow,
            And aye betweene the cups, she did prepare
            Way to her love, and secret darts did throw;
        But *Britomart* would not such guilfull message know.

52   So when they slaked had the fervent heat
            Of appetite with meates[9] of every sort,
            The Lady did faire *Britomart* entreat,
            Her to disarme, and with delightfull sport
            To loose her warlike limbs and strong effort,
            But when shee mote not thereunto be wonne,
            (For shee her sexe under that straunge purport
            Did use to hide, and plaine apparaunce shonne:)[10]
        In playner wise to tell her grievaunce she[11] begonne.

---

[1] **skill:** have knowledge.

[2] **at her:** at Britomart.

[3] Britomart pretends not to notice that her hostess is burning with love.

[4] **dight:** prepared.

[5] *Ceres:* goddess of grain; **Lyæus:** god of wine.

[6] **spight:** grudge.

[7] **dainty:** precious; choice.

[8] **aye:** constantly, always.

[9] **meates:** food.

[10] Britomart will not disarm, because she still wants everyone to believe she is a man.

[11] The Lady—though this is one of the passages in which Spenser bounces us from pronoun to pronoun until we must fight to keep our place. Here, the confused pronouns might make us wonder whether the distinction that the narrator is making between the two women is, after all, absolute.

53   And all attonce discovered her desire
           With sighes, and sobs, and plaints, and piteous griefe,
           The outward sparkes of her inburning fire;
           Which spent in vaine, at last she told her briefe,
           That but if[1] she did lend her short reliefe,
           And doe her comfort, she mote algates[2] dye.
           But the chaste damzell, that had never priefe[3]
           Of such malengine[4] and fine forgerye,
       Did easely beleeve her strong extremitye.

54   Full easy was for her to have beliefe,
           Who by self-feeling of her feeble sexe,
           And by long triall of the inward griefe,
           Wherewith imperious love her hart did vexe,
           Could judge what paines doe loving harts perplexe.[5]
           Who meanes no guile, be-guiled soonest shall,
           And to faire semblaunce doth light faith annexe;
           The bird, that knowes not the false fowlers call,
       Into his hidden nett full easely doth fall.

55   For thy[6] she would not in discourteise wise,
           Scorne the faire offer of good will profest;
           For great rebuke it is, love to despise,
           Or rudely sdeigne a gentle harts request;
           But with faire countenaunce, as beseemed best,
           Her entertaynd; nath'lesse shee inly deemd
           Her love too light, to wooe a wandring guest:
           Which she misconstruing, thereby esteemd
       That from like inward fire that outward smoke had steemd.[7]

---

[1] **but if:** unless.

[2] **her comfort:** satisfy her desire; **algates:** at any rate.

[3] **priefe:** experience.

[4] **malengine:** evil machination.

[5] It is easy for Britomart to believe that the Lady is burning with the same sort of love that Britomart feels (for someone else). Thus Britomart's very innocence makes her vulnerable to the Lady's lustful plotting.

[6] **For thy:** therefore.

[7] As befits a courtly knight, Britomart does not insult the Lady by refusing her outright; and even though Britomart privately considers the Lady too forward, Britomart's own experiences with burning love make her believe that the Lady's intentions match her own chaste ones. The picture of Britomart's innocence is complicated, however, by Britomart's dissembling in this passage (pretending to be a man) and by her inability in the following canto to understand the moral status of her own erotic desires.

56   Therewith a while she her flit[1] fancy fedd,
            Till she mote winne fit time for her desire,
            But yet her wound still inward freshly bledd,
            And through her bones the false instilled fire
            Did spred it selfe, and venime close inspire.
            Tho[2] were the tables taken all away,
            And every knight, and every gentle Squire
            Gan choose his dame with *Bascimano*[3] gay,
        With whom he ment to make his sport and courtly play.

57   Some fell to daunce, some fel to hazardry,[4]
            Some to make love, some to make meryment,
            As diverse witts to diverse things apply;
            And all the while faire *Malecasta*[5] bent
            Her crafty engins[6] to her close intent.
            By this th'eternall lampes,[7] wherewith high *Jove*
            Doth light the lower world, were halfe yspent,
            And the moist daughters of huge *Atlas*[8] strove
        Into the *Ocean* deepe to drive their weary drove.

58   High time it seemed then for everie wight
            Them to betake unto their kindly rest;
            Eftesoones long waxen torches weren light,
            Unto their bowres to guyden every guest:
            Tho when the Britonesse saw all the rest
            Avoided quite, she gan her selfe despoile,[9]

---

[1] **she:** the Lady's, but the pronouns are doing a dance; **flit:** fleeting, inconstant.

[2] **Tho:** then.

[3] *Bascimano:* Italian *bascio le mani,* kissing the hands.

[4] **hazardry:** playing at dice.

[5] *Malecasta:* for the first time, we read the Lady's name; it means, in Italian, "badly chaste." Although Spenser often waits to reveal a character's name until we have begun to figure out from the character's actions what sort of virtues or vices he or she embodies, more development of the character often follows. In this case, we know by now just how bad Malecasta is. The critical question is whether this evil portrait is sharpened by the remainder of this canto, or whether her nature becomes less clear.

[6] **engins:** machinations.

[7] **lampes:** stars.

[8] **moist daughters of huge *Atlas:*** the Hyades, a group of stars traditionally thought to bring rain.

[9] **Avoided:** having exited the room; **despoile:** undress. This is the word most often used to describe taking a foe's armor as a trophy after killing him. Allegorically, she is letting down her guard.

And safe committ to her soft fethered nest,
Wher through long watch, and late daies weary toile,
She soundly slept, and carefull thoughts did quite assoile.[1]

59   Now whenas all the world in silence deepe
      Yshrowded was, and every mortall wight
      Was drowned in the depth of deadly sleepe,[2]
      Faire *Malecasta*, whose engrieved spright[3]
      Could find no rest in such perplexed plight,
      Lightly arose out of her wearie bed,
      And under the blacke vele of guilty Night,
      Her with a scarlott mantle covered,
    That was with gold and Ermines[4] faire enveloped.

60   Then panting soft, and trembling every joynt,
      Her fearfull feete towards the bowre she mov'd.
      Where she for secret purpose did appoynt
      To lodge the warlike maide[5] unwisely loov'd,
      And to her bed approching, first she proov'd,[6]
      Whether she slept or wakte, with her softe hand
      She softely felt, if any member[7] moov'd,
      And lent her wary eare to understand,
    If any puffe of breath, or signe of sence shee fond.

61   Which whenas none she fond, with easy shifte,[8]
      For feare least her unwares she should abrayd,[9]
      Th'embroderd quilt she lightly up did lifte,

---

[1] **assoile:** set free. The passage is also peripherally informed by other meanings of the word: to acquit; to absolve.

[2] The round vowels and liquid consonants convey the drowsy mood.

[3] **spright:** spirit.

[4] Ermines were emblems both of chastity and of sexual incontinence; Spenser uses them in both senses in Britomart's book. Ermines were traditionally worn by royalty, and they had become especially associated with the Virgin Queen.

[5] **maide:** virgin; unmarried woman (presumed virginal).

[6] **proov'd:** tested.

[7] **member:** limb, but with the obvious double entendre. Malecasta is afraid the knight will move his limbs at her touch, awaken, and wish her gone; but Malecasta wouldn't mind if the knight's specifically male member were to move, signifying the knight's desire for her to stay. The eroticism of this passage comes partly from the heterosexual image in Malecasta's head and partly from an entirely hypothetical image available only to us: that of the female Britomart waking and feeling lust for the female Malecasta. We know this will not happen, but Spenser teases us to imagine it.

[8] **easy shifte:** careful motion.

[9] **abrayd:** startle.

And by her side her selfe she softly layd,
Of every finest fingers touch affrayd;
Ne any noise she made, ne word she spake,
But inly sigh'd.[1] At last the royall Mayd
Out of her quiet slomber did awake,
And chaungd her weary side,[2] the better ease to take.

62   Where feeling one close couched by her side,
    She lightly lept out of her filed[3] bedd,
    And to her weapon ran, in minde to gride[4]
    The loathed leachour. But the Dame[5] halfe dedd
    Through suddein feare and ghastly drerihedd,[6]
    Did shrieke alowd, that through the hous it rong,
    And the whole family therewith adredd,
    Rashly out of their rouzed couches[7] sprong,
And to the troubled chamber all in armes did throng.

63   And those six knights that ladies Champions,
    And eke the *Redcrosse* knight ran to the stownd,
    Halfe armd and halfe unarmd, with them attons:[8]
    Where when confusedly they came, they fownd
    Their lady lying on the sencelesse grownd;
    On thother side, they saw the warlike Mayd
    Al in her snow-white smocke,[9] with locks unbownd,
    Threatning the point of her avenging blaed,
That with so troublous terror they were all dismayd.[10]

64   About their Ladye first they flockt arownd,
    Whom having laid in comfortable couch,
    Shortly they reard out of her frosen swownd;[11]
    And afterwardes they gan with fowle reproch

---

[1] The stanza slows to a quiet halt, the calm before the storm.

[2] I.e., turned over.

[3] **filed:** defiled.

[4] **gride:** pierce through.

[5] **Dame:** Malecasta.

[6] **drerihedd:** dreariness.

[7] **rouzed couches:** Spenser is a master of transferred epithets: "wearie bed," "guilty Night," "rouzed couches," "sencelesse grownd."

[8] **attons:** all at once

[9] **smocke:** though no longer in her armor of chastity, Britomart still wears a virginal white smock (an undergarment used by both sexes as sleeping attire).

[10] **dismayd:** defeated; appalled; discouraged. But again, the word puns on "dis-maid."

[11] **swownd:** swoon.

To stirre up strife, and troublous contecke[1] broch:
But by ensample of the last dayes losse,
None of them rashly durst to her approch,
Ne in so glorious spoile themselves embosse,[2]
Her succourd eke the Champion of the bloody Crosse.[3]

65   But one of those six knights, *Gardante* hight,
Drew out a deadly bow and arrow keene,
Which forth he sent with felonous despight,
And fell intent against the virgin sheene:[4]
The mortall steele stayd not, till it was seene
To gore her side, yet was the wound not deepe,
But lightly rased[5] her soft silken skin,
That drops of purple blood thereout did weepe,
Which did her lilly smock with staines of vermeil steep.[6]

66   Wherewith enrag'd, she fiercely at them flew,
And with her flaming sword about her layd,
That none of them foule mischiefe could eschew,[7]
But with her dreadfull strokes were all dismayd:
Here, there, and every where about her swayd
Her wrathfull steele, that none mote it abyde;
And eke the *Redcrosse* knight gave her good ayd,
Ay joyning foot to foot, and syde to syde,
That in short space their foes they have quite terrifyde.

67   Tho[8] whenas all were put to shamefull flight,
The noble *Britomartis* her arayd,

---

[1] **contecke:** contention.

[2] **spoile:** booty; **embosse:** cover themselves (in the glory of conquering her virginity).

[3] Redcrosse comes to her aid.

[4] **sheene:** shining, gorgeous.

[5] **rased:** grazed.

[6] The plot eventually makes it clear that Britomart has not actually lost her virginity, but this wound, however slight, is clearly sexual. As the next canto will show, Spenser's ideas of chastity can accommodate both erotic desire and the emotional wounds that result from such desire. Critics debate the extent to which Spenser wants us to imagine any fault in Britomart's responses to Malecasta's invasion of her bed. In a world in which virginity is considered an unmarried woman's most precious commodity, is Britomart to be commended for her vigorous defense of her person, or are we meant to smile at her naïve belief that Malecasta is utterly monstrous? And what is the relationship of this wound to Adonis's wound—or to Amoret's wounds in xii.19–21 and IV.vii.27?

[7] **eschew:** escape.

[8] **Tho:** then.

And her bright armes about her body dight:
For nothing would she lenger there be stayd,
Where so loose life, and so ungentle trade[1]
Was usd of knights and Ladies seeming gent:
So earely ere the grosse Earthes gryesy[2] shade,
Was all disperst out of the firmament,
They tooke their steeds, and forth upon their journey went.

---

[1] **ungentle trade:** interactions inappropriate for gentlemen and gentlewomen.

[2] **gryesy:** gray and grim.

Canto Two

The Redcrosse knight to Britomart
describeth Artegall:
The wondrous myrrhour, by which she
in love with him did fall.

1   Here have I cause, in men just blame to find,
        That in their proper[1] praise too partiall bee,
        And not indifferent[2] to woman kind,
        To whom no share in armes and chevalree,
        They doe impart, ne maken memoree
        Of their brave gestes[3] and prowesse martiall;
        Scarse doe they spare to one or two or three,[4]
        Rowme in their writtes; yet the same writing small[5]
    Does all their deedes deface, and dims their glories all,

2   But by record of antique times I finde,
        That wemen wont in warres to beare most sway,
        And to all great exploites them selves inclind:
        Of which they still the girlond[6] bore away,
        Till envious Men fearing their rules decay,
        Gan coyne streight[7] lawes to curb their liberty,
        Yet sith they warlike armes have laide away,
        They have exceld in artes and pollicy,[8]
    That now we foolish men that prayse gin[9] eke t'envy.

3   Of warlike puissaunce in ages spent,[10]
        Be thou faire *Britomart*, whose prayse I wryte,
        But of all wisedom bee thou precedent,

---

[1] **proper:** own.

[2] **indifferent:** impartial.

[3] **gestes:** exploits; stories about their exploits.

[4] One thinks of Penthesilea and Camilla in Virgil's *Aeneid*, of Bradamante in Ariosto's *Orlando Furioso*, and of Clorinda in Tasso's *Gerusalemme Liberata*.

[5] **writtes:** writings; **small:** the same sparse treatment; the same belittling treatment.

[6] **girlond:** the victor's wreath.

[7] **streight:** strait, restrictively narrow.

[8] **pollicy:** government.

[9] **gin:** begin.

[10] **spent:** passed.

O soveraine Queene,[1] whose prayse I would endyte,
  Endite I would as dewtie doth excyte;
  But ah my rymes too rude and rugged arre,
  When in so high an object they doe lyte,
  And striving, fit to make,[2] I feare doe marre:
Thy selfe thy prayses tell, and make them knowen farre.

4 She traveiling with *Guyon*[3] by the way,
    Of sondry thinges faire purpose[4] gan to find,
    T'abridg their journey long, and lingring day;
    Mongst which it fell into that Fairies[5] mind,
    To aske this Briton Maid, what uncouth wind,
    Brought her into those partes, and what inquest[6]
    Made her dissemble her disguised kind:[7]
    Faire Lady she him seemd, like Lady drest,
But fairest knight alive, when armed was her brest.

5 Thereat she sighing softly, had no powre
    To speake a while, ne ready answere make,
    But with hart-thrilling throbs and bitter stowre,[8]
    As if she had a fever fitt, did quake,
    And every daintie limbe with horrour shake,
    And ever and anone the rosy red,
    Flasht through her face, as it had beene a flake[9]
    Of lightning, through bright heven fulmined;[10]
At last the passion past she thus him answered.

6 "Faire Sir, I let you weete,[11] that from the howre
    I taken was from nourses tender pap,[12]
    I have beene trained up in warlike stowre,
    To tossen speare and shield, and to affrap[13]

---

[1] **soveraine Queene:** Elizabeth I, for whom *The Faerie Queene* is an elaborate compliment.

[2] Poets were sometimes called "makers."

[3] **She:** Britomart; *Guyon:* this name is clearly an error for "Redcrosse."

[4] **purpose:** conversation.

[5] **Fairies:** Redcrosse's.

[6] **inquest:** quest, with the implication that Britomart's quest is an inner one.

[7] **kind:** sex (female).

[8] **thrilling:** piercing; **stowre:** tumult.

[9] **flake:** flash.

[10] **fulmined:** flashed forth.

[11] **I let you weete:** I'll let you know.

[12] **pap:** breast (that of a wet nurse).

[13] **affrap:** strike. This is one of Spenser's wonderfully backward-looking neologisms —more Chaucerian than Elizabethan, yet new to the world. He is thinking of the Italian *affrappare*, but his version is sturdily Anglo-Saxon in sound.

The warlike ryder to his most mishap;[1]
Sithence I loathed have my life to lead,
As Ladies wont, in pleasures wanton lap,
To finger the fine needle and nyce[2] thread;
Me lever were[3] with point of foemans speare be dead.

7   "All my delight on deedes of armes is sett,
    To hunt out perilles and adventures hard,
    By sea, by land, where so they may be mett,
    Onely for honour and for high regard,
    Without respect of richesse or reward.
    For such intent into these partes I came,
    Withouten compasse, or withouten card,
    Far fro my native soyle, that is by name
The greater *Brytayne*,[4] here to seeke for praise and fame.

8   "Fame blazed hath, that here in Faery lond
    Doe many famous knightes and Ladies wonne,[5]
    And many straunge adventures to bee fond,
    Of which great worth and worship[6] may be wonne;
    Which I to prove, this voyage have begonne.
    But mote I weet[7] of you, right courteous knight,
    Tydings of one, that hath unto me donne
    Late foule dishonour and reprochfull spight,[8]
The which I seeke to wreake, and *Arthegall*[9] he hight."

---

[1] **mishap:** misfortune.

[2] **nyce:** fine, with ironic overtones of uselessness.

[3] **Me lever were:** I would rather.

[4] **greater *Brytayne*:** to distinguish it from the lesser Britain, i.e., Brittany (a region of France). Here, the term refers to Wales (rather than to England or to all of the territory formerly inhabited by the Britons).

[5] **wonne:** dwell.

[6] **worship:** admiration.

[7] **weet:** learn.

[8] Doing dishonor to a male knight can mean any of a number of things; however, now that Redcrosse knows Britomart is a woman (having seen her in her smock in Malecasta's house), her claim that Artegall has done her dishonor can mean only one of two things: that he tried to rape her or that he succeeded in doing so. As the next stanza indicates, she is lying here, and indeed, her whole account of her childhood is a lie. Spenser deftly manages the psychological nuances of this passage, reminding us of just how much Britomart still has to learn: she is like a fifth-grader who declares largely that she hates boys, especially that particular boy—just so she can have the excuse to say that boy's name. Then again, there is a large element of truth in Britomart's story, given that the image of Artegall has erotically penetrated and wounded her heart. We learn the details of this wounding in stanzas 22 through 39; see especially 29 through 39.

[9] ***Arthegall:*** also spelled "Artegall." His name includes elements of "Arthur" (implying a relationship to, though not identity with, Prince Arthur) and of "equality"

9   The word gone out, she backe againe would call,
      As her repenting so to have missayd,
      But that he it uptaking ere the fall,
      Her shortly answered; "Faire martiall Mayd
      Certes ye misavised beene, t'upbrayd,
      A gentle[1] knight with so unknightly blame:
      For weet ye well of all, that ever playd
      At tilt or tourney, or like warlike game,
    The noble *Arthegall* hath ever borne the name.[2]

10   "For thy[3] great wonder were it, if such shame
      Should ever enter in his bounteous thought,
      Or ever doe, that[4] mote deserven blame:
      The noble corage[5] never weeneth ought,
      That may unworthy of it selfe be thought.
      Therefore, faire Damzell, be ye well aware,
      Least[6] that too farre ye have your sorrow sought:
      You and your countrey both I wish welfare,[7]
    And honour both; for each of other worthy are."

11   The royall Maid woxe inly wondrous glad,
      To heare her Love so highly magnifyde,
      And joyd that ever she affixed had,
      Her hart on knight so goodly glorifyde,
      How ever finely[8] she it faind to hyde:
      The loving mother, that nine monethes did beare,
      In the deare closett[9] of her painefull syde,
      Her tender babe, it seeing safe appeare,
    Doth not so much rejoyce, as she rejoyced theare.[10]

(since he will turn out to be the hero of the Book of Justice, Book Five). Spenser also signals the couple's appropriateness for each other by beginning Artegall's name where Britomart's ends, with "art."

[1] **gentle:** noble, virtuous.

[2] I.e., for understand this well, that from all challengers who ever played in any tournament, the noble Artegall has always won the prize. Here Redcrosse equates martial prowess with moral goodness, implying that no one so courageous in tournaments could be so low as to commit a rape.

[3] **For thy:** therefore.

[4] **that:** that which.

[5] **corage:** heart as the seat of emotion and thought, but with puns on the meanings "sexual vigor" and "lust."

[6] **Least:** lest.

[7] **welfare:** fare well.

[8] **finely:** cleverly.

[9] **closett:** private room; womb.

[10] After months of wondering whether Artegall is merely a figment of her own imagination, Britomart is relieved to see

12   But to occasion him to further talke,
        To feed her humor with his pleasing style,
        Her list in stryfull termes with him to balke,[1]
        And thus replyde, "How ever, Sir, ye fyle[2]
        Your courteous tongue, his prayses to compyle,
        It ill beseemes a knight of gentle sort,
        Such as ye have him boasted, to beguyle
        A simple maide, and worke so hainous tort,
    In shame of knighthood, as I largely can report.

13   "Let bee therefore my vengeaunce to disswade,
        And read, where I that faytour[3] false may find."
        "Ah, but if reason faire might you perswade,
        To slake your wrath, and mollify your mind,"
        (Said he) "perhaps ye should it better find:
        For hardie thing it is, to weene by might,
        That man to hard conditions to bind,
        Or ever hope to match in equall fight,
    Whose prowesse paragone saw never living wight.

14   "Ne soothlich is it easie for to read,[4]
        Where now on earth, or how he may be fownd;
        For he ne wonneth in one certeine stead,[5]
        But restlesse walketh all the world arownd,
        Ay[6] doing thinges, that to his fame redownd,
        Defending Ladies cause, and Orphans right,
        Where so he heares, that any[7] doth confownd
        Them comfortlesse, through tyranny or might;
    So is his soveraine[8] honour raisde to hevens hight."

---

that he exists outside of her, as proven by the fact that Redcrosse knows him. Artegall appears to readers by degrees, as well: we catch hints of him in Canto One (blurred by their uncertain reflection in Malecasta's version of desire), and we hear certainly of his existence here, but it will be several more stanzas before we can even begin to understand who he is or how Britomart knows about him.

[1] **to balke:** to object to his arguments.

[2] **fyle:** moral pamphlets often accused seducers and confidence men of metaphorically filing their tongues to make smooth talk.

[3] **read:** inform me; **faytour:** impostor.

[4] **soothlich:** truly, forsooth; **read:** find out.

[5] **ne wonneth:** does not dwell; **stead:** place.

[6] **Ay:** always.

[7] **any:** anyone.

[8] **soveraine:** excellent.

15　His feeling wordes her feeble sence much pleased,
　　　　And softly sunck into her molten hart;
　　　　Hart that is inly hurt, is greatly eased
　　　　With hope of thing, that may allegge his[1] smart;
　　　　For pleasing wordes are like to Magick art,
　　　　That doth the charmed Snake in slomber lay:
　　　　Such secrete ease felt gentle *Britomart,*
　　　　Yet list the same efforce with faind gainesay;[2]
　　So dischord ofte in Musick makes the sweeter lay.[3]

16　And sayd, "Sir knight, these ydle termes forbeare,
　　　　And sith it is uneath[4] to finde his haunt,
　　　　Tell me some markes, by which he may appeare,
　　　　If chaunce I him encounter paravaunt;[5]
　　　　For perdy[6] one shall other slay, or daunt:
　　　　What shape, what shield, what armes, what steed, what stedd,[7]
　　　　And what so else his person most may vaunt?"[8]
　　　　All which the *Redcrosse* knight to point aredd,[9]
　　And him in everie part before her fashioned.

17　Yet him in everie part before she knew,
　　　　How ever list her now her knowledge fayne,[10]
　　　　Sith him whylome[11] in *Brytayne* she did vew,
　　　　To her revealed in a mirrhour playne,
　　　　Whereof did grow her first engraffed[12] payne,
　　　　Whose root and stalke so bitter yet did taste,
　　　　That but[13] the fruit more sweetnes did contayne,
　　　　Her wretched dayes in dolour she mote waste,
　　And yield the pray[14] of love to lothsome death at last.

---

[1] **allegge:** alleviate; **his:** its.

[2] I.e., yet wanted to struggle against that secret sense of relief by pretending that she did not feel it.

[3] **lay:** song.

[4] **uneath:** difficult.

[5] **paravaunt:** by chance.

[6] **perdy:** by God.

[7] **stedd:** mark, as for example an heraldic device.

[8] **vaunt:** proudly show.

[9] **to point:** precisely; **aredd:** explained.

[10] **fayne:** feign.

[11] **whylome:** while.

[12] **engraffed:** engrafted.

[13] **but:** unless.

[14] **pray:** prey.

18 By straunge occasion[1] she did him behold,
    And much more straungely gan to love his sight,
    As it in bookes hath written beene of old.
    In *Deheubarth* that now South-wales is hight,
    What time king *Ryence*[2] raign'd, and dealed right,
    The great Magitien *Merlin*[3] had deviz'd,
    By his deepe science, and hell-dreaded might,
    A looking glasse, right wondrously aguiz'd,[4]
  Whose vertues through the wyde worlde soone were solemniz'd.

19 It vertue had, to shew in perfect sight,
    What ever thing was in the world contaynd,
    Betwixt the lowest earth and hevens hight,
    So that[5] it to the looker appertaynd;
    What ever foe had wrought, or frend had faynd,
    Therein discovered was, ne ought[6] mote pas,
    Ne ought in secret from the same remaynd;
    For thy[7] it round and hollow shaped was,
  Like to the world it selfe, and seemd a world of glas.

20 Who wonders not, that reades[8] so wonderous worke?
    But who does wonder, that has red the Towre,
    Wherein th'Aegyptian *Phao*[9] long did lurke
    From all mens vew, that none might her discovre,
    Yet she might all men vew out of her bowre?

---

[1] **occasion:** circumstance.

[2] *Ryence:* Britomart's father. In Malory's *Le Morte D'Arthur,* King Ryons of North Wales trims a cloak with the beards of other kings, signifying that he has robbed them of their manhood (1.26).

[3] *Merlin:* in Arthurian legend and in Geoffrey of Monmouth's history, Merlin uses his knowledge of the art of magic to help King Uther Pendragon and his son, the famous Arthur. Among other feats, Merlin brings the stones to Stonehenge and makes the Round Table for Uther's knights. Merlin's name may have originated from Myrddhin, a semilegendary Welsh bard.

[4] **looking glasse:** called "*Venus* looking glas" at i.8.9. It is described in two ways: first as a mirror, then as a crystal ball. Queen Elizabeth regularly consulted an astrologer, John Dee, who used a crystal ball that is now in the British Museum; **aguiz'd:** guised, fashioned.

[5] **So that:** so long as, with the proviso that.

[6] **discovered:** disclosed; **ought:** aught, anything.

[7] **For thy:** because.

[8] **reades:** sees—but with a pun on reading a text. Spenser's poem, like Merlin's crystal ball, is a prophetic world in miniature.

[9] *Phao:* her name comes from the Greek verb meaning "to shine." See next note.

Great *Ptolomæe* it for his lemans[1] sake
Ybuilded all of glasse, by Magicke powre,
And also it impregnable did make;
Yet when his love was false, he with a peaze[2] it brake.

21 Such was the glassy globe that *Merlin* made,
  And gave unto king *Ryence* for his gard,
  That never foes his kingdome might invade,
  But he it knew at home before he hard[3]
  Tydings thereof, and so them still debar'd.[4]
  It was a famous Present for a Prince,
  And worthy worke of infinite reward,
  That treasons could bewray, and foes convince;[5]
Happy this Realme, had[6] it remayned ever since.

22 One day it fortuned, fayre *Britomart*
  Into her fathers closet[7] to repayre;
  For nothing he from her reserv'd apart,
  Being his onely daughter and his hayre:[8]
  Where when she had espyde that mirrhour fayre,
  Her selfe awhile therein she vewd in vaine;
  Tho her avizing[9] of the vertues rare,
  Which thereof spoken were, she gan againe
Her to bethinke of, that[10] mote to her selfe pertaine.

23 But as it falleth,[11] in the gentlest harts
  Imperious Love hath highest set his throne,
  And tyrannizeth in the bitter smarts
  Of them, that to him buxome are and prone:[12]

---

[1] *Ptolomæe:* second-century Greek astronomer in Alexandria, who experimented with optics to explore the properties of light. Spenser imagines that Ptolemy had a beloved, Phao, for whom he built a glass tower—the magical optics of which allowed her to see out while preventing others from seeing in; **lemans:** beloved's.

[2] **peaze:** strong blow.

[3] **But he it knew:** but that he would know it; **hard:** heard.

[4] **still debar'd:** always barred their way.

[5] **bewray:** disclose; **convince:** prove guilty.

[6] **had:** if it had.

[7] **closet:** private room.

[8] **hayre:** heir.

[9] **avizing:** reminding herself.

[10] **that:** whatever.

[11] **falleth:** happens.

[12] **buxome:** favorable, welcoming; morally easy to bend; **prone:** inclined. The sexual overtones of these two terms in combination may be more evident to modern readers

So thought this Mayd (as maydens use to done)
Whom fortune for her husband would allot,
Not that she lusted after any one;[1]
For she was pure from blame of sinfull blot,[2]
Yet wist her life at last must lincke in that same knot.[3]

24 Eftsoones there was presented to her eye
    A comely knight, all arm'd in complete wize,
    Through whose bright ventayle[4] lifted up on hye
    His manly face, that did his foes agrize,[5]
    And frends to termes of gentle truce entize,
    Lookt foorth, as *Phœbus* face out of the east,
    Betwixt two shady mountaynes doth arize;
    Portly[6] his person was, and much increast
Through his Heroicke grace, and honorable gest.[7]

25 His crest was covered with a couchant[8] Hownd,
    And all his armour seemd of antique mould,[9]
    But wondrous massy and assured sownd,
    And round about yfretted[10] all with gold,
    In which there written was with cyphres[11] old,
    "Achilles armes, which Arthogall did win."

---

than to those in the sixteenth century, when "buxom" had barely begun to acquire the additional meanings "full of health . . . well-favored, plump and comely" (OED a4).

[1] **any one:** any particular person.

[2] Sixteenth-century England was less repressive about women's sexuality than was, say, England during the Victorian period. Romantic comedies celebrated unmarried women's ability to love, even though such ability was generally couched in terms of its transgressive nature. According to many moral pamphlets, however, a woman was not supposed to feel erotic longing until after marriage—at which point it was actually thought necessary for her to experience sexual climax in order to conceive a child.

In this canto, Spenser raises questions about how we can define ideal chastity. Ultimately, he envisions chastity as a dynamic series of interactions with others and with oneself, rather than as a fixed state of mind and body.

[3] **knot:** marriage union.

[4] **ventayle:** visor and/or lower part of the helmet.

[5] **agrize:** cause to shudder.

[6] **Portly:** carried with dignity.

[7] **gest:** bearing.

[8] **couchant:** in heraldry, signifies an animal crouching and ready to pounce.

[9] **mould:** pattern, style.

[10] **yfretted:** ornamentally interlaced.

[11] **cyphres:** letters.

And on his shield enveloped sevenfold
He bore a crowned litle Ermilin,[1]
That deckt the azure field with her fayre pouldred[2] skin.

26   The Damzell well did vew his Personage,
    And liked well, ne further fastned not,[3]
    But went her way; ne her unguilty age
    Did weene, unwares, that her unlucky lot
    Lay hidden in the bottome of the pot;
    Of hurt unwist most daunger doth redound:
    But the false Archer,[4] which that arrow shot
    So slyly, that she did not feele the wound,
Did smyle full smoothly at her weetlesse[5] wofull stound.

27   Thenceforth the fether in her lofty crest,[6]
    Ruffed of love, gan lowly to availe,[7]
    And her prowd portaunce, and her princely gest,[8]
    With which she earst[9] tryumphed, now did quaile:
    Sad, solemne, sowre, and full of fancies fraile
    She woxe;[10] yet wist she nether how, nor why,
    She wist not, silly Mayd, what she did aile,[11]
    Yet wist, she was not well at ease perdy,
Yet thought it was not love, but some melancholy.[12]

28   So soone as Night had with her pallid[13] hew
    Defaste[14] the beautie of the shyning skye,
    And reft from men the worldes desired vew,
    She with her Nourse[15] adowne to sleepe did lye;
    But sleepe full far away from her did fly:
    In stead thereof sad sighes, and sorrowes deepe

---

[1] **Ermilin:** see i.59.n.

[2] **pouldred:** powdered (white).

[3] **ne further fastned not:** thought no more of him (at least not consciously).

[4] **Archer:** Cupid.

[5] **weetlesse:** unwitting.

[6] **crest:** (on her helmet).

[7] **Ruffed of:** ruffled by; **availe:** droop.

[8] **portaunce:** carriage, mien; **gest:** bearing.

[9] **earst:** previously.

[10] **woxe:** waxed, grew.

[11] **silly:** helpless; innocent; **what she did aile:** what ailed her.

[12] **melancholy:** the early modern medical term for depression, supposed to be characteristic of lovers and of poets.

[13] **pallid:** pale.

[14] **Defaste:** defaced.

[15] In the richer families, a woman who nursed the children while they were young might remain as a companion and upper servant in later years.

Kept watch and ward[1] about her warily,
That nought she did but wayle, and often steepe
Her dainty couch with teares, which closely[2] she did weepe.

29   And if that any drop of slombring rest
        Did chaunce to still[3] into her weary spright,
        When feeble nature felt her selfe opprest,
        Streight way with dreames, and with fantastick sight
        Of dreadfull things the same was put to flight,
        That oft out of her bed she did astart,
        As one with vew of ghastly feends affright:
        Tho gan she to renew her former smart,
And thinke of that fayre visage, written in her hart.

30   One night, when she was tost with such unrest,
        Her aged Nourse, whose name was *Glauce*[4] hight,
        Feeling her leape out of her loathed nest,
        Betwixt her feeble armes her quickly keight,[5]
        And downe againe her in her warme bed dight;
        "Ah my deare daughter, ah my dearest dread,[6]
        What uncouth[7] fit" (sayd she) "what evill plight
        Hath thee opprest, and with sad drearyhead
Chaunged thy lively cheare, and living made thee dead?[8]

31   "For not of nought these suddein ghastly feares
        All night afflict thy naturall repose,
        And all the day, when as thine equall peares,
        Their fit disports with faire delight doe chose,
        Thou in dull corners doest thy selfe inclose,
        Ne tastest Princes[9] pleasures, ne doest spred

---

[1] **ward:** guard.

[2] **couch:** bed; **closely:** privately.

[3] **still:** distil.

[4] *Glauce:* the name resembles the Greek words for "gray" and for "owl" (a bird emblematic of the warrior goddess Minerva). It is also one name for the goddess Diana's mother.

[5] **keight:** caught.

[6] **my dearest dread:** this lovely phrase conveys Glauce's competing feelings: she is in awe of Britomart, who is, after all, her mistress; but she also loves Britomart

protectively, fearing that harm might come to her.

[7] **uncouth:** unknown, mysterious.

[8] **living made thee dead:** made you, while yet living, look deathly.

[9] **Princes:** those of rulers. A Prince could be either male or female; Queen Elizabeth was called a Prince. Glauce means that Britomart has not been availing herself of the privileged leisure and entertainments that are hers by right of her royal birth. Nonetheless, there is a hint of a double entendre: the idea that Britomart has not been

Abroad thy fresh youths fayrest flowre, but lose
Both leafe and fruite, both too untimely shed,
As one in wilfull bale[1] for ever buried.

32   "The time,[2] that mortall men their weary cares
      Do lay away, and all wilde beastes do rest,
      And every river eke his[3] course forbeares,
      Then doth this wicked evill thee infest,
      And rive with thousand throbs thy thrilled[4] brest;
      Like an huge *Aetn'*[5] of deepe engulfed gryefe,
      Sorrow is heaped in thy hollow chest,
    Whence foorth it breakes in sighes and anguish ryfe,
As smoke and sulphure mingled with confused stryfe.

33   "Ay me, how much I feare, least love it bee,[6]
      But if that love it be, as sure I read
      By knowen signes and passions, which I see,
      Be it worthy of thy race[7] and royall sead,
      Then I avow by this most sacred head
      Of my deare foster childe, to ease thy griefe,
      And win thy will: Therefore away doe[8] dread;
      For death nor daunger from thy dew reliefe
Shall me debarre; tell me therefore my liefest liefe."[9]

34 So having sayd, her twixt her armes twaine
      Shee streightly straynd, and colled tenderly,[10]
      And every trembling joynt, and every vaine
      Shee softly felt, and rubbed busily,
      To doe the frosen cold away to fly;
      And her faire deawy eies with kisses deare
      Shee ofte did bathe, and ofte againe did dry;
      And ever her importund, not to feare
To let the secret of her hart to her appeare.

---

tasting the joys of disporting herself with male princes.

[1] **bale:** torment; evil.

[2] **The time:** i.e., nighttime.

[3] **his:** its.

[4] **rive:** cleave; **thrilled:** penetrated, pierced.

[5] *Aetn':* Aetna, volcano.

[6] **least:** lest. Glauce gives no indication of thinking that love is wrong, but she knows that it causes pain.

[7] **race:** lineage.

[8] **win thy will:** help you achieve your desire; **away doe:** do away with.

[9] **liefest liefe:** dearest dear.

[10] I.e., tightly held and hugged tenderly.

35   The Damzell pauzd, and then thus fearfully;
        "Ah Nurse, what needeth thee to eke[1] my paine?
        Is not enough, that I alone doe dye,
        But it must doubled bee with death of twaine?
        For nought for me, but death there doth remaine."
        "O daughter deare" (said she) "despeire no whit,
        For never sore, but might[2] a salve obtaine:
        That blinded God, which hath ye blindly smit,
Another arrow hath your lovers hart to hit."

36   "But mine is not" (quoth she) "like others wownd;
        For which no reason can finde remedy."[3]
        "Was never such, but mote the like be fownd,"[4]
        (Said she) "and though no reason may apply
        Salve to your sore, yet love can higher stye,[5]
        Then reasons reach, and oft hath wonders donne."
        "But neither God of love, nor God of skye
        Can doe" (said she) "that, which cannot be donne."
"Things ofte impossible" (quoth she) "seeme ere begonne."

37   "These idle wordes" (said she) "doe nought aswage
        My stubborne smart, but more annoiaunce breed.
        For no no usuall fire, no usuall rage
        Yt is, O Nourse, which on my life doth feed,
        And sucks the blood, which from my hart doth bleed.
        But since thy faithfull zele lets me not hyde
        My crime, (if crime it be) I will it reed.
        Nor Prince, nor pere it is, whose love hath gryde[6]
My feeble brest of late, and launched[7] this wound wyde.

38   "Nor man it is, nor other living wight;
        For then some hope I might unto me draw,
        But th'only shade[8] and semblant of a knight,

---

[1] **eke:** augment.

[2] **never sore, but might:** there is never a sore that cannot.

[3] Unlike other people, she has fallen in love not with a person but with a mere image, so she believes herself unique in having a desire that is impossible to satisfy. In another sense, however, she is just like any love-smitten teenager, certain that no one else in the history of the world has felt her degree of pain.

[4] I.e., there has never existed a wound of this sort for which it is impossible to find a remedy.

[5] **stye:** rise, surmount.

[6] **gryde:** pierced.

[7] **launched:** lanced.

[8] **shade:** insubstantial image; spirit.

Whose shape[1] or person yet I never saw,
Hath me subjected to loves cruell law:
The same one day, as me misfortune led,
I in my fathers wondrous mirrhour saw,
And pleased with that seeming goodly-hed,[2]
Unwares the hidden hooke with baite I swallowed.

39 "Sithens[3] it hath infixed faster hold
Within my bleeding bowells, and so sore
Now ranckleth in this same fraile fleshly mould,
That all mine entrailes flow with poisnous gore,
And th'ulcer groweth daily more and more;
Ne can my ronning sore finde remedee,
Other then my hard fortune to deplore,
And languish as the leafe faln from the tree,
Till death make one end of my daies and miseree."

40 "Daughter" (said she) "what[4] need ye be dismayd,
Or why make ye such Monster of your minde?[5]
Of much more uncouth[6] thing I was affrayd;
Of filthy lust, contrary unto kinde:[7]
But this affection nothing straunge I finde;
For who with reason can you aye[8] reprove,
To love the semblaunt[9] pleasing most your minde,
And yield your heart, whence ye cannot remove?
No guilt in you, but in the tyranny of love.

41 "Not so th'*Arabian Myrrhe*[10] did sett her mynd,
Nor so did *Biblis* spend her pining hart,

---

[1] **shape:** i.e., appearance in person, rather than in a crystal ball.

[2] **goodly-hed:** goodlihead, promising appearance.

[3] **Sithens:** since then.

[4] **what:** why, for what reason.

[5] I.e., why do you conceive that your thoughts are monstrous? Cf. Britomart's responding to Malecasta in Canto One as though Malecasta were a monster—or as though having anything to do with Malecasta would make Britomart herself into a monster.

[6] **uncouth:** outlandish, inexplicable.

[7] **contrary unto kinde:** contrary to what is proper for a human being.

[8] **aye:** ever.

[9] **semblaunt:** appearance.

[10] Glauce gives examples of women in Roman mythology whose desires were shameful: Myrrha committed incest with her father, Biblis desired her brother, and Pasiphaë had intercourse with a bull. Ovid's account of Myrrha's attempts to fight her incestuous desires and of her confiding in her nurse strongly resembles Spenser's

But lov'd their native flesh against al kynd,[1]
And to their purpose used wicked art:
Yet playd *Pasiphaë* a more monstrous part,
That lov'd a Bul, and learnd a beast to bee;
Such shamefull lusts who loaths not, which depart
From course of nature and of modestee?
Swete love such lewdnes bands from his faire companee.

42   "But thine my Deare (welfare thy heart[2] my deare)
Though straunge beginning had, yet fixed is
On one, that worthy may perhaps appeare;
And certes seemes bestowed not amis:
Joy thereof have thou and eternall blis."
With that upleaning on her elbow weake,
Her alablaster brest she soft did kis,
Which all that while shee felt to pant and quake,
As it an Earth-quake were, at last she thus bespake.

43   "Beldame,[3] your words doe worke me litle ease;
For though my love be not so lewdly bent,[4]
As those ye blame, yet may it nought appease
My raging smart, ne ought[5] my flame relent,
But rather doth my helpelesse griefe augment.
For they, how ever shamefull and unkinde,
Yet did possesse their horrible intent:
Short end of sorowes they therby did finde;
So was their fortune good, though wicked were their minde.[6]

44   "But wicked fortune mine, though minde be good,
Can have no end,[7] nor hope of my desire,
But feed on shadowes, whiles I die for food,

---

account in this canto, except that Brito-
mart's desires turn out to be far less shame-
ful than her nurse had feared, whereas the
reverse is true in Myrrha's case (*Metamor-
phoses*, 10.298–501).

[1] **native flesh:** members of their own fam-
ilies; **against al kynd:** unnaturally for hu-
mankind.

[2] **welfare thy heart:** may your heart be
well.

[3] **Beldame:** elderly woman, literally
"grandmother."

[4] **lewdly bent:** wickedly inclined.

[5] **ought:** at all.

[6] Despite being a paragon of chastity, Brit-
omart is still youthful enough for self-cen-
tered melodrama: ignoring the weighty
moral component of Glauce's advice, Brit-
omart responds petulantly, "Well, at least
those women who committed incest and
bestiality got what they wanted, so they
were luckier than I am."

[7] **end:** goal; ending.

And like a shadow wexe,[1] whiles with entire
Affection, I doe languish and expire.
I fonder, then *Cephisus* foolish chyld,[2]
Who having vewed in a fountaine shere
His face, was with the love thereof beguyld;
I fonder love a shade, the body far exyld."

45   "Nought like"[3] (quoth shee) "for that same wretched boy
Was of him selfe the ydle Paramoure;
Both love and lover, without hope of joy,
For which he faded to a watry flowre.
But better fortune thine, and better howre,[4]
Which lov'st the shadow[5] of a warlike knight;
No shadow, but a body hath in powre:
That body, wheresoever that it light,
May learned be by cyphres, or by Magicke might.[6]

46   "But if thou may with reason yet represse
The growing evill, ere it strength have gott,
And thee abandond wholy doe possesse,
Against it strongly strive,[7] and yield thee nott,
Til thou in open fielde adowne be smott.[8]
But if the passion mayster thy fraile might,
So that needs[9] love or death must bee thy lott,
Then I avow to thee, by wrong or right
To compas[10] thy desire, and find that loved knight."

47   Her chearefull words much cheard the feeble spright
Of the sicke virgin, that her downe she layd
In her warme bed to sleepe, if that she might;

---

[1] **wexe:** grow, become.

[2] **fonder:** more foolish; **chyld:** Narcissus, a mythological boy who fell in love with his own reflection in a pool and pined away gazing at it, ultimately turning into the narcissus flower.

[3] **Nought like:** i.e., you are nothing like him.

[4] **howre:** hour, time.

[5] **shadow:** insubstantial image; reflection.

[6] I.e., no matter where that knight's body is, signs or magic will show us its location.

[7] I.e., but if, before your desire grows strong enough to possess you utterly, you are able to use the power of reason to repress it, do struggle against it.

[8] **open fielde:** field of battle; **smott:** smitten.

[9] **needs:** necessarily.

[10] **compas:** achieve; embrace; work machinations for; understand.

And the old-woman carefully displayd
The clothes about her round with busy ayd,
So that at last a litle creeping sleepe
Surprisd her sence: Shee therewith well apayd,
The dronken[1] lamp down in the oyl did steepe,
And sett her by to watch, and sett her by to weepe.[2]

48　Earely the morrow next, before that day
　　His joyous face did to the world revele,
　　They both uprose, and tooke their ready way
　　Unto the Church, their praiers to appele,[3]
　　With great devotion, and with litle zele:
　　For the faire Damzell from the holy herse[4]
　　Her love-sicke hart to other thoughts did steale;
　　And that old Dame said many an idle verse,
Out of her daughters hart fond fancies to reverse.[5]

49　Retourned home, the royall Infant[6] fell
　　Into her former fitt; for why[7] no powre,
　　Nor guidaunce of her selfe in her did dwell.[8]
　　But th'aged Nourse her calling to her bowre,
　　Had gathered Rew, and Savine,[9] and the flowre
　　Of *Camphora*, and Calamint, and Dill,
　　All which she in a earthen Pot did poure,
　　And to the brim with Colt wood did it fill,
And many drops of milk and blood through it did spill.

---

[1] **dronken:** i.e., drunk with lamp oil. This is not precisely a transferred epithet, given that Glauce is not drunk, but she is indeed feeling overwhelmed by a flood of cares.

[2] Glauce is saddened that her foster daughter is now old enough to feel pain in love. The nurse's anxious ministrations also suggest a sadness arising from no longer being able to understand or govern Britomart fully.

[3] **appele:** appeal.

[4] **herse:** liturgy.

[5] I.e., in order to purge her daughter's heart of foolish fancies.

[6] **Infant:** youth of noble birth.

[7] **for why:** because.

[8] Cf. the slightly older Britomart's declaration to Malecasta's knights: "Ne may love be compeld by maistery; / For soone as maistery comes, sweet love anone / Taketh his nimble winges, and soone away is gone" (i.25).

[9] **Rew, and Savine:** these, along with camphor, mint, dill, and colt wood, are herbs used to soothe the intestines, purge bad humors, and stanch bleeding. They were regarded as especially useful in abating lust and preventing pregnancy.

50 Then taking thrise three heares from off her head,
    Them trebly breaded in a threefold lace,
    And round about the Pots mouth, bound the thread,[1]
    And after having whispered a space
    Certein sad[2] words, with hollow voice and bace,
    Shee to the virgin sayd, thrise sayd she itt;
    "Come daughter come, come; spit upon my face,
    Spitt thrise upon me, thrise upon me spitt;
Th'uneven nomber for this busines is most fitt."[3]

51 That sayd, her rownd about she from her turnd,
    She turned her contrary to the Sunne,
    Thrise she her turnd contrary, and returnd,
    All contrary; for she the right did shunne,
    And ever what she did, was streight undonne.
    So thought she to undoe her daughters love:
    But love, that is in gentle brest begonne,
    No ydle charmes so lightly may remove,
That well can witnesse, who by tryall it does prove.[4]

52 Ne ought[5] it mote the noble Mayd avayle,
    Ne slake the fury of her cruell flame,
    But that shee still did waste, and still did wayle,
    That through long languour, and hart-burning brame[6]
    She shortly like a pyned ghost became,
    Which long hath waited by the Stygian strond.[7]
    That when old *Glauce* saw, for feare least[8] blame
    Of her miscarriage should in her be fond,[9]
She wist not how t'amend, nor how it[10] to withstond.

---

[1] Glauce is practicing magic.

[2] **sad:** solemn.

[3] We must ask ourselves whether the poem is asking us to be touched at Glauce's earnest efforts or whether it is asking us to find those efforts amusing. Certainly Glauce's magic does not seem evil, but its mystery is less powerful than that of love itself.

[4] **prove:** test.

[5] **ought:** aught, at all.

[6] **brame:** longing.

[7] **Stygian strond:** the shores of the river Styx. In Greek and Roman mythology, spirits of the dead waited by this river longingly until allowed to cross over into the underworld.

[8] **least:** lest.

[9] **miscarriage:** ill management; **fond:** found.

[10] The reference of "it" broadens further the longer one looks at it: Britomart's desire, the effects of Britomart's desire, the whole future that opens up because of Britomart's desire, the condition of the desiring human race.

Canto Three

Merlin bewrayes[1] to Britomart,
The state of Arthegall.
And shews the famous Progeny
Which from them springen shall.

1   Most sacred fyre, that burnest mightily
    In living brests, ykindled first above,
    Emongst th'eternall spheres and lamping[2] sky,
    And thence[3] pourd into men, which men call Love;
    Not that same, which doth base affections[4] move
    In brutish mindes, and filthy lust inflame,
    But that sweete fit, that doth true beautie love,
    And choseth vertue for his dearest Dame,
Whence spring all noble deedes and never dying fame:

2   Well did Antiquity a God thee deeme,
        That over mortall mindes hast so great might,
        To order them, as best to thee doth seeme,
        And all their actions to direct aright;
        The fatall[5] purpose of divine foresight,
        Thou doest effect in destined descents,[6]
        Through deepe impression of thy secret might,
        And stirredst up th'Heroes high intents,
Which the late world admyres for wondrous moniments.[7]

3   But thy dredd dartes in none doe triumph more,
        Ne braver[8] proofe in any, of thy powre
        Shew'dst thou, then in this royall Maid of yore,
        Making her seeke an unknowne Paramoure,
        From the worlds end, through many a bitter stowre:

---

[1] **bewrayes:** reveals.

[2] **lamping:** flashing, resplendent. One of Spenser's neologisms.

[3] **thence:** from there.

[4] **affections:** emotions; passions.

[5] **fatall:** determined by fate.

[6] **destined descents:** lines of progeny determined by destiny.

[7] **late:** old; advanced; tardy; recent; **moniments:** marks of Love's power and/or evidence of the heroes' virtues.

[8] **braver:** more splendid; worthier.

From whose two loynes[1] thou afterwardes did rayse
  Most famous fruites of matrimoniall bowre,
  Which through the earth have spredd their living prayse,
That fame in tromp[2] of gold eternally displayes.

4   Begin then, O my dearest sacred Dame,
      Daughter of *Phœbus* and of *Memorye*,[3]
      That doest ennoble with immortall name
      The warlike Worthies,[4] from antiquitye,
      In thy great volume of Eternitye:
      Begin, O *Clio*, and recount from hence
      My glorious Soveraines goodly auncestrye,
    Till that by dew degrees and long protense,[5]
Thou have it lastly brought unto her Excellence.

5   Full many wayes within her troubled mind,
      Old *Glauce* cast, to cure this Ladies griefe:
      Full many waies she sought, but none could find,
      Nor herbes, nor[6] charmes, nor counsel that is chiefe,
      And choisest med'cine for sick harts reliefe:
      For thy great care she tooke, and greater feare,
      Least that it should her turne to fowle repriefe,[7]
    And sore reproch, when so her father deare
Should of his dearest daughters hard misfortune heare.[8]

6   At last she her avisde,[9] that he, which made
      That mirrhour, wherein the sicke Damosell
      So straungely vewed her straunge[10] lovers shade,

---

[1] **loynes:** loins.

[2] **tromp:** trumpet. Cf. Spenser's metaphorizing his poem as "trumpets sterne" in I.Pr.1.

[3] The speaker calls upon his muse to help him write poetry. Clio, one of the nine muses, is the daughter of Apollo (Phoebus) and Mnemosyne (Memory).

[4] **Worthies:** the Nine Worthies were nine men—three pagans, three Jews, and three Christians—famed for their deeds throughout history. The precise list of names varies according to source.

[5] **dew degrees:** legitimate steps. Elizabeth's father, Henry VIII, had declared her a bastard in her youth, so it was important for her to establish legitimacy as an adult; **protense:** duration.

[6] **Nor . . . nor:** neither . . . nor.

[7] **Least:** lest; **repriefe:** reproof.

[8] For all that he is mentioned, Britomart's father never makes an appearance in the poem. Spenser gives Britomart legitimacy through her own virtues, through her identification as Elizabeth's ancestor, and through her resemblance to the goddess Minerva as much as through her ties to various Welsh and English kings.

[9] **avisde:** recalled.

[10] **straunge:** unknown, foreign.

To weet,[1] the learned *Merlin*, well could tell,
Under what coast[2] of heaven the man did dwell,
And by what means his love might best be wrought:
For though beyond the *Africk Ismael*,[3]
Or th'Indian *Peru* he were, she thought
Him forth through infinite endevour to have sought.

7   Forthwith them selves disguising both in straunge
And base atyre, that none might them bewray,
To *Maridunum*, that is now by chaunge
Of name *Cayr-Merdin*[4] cald, they tooke their way:
There the wise *Merlin* whylome wont (they[5] say)
To make his wonne,[6] low underneath the ground,
In a deepe delve,[7] farre from the vew of day,
That of no living wight he mote be found,
When so he counseld with his sprights encompast round.

8   And if thou ever happen that same way
To traveill, go to see that dreadfull place:
It is an hideous hollow cave (they say)
Under a Rock that lyes a litle space
From the swift *Barry*,[8] tombling downe apace,
Emongst the woody hilles of *Dynevowre*:[9]
But dare thou not, I charge, in any cace,
To enter into that same balefull Bowre,
For fear the cruell Feendes should thee unwares devowre.

9   But standing high aloft, low lay thine eare,
And there such ghastly noyse of yron chaines,
And brasen[10] Caudrons thou shalt rombling heare,
Which thousand sprights with long enduring paines
Doe tosse, that it will stonn thy feeble braines,
And oftentimes great grones, and grievous stownds,

---

[1] **To weet:** to wit, that is.

[2] **coast:** region.

[3] ***Africk Ismael:*** northern Africa, whose inhabitants were thought to have descended from Ishmael.

[4] ***Cayr-Merdin:*** Carmarthen in Wales.

[5] **they:** in this canto, Spenser makes extensive use of chronicles written by Geoffrey of Monmouth and by Holinshed, among others, as well as of Malory's *Le Morte D'Arthur*.

[6] **wonne:** dwelling.

[7] **delve:** excavated cave.

[8] ***Barry:*** the river Cadoxton in Wales.

[9] ***Dynevowre:*** Dynevor Castle.

[10] **brasen:** brass.

When too huge toile and labour them constraines:
And oftentimes loud strokes, and ringing sowndes
From under that deepe Rock most horribly rebowndes.

10   The cause some say is this: A litle whyle
         Before that *Merlin* dyde, he did intend,
         A brasen wall in compas to compyle
         About *Cairmardin,* and did it commend
         Unto these Sprights, to bring to perfect end.[1]
         During which worke the Lady of the Lake,
         Whom long he lov'd, for him in hast did send,
         Who thereby forst his workemen to forsake,
Them bownd till his retourne, their labour not to slake.

11   In the meane time through that false Ladies traine,[2]
         He was surprisd, and buried under beare,[3]
         Ne ever to his worke returnd againe:
         Nath'lesse those feends may not their work forbeare,
         So greatly his commandement they feare,
         But there doe toyle and traveile day and night,
         Untill that brasen wall they up doe reare:
         For *Merlin* had in Magick more insight,
Then ever him before or after living wight.

12   For he by wordes could call out of the sky
         Both Sunne and Moone, and make them him obay:
         The Land to sea, and sea to maineland dry,
         And darksom night he eke could turne to day:
         Huge hostes of men he could alone[4] dismay,
         And hostes of men of meanest thinges could frame,[5]
         When so him list his enimies to fray:[6]
         That to this day for terror of his fame,
The feends do quake, when any him to them does name.

13   And sooth, men say that he was not the sonne
         Of mortall Syre, or other living wight,
         But wondrously begotten, and begonne

---

[1] **end:** fulfillment, completion.

[2] **traine:** wiles, machinations.

[3] **beare:** bier.

[4] **alone:** single-handedly.

[5] **meanest:** most ignoble; basest; **frame:** form. Merlin conjures armies out of everyday materials.

[6] **fray:** frighten.

By false illusion of a guilefull Spright,
On a faire Ladie Nonne,[1] that whilome hight
Matilda, daughter to *Pubidius,*
Who was the Lord of *Mathraval*[2] by right,
And coosen unto king *Ambrosius:*
Whence he indued was with skill so marveilous.

14 They here ariving, staid a while without,
  Ne durst adventure rashly in to wend,
  But of their first intent gan make new dout
  For dread of daunger, which it might portend:
  Untill the hardy Mayd (with love to frend[3])
  First entering, the dreadfull Mage[4] there fownd
  Deepe busied bout worke of wondrous end,
  And writing straunge characters[5] in the grownd,
With which the stubborne[6] feendes he to his service bownd.

15 He nought was moved at their entraunce bold:
  For of their comming well he wist afore,
  Yet list[7] them bid their businesse to unfold,
  As if ought in this world in secrete store
  Were from him hidden, or unknowne of yore.
  Then *Glauce* thus, "Let not it thee offend,
  That we thus rashly through thy darksom dore,
  Unwares have prest: for either fatall end,[8]
Or other mightie cause us two did hether send."

16 He bad[9] tell on; And then she thus began.
  "Now have three Moones with borrowd brothers light,
  Thrise shined faire, and thrise seemd dim and wan,
  Sith a sore evill, which this virgin bright
  Tormenteth, and doth plonge in dolefull plight,
  First rooting tooke; but what thing it mote bee,
  Or whence it sprong, I can not read aright:
  But this I read, that but if[10] remedee,
Thou her afford, full shortly I her dead shall see."

---

[1] **Nonne:** nun.

[2] *Mathraval:* the seat of the Welsh kings of Powys.

[3] **to frend:** as a friend.

[4] **Mage:** magician, sorcerer.

[5] **characters:** letters.

[6] **stubborne:** difficult to tame.

[7] **list:** desired, requested.

[8] **fatall end:** goal determined by fate.

[9] **bad:** bade her.

[10] **but if:** unless.

17   Therewith th'Enchaunter softly gan to smyle
        At her smooth speeches, weeting inly[1] well,
        That she to him dissembled womanish guyle,
        And to her said, Beldame, by that[2] ye tell,
        More neede of leach-crafte[3] hath your Damozell,
        Then of my skill: who helpe may have elswhere,
        In vaine seekes wonders out of Magick spell."
        Th'old woman wox[4] half blanck, those words to heare;
    And yet was loth to let her purpose plaine appeare.

18   And to him said, "Yf any leaches skill,
        Or other learned meanes could have redrest
        This my deare daughters deepe engraffed[5] ill,
        Certes[6] I should be loth thee to molest:
        But this sad evill, which doth her infest,
        Doth course of naturall cause farre exceed,
        And housed is within her hollow brest,
        That either seemes some cursed witches deed,
    Or evill spright, that in her doth such torment breed."

19   The wisard could no lenger beare her bord,[7]
        But brusting forth in laughter, to her sayd;
        "*Glauce*, what needes this colourable[8] word,
        To cloke the cause, that hath it selfe bewrayd?
        Ne ye fayre *Britomartis*, thus arayd,
        More hidden are, then Sunne in cloudy vele;
        Whom thy good fortune, having fate obayd,
        Hath hether brought, for succour to appele:
    The which the powres to thee are pleased to revele."

20   The doubtfull[9] Mayd, seeing her selfe descryde,
        Was all abasht, and her pure yvory[10]
        Into a cleare Carnation suddeine dyde;
        As fayre *Aurora* rysing hastily,

[1] **inly:** inwardly.

[2] **Beldame:** elderly woman, "grandmother"; **by that:** according to that which.

[3] **leach-crafte:** skill of a physician. (Physicians used leeches to draw blood, in order to bring patients' humors back into balance.)

[4] **wox:** waxed, grew.

[5] **engraffed:** engrafted.

[6] **Certes:** certainly.

[7] **bord:** bourd, nonsense, silly story.

[8] **colourable:** specious.

[9] **doubtfull:** full of doubt; hesitating.

[10] **yvory:** i.e., complexion.

Doth by her blushing tell, that she did lye
All night in old *Tithonus* frosen bed,[1]
Whereof she seemes ashamed inwardly.
But her olde Nourse was nought dishartened,
But vauntage made of that, which *Merlin* had ared.[2]

21   And sayd, "Sith then thou knowest all our griefe,
          (For what doest not thou knowe?) of grace I pray,
          Pitty our playnt, and yield us meet reliefe."
          With that the Prophet still awhile did stay,[3]
          And then his spirite thus gan foorth display;
          "Most noble Virgin, that by fatall lore
          Hast learn'd to love, let no whit thee dismay
          The hard beginne, that meetes thee in the dore,
And with sharpe fits thy tender hart oppresseth sore.

22   "For so must all things excellent begin,
          And eke enrooted deepe must be that Tree,
          Whose big embodied braunches shall not lin,[4]
          Till they to hevens hight forth stretched bee.
          For from thy wombe a famous Progenee
          Shall spring, out of the auncient *Trojan* blood,[5]
          Which shall revive the sleeping memoree
          Of those same antique Peres,[6] the hevens brood,
Which *Greeke* and *Asian* rivers stayned with their blood.

23   "Renowmed kings, and sacred Emperours,
          Thy fruitfull Ofspring, shall from thee descend;
          Brave Captaines, and most mighty warriours,

---

[1] *Tithonus* **frosen bed:** in Greek and Roman mythology, Aurora (the Dawn, Eos) loved a mortal man, Tithonus. She begged Zeus to make her lover immortal, which wish he granted; but because she had forgotten to ask that he remain young, Tithonus grew continuously older.

[2] **vauntage:** advantage; **ared:** interpreted; discerned, saw; understood; predicted; guessed; named; declared; taught; advised; decreed.

[3] **stay:** wait.

[4] **embodied:** laden with, or composed of, bodies; **lin:** cease.

[5] *Trojan* **blood:** partly because of the ancient Roman occupation of Britain, the English of Spenser's day believed their ancestry traced back to Aeneas, a Trojan prince who left Troy as it burned and went on to found the Roman race. According to Geoffrey of Monmouth, Aeneas's great-grandson Brute traveled to Britain and founded Troynovant, or London. See ix.34.9.n.

[6] **Peres:** Homeric heroes.

That shall their conquests through all lands extend,
And their decayed kingdomes shall amend:
The feeble Britons, broken with long warre,
They shall upreare, and mightily defend
Against their forren foe, that commes from farre,
Till universall peace compound all civill jarre.[1]

24   "It was not, *Britomart*, thy wandring eye,
Glauncing unwares in charmed looking glas,
But the streight[2] course of hevenly destiny,
Led with eternall providence, that has
Guyded thy glaunce, to bring his will to pas:
Ne is thy fate, ne is thy fortune ill,
To love the prowest[3] knight, that ever was.
Therefore submit thy wayes unto his will,
And doe by all dew meanes thy destiny fulfill."

25   "But read" (said *Glauce*) "thou Magitian
What meanes shall she out seeke, or what waies take?
How shall she know, how shall she finde the man?
Or what needes her to toyle, sith fates can make
Way for themselves, their purpose to pertake?"[4]
Then *Merlin* thus, "Indeede the fates are firme,
And may not shrinck, though all the world do shake:
Yet ought mens good endevours them confirme,
And guyde the heavenly causes to their constant terme.[5]

26   "The man whom heavens have ordaynd to bee
The spouse of *Britomart*, is *Arthegall*:[6]

---

[1] **jarre:** strife.

[2] **streight:** strait, confined, strict. In contrast, compare this book's images of wandering and erring.

[3] **prowest:** most worthy, most valiant.

[4] **pertake:** partake, obtain.

[5] **constant terme:** fixed conclusion.

[6] Merlin's prophecy is the second of three recountings of Britain's history in *The Faerie Queene,* although the three parts are not presented in chronological order. Two-thirds of the way through Book Three,

Paridell's account of his family's history will begin at the beginning, with Paris' rape of Helen, which led to the Trojan War (III.ix.33–52). In Book Two, Sir Guyon found a book that told the history of Britain from the arrival of Brute, a legendary descendant of the Trojans who fled the fallen city, to the rule of Arthur's father (II.ix.60–x.77). In the present canto, Merlin tells Britomart the final installment when he predicts the future of her and Artegall's descendants. By having Merlin utter this prophesy, Spenser is actually recounting the past: Merlin's prophecy will end with

He wonneth in the land of *Fayeree*,[1]
Yet is no *Fary* borne, ne sib[2] at all
To Elfes,[3] but sprong of seed terrestriall,
And whylome by false *Faries* stolne away,
Whyles yet in infant cradle he did crall;[4]
Ne other[5] to himselfe is knowne this day,
But that he by an Elfe was gotten[6] of a Fay.

27   "But sooth he is the sonne of *Gorlois*,[7]
And brother unto *Cador* Cornish king,
And for his warlike feates renowmed is,
From where the day out of the sea doth spring,
Untill the closure of the Evening.
From thence, him firmely bound with faithfull band,[8]
To this his native soyle thou backe shalt bring,
Strongly to ayde his countrey, to withstand
The powre of forreine Paynims,[9] which invade thy land.

28   "Great ayd thereto his mighty puissaunce,[10]
And dreaded name shall give in that sad day:
Where also proofe of thy prow[11] valiaunce
Thou then shalt make, t'increase thy lovers pray.[12]

Elizabeth's rule, depicted by Merlin as the glorious culmination of one thousand years of hope and struggle after Britomart's and Artegall's deaths. For all three histories, Spenser relies heavily upon the most respected chronicles of his day: Geoffrey of Monmouth, John Hardyng, John Stow, and Raphael Holinshed.

[1] *Fayeree:* see Introduction, 2.

[2] **sib:** sibling.

[3] **Elfes:** faeries.

[4] **crall:** crawl.

[5] **Ne other:** i.e., no other version of his past.

[6] **gotten:** begotten.

[7] **sooth:** truly; *Gorlois:* Prince of Cornwall, whose wife, Igerne, slept with Uther Pendragon and as a result gave birth to Arthur. Spenser thus implicitly makes Artegall the stepbrother of Arthur. If the 25

stanzas that name the generations sometimes seem wearisome to modern readers, we would do well to remember that in the sixteenth century—and indeed, up through the nineteenth—whenever one met or heard of a stranger, the first thing one wanted to know was who that person's parents and grandparents were. Merlin's prophecy gives information about the boy who has, so to speak, shown up to take Glauce's daughter on a date—but it is also proof of national identity, and it grounds that identity in the Tudor bloodline.

[8] **thence:** Faerie Land; **faithfull band:** bond of matrimony.

[9] **Paynims:** pagans (the Saxon invaders of Britain).

[10] **puissaunce:** strength.

[11] **proofe:** test, experience; **prow:** worthy.

[12] **pray:** prey.

Long time ye both in armes shall beare great sway,
Till thy wombes burden thee from them do call,
And his last fate him from thee take away,
Too rathe[1] cut off by practise criminall,
Of secrete foes, that him shall make in mischiefe fall.

29   "With thee yet shall he leave for memory
Of his late puissaunce, his ymage dead,[2]
That living him in all activity
To thee shall represent. He[3] from the head
Of his coosen *Constantius* without dread
Shall take the crowne, that was his fathers right,
And therewith crowne himselfe in th'others stead:
Then shall he issew forth with dreadfull might,
Against his Saxon foes in bloody field to fight.

30   "Like as a Lyon, that in drowsie cave
Hath long time slept, himselfe so shall he shake,
And comming forth, shall spred his banner brave
Over the troubled South, that it shall make
The warlike *Mertians*[4] for feare to quake:
Thrise shall he fight with them, and twise shall win,
But the third time shall fayre accordaunce[5] make:
And if he then with victorie can lin,[6]
He shall his dayes with peace bring to his earthly In.[7]

31   "His sonne, hight *Vortipore,* shall him succeede
In kingdome, but not in felicity;[8]
Yet shall he long time warre with happy speed,[9]
And with great honour many batteills try:

---

[1] **rathe:** quickly, soon.

[2] **his ymage dead:** the picture of a live Artegall after his death. This image of Artegall is his son; children were thought of as pictures of their parents. Spenser does not name the son, although the chroniclers gave his name as Conan.

[3] **To thee shall represent:** i.e., who will represent Artegall to you as he was when he was alive and active; **He:** Artegall's son.

[4] *Mertians:* inhabitants of Mercia, an Anglo-Saxon kingdom in south-central England.

[5] **accordaunce:** treaty.

[6] **lin:** leave it at that.

[7] **In:** inn, abode.

[8] Stanzas 31 through 50 recount essentially what every student learned about England's history, from the chroniclers Geoffrey of Monmouth and Holinshed.

[9] **speed:** success.

But at the last to th'importunity[1]
Of froward[2] fortune shall be forst to yield.
But his sonne *Malgo* shall full mightily
Avenge his fathers losse, with speare and shield,
And his proud foes discomfit in victorious field.

32   "Behold the man,[3] and tell me *Britomart,*
If ay[4] more goodly creature thou didst see;
How like a Gyaunt in each manly part
Beares he himselfe with portly majestee,
That one of th'old *Heroes* seemes to bee:
He the six Islands, comprovinciall[5]
In auncient times unto great Britainee,
Shall to the same reduce,[6] and to him call
Their sondry kings to doe their homage severall.[7]

33   "All which his sonne *Careticus* awhile
Shall well defend, and *Saxons* powre suppresse,
Untill a straunger king from unknowne soyle
Arriving, him with multitude oppresse;
Great *Gormond,* having with huge mightinesse
Ireland subdewd, and therein fixt his throne,
Like a swift Otter, fell through emptinesse,[8]
Shall overswim the sea with many one
Of his Norveyses, to assist the Britons fone.[9]

34   "He in his furie all shall overronne,
And holy Church with faithlesse handes deface,
That thy sad people utterly fordonne,
Shall to the utmost mountaines fly apace:

---

[1] **importunity:** demands.

[2] **froward:** adverse; uncooperative; inimical.

[3] **Behold the man:** we are not told whether Merlin is conjuring pictures in the air or whether he depends solely upon the magic of words to bring his subjects before Britomart's mind's eye.

[4] **ay:** ever.

[5] **six Islands:** Ireland, Iceland, Gothland, the Orkneys, Norway, and Denmark, which were said by the chroniclers to have become British possessions in this early period; **comprovinciall:** of the same province.

[6] **reduce:** subdue.

[7] **severall:** each, individually.

[8] **fell through emptinesse:** cruel because of hunger.

[9] **Norveyses:** Norwegians; **fone:** foes.

Was never so great waste in any place,
Nor so fowle outrage doen by living men:
For all thy Citties they shall sacke and race,[1]
And the greene grasse, that groweth, they shall bren,[2]
That even the wilde beast shall dy in starved den.[3]

35   "Whiles thus thy Britons doe in languour pine,
Proud *Etheldred* shall from the North arise,
Serving th'ambitious will of *Augustine*,[4]
And passing *Dee*[5] with hardy enterprise,
Shall backe repulse the valiaunt *Brockwell* twise,
And *Bangor* with massacred Martyrs fill;
But the third time shall rew his foolhardise:
For *Cadwan* pittying his peoples ill,
Shall stoutly him defeat, and thousand *Saxons* kill.

36   "But after him, *Cadwallin*[6] mightily
On his[7] sonne *Edwin* all those wrongs shall wreake;
Ne shall availe the wicked sorcery
Of false *Pellite*, his purposes to breake,
But him shall slay, and on a gallowes bleak
Shall give th'enchaunter his unhappy hire:[8]
Then shall the Britons, late dismayd and weake,
From their long vassallage gin to respire,
And on their Paynim foes avenge their ranckled ire.

37   "Ne shall he yet his wrath so mitigate,
Till both the sonnes of *Edwin* he have slayne,
Offricke and *Osricke*, twinnes unfortunate,
Both slaine in battaile upon Layburne playne,
Together with the king of *Louthiane*,[9]
Hight *Adin*, and the king of *Orkeny*,

---

[1] **race:** raze.

[2] **bren:** burn.

[3] **in starved den:** a transferred epithet here meaning either "starved in its den" or "dead in its den."

[4] *Augustine:* not the theologian of the same name, but the first Archbishop of Canterbury, sent by the pope to convert the Anglo-Saxons to Catholicism.

[5] *Dee:* river in northern Wales and western England.

[6] *Cadwallin:* Cadwan's son.

[7] **his:** Etheldred's.

[8] **hire:** deserts.

[9] *Louthiane:* Scotland.

Both joynt partakers of their fatall payne:
But *Penda,* fearefull of like desteny,
Shall yield him selfe his liegeman, and sweare fealty.

38   "Him shall he make his fatall Instrument,
            T'afflict the other *Saxons* unsubdewd;
            He marching forth with fury insolent
            Against the good king *Oswald,* who indewd
            With heavenly powre, and by Angels reskewd,
            Al holding crosses in their hands on hye,
            Shall him defeate withouten blood imbrewd:[1]
            Of which, that field for endlesse memory,
        Shall *Hevenfield* be cald to all posterity.

39   "Whereat *Cadwallin* wroth, shall forth issew,
            And an huge hoste into Northumber lead,
            With which he godly *Oswald* shall subdew,
            And crowne with martiredome his sacred head.
            Whose brother *Oswin,* daunted with like dread,
            With price of silver shall his kingdome buy,
            And *Penda* seeking him adowne to tread,
            Shall tread adowne, and doe him fowly dye,[2]
        But shall with guifts his Lord *Cadwallin* pacify.

40   "Then shall *Cadwallin* die, and then the raine
            Of *Britons* eke with him attonce shall dye;
            Ne shall the good *Cadwallader*[3] with paine,
            Or powre, be hable[4] it to remedy,
            When the full time prefixt by destiny,
            Shalbe expird of *Britons* regiment.[5]
            For heven it selfe shall their successe envy,
            And them with plagues and murrins[6] pestilent
        Consume, till all their warlike puissaunce be spent.

41   "Yet after all these sorrowes, and huge hills
            Of dying people, during eight yeares space,
            Cadwallader not yielding to his ills,

---

[1] **imbrewd:** having stained their hands.

[2] I.e., and Penda, seeking to tread Oswin down, will be himself tread down by Oswin, who will hideously kill him.

[3] *Cadwallader:* Cadwallin's son.

[4] **hable:** able.

[5] **regiment:** rule.

[6] **murrins:** plagues.

From *Armoricke,*[1] where long in wretched cace
He liv'd, retourning to his native place,
Shalbe by vision staide from his intent:
For th'heavens have decreed, to displace
The *Britons,* for their sinnes dew punishment,
And to the *Saxons* over-give their government.

42   "Then woe, and woe, and everlasting woe,
Be to the Briton babe, that shalbe borne,
To live in thraldome of his fathers foe;
Late[2] king, now captive, late lord, now forlorne,
The worlds reproch, the cruell victors scorne,
Banisht from princely bowre to wasteful[3] wood:
O who shal helpe me to lament, and mourne
The royall seed, the antique *Trojan* blood,
Whose empire lenger here, then ever any stood."

43   The Damzell[4] was full deepe empassioned,
Both for his griefe, and for her peoples sake,
Whose future woes so plaine he fashioned,[5]
And sighing sore, at length him thus bespake;
"Ah but will hevens fury never slake,
Nor vengeaunce huge relent it selfe at last?
Will not long misery late mercy make,
But shall their name for ever be defaste,
And quite from off the earth their memory be raste?"[6]

44   "Nay but the terme" (sayd he) "is limited,
That in this thraldome *Britons* shall abide,
And the just revolution[7] measured,
That they as Straungers shalbe notifide.[8]
For twise fowre hundreth yeares shalbe supplide,[9]
Ere they unto their former rule restor'd shalbee,[10]

---

[1] *Armoricke:* Brittany.
[2] **Late:** lately, recently.
[3] **wasteful:** deserted, wild.
[4] **Damzell:** Britomart.
[5] **fashioned:** described.
[6] **raste:** erased.

[7] **just revolution:** full cycle.
[8] **Straungers:** figuratively, wanderers in their own land; **notifide:** denoted.
[9] **supplide:** completed.
[10] I.e., when the first Tudor, Henry VII, ascends the English throne in 1485.

And their importune[1] fates all satisfide:
Yet during this their most obscuritee,
Their beames shall oft breake forth, that men then faire may see.

45   "For *Rhodoricke,* whose surname shalbe Great,
Shall of him selfe a brave ensample shew,
That Saxon kings his frendship shall intreat;
And *Howell Dha* shall goodly well indew
The salvage minds with skill of just and trew;[2]
Then *Griffyth Conan* also shall up reare
His dreaded head, and the old sparkes renew
Of native corage, that his foes shall feare,
Least back againe the kingdom he from them should beare.

46   "Ne shall the Saxons selves all peaceably
Enjoy the crowne, which they from Britons wonne
First ill,[3] and after ruled wickedly:
For ere two hundred yeares be full outronne,
There shall a Raven[4] far from rising Sunne,
With his wide wings upon them fiercely fly,
And bid his faithlesse chickens overonne
The fruitfull plaines, and with fell cruelty,
In their avenge, tread downe the victors surquedry.[5]

47   "Yet shall a third both these, and thine subdew;
There shall a Lion from the sea-bord wood
Of *Neustria* come roring, with a crew[6]
Of hungry whelpes, his battailous bold brood,
Whose clawes were newly dipt in cruddy[7] blood,
That from the Daniske Tyrants head shall rend
Th'usurped crowne, as if that he were wood,[8]
And the spoile[9] of the countrey conquered
Emongst his young ones shall divide with bountyhed.

---

[1] **importune:** burdensome, severe.

[2] **salvage:** savage, brutish; wild; **skill of just and trew:** knowledge of justice and truth.

[3] **ill:** badly.

[4] **Raven:** the Danish standard depicted a Raven.

[5] **surquedry:** arrogance.

[6] *Neustria:* Normandy, the realm of William the Conqueror; **crew:** bunch; gang; mob; group.

[7] **cruddy:** curdled.

[8] **wood:** insane (with lust for war).

[9] **spoile:** booty.

48 "Tho when the terme is full accomplishid,
      There shall a sparke of fire, which hath long-while
      Bene in his ashes raked up, and hid,
      Bee freshly kindled in the fruitfull Ile
      Of *Mona*,[1] where it lurked in exile;
      Which shall breake forth into bright burning flame,
      And reach into the house, that beares the stile[2]
      Of roiall majesty and soveraine name;
   So shall the Briton blood their crowne agayn reclame.

49 "Thenceforth eternall union shall be made
      Betweene the nations different afore,
      And sacred Peace shall lovingly persuade
      The warlike minds, to learne her goodly lore,
      And civile armes[3] to exercise no more:
      Then shall a royall Virgin[4] raine, which shall
      Stretch her white rod over the *Belgicke*[5] shore,
      And the great Castle smite so sore with all,[6]
   That it shall make him shake, and shortly learn to fall.

50 "But yet the end is not."[7] There *Merlin* stayd,
      As overcomen of the spirites powre,
      Or other ghastly spectacle dismayd,

---

[1] *Mona:* Anglesey, an island off the coast of Wales, where Henry VII was born.

[2] **stile:** title.

[3] **civile armes:** arms used in civil war or in disputes between the civilians of England and of Wales.

[4] Elizabeth Tudor, the Virgin Queen.

[5] *Belgicke:* Belgian. Spenser uses the name to refer collectively to the Low Countries, including the Netherlands and Belgium, which had harbors that provided dangerously easy access to England. Spain had controlled the Low Countries for decades, making Elizabeth nervous. Yet there were Dutch Protestants who started a rebellion against Spain's Catholic rule. After years of ambiguously supporting the Dutch rebels, Elizabeth finally sent in an army in 1585. Relations with Spain worsened to the point at which Spain attempted to invade England in 1588. Although the Spanish Armada was defeated primarily by a storm, rather than by direct battle, the English victory cemented Elizabeth's power in her own country. She had proven herself a warlike maid, a virgin in armor.

[6] **sore:** violently; **with all:** therewith (OED 2).

[7] **But yet the end is not:** but the end (of this story) has not yet been told—or has not yet occurred. The phrase negotiates between Merlin's position—living before these events have occurred, while nevertheless being able to predict most of them—and Spenser's position—living after these events have occurred, but hopeful of even more glorious things to come in Elizabeth's reign. Merlin's words also echo those of Jesus to the disciples in Matt. 24.6.

That secretly he saw, yet note[1] discovre:
Which suddein fitt, and halfe extatick stoure[2]
When the two fearefull wemen saw, they grew
Greatly confused in behaveoure;
At last the fury past, to former hew[3]
Hee turnd againe, and chearfull looks did shew.

51   Then, when them selves they well instructed had
Of all, that needed them to be inquird,[4]
They both conceiving hope of comfort glad,
With lighter hearts unto their home retird;
Where they in secret counsell close conspird,
How to effect so hard an enterprize,
And to possesse the purpose they desird:
Now this, now that twixt them they did devize,
And diverse plots did frame, to maske in strange disguise.

52   At last the Nourse in her foolhardy wit
Conceivd a bold devise,[5] and thus bespake;
"Daughter, I deeme that counsel aye most fit,
That of the time doth dew advauntage take;
Ye see that good king *Uther* now doth make
Strong warre upon the Paynim brethren, hight
Octa and *Oza*, whom he lately brake
Beside *Cayr Verolame*,[6] in victorious fight,
That now all *Britany* doth burne in armes bright.

53   "That therefore nought our passage may empeach,[7]
Let us in feigned armes our selves disguize,
And our weake hands (need makes good schollers) teach
The dreadful speare and shield to exercize:
Ne certes daughter that same warlike wize
I weene, would you misseeme;[8] for ye beene tall,

---

[1] **note:** did not.

[2] **extatick stoure:** visionary trance. The implication is that Merlin sees something either so wonderful or so horrifying that he cannot relate it to Britomart and Glauce. Spenser, of course, does not know what will happen next.

[3] **hew:** appearance; condition.

[4] I.e., about everything they needed to ask.

[5] **devise:** device, clever plan.

[6] *Cayr Verolame:* St. Albans, a town north of London. Uther fought the Jutes Octa and Oza around the time when Arthur first appears in the chronicles.

[7] **empeach:** impede.

[8] **you misseeme:** misbecome you, seem inappropriate on you.

And large of limbe, t'atchieve an hard emprize,[1]
Ne ought ye want, but skil, which practize small
Wil bring, and shortly make you a mayd Martiall.

54   "And sooth, it ought your corage much inflame,
     To heare so often, in that royall hous,
     From whence to none inferior ye came:
     Bards tell of many wemen valorous,
     Which have full many feats adventurous,
     Performd, in paragone[2] of proudest men:
     The bold *Bunduca*,[3] whose victorious
     Exployts made *Rome* to quake, stout *Guendolen*,[4]
  Renowmed *Martia*, and redoubted *Emmilen*.[5]

55   "And that, which more then all the rest may sway,
     Late dayes ensample, which these eyes beheld,
     In the last field before *Menevia*[6]
     Which *Uther* with those forrein Pagans held,
     I saw a *Saxon* Virgin, the which feld
     Great *Ulfin*[7] thrise upon the bloodly playne,
     And had not *Carados*[8] her hand withheld
     From rash revenge, she had him surely slayne,
  Yet *Carados* himselfe from her escapt with payne."

---

[1] **emprize:** enterprise.

[2] **paragone:** emulation.

[3] *Bunduca:* Queen Boadicea, whose realm was in eastern Britain. She led an unsuccessful revolt against the Roman occupation in the first century CE.

[4] **stout:** proud; brave; hardy; *Guendolen:* her husband, Locrine, King of Cornwall, put Guendolen aside and took up with another woman, Estrild. Guendolen sent an army against her husband, had him killed, and ordered that Estrild and her daughter be thrown into the Severn River. Guendolen then ruled as Queen of Cornwall for many years.

[5] *Martia:* Dame Mertia, mentioned in II.x.42 as being the wife of King Guitheline, possibly a fairy, and worthy of praise for her proposals of many good laws;

redoubted: formidable; *Emmilen:* identity uncertain.

[6] *Menevia:* St. David's, on the most western tip of Wales. Here Uther fought the Saxons.

[7] *Ulfin:* ally of Uther. When Uther lusted after a married woman, Ygerne, Ulfin advised him to consult Merlin. The magician disguised Uther and Ulfin as Ygerne's husband, Gorlois, and Gorlois' friend Jordan, so that they could gain access to Ygerne's castle. After Uther slept with Ygerne, she gave birth to Arthur. In the following stanzas, Britomart and Glauce will insert Britomart symbolically into this unchaste story by disguising her as Uther's enemy, the virginal Saxon warrior named Angela.

[8] *Carados:* identity uncertain. Perhaps a king of Scotland.

56   "Ah read," (quoth *Britomart*) "how is she[1] hight?"
           "Fayre *Angela*"[2] (quoth she) "men do her call,
           No whit lesse fayre,[3] then terrible in fight:
           She hath the leading of a Martiall
           And mightie people, dreaded more then all
           The other *Saxons,* which doe for her sake
           And love, themselves of her name *Angles* call.
           Therefore faire Infant her ensample make
     Unto thy selfe, and equall corage[4] to thee take."

57   Her harty wordes so deepe into the mynd
           Of the yong Damzell sunke, that great desire
           Of warlike armes in her forthwith they tynd,[5]
           And generous stout courage did inspyre,
           That she resolv'd, unweeting to her Syre,[6]
           Advent'rous knighthood on her selfe to don,
           And counseld with her Nourse, her Maides attyre
           To turne into a massy habergeon,[7]
     And bad her all things put in readinesse anon.

58   Th'old woman nought, that needed, did omit;
           But all thinges did conveniently purvay:[8]
           It fortuned (so time their turne did fitt)
           A band of Britons ryding on forray
           Few dayes before, had gotten a great pray[9]
           Of Saxon goods, emongst the which was seene
           A goodly Armour, and full rich aray,
           Which long'd[10] to *Angela,* the Saxon Queene,
     All fretted round with gold, and goodly wel beseene.[11]

59   The same, with all the other ornaments,
           King *Ryence* caused to be hanged hy

---

[1] **she:** the Saxon virgin.

[2] *Angela:* Spenser invented this character, whose name is derived from the Latin name for England: Anglia.

[3] **fayre:** beautiful.

[4] I.e., therefore, beautiful noblewoman, take her as your example; **corage:** heart, but with puns on the meanings "sexual vigor" and "lust."

[5] **tynd:** ignited, kindled.

[6] **unweeting:** unknown; **Syre:** father.

[7] **massy habergeon:** weighty chain-mail tunic.

[8] **purvay:** see to, arrange, provide.

[9] **pray:** plunder

[10] **long'd:** belonged.

[11] **beseene:** appearing.

In his chiefe Church, for endlesse moniments[1]
Of his successe and gladfull victory:
Of which her selfe avising[2] readily,
In th'evening late old *Glauce* thether led
Faire *Britomart,* and that same Armory
Downe taking, her therein appareled,
Well as she might, and with brave bauldrick[3] garnished.

60 Beside those armes there stood a mightie speare,
Which *Bladud*[4] made by Magick art of yore,
And usd the same in batteill aye to beare;
Sith which it had beene here preserv'd in store,
For his great vertues proved long afore:
For never wight so fast in sell[5] could sit,
But him perforce unto the ground it bore:[6]
Both speare she tooke, and shield, which hong by it;
Both speare and shield of great powre, for her purpose fit.

61 Thus when she[7] had the virgin all arayd,
Another harnesse,[8] which did hang thereby,
About her selfe she dight, that the young Mayd
She might in equall armes accompany,
And as her Squyre attend her carefully:
Tho to their ready Steedes they clombe full light,[9]
And through back waies, that none might them espy,
Covered with secret cloud of silent night,
Themselves they forth convaid, and passed forward right.

62 Ne rested they, till that to Faery lond
They came, as *Merlin* them directed late:
Where meeting with this *Redcrosse* knight, she fond[10]
Of diverse thinges discourses to dilate,[11]

---

[1] **moniments:** monuments, trophies.

[2] **avising:** reminding.

[3] **brave:** resplendent; **bauldrick:** a highly decorated belt or sash, worn across the chest and over one shoulder, used to hang one's shield.

[4] ***Bladud:*** Briton king famed for his magical knowledge; see II.x.25–6. Note that Britomart's armor has both Saxon and Briton origins.

[5] **sell:** saddle.

[6] We have already seen the spear's power in i.6, with the unseating of Guyon.

[7] **she:** Glauce.

[8] **harnesse:** suit of armor.

[9] **clombe:** climbed; **light:** lightly.

[10] **fond:** found.

[11] **dilate:** elaborate upon.

But most of *Arthegall,* and his estate.[1]
At last their wayes so fell, that they mote part:
Then each to other well affectionate,
Friendship professed with unfained hart,
The *Redcrosse* knight diverst,[2] but forth rode *Britomart.*

---

[1] **estate:** state, fortune.   [2] **diverst:** diverted his course.

Canto Four

Bold Marinell of Britomart,
Is throwne on the Rich strond:[1]
Faire Florimell of[2] *Arthure is*
Long followed, but not fond.

1   Where is the Antique glory now become,[3]
       That whylome wont in wemen to appeare?
       Where be the brave atchievements doen by some?
       Where be the batteilles, where the shield and speare,
       And all the conquests, which them high did reare,
       That matter made for famous Poets verse,
       And boastfull men so oft abasht to heare?
       Beene they all dead, and laide in dolefull herse?[4]
       Or doen they onely sleepe, and shall againe reverse?[5]

2   If they be dead, then woe is me therefore:
       But if they sleepe, O let them soone awake:
       For all too long I burne with envy[6] sore,
       To heare the warlike feates, which *Homere*[7] spake
       Of bold *Penthesilee*,[8] which made a lake
       Of *Greekish* blood so ofte in *Trojan* plaine;
       But when I reade, how stout *Debora*[9] strake

---

[1] **strond:** shore.

[2] **of:** by.

[3] **become:** come to be.

[4] **herse:** funeral ceremonies; funeral poem.

[5] **reverse:** turn themselves back (toward life); return (to life).

[6] **envy:** admiration, with overtones of mortification at one's own inferiority.

[7] **Homere:** although neither the *Iliad* nor the *Odyssey* mentions Penthesilea, other poems were attributed to Homer, including

Aethiopis, which describes Penthesilea's death at Achilles' hands. Virgil also mentions Penthesilea in the *Aeneid* (1.490–93 and 11.661–3).

[8] **Penthesilee:** Penthesilea, virginal warrior queen of the Amazons, who joined the Trojans in fighting the Greeks. Achilles finally slew her, but he then grieved for her.

[9] **Debora:** in Judg. 4–5, Debora accompanies an army of Israelites and is able, through God's help, to deliver Sisera, a Canaanite general, into their hands.

Proud *Sisera,* and how *Camill'*[1] hath slaine
The huge *Orsilochus,* I swell with great disdaine.[2]

3   Yet these, and all that els had puissaunce,
        Cannot with noble *Britomart* compare,
        Aswell for glorie of great valiaunce,
        As for pure chastitie[3] and vertue rare,
        That all her goodly deedes do well declare.
        Well worthie stock, from which the branches sprong,
        That in late yeares so faire a blossome bare,
        As thee, O Queene, the matter[4] of my song,
    Whose lignage from this Lady I derive along.[5]

4   Who when through speaches with the *Redcrosse* knight,
        She learned had th'estate[6] of *Arthegall,*
        And in each point[7] her selfe informd aright,
        A frendly league of love perpetuall
        She with him bound, and *Congé* tooke withall.[8]
        Then he forth on his journey did proceede,
        To seeke adventures, which mote him befall,
        And win him worship[9] through his warlike deed,
    Which alwaies of his paines he made the chiefest meed.[10]

5   But *Britomart* kept on her former course,
        Ne ever dofte her armes,[11] but all the way
        Grew pensive through that amarous discourse,
        By which the *Redcrosse* knight did earst display

---

[1] *Camill':* Camilla, a virginal warrior princess who never learned to spin wool (thus distinguishing herself from every proper woman in the Roman world), lived in the woods, and served Diana. She came to Aeneas' aid and slew many of his enemies before herself being slain by Arruns, who had Apollo's aid (*Aeneid,* 7.803 and 11.432–898).

[2] *Orsilochus:* a Trojan general. See *Aeneid,* 11.690–91; **disdaine:** contempt; indignation (toward the slain men).

[3] **chastitie:** this is the first time that the speaker has explicitly called Britomart chaste.

[4] **O Queene:** Elizabeth Tudor; **matter:** subject.

[5] **along:** from one end to the other.

[6] **estate:** state, condition, fortune.

[7] **each point:** each detail.

[8] **him:** Redcrosse; *Congé:* courteous goodbyes; **withall:** in addition, moreover.

[9] **worship:** honor, a good reputation.

[10] I.e., which (honor) he always considered the chief reward for his efforts.

[11] In Malecasta's castle, Britomart learned her lesson about keeping her armor on.

Her lovers shape, and chevalrous aray;
A thousand thoughts she fashiond in her mind,
And in her feigning[1] fancie did pourtray
Him such, as fittest she for love could find,
Wise, warlike, personable, courteous, and kind.

6   With such selfe-pleasing thoughts her wound she fedd,
And thought so to beguile[2] her grievous smart;
But so her smart was much more grievous bredd,
And the deepe wound more deep engord her hart,
That nought but death her dolour mote depart.[3]
So forth she rode without repose or rest,
Searching all lands and each remotest part,
Following the guydaunce of her blinded guest,[4]
Till that to the seacoast at length she her addrest.[5]

7   There she alighted from her light-foot beast,
And sitting downe upon the rocky shore,
Badd her old Squyre unlace her lofty creast;
Tho having vewd a while the surges hore,[6]
That gainst the craggy clifts did loudly rore,
And in their raging surquedry disdaynd,[7]
That the fast earth affronted them so sore,
And their devouring covetize[8] restraynd,
Thereat she sighed deepe, and after thus complaynd.[9]

---

[1] **feigning:** a pun on "fain" and "feign"; her fancy is both desiring and—thus far—the creator of that which it desires.

[2] **beguile:** charm away; divert (her) attention from.

[3] **dolour:** physical or mental suffering; **depart:** send away.

[4] **her blinded guest:** Cupid, who wears a blindfold and shoots people at random with the darts of love (and, in some sources, with the darts of hate).

[5] **her addrest:** directed her course.

[6] **surges hore:** hoary wave (hoary presumably from white foam).

[7] **surquedry:** arrogance; **disdaynd:** were indignant.

[8] **covetize:** covetousness.

[9] Britomart's complaint takes the form of a well-known genre of poetry, the plaint, in which the speaker, usually in a monologue, complains about unrequited love or the world's unfairness and asks for relief. The Renaissance plaint often uses Petrarchan devices, such as the pathetic fallacy (the projection of the speaker's emotion onto his or her natural surroundings). Cf. Cymoent's plaint at stanzas 36 through 39 and Arthur's at stanzas 55 through 60.

8   "Huge sea of sorrow, and tempestuous griefe,
        Wherein my feeble barke[1] is tossed long,
        Far from the hoped haven of reliefe,
        Why doe thy cruel billowes beat so strong,
        And thy moyst mountaines each on others throng,
        Threatning to swallow up my fearefull lyfe?
        O doe thy cruell wrath and spightfull wrong
        At length allay, and stint[2] thy stormy stryfe,
      Which in thy troubled bowels raignes, and rageth ryfe.

9   "For els my feeble vessell crazd,[3] and crackt
        Through thy strong buffets and outrageous blowes,
        Cannot endure, but needes it must be wrackt[4]
        On the rough rocks, or on the sandy shallowes,
        The whiles that love it steres, and fortune rowes;
        Love my lewd[5] Pilott hath a restless minde
        And fortune Boteswaine no assuraunce knowes,
        But saile withouten starres, gainst tyde and winde:
      How can they other doe, sith both are bold and blinde?[6]

10   "Thou God of windes, that raignest[7] in the seas,
        That raignest also in the Continent,[8]
        At last blow up some gentle gale of ease,
        The which may bring my ship, ere it be rent,[9]
        Unto the gladsome port of her[10] intent:
        Then when I shall my selfe in safety see,
        A table[11] for eternall moniment
        Of thy great grace, and my great jeopardee,
      Great *Neptune*,[12] I avow to hallow unto thee."

---

[1] **barke:** boat.

[2] **stint:** cease.

[3] **crazd:** cracked (with or without being broken apart).

[4] **wrackt:** wrecked.

[5] **lewd:** ignorant; evil; unchaste. Imagine commas before "my" and after "Pilott," making the phrase an appositive to "Love."

[6] These are all common Petrarchan similes.

[7] **raignest:** pun on "reigns" and "rains."

[8] **Continent:** land, but with a pun on the meaning "sexually self-restrained."

[9] **rent:** torn asunder.

[10] **her:** the ship's.

[11] **table:** votive tablet often dedicated to a god by a mariner who had come home safely.

[12] ***Neptune:*** god of the sea.

11   Then sighing softly sore, and inly deepe,
        She shut up all her plaint in privy[1] griefe;
        For her great courage would not let her weepe,
        Till that old *Glauce* gan with sharpe repriefe,[2]
        Her to restraine, and give her good reliefe,
        Through hope of those, which *Merlin* had her told
        Should of her name and nation be chiefe,
        And fetch their being from the sacred mould
Of her immortall womb, to be in heaven enrold.

12   Thus as she her recomforted, she[3] spyde,
        Where far away one all in armour bright,
        With hasty gallop towards her did ryde;[4]
        Her dolour[5] soone she ceast, and on her dight
        Her Helmet, to her Courser mounting light:
        Her former sorrow into suddein wrath,
        Both coosen passions of distroubled[6] spright,
        Converting, forth she beates the dusty path;
Love and despight attonce her courage kindled hath.

13   As when a foggy mist hath overcast
        The face of heven, and the cleare ayre engroste,[7]
        The world in darkenes dwels, till that at last
        The watry Southwinde from the seabord coste
        Upblowing, doth disperse the vapour lo'ste,[8]
        And poures it selfe forth in a stormy showre;
        So the fayre *Britomart* having disclo'ste[9]
        Her clowdy care into a wrathfull stowre,
The mist of griefe dissolv'd, did into vengeance powre.

14   Eftsoones her goodly shield addressing fayre,[10]
        That mortall speare she in her hand did take,
        And unto battaill did her selfe prepayre.

[1] **privy:** private.

[2] **repriefe:** reproof.

[3] The first "she" is Glauce; the second, Britomart.

[4] Allegorically speaking, she is bound to be confronted by an angry stranger at this point, because she is ready for one to appear. Her distress over her unremitting inner pain is transferred, in psychologically understandable fashion, into a readiness to punch someone, anyone.

[5] **dolour:** suffering; expression of suffering.

[6] **distroubled:** very troubled.

[7] **engroste:** condensed.

[8] **lo'ste:** loosed.

[9] **disclo'ste:** disclosed, opened up, freed.

[10] **addressing fayre:** directing well.

The knight approching, sternely her bespake;
"Sir knight, that doest thy voyage rashly make
By this forbidden way in my despight,[1]
Ne doest by others death ensample[2] take,
I read thee soone retyre, whiles thou hast might,
Least afterwards it be too late to take thy flight."

15   Ythrild with deepe disdaine of his proud threat,
        She shortly thus; "Fly they, that need to fly;
        Wordes fearen babes.[3] I meane not thee entreat
        To passe; but maugre[4] thee will passe or dy."
        Ne lenger stayd for th'other to reply,
        But with sharpe speare the rest[5] made dearly knowne.
        Strongly the straunge knight ran, and sturdily
        Strooke her full on the brest, that made her downe
Decline her head, and touch her crouper[6] with her crown.

16   But she againe him in the shield did smite
        With so fierce furie and great puissaunce,
        That through his threesquare scuchin[7] percing quite,
        And through his mayled hauberque, by mischaunce[8]
        The wicked steele through his left side[9] did glaunce;
        Him so transfixed she before her bore
        Beyond his croupe,[10] the length of all her launce,
        Till sadly soucing[11] on the sandy shore,
He tombled on an heape, and wallowd in his gore.

17   Like as the sacred Oxe, that carelesse[12] stands,
        With gilden hornes, and flowry girlonds crownd,[13]
        Proud of his dying honor and deare bandes,[14]

---

[1] **in my despight:** in contempt of me.

[2] **ensample:** example.

[3] I.e., words frighten (only) babies.

[4] **maugre:** despite.

[5] **the rest:** i.e., the rest of what she had to say.

[6] **crouper:** horse's rump.

[7] **threesquare scuchin:** triangular escutcheon (shield).

[8] **mayled hauberque:** chain-mail tunic; **mischaunce:** bad luck.

[9] Note that his left side is near his heart.

[10] **croupe:** crouper.

[11] **sadly soucing:** heavily thumping; fully soaking (himself) with water.

[12] **carelesse:** without cares.

[13] In the ancient world, an ox intended for sacrifice was decked with gold and flowers.

[14] **dying honor:** honor that attends his dying (as a sacrifice); **deare bandes:** precious garlands or bonds.

Whiles th'altars fume with frankincense arownd,
All suddeinly with mortall stroke astownd,[1]
Doth groveling fall, and with his streaming gore
Distaines[2] the pillours, and the holy grownd,
And the faire flowres, that decked him afore;
So fell proud *Marinell*[3] upon the pretious shore.

18   The martiall Mayd stayd not him to lament,
      But forward rode, and kept her ready[4] way
      Along the strond, which as she over-went,
      She saw bestrowed all with rich aray
      Of pearles and pretious stones of great assay,[5]
      And all the gravell mixt with golden owre;
      Whereat she wondred much, but would not stay
      For gold, or perles, or pretious stones an howre,
But them despised all; for all was in her powre.[6]

19   Whiles thus he lay in deadly stonishment,
      Tydings hereof came to his mothers eare;
      His mother was the blacke-browd *Cymoent*,
      The daughter of great *Nereus*,[7] which did beare
      This warlike sonne unto an earthly peare,[8]
      The famous *Dumarin;* who on a day[9]
      Finding the Nymph a sleepe in secret wheare,[10]
      As he by chaunce did wander that same way,
Was taken with her love, and by her closely lay.

20   There he this knight of her begot, whom borne
      She of his father *Marinell* did name,
      And in a rocky cave as wight[11] forlorne,

---

[1] **astownd:** astounded, stunned.

[2] **Distaines:** stains.

[3] *Marinell:* the opposing knight's name, which connects him with the sea—and with Florimell, whose investment in Marinell will be revealed at v.8–10.

[4] **ready:** direct, straight.

[5] **assay:** value.

[6] This is a phrase ripe for interpretation. We must ask ourselves what the relationship is among her power of chastity, her power of resisting diversions, and her power of scorning riches.

[7] *Nereus:* a god of the sea.

[8] I.e., who was impregnated by a mortal mate.

[9] *Dumarin:* of the sea; seaworthy; like a mariner; **on a day:** one day.

[10] **wheare:** place (as in "somewhere").

[11] **rocky cave:** Spenser's caves are often linked with hidden passions or perplexing emotional states; **wight:** person.

Long time she fostred up, till he became
A mighty man at armes, and mickle[1] fame
Did get through great adventures by him donne:
For never man he suffred[2] by that same
Rich strond to travell, whereas[3] he did wonne,
But that he must do battail with the Sea-nymphes sonne.

21   An hundred knights of honorable name
He had subdew'd, and them his vassals made,
That through all Farie lond his noble fame
Now blazed[4] was, and feare did all invade,
That none durst passen through that perilous glade.
And to advaunce his name and glory more,
Her Sea-god syre she dearely did perswade,[5]
T'endow her sonne with threasure and rich store,
Bove[6] all the sonnes, that were of earthly wombes ybore.

22   The God did graunt his daughters deare[7] demaund,
To doen his Nephew[8] in all riches flow;
Eftsoones his heaped waves he did commaund,
Out of their hollow bosome forth to throw
All the huge threasure, which the sea below
Had in his greedy gulfe devoured deepe,
And him enriched through the overthrow
And wreckes[9] of many wretches, which did weepe,
And often wayle their wealth, which he from them did keepe.

23   Shortly upon that shore there heaped was,
Exceeding riches and all pretious things,
The spoyle of all the world, that it did pas
The wealth of th'East, and pompe of *Persian* kings;
Gold, amber, yvorie, perles, owches,[10] rings,
And all that els was pretious and deare,

---

[1] **mickle:** much, great (quantity).

[2] **suffred:** allowed.

[3] **whereas:** where.

[4] **blazed:** proclaimed.

[5] **perswade:** intreat.

[6] **Bove:** above.

[7] **deare:** expensive.

[8] **Nephew:** grandson.

[9] **wreckes:** shipwrecks.

[10] **amber:** alloy of four parts gold to one of silver; amber, the precious resin; **owches:** brooches (often set with precious stones).

The sea unto him voluntary brings,
That shortly he a great Lord did appeare,
As was in all the lond of Faery, or else wheare.

24 Thereto he was a doughty[1] dreaded knight,
Tryde often to the scath of many Deare,[2]
That none in equall armes him matchen might,
The which his mother seeing, gan to feare
Least his too haughtie hardines might reare[3]
Some hard mishap, in hazard of his life:
For thy she oft him counseld to forbeare
The bloody batteill, and to stirre up strife,
But after all his warre, to rest his wearie knife.

25 And for his more assuraunce,[4] she inquir'd
One day of *Proteus* by his mighty spell,
(For *Proteus* was with prophecy inspir'd)
Her deare sonnes destiny to her to tell,
And the sad end of her sweet *Marinell.*
Who through foresight of his[5] eternall skill,
Bad her from womankind to keepe him well:
For of a woman he should have much ill,
A virgin straunge and stout him should dismay,[6] or kill.

26 For thy she gave him warning every day,
The love of women not to entertaine;
A lesson too too hard for living clay,[7]
From love in course of nature to refraine:
Yet he his mothers lore did well retaine,
And ever from fayre Ladies love did fly;
Yet many Ladies fayre did oft complaine,
That they for love of him would algates[8] dy:
Dy, who so list[9] for him, he was loves enimy.

---

[1] **Thereto:** additionally; **doughty:** valiant, worthy.

[2] I.e., often proved to be severely injurious to many.

[3] **hardines:** courage; **reare:** cause.

[4] **assuraunce:** safety.

[5] **his:** Proteus'.

[6] **straunge:** unknown; foreign; **dismay:** defeat.

[7] **clay:** referring to the Biblical notion that humans come from earth and are, like everything that comes from the earth, imperfect and impermanent.

[8] **algates:** at any rate; notwithstanding; otherwise.

[9] **list:** wished.

27　　But ah, who can deceive his destiny,
　　　　　Or weene by warning to avoyd his fate?
　　　　That when he sleepes in most security,
　　　　And safest seemes, him soonest doth amate,[1]
　　　　And findeth dew effect or soone or[2] late.
　　　　So feeble is the powre of fleshly arme.
　　　　His mother bad him wemens love to hate,
　　　　For she of womans force did feare no harme;[3]
　　So weening[4] to have arm'd him, she did quite disarme.

28　　This was that woman, this that deadly wownd,
　　　　　That *Proteus* prophecide should him dismay,
　　　　The which his mother vainely did expownd,
　　　　To be hart-wownding love, which should assay[5]
　　　　To bring her sonne unto his last decay.[6]
　　　　So ticle be the termes of mortall state,[7]
　　　　And full of subtile sophismes,[8] which doe play
　　　　With double sences, and with false debate,
　　T'approve the unknowen purpose of eternall fate.

29　　Too true the famous *Marinell* it fownd,
　　　　　Who through late triall, on that wealthy Strond
　　　　Inglorious now lies in sencelesse swownd,[9]
　　　　Through heavy stroke of *Britomartis* hond.[10]
　　　　Which when his mother deare did understond,
　　　　And heavy tidings heard, whereas she playd
　　　　Amongst her watry sisters[11] by a pond,
　　　　Gathering sweete daffadillyes, to have made
　　Gay girlonds,[12] from the Sun their forheads fayr to shade,

30　　Eftsoones both flowres and girlonds far away
　　　　　Shee flong, and her faire deawy locks yrent,
　　　　To sorrow huge she turnd her former play,

---

[1] **amate:** overwhelm.

[2] **or . . . or:** either . . . or.

[3] I.e., she feared women's love but not their martial might.

[4] **weening:** believing.

[5] **assay:** try.

[6] **decay:** death.

[7] **ticle:** not steadfast, fickle; insecure; **mortall state:** life on earth.

[8] **sophismes:** sophistry.

[9] **swownd:** swoon.

[10] **hond:** hand.

[11] **watry sisters:** the Nereids, sea nymphs and daughters of the sea god Nereus.

[12] **girlonds:** garlands.

And gamesome merth to grievous dreriment:[1]
Shee threw her selfe downe on the Continent,[2]
Ne word did speake, but lay as in a swownd,
Whiles al her sisters did for her lament,
With yelling outcries, and with shrieking sowne;
And every one did teare her girlond from her crowne.

31   Soone as shee up out of her deadly fitt
     Arose, shee bad her charett[3] to be brought,
     And all her sisters, that with her did sitt,
     Bad eke attonce their charetts to be sought;
     Tho full of bitter griefe and pensife thought,
     She to her wagon clombe; clombe all the rest,
     And forth together went, with sorow fraught.
     The waves obedient to theyr beheast,
Them yielded ready passage, and their rage surceast.

32   Great *Neptune* stoode amazed at their sight,
     Whiles on his broad rownd backe they softly slid
     And eke him selfe mournd at their mournfull plight,
     Yet wist[4] not what their wailing ment, yet did
     For great compassion of their sorow, bid
     His mighty waters to them buxome[5] bee:
     Eftesoones the roaring billowes still abid,[6]
     And all the griesly Monsters of the See
Stood gaping at their gate,[7] and wondred them to see.

33   A teme of Dolphins raunged in aray,
     Drew the smooth charett of sad *Cymoent;*
     They were all taught by *Triton*,[8] to obay
     To the long raynes, at her commaundement:
     As swifte as swallowes, on the waves they went,
     That their brode flaggy[9] finnes no fome did reare,
     Ne bubling rowndell[10] they behinde them sent;
     The rest of other fishes drawen weare,
Which with their finny oars the swelling sea did sheare.

---

[1] **dreriment:** dreariness.

[2] **Continent:** see note at 10.2.

[3] **charett:** chariot.

[4] **wist:** knew.

[5] **buxome:** favorable, welcoming.

[6] **abid:** became and/or remained still.

[7] **gate:** passage; manner of going.

[8] *Triton:* sea god, son of Neptune, and part dolphin.

[9] **flaggy:** drooping.

[10] **rowndell:** swirls of foam.

34   Soone as they bene arriv'd upon the brim
          Of the *Rich strond,* their charets they forlore,[1]
          And let their temed fishes softly swim
          Along the margent of the fomy shore,
          Least they their finnes should bruze, and surbate[2] sore
          Their tender feete upon the stony grownd:
          And comming to the place, where all in gore
          And cruddy[3] blood enwallowed they fownd
      The lucklesse *Marinell,* lying in deadly swownd;

35   His mother swowned thrise, and the third time
          Could scarce recovered bee out of her paine;
          Had she not beene devoide of mortall slime,
          Shee should not then have bene relyv'd againe;
          But soone as life recovered had the raine,[4]
          Shee made so piteous mone and deare wayment,[5]
          That the hard rocks could scarse from tears refraine,
          And all her sister Nymphes with one consent[6]
      Supplide her sobbing breaches[7] with sad complement.

36   "Deare image of my selfe," (she sayd) "that is,
          The wretched sonne of wretched mother borne,
          Is this thine high advauncement, O is this
          Th'immortall name, with which thee yet unborne
          Thy Gransire *Nereus* promist to adorne?
          Now lyest thou of life and honor refte;[8]
          Now lyest thou a lumpe of earth forlorne,
          Ne of thy late life memory is lefte,
      Ne can thy irrevocable desteny bee wefte?[9]

[1] **forlore:** left; abandoned.
[2] **surbate:** bruise.
[3] **cruddy:** curdled.
[4] **raine:** reign.
[5] **wayment:** wailing.
[6] **consent:** accord.
[7] **breaches:** pauses (between sobs).
[8] **refte:** bereft.

[9] **wefte:** done away with or avoided. The meaning is clear from the context, although the OED does not give an appropriate definition for this time period. But Spenser's *weft* may be an alternative spelling for *wafte,* a past tense of *waive,* "to avoid" (OED v[1]6a). Given that *weft* is also an alternative spelling for *waft* (sb[1]), one might speculate that it could serve as a past participle of *waft* (v[1]2), "convey safely by water," appropriate for Marinell's destiny.

37   "Fond[1] *Proteus,* father of false prophecis,
      And they more fond, that credit to thee give,
      Not this the worke of womans hand ywis,[2]
      That so deepe wound through these deare members[3] drive.
      I feared love: but they that love doe live,
      But they that dye, doe nether love nor hate.
      Nath'lesse to thee thy folly I forgive,
      And to my selfe, and to accursed fate
    The guilt I doe ascribe: deare wisedom bought too late.

38   "O what availes it of immortall seed
      To beene ybredd and never borne to dye?
      Farre better I it deeme to die with speed,
      Then waste in woe and waylfull miserye.
      Who dyes the utmost dolor doth abye,[4]
      But who that lives, is lefte to waile his losse:
      So life is losse, and death felicity.
      Sad life worse then[5] glad death: and greater crosse
    To see frends grave, then dead the grave self to engrosse.

39   "But if the heavens did his dayes envie,
      And my short blis maligne,[6] yet mote they well
      Thus much afford[7] me, ere that he did die
      That the dim eies of my deare *Marinell*
      I mote have closed, and him bed farewell,
      Sith other offices for mother meet[8]
      They would not graunt.[9]
      Yett maulgre[10] them farewell, my sweetest sweet;
    Farewell my sweetest sonne, till we againe may meet."

40   Thus when they all had sorowed their fill,
      They softly gan to search his griesly wownd:
      And that they might him handle more at will,
      They him disarmd, and spredding on the grownd

---

[1] **Fond:** foolish.

[2] **ywis:** I know.

[3] **members:** limbs.

[4] **abye:** abide, endure.

[5] **then:** than.

[6] **maligne:** resent; contrive against.

[7] **afford:** grant.

[8] **meet:** appropriate.

[9] The incomplete line may represent Cymoent's breaking off to weep or to grieve silently.

[10] **maulgre:** despite.

Their watchet[1] mantles frindgd with silver rownd,
They softly wipt away the gelly blood
From th'orifice; which having well upbownd,
They pourd in soveraine[2] balme, and Nectar good,
Good both for erthly med'cine, and for hevenly food.

41   Tho when the lilly handed *Liagore,*
        (This *Liagore* whilome had learned skill
        In leaches craft, by great *Appolloes* lore,[3]
        Sith her whilome upon high *Pindus* hill,
        He loved, and at last her wombe did fill
        With hevenly seed, whereof wise *Pæon*[4] sprong)
        Did feele his pulse, shee knew there staied still
        Some litle life his feeble sprites emong;
Which to his mother told, despeyre she from her flong.

42   Tho up him taking in their tender hands,
        They easely unto her charett beare:
        Her teme at her commaundement quiet stands,
        Whiles they the corse[5] into her wagon reare,
        And strowe with flowres the lamentable beare:[6]
        Then all the rest into their coches clim,[7]
        And through the brackish waves their passage shear;
        Upon great *Neptunes* necke they softly swim,
And to her watry chamber swiftly carry him.

43   Deepe in the bottome of the sea, her bowre
        Is built of hollow billowes heaped hye,[8]
        Like to thicke clouds, that threat a stormy showre,
        And vauted[9] all within, like to the Skye,
        In which the Gods doe dwell eternally:
        There they him laide in easy couch[10] well dight;

---

[1] **watchet:** light blue.

[2] **soveraine:** supremely efficacious.

[3] **leaches:** physician's; **lore:** learning.

[4] **Pæon:** physician to the gods.

[5] **corse:** body (not necessarily dead).

[6] **beare:** bier, stretcher.

[7] **clim:** climb.

[8] Compare Spenser's bowers with his caves.

[9] **vauted:** vaulted.

[10] **couch:** bed.

And sent in haste for *Tryphon*,[1] to apply
Salves to his wounds, and medicines of might:
For *Tryphon* of sea gods the soveraine leach[2] is hight.

44   The whiles the *Nymphes* sitt all about him rownd,
Lamenting his mishap and heavy plight;
And ofte his mother vewing his wide wownd,
Cursed the hand, that did so deadly smight
Her dearest sonne, her dearest harts delight.
But none of all those curses overtooke
The warlike Maide, th'ensample of that might,
But fairely well shee thryvd, and well did brooke[3]
Her noble deeds, ne her right course for ought forsooke.

45   Yet did false *Archimage*[4] her still pursew,
To bring to passe his mischievous intent,
Now that he had her singled from the crew[5]
Of courteous knights, the Prince, and Fary gent,[6]
Whom late in chace of beauty excellent
Shee lefte,[7] pursewing that same foster strong;
Of whose fowle outrage they impatient,
And full of firy zele, him followed long,
To reskew her from shame, and to revenge her wrong.

46   Through thick and thin, through mountains and through playns,
Those two gret champions did attonce[8] pursew
The fearefull damzell, with incessant payns:
Who from them fled, as light-foot hare from vew
Of hunter swifte, and sent of howndes trew.[9]

---

[1] *Tryphon:* brother of the immortal physician Aesculapius.

[2] **leach:** physician.

[3] **thryvd:** thrived; **brooke:** bear.

[4] *Archimage:* Archimago is one of the main villains of Books One and Two, disguising himself in order to pursue, tempt, and plot against Redcrosse, Sir Guyon, and their allies. He represents hypocrisy and is sometimes associated with Roman Catholicism. This is his last appearance in the poem, and the fact that his presence here seems pointless may be the result of Spenser's unfin-

ished plotting. Nonetheless, his almost random intrusion adds to the sense that Britomart is only partly aware of the perils that surround her. Her conscious anxieties are overdetermined.

[5] **crew:** group.

[6] I.e., Arthur and Sir Guyon; **gent:** having the qualities of a gentle-born person.

[7] See i.15–19; **foster:** forester; see i.17.

[8] **attonce:** together.

[9] **trew:** accurate (hounds) or certain (scent).

At last they came unto a double way,[1]
Where, doubtfull which to take, her to reskew,
Themselves they did dispart, each to assay,[2]
Whether more happy were, to win so goodly pray.[3]

47   But *Timias,* the Princes gentle Squyre,
        That Ladies love unto his Lord forlent,[4]
        And with proud envy, and indignant yre,
        After that wicked foster fiercely went.
        So beene they three three sondry wayes ybent.[5]
        But fayrest fortune to the Prince befell,
        Whose chaunce it was, that soone he did repent,
        To take that way, in which that Damozell
Was fledd afore, affraid of him, as feend of hell.

48   At last of her far off he gained vew:
        Then gan he freshly pricke his fomy steed,
        And ever as he nigher[6] to her drew,
        So evermore he did increase his speed,
        And of each turning still kept wary heed:
        Alowd to her he oftentimes did call,
        To doe away[7] vaine doubt, and needlesse dreed:
        Full myld to her he spake, and oft let fall
Many meeke wordes, to stay and comfort her withall.

49   But nothing might relent[8] her hasty flight;
        So deepe the deadly feare of that foule swaine[9]
        Was earst impressed in her gentle spright:
        Like as a fearefull Dove, which through the raine,
        Of the wide ayre her way does cut amaine,
        Having farre off espyde a Tassell[10] gent,

---

[1] **double way:** fork in the path.

[2] **dispart:** split up; **assay:** test.

[3] **Whether:** which; **pray:** prey.

[4] **forlent:** gave up entirely.

[5] **ybent:** directed.

[6] **nigher:** closer.

[7] **To doe away:** to do away with.

[8] **relent:** abate.

[9] **swaine:** man; man of low degree; laborer; wooer. Although the word clearly applies to the Forester in this context, it is important that it can also obliquely apply to Arthur, who is, after all, also chasing Florimell.

[10] **Tassell:** male falcon, a bird of prey tamed and used by hunters to bring down other birds.

Which after her his nimble winges doth straine,
Doubleth her hast for feare to bee for-hent,[1]
And with her pineons cleaves the liquid[2] firmament.

50   With no lesse hast, and eke with no lesse dreed,
    That fearefull Ladie fledd from him, that ment
    To her no evill thought, nor evill deed;
    Yet former feare of being fowly shent,[3]
    Carried her forward with her first intent:
    And though oft looking backward, well she vewde,
    Her selfe freed from that foster insolent,[4]
    And that it was a knight, which now her sewde,[5]
Yet she no lesse the knight feard, then that villein[6] rude.

51   His uncouth[7] shield and straunge armes her dismayd,
    Whose like in Faery lond were seldom seene,
    That fast she from him fledd, no lesse afrayd,
    Then of wilde beastes if she had chased beene:
    Yet he her followd still with corage[8] keene,
    So long that now the golden *Hesperus*[9]
    Was mounted high in top of heaven sheene,[10]
    And warnd his other brethren joyeous,
To light their blessed lamps in *Joves*[11] eternall hous.

---

[1] **for-hent:** seized.

[2] **liquid:** transparent like water; fluid like water.

[3] **shent:** disgraced; defiled.

[4] **insolent:** presumptuously insulting; immoderate.

[5] **sewde:** pursued (with a pun on "sued," courted).

[6] **villein:** originally a serf; by the sixteenth century, it was nearly impossible to tell whether the speaker meant "serf" or "base-minded wretch," given that the two social categories were both cause for contempt.

[7] **uncouth:** unusual. Arthur keeps his shield covered, presumably with a cloth. Merlin fashioned it of pure diamond, and not only is it impervious to weapons, but its brightness daunts monsters on the rare occasions when Arthur pulls aside its veil. It reveals foes' disguises, turns rascals into stones, turns stones into dust, turns dust into nothing, and blinds the proud (I.vii.33–35).

[8] **corage:** heart; lust. The second definition is especially important here, though the surrounding praise of Arthur points toward the first definition as primary.

[9] *Hesperus:* the evening star, which Spenser calls "the lampe of love" in his poem the *Epithalamion* (288).

[10] **sheene:** beautiful; shining.

[11] *Joves:* belonging to the king of the Roman gods.

52   All suddeinly dim wox the dampish ayre,
      And griesly shadowes covered heaven bright,
      That now with thousand starres was decked fayre;
      Which when the Prince beheld, a lothfull sight,
      And that perforce, for want[1] of lenger light,
      He mote surceasse his suit, and lose the hope
      Of his long labour, he gan fowly wyte[2]
      His wicked fortune, that had turnd aslope,[3]
And cursed night, that reft from him so goodly scope.[4]

53   Tho when her wayes he could no more descry,
      But to and fro at disaventure[5] strayd;
      Like as a ship, whose Lodestar suddeinly
      Covered with cloudes, her Pilott hath dismayd;
      His wearisome pursuit perforce[6] he stayd,
      And from his loftie steed dismounting low,
      Did let him forage. Downe himselfe he layd
      Upon the grassy ground, to sleepe a throw;[7]
The cold earth was his couch, the hard steele his pillow.

54   But gentle Sleepe envyde him any rest;
      In stead thereof sad sorow, and disdaine
      Of his hard hap did vexe his noble brest,
      And thousand fancies bett[8] his ydle brayne
      With their light wings, the sights of semblants vaine:[9]
      Oft did he wish, that Lady faire mote bee
      His faery Queene, for whom he did complaine:[10]
      Or that his Faery Queene were such, as shee:[11]
And ever hastie Night he blamed bitterlie.

---

[1] **want:** lack.

[2] **wyte:** blame.

[3] **aslope:** aslant, athwart.

[4] **scope:** view.

[5] **at disaventure:** according to mischance; aimlessly and with poor results.

[6] **perforce:** of necessity.

[7] **a throw:** a while.

[8] **bett:** beat.

[9] **semblants vaine:** useless images.

[10] Arthur is in love with, and is searching for, the Faerie Queen, Gloriana, whom he has seen only in an erotic dream (I.ix.13–16). He complains for her not on her behalf, but with frustrated desire for her.

[11] **shee:** the woman whom he wants to rescue from the Forester.

55   "Night thou foule Mother of annoyaunce sad,
      Sister of heavie death, and nourse of woe,
      Which wast begot in heaven, but for thy bad
      And brutish shape thrust downe to hell below,
      Where by the grim floud of *Cocytus*[1] slow
      Thy dwelling is, in *Herebus*[2] black hous,
      (Black *Herebus* thy husband is the foe
      Of all the Gods) where thou ungratious,
 Halfe of thy dayes doest lead in horrour hideous.

56   "What had th'eternall Maker need of thee,
      The world in his continuall course to keepe,
      That doest all thinges deface, ne lettest see
      The beautie of his worke? Indeed in sleepe
      The slouthfull body, that doth love to steep
      His lustlesse limbes, and drowne his baser mind,[3]
      Doth praise thee oft, and oft from *Stygian*[4] deepe
      Calles thee, his goddesse in his errour blind,
 And great Dame Natures handmaide, chearing every kind.

57   "But well I wote,[5] that to an heavy hart
      Thou art the roote and nourse of bitter cares,
      Breeder of new, renewer of old smarts:
      In stead of rest thou lendest rayling[6] teares,
      In stead of sleepe thou sendest troublous feares,
      And dreadfull visions, in the which alive
      The dreary image of sad death appeares:
      So from the wearie spirit thou doest drive
 Desired rest, and men of happinesse deprive.

58   "Under thy mantle blacke there hidden lye,
      Light-shonning thefte, and traiterous intent,
      Abhorred bloodshed, and vile felony,
      Shamefull deceipt, and daunger imminent;
      Fowle horror, and eke hellish dreriment:
      All these I wote in thy protection bee,

---

[1] *Cocytus:* the river of lamentation in hell.

[2] *Herebus:* Erebus, god of darkness.

[3] **lustlesse:** listless; **baser:** too base.

[4] *Stygian:* of Styx, a river in hell; of hell.

[5] **wote:** wot, know.

[6] **rayling:** gushing; loudly complaining.

And light doe shonne, for feare of being shent:[1]
For light ylike is loth'd of them and thee,
And all that lewdnesse love, doe hate the light to see.

59　　"For day discovers all dishonest wayes,
　　　　And sheweth each thing, as it is in deed:
　　　　The prayses of high God he faire displayes,
　　　　And his large bountie rightly doth areed.
　　　　The children of day[2] be the blessed seed,
　　　　Which darknesse shall subdue, and heaven win:
　　　　Truth is his daughter; he her first did breed,
　　　　Most sacred virgin, without spot of sinne.
　　Our life is day, but death with darknesse doth begin.

60　　"O when will day then turne to me againe,
　　　　And bring with him his long expected light?
　　　　O *Titan,* hast to reare thy joyous waine:[3]
　　　　Speed thee to spred abroad thy beames bright,
　　　　And chace away this too long lingring night,
　　　　Chace her away, from whence she came, to hell.
　　　　She, she it is, that hath me done despight:
　　　　There let her with the damned spirits dwell,
　　And yield her rowme to day, that can it governe well."

61　　Thus did the Prince that wearie night outweare,
　　　　In restlesse anguish and unquiet paine:
　　　　And earely, ere the morrow did upreare
　　　　His deawy head out of the *Ocean* maine,
　　　　He up arose, as halfe in great disdaine,
　　　　And clombe[4] unto his steed. So forth he went,
　　　　With heavy looke and lumpish[5] pace, that plaine
　　　　In him bewraid great grudge and maltalent:[6]
　　His steed eke seemd t'apply his steps to his intent.

---

[1] **shent:** digraced.

[2] "Dayes dearest children" (1596 ed.). Cf. 1 Thess. 5.4–8.

[3] *Titan:* the sun god; **waine:** chariot; wagon.

[4] **clombe:** climbed.

[5] **lumpish:** lethargic.

[6] **bewraid:** revealed; **maltalent:** ill temper.

Canto Five

Prince Arthur heares of Florimell:
three fosters[1] Timias wound,
Belphebe findes him almost dead,
and reareth out of sownd.[2]

1   Wonder it is to see, in diverse mindes,
      How diversly love doth his pageaunts play,[3]
      And shewes his powre in variable kindes:[4]
      The baser wit, whose ydle thoughts alway
      Are wont to cleave[5] unto the lowly clay,
      It stirreth up to sensuall desire,
      And in lewd slouth to wast his carelesse day:
      But in brave sprite it kindles goodly fire,
    That to all high desert and honour doth aspire.

2   Ne suffereth[6] it uncomely idlenesse,
      In his free thought to build her sluggish nest:
      Ne suffereth it thought of ungentlenesse,
      Ever to creepe into his noble brest,
      But to the highest and the worthiest
      Lifteth it up, that els would lowly fall:
      It lettes not fall, it lettes it not to rest:
      It lettes not scarse this Prince to breath at all,
    But to his first poursuit[7] him forward still doth call.

3   Who long time wandred through the forest wyde,
      To finde some issue thence,[8] till that at last
      He met a Dwarfe, that seemed terrifyde
      With some late perill, which he hardly past,
      Or other accident, which him aghast;

---

[1] **fosters:** foresters.

[2] **sownd:** swoon.

[3] I.e., puts on various disguises, acting out various roles.

[4] **kindes:** natures.

[5] **wont to cleave:** used to cling.

[6] **suffereth:** allows.

[7] I.e., his quest to find the Faerie Queen.

[8] I.e., to find a way out.

> Of whom he asked, whence he lately came,
> And whether[1] now he traveiled so fast:
> For sore he swat,[2] and ronning through that same
> Thicke forest, was bescracht, and both his feet nigh[3] lame.

4   Panting for breath, and almost out of hart,
>   The Dwarfe him answerd, "Sir, ill[4] mote I stay
>   To tell the same. I lately did depart
>   From Faery court, where I have many a day
>   Served a gentle Lady of great sway,[5]
>   And high accompt through out all Elfin[6] land,
>   Who lately left the same, and tooke this way:
>   Her now I seeke, and if ye understand
> Which way she fared hath, good Sir tell out of hand."

5   "What mister[7] wight" (saide he) "and how arayd?"
>   "Royally clad" (quoth he) "in cloth of gold,
>   As meetest may beseeme[8] a noble mayd;
>   Her faire lockes in rich circlet be enrold,[9]
>   A fayrer wight did never Sunne behold,
>   And on a Palfrey rydes more white then snow,
>   Yet she her selfe is whiter manifold:
>   The surest signe, whereby ye may her know,
> Is, that she is the fairest wight alive, I trow."

6   "Now certes swaine" (saide he) "such one I weene,
>   Fast flying through this forest from her fo,
>   A foule ill favoured foster, I have seene;
>   Her selfe, well as I might, I reskewd tho,
>   But could not stay; so fast she did foregoe,
>   Carried away with wings of speedy feare."

---

[1] **whether:** whither.

[2] **swat:** sweated.

[3] **bescracht:** thoroughly scratched; **nigh:** nearly.

[4] **ill:** scarcely; with bad results.

[5] **sway:** power, influence.

[6] **accompt:** account, reputation; **Elfin:** Faerie.

[7] **mister:** sort, type.

[8] **meetest:** most appropriately; **beseeme:** appear (on).

[9] **circlet:** ornamental metal or ribbon band worn around the head; circle of twisted or braided hair; **enrold:** coiled; braided.

"Ah dearest God" (quoth he) "that is great woe,
And wondrous ruth[1] to all, that shall it heare.
But can ye read Sir, how I may her finde, or where?"

7   "Perdy me lever were[2] to weeten that,"
    (Saide he) "then ransome of the richest knight,
    Or all the good that ever yet I gat:
    But froward fortune, and too forward[3] Night
    Such happinesse did, maulgre,[4] to me spight,
    And fro me reft both life and light attone.
    But Dwarfe aread, what is that Lady bright,
    That through this forrest wandreth thus alone;
For of her errour[5] straunge I have great ruth and mone."

8   "That Ladie is" (quoth he) "where so she bee,
    The bountiest virgin, and most debonaire,[6]
    That ever living eye I weene did see;
    Lives none this day, that may with her compare
    In stedfast chastitie and vertue rare,
    The goodly ornaments of beautie bright;
    And is ycleped *Florimell*[7] the fayre,
    Faire *Florimell* belov'd of many a knight,
Yet she loves none but one, that *Marinell* is hight.

9   "A Sea-nymphes sonne, that *Marinell* is hight,
    Of my deare Dame is loved dearely well;
    In other none, but him, she sets delight,
    All her delight is set on *Marinell;*
    But he sets nought at all by *Florimell.*[8]
    For Ladies love his mother long ygoe
    Did him, they say, forwarne through sacred spell.
    But fame[9] now flies, that of a forreine foe
He is yslaine, which is the ground[10] of all our woe.

---

[1] **ruth:** cause of compassion or sorrow.

[2] **Perdy:** by God; **me lever were:** I had rather.

[3] **froward:** adverse, untoward, counter to what is reasonable or desirable; inimical; **forward:** arriving too quickly.

[4] **maulgre:** a generalized curse, like "dammit!"

[5] **errour:** wandering.

[6] **debonaire:** gracious.

[7] Florimell first entered the poem as the "goodly Lady" of i.15. Her name links her to Marinell, as well as to flowers.

[8] I.e., he does not care for her.

[9] **fame:** rumor.

[10] **ground:** foundation, reason.

10   "Five daies there be, since he (they say) was slaine,
         And fowre, since *Florimell* the Court forwent,[1]
         And vowed never to returne againe,
         Till him alive or dead she did invent.[2]
       Therefore, faire Sir, for love of knighthood gent,
         And honour of trew Ladies, if ye may
         By your good counsell, or bold hardiment,
         Or succour her, or[3] me direct the way,
       Do one, or other good, I you most humbly pray.

11   "So may ye gaine to you full great renowme,
         Of all good Ladies through the world so wide,
         And haply in her hart finde highest rowme,[4]
         Of whom ye seeke to be most magnifide:[5]
       At least eternall meede shall you abide."[6]
       To whom the Prince; "Dwarfe, comfort to thee take,
         For till thou tidings learne, what her betide,
         I here avow thee never to forsake.
       Ill weares he armes, that nill them use for Ladies sake."

12   So with the Dwarfe he backe retourn'd againe,
         To seeke his Lady, where he mote her finde;
         But by the way he greatly gan complaine
         The want of his good Squire late left behinde,[7]
       For whom he wondrous pensive grew in minde,
         For doubt of daunger, which mote him betide;[8]
         For him he loved above all mankinde,
         Having him trew and faithfull ever tride,
       And bold, as ever Squyre that waited by knights side.

13   Who all this while full hardly was assayd[9]
         Of deadly daunger, which to him betidd;[10]
         For whiles his Lord pursewd that noble Mayd,

---

[1] **forwent:** left.

[2] **invent:** come upon, find.

[3] **Or . . . or:** either . . . or.

[4] **rowme:** room, place.

[5] **magnifide:** praised.

[6] **meede:** reward; **shall you abide:** shall
wait for you.

[7] See i.18.6–9.

[8] **doubt:** apprehensiveness, worry, fear;
betide: befall.

[9] **Who:** Arthur's squire, Timias. Spenser is
fond of transporting the narrative across
time and space by the expedient of one rel-
ative pronoun; **assayd:** assailed.

[10] **betidd:** befell.

After that foster fowle he fiercely ridd,[1]
To bene avenged of the shame, he did
To that faire Damzell: Him he chaced long
Through the thicke woods, wherein he would have hid
His shamefull head from his avengement strong,
And oft him threatned death for his outrageous wrong.

14   Nathlesse the villein[2] sped himselfe so well,
Whether through swiftnesse of his speedie beast,
Or knowledge of those woods, where he did dwell,
That shortly he from daunger was releast,
And out of sight escaped at the least;[3]
Yet not escaped from the dew reward
Of his bad deedes, which daily he increast,
Ne ceased not, till him oppressed hard
The heavie plague,[4] that for such leachours is prepard.

15   For soone as he was vanisht out of sight,
His[5] coward courage gan emboldned bee,
And cast t'avenge him of that fowle despight,
Which he had borne of his bold enimee.
Tho to his brethren came: for they were three
Ungratious[6] children of one gracelesse syre,
And unto them complayned, how that he
Had used beene of that foolehardie Squyre;
So them with bitter words he stird to bloodie yre.

16   Forthwith themselves with their sad[7] instruments
Of spoyle and murder they gan arme bylive,[8]
And with him foorth into the forrest went,
To wreake the wrath, which he did earst revive
In their sterne brests, on him which late did drive
Their brother to reproch and shamefull flight:
For they had vow'd, that never he alive
Out of that forest should escape their might;
Vile rancour their rude harts had fild with such despight.

---

[1] **ridd:** rode.

[2] **villein:** base character; serf.

[3] **at the least:** at last.

[4] **plague:** blow or wound.

[5] **His:** the Forester's.

[6] **Ungratious:** lacking spiritual grace.

[7] **sad:** capable of causing sorrow.

[8] **bylive:** speedily.

17   Within that wood there was a covert glade,
          Foreby a narrow foord,[1] to them well knowne,
          Through which it was uneath[2] for wight to wade,
          And now by fortune it was overflowne:[3]
          By that same way they knew that Squyre unknowne
          Mote algates passe; for thy themselves they set
          There in await, with thicke woods over growne,
          And all the while their malice they did whet
    With cruell threats, his passage through the ford to let.[4]

18   It fortuned, as they devized had,
          The gentle Squyre came ryding that same way,
          Unweeting of their wile and treason bad,
          And through the ford to passen did assay;
          But that fierce foster, which late fled away,
          Stoutly[5] foorth stepping on the further shore,
          Him boldly bad his passage there to stay,
          Till he had made amends, and full restore[6]
    For all the damage, which he had him doen afore.

19   With that at him a quiv'ring dart he threw,
          With so fell force and villeinous despite,
          That through his habericon[7] the forkehead flew,
          And through the linked mayles[8] empierced quite,
          But had no powre in his soft flesh to bite:
          That stroke the hardy Squire did sore displease,
          But more that him he could not come to smite;[9]
          For by no meanes the high banke he could sease,[10]
    But labour'd long in that deepe ford with vaine disease.[11]

20   And still the foster with his long bore-speare
          Him kept from landing at his wished will;
          Anone one sent out of the thicket neare

---

[1] I.e., close by a narrow ford.

[2] **uneath:** difficult.

[3] **overflowne:** overflowed, flooded.

[4] **let:** prevent. Waiting for an enemy beside a narrow ford was a technique used by the Irish and known to Spenser.

[5] **Stoutly:** with bravery.

[6] **restore:** restitution.

[7] **habericon:** habergeon, chain-mail tunic.

[8] **mayles:** individual links that make up chain mail.

[9] I.e., it displeased the Squire even more that he could not get close enough to them to strike a blow.

[10] **sease:** seize (i.e., climb to).

[11] **disease:** uneasiness; trouble.

A cruell shaft, headed with deadly ill,
And fethered with an unlucky quill;
The wicked steele stayd not, till it did light
In his left thigh, and deepely did it thrill:[1]
Exceeding griefe that wound in him empight,[2]
But more that with his foes he could not come to fight.

21   At last through wrath and vengeaunce making way,
He on the bancke arryvd with mickle payne,[3]
Where the third brother him did sore assay,
And drove at him with all his might and mayne
A forest bill,[4] which both his hands did strayne;
But warily he did avoide the blow,
And with his speare requited him agayne,
That both his[5] sides were thrilled with the throw,
And a large streame of bloud out of the wound did flow.

22   He tombling downe, with gnashing teeth did bite
The bitter earth, and bad to lett him in
Into the balefull house of endlesse night,
Where wicked ghosts doe waile their former sin.
Tho gan the battaile freshly to begin;
For nathemore for that spectacle bad,
Did th'other two their cruell vengeaunce blin,[6]
But both attonce on both sides him bestad,[7]
And load upon him layd, his life for to have had.

23   Tho when that villayn he aviz'd,[8] which late
Affrighted had the fairest *Florimell,*
Full of fiers fury, and indignant hate,
To him he turned, and with rigor fell
Smote him so rudely on the Pannikell,[9]

---

[1] **his:** Timias'; **thrill:** pierce. "Thigh" is often a poetic euphemism for, or allegorical pointer to, "groin." If that interpretation at first seems unlikely, it makes perfect sense the next time the location of Timias' wound is mentioned, in stanza 42.

[2] **empight:** emplanted.

[3] **mickle payne:** much effort.

[4] **forest bill:** tool used for pruning, with a long, concave blade sometimes ending in a hook.

[5] **his:** those of the Forester's second brother.

[6] **blin:** cease.

[7] **bestad:** beset.

[8] **he:** Timias; **aviz'd:** saw, took note of; i.e., when Timias saw the Forester.

[9] **Pannikell:** pate, skull.

That to the chin he clefte his head in twaine:
Downe on the ground his carkas groveling fell;
His sinfull sowle with desperate disdaine,
Out of her fleshly ferme[1] fled to the place of paine.

24   That seeing now the only last of three,
      Who with that wicked shafte him wounded had,
      Trembling with horror, as that did foresee
      The fearefull end of his avengement sad,
      Through which he follow should his brethren bad,
      His bootelesse[2] bow in feeble hand upcaught,
      And therewith shott an arrow at the lad;
      Which fayntly fluttring, scarce his helmet raught,[3]
And glauncing fel to ground, but him annoyed naught.

25   With that he would have fled into the wood;
      But *Timias* him lightly overhent,[4]
      Right as he entring was into the flood,
      And strooke at him with force so violent,
      That headlesse him into the foord he sent:
      The carcas with the streame was carried downe,
      But th'head fell backeward on the Continent.
      So mischief fel upon the meaners crowne;[5]
They three be dead with shame, the Squire lives with renowne.

26   He lives, but takes small joy of his renowne;
      For of that cruell wound he bled so sore,
      That from his steed he fell in deadly swowne;
      Yet still the blood forth gusht in so great store,
      That he lay wallowd all in his owne gore.
      Now God thee keepe, thou gentlest squire alive,

---

[1] **ferme:** As Roche suggests in his note to this line, Spenser may mean "enclosure," from the French verb "fermer," "to close." Alternatively, this may be the first instance of the use of a rare English word recorded by the OED only in 1620 and 1688, meaning "hole; cave; hiding place." The body was often referred to piously as the prison of the soul, whose proper home was heaven. Here, Spenser may be going a step further to imply that the Forester's body is a lair for his beastly soul.

[2] **bootelesse:** useless.

[3] **raught:** reached.

[4] **overhent:** overtook.

[5] **meaners crowne:** the head of one who intended mischief.

Els shall thy loving Lord[1] thee see no more,
But both of comfort him thou shalt deprive,
And eke thy selfe of honor, which thou didst atchive.

27   Providence hevenly passeth[2] living thought,
      And doth for wretched mens reliefe make way;
      For loe great grace or fortune thether[3] brought
      Comfort to him, that comfortlesse now lay.
      In those same woods, ye well remember may,
      How that a noble hunteresse did wonne,
      Shee, that base *Braggadochio* did affray,
      And made him fast out of the forest ronne;
Belphœbe was her name, as faire as *Phœbus* sunne.[4]

28   She on a day, as shee pursewd the chace
      Of some wilde beast, which with her arrowes keene
      She wounded had, the same along did trace
      By tract[5] of blood, which she had freshly seene,
      To have besprinckled all the grassy greene,
      By the great persue,[6] which she there perceav'd,
      Well hoped shee the beast engor'd had beene,
      And made more haste, the life to have bereav'd:[7]
But ah, her expectation greatly was deceav'd.

29   Shortly she came, whereas that woefull Squire
      With blood deformed,[8] lay in deadly swownd:
      In whose faire eyes, like lamps of quenched fire,

[1] **Lord:** Arthur.

[2] **passeth:** surpasses.

[3] **thether:** thither.

[4] Belphoebe is Spenser's invention, though he aligns her with Diana, the chaste goddess of the hunt. In "The Letter to Raleigh," Spenser explicitly names Belphoebe as one of the characters who represent aspects of Elizabeth Tudor. When Belphoebe makes her first appearance in Book Two, the narrator describes her as "borne of heavenly birth," "Hable to heale the sick, and to revive the ded," surpassingly beautiful, and having eyes that radiate "dredd Majestie" (II.iii.22–23). The bragging and cowardly Braggadocchio attempts to embrace her; she vigorously repels him with her javelin and flees; he and his friend, Trompart, then quickly leave, as well (II.iii.34–46). The earlier passage could be interpreted as meaning that he and Trompart left quickly because they were reluctant to run into Belphoebe again.

[5] **tract:** track. Timias has become the huntress' quarry.

[6] **persue:** the track of blood left by a wounded animal, such as a deer.

[7] **bereav'd:** taken from the beast.

[8] **deformed:** disfigured.

The Christall humor[1] stood congealed rownd;
His locks, like faded leaves fallen to grownd,
Knotted with blood, in bounches rudely[2] ran,
And his sweete lips, on which before that stownd
The bud of youth to blossome faire began,
Spoild of their rosy red, were woxen pale and wan.

30   Saw never living eie more heavy sight,
      That could have made a rocke of stone to rew,[3]
    Or rive in twaine: which when that Lady bright
    Besides all hope[4] with melting eies did vew,
    All suddeinly abasht shee chaunged hew,
    And with sterne horror backward gan to start:
    But when shee better him beheld, shee grew
    Full of soft passion and unwonted smart:
The point of pitty perced through her tender hart.

31   Meekely shee bowed downe, to weete if life
      Yett in his frosen members did remaine,
    And feeling by his pulses beating rife,
    That the weake sowle her seat did yett retaine,
    She cast to comfort him with busy paine:
    His double folded necke she reard upright,
    And rubd his temples, and each trembling vaine;
    His mayled habericon she did undight,
And from his head his heavy burganet[5] did light.

32   Into the woods thenceforth in haste shee went,
      To seeke for hearbes, that mote him remedy;
    For shee of herbes had great intendiment,[6]
    Taught of the Nymphe, which from her infancy
    Her nourced had in trew Nobility:
    There, whether yt divine *Tobacco*[7] were,

---

[1] **Christall humor:** crystal-clear liquid in the eye.

[2] **rudely:** in a disorderly fashion.

[3] **rew:** rue, pity.

[4] **Besides all hope:** having no hope that he was alive.

[5] **burganet:** helmet with visor.

[6] **intendiment:** understanding.

[7] *Tobacco:* introduced from the Americas by Raleigh in 1584 and at first thought to be healthful in its purging the body of phlegm. This is the first reference to tobacco in English imaginative literature.

Or *Panachœa*, or *Polygony*,[1]
Shee fownd, and brought it to her patient deare[2]
Who al this while lay bleeding out his hart-blood neare.

33   The soveraine weede betwixt two marbles[3] plaine
    Shee pownded small, and did in peeces bruze,
    And then atweene her lilly handes twaine,
    Into his wound the juice thereof did scruze,[4]
    And round about, as she could well it uze,
    The flesh therewith shee suppled[5] and did steepe,
    T'abate all spasme, and soke the swelling bruze,
    And after having searcht the intuse[6] deepe,
She with her scarf did bind the wound from cold to keepe.

34   By this he had sweet life recur'd[7] agayne,
    And groning inly deepe, at last his eies,
    His watry eies, drizling like deawy rayne,
    He up gan lifte toward the azure skies,
    From whence descend all hopelesse[8] remedies:
    Therewith he sigh'd, and turning him aside,
    The goodly Maide ful of divinities,
    And gifts of heavenly grace he by him spide,
Her bow and gilden quiver lying him beside.

35   "Mercy deare Lord" (said he) "what grace is this,
    That thou hast shewed to me sinfull wight,
    To send thine Angell from her bowre of blis,[9]
    To comfort me in my distressed plight?
    Angell, or Goddesse doe I call thee right?
    What service may I doe unto thee meete,
    That hast from darkenes me returnd to light,
    And with thy hevenly salves and med'cines sweete,
Hast drest my sinfull wounds? I kisse thy blessed feete."

---

[1] *Panachœa:* panacea, the herb Heal-All; *Polygony:* an herb used in treating wounds.

[2] **deare:** note the pun on her more usual quarry.

[3] **marbles:** flat pieces of marble.

[4] **scruze:** squeeze.

[5] **suppled:** softened; massaged.

[6] **intuse:** bruise.

[7] **recur'd:** recovered.

[8] **hopelesse:** unhoped for, unexpected; for those who are (otherwise) hopeless.

[9] Cf. Acrasia's Bower of Bliss in II.vi and II.xii.

36   Thereat she blushing said, "Ah gentle Squire,
          Nor Goddesse I, nor Angell, but the Mayd,
          And daughter of a woody Nymphe, desire
          No service, but thy safety and ayd,
          Which if thou gaine, I shalbe well apayd.
          Wee mortall wights, whose lives and fortunes bee
          To commun accidents[1] stil open layd,
          Are bownd with commun bond of frailtee,
     To succor wretched wights, whom we captived see."

37   By this[2] her Damzells, which the former chace
          Had undertaken after her, arryv'd,
          As did *Belphœbe,* in the bloody place,
          And thereby deemd the beast had bene depriv'd
          Of life, whom late their ladies arrow ryv'd:
          For thy the bloody tract they followd fast,
          And every one to ronne the swiftest stryv'd;
          But two of them the rest far overpast,
     And where their Lady was, arrived at the last.

38   Where when they saw that goodly boy, with blood
          Defowled, and their Lady dresse his wownd,
          They wondred much, and shortly understood,
          How him in deadly case theyr Lady fownd,
          And reskewed out of the heavy stownd.
          Eftsoones his warlike courser, which was strayd
          Farre in the woodes, whiles that he lay in swownd,
          She made those Damzels search, which being stayd,[3]
     They did him[4] set thereon, and forth with them convayd.

39   Into that forest farre they thence[5] him led,
          Where was their dwelling, in a pleasant glade,
          With mountaines rownd about environed,[6]
          And mightie woodes, which did the valley shade,
          And like a stately Theatre[7] it made,
          Spreading it selfe into a spatious plaine.

---

[1] **accidents:** chance occurrences.

[2] **By this:** by this time, at this time.

[3] **search:** search for; **stayd:** stopped; taken captive.

[4] **him:** Timias.

[5] **thence:** from there.

[6] **environed:** encircling.

[7] **Theatre:** natural amphitheater.

And in the midst a little river plaide
Emongst the pumy[1] stones, which seemd to plaine
With gentle murmure, that his cours they did restraine.

40   Beside the same a dainty[2] place there lay,
        Planted with mirtle[3] trees and laurells greene,
        In which the birds song many a lovely lay[4]
        Of gods high praise, and of their loves sweet teene,[5]
        As it an earthly Paradize had beene:
        In whose enclosed shadow there was pight[6]
        A faire Pavilion, scarcely to be seene,[7]
        The which was al within most richly dight,
    That greatest Princes living it mote well delight.

41   Thether they brought that wounded Squyre, and layd
        In easie couch[8] his feeble limbes to rest.
        He rested him a while, and then the Mayd
        His readie[9] wound with better salves new drest;
        Daily she dressed him,[10] and did the best
        His grievous hurt to guarish,[11] that she might,
        That shortly she his dolour hath redrest,
        And his foule sore reduced to faire plight:[12]
    It she reduced, but himselfe destroyed quight.[13]

42   O foolish physick, and unfruitfull paine,[14]
        That heales up one and makes another wound:
        She his hurt thigh to him recurd[15] againe,

---

[1] **pumy:** pumice.

[2] **dainty:** delightful; choice.

[3] **mirtle:** myrtles are sacred to Venus.

[4] **lay:** song, usually about love.

[5] **teene:** affliction; vexation; injury; suffering.

[6] **pight:** pitched (as a tent).

[7] Cf. Spenser's other bowers, caves, and secret circular places—all the way to Mount Acidale in VI.x.5–31. They do not all serve the same allegorical function, but they play against each other.

[8] **easie:** comfortable, conducive to ease; **couch:** bed.

[9] **readie:** prepared; dressed.

[10] I.e., his wound.

[11] **guarish:** cure.

[12] **reduced:** brought back; restored—but given stanza 42, there is a peripheral pun here on the sense "brought under subjection"; **faire plight:** good condition, with peripheral puns on the senses "peril," "guilt," and even "pledge of marriage engagement."

[13] Compare Timias' condition with that of the beast in stanza 37.

[14] **physick:** medicine; medical care; **unfruitfull:** producing no good results; producing no child; **paine:** care or labor, with an obvious pun.

[15] **thigh:** the possibility that this is a euphemism for "groin" in stanza 20 becomes clear here; **recurd:** recovered.

But hurt his hart, the which before was sound,[1]
Through an unwary dart, which did rebownd[2]
From her faire eyes and gratious countenaunce.
What bootes[3] it him from death to be unbownd,
To be captived in endlesse duraunce[4]
Of sorrow and despeyre without aleggeaunce?[5]

43   Still as his wound did gather, and grow hole,[6]
So still his hart woxe sore, and health decayd:
Madnesse to save a part, and lose the whole.
Still whenas he beheld the heavenly Mayd,
Whiles dayly playsters[7] to his wownd she layd,
So still his Malady the more increast,
The whiles her matchlesse beautie him dismayd.
Ah God, what other could he doe at least,
But love so fayre a Lady, that his life releast?[8]

44   Long while he strove in his corageous brest,
With reason dew[9] the passion to subdew,
And love for to dislodge out of his nest:
Still when her excellencies he did vew,
Her soveraine bountie, and celestiall hew,[10]
The same to love he strongly was constraynd:

---

[1] **sound:** healthy.

[2] **rebownd:** leap out or arise from; bounce. The context suggests the former definition, but the latter is more common in sixteenth-century texts, and it works well here as a pun. Light was thought to proceed from eyes; however, with the second sense of "rebownd," Cupid's dart does not proceed from Belphoebe's eyes to Timias' heart but bounces on her eyes and back out. This suggests that it originates with Timias, fails to hurt her, and returns to hurt him. It is relevant that sixteenth- and seventeenth-century poets were fascinated with the reflection of oneself that one could see in a beloved's eyes when up close. Petrarchan poets had explored the idea that a despairing wooer constructs his own version of his beloved inside his mind and loves that construction more than he loves any woman out in the world around him.

[3] **bootes:** avails.

[4] **duraunce:** imprisonment.

[5] **aleggeaunce:** alleviation, with a possible pun on the sense "presenting proof in court," given that Timias cannot plead his case to Belphoebe.

[6] The puns nicely convey Timias' paradoxical state: his physical wound gathers (as its sides grow together) and becomes whole; his emotional wound gathers (becomes infected) and becomes a hole.

[7] **playsters:** bandages.

[8] I.e., from death's clutches.

[9] **dew:** due, appropriate.

[10] **hew:** hue, complexion; appearance.

But when his meane estate he did revew,
He from such hardy boldnesse was restraynd,
And of his lucklesse lott and cruell love thus playnd.

45   "Unthankfull wretch" (said he) "is this the meed,[1]
    With which her soverain mercy thou doest quight?[2]
    Thy life she saved by her gratious deed,
    But thou doest weene with villeinous despight,
    To blott her honour, and her heavenly light.
    Dye rather, dye, then so disloyally
    Deeme of her high desert, or seeme so light:[3]
    Fayre death it is to shonne more shame, to dy:[4]
Dye rather, dy, then ever love disloyally.

46   "But if to love disloyalty it bee,[5]
    Shall I then hate her, that from deathes dore
    Me brought? ah farre be such reproch fro mee.
    What can I lesse doe, then her love therefore,
    Sith I her dew reward cannot restore:
    Dye rather, dye,[6] and dying doe her serve,
    Dying her serve, and living her adore;
    Thy life she gave, thy life she doth deserve:
Dye rather, dye, then ever from her service swerve.

---

[1] **meed:** reward; repayment; Timias is speaking to himself.

[2] **quight:** requite. Timias would not need to feel so guilty at loving her chastely without expectation of return; his guilt indicates that he is also having lustful thoughts.

[3] I.e., to form such a disloyal opinion of—or such a disloyal expectation of—her lofty worthiness, or to seem so shallow-minded.

[4] I.e., it will be good for you (speaking to himself) to die if by doing so you avoid incurring still more shame. There are puns on both "dye" (common slang for "have an orgasm") and "serve" (common slang for "service someone sexually").

[5] I.e., if it is disloyal to love.

[6] This contrived refrain is not necessarily a sign that the poem is asking its readers to consider Timias as more self-consciously artful than sincere. Sixteenth-century poets often used highly artificial language to convey the intense emotion attendant upon times of great stress or of great sincerity. Nor was this merely a poetic strategy; in his handbook for courtiers, Castiglione at times apparently leans toward the opinion that people who are noble in every sense of the word find it easy to learn how to speak nobly and can thus be recognized as noble through their easy but elegant manner of speaking. See Introduction, 1.

47   "But foolish boy, what bootes[1] thy service bace
     To her, to whom the hevens doe serve and sew?[2]
     Thou a meane Squyre, of meeke and lowly place,[3]
     She hevenly borne, and of celestiall hew.
     How then? of all love taketh equall vew:[4]
     And doth not highest God vouchsafe[5] to take
     The love and service of the basest crew?[6]
     If she will not, dye meekly for her sake;
  Dye rather, dye, then ever so faire love forsake."

48   Thus warreid[7] he long time against his will,
     Till that[8] through weaknesse he was forst at last,
     To yield himselfe unto the mightie ill:
     Which as a victour proud, gan ransack fast
     His inward partes, and all his entrayles wast,[9]
     That neither blood in face, nor life in hart
     It left, but both did quite drye up, and blast;[10]
     As percing levin,[11] which the inner part
  Of every thing consumes, and calcineth by art.[12]

49   Which seeing[13] fayre *Belphoebe,* gan to feare,
     Least[14] that his wound were inly well not heald,
     Or that the wicked steele empoysned were:
     Litle shee weend, that love he close conceald;
     Yet still he wasted, as the snow congeald,
     When the bright sunne his beams thereon doth beat;
     Yet never he his hart to her reveald,
     But rather chose to dye for sorow great,
  Then with dishonorable termes her to entreat.

---

[1] **bootes:** avails, profits.

[2] **sew:** attend upon; take as a guide; court; apply to for favor.

[3] **meane:** inferior; low; **place:** occupation; status.

[4] I.e., love looks alike on everyone.

[5] **vouchsafe:** grant.

[6] **crew:** bunch; gang; mob.

[7] **warreid:** warred.

[8] **Till that:** until.

[9] **wast:** waste.

[10] **blast:** wither.

[11] **levin:** lightning.

[12] **calcineth by art:** reduces to powder by alchemical means.

[13] Imagine a comma here; Belphoebe is doing the seeing.

[14] **Least:** lest.

50   She gracious Lady, yet no paines did spare,
        To doe him ease, or doe him remedy:
        Many Restoratives of vertues[1] rare,
        And costly Cordialles[2] she did apply,
        To mitigate his stubborne malady:
        But that sweet Cordiall, which can restore
        A love-sick hart, she did to him envy;[3]
        To him, and to all th'unworthy world forlore[4]
    She did envy that soveraine[5] salve, in secret store.

51   That daintie Rose,[6] the daughter of her Morne,
        More deare then life she tendered, whose flowre
        The girlond[7] of her honour did adorne:
        Ne suffred she the Middayes scorching powre,
        Ne the sharp Northerne wind thereon to showre,
        But lapped up her silken leaves most chayre,[8]
        When so the froward skye began to lowre;[9]
        But soone as calmed was the christall ayre,
    She did it fayre dispred,[10] and let to florish fayre.

[1] **vertues:** healing qualities.

[2] **Cordialles:** restorative beverage, usually made by the lady of the house, consisting of sweetened spirits with or without herbs or other medicinal ingredients (sugar being itself thought medicinal). Etymologically, medicine that restores the heart.

[3] **envy:** deny; begrudge.

[4] **forlore:** miserable; forlorn.

[5] **soveraine:** superlatively efficacious.

[6] **Rose:** her chastity and/or her virginity. Clearly Spenser is using the character of Belphoebe to comment upon, and at least ostensibly to praise, the Virgin Queen. However, the stanza's concrete descriptions tip the rose metaphor dangerously toward equating the rose neither with chastity nor virginity but with Belphoebe's unbroken hymen. If the metaphor tips all the way in that direction, several of the stanza's images become nothing short of bizarre. But with or without the rose metaphor, Belphoebe's denying Timias the one thing that would cure him is ambiguously represented: is she virtue personified, or is she cold-hearted and even selfish? In a world in which a barrage of parental lectures, sermons, pamphlets, books, letters, and passing remarks teach unmarried women that their highest aspiration to virtue consists of preserving their virginity until marriage, the question of whether Spenser is purely praising or partly condemning Belphoebe is not an easy one. Shakespeare recognized the moral dilemma when he wrote about Isabella, Claudio, and Angelo in *Measure for Measure*.

[7] **girlond:** garland.

[8] **lapped:** folded up; **chayre:** charily, carefully; frugally.

[9] **froward:** uncooperative; inimical; **lowre:** lower, scowl—i.e., become overcast.

[10] **dispred:** spread out; spread around.

52   Eternall God in his almightie powre,
             To make ensample of his heavenly grace,
             In Paradize whylome did plant this flowre;
             Whence he it fetcht out of her native place,
             And did in stocke of earthly flesh enrace,[1]
             That mortall men her glory should admyre:
             In gentle Ladies breste, and bounteous race
             Of woman kind it fayrest flowre doth spyre,[2]
     And beareth fruit of honour and all chast desyre.

53   Fayre ympes[3] of beautie, whose bright shining beames
             Adorne the world with like to heavenly light,
             And to your willes both royalties and Reames[4]
             Subdew, through conquest of your wondrous might,
             With this fayre flowre your goodly girlonds dight,
             Of chastity and vertue virginall,
             That shall embellish more your beautie bright,
             And crowne your heades with heavenly coronall,
     Such as the Angels weare before Gods tribunall.

54   To youre faire selves a faire ensample frame,[5]
             Of this faire virgin, this *Belphebe* fayre,
             To whom in perfect love, and spotlesse fame
             Of chastitie, none living[6] may compayre:
             Ne poysnous Envy justly can empayre
             The prayse of her fresh flowring Maydenhead;
             For thy she standeth on the highest stayre[7]
             Of th'honorable stage of womanhead,
     That Ladies all may follow her ensample dead.[8]

---

[1] **enrace:** implant.

[2] **spyre:** put forth (as a plant puts forth spires of new growth).

[3] **ympes:** offspring.

[4] **Reames:** realms.

[5] **frame:** fashion.

[6] **none living:** Anderson argues that this phrase would tend to turn Belphoebe into a pure ideal rather than into a living example (56). The phrase is at least ambiguous, given that Belphoebe is still living when the fictional action of the stanza is taking place and that Elizabeth is still living when Spenser writes these lines.

[7] **stayre:** step; degree.

[8] **her ensample dead:** her example after she is dead. Anderson points out that the phrase also conveys the ironic meaning "her lifeless example." Again, the poem leaves open the possibility that Belphoebe's flourishing chastity is cold and inhumane.

55	In so great prayse of stedfast chastity,
	Nathlesse she was so courteous and kynde,
	Tempred with grace, and goodly modesty,
	That seemed those two vertues strove to fynd
	The higher place in her Heroick mynd:
	So striving each did other more augment,
	And both encreast the prayse of woman kynde,
	And both encreast her beautie excellent;
So all did make in her a perfect complement.[1]

---

[1] **complement:** completion; fulfillment;
consummation.

Canto Six

The birth of fayre Belphoebe and
Of Amorett is told.
The Gardins of Adonis fraught[1]
With pleasures manifold.

1   Well may I weene, faire Ladies, all this while
       Ye wonder, how this noble Damozell[2]
       So great perfections did in her compile,
       Sith that in salvage forests she did dwell,
       So farre from court and royall Citadell,
       The great schoolmaistresse of all courtesy:[3]
       Seemeth[4] that such wilde woodes should far expell
       All civile usage and gentility,
    And gentle sprite deforme with rude rusticity.

2   But to this faire *Belphœbe* in her berth[5]
       The hevens so favorable were and free,[6]
       Looking with myld aspect[7] upon the earth,
       In th'*Horoscope* of her nativitee,
       That all the gifts of grace and chastitee
       On her they poured forth of plenteous horne;[8]

---

[1] **fraught:** freighted, laden. The plural of *"Gardins"* emphasizes that the one garden described in this canto is closely tied to the many little gardens (or pots of quickly blooming flowers) grown by Greek followers of the Cult of Adonis.

[2] I.e., Belphoebe.

[3] **great schoolmaistresse:** the court, which was supposed to be the definition and origin of courtesy; **courtesy:** not only courtesy in the modern sense, but the whole panoply of good manners, talents, and virtues to which any knight, lord, or lady serving at court was supposed to aspire. The lower classes were not usually considered capable of true courtesy, although humanists gestured toward the idea that education was as important as lineage in determining noble virtue.

[4] **Seemeth:** it seems; it would seem.

[5] **berth:** birth.

[6] **free:** generous.

[7] **myld aspect:** favorable astrological relationships.

[8] **plenteous horne:** cornucopia, horn of plenty.

Jove laught on *Venus* from his soverayne see,[1]
And *Phœbus* with faire beames did her adorne,[2]
And all the *Graces* rockt her cradle being borne.

3   Her berth was of the wombe of Morning dew,[3]
    And her conception of the joyous Prime,[4]
    And all her whole creation did her shew
    Pure and unspotted from all loathly crime,
    That is ingenerate in fleshly slime.[5]
    So was this virgin borne, so was she bred,
    So was she trayned up from time to time,[6]
    In all chaste vertue, and true bounti-hed
Till to her dew perfection she was ripened.

4   Her mother was the faire *Chrysogonee*,[7]
    The daughter of *Amphisa*,[8] who by race
    A Faerie was, yborne of high degree,
    She bore *Belphœbe*, she bore in like cace[9]
    Fayre *Amoretta* in the second place:
    These two were twinnes, and twixt them two did share
    The heritage of all celestiall grace.
    That all the rest it seemd they robbed bare
Of bounty, and of beautie, and all vertues rare.

5   It were a goodly storie, to declare,
    By what straunge accident[10] faire *Chrysogone*
    Conceiv'd these infants, and how them she bore,
    In this wilde forrest wandring all alone,
    After she had nine moneths fulfild and gone:
    For not as other wemens commune brood,

---

[1] **see:** seat, throne.

[2] I.e., the planets were favorably aligned at her birth.

[3] Cf. Ps. 110.3.

[4] **Prime:** springtime.

[5] I.e., unlike all other mortals except for Jesus and his mother, Mary, Belphoebe is born without original sin—the general sin made inherent in the human race by Adam and Eve's specific sin.

[6] **from time to time:** continuously.

[7] *Chrysogonee:* Greek "golden-born." The name links her with Danaë, a mythological character who conceived when Jove came to her in the form of a shower of gold.

[8] *Amphisa:* Greek "of double nature."

[9] **in like cace:** by the same means; at the same (or much the same) time.

[10] **accident:** chance.

They were enwombed in the sacred throne
Of her chaste bodie, nor with commune food,
As other wemens babes, they sucked vitall blood.[1]

6   But wondrously they were begot, and bred
Through influence of th'hevens fruitfull ray,
As it in antique bookes is mentioned.[2]
It was upon a Sommers shinie day,
When *Titan*[3] faire his beames did display,
In a fresh fountaine,[4] far from all mens vew,
She bath'd her brest, the boyling heat t'allay;
She bath'd with roses red, and violets blew,[5]
And all the sweetest flowres, that in the forrest grew.

7   Till faint through yrkesome wearines, adowne
Upon the grassy ground her selfe she layd
To sleepe, the whiles a gentle slombring swowne
Upon her fell all naked bare displayd;
The sunbeames bright upon her body playd,
Being through former bathing mollifide,[6]
And pierst into her wombe, where they embayd[7]
With so sweet sence[8] and secret power unspide,
That in her pregnant flesh they shortly fructifide.

---

[1] Given that fetuses were believed to be nurtured by their mothers' blood in the womb, these lines cannot be saying that unlike other fetuses, these sucked vital blood. Mothers' milk was thought to be concocted from mothers' blood, which thus differs from "vital" blood; yet it is difficult to believe that Spenser wants us to imagine the two newborn babies sucking blood at their comatose mother's breast, especially since their birth has yet to be described. Zurcher has argued persuasively that lines 5.6–9 are a *précis* of the rest of the canto, in which we learn that the babies are nursed in an uncommon *manner*—by nymphs—and that Amoret is reared in a garden that contains decidedly uncommon means of nourishment for babies. Commenting upon Spenser's discomfort with the pregnant body, Adelman observes that his giving Belphoebe and Amoret a miraculous form of nursing is "giving back with one hand what he has just taken away with the other, i.e., the miraculousness of conception even by ordinary means."

[2] Although Chrysogone is Spenser's invention, "antique books" do, of course, mention other cases of conception by divine influence. But the phrase is intended to give a transparently fictional authority to Spenser's story.

[3] ***Titan:*** the sun god.

[4] **fountaine:** spring.

[5] In the language of flowers, roses represented romantic love; violets represented virginity.

[6] **mollifide:** softened; made receptive.

[7] **embayd:** steeped.

[8] **sence:** sensation.

8   Miraculous may seeme to him,[1] that reades
      So straunge ensample of conception,
      But reason teacheth that the fruitfull seades
      Of all things living, through impression
      Of the sunbeames in moyst complexion,[2]
      Doe life conceive and quickned are by kynd:[3]
      So after *Nilus* inundation,
      Infinite shapes[4] of creatures men doe fynd,
      Informed[5] in the mud, on which the Sunne hath shynd.

9   Great father he of generation
      Is rightly cald, th'authour of life and light;
      And his faire sister[6] for creation
      Ministreth matter fit, which tempred right
      With heate and humour,[7] breedes the living wight.
      So sprong these twinnes in wombe of *Chrysogone,*
      Yet wist she nought thereof, but sore affright,
      Wondred to see her belly so upblone,
      Which still[8] increast, till she her terme had full outgone.

---

[1] **him:** i.e., anyone.

[2] I.e., when the woman's body is primarily of a moist humor. Every body was believed to be made up of four humors—blood, black bile, yellow bile, and phlegm—the balance of which determined the person's physical and mental constitution. Each of the humors corresponded to one of the four elements and had its properties; phlegm corresponded to water and was moist. In general, women were primarily cold and moist, which made them both fruitful and less able than men to think or act vigorously. Even their fruitfulness was of a phlegmatic sort, being that of a receptive earth in which men planted their active seed. Women's wombs were usually thought of as containers, not creators of life (though see 47.8.n.). Spenser underscores this idea by having Chrysogone actually asleep both when she conceives and when she gives birth (stanza 27)—and by comparing her body at conception to the riparian zone of the Nile River when the annual flood has left it moist. There had long been a belief that the Nile and the sun could combine forces to generate living creatures from earth; see, e.g., *Metamorphoses,* 1.416–29, in which Ovid compares the fertile mud left by the receding Nile after a flood to the moist fertility of a woman's uterus. Cf. *FQ* I.i.21 and III.vi.35. See also III.ix.6.9.n.

[3] **quickned are by kynd:** are brought to life naturally; are brought to life according to their species.

[4] **Infinite shapes:** cf. the infinite shapes in the Garden of Adonis (vi.35) and in Alma's brain (II.ix.50).

[5] **Informed:** formed inside.

[6] **sister:** the moon, thought to influence women's wombs.

[7] **humour:** moisture.

[8] **still:** constantly.

10   Whereof conceiving[1] shame and foule disgrace,
           Albe[2] her guiltlesse conscience her cleard,
           She fled into the wildernesse a space,
           Till that unweeldy burden she had reard,[3]
           And shund dishonor, which as death she feard:
           Where wearie of long traveill, downe to rest
           Her selfe she set, and comfortably cheard;
           There a sad cloud of sleepe her overkest,[4]
       And seized every sence with sorrow sore opprest.

11   It fortuned, faire *Venus* having lost
           Her little sonne, the winged god of love,[5]
           Who for some light displeasure, which him crost,
           Was from her fled, as flit as ayery Dove,[6]
           And left her blisfull bowre of joy above,
           (So from her often he had fled away,
           When she for ought him sharpely did reprove,
           And wandred in the world in straunge aray,
       Disguiz'd in thousand shapes, that none might him bewray.)

12   Him for to seeke, she left her heavenly hous,
           The house of goodly formes and faire aspects,[7]
           Whence all the world derives the glorious
           Features of beautie, and all shapes select,
           With which high God his workmanship hath deckt;
           And searched everie way, through which his wings
           Had borne him, or his tract[8] she mote detect:
           She promist kisses sweet, and sweeter things,
       Unto the man, that of him tydings to her brings.

13   First she him sought in Court, where most he us'd
           Whylome to haunt, but there she found him not;
           But many there she found, which sore accus'd
           His falshood, and with fowle infamous blot

---

[1] The pun is obvious.

[2] **Albe:** although.

[3] **reard:** brought forth.

[4] **overkest:** overcast.

[5] Inspired by Moschus' second-century BCE poem *Eros drapetes,* many Renaissance authors wrote about Venus searching through the forest for Cupid.

[6] **flit:** fleet; inconstant; **Dove:** a bird associated with Venus.

[7] **formes:** the shapes given to chaotic matter; **aspects:** astrological positions of the planet Venus. See 47.8.n. for a discussion of Venus' relationship to heavenly forms.

[8] **tract:** trace; track.

His cruell deedes and wicked wyles did spot:[1]
Ladies and Lordes she every where mote heare
Complayning, how with his empoysned shot
Their wofull harts he wounded had whyleare,[2]
And so had left them languishing twixt hope and feare.

14   She then the Cities sought from gate to gate,
      And everie one did aske, did he him see;
      And everie one her answerd, that too late[3]
      He had him seene, and felt the crueltee
      Of his sharpe dartes and whot artilleree;[4]
      And every one threw forth reproches rife
      Of his mischievous deedes, and sayd, That hee
      Was the disturber of all civill life,
The enimy of peace, and authour of all strife.

15   Then in the countrey she abroad[5] him sought,
      And in the rurall cottages inquir'd,
      Where also many plaintes to her were brought,
      How he their heedelesse harts with love had fir'd,
      And his false venim through their veines inspir'd;[6]
      And eke the gentle Shepheard swaynes,[7] which sat
      Keeping their fleecy flockes, as they were hyr'd,
      She sweetly heard complaine, both how and what
Her sonne had to them doen; yet she did smile thereat.

16   But when in none of all these she him got,
      She gan avize, where els he mote him hyde:
      At last she her bethought, that she had not
      Yet sought the salvage woods and forests wyde,
      In which full many lovely Nymphes abyde,
      Mongst whom might be, that he did closely[8] lye,
      Or that the love of some of them him tyde:
      For thy she thether cast[9] her course t'apply,
To search the secret haunts of *Dianes* company.

---

[1] **spot:** besmirch; vilify.

[2] **whyleare:** erewhile, some time previously.

[3] I.e., too late to take evasive action.

[4] **whot artilleree:** hot weapons.

[5] **abroad:** widely; out in the open air.

[6] **inspir'd:** breathed.

[7] **swaynes:** country workers; country lovers.

[8] **closely:** covertly.

[9] **cast:** resolved.

17   Shortly unto the wastefull[1] woods she came,
           Whereas she found the Goddesse with her crew,
           After late chace of their embrewed[2] game,
           Sitting beside a fountaine in a rew,[3]
           Some of them washing with the liquid dew
           From off their dainty limbs the dusty sweat,
           And soyle which did deforme their lively hew,[4]
           Others lay shaded from the scorching heat;
       The rest upon her person gave attendance great.

18   She having hong upon a bough on high
           Her bow and painted quiver, had unlaste
           Her silver buskins[5] from her nimble thigh,
           And her lanck loynes ungirt, and brests unbraste,[6]
           After her heat the breathing cold to taste;
           Her golden lockes, that late in tresses bright
           Embreaded[7] were for hindring of her haste,
           Now loose about her shoulders hong undight,
       And were with sweet *Ambrosia*[8] all besprinckled light.

19   Soone as she *Venus* saw behinde her backe,
           She was asham'd to be so loose surpriz'd,
           And woxe halfe wroth against her damzels slacke,
           That had not her thereof before aviz'd,
           But suffred her so carelesly disguiz'd[9]
           Be overtaken. Soone her garments loose
           Upgath'ring, in her bosome she compriz'd,[10]
           Well as she might, and to the Goddesse rose,
       Whiles all her Nymphes did like a girlond her enclose.[11]

---

[1] **wastefull:** deserted.

[2] **embrewed:** soaked in blood.

[3] **fountaine:** spring; **rew:** row.

[4] **deforme:** disfigure; **hew:** countenances.

[5] **buskins:** boots.

[6] **lanck loynes:** slim hips; **unbraste:** un-braced, loosened from clothing.

[7] **Embreaded:** braided.

[8] *Ambrosia:* a perfume worn only by the gods.

[9] **suffred:** allowed; **disguiz'd:** unclothed.

[10] **compriz'd:** gathered together.

[11] Spenser's garlands are worth examining. Cf. I.ii.37, I.vii.4, I.x.54, ii.2, iv.17, v.51, vi.43, IV.i.24, VI.ix.8, VI.ix.43, and VI.x.12, just for starters.

20   Goodly she gan faire *Cytherea*[1] greet,
            And shortly[2] asked her, what cause her brought
            Into that wildernesse for her unmeet,
            From her sweete bowres, and beds with pleasures fraught:
            That suddein chaung she straung adventure[3] thought.
            To whom halfe weeping, she thus answered,
            That she her dearest sonne *Cupido* sought,
            Who in his frowardnes from her was fled;
        That she repented sore, to have him angered.

21   Thereat *Diana* gan to smile, in scorne
            Of her vaine playnt, and to her scoffing sayd;
            "Great pitty sure, that ye be so forlorne[4]
            Of your gay sonne, that gives ye so good ayd
            To your disports: ill mote ye bene apayd,"[5]
            But she was more engrieved, and replide;
            "Faire sister, ill beseemes it to upbrayd
            A dolefull heart with so disdainfull pride;
        The like that mine, may be your paine another tide.[6]

22   "As you in woods and wanton[7] wildernesse
            Your glory sett, to chace the salvage beasts,
            So my delight is all in joyfulnesse,
            In beds, in bowres, in banckets,[8] and in feasts:
            And ill becomes you with your lofty creasts,[9]
            To scorne the joy, that *Jove* is glad to seeke;
            We both are bownd to follow heavens beheasts,
            And tend our charges with obeisaunce meeke:
        Spare, gentle sister, with reproch my paine to eeke.[10]

23   "And tell me, if that ye my sonne have heard,
            To lurke emongst your Nimphes in secret wize;[11]
            Or keepe their cabins: much I am affeard,

---

[1] **Goodly:** courteously; *Cytherea:* another name for Venus, who was born from the sea off the island of Cythera.

[2] **shortly:** quickly; curtly.

[3] **adventure:** chance.

[4] **forlorne:** bereft.

[5] I.e., your son helps you in your bad sport (of infecting people with painful love); may you be repaid with similar unhappiness.

[6] I.e., the pain that I am feeling may at another time be what you feel.

[7] **wanton:** undisciplined, wild—but with an ironic pun on the meaning "unchaste."

[8] **banckets:** banquets; special-occasion meals of sweets.

[9] **creasts:** helmets; crests on a helmet.

[10] **eeke:** increase.

[11] **wize:** manner.

Least[1] he like one of them him selfe disguize,
And turne his arrowes to their exercize:[2]
So may he long him selfe full easie[3] hide:
For he is faire and fresh in face and guize,[4]
As any Nimphe (let not it be envide.)"
So saying every Nimph full narrowly shee eide.

24   But *Phœbe* therewith sore was angered,
        And sharply saide, "Goe Dame, goe seeke your boy,
        Where you him lately lefte, in *Mars* his[5] bed;
        He comes not here, we scorne his foolish joy,
        Ne lend we leisure to his idle toy:[6]
        But if I catch him in this company,
        By *Stygian* lake I vow, whose sad annoy[7]
        The Gods doe dread, he dearly shall abye:[8]
Ile clip his wanton[9] wings, that he no more shall flye."

25   Whom whenas *Venus* saw so sore displeasd,
        Shee inly[10] sory was, and gan relent,
        What shee had said: so her she soone appeasd,
        With sugred words and gentle blandishment,
        From which a fountaine from her sweete lips went,
        And welled goodly forth, that in short space
        She[11] was well pleasd, and forth her damzells sent
        Through all the woods, to search from place to place,
If any tract[12] of him or tidings they mote trace.

26   To search[13] the God of love her Nimphes she sent,
        Throughout the wandring forest every where:
        And after them her selfe eke with her went

---

[1] **Least:** lest.

[2] I.e., he may disguise himself as one of them and go hunting with them, or he may disguise himself as one of them and hunt them with his arrows (which would make them turn away from Diana's chaste rules).

[3] **full easie:** quite easily.

[4] **guize:** appearance.

[5] ***Mars* his:** Mars'.

[6] **toy:** game; foolishness.

[7] ***Stygian:*** of the river Styx, in hell. Even the gods regarded oaths taken upon Styx as sacrosanct; **sad annoy:** serious annoyance.

[8] **abye:** pay the penalty.

[9] **wanton:** undisciplined, with pun on "unchaste."

[10] **inly:** inwardly.

[11] **She:** Diana.

[12] **tract:** trace, track.

[13] **search:** search for.

To seeke the fugitive.[1]
So long they sought, till they arrived were
In that same shady covert, whereas lay
Faire *Crysogone* in slombry traunce whilere:[2]
Who in her sleepe (a wondrous thing to say)
Unwares had borne two babes, as faire as springing[3] day.

27   Unwares she them conceivd, unwares she bore:
      She bore withouten paine, that she conceiv'd
      Withouten pleasure: ne her need implore
      Lucinaes[4] aide: which when they both perceiv'd,
      They were through wonder nigh of sence berev'd,
      And gazing each on other, nought bespake:
      At last they both agreed, her seeming griev'd
      Out of her heavie swowne not to awake,
But from her loving side[5] the tender babes to take.

28   Up they them tooke, eachone a babe uptooke,
      And with them carried, to be fostered;
      Dame *Phœbe* to a Nymphe her babe betooke,[6]
      To be upbrought in perfect Maydenhed,
      And of her selfe her name *Belphœbe* red:
      But *Venus* hers thence far away convayd,
      To be upbrought in goodly womanhed,
      And in her litle loves stead, which was strayd,
Her *Amoretta*[7] cald, to comfort her dismayd.

---

[1] This line is incomplete in the 1590 edition; for the 1596 edition, Spenser emended the line to read, "To seeke the fugitive, both farre and nere."

[2] **whilere:** a while previously.

[3] **springing:** dawning.

[4] *Lucinaes:* a name applied both to Diana and to Juno, each in her role as the protector of women in labor.

[5] **loving side:** as Hamilton explains in his note, the fact that "side" could mean "womb" suggests that Diana and Venus either take the babies from beside Chrysogone or that they help her complete the delivery (Hamilton, *FQ* III.vi.27.9.n.). Gross argues that the words "loving side" take the love that Chrysogone will never be able to give her children and transfer it to her unfeeling side in the very moment in which the babies are taken from her.

[6] **betooke:** gave to care for. Quitslund points out that English attitudes toward wet nursing are relevant to this passage (2006). It was the practice among those who could afford it to give a baby to a wet nurse until it was weaned. Despite the ubiquity of this practice, anxieties surrounded the choice of a wet nurse, since it was believed that she could harm the child not only by taking insufficient care of it but also by transferring her character to it through her milk. In *A View of the Present State of Ireland,* Spenser discusses the evils of the English in Ireland taking on Irish wet nurses (*View*, 67–8).

[7] *Amoretta:* from the Italian "amoretto," meaning "little love."

29   Shee brought her to her joyous Paradize,
          Wher most she wonnes, when she on earth does dwell.
          So faire a place, as Nature can devize:
          Whether in *Paphos,* or *Cytheron* hill,
          Or it in *Gnidus*[1] bee, I wote not well;
          But well I wote by triall,[2] that this same
          All other pleasant places doth excell,
          And called is by her lost lovers name,
       The *Gardin* of *Adonis,* far renowmd by fame.[3]

30   In that same Gardin all the goodly flowres,
          Wherewith dame Nature doth her beautify,
          And decks the girlonds of her Paramoures,
          Are fetcht: there is the first seminary[4]
          Of all things, that are borne to live and dye,
          According to their kynds. Long worke it were,[5]
          Here to account[6] the endlesse progeny
          Of all the weeds,[7] that bud and blossome there;
       But so much as doth need, must needs be counted here.[8]

31   It sited[9] was in fruitfull soyle of old,
          And girt[10] in with two walls on either side;
          The one of yron, the other of bright gold,
          That none might thorough breake, nor over-stride:
          And double gates it had, which opened wide,
          By which both in and out men moten pas;

---

[1] Paphos, Gnidus, and Cytheron Hill were places in Cyprus and Greece that were supposed to have worshipped Venus (as Aphrodite). Cytheron Hill may be either the island of Cythera or Mount Cytheron.

[2] **triall:** experience. Of love? Of sexual dalliance? Of life (given that the Garden of Adonis is the source of life)?

[3] In ancient Greece, devotees of the cult of Adonis grew forcing gardens of herbs in pots; these were called Gardens of Adonis and symbolized both ephemerality and cyclical life. However, the idea that a larger Garden of Adonis is the source of all life and the home of Venus and Adonis is Spenser's invention. See i.34.5.n. for the most common versions of their story.

[4] **seminary:** seed bed.

[5] **kynds:** natural types; species; **it were:** it would be.

[6] **to account:** to recount.

[7] **weeds:** plants—though in other contexts, the word could also have its modern meaning of "undesirable plants," and this meaning may press ironically upon the text here.

[8] I.e., but this poem must recount as many of these progeny here as are necessary to recount.

[9] **sited:** situated; placed (on a site).

[10] **girt:** girded, encircled.

Th'one[1] faire and fresh, the other old and dride:
Old *Genius* the porter of them was,
Old *Genius,* the which a double nature has.[2]

32   He letteth in, he letteth out to wend,[3]
      All that to come into the world desire;
      A thousand thousand naked babes[4] attend
      About him day and night, which doe require,
      That he with fleshly weeds[5] would them attire:
      Such as him list, such as eternall fate
      Ordained hath, he clothes with sinfull mire,[6]
      And sendeth forth[7] to live in mortall state,
   Till they agayn returne backe by the hinder[8] gate.

33   After that they againe retourned beene,
      They in that Gardin planted bee agayne;
      And grow afresh, as they had never seene
      Fleshly corruption, nor mortall payne.
      Some thousand yeares so doen they there remayne,
      And then of him are clad with other hew,[9]
      Or[10] sent into the chaungefull world agayne,
      Till thether they retourne, where first they grew:
   So like a wheele arownd they ronne from old to new.[11]

---

[1] **Th'one:** i.e., the one gate.

[2] Genius is the god of birth and death, sending people out into the world and bringing them back to the garden of generation and regeneration.

[3] **wend:** travel; betake oneself to something different; depart; turn from one condition or form to another; perish. Genius' nature is beautifully encapsulated in this one word; he is the porter of a garden that, in being the source of mortal life, must also in some sense be the source of death.

[4] **naked babes:** it is not certain exactly what these naked babes represent. They may be souls before they are born into earthly bodies; tiny people (*homunculi*) that exist in semen and can grow into fetuses in women's wombs; or what Spenser calls "substaunces" in stanzas 36 and 37. In one sense, Amoret is one of these babes, raised in the garden.

[5] **weeds:** clothing—and by metaphorical extension, the bodies that clothe souls when they enter the world.

[6] **mire:** mud—and by metaphorical extension, the earthly bodies that souls must inhabit for a time, despite those bodies' infection with original sin.

[7] I.e., forth from the garden, into the mortal world.

[8] **hinder:** back, rear.

[9] **hew:** appearance; fleshly form.

[10] **Or:** one would expect "and" here.

[11] The Garden of Adonis facilitates the transmigration of souls—or at least the generative and formative parts of the souls—from one earthly body to another,

34   Ne needs there Gardiner to sett, or sow,
          To plant or prune: for of their owne accord
          All things, as they created were, doe grow,
          And yet remember well the mighty word,
          Which first was spoken by th'Almighty lord,
          That bad them to increase and multiply:
          Ne doe they need with water of the ford,
          Or of the clouds to moysten their roots dry;
          For in themselves eternall moisture they imply.[1]

35   Infinite shapes[2] of creatures there are bred,
          And uncouth[3] formes, which none yet ever knew,
          And every sort is in a sondry[4] bed
          Sett by it selfe, and ranckt in comely rew:[5]
          Some fitt for reasonable sowles[6] t'indew,
          Some made for beasts, some made for birds to weare,

---

with a thousand years between (see Quit-slund, 201–2). At the same time, the Garden represents the idea of eternity in mutability, a notion to which Spenser's poetry returns time and again. The standard version of this philosophy comes most directly from *De consolatione philosophiae* (*The Consolation of Philosophy*), by the neoplatonic Roman philosopher Boethius, who lived in the late fifth and early sixth century CE. Boethius argues that whereas everything on earth is impermanent, corruptible, and fleeting, the larger picture seen by God is that all change occurs in cyclical patterns, which themselves do not change and thus form part of the eternal, divine plan. In neoplatonist philosophy, "form" designates a perfect, transcendent idea of which earthly matter is only an imperfect representation. Yet in Spenser's version, surprisingly, forms change while matter remains eternal. Spenser is not simply reversing the usual terminology, since for him, "forms" are both the heavenly forms that come from Venus and the outward, visible shapes that descend from those heavenly forms—the shapes given to lumps of matter before those lumps are endowed with souls. Spenser's version becomes more abstract

and comprehensive in the "Cantos of Mutabilitie," with which *The Faerie Queene* ends; those cantos argue that all things work toward a larger perfection in the eternal plan, even while seeming to waver and decay when viewed by mortals, who are confined to earthly time.

[1] **imply:** enclose.

[2] **Infinite shapes:** see also the analogy between Chrysogone's fertility and the Nile's ability to generate infinite shapes when warmed by the sun (st.8), the infinite shapes in Alma's brain (II.ix.50), and the comparison of Errour's spawn to "Ten thousand kindes of creatures" bred by the Nile (I.i.21).

[3] **uncouth:** strange.

[4] **sondry:** different—i.e., each species in its own bed.

[5] **rew:** row.

[6] **reasonable sowles:** souls of reasoning creatures. Plants had vegetable souls, capable only of reproducing, nourishing, and growing. Animals had sensible souls, which could do the above and also perceive and desire. Only humans had souls that could reason.

And all the fruitfull spawne of fishes hew[1]
In endlesse rancks along enraunged were,
That seemd the *Ocean* could not containe them there.

36   Daily they grow, and daily forth are sent
    Into the world, it to replenish more,
    Yet is the stocke not lessened, nor spent,
    But still[2] remaines in everlasting store,
    As it at first created was of yore.
    For in the wide wombe of the world there lyes,
    In hatefull darknes and in deepe horrore,
    An huge eternal *Chaos*, which supplyes
The substaunces[3] of natures fruitfull progenyes.

37   All things from thence doe their first being fetch,
    And borrow matter, whereof they are made,
    Which whenas forme and feature it does ketch,[4]
    Becomes a body, and doth then invade
    The state of life, out of the griesly shade.
    That substaunce is eterne, and bideth[5] so,
    Ne when the life decayes, and forme does fade,
    Doth it consume,[6] and into nothing goe,
But chaunged is, and often altred to and froe.

38   The substaunce is not chaungd, nor altered,
    But th'only forme and outward fashion;[7]
    For every substaunce is conditioned
    To chaunge her hew,[8] and sondry formes to don
    Meet for her temper and complexion:
    For formes are variable and decay,
    By course of kinde,[9] and by occasion;
    And that faire flowre of beautie fades away,
As doth the lilly fresh before the sunny ray.

---

[1] **hew:** fleshly form.

[2] **still:** always.

[3] **substaunces:** matter that does not yet have form. How the products of Chaos differ from those of the Garden is an interpretive issue.

[4] **ketch:** catch, take.

[5] **bideth:** remains.

[6] I.e., nor is the substance consumed when life leaves it.

[7] I.e., the matter does not change, though its form and appearance do change.

[8] **her hew:** the substance's form and appearance.

[9] **kinde:** nature; species.

39   Great enimy to it, and to all the rest,
           That in the *Gardin of Adonis* springs,
           Is wicked *Tyme,* who with his scyth addrest,[1]
           Does mow the flowring herbes[2] and goodly things,
           And all their glory to the ground downe flings,
           Where they do wither, and are fowly mard:[3]
           He flyes about, and with his flaggy[4] winges
           Beates downe both leaves and buds without regard,
       Ne ever pitty may relent[5] his malice hard.

40   Yet pitty often did the gods relent,
           To see so faire thinges mard, and spoiled quight:
           And their great mother *Venus* did lament
           The losse of her deare brood, her deare delight:
           Her hart was pierst with pitty at the sight,
           When walking through the Gardin, them she spyde,
           Yet no'te[6] she find redresse for such despight:
           For all that lives, is subject to that law:
       All things decay in time, and to their end doe draw.[7]

41   But were it not, that *Time* their troubler is,
           All that in this delightfull Gardin growes,
           Should happy bee, and have immortall blis:
           For here all plenty, and all pleasure flowes,
           And sweete love gentle fitts[8] emongst them throwes,
           Without fell rancor, or fond gealosy;

---

[1] *Tyme:* Time, here conventionally personified as a man with a scythe; **addrest:** made ready; aimed. The presence of Time makes it clear that Spenser is not thinking of the Garden of Adonis as having heavenly perfection or even Edenic immortality. Time may at first seem out of place, but in fact the entire description of the Garden has emphasized time: in time, each substance takes a form, and in time, each form grows until it is ready to leave the Garden. The eternity of the Garden consists of the Garden's persistent use and reuse of the same matter, rather than of its being protected from change. Nonetheless, the destructive figure of Time is designed to take us by surprise.

[2] **herbes:** any nonwoody green plants.

[3] **mard:** marred.

[4] **flaggy:** drooping.

[5] **relent:** cause to relent.

[6] **no'te:** could not; did not know how to.

[7] In the Cantos of Mutabilitie, Spenser develops an answer to this apparent dilemma: that individual beings die precisely in order to bring their species to perfection, in a larger pattern that is eternal.

[8] **fitts:** i.e., fits of amorous desire.

Franckly each Paramor his leman knowes,[1]
Each bird his mate, ne any does envy
Their goodly meriment, and gay felicity.

42   There is continuall Spring, and harvest there
      Continuall, both meeting at one tyme:[2]
      For both the boughes doe laughing blossoms beare,
      And with fresh colours decke the wanton Pryme,[3]
      And eke attonce the heavenly trees they clyme,
      Which seeme to labour under their fruites lode:
      The whiles the joyous birdes make their pastyme
      Emongst the shady leaves, their sweet abode,
And their trew loves without suspition tell abrode.[4]

43   Right in the middest of that Paradise,
      There stood a stately Mount,[5] on whose round top
      A gloomy grove of mirtle trees did rise,
      Whose shady boughes sharpe steele did never lop,[6]
      Nor wicked beastes their tender buds did crop,
      But like a girlond compassed[7] the hight,
      And from their fruitfull sydes sweet gum did drop,
      That all the ground with pretious deaw bedight,
Threw forth most dainty odours, and most sweet delight.

44   And in the thickest covert of that shade,
      There was a pleasaunt Arber, not by art,
      But of the trees owne inclination made,[8]

[1] I.e., each wooer freely and openly has sexual intercourse with his beloved.

[2] Descriptions of the mythical Golden Age frequently included descriptions of springtime and harvest lasting year-round—an especially attractive vision in cultures in which most preserved food was tough and salty, and in which a poor harvest could lead to winter famine.

[3] **Pryme:** springtime.

[4] **tell:** declare or reveal; **abrode:** out in the open air; all around.

[5] **Mount:** in describing the hill on which Venus and Adonis lie with each other, Spenser could expect his readers to know that *mons veneris* was Latin for "Mount of Venus," the anatomical term for the hair-covered protuberance in the center of a woman's pubis. Succeeding lines reinforce the allegorical image with its description of a circle of trees that drop sweet gum and provide sweet delight.

[6] **lop:** prune; cut down.

[7] **compassed:** encircled.

[8] **inclination:** physical leaning; natural disposition. The absence of art distinguishes this arbor from the highly artificial Bower of Bliss (II.v.29; II.xii.42–77). It is well to remember, however, that English Romanticism would not be invented for another two hundred years. The English Renaissance celebrated artifice (the skilled work of human hands) at least as much as it vilified

Which knitting their rancke[1] braunches part to part,
With wanton yvie twyne entrayld athwart,[2]
And Eglantine, and Caprifole[3] emong,
Fashiond above within their[4] inmost part,
That nether *Phœbus*[5] beams could through them throng,
Nor *Aeolus*[6] sharp blast could worke them any wrong.

45   And all about grew every sort of flowre,
       To which sad lovers were transformde of yore;
       Fresh *Hyacinthus, Phœbus* paramoure,[7]
       Foolish *Narcisse*, that likes the watry shore,[8]
       Sad *Amaranthus*, made a flowre but late,[9]
       Sad *Amaranthus*, in whose purple gore
       Me seemes I see *Amintas*[10] wretched fate,
    To whom sweet Poets verse hath given endlesse date.[11]

---

its opposition to nature, and untamed nature was still most likely to be associated with wild incivility or bestiality. Here, Venus' Mount has the best of both conditions: the trees have not been pruned and trained, but they look as if they had been. Their natural growth habit weaves a bower for the lovers' comfort.

[1] **rancke:** profusely growing.

[2] **yvie twyne entrayld athwart:** ivy vine entwined across.

[3] **Caprifole:** honeysuckle.

[4] **their:** the trees'.

[5] *Phœbus:* the sun's.

[6] *Aeolus:* the wind's.

[7] *Hyacinthus:* a young man who was beloved of Phoebus Apollo. Zephyrus, the west wind, also fancied Hyacinthus and became jealous. When Apollo and Hyacinthus were throwing the discus, Zephyrus hurled the discus back at the youth's head, killing him. After trying vainly to bring his beloved back to life, Apollo noticed that the youth's head drooped on his neck like a broken flower. Apollo made a hyacinth flower spring from Hyacinthus' blood, and on the petals Apollo inscribed the letters "AI, AI," representing the sound of a mourner wailing (Ovid, *Metamorphoses,*

10.162–219, where Hyacinthus is also called Amyclides).

[8] *Narcisse:* At age sixteen, Narcissus was too proud to return anyone's love; he fled from the nymph Echo, who could show her love only by repeating what he said to her. A curse pronounced upon him by a rejected young man came true: Narcissus fell in love with his own reflection in a spring and stayed there, attempting to clasp his own image, until he died from hunger. Even in the underworld, he continued to gaze at his image in the Stygian waters. On earth, his body disappeared and a narcissus flower took its place (*Metamorphoses*, 3.339–510).

[9] *Amaranthus:* an imaginary flower that never fades; its name means "unfading" in Greek and is the same word used to describe an unfading crown of glory in 1 Pet. 5.4—but see next note; **but late:** only recently.

[10] *Amintas:* probably refers to Spenser's friend Sir Philip Sidney, who had recently died at a young age, of a war wound. A contemporary poem describes Amintas as pining away for love of Phyllis and subsequently being changed into the purple amaranthus flower (Fraunce, *Lamentations*).

[11] **endlesse date:** endless term of life; eternal life. Note the eight-line stanza.

46   There wont fayre *Venus* often to enjoy[1]
        Her deare *Adonis* joyous company,
        And reape sweet pleasure of the wanton boy:
        There yet, some say, in secret he does ly,
        Lapped in flowres and pretious spycery,[2]
        By her hid from the world, and from the skill[3]
        Of *Stygian* Gods,[4] which doe her love envy;
        But she her selfe, when ever that she will,
   Possesseth him, and of his sweetnesse takes her fill.[5]

47   And sooth it seemes they say:[6] for he may not
        For ever dye, and ever buried bee
        In balefull night, where all thinges are forgot;
        All be he[7] subject to mortalitie,
        Yet is eterne[8] in mutabilitie,
        And by succession made perpetuall,
        Transformed oft, and chaunged diverslie:
        For him the Father of all formes they call;[9]
   Therefore needs mote he live, that living gives to all.

48   There now he liveth in eternall blis,
        Joying his goddesse, and of her enjoyd:
        Ne feareth he henceforth that foe of his,

---

[1] **wont:** used; **enjoy:** have sex with.

[2] **spycery:** spices, associated with luxury since many of them were expensive imported products.

[3] **skill:** knowledge.

[4] **Stygian Gods:** gods of the underworld. See i.34.5.n. for their claim on Adonis.

[5] **Possesseth:** takes sexually; **takes her fill:** at least two puns are obvious, depending upon whether one is thinking of intercourse or of oral sex.

[6] I.e., what they say seems true.

[7] **All be he:** although he is; even if he is.

[8] **eterne:** eternal. See 33.9.n.

[9] Stanza 12.1–4 would seem to identify Venus as the originator of forms, while this stanza declares, in apparent contradiction, that Adonis is the originator of forms. As Miller writes, medieval allegorists such as Bernard Silvestris posited "a continuity between the descent of forms from heaven and their transmission in the work of generation. A phallic Adonis might still be the Father of all generated or embodied forms without being their absolute origin; they may descend to him from a heavenly source associated with Venus" (2006). By aligning the female with transcendent form while aligning the male with its earthly embodiment, this allegory inverts the common Renaissance belief that women were more earthbound than men, less cerebral, and less given to abstract thought. One theory about male and female roles in generation was that the man gave life to the fetus, whereas the woman contributed only matter. Another was that both partners contributed seed, which contained spirit.

Which with his cruell tuske him deadly cloyd:[1]
For that wilde Bore, the which him once annoyd,[2]
She firmely hath emprisoned for ay,[3]
That her sweet love his malice mote[4] avoyd,
In a strong rocky Cave, which is they say,
Hewen underneath that Mount, that none him losen may.[5]

49   There now he lives in everlasting joy,
      With many of the Gods in company,
      Which thether haunt, and with the winged boy[6]
      Sporting him selfe in safe felicity:
      Who when he hath with spoiles and cruelty
      Ransackt the world, and in the wofull harts
      Of many wretches set his triumphes hye,
      Thether resortes, and laying his sad dartes
    Asyde, with faire *Adonis* playes his wanton partes.[7]

50   And his trew love faire *Psyche*[8] with him playes,
      Fayre *Psyche* to him lately reconcyld,

[1] **cloyd:** gored, with obviously sexual imagery.

[2] **annoyd:** injured.

[3] **for ay:** for always.

[4] **mote:** might.

[5] The image of the furious boar imprisoned in a cave beneath Venus' Mount (or *mons veneris*) lends itself to various interpretations: is Venus keeping a threatening aspect of Adonis' phallic power in check, imprisoning his sexual energy so that she may enjoy it whenever she wishes, reining in her own dangerous desires, causing him to fear her controlling sexuality, convincing herself that her transgressive desires are actually his, or participating in a tableau that allegorizes the violence lurking beneath ordinary sex acts? No matter which interpretation we choose, our experience of this passage is unsettled by our knowledge that several other imprisoned monsters in the poem manage to break loose or otherwise threaten peace after apparently being conquered.

[6] **haunt:** frequent; spend time; **winged boy:** Cupid.

[7] Like many Renaissance authors, Spenser seems to have been fascinated with homoerotics even while constructing heteronormative fictional worlds. See Introduction, 5e.

[8] *Psyche:* The Algerian-born author Apuleius, who lived in the second century CE, tells the story of Cupid and Psyche in his *Metamorphoses seu de Asino Aureo (The Golden Ass)*. The princess Psyche was so beautiful that people confused her with Venus, which angered Venus so much that she told her son, Cupid, to wound Psyche with an arrow. An oracle said that Psyche's future husband was a serpent and that she must put on mourning and go to a mountaintop for her funereal marriage. On the mountain, a breeze carried her into a paradisiacal valley where she was surrounded by luxuries and visited each night by a husband whom she could not see in the dark. Her jealous sisters convinced her that her hus-

After long troubles and unmeet upbrayes,[1]
With which his mother *Venus* her revyld,
And eke himselfe her cruelly exyld:
But now in stedfast love and happy state
She with him lives, and hath him borne a chyld,
Pleasure, that doth both gods and men aggrate,[2]
Pleasure, the daughter of *Cupid* and *Psyche* late.[3]

51   Hether great *Venus* brought this infant[4] fayre,
The yonger daughter of *Chrysogonee,*
And unto *Psyche* with great trust and care
Committed her, yfostered to bee,
And trained up in trew feminitee:
Who no lesse carefully her tendered,
Then her owne daughter *Pleasure,* to whom shee
Made her companion, and her lessoned[5]
In all the lore[6] of love, and goodly womanhead.

52   In which when she to perfect ripenes[7] grew,
Of grace and beautie noble Paragone,
She brought her forth into the worldes vew,
To be th'ensample of true love alone,[8]
And Lodestarre[9] of all chaste affection,
To all fayre Ladies, that doe live on grownd.[10]

---

band was a monstrous snake, whereupon she lay in wait for him with a knife and a lamp. In the lamplight she saw that he was the glorious Cupid, but when a drop of lamp oil burned his shoulder and woke him up, he flew away. Psyche spent the rest of her earthly life searching for Cupid and performing unpleasant tasks set by the angry Venus. Cupid begged Jupiter to help Psyche, whereupon the gods gave her a cup of nectar to make her immortal so that she and Cupid could live together. Psyche gave birth to a child named *Voluptas,* meaning pleasure (especially sensual pleasure). Spenser may have read only Boccaccio's translation of the story, in which Boccaccio allegorizes Psyche as the Soul, which must endure trials before attaining eternal joy.

[1] **upbrayes:** upbraidings.

[2] **aggrate:** please, gratify.

[3] **late:** recently (born).

[4] **this infant:** Amoret.

[5] **lessoned:** instructed.

[6] **lore:** doctrine; advice; body of knowledge.

[7] **ripenes:** maturity.

[8] I.e., the only example of true love.

[9] **Lodestarre:** guiding star; cynosure.

[10] **on grownd:** on earth.

To Faery court she came, where many one
Admyrd her goodly haveour,[1] and fownd
His feeble hart wide launched with loves cruel wownd.[2]

53   But she to none of them her love did cast,
Save to the noble knight *Sir Scudamore*,[3]
To whom her loving hart she linked fast
In faithfull love, t'abide for evermore,
And for his dearest sake endured sore,
Sore trouble of an hainous enimy,
Who her would forced have to have forlore[4]
Her former love, and stedfast loialty,
As ye may elswhere reade that ruefull history.[5]

54   But well I weene, ye first desire to learne,
What end unto that fearefull Damozell,[6]
Which fledd so fast from that same foster stearne,[7]
Whom with his brethren *Timias* slew, befell:[8]
That was to weet,[9] the goodly *Florimell*,
Who wandring for to seeke her lover deare,
Her lover deare, her dearest *Marinell*,
Into misfortune fell, as ye did heare,
And from Prince *Arthure* fled with wings of idle feare.[10]

---

[1] **haveour:** deportment (originally "possession," then "self-possession").

[2] **launched:** lanced, pricked; **wownd:** wound.

[3] *Sir Scudamore:* Italian *scudo* (shield) and *amore* (love). His name ends where Amoret's begins.

[4] **forlore:** forsaken.

[5] Scudamore's part in the narrative will get fully underway at xi.7.

[6] **fearefull Damozell:** Florimell, last seen at iv.51.

[7] **foster stearne:** cruel forester (see i.17).

[8] Timias killed the Forester and his two brothers at v.15–25; **befell:** i.e., "what end . . . befell" the "fearefull Damozell."

[9] **to weet:** to wit; namely.

[10] At iv.49–53.

Canto Seven

The witches sonne loves Florimell:
She flyes, he faines to dy.
Satyrane[1] saves the Squyre of Dames
From Gyaunts tyranny.

1   Like as an Hynd[2] forth singled from the heard,
        That hath escaped from a ravenous beast,
        Yet flyes away of her owne feete afeard,
        And every leafe, that shaketh with the least[3]
        Murmure of winde, her terror hath encreast;
        So fledd fayre *Florimell* from her vaine feare,
        Long after she from perill was releast:
        Each shade she saw, and each noyse she did heare,
    Did seeme to be the same, which she escapt whileare.

2   All that same evening she in flying spent,
        And all that night her course continewed:
        Ne did she let dull sleepe once to relent,
        Nor wearinesse to slack her hast, but fled
        Ever alike, as if her former dred
        Were hard behind, her ready to arrest:
        And her white Palfrey having conquered
        The maistring raines out of her weary wrest,[4]
    Perforce her carried, where ever he thought best.

---

[1] **Satyrane:** first introduced at I.vi.20, this "noble warlike knight" was the offspring of a married woman and a satyr (half man, half goat, and infamously lecherous). Thyamis' husband habitually ignored her in order to go hunting, so she wandered into the forest in search of him. A satyr abducted her, impregnated her, kept her until the boy was born, and then let her go but kept the boy. He raised Satyrane in the woods, teaching him to overpower and tame wild beasts.

[2] **Hynd:** female red deer.

[3] An unusually strong enjambment for Spenser.

[4] I.e., her white horse having taken the mastering reins out of her weary grasp. In emblem books of the period, a runaway horse symbolizes emotion acting without the guidance of reason.

129

3   So long as breath, and hable puissaunce[1]
               Did native corage unto him supply,
               His pace he freshly forward did advaunce,
               And carried her beyond all jeopardy,
               But nought that wanteth rest, can long aby.[2]
               He having through incessant traveill[3] spent
               His force, at last perforce adowne did ly,
               Ne foot could further move: The Lady gent
          Thereat was suddein strook with great astonishment.

4   And forst t'alight, on foot mote algates[4] fare,
               A traveiler unwonted[5] to such way:
               Need teacheth her this lesson hard and rare,
               That fortune all in equall launce doth sway,[6]
               And mortall miseries doth make her play.[7]
               So long she traveild, till at length she came
               To an hilles side, which did to her bewray[8]
               A litle valley, subject to[9] the same,
          All coverd with thick woodes, that quite it overcame.[10]

5   Through the tops of the high trees she did descry
               A litle smoke, whose vapour thin and light,
               Reeking[11] aloft, uprolled to the sky:
               Which, chearefull signe did send unto her sight,
               That in the same did wonne some living wight.
               Eftsoones her steps she thereunto applyd,[12]
               And came at last in weary wretched plight[13]
               Unto the place, to which her hope did guyde,
          To finde some refuge there, and rest her wearie syde.

---

[1] **hable puissaunce:** able strength.

[2] **aby:** abide.

[3] **traveill:** labor.

[4] **algates:** always; at any rate.

[5] **unwonted:** unused.

[6] **launce:** balance; **sway:** rule.

[7] I.e., humans' miseries provide Fortune with amusement.

[8] **bewray:** reveal.

[9] **subject to:** beneath.

[10] **overcame:** covered.

[11] **Reeking:** billowing, rising (almost always used to describe the emission of smoke, vapor, or blood).

[12] **applyd:** directed.

[13] **plight:** condition.

6   There in a gloomy hollow glen she found
        A little cottage, built of stickes and reedes
        In homely[1] wize, and wald with sods around,
        In which a witch did dwell, in loathly weedes,[2]
        And wilfull want,[3] all carelesse of her needes,
        So choosing solitarie to abide,
        Far from all neighbours, that her divelish deedes
        And hellish arts from people she might hide,
And hurt far off unknowne, whom ever she envide.

7   The Damzell there arriving entred in;
        Where sitting on the flore the Hag she found,
        Busie (as seem'd) about some wicked gin:[4]
        Who soone as she beheld that suddein stound,[5]
        Lightly upstarted from the dustie ground,
        And with fell looke and hollow deadly gaze
        Stared on her awhile, as one astound,
        Ne had one word to speake, for great amaze,
But shewd by outward signes, that dread her sence did daze.

8   At last turning her feare to foolish wrath,
        She askt, what devill had her thether brought,
        And who she was, and what unwonted path
        Had guided her, unwelcomed, unsought.
        To which the Damzell full of doubtfull[6] thought,
        Her mildly answer'd; "Beldame be not wroth
        With silly Virgin by adventure[7] brought
        Unto your dwelling, ignorant and loth,[8]
That crave but rowme to rest, while tempest overblo'th."

9   With that adowne out of her christall eyne[9]
        Few trickling teares she softly forth let fall,
        That like two orient[10] perles, did purely shyne
        Upon her snowy cheeke; and therewithall[11]

---

[1] **homely:** homelike.

[2] **weedes:** clothing.

[3] **wilfull want:** intentional poverty.

[4] **gin:** stratagem, plot.

[5] **stound:** shocking event; sudden attack (Florimell's unexpected entry).

[6] **doubtfull:** anxious.

[7] **adventure:** accident, chance.

[8] **loth:** loath, reluctant.

[9] **eyne:** eyes.

[10] **orient:** from the east; precious; lustrous.

[11] **therewithall:** in addition to that, besides.

She sighed soft, that none so bestiall,
Nor salvage hart, but ruth[1] of her sad plight
Would make to melt, or pitteously appall;[2]
And that vile Hag, all were her whole delight
In mischiefe,[3] was much moved at so pitteous sight.

10   And gan recomfort her in her rude[4] wyse,
With womanish compassion of her plaint,
Wiping the teares from her suffused eyes,
And bidding her sit downe, to rest her faint
And wearie limbs a while. She nothing quaint[5]
Nor s'deignfull of so homely fashion,
Sith brought she was now to so hard constraint,[6]
Sate downe upon the dusty ground anon,[7]
As glad of that small rest, as Bird of[8] tempest gon.

11   Tho gan she gather up her garments rent,
And her loose lockes to dight in order dew,
With golden wreath and gorgeous ornament;
Whom such whenas the wicked Hag did vew,
She was astonisht at her heavenly hew,
And doubted her to deeme an earthly wight,
But or some Goddesse, or of *Dianes* crew,
And thought her to adore with humble spright;
T'adore thing so divine as beauty, were but right.

12   This wicked woman had a wicked sonne,
The comfort of her age and weary dayes,
A laesy loord, for nothing good to donne,[9]
But stretched forth in ydlenesse alwayes,
Ne ever cast his mind to covet[10] prayse,
Or ply[11] him selfe to any honest trade,

---

[1] **ruth:** pity.

[2] **appall:** make pale or feeble (with pity); check or quell.

[3] I.e., even though her only delight consisted of doing mischief.

[4] **rude:** unsophisticated, crude.

[5] **quaint:** choosy.

[6] **constraint:** necessity; affliction.

[7] **anon:** immediately.

[8] **of:** out of.

[9] I.e., lazy lout, good for nothing.

[10] **covet:** wish for.

[11] **ply:** apply.

But all the day before the sunny rayes
He us'd to slug,[1] or sleepe in slothfull shade:
Such laesinesse both lewd[2] and poore attonce him made.

13   He comming home at undertime,[3] there found
      The fayrest creature, that he ever saw,
      Sitting beside his mother on the ground;
      The sight whereof did greatly him adaw,[4]
      And his base thought with terrour and with aw
      So inly smot, that as one, which hath gaz'd
      On the bright Sunne unwares, doth soone withdraw
      His feeble eyne, with too much brightnes daz'd,
So stared he on her, and stood long while amaz'd.

14   Softly at last he gan his mother aske,
      What mister[5] wight that was, and whence deriv'd,
      That in so straunge disguizement there did maske,
      And by what accident she there arriv'd:
      But she, as one nigh of her wits depriv'd,
      With nought but ghastly lookes him answered,
      Like to a ghost, that lately is reviv'd
      From *Stygian* shores, where late it wandered;
So both at her, and each at other wondered.

15   But the fayre Virgin was so meeke and myld,
      That she to them vouchsafed to embace[6]
      Her goodly port,[7] and to their senses vyld,
      Her gentle speach applyde, that in short space
      She grew familiare in that desert[8] place.
      During which time, the Chorle[9] through her so kind
      And courteise use conceiv'd affection bace,
      And cast to love her in his brutish mind;
No love, but brutish lust, that was so beastly tind.[10]

---

[1] **slug:** idle around.

[2] **lewd:** ignorant.

[3] **undertime:** undern-time, which denoted various hours of the day: 9:00 AM, noon, or afternoon; a meal taken at any of these times.

[4] **adaw:** overawe, daunt; subdue.

[5] **mister:** sort of, kind of.

[6] **embace:** lower, condescend, humble.

[7] **port:** carriage; demeanor.

[8] **familiare:** friendly; **desert:** deserted.

[9] **Chorle:** churl.

[10] **tind:** ignited.

16   Closely the wicked flame his bowels brent,[1]
       And shortly grew into outrageous fire;
       Yet had he not the hart, nor hardiment,[2]
       As unto her to utter his desire;
       His caytive thought durst[3] not so high aspire,
       But with soft sighes, and lovely semblaunces,[4]
       He ween'd that his affection entire
       She should aread; many resemblaunces[5]
     To her he made, and many kinde remembraunces.[6]

17   Oft from the forrest wildings[7] he did bring,
       Whose sides empurpled[8] were with smyling red,
       And oft young birds, which he had taught to sing
       His maistresse praises, sweetly caroled,
       Girlonds of flowres sometimes for her faire hed
       He fine would dight; sometimes the squirrell wild
       He brought to her in bands, as conquered
       To be her thrall, his fellow servant[9] vild;
     All which, she of him tooke with countenance meeke and mild.

18   But past awhile, when she fit season[10] saw
       To leave that desert mansion,[11] she cast
       In secret wize her selfe thence to withdraw,
       For feare of mischiefe, which she did forecast
       Might by the witch or by her sonne compast:[12]
       Her wearie Palfrey closely, as she might,[13]

---

[1] **Closely:** secretly; **brent:** burned.

[2] **hardiment:** courage.

[3] **caytive:** vile, wretched (literally "captive"; to call someone a "slave" was a serious insult); **durst:** dared.

[4] **semblaunces:** shows, empty demonstrations of love (empty because what the loutish son feels is mere lust). Compare Timias' resolute silence about his love for Belphoebe (v.44–48).

[5] **resemblaunces:** shows, empty demonstrations of love.

[6] **remembraunces:** keepsakes.

[7] **wildings:** wild crabapples; wild fruit of various kinds.

[8] **empurpled:** in poetic terms, "purple" often means "red."

[9] **servant:** suitor; wooer professing service to his lady.

[10] **past awhile:** after a while had passed; **season:** time.

[11] **mansion:** dwelling.

[12] **compast:** compassed, devised.

[13] **closely, as she might:** as secretly as she could.

Now well recovered after long repast,
In his proud furnitures[1] she freshly dight,
His late miswandred wayes now to remeasure[2] right.

19   And earely ere the dawning day appeard,
      She forth issewed, and on her journey went;
      She went in perill, of each noyse affeard,
      And of each shade, that did it selfe present;
      For still she feared to be overhent,[3]
      Of that vile hag, or her uncivile sonne:
      Who when too late awaking, well they kent,[4]
      That their fayre guest was gone, they both begonne
To make exceeding mone, as they had beene undonne.

20   But that lewd lover did the most lament
      For her depart,[5] that ever man did heare;
      He knockt his brest with desperate intent,
      And scratcht his face, and with his teeth did teare
      His rugged flesh, and rent his ragged heare:
      That his sad mother seeing his sore plight,
      Was greatly woe begon, and gan to feare,
      Least his fraile senses were emperisht[6] quight,
And love to frenzy turnd, sith love is franticke hight.[7]

21   All wayes shee sought, him to restore to plight,[8]
      With herbs, with charms, with counsel, and with teares,
      But tears, nor charms,[9] nor herbs, nor counsell might
      Asswage the fury, which his entrails teares:
      So strong is passion, that no reason heares.
      Tho when all other helpes she saw to faile,
      She turnd her selfe backe to her wicked leares[10]
      And by her divelish arts thought to prevaile,
To bring her backe againe, or worke her finall bale.[11]

---

[1] **furnitures:** saddle, reins, and other equipment.

[2] **remeasure:** retrace.

[3] **overhent:** overtaken.

[4] **kent:** kenned, knew.

[5] **depart:** departure.

[6] **emperisht:** empaired.

[7] I.e., since love is called madness.

[8] **plight:** healthy condition.

[9] I.e., neither tears nor charms.

[10] **leares:** lore, learning—in this case, witchcraft.

[11] **finall bale:** final harm, i.e., death.

22   Eftesoones out of her hidden cave she cald
     An hideous beast, of horrible aspect,
     That could the stoutest corage have appald;
     Monstrous, mishapt, and all his backe was spect
     With thousand spots of colours queint elect,[1]
     Thereto so swifte, that it all beasts did pas:[2]
     Like never yet did living eie detect;
     But likest it to an *Hyena*[3] was,
That feeds on wemens flesh, as others feede on gras.

23   It forth she cald, and gave it streight[4] in charge,
     Through thicke and thin her[5] to poursew apace,
     Ne once to stay to rest, or breath[6] at large,
     Till her he had attaind, and brought in place,[7]
     Or quite devourd her beauties scornefull grace.
     The Monster swifte as word, that from her went,
     Went forth in haste, and did her footing trace
     So sure and swiftly, through his perfect sent,[8]
And passing[9] speede, that shortly he her overhent.

24   Whom when the fearefull Damzell nigh[10] espide,
     No need to bid her fast away to flie;
     That ugly shape so sore her terrifide,
     That it she shund no lesse, then dread to die,
     And her flitt[11] Palfrey did so well apply
     His nimble feet to her conceived feare,
     That whilest his breath did strength to him supply,
     From perill free he her away did beare:
But when his force gan faile, his pace gan wex areare.[12]

25   Which whenas she perceiv'd, she was dismayd
     At that same last extremity ful sore,
     And of her safety greatly grew afrayd;

---

[1] **queint elect:** ingeniously chosen (for camouflage or for a horrible appearance).

[2] **Thereto:** moreover; **pas:** surpass.

[3] *Hyena:* traditionally associated with witches and with treacherous violence.

[4] **streight:** strictly; straightway.

[5] **her:** Florimell.

[6] **breath:** rest.

[7] **in place:** here (to the witch's cottage).

[8] **sent:** scent, sense of smell.

[9] **passing:** surpassing.

[10] **nigh:** nearby.

[11] **flitt:** fleet, swift.

[12] **wex areare:** grow backward, i.e., become slower.

And now she gan approch to the sea shore,
As it befell,[1] that she could flie no more,
But yield her selfe to spoile[2] of greedinesse.
Lightly she leaped, as a wight forlore,[3]
From her dull horse, in desperate distresse,
And to her feet betooke her doubtfull sickernesse.[4]

26   Not halfe so fast the wicked *Myrrha*[5] fled
From dread of her revenging fathers hond:
Nor halfe so fast to save her maydenhed,
Fled fearfull *Daphne*[6] on th'*AEgaean* strond,
As *Florimell* fled from that Monster yond,[7]
To reach the sea, ere she of him were raught:[8]
For in the sea to drowne her selfe she fond,[9]
Rather then of the tyrant to be caught:
Thereto fear gave her wings, and need her corage taught.

27   It fortuned (high God did so ordaine)
As shee arrived on the roring shore,
In minde to leape into the mighty maine,[10]
A little bote lay hoving[11] her before,
In which there slept a fisher old and pore,
The whiles his nets were drying on the sand:
Into the same shee lept, and with the ore
Did thrust the shallop from the floting strand:[12]
So safety fownd at sea, which she fownd not at land.

---

[1] **befell:** happened.

[2] **spoile:** despoilation.

[3] **forlore:** lost.

[4] **doubtfull sickernesse:** unlikely safety.

[5] *Myrrha:* tricked her father into committing incest; see ii.41.1.n.

[6] *Daphne:* rejected all suitors because she did not want to be controlled by a husband; Apollo fell in love with her and pursued her through the forest, whereupon she asked her father, a river god, to destroy her beauty. He changed her into a laurel tree, completely unlike her former self *except* for its beauty. Apollo made a wreath for his head from her leaves (Ovid, *Metamorphoses,* 1.452–567).

[7] **yond:** furious; savage.

[8] **of him:** by him; **raught:** snatched.

[9] **fond:** undertook (OED "fand" v6).

[10] **maine:** sea.

[11] **hoving:** lying at anchor.

[12] I.e., thrust the little boat from the shore off which it was floating.

28   The Monster ready on the pray to sease,[1]
    Was of his forward[2] hope deceived quight,
    Ne durst assay[3] to wade the perlous seas,
    But greedily long gaping at the sight,
    At last in vaine was forst to turne his flight,
    And tell the idle tidings[4] to his Dame:
    Yet to avenge his divelishe despight,
    He sett upon her Palfrey tired lame,
And slew him cruelly, ere any reskew came.

29   And after having him embowelled,
    To fill his hellish gorge, it chaunst a knight
    To passe that way, as forth he traveiled;
    Yt was a goodly Swaine,[5] and of great might,
    As ever man that bloody field did fight;
    But in vain sheows, that wont yong knights bewitch,
    And courtly services tooke no delight,
    But rather joyd to bee, then seemen sich:
For both to be and seeme to him was labor lich.[6]

30   It was to weete the good Sir *Satyrane*,[7]
    That raungd abrode to seeke adventures wilde,
    As was his wont in forest, and in plaine;
    He was all armd in rugged steele unfilde,[8]
    As in the smoky forge it was compilde,[9]
    And in his Scutchin bore a Satyres hedd:[10]
    He comming present, where the Monster vilde
    Upon that milke-white Palfreyes carcas fedd,
Unto his reskew ran, and greedily him spedd.[11]

---

[1] **on the pray to sease:** to seize on the prey.

[2] **forward:** imminent; foremost.

[3] **assay:** attempt.

[4] **idle tidings:** worthless news.

[5] **Swaine:** young man.

[6] **lich:** like. It was just as much work for him to seem to be a good knight as actually to be one.

[7] **to weete:** to wit, namely; *Satyrane:* see Argument, note.

[8] **unfilde:** unpolished; crude.

[9] **compilde:** constructed.

[10] **Scutchin:** escutcheon, shield on which a coat of arms is depicted; **Satyres hedd:** see Argument, note.

[11] **his:** the horse's; **greedily:** eagerly; **him spedd:** succeeded; hurried himself; made the hyena run away.

31   There well perceivd he, that it was the horse,
          Whereon faire *Florimell* was wont to ride,
          That of that feend was rent without remorse:
          Much feared he, least ought did ill betide
          To that faire Maide, the flowre of wemens pride;
          For her he dearely loved,[1] and in all
          His famous conquests highly magnifide:[2]
          Besides her golden girdle,[3] which did fall
      From her in flight, he fownd, that did him sore apall.

32   Full of sad feare, and doubtfull agony,
          Fiercely he flew upon that wicked feend,
          And with huge strokes, and cruell battery
          Him forst to leave his pray, for to attend
          Him selfe from deadly daunger to defend:
          Full many wounds in his corrupted flesh
          He did engrave, and muchell blood did spend,
          Yet might not doe him die, but aie[4] more fresh
      And fierce he still appeard, the more he did him thresh.[5]

33   He wist not, how him to despoile of life,
          Ne how to win the wished victory,
          Sith him he saw still stronger grow through strife,
          And him selfe weaker through infirmity;
          Greatly he grew enrag'd, and furiously
          Hurling his sword away, he lightly lept
          Upon the beast, that with great cruelty
          Rored, and raged to be underkept:[6]
      Yet he perforce him held, and strokes upon him hept.[7]

34   As he that strives to stop a suddein flood,
          And in strong bancks his violence enclose,
          Forceth it swell above his wonted mood,
          And largely overflow the fruitfull plaine,
          That all the countrey seemes to be a Maine,[8]

---

[1] So Satyrane loves Florimell, who loves
Marinell, who loves no one.

[2] **magnifide:** glorified her by fighting in
her name.

[3] **girdle:** sash.

[4] **aie:** aye, always.

[5] **thresh:** thrash.

[6] **underkept:** kept down; subjected.

[7] **hept:** heaped.

[8] **Maine:** sea.

And the rich furrowes flote, all quite fordonne:[1]
The wofull husbandman doth lowd complaine,
To see his whole yeares labor lost so soone,
For which to God he made so many an idle boone.[2]

35   So him he held, and did through might amate:[3]
So long he held him, and him bett[4] so long,
That at the last his fiercenes gan abate,
And meekely stoup unto the victor strong:
Who to avenge the implacable wrong,
Which he supposed donne to *Florimell,*
Sought by all meanes his dolor to prolong,
Sith dint of steele his carcas could not quell:
His maker with her charmes had framed him so well.

36   The golden ribband,[5] which that virgin wore
About her sclender waste, he tooke in hand,
And with it bownd the beast, that lowd did rore
For great despight of that unwonted band,[6]
Yet dared not his victor to withstand,
But trembled like a lambe, fled from the pray,[7]
And all the way him followd on the strand,
As he had long bene learned[8] to obay;
Yet never learned he such service, till that day.

37   Thus as he led the Beast along the way,
He spide far off a mighty Giauntesse,
Fast flying on a Courser[9] dapled gray,
From a bold knight, that with great hardinesse
Her hard pursewd, and sought for to suppresse;
She bore before[10] her lap a dolefull Squire,
Lying athwart her horse in great distresse,
Fast bounden hand and foote with cords of wire,[11]
Whom she did meane to make the thrall of her desire.

---

[1] **fordonne:** done in, destroyed.

[2] **boone:** prayer of petition.

[3] **amate:** overwhelm.

[4] **bett:** beat.

[5] **ribband:** ribbon.

[6] **band:** bond.

[7] **pray:** one who preys upon another.

[8] **learned:** taught.

[9] **Courser:** swift horse.

[10] **before:** in front of.

[11] As Hamilton points out, every other time when Spenser uses the word "wire," he is comparing a beautiful woman's hair with golden wire. Implicitly, then, the doleful Squire is bound by a woman's

38   Which whenas *Satyrane* beheld, in haste
        He lefte his captive Beast at liberty,
        And crost the nearest way, by which he cast
        Her to encounter, ere she passed by:
        But she the way shund nathemore for thy,[1]
        But forward gallopt fast, which when he spyde,
        His mighty speare he couched[2] warily,
        And at her ran: she having him descryde,
    Her selfe to fight addrest, and threw her lode aside.

39   Like as a Goshauke,[3] that in foote doth beare
        A trembling Culver,[4] having spide on hight
        An Eagle, that with plumy[5] wings doth sheare
        The subtile ayre, stouping[6] with all his might,
        The quarrey throwes to ground with fell despight,
        And to the batteill doth her selfe prepare:
        So ran the Geauntesse unto the fight;
        Her fyrie eyes with furious sparkes did stare,[7]
    And with blasphemous bannes[8] high God in peeces tare.

40   She caught in hand an huge great yron mace,
        Wherewith she many had of life depriv'd,
        But ere the stroke could seize his[9] aymed place,
        His speare amids her sun-brode[10] shield arriv'd,
        Yet nathemore the steele a sonder riv'd,[11]
        All were the beame[12] in bignes like a mast,
        Ne her out of the stedfast sadle driv'd,
        But glauncing on the tempred metall, brast
    In thousand shivers, and so forth beside her past.

---

charms, and his desire has become mon-
strous (Hamilton, *FQ* III.vii.37.8.n.).

[1] **for thy:** therefore, because of that.

[2] **couched:** lowered to the position for at-
tack.

[3] **Goshauke:** goshawk, a particular type of
hawk.

[4] **Culver:** dove.

[5] **plumy:** feathery.

[6] **subtile:** rarefied, thin; **stouping:** diving
for the kill.

[7] **stare:** shine; stare.

[8] **bannes:** curses.

[9] **his:** its.

[10] **sun-brode:** as broad as the sun.

[11] **a sonder riv'd:** cleaved asunder.

[12] **All were the beame:** even though the
spear's shaft was.

41   Her Steed did stagger with that puissaunt strooke;
              But she no more was moved with that might,
              Then it[1] had lighted on an aged Oke;
              Or on the marble Pillour, that is pight
              Upon the top of Mount *Olympus* hight,
              For the brave youthly Champions to assay,
              With burning charet wheeles it nigh to smite:
              But who that smites it, mars his joyous play,
        And is the spectacle of ruinous decay.[2]

42   Yet therewith sore enrag'd, with sterne regard
              Her dreadfull weapon she to him addrest,
              Which on his helmet martelled[3] so hard,
              That made him low incline his lofty crest,
              And bowd his battred visour to his brest:
              Wherewith hee was so stund, that he n'ote[4] ryde
              But reeled to and fro from east to west:[5]
              Which when his cruell enimy espyde,
        She lightly unto him adjoyned syde to syde;[6]

43   And on his collar laying puissaunt hand,
              Out of his wavering seat him pluckt perforse,[7]
              Perforse him pluckt, unable to withstand,
              Or helpe himselfe, and laying thwart her horse,
              In loathly wise like to a carrion corse,[8]
              She bore him fast away. Which when the knight,
              That her pursewed, saw with great remorse,[9]
              He nere was touched in his noble spright,
        And gan encrease his speed, as she encreast her flight.

---

[1] **Then it:** than if it.

[2] In the ancient Olympic games, imagined by Spenser's contemporaries to have been held on Mount Olympus, chariots ran a race in which they had to reverse course around a pillar, coming close to it in order not to lose time but not coming close enough to crash into it.

[3] **martelled:** hammered.

[4] **n'ote:** could not.

[5] This is the sort of scene understandably beloved of Monty Python—and indeed, the entire story of the Squire on the Giantesse's lap has a parodic edge.

[6] I.e., approached alongside.

[7] **perforse:** by force.

[8] **corse:** corpse.

[9] **remorse:** compassion.

44　Whom when as nigh approching she espyde,
　　　She threw away her burden angrily;
　　　For she list not the batteill to abide,[1]
　　　But made her selfe more light, away to fly:
　　　Yet her the hardy knight pursewd so nye
　　　That almost in the backe he oft her strake:[2]
　　　But still when him at hand she did espy,
　　　She turnd, and semblaunce of faire fight did make;
　　But when he stayd, to flight againe she did her take.

45　By this[3] the good Sir *Satyrane* gan wake
　　　Out of his dreame, that did him long entraunce,[4]
　　　And seeing none in place,[5] he gan to make
　　　Exceeding mone, and curst that cruell chaunce,
　　　Which reft from him so faire a chevisaunce:[6]
　　　At length he spyde, whereas that wofull Squyre,
　　　Whom he had reskewed from captivaunce
　　　Of his strong foe, lay tombled in the myre,
　　Unable to arise, or foot or hand to styre.[7]

46　To whom approching, well he mote perceive
　　　In that fowle plight a comely[8] personage,
　　　And lovely face, made fit for to deceive
　　　Fraile Ladies hart with loves consuming rage,
　　　Now in the blossome of his freshest age:
　　　He reard him up, and loosd his yron bands,[9]
　　　And after gan inquire his parentage,
　　　And how he fell into the Gyaunts hands,
　　And who that was, which chaced her along the lands.

47　Then trembling yet through feare, the Squire bespake,
　　　"That Geauntesse *Argante*[10] is behight,
　　　A daughter of the *Titans* which did make

---

[1] **abide:** continue.

[2] **strake:** struck.

[3] **By this:** by this time.

[4] I.e., being struck so hard that he reeled from east to west (42.7).

[5] **in place:** right there.

[6] **chevisaunce:** chivalric deed; goal; booty.

[7] **styre:** stir.

[8] **comely:** handsome.

[9] **yron bands:** cf. "cords of wire," 37.8.

[10] In Tasso's *Gerusalemme Liberata* (1581), a romanticized account of the First Crusade, Argantes is a Circassian warrior who fights against the Christians. In Layamon's *Brut,* Argante is a name for Morgan le Fay, the fairy who sometimes helps and sometimes harms King Arthur.

Warre against heven, and heaped hils on hight,
To scale the skyes, and put *Jove* from his right:[1]
Her syre *Typhoeus*[2] was, who mad through merth,
And dronke with blood of men, slaine by his might,
Through incest, her of his owne mother Earth
Whylome begot, being but halfe twin of that berth.

48   "For at that berth another Babe she bore,
To weet the mightie *Ollyphant*,[3] that wrought
Great wreake to many errant knights of yore,[4]
Till him Chylde *Thopas* to confusion[5] brought.
These twinnes, men say, (a thing far passing[6] thought)
Whiles in their mothers wombe enclosd they were,
Ere they into the lightsom[7] world were brought,
In fleshly lust were mingled both yfere,[8]
And in that monstrous wise did to the world appere.

49   "So liv'd they ever after in like sin,
Gainst natures law, and good behaveoure:
But greatest shame was to that maiden twin,
Who not content so fowly to devoure
Her native flesh, and staine her brothers bowre,
Did wallow in all other fleshly myre,
And suffred beastes her body to deflowre:
So whot she burned in that lustfull fyre,
Yet all that might not slake her sensuall desyre.

---

[1] The ultimately unsuccessful war of the Giants against Zeus and the other Olympians is found in many sources of Greek myth, though Spenser seems to have invented Argante's place in it. Hesiod and Ovid differ somewhat in their descriptions of the time and nature of the revolt; see *Theogony* (617–735) and *Metamorphoses* (1.151–62).

[2] *Typhoeus:* a giant who is also a powerful wind.

[3] *Ollyphant:* not found in Greek myth. The name, which comes from Chaucer's "Tale of Sir Thopas" (807–9), means "ele-phant," with the standard phallic association.

[4] **wreake:** harm; **yore:** olden times.

[5] **Till him Chylde *Thopas* to:** "And many hath to foule" (1596). Because Chaucer left "The Tale of Sir Thopas" unfinished, he did not actually write about the inevitable slaying of Sir Oliphant by Sir Thopas. **Chylde:** courtesy title for a youth of gentle birth; **confusion:** downfall.

[6] **passing:** surpassing.

[7] **lightsom:** filled with light.

[8] **yfere:** as companions.

50   "But over all the countrie she did raunge,
        To seeke young men, to quench her flaming thurst,
        And feed her fancy with delightfull chaunge:[1]
        Whom so[2] she fittest findes to serve her lust,
        Through her maine[3] strength, in which she most doth trust,
        She with her bringes into a secret Ile,[4]
        Where in eternall bondage dye he must,
        Or be the vassall[5] of her pleasures vile,
    And in all shamefull sort him selfe with her defile.

51   "Me seely wretch she so at vauntage caught,[6]
        After she long in waite for me did lye,
        And meant unto her prison to have brought,
        Her lothsom pleasure there to satisfye;
        That thousand deathes me lever were[7] to dye,
        Then breake the vow, that to faire *Columbell*[8]
        I plighted[9] have, and yet keepe stedfastly:
        As for my name, it mistreth not[10] to tell;
    Call me the *Squyre of Dames* that me beseemeth[11] well.

52   "But that bold knight, whom ye pursuing saw
        That Geauntesse, is not such, as she seemd,
        But a faire virgin, that in martiall law,
        And deedes of armes above all Dames is deemd,
        And above many knightes is eke esteemd,
        For her great worth; She *Palladine*[12] is hight:
        She you from death, you me from dread redeemd.
        Ne any may that Monster match in fight,
    But she, or such as she, that is so chaste a wight."[13]

---

[1] **chaunge:** women were often called changeable when being accused of having fickle and immodest sexual appetites.

[2] **Whom so:** whomever.

[3] **maine:** sheer.

[4] **Ile:** isle.

[5] **vassall:** sworn servant.

[6] I.e., she caught me, pitiful wretch, at a moment when she had the advantage (or by chance).

[7] **me lever were:** I would rather.

[8] *Columbell:* French for "dove."

[9] **plighted:** pledged.

[10] **it mistreth not:** it is unnecessary (OED "mister" v[1]1).

[11] *Squyre of Dames:* a title (possibly invented by Spenser) that parodies the "Squire of the Body," a personal servant of a king, queen, or other dignitary; **beseemeth:** suits.

[12] *Palladine:* from "paladin," a paragon of chivalry.

[13] For those readers who may have lost track of the rapid sequence of events (a not uncommon experience while reading *The*

53   "Her well beseemes that Quest" (quoth *Satyrane*)
      "But read, thou *Squyre of Dames,* what vow is this,
      Which thou upon thy selfe hast lately ta'ne?"
      "That shall I you recount" (quoth he) "ywis,[1]
      So be ye pleasd to pardon all amis.[2]
      That gentle Lady, whom I love and serve,
      After long suit and wearie servicis,[3]
      Did aske me, how I could her love deserve,
      And how she might be sure, that I would never swerve.

54   "I glad by any meanes her grace[4] to gaine,
      Badd her commaund my life to save, or spill.[5]
      Eftsoones she badd me, with incessaunt paine[6]
      To wander through the world abroad at will,
      And every where, where with my power or skill
      I might doe service[7] unto gentle Dames,
      That I the same should faithfully fulfill,
      And at the twelve monethes end should bring their names
      And pledges;[8] as the spoiles of my victorious games.

Faerie Queene), a summary of Florimell's story may be in order: Florimell, in search of Marinell, is pursued by a lustful Forester, who is driven off by Timias and Arthur. Florimell continues to flee from Arthur, takes refuge in a witch's house, and is figuratively pursued by the witch's lustful son. When Florimell flees the house, the witch sends a hyena after her, so Florimell jumps into a little boat, leaving her horse behind to be eaten by the hyena. Satyrane, who loves Florimell, sees the hyena with Florimell's horse and fears the hyena has also eaten Florimell. After subduing the hyena and putting it on a leash, he sees a Giantess with a trussed-up Squire across her saddle, pursued by another knight. Satyrane and the Giantess square off, and she throws the bound Squire to the ground so he will not get in the way. Satyrane strikes the Giantess, who, undaunted, gives him such a blow that it makes him reel in a daze. She slings him across her saddle. The unnamed knight who had been pursuing her now resumes pursuit, at which she flees, tossing

Satyrane to the ground to lighten her load. Satyrane revives, releases the Squire from his bands, and listens to his story. The Squire of Dames reveals that the knight who pursued the Giantess Argante was Palladine, a woman in armor, and that only a woman could have subdued Argante. Palladine never appears in the poem again.

[1] **ywis:** certainly.

[2] I.e., to pardon anything in my tale that is inappropriate.

[3] **servicis:** services, sexual or otherwise.

[4] **grace:** favor.

[5] **Badd:** bade; **spill:** destroy.

[6] **paine:** labor; trouble; care.

[7] **doe service:** a transparent double entendre: a wooer was supposed to serve his beloved, and a knight was supposed to serve any lady in need, but to "do service" for a woman was to have sex with her.

[8] **pledges:** love tokens (such as handkerchiefs or locks of hair); oral or written promises of love.

55   "So well I to faire Ladies service did,
           And found such favour in their loving hartes,
           That ere the yeare his course had compassid,
           Three hundred pledges for my good desartes,[1]
           And thrise three hundred thanks for my good partes[2]
           I with me brought, and did to her present:
           Which when she saw, more bent to eke my smartes,[3]
           Then to reward my trusty true intent,
       She gan for me devise a grievous punishment.

56   "To weet, that I my traveill should resume,
           And with like labour walke the world arownd,
           Ne ever to her presence should presume,
           Till I so many other Dames had fownd,
           The which, for all the suit I could propownd,[4]
           Would me refuse their pledges to afford,[5]
           But did abide for ever chaste and sownd."
           "Ah gentle Squyre" (quoth he) "tell at one word,
       How many fowndst thou such to put in thy record?"

57   "In deed Sir knight" (said he) "one word may tell
           All, that I ever fownd so wisely stayd;[6]
           For onely three they were disposd so well,
           And yet three yeares I now abrode have strayd,
           To fynd them out." "Mote I" (then laughing sayd
           The knight) "inquire of thee, what were those three,
           The which thy proffred curtesie denayd?
           Or[7] ill they seemed sure avizd to bee,
       Or brutishly brought up, that nev'r did fashions see."[8]

58   "The first which then refused me" (said hee)
           "Certes was but a common Courtisane,[9]
           Yet flat refusd to have a doe[10] with mee,

---

[1] **desartes:** deserts.

[2] **partes:** characteristics, but with a pun on genitalia.

[3] **bent:** inclined; **eke:** augment; **smartes:** torment.

[4] I.e., for all the requests I could propose.

[5] **afford:** give, provide.

[6] **stayd:** steadied, immovable (characteristic of a virtuous woman, as opposed to being changeable).

[7] **Or:** either.

[8] Satyrane humorously suggests that chastity is not currently fashionable.

[9] **common Courtisane:** prostitute (as opposed to a court mistress, who could also be called a courtesan).

[10] **have a doe:** have it off with, have sex with.

Because I could not give her many a Jane."[1]
(Thereat full hartely laughed *Satyrane*)
"The second was an holy Nunne to chose,[2]
Which would not let me be her Chappellane,[3]
Because she knew, she sayd, I would disclose
Her counsell, if she should her trust in me repose.[4]

59   "The third a Damzell was of low degree,[5]
    Whom I in countrey cottage fownd by chaunce;
    Full litle weened I, that chastitee
    Had lodging in so meane a maintenaunce,[6]
    Yet was she fayre, and in her countenaunce
    Dwelt simple truth in seemely fashion.
    Long thus I woo'd her with dew observaunce,
    In hope unto my pleasure to have won,
But was as far[7] at last, as when I first begon.

60   "Safe[8] her, I never any woman found,
    That chastity did for it selfe embrace,[9]
    But were for other causes firme and sound,
    Either for want of handsome[10] time and place,
    Or else for feare of shame and fowle disgrace.
    Thus am I hopelesse ever to attaine
    My Ladies love, in such a desperate case,
    But all my dayes am like to waste in vaine,
Seeking to match the chaste with th'unchaste Ladies traine."[11]

---

[1] **Jane:** silver half-penny.

[2] **to chose:** by choice (OED "choose" v12, adv. sense); devoted to her calling (OED "choose" v10).

[3] **Chappellane:** chaplain, confessor—with the common Protestant insinuation that nuns had sex with their confessors.

[4] A priest was not supposed to disclose anything told in the confessional; the nun fears that the Squire of Dames will kiss and tell, so to speak.

[5] **degree:** social status.

[6] **maintenaunce:** state of living.

[7] **as far:** i.e., as far from succeeding.

[8] **Safe:** save, except for.

[9] I.e., who chose chastity for the sake of chastity itself.

[10] **handsome:** convenient.

[11] I.e., seeking to find a match for the chastity of my Lady in the unchastity of a series of other ladies; seeking to fit my Lady's chaste plot to the unchaste plots of other ladies.

61   "Perdy," (sayd *Satyrane*) "thou *Squyre of Dames,*
        Great labour fondly hast thou hent[1] in hand,
        To get small thankes, and therewith many blames,
        That may emongst *Alcides*[2] labours stand."
        Thence backe returning to the former land,
        Where late he left the Beast, he overcame,[3]
        He found him not; for he had broke his band,
        And was returnd againe unto his Dame,[4]
        To tell what tydings[5] of fayre *Florimell* became.

---

[1] **hent:** taken, grasped.

[2] ***Alcides:*** Hercules. An oracle directed him to do whatever King Eurystheus required of him, which turned out to be twelve "labors," each a seemingly impossible task that he nevertheless performed successfully.

[3] **the Beast, he overcame:** the hyena that he had overcome.

[4] I.e., after breaking the golden sash with which Satyrane had bound him (stanza 36), the hyena had returned to his mistress, the witch.

[5] **tydings:** news.

Canto Eight

The Witch creates a snowy Lady,
like to Florimell,
Who wrongd by Carle by Proteus[1] sav'd,
is sought by Paridell.[2]

1   So oft as I this history[3] record,
My hart doth melt with meere[4] compassion,
To thinke, how causelesse of her owne accord[5]
This gentle Damzell, whom I write upon,
Should plonged be in such affliction,
Without all hope of comfort or reliefe,[6]
That sure I weene, the hardest hart of stone,
Would hardly finde to[7] aggravate her griefe;
For misery craves rather mercy, then repriefe.[8]

2   But that accursed Hag, her hostesse late,
Had so enranckled[9] her malitious hart,
That she desyrd th'abridgement of her fate,[10]
Or long enlargement of her painefull smart.
Now when the Beast,[11] which by her wicked art
Late foorth she sent, she backe retourning spyde,
Tyde with her[12] golden girdle, it a part
Of her rich spoyles, whom he had earst destroyd,[13]
She weend, and wondrous gladnes to her hart applyde.

---

[1] **Carle:** churl; **Proteus:** a sea god capable of assuming any shape.

[2] **Paridell:** a name that associates him with Paris, whose abduction of Helen caused the Trojan War.

[3] **history:** a narrative of fictional or factual events, though the word was increasingly used in the latter sense.

[4] **meere:** pure, unmixed.

[5] I.e., through no blame of her own—or for no reason, of her own accord.

[6] With wide-eyed innocence, Spenser's narrator deplores the fact that a maiden as gen-teel as Florimell has ended up in such a sea of troubles. The cause of those troubles is, of course, Spenser (cf. 43.8 and IV.i.1).

[7] **finde to:** find the will or desire to.

[8] **repriefe:** reproof.

[9] **enranckled:** rankled in, festered in.

[10] **her fate:** the span of life alloted to Florimell by the Fates, goddesses who determined each baby's lifespan at birth.

[11] **the Beast:** the hyena.

[12] **her:** Florimell's.

[13] I.e., that the sash was a part of Florimell's goods, which the hyena got after killing her.

3   And with it ronning hast'ly to her sonne,
        Thought with that sight him much to have reliv'd;[1]
        Who thereby deeming sure the thing as donne,
        His former griefe with furie fresh reviv'd,
        Much more then earst, and would have algates riv'd[2]
        The hart out of his brest: for sith her dedd
        He surely dempt,[3] himselfe he thought depriv'd
        Quite of all hope, wherewith he long had fedd
His foolish malady, and long time had misledd.

4   With thought whereof, exceeding mad he grew,
        And in his rage his mother would have slaine,
        Had she not fled into a secret mew,[4]
        Where she was wont her Sprightes to entertaine
        The maisters of her art: there was she faine[5]
        To call them all in order to her ayde,
        And them conjure upon eternall paine,[6]
        To counsell her so carefully[7] dismayd,
How she might heale her sonne, whose senses were decayd.

5   By their device,[8] and her owne wicked wit,
        She there deviz'd a wondrous worke to frame,[9]
        Whose like on earth was never framed yit,
        That even Nature selfe envide the same,
        And grudg'd to see the counterfet should shame
        The thing it selfe: In hand she[10] boldly tooke
        To make another like the former Dame,
        Another *Florimell*, in shape and looke
So lively and so like,[11] that many it mistooke.

---

[1] **reliv'd:** revived, reinvigorated.

[2] **riv'd:** torn.

[3] **dempt:** deemed.

[4] **mew:** hiding place.

[5] **The maisters of her art:** an appositive to "her Sprights"; they are her familiars, demons that a witch can command to perform magic that she could not perform without them; **faine:** disposed; wont, used.

[6] **conjure:** command; **upon eternall paine:** under the threat of eternal pain.

[7] **carefully:** with care, grievously.

[8] **device:** machination.

[9] **to frame:** to construct.

[10] **she:** the witch.

[11] **So lively and so like:** so lifelike and so like Florimell.

6   The substance,[1] whereof she the body made,
           Was purest snow in massy mould[2] congeald,
           Which she had gathered in a shady glade
           Of the *Riphœan* hils,[3] to her reveald
           By errant[4] Sprights, but from all men conceald:
           The same she tempred with fine Mercury,
           And virgin wex,[5] that never yet was seald,
           And mingled them with perfect vermily,[6]
       That like a lively sanguine[7] it seemd to the eye.

7   In stead of eyes two burning lampes she set
           In silver sockets, shyning like the skyes,
           And a quicke moving Spirit did arret[8]
           To stirre and roll[9] them, like to womens eyes;
           In stead of yellow lockes she did devyse,
           With golden wyre to weave her curled head;
           Yet golden wyre was not so yellow thryse[10]
           As *Florimells* fayre heare: and in the stead
       Of life, she put a Spright to rule the carcas dead.[11]

8   A wicked Spright yfraught[12] with fawning guyle,
           And fayre resemblance above all the rest,
           Which with the Prince of Darkenes fell somewhyle,[13]
           From heavens blis and everlasting rest,[14]

[1] **substance:** a common word that has taken on wider meaning after our reading of Canto Six.

[2] **massy mould:** solid form. "Mould" also puns on "earth," the substance from which Adam was made and therefore a metaphorical term for all mortal flesh (in contrast to the Snowy Florimell's frozen substance, which is not alive).

[3] *Riphœan* **hils:** Riphean Mountains, the name used by early geographers for Russia's Ural Mountains (Paradise, 193–4).

[4] **errant:** physically wandering, but with a pun on moral wandering.

[5] **wex:** sealing wax.

[6] **vermily:** vermilion.

[7] **sanguine:** blood; the color of blood. One of the four humors, its predominance in the body causes a lecherous character.

[8] **quicke:** living; **arret:** appoint.

[9] A woman was criticized for having rolling eyes—meaning that she glanced from side to side flirtatiously.

[10] **thryse:** thrice; i.e., Florimell's hair was three times as yellow as golden wire.

[11] The stanza parodies the standard Petrarchan blazon, in which the beloved's features are admiringly described, one by one, and compared to beautiful objects—hair like golden wire, cheeks like cherries, eyes like stars, and so on.

[12] **yfraught:** laden.

[13] **somewhyle:** at some time.

[14] According to Revelation, a red dragon (later identified with Satan) warred against the faithful angels in heaven, for which he and the angels who had fought on his side were thrown down to earth (12.3–9).

Him needed not instruct, which way were best
Him selfe to fashion likest *Florimell,*
Ne how to speake, ne how to use his gest;[1]
For he in counterfesaunce[2] did excell,
And all the wyles of wemens wits knew passing well.

9   Him shaped[3] thus, she deckt in garments gay,
     Which *Florimell* had left behind her late,
     That who so then her saw, would surely say,
     It was her selfe, whom it did imitate,
     Or fayrer then her selfe, if ought algate
     Might fayrer be. And then she forth her brought
     Unto her sonne, that lay in feeble state;
     Who seeing her gan streight[4] upstart, and thought
She was the Lady selfe, who he so long had sought.

10   Tho fast her clipping twixt his armes twayne,
     Extremely joyed in so happy sight,
     And soone forgot his former sickely payne;
     But she,[5] the more to seeme such as she hight,
     Coyly rebutted his embracement light;[6]
     Yet still with gentle countenaunce retain'd,
     Enough to hold a foole in vaine delight:
     Him long she so with shadowes entertain'd,[7]
As her Creatresse had in charge to her ordain'd.

11   Till on a day,[8] as he disposed was
     To walke the woodes with that his Idole faire,
     Her to disport,[9] and idle time to pas,
     In th'open freshnes of the gentle aire,
     A knight that way there chaunced to repaire;
     Yet knight he was not, but a boastfull swaine,

---

[1] **gest:** comportment, manner.

[2] **counterfesaunce:** counterfeiting.

[3] **shaped:** naturally fitted; transformed; directed (perhaps with a pun on the common saying that God shapes human lives).

[4] **streight:** straightway.

[5] An ironic "she," given that "she" is animated by a male spirit.

[6] **rebutted:** rebuffed; **light:** deftly (referring to her action) or wanton (referring to his embrace).

[7] She is a shadow herself, but Spenser is also implying that flirtation is show without substance.

[8] **on a day:** one day.

[9] **disport:** entertain (with sexual overtones).

That deedes of armes had ever in despaire,[1]
Proud *Braggadocchio,* that in vaunting vaine[2]
His glory did repose, and credit[3] did maintaine.

12   He seeing with that Chorle so faire a wight,
       Decked with many a costly ornament,
       Much merveiled thereat, as well he might,
       And thought that match a fowle disparagement:[4]
       His bloody speare eftesoones he boldly bent
       Against the silly clowne,[5] who dead through feare,
       Fell streight to ground in great astonishment;
       "Villein" (sayd he)[6] "this Lady is my deare,
       Dy, if thou it gainesay: I will away her beare."

13   The fearefull Chorle durst not gainesay, nor dooe,[7]
       But trembling stood, and yielded him the pray;
       Who finding litle leasure her to wooe,
       On *Tromparts* steed her mounted without stay,[8]
       And without reskew led her quite away.
       Proud man himselfe then *Braggadochio* deem'd,

---

[1] I.e., who despaired of ever performing great feats of war.

[2] *Braggadocchio:* from the English "braggart" and the Italian suffix *occio,* an intensifier. Spenser invented the name, which is now used generically to refer to anyone like this character. See v.27.9.n.; **vaunting vaine:** empty boasting.

[3] **credit:** reputation. The relationship between credit as personal reputation and credit as reputation for financial solvency had become a crucial social issue by the late Middle Ages and early Renaissance, as the feudal economy of fixed inheritance and farming changed slowly into an investment economy. A person's financial credit was established largely by personal reputation and connections, which meant that one had to put on an expensive show in order to prove oneself worthy to borrow money. The result was often bankruptcy, even for aristocrats and previously wealthy members of the merchant class. In Braggadocchio,

Spenser paints a character whose very being is bankrupt.

[4] **disparagement:** insult to the lady, who should have been married to someone of a higher station. (Braggadocchio carries arms and scorns the peasant, yet he has no title, so he must be of a middling class.)

[5] **clowne:** peasant; country bumpkin.

[6] **Villein:** serf; base character; **he:** Braggadocchio.

[7] **durst:** dared; **dooe:** do anything to resist.

[8] *Tromparts:* Trompart is Braggadocchio's vassal; his name implies deception (a "trumper" was a deceiver) and likens him to a trumpet in his flattering willingness to "blow the bellowes to [Braggadocchio's] swelling vanity" (II.iii.9.9). One cannot help thinking of Hieronymus Bosch's late fifteenth- or early sixteenth-century painting of the Last Judgment, in which one of the damned plays a trumpet with his anus; **stay:** delay; hindrance.

And next to none,[1] after that happy day,
Being possessed of that spoyle, which seem'd
The fairest wight on ground, and most of men esteem'd.

14   But when hee saw him selfe free from poursute,
He gan make gentle purpose[2] to his Dame,
With termes of love and lewdnesse dissolute;
For he could well his glozing speaches frame[3]
To such vaine uses, that him best became:
But she thereto would lend but light regard,
As seeming sory, that she ever came
Into his powre, that used her so hard,
To reave[4] her honor, which she more then life prefard.

15   Thus as they two of kindnes treated[5] long,
There them by chaunce encountred on the way
An armed knight, upon a courser[6] strong,
Whose trampling feete upon the hollow lay[7]
Seemed to thunder, and did nigh affray[8]
That Capons[9] corage: yet he looked grim,
And faynd[10] to cheare his lady in dismay,
Who seemd for feare to quake in every lim,[11]
And her to save from outrage, meekely prayed him.[12]

16   Fiercely that straunger forward came, and nigh
Approching, with bold words and bitter threat,
Bad that same boaster, as he mote, on high[13]
To leave to him that lady for excheat,[14]
Or bide him batteill without further treat.[15]

---

[1] **next to none:** i.e., second to none.

[2] **gentle purpose:** genteel conversation.

[3] **glozing:** flattering; **frame:** adapt; direct.

[4] **reave:** tear away.

[5] **treated:** discussed.

[6] **courser:** swift horse.

[7] **lay:** ground.

[8] **affray:** frighten.

[9] **Capons:** a capon is a rooster that has been castrated to make the meat tender; by extension, the term meant "eunuch" and was used as a term of contempt for a man deemed insufficiently manly.

[10] **faynd:** wanted; attempted; with a pun on the sense "feign," spelled the same way.

[11] **lim:** limb.

[12] I.e., meekly asked him to save her from being raped by the strange knight.

[13] **Bad:** bade; **on high:** loudly.

[14] **excheat:** forfeit.

[15] I.e., endure battle with him, without any further ado.

That challenge did too peremptory seeme,
And fild his senses with abashment great;
Yet seeing nigh him jeopardy extreme,
He it dissembled well, and light[1] seemd to esteeme.

17   Saying, "Thou foolish knight, that weenst with words
      To steale away, that[2] I with blowes have wonne,
      And broght throgh points of many perilous swords:
      But if thee list to see thy Courser ronne,
      Or prove thy selfe, this sad encounter shonne,
      And seeke els[3] without hazard of thy hedd."
      At those prowd words that other knight begonne
      To wex exceeding wroth, and him aredd
To turne his steede about, or sure he should be dedd.

18   "Sith then" (said *Braggadochio*) "needes thou wilt[4]
      Thy daies abridge, through proofe[5] of puissaunce,
      Turne we our steeds, that both in equall tilt[6]
      May meete againe, and each take happy chaunce."[7]
      This said, they both a furlongs mountenaunce[8]
      Retird their steeds, to ronne in even race:
      But *Braggadochio* with his bloody launce
      Once having turnd, no more returnd[9] his face,
But lefte his love to losse, and fled him selfe apace.[10]

19   The knight him seeing flie, had no regard[11]
      Him to poursew, but to the lady rode,
      And having her from *Trompart* lightly[12] reard,
      Upon his Courser sett the lovely lode,
      And with her fled away without abode.[13]
      Well weened he, that fairest *Florimell*

---

[1] **light:** unimportant.

[2] **that:** that which.

[3] **els:** elsewhere.

[4] **needes thou wilt:** necessarily you will.

[5] **proofe:** trial.

[6] **tilt:** jousting (running at each other on horseback, with lances pointing forward).

[7] **happy chaunce:** whatever fortune happens to bring.

[8] **furlongs mountenaunce:** the measure of a furlong, about one-eighth of a mile; loosely used to mean "a short way."

[9] **returnd:** turned back.

[10] **apace:** speedily.

[11] **regard:** inclination; interest.

[12] **lightly:** easily; deftly.

[13] **abode:** delay.

It was, with whom in company he yode,[1]
And so her selfe did alwaies to him tell;
So made him thinke him selfe in heven, that was in hell.

20   But *Florimell* her selfe was far away,
       Driven to great distresse by fortune straunge,
       And taught the carefull Mariner to play,[2]
       Sith late mischaunce[3] had her compeld to chaunge
       The land for sea, at randon there to raunge:[4]
       Yett there that cruell Queene[5] avengeresse,
       Not satisfyde so far her to estraunge
       From courtly blis and wonted happinesse,
Did heape on her new waves of weary wretchednesse.

21   For being fled into the fishers bote,
       For refuge from the Monsters cruelty,
       Long so she on the mighty maine did flote,
       And with the tide drove forward carelesly,
       For th'ayre was milde, and cleared was the skie,
       And all his windes *Dan Aeolus*[6] did keepe,
       From stirring up their stormy enmity,
       As pittying to see her waile and weepe;
But all the while the fisher did securely sleepe.

22   At last when droncke with drowsinesse, he woke,
       And saw his drover drive along the streame,[7]
       He was dismayd, and thrise his breast he stroke,
       For marveill of that accident extreame;
       But when he saw, that blazing beauties beame,
       Which with rare light his bote did beautifye,
       He marveild more, and thought he yet did dreame
       Not well awakte, or that some extasye[8]
Assotted[9] had his sence, or dazed was his eye.

---

[1] **yode:** went.

[2] I.e., fortune had taught her to put on the role of mariner (when she jumped into the little boat to escape the hyena (vii.27).

[3] **mischaunce:** misfortune.

[4] **randon:** random; **raunge:** drift; wander.

[5] I.e., Fortune.

[6] ***Dan:*** courtesy title for a male member of a religious order or for a male scholar, knight, poet, or deity; ***Aeolus:*** a god of the winds, who sometimes keeps them shut up in his cave.

[7] **drover:** fishing boat; **streame:** current.

[8] **extasye:** trance; temporary condition of being out of touch with reality.

[9] **Assotted:** befooled; infatuated.

23   But when her well avizing, hee perceiv'd
        To be no vision, nor fantasticke[1] sight,
        Great comfort of her presence he conceiv'd,
        And felt in his old corage[2] new delight
        To gin awake, and stir his frosen spright:[3]
        Tho rudely askte her, how she thether came.
        "Ah" (sayd she) "father I note read aright,
        What hard misfortune brought me to this same;
    Yet am I glad that here I now in safety ame.

24   "But thou good man, sith far in sea we bee,
        And the great waters gin apace to swell,[4]
        That now no more we can the mayn-land see,
        Have care, I pray, to guide the cock-bote[5] well,
        Least worse on sea then us on land befell."
        Thereat th'old man did nought but fondly[6] grin,
        And saide, his boat the way could wisely tell:
        But his deceiptfull eyes did never lin,[7]
    To looke on her faire face, and marke[8] her snowy skin.

25   The sight whereof[9] in his congealed flesh,
        Infixt such secrete sting of greedy lust,
        That the drie withered stocke[10] it gan refresh,
        And kindled heat, that soone in flame forth brust:
        The driest wood is soonest burnt to dust.
        Rudely to her he lept, and his rough hand
        Where ill became him, rashly would have thrust,
        But she with angry scorne him did withstond,
    And shamefully reprov'd for his rudenes fond.

[1] **fantasticke:** produced by fantasy; imaginary.

[2] **corage:** spirit, with a pun on sexual powers.

[3] **frosen spright:** according to sixteenth-century medical knowledge, a man's semen contained spirits which needed heat to stir themselves.

[4] Florimell does not realize that the fisher will hear a bawdy double meaning in her words; his "waters" are also beginning to swell.

[5] **cock-bote:** very small, light boat. According to the OED, the first recorded use of "cock" to mean "penis" was in 1618 (sb[1]20), so Spenser may or may not be punning here.

[6] **fondly:** foolishly.

[7] **lin:** leave off, cease.

[8] **marke:** take note of.

[9] **whereof:** of which.

[10] **stocke:** anyone or anything devoid of sensation, such as a stick of wood (with implied allusion to the penis); trunk of the body; progenitor.

26 But he, that never good nor maners knew,
  Her sharpe rebuke full litle did esteeme;
  Hard is to teach an old horse amble trew.
  The inward smoke, that did before but steeme,
  Broke into open fire and rage[1] extreme,
  And now he strength gan adde unto his will,
  Forcying to doe, that[2] did him fowle misseeme:
  Beastly he threwe her downe, ne car'd to spill[3]
Her garments gay with scales of fish,[4] that all did fill.

27 The silly[5] virgin strove him to withstand,
  All that she might, and him in vaine revild:
  Shee strugled strongly both with foote and hand,
  To save her honor from that villaine vilde,
  And cride to heven, from humane helpe exild.
  O ye brave knights, that boast this Ladies love,
  Where be ye now, when she is nigh defild
  Of filthy wretch? well may she you reprove
Of falsehood or of slouth, when most it may behove.[6]

28 But if that thou, Sir *Satyran,* didst weete,
  Or thou, Sir *Peridure,*[7] her sory state,
  How soone would yee assemble many a fleete,
  To fetch from sea, that[8] ye at land lost late;
  Towres, citties, kingdomes ye would ruinate,[9]
  In your avengement and dispiteous[10] rage,
  Ne ought[11] your burning fury mote abate;
  But if Sir *Calidore* could it presage,[12]
No living creature could his cruelty asswage.

---

[1] **rage:** sexual fury.

[2] **that:** that which.

[3] **ne car'd to spill:** nor cared whether he spoiled.

[4] I.e., "spill . . . with scales of fish" (her gay garments are spoiled by being smeared with fish scales).

[5] **silly:** defenceless.

[6] I.e., when it would be most appropriate for you to help her.

[7] **Sir *Peridure*:** mentioned briefly in the chronicle of British kings in Book Two; otherwise, he does not appear in the poem (II.x.44.9).

[8] **that:** that which.

[9] **ruinate:** lay waste.

[10] **dispiteous:** lacking pity, merciless.

[11] **ought:** aught, anything.

[12] **presage:** feel a foreboding about; predict intuitively.

29   But sith that none of all her knights is nye,
          See how the heavens of voluntary grace,
          And soveraine favor towards chastity,
          Doe succor send to her distressed cace:
       So much high God doth innocence embrace.
          It fortuned, whilest thus she stifly[1] strove,
          And the wide sea importuned[2] long space
          With shrilling shriekes, *Proteus*[3] abrode did rove,
       Along the fomy waves driving his finny drove.

30   *Proteus* is Shepheard of the seas of yore,
          And hath the charge of *Neptunes* mighty heard,[4]
          An aged sire with head all frowy hore,[5]
          And sprinckled frost upon his deawy beard:
       Who when those pittifull outcries he heard,
          Through all the seas so ruefully resownd,
          His charett[6] swifte in hast he thether steard,
          Which with a teeme of scaly *Phocas*[7] bownd
       Was drawne upon the waves, that fomed him arownd.

31   And comming to that Fishers wandring bote,
          That went at will, withouten card[8] or sayle,
          He therein saw that yrkesome sight, which smote
          Deepe indignation and compassion frayle[9]
       Into his hart attonce: streight did he hayle
          The greedy villein from his hoped pray,
          Of which he now did very litle fayle,[10]
          And with his staffe, that drives his heard astray,
       Him bett so sore, that life and sence did much dismay.

32   The whiles the pitteous Lady up did ryse,
          Ruffled and fowly raid[11] with filthy soyle,
          And blubbred[12] face with teares of her faire eyes:

---

[1] **stifly:** resolutely.

[2] I.e., pleaded to the wide sea.

[3] *Proteus:* see Argument, note.

[4] *Neptunes:* belonging to the chief god of the ocean; **heard:** herd (of fish).

[5] **frowy:** dank; perhaps an error for "frory," meaning "frosty" or "frothy," as at 35.2; **hore:** hoary, greyish-white (hair) or covered with frost.

[6] **charett:** chariot.

[7] *Phocas:* seals.

[8] **at will:** in the manner of lust on the loose; **card:** chart or compass card.

[9] **frayle:** tender.

[10] I.e., the fisher was very short of succeeding in taking possession of her.

[11] **raid:** smeared (OED "ray" v²5).

[12] **blubbred:** swollen with weeping.

Her heart nigh broken was with weary toyle,
To save her selfe from that outrageous spoyle,
But when she looked up, to weet, what wight
Had her from so infamous fact assoyld,[1]
For shame, but more for feare of his grim sight,
Downe in her lap she hid her face, and lowdly shright.[2]

33   Herselfe not saved yet from daunger dredd
    She thought, but chaung'd from one to other feare;
    Like as a fearefull partridge, that is fledd
    From the sharpe hauke, which her attached neare,[3]
    And fals to ground, to seeke for succor theare,
    Whereas the hungry Spaniells she does spye,
    With greedy jawes her ready for to teare;
    In such distresse and sad perplexity
Was *Florimell,* when *Proteus* she did see her by.

34   But he endevored with speaches milde
    Her to recomfort, and accourage bold,[4]
    Bidding her feare no more her foeman vilde,
    Nor doubt himselfe; and who he was her told.
    Yet all that could not from affright her hold,
    Ne to recomfort her at all prevayld;
    For her faint hart was with the frosen cold
    Benumbd so inly, that her wits nigh fayld,
And all her sences with abashment quite were quayld.

35   Her up betwixt his rugged hands he reard,
    And with his frory lips full[5] softly kist,
    Whiles the cold ysickles from his rough beard,
    Dropped adowne upon her yvory brest:
    Yet he him selfe so busily addrest,[6]
    That her out of astonishment[7] he wrought,
    And out of that same fishers filthy nest
    Removing her, into his charet brought,
And there with many gentle termes her faire besought.[8]

---

[1] **assoyld:** released.

[2] **shright:** shrieked.

[3] **attached neare:** nearly seized.

[4] **accourage bold:** boldy take heart.

[5] **frory:** frosty; frothy; **full:** very, quite.

[6] **addrest:** applied.

[7] **astonishment:** stunned condition; stupor.

[8] **besought:** entreated; attempted to gain.

36   But that old leachour,[1] which with bold assault
    That beautie durst presume to violate,
    He cast to punish for his hainous fault;
    Then tooke he him yet trembling sith of late,
    And tyde behind his charet, to aggrate[2]
    The virgin, whom he[3] had abusde so sore:
    So drag'd him through the waves in scornfull state,
    And after cast him up, upon the shore;
But *Florimell* with him unto his bowre he bore.

37   His bowre is in the bottom of the maine,
    Under a mightie rocke, gainst which doe rave
    The roring billowes in their proud disdaine,
    That with the angry working of the wave,
    Therein is eaten out an hollow cave,
    That seemes rough Masons hand with engines keene
    Had long while laboured it to engrave:
    There was his wonne, ne living wight was seene,
Save one old *Nymph,* hight *Panope* to keepe it cleane.

38   Thether he brought the sory *Florimell,*
    And entertained[4] her the best he might
    And *Panope* her entertaind eke well,
    As an immortall mote a mortall wight,
    To winne her liking unto his delight:
    With flattering wordes he sweetly wooed her,
    And offered faire guiftes, t'allure her sight,
    But she both offers and the offerer
Despysde, and all the fawning of the flatterer.

39   Dayly he tempted her with this or that,
    And never suffred[5] her to be at rest:
    But evermore she him refused flat,
    And all his fained kindnes did detest.
    So firmely she had sealed up her brest.
    Sometimes he boasted, that a God he hight:

---

[1] I.e., the fisher.

[2] **aggrate:** please.

[3] **he:** the fisher.

[4] **entertained:** treated.

[5] **suffred:** allowed.

But she a mortall creature loved best:
Then he would make him selfe a mortall wight;
But then she said she lov'd none, but a Faery knight.

40   Then like a Faerie knight him selfe he drest;
For every shape on him he could endew:[1]
Then like a king he was to her exprest,[2]
And offred kingdoms unto her in vew,
To be his Leman[3] and his Lady trew:
But when all this he nothing saw prevaile,
With harder meanes he cast her to subdew,
And with sharpe threates her often did assayle,
So thinking for to make her stubborne corage quayle.

41   To dreadfull shapes he did him selfe transforme,
Now like a Gyaunt, now like to a feend,
Then like a Centaure,[4] then like to a storme,
Raging within the waves: thereby he weend
Her will to win unto his wished eend.[5]
But when with[6] feare, nor favour, nor with all
He els could doe, he saw him selfe esteemd,
Downe in a Dongeon deepe he let her fall,
And threatned there to make her his eternall thrall.

42   Eternall thraldome was to her more liefe,[7]
Then losse of chastitie, or chaunge of love:[8]
Dye had she rather in tormenting griefe,
Then any should of falseness[9] her reprove,
Or loosenes, that she lightly did remove.[10]
Most vertuous virgin, glory be thy meed,
And crowne of heavenly prayse with Saintes above,
Where most sweet hymmes of this thy famous deed
Are still emongst them song, that far my rymes exceed.[11]

---

[1] **endew:** endue, put on.

[2] **exprest:** manifested; represented, portrayed.

[3] **Leman:** beloved; paramour, mistress.

[4] **Centaure:** half man, half horse, and known for lust.

[5] **eend:** end, goal.

[6] **with:** neither with.

[7] **more liefe:** preferable.

[8] Cf. Belphoebe's resolute chastity in the face of Timias' need.

[9] **falseness:** infidelity.

[10] **remove:** i.e., remove her affections from one man to transfer them to another.

[11] I.e., that far exceed my rymes.

43   Fit song of Angels caroled to bee,
            But yet what so[1] my feeble Muse can frame,
            Shalbe t'advance[2] thy goodly chastitee,
            And to enroll[3] thy memorable name,
            In th'heart of every honourable[4] Dame,
            That they thy vertuous deedes may imitate,
            And be partakers of thy endlesse fame.
        Yt yrkes me, leave thee in this wofull state,[5]
    To tell of *Satyrane,* where I him left of late.

44   Who having ended with that *Squyre of Dames*
            A long discourse of his adventures vayne,[6]
            The which himselfe, then Ladies more defames,
            And finding not th'*Hyena* to be slayne,[7]
            With that same *Squyre,* retourned back agayne
            To his first way.[8] And as they forward went,
            They spyde a knight fayre pricking[9] on the playne,
            As if he were on some adventure bent,
        And in his port[10] appeared manly hardiment.

45   Sir *Satyrane* him towardes did addresse,
            To weet, what wight he was, and what his quest:
            And comming nigh, eftsoones he gan to gesse
            Both by the burning hart, which on his brest
            He bare,[11] and by the colours in his crest,
            That *Paridell*[12] it was. Tho to him yode,
            And him saluting, as beseemed best,
        Gan first inquire of tydinges[13] farre abrode;
    And afterwardes, on what adventure now he rode.

---

[1] **what so:** whatever.

[2] **advance:** praise publicly, extol.

[3] **enroll:** record as a way of honoring.

[4] When applied to a woman, the word "honorable" means "chaste and faithful."

[5] I.e., it irks me to leave you in this woeful condition. The poem's speaker is being wide-eyed with innocence, again (cf. 1.6.n.).

[6] **vayne:** useless, i.e., the Squire of Dames' search for chaste women.

[7] **to be slayne:** to slay it.

[8] **his first way:** his original quest (see vii.30).

[9] **pricking:** spurring his horse onward.

[10] **port:** carriage of himself.

[11] I.e., he bore a representation of a burning heart on the front of his tunic.

[12] See Arg.4.n.

[13] **tydinges:** news.

46   Who thereto answering, said, "The tydinges bad,
        Which now in Faery court all men doe tell,
        Which turned hath great mirth, to mourning sad,
        Is the late ruine of proud *Marinell,*
        And suddein parture[1] of faire *Florimell,*
        To find him forth: and after her are gone
        All the brave knightes, that doen[2] in armes excell,
        To savegard[3] her, ywandred all alone;
    Emongst the rest my lott (unworthy) is to be one."

47   "Ah gentle knight" (said then Sir *Satyrane*)
        "Thy labour all is lost, I greatly dread,
        That hast a thanklesse service on thee ta'ne,
        And offrest sacrifice unto the dead:
        For dead, I surely doubt,[4] thou maist aread
        Henceforth for ever *Florimell* to bee,
        That all the noble knights of *Maydenhead,*[5]
        Which her ador'd, may sore repent[6] with mee,
    And all faire Ladies may for ever sory bee."

48   Which wordes when *Paridell* had heard, his hew
        Gan greatly chaung and seemd dismaid to bee,
        Then said, "Fayre Sir, how may I weene it trew,
        That[7] ye doe tell in such uncerteintee?
        Or speake ye of report,[8] or did ye see
        Just[9] cause of dread, that makes ye doubt so sore?
        For perdie elles[10] how mote it ever bee,
        That ever hand should dare for to engore
    Her noble blood? the hevens such crueltie abhore."

---

[1] **parture:** departure.

[2] **doen:** do.

[3] **savegard:** safeguard.

[4] **doubt:** fear.

[5] **knights of *Maydenhead*:** an order of knights invented by Spenser to serve Gloriana, in a tribute to the actual Knights of the Garter, who served the Virgin Queen, Elizabeth. As in the Elizabethan court, the political relationship of Gloriana to her knights is articulated in the same sorts of terms as those used by a chaste Petrarchan mistress and her suitors, even when the knights are actually in love with other women.

[6] **repent:** mourn; regret; feel guilty about.

[7] **That:** that which.

[8] **report:** rumor.

[9] **Just:** reliable.

[10] **elles:** otherwise.

49   "These eyes did see, that they will ever¹ rew
          To have seene," (quoth he) "when as a monstrous beast
          The Palfrey, whereon she did travell, slew,
          And of his bowels made his bloody feast:
          Which speaking token² sheweth at the least
          Her certeine losse, if not her sure decay:
          Besides, that more suspicion encreast,
          I found her golden girdle cast astray,
Distaynd with durt and blood, as relique³ of the pray."

50   "Ay me," (said *Paridell*) "the signes be sadd,
          And but God turne the same to good sooth say,⁴
          That Ladies safetie is sore to be dradd:
          Yet will I not forsake my forward way,
          Till triall⁵ doe more certeine truth bewray."
          "Faire Sir" (quoth he) "well may it you succeed,
          Ne long shall *Satyrane* behind you stay,
          But to the rest, which⁶ in this Quest proceed
My labour adde, and be partaker of their speed."⁷

51   "Ye noble knights" (said then the *Squyre of Dames*)
          "Well may yee speede in so praiseworthy payne:
          But sith the Sunne now ginnes to slake his beames,
          In deawy vapours of the westerne mayne,
          And lose the teme out of his weary wayne,⁸
          Mote not mislike you⁹ also to abate
          Your zealous hast, till morrow next againe
          Both light of heven, and strength of men relate:¹⁰
Which if ye please, to yonder castle turne your gate."

52   That counsell pleased well; so all yfere¹¹
          Forth marched to a Castle them before,
          Where soone arryving, they restrained were

---

¹ **that:** that which; **ever:** always.

² **speaking token:** significant sign.

³ **Distaynd:** defiled; **relique:** relic, venerated token; remnant.

⁴ I.e., unless God turns these signs (most specifically, this sash) into a good omen.

⁵ **triall:** direct experience.

⁶ **which:** who.

⁷ **speed:** success; speed.

⁸ I.e., unharness the team of horses that draw the wain—the wagon—of the Sun.

⁹ **Mote not mislike you:** may it not displease you.

¹⁰ **relate:** restore.

¹¹ **yfere:** in a friendly company.

Of ready entraunce, which ought evermore
To errant knights be commune:[1] wondrous sore
Thereat displeasd they were, till that young Squyre
Gan them informe the cause, why that same dore
Was shut to all, which[2] lodging did desyre:
The which to let you weet, will further time requyre.

[1] In a world with very few inns, it was expected that respectable-looking strangers should be able to knock on the door of any house but the most poverty-stricken and be given food and shelter for the night.

[2] **which:** who.

Canto Nine

Malbecco[1] will no straunge knights host,
For peevish[2] gealosy:
Paridell giusts[3] with Britomart:
both shew their auncestry.

1   Redoubted[4] knights, and honorable Dames,
            To whom I levell[5] all my labours end,
            Right sore I feare, least with unworthie blames
            This odious argument my rymes should shend,[6]
            Or ought[7] your goodly patience offend,
            Whiles of a wanton Lady I doe write,
            Which with her loose incontinence doth blend[8]
            The shyning glory of your soveraine light,
      And knighthood fowle defaced by a faithlesse knight.

2   But never let th'ensample of the bad
            Offend the good: for good by paragone[9]
            Of evill, may more notably be rad,[10]
            As white seemes fayrer, macht with blacke attone;[11]
            Ne all are shamed by the fault of one:
            For lo in heven, whereas[12] all goodnes is,
            Emongst the Angels, a whole legione[13]
            Of wicked Sprightes did fall from happy blis;[14]
      What wonder then, if one of women all did mis?[15]

---

[1] **Malbecco:** Latin *malus* (bad) + Italian *becco* (male goat; cuckold).

[2] **peevish:** senseless; insane; spiteful; perverse; morose.

[3] **giusts:** jousts.

[4] **Redoubted:** respected.

[5] **levell:** direct.

[6] **argument:** subject; **rymes:** poetry; **shend:** shame.

[7] **ought:** at all.

[8] **blend:** dilute; obscure.

[9] **paragone:** comparison.

[10] **rad:** (form of "read") understood; perceived.

[11] **macht:** matched; **attone:** together.

[12] **whereas:** where.

[13] **legione:** vast number in a mass; army.

[14] The fallen angels who conspired with Satan to overthrow God were punished by being thrown out of heaven.

[15] **mis:** err; sin.

3   Then listen Lordings,[1] if ye list to weet
       The cause, why *Satyrane* and *Paridell*
       Mote not be entertaynd,[2] as seemed meet,
       Into that Castle (as that Squyre does tell.)
       "Therein a cancred crabbed Carle[3] does dwell,
       That has no skill of Court nor courtesie,[4]
       Ne cares, what men say of him ill or well;
       For all his dayes he drownes in privitie,[5]
    Yet has full large[6] to live, and spend at libertie.

4   "But all his mind is set on mucky pelfe,[7]
       To hoord up heapes of evill gotten masse,
       For which he others wrongs and wreckes himselfe;
       Yet is he lincked to a lovely lasse,
       Whose beauty doth her bounty far surpasse,
       The which to him both far unequall yeares,[8]
       And also far unlike conditions has;
       For she does joy to play emongst her peares,[9]
    And to be free from hard restraynt and gealous feares.

5   "But he is old, and withered like hay,
       Unfit faire Ladies service[10] to supply,
       The privie guilt whereof makes him alway

---

[1] Having warned that the subject matter will be racy, the speaker is no longer inviting women to listen—yet the chief audience presumed by the poem is always Elizabeth. There has been quite racy subject matter in the poem before this point, of course. Perhaps by the time he was writing these lines, Spenser had already begun to receive the criticism to which he will allude at the beginning of the 1596 edition (IV.Pr); but it is just as likely that these stanzas here in Book Three are humorously arch.

[2] **entertaynd:** courteously admitted.

[3] **cancred crabbed Carle:** churlish churlish churl. The *c*'s emphasize his constipated disposition.

[4] **skill:** knowledge; **courtesie:** see vi.1.6.n.

[5] **privitie:** seclusion; secret plans; personal affairs—with puns on "intimacy," "private parts," and "the legal bond of marriage," and with an oblique invocation of "privation." All of these are significant for Malbecco's story.

[6] **large:** largesse, bounty (normally designating the quality of being bountiful; here designating merely the financial potential to be so).

[7] **mucky:** filthy; **pelfe:** money; property; stolen goods—with additional resonance from the meaning "rubbish."

[8] I.e., they are of very different ages.

[9] **peares:** peers.

[10] **service:** sexual servicing, a subject on which the Squire of Dames is something of an authority (see vii.53–55).

Suspect her truth,[1] and keepe continuall spy
Upon her with his other blincked eye;[2]
Ne suffreth he resort[3] of living wight
Approch to her, ne keepe her company,
But in close bowre her mewes[4] from all mens sight,
Depriv'd of kindly[5] joy and naturall delight.

6   "*Malbecco* he, and *Hellenore*[6] she hight,
Unfitly yokt together in one teeme,[7]
That is the cause, why never any knight
Is suffred here to enter, but he seeme
Such, as no doubt of him he neede misdeeme."[8]
Thereat Sir *Satyrane* gan smyle, and say;
"Extremely mad[9] the man I surely deeme,
That weenes with watch and hard restraynt to stay[10]
A womans will, which is disposd to go astray.[11]

7   "In vaine he feares that, which he cannot shonne:
For who wotes not, that womans subtiltyes
Can guylen *Argus*,[12] when she list misdonne?
It is not yron bandes, nor hundred eyes,
Nor brasen walls, nor many wakefull spyes,
That can withhold her wilfull wandring feet,

---

[1] **Suspect her truth:** be suspicious about her chastity (i.e., her possible loss of it).

[2] I.e., his one eye or his left eye, which is partly blinded or subject to blinking.

[3] **suffreth:** allows; **resort:** company; access.

[4] **mewes:** pens up.

[5] **kindly:** natural.

[6] *Malbecco:* see Arg.1.n.; *Hellenore:* a name evoking Helen of Troy; Fowler suggests that Elizabethans might have heard "Helen-whore" (Fowler 1959, 585, n. 3).

[7] **teeme:** team, as of oxen.

[8] **doubt:** fear; suspicion; **misdeeme:** suspect.

[9] **mad:** crazed.

[10] **stay:** restrain.

[11] It was believed that women's cold, moist humors and unstable wombs (which could wander about inside their bodies if diseased and which, in any case, were influenced by the changeable moon) made them inherently disposed to err morally and kept them from establishing firm lines of thought or firm purposes. See also vi.8.5.n.

[12] **guylen:** beguile; hoodwink; *Argus:* in Greek mythology, a giant with a hundred eyes, only two of which slept at any given time. Juno was jealous of Jove's current in-*amorata* and rape victim, the beautiful Io, so Jove changed Io into a white heifer. Juno set Argus to guard Io with his hundred eyes, keeping her miserably lonely. Taking pity on Io, Mercury played his pipe to Argus until all hundred eyes were lulled asleep; then Mercury cut off Argus' head, and Juno put the giant's eyes into a peacock's tail (Ovid, *Metamorphoses*, 1.583–723).

But fast goodwill with gentle courtesyes,
And timely service to her pleasures meet
May her perhaps containe, that else would algates fleet."[1]

8   "Then is he not more mad" (sayd *Paridell*)
      "That hath himselfe unto such service sold,
      In dolefull thraldome all his dayes to dwell?
      For sure a foole I doe him firmely hold,
      That loves his fetters, though they were of gold.
      But why doe wee devise of[2] others ill,
      Whyles thus we suffer this same dotard[3] old,
      To keepe us out, in scorne of his owne will,
And rather do not ransack all, and him selfe kill?"[4]

9   "Nay let us first" (sayd *Satyrane*) "entreat
      The man by gentle meanes, to let us in,
      And afterwardes affray[5] with cruell threat,
      Ere that we to efforce it doe begin:
      Then if all fayle, we will by force it win,
      And eke reward the wretch for his mesprise,[6]
      As may be worthy of his haynous sin."
      That counsell pleasd: then *Paridell* did rise,
And to the Castle gate approcht in quiet wise.

10   Whereat soft knocking, entrance he desyrd.
      The good man selfe, which then the Porter playd,[7]
      Him answered, that all were now retyrd
      Unto their rest, and all the keyes convayd
      Unto their maister, who in bed was layd,
      That none him durst awake out of his dreme;
      And therefore them of patience gently prayd.
      Then *Paridell* began to chaunge his theme,
And threatned him with force and punishment extreme.

---

[1] **fleet:** flee.

[2] **devise of:** converse about.

[3] **dotard:** senile person.

[4] As usual, Paridell is impetuous and hot-headed.

[5] **affray:** frighten.

[6] **mesprise:** mistake; offense; contempt; failure to recognize someone's worth.

[7] **good man:** head of the household; **the Porter playd:** i.e., Malbecco pretended to be his own porter, coming to answer the door.

11   But all in vaine; for nought mote him relent,
         And now so long before the wicket fast[1]
         They wayted, that the night was forward[2] spent,
         And the faire welkin[3] fowly overcast,
         Gan blowen up a bitter stormy blast,
         With showre and hayle so horrible and dred,
         That this faire many[4] were compeld at last,
         To fly for succour[5] to a little shed,
     The which beside the gate for swyne was ordered.[6]

12   It fortuned, soone after they were gone,
         Another knight, whom tempest thether brought,
         Came to that Castle, and with earnest mone,
         Like as the rest, late entrance deare[7] besought;
         But like so as the rest he prayd for nought,
         For flatly he of entrance was refusd.
         Sorely thereat he was displeasd, and thought
         How to avenge himselfe so sore abusd,
     And evermore the Carle of courtesie accusd.[8]

13   But to avoyde th'intollerable stowre,[9]
         He was compeld to seeke some refuge neare,
         And to that shed, to shrowd him from the showre,
         He came, which full of guests he found whyleare,[10]
         So as he was not let to enter there:[11]
         Whereat he gan to wex exceeding wroth,
         And swore, that he would lodge with them yfere,
         Or them dislodg, all were they liefe or loth;[12]
     And so defyde them each, and so defyde them both.[13]

---

[1] **wicket fast:** locked gate.

[2] **forward:** far.

[3] **welkin:** sky.

[4] **faire many:** worthy group.

[5] **succour:** refuge.

[6] **swyne:** swine; **ordered:** placed.

[7] **deare:** dearly, earnestly.

[8] I.e., accused him in the name of courtesy.

[9] **stowre:** storm.

[10] **whyleare:** modifies "full"; the pigsty was filled previous to his coming.

[11] **let:** allowed. Although the pigsty is already filled with Paridell, Satyrane, and their two horses, these two knights are, in their own way, being as inhospitable as Malbecco. A certain grumpiness pervades this entire canto, undercutting all of the knights' accustomed dignity, including that of the stranger soaking in the rain.

[12] **liefe or loth:** willing or not.

[13] The repetition emphasizes the humor of the stranger's not being satisfied with one all-encompassing oath, instead furiously breaking the imprecation down into sub-headings.

14   Both were full loth to leave that needfull tent,[1]
     And both full loth in darkenesse to debate;
     Yet both full liefe[2] him lodging to have lent,
     And both full liefe his boasting to abate;[3]
     But chiefely *Paridell* his hart did grate,[4]
     To heare him threaten so despightfully,
     As if he did a dogge in kenell rate,[5]
     That durst not barke; and rather had he dy,
 Then when he was defyde, in coward corner ly.

15   Tho hastily remounting to his steed,
     He forth issew'd; like as a boystrous winde,
     Which in th'earthes hollow caves hath long ben hid,
     And shut up fast within her prisons blind,
     Makes the huge element against her kinde[6]
     To move, and tremble as it were aghast,
     Untill that it an issew forth may finde;
     Then forth it breakes, and with his furious blast
 Confounds both land and seas, and skyes doth overcast.[7]

16   Their steel-hed speares they strongly coucht, and met
     Together with impetuous rage and forse,
     That with the terrour of their fierce affret,[8]
     They rudely[9] drove to ground both man and horse,

---

[1] Again the description is droll: Paridell and Satyrane want to do a great deed by teaching the strange knight a lesson, but they would prefer not to have to do it in the rain.

[2] **liefe:** either they are hypocritically assuring themselves, each other, or the strange knight that they would let him in if they could, or else this word is a mistake for "loath," given the next line, 13.5, and all of 16.

[3] **abate:** stop.

[4] *Paridell* **his:** Paridell's; **grate:** fret.

[5] I.e., as if he taunted a dog in a kennel.

[6] I.e., makes the huge earth, against her nature.

[7] After a rare earthquake had occurred in England in 1580, Gabriel Harvey and Spenser wrote to each other—and subsequently published—"Three proper wittie familiar Letters, lately passed betwene two Universitie men, touching the Earthquake in April last, and our English reformed Versifying." Harvey opined that earthquakes resulted from a wind, shut up in the earth, breaking out violently in a "forcible Eruption, and strong breath" (Spenser 1912, 616). In that passage, as in the description of Paridell's suddenly issuing from the pigsty, it is well to remember that "wind" was the most common Elizabethan word for "fart."

[8] **affret:** attack (a Spenserian neologism).

[9] **rudely:** violently.

That each awhile lay like a sencelesse corse.[1]
But *Paridell* sore brused with the blow,
Could not arise, the counterchaunge to scorse,[2]
Till that young Squyre him reared from below;
Then drew he his bright sword, and gan about him throw.[3]

17   But *Satyrane* forth stepping, did them stay
And with faire treaty[4] pacifide their yre;
Then when they were accorded[5] from the fray,
Against that Castles Lord they gan conspire,
To heape on him dew vengeaunce for his hire.[6]
They beene agreed, and to the gates they goe
To burne the same with unquenchable fire,
And that uncurteous Carle their commune foe
To doe fowle death to die, or wrap in grievous woe.

18   *Malbecco* seeing them resolvd in deed
To flame the gates, and hearing them to call
For fire in earnest, ran with fearfull speed,
And to them calling from the castle wall,
Besought them humbly, him to beare with all,[7]
As ignorant of servants bad abuse,
And slacke attendaunce unto straungers call.[8]
The knights were willing all things to excuse,
Though nought belev'd, and entraunce late did not refuse.

19   They beene ybrought into a comely bowre,[9]
And servd of all things that mote needfull bee;
Yet secretly their hoste did on them lowre,[10]
And welcomde more for feare, then charitee;

---

[1] This would have been a common enough phenomenon on a late medieval battlefield: a knight in heavy armor who fell off his horse would have trouble getting to his feet on his own. Nonetheless, in the context of this passage, the image of Paridell and the stranger lying on their backs in the mud, staring dazedly at the sky because of an argument over a pigsty, is less than noble.

[2] **counterchaunge:** requital; **scorse:** exchange.

[3] **throw:** brandish.

[4] **treaty:** entreaty.

[5] **accorded:** reconciled.

[6] **hire:** reward, payback.

[7] I.e., to bear with him.

[8] Malbecco pretends that it was a servant rather than himself who previously denied them entrance.

[9] **comely bowre:** handsome room.

[10] **lowre:** lower, look gloomily.

But they dissembled, what they did not see,[1]
And welcomed themselves. Each gan undight
Their garments wett, and weary armour free,
To dry them selves by *Vulcanes* flaming light,[2]
And eke their lately bruzed parts to bring in plight.[3]

20 And eke that straunger knight emongst the rest,
Was for like need enforst to disaray:
Tho whenas vailed was her[4] lofty crest,
Her golden locks, that were in tramells[5] gay
Upbounden, did them selves adowne display,
And raught unto her heeles; like sunny beames,
That in a cloud their light did long time stay,
Their vapour vaded,[6] shewe their golden gleames,
And through the persant aire[7] shoote forth their azure streames.

21 Shee also dofte her heavy haberjeon,[8]
Which the faire feature of her limbs did hyde,
And her well plighted[9] frock, which she did won
To tucke about her short, when she did ryde,
Shee low let fall, that flowd from her lanck[10] syde
Downe to her foot, with carelesse[11] modestee.
Then of them all she plainly was espyde,
To be a woman wight, unwist to bee,[12]
The fairest woman wight, that ever eie did see.

---

[1] I.e., they pretended not to notice that Malbecco's hospitality was not genuine.

[2] by *Vulcanes* flaming light: by the fire. Vulcan, the god of fire, was cuckolded by his wife, Venus.

[3] in plight: into healthy condition.

[4] vailed: removed; her: we find out that "he" is a "she" at the very moment when this fact is revealed to Paridell, Scudamour, and the others. Until now, Spenser has been using masculine pronouns for the stranger.

[5] tramells: braids.

[6] Their: the clouds'; vaded: dispersed.

[7] persant aire: piercing air—though "piercing" may be a transferred epithet belonging more logically to the "sunny beames." Alternatively, and more logically still, "persant" and "azure" may have been inadvertently switched by the compositor (a suggestion made by Collier in his gloss).

[8] haberjeon: habergeon, chain-mail tunic.

[9] plighted: pleated.

[10] lanck: slim.

[11] carelesse: artless.

[12] I.e, which they previously had not known.

22   Like as *Bellona*,[1] being late returnd
            From slaughter of the Giaunts conquered;
            Where proud *Encelade*, whose wide nosethrils[2] burnd
            With breathed flames, like to a furnace redd,
            Transfixed with her speare, downe tombled dedd
            From top of *Hemus*,[3] by him heaped hye;
            Hath loosd her helmet from her lofty hedd,
            And her *Gorgonian*[4] shield gins to untye
From her lefte arme, to rest in glorious victorye.

23   Which whenas they beheld, they smitten were
            With great amazement of so wondrous sight,
            And each on other, and they all on her
            Stood gazing, as if suddein great affright
            Had them surprizd. At last avizing right,
            Her goodly personage and glorious hew,
            Which they so much mistooke, they tooke delight
            In their first error, and yett still anew
With wonder of her beauty fed their hongry vew.

24   Yet note[5] their hongry vew be satisfide,
            But seeing still the more desir'd to see,
            And ever firmely fixed[6] did abide
            In contemplation of divinitee:
            But most they mervaild at her chevalree,
            And noble prowesse, which they had approv'd,[7]
            That much they faynd[8] to know, who she mote bee;
            Yet none of all them her thereof amov'd,
Yet every one her likte, and every one her lov'd.

---

[1] *Bellona*: goddess of war, Minerva, whose picture of Medusa's snaky head (or, in some versions, the head itself) on her breastplate or shield turned her male enemies into stone when they looked at it.

[2] *Encelade*: one of Minerva's opponents; **nosethrils**: nostrils.

[3] *Hemus*: Mount Haemus.

[4] *Gorgonian*: pertaining to the Gorgons, Medusa and her sisters. Britomart does not actually have Medusa on her shield, but her chastity is gorgonian in its ability to keep men at a distance. Cf. i.46, where Britomart's beauty attracts her admirers while her forbidding aspect makes them regret their interest.

[5] **note**: could not.

[6] Like the men who view Medusa's head— except that here they do not die.

[7] **approv'd**: tested, observed.

[8] **faynd**: desired.

25   And *Paridell* though partly discontent
        With his late fall, and fowle indignity,[1]
        Yet was soone wonne his malice to relent,
        Through gratious regard of her faire eye,
        And knightly worth, which he too late did try,
        Yet tried did adore. Supper was dight;
        Then they *Malbecco* prayd of courtesy,
        That of his lady they might have the sight,
    And company at meat,[2] to doe them more delight.

26   But he to shifte their curious request,[3]
        Gan causen, why she could not come in place;[4]
        Her crased[5] helth, her late recourse to rest,
        And humid evening ill for sicke folkes cace,
        But none of those excuses could take place;[6]
        Ne would they eate, till she in presence came.
        Shee came in presence with right comely grace,
        And fairely them saluted, as became,[7]
    And shewd her selfe in all a gentle courteous Dame.

27   They sate to meat, and *Satyrane* his chaunce,[8]
        Was her before, and *Paridell* beside;
        But he him selfe[9] sate looking still askaunce,
        Gainst *Britomart*, and ever closely eide
        Sir *Satyrane*, that glaunces might not glide:[10]
        But his blinde eie, that sided *Paridell*,
        All his demeasnure[11] from his sight did hide:
        On her faire face so did he feede his fill,
    And sent close messages of love to her at will.[12]

---

[1] **indignity:** although Paridell and the strange knight became friends at 17.3, Paridell's anger renews at the embarrassing discovery that he was defeated by a woman.

[2] **at meat:** at the meal.

[3] **shifte:** sidestep; **curious request:** request asked out of curiosity.

[4] **causen:** explain, give causes; **in place:** there.

[5] **crased:** broken.

[6] **take place:** find acceptance.

[7] I.e., courteously kissed them, as was fitting (a common greeting for guests).

[8] **his chaunce:** according to his lot.

[9] **he him selfe:** Malbecco.

[10] Malbecco keeps a suspicious watch on Britomart as well as on Satyrane, fearing that anyone and everyone could seduce his wife.

[11] **demeasnure:** demeanor, behavior.

[12] **close:** secret. Because of Malbecco's blind eye, he cannot keep watch on Paridell, who casts flirtatious glances in the direction of Malbecco's wife. Thus this new Paris and new Helen stir up new trouble.

28   And ever and anone, when none was ware,[1]
        With speaking lookes, that close embassage[2] bore,
        He rov'd[3] at her, and told his secret care:
        For all that art he learned had of yore.
        Ne was she ignoraunt of that leud lore,[4]
        But in his eye his meaning wisely redd,
        And with the like him aunswerd evermore:
        Shee sent at him one fyrie dart, whose hedd
Empoisned was with privy lust, and gealous dredd.[5]

29   He from that deadly throw made no defence,
        But to the wound his weake heart opened wyde;
        The wicked engine through false influence,[6]
        Past through his eies, and secretly did glyde
        Into his heart, which it did sorely gryde.[7]
        But nothing new to him was that same paine,
        Ne paine at all; for he so ofte had tryde[8]
        The powre thereof, and lov'd so oft in vaine,
That thing of course[9] he counted, love to entertaine.

30   Thenceforth to her he sought to intimate
        His inward griefe, by meanes to him well knowne,
        Now *Bacchus* fruit[10] out of the silver plate
        He on the table dasht, as overthrowne,
        Or of the fruitfull liquor overflowne,
        And by the dauncing bubbles did divine,[11]
        Or therein write to lett his love be showne;
        Which well she redd out of the learned line,
A sacrament prophane in mistery of wine.[12]

---

[1] **ware:** aware.

[2] **embassage:** messages.

[3] **rov'd:** shot glances.

[4] **leud lore:** knowledge of flirtation.

[5] The dart causes the former in Paridell and the latter in Malbecco.

[6] **engine:** tool; treachery; **false influence:** deceptive influx.

[7] **gryde:** pierce through.

[8] **tryde:** experienced.

[9] **of course:** as a matter of course, as no surprise. The vivid and painful imagery of

fire, poison, and serious wounding here descends bathetically into no big deal; he is used to falling in love and knows how to be appropriately despairing.

[10] *Bacchus* fruit: wine. Bacchus was the god of wine and revelry.

[11] **divine:** discern; tell (someone's) fortune.

[12] They are playing a flirtatious game in which someone writes another person's name in wine on the table. Castiglione and Harington—neither one of them categorically against games of love—had condemned this game as being sluttish

31   And when so of his hand the pledge she raught,[1]
       The guilty cup she fained to mistake,[2]
       And in her lap did shed her idle draught,[3]
       Shewing desire her inward flame to slake:
       By such close signes they secret way did make
       Unto their wils, and one eies watch[4] escape;
       Two eies him needeth, for to watch and wake,
       Who lovers will deceive. Thus was the ape,
    By their faire handling, put into *Malbeccoes* cape.[5]

32   Now when of meats and drinks they had their fill,
       Purpose was moved[6] by that gentle Dame,
       Unto those knights adventurous, to tell
       Of deeds of armes, which unto them became,[7]
       And every one his kindred, and his name.
       Then *Paridell,* in whom a kindly[8] pride
       Of gratious speach, and skill his words to frame[9]
       Abounded, being yglad of so fitte tide[10]
    Him to commend to her, thus spake, of al well eide.

33   "*Troy,* that art now nought, but an idle name,
       And in thine ashes buried low dost lie,[11]
       Though whilome far much greater then thy fame,
       Before that angry Gods, and cruell skie
       Upon thee heapt a direfull destinie,[12]

(Hamilton, *FQ* III.ix.30.n.; Castiglione, 252; Harington, 12).

[1] **pledge:** token, in the form of the cup of wine. Although one cup might properly be shared by two or more people who were only casual acquaintances, it was proper for the man to put the cup down onto the table and for the woman then to pick it up from the table, rather than taking it from his hand.

[2] **fained to mistake:** feigned to fumble.

[3] **draught:** drink.

[4] **one eies watch:** i.e., observation by Malbecco's one eye.

[5] Apes were symbols of idiocy. If one spoke of putting an ape into a man's hood, one meant that he was being tricked.

[6] **Purpose was moved:** conversation was proposed.

[7] **became:** was fitting; befell.

[8] **kindly:** innate.

[9] **frame:** compose.

[10] **tide:** time; opportunity.

[11] Paridell's (and subsequently Britomart's) history of the siege and fall of Troy is the third of three recountings of Britain's history in *The Faerie Queene;* see iii.22.6.n., iii.26.2.n., and the following stanzas for information about Britain's relationship to Troy.

[12] Various gods and goddesses took sides in the war between the Greeks and the Trojans, sending aid to their favorites.

What boots it boast thy glorious descent,
And fetch from heven thy great genealogie,
Sith all thy worthie prayses being blent,[1]
Their ofspring hath embaste, and later glory shent.[2]

34   "Most famous Worthy of the world,[3] by whome
      That warre was kindled, which did *Troy* inflame,
      And stately towres of *Ilion*[4] whilome
      Brought unto balefull ruine, was by name
      Sir *Paris* far renowmd through noble fame,
      Who through great prowesse and bold hardinesse,
      From *Lacedaemon*[5] fetcht the fayrest Dame,
      That ever *Greece* did boast, or knight possesse,
      Whom *Venus* to him gave for meed of worthinesse.[6]

35   "Fayre *Helene,* flowre of beautie excellent,
      And girlond[7] of the mighty Conquerours,
      That madest many Ladies deare lament
      The heavie losse of their brave Paramours,
      Which they far off beheld from *Trojan* toures,
      And saw the fieldes of faire *Scamander*[8] strowne

[1] **blent:** blemished (OED "blench" v[2]); polluted (OED "blend" v[2]2).

[2] **embaste:** made base; **shent:** disgraced.

[3] The Nine Worthies were a specific list of heroes of the past (three pagans from the ancient world, three Jews, and three Christians), and Paris was not among them. Paridell elevates his ancestor beyond his deserts.

[4] *Ilion:* Another name for Troy.

[5] *Lacedaemon:* Sparta, in Greece.

[6] According to the myth, the Goddess of Discord wrote "To the Fairest" on an apple and threw it among the guests attending the wedding of Peleus and Thetis. Juno, Minerva, and Venus each thought she deserved the apple, so they asked Paris, a mortal prince of Troy, to decide the matter. He chose Venus, after she promised to give him the most beautiful woman in the world as a reward. The most beautiful woman in the world was Helen, wife of the Spartan king Menelaus, so Paris traveled to Greece, seduced Helen, and took her back to Troy. Menelaus called his fellow kings throughout Greece to mount an expedition to attack Troy. The siege of Troy lasted ten years, with the battle going one way and another, but finally the Greeks tricked the Trojans into pulling a gigantic, hollow wooden horse into the city. That night, Greek soldiers poured out of the hollow horse, opened the city gates, and burned Troy to the ground. Aeneas, another Trojan prince, escaped with members of his family and went on to establish the lineage that ultimately founded Rome and, generations later, London. (Although there may have been a Trojan war, the rest is fiction, but at least some of it was taken as fact in the sixteenth century.)

[7] **girlond:** garland, i.e., crown.

[8] *Scamander:* river of Troy.

With carcases of noble warrioures,
Whose fruitlesse lives were under furrow sowne,
And *Xanthus*[1] sandy bankes with blood all overflowne.

36   "From him my linage I derive aright,[2]
Who long before the ten yeares siege of *Troy,*
Whiles yet on *Ida*[3] he a shepeheard hight,
On faire *Oenone* got[4] a lovely boy,
Whom for remembrance of her passed joy,
She of his Father *Parius* did name;
Who, after *Greekes* did *Priams*[5] realme destroy,
Gathred the *Trojan* reliques sav'd from flame,
And with them sayling thence, to th'Isle of *Paros* came.

37   "That was by him cald *Paros,* which before
Hight *Nausa,* there he many yeares did raine,
And built *Nausicle* by the *Pontick* shore,
The which he dying lefte next in remaine[6]
To *Paridas* his sonne.[7]
From whom I *Paridell* by kin descend;
But for faire ladies love, and glories gaine,
My native soile have lefte, my dayes to spend
In seewing[8] deeds of armes, my lives and labors end."

38   Whenas the noble *Britomart* heard tell
Of *Trojan* warres, and *Priams* citie sackt,
The ruefull story of Sir *Paridell,*
She was empassiond at that piteous[9] act,
With zelous envy of Greekes cruell fact,[10]
Against that nation, from whose race of old
She heard, that she was lineally extract:[11]
For noble *Britons* sprong from *Trojans* bold,
And *Troynovant*[12] was built of old *Troyes* ashes cold.

---

[1] *Xanthus:* the gods' name for the above river.

[2] **aright:** directly; legitimately.

[3] **Ida:** Mount Ida.

[4] *Oenone:* a nymph; **got:** begot.

[5] Priam was King of Troy.

[6] **next in remaine:** next in succession.

[7] The line is unfinished—or intentionally short—in both the 1590 and 1596 editions.

[8] **seewing:** pursuing.

[9] **piteous:** pitiful, worthy of compassion.

[10] **fact:** deed.

[11] **extract:** descended.

[12] *Troynovant:* New Troy, a popular nickname for London. See 34.9.n.

39   Then sighing soft awhile, at last she thus:
　　　　"O lamentable fall of famous towne,
　　　　Which raignd so many yeares victorious,
　　　　And of all *Asie*[1] bore the soveraine crowne,
　　　　In one sad night consumd, and throwen downe:
　　　　What stony hart, that heares thy haplesse fate,
　　　　Is not empierst with deepe compassiowne,
　　　　And makes ensample[2] of mans wretched state,
　　That floures so fresh at morne, and fades at evening late?

40   "Behold, Sir, how your pitifull[3] complaint
　　　　Hath fownd another partner of your payne:
　　　　For nothing may impresse so deare constraint,[4]
　　　　As countries cause, and commune foes disdayne.
　　　　But if it should not grieve you, backe agayne
　　　　To turne your course, I would to heare desyre,
　　　　What to *Aeneas* fell;[5] sith that men sayne
　　　　He was not in the cities wofull fyre
　　Consum'd, but did him selfe to safety retyre."

41   "*Anchyses* sonne begott of *Venus* fayre,"[6]
　　　　Said he, "out of the flames for safegard fled,
　　　　And with a remnant did to sea repayre,[7]
　　　　Where he through fatall errour[8] long was led
　　　　Full many yeares, and weetlesse wandered
　　　　From shore to shore, emongst the Lybick[9] sandes,
　　　　Ere rest he fownd. Much there he suffered,[10]
　　　　And many perilles past in forreine landes,
　　To save his people sad from victours vengefull handes.

---

[1] *Asie:* Asia.

[2] **makes ensample:** takes as a cautionary example.

[3] **pitifull:** compassionate.

[4] **deare constraint:** great extremity.

[5] **fell:** befell, happened.

[6] Aeneas had a mortal father and an immortal mother.

[7] **repayre:** go; take refuge.

[8] **fatall errour:** fated wanderings—from *fato profugus*, "exiled by fate," *Aeneid,* 1.2 (Hamilton, *FQ* III.ix.41–43.n.).

[9] **Lybick:** Libyan.

[10] Paridell glosses over what happened in Libya: Aeneas, his former wife having died, fell in love with Queen Dido, who returned the passion with interest. After the gods told Aeneas he had to leave, since his duty lay in founding the Roman race, Aeneas tried to sneak away without telling Dido. She saw the preparations and immolated herself on a funeral pyre (*Aeneid,* IV).

42   "At last in *Latium*[1] he did arryve,
        Where he with cruell warre was entertaind[2]
        Of th'inland folke, which sought him backe to drive,
        Till he with old *Latinus*[3] was constraind,
        To contract wedlock: (so the fates ordaind.)
        Wedlocke contract in blood, and eke in blood
        Accomplished, that many deare complaind:
        The rivall slaine, the victour through the flood[4]
    Escaped hardly, hardly praisd his wedlock good.

43   "Yet after all, he victour did survive,
        And with *Latinus* did the kingdom part.
        But after, when both nations gan to strive,
        Into their names the title to convart,[5]
        His sonne *Julus* did from thence depart,
        With all the warlike youth of Trojans bloud,
        And in long *Alba*[6] plast his throne apart,
        Where faire it florished, and long time stoud,
    Till *Romulus*[7] renewing it, to *Rome* removd."

44   "There there"[8] (said *Britomart*) "a fresh appeard
        The glory of the later world to spring,
        And *Troy* againe out of her dust was reard,
        To sitt in second seat of soveraine king,
        Of all the world under her governing.
        But a third kingdom yet is to arise,
        Out of the *Trojans* scattered ofspring,
        That in all glory and great enterprise,
    Both first and second *Troy* shall dare to equalise.[9]

---

[1] *Latium:* a region in Italy.

[2] **entertaind:** received.

[3] *Latinus:* King of Latium, who made peace conditional upon a marriage between his daughter, Lavinia, and Aeneas.

[4] **rivall:** Turnus, who also wanted Lavinia's hand; **flood:** the battles between the two peoples, during which blood flowed.

[5] I.e., to have the country named after them.

[6] **long *Alba*:** Alba Longa, in Latium.

[7] *Romulus:* a descendant of Aeneas, more than three hundred years after the fall of Troy.

[8] **There there:** not a soothing phrase but an expression of awe at what one has heard: Lo, lo!

[9] **equalise:** match itself against; be the equal of.

45   "It *Troynovant* is hight, that with the waves
          Of wealthy *Thamis*[1] washed is along,
          Upon whose stubborne neck whereat he raves
          With roring rage, and sore him selfe does throng,[2]
          That all men feare to tempt[3] his billowes strong,
          She fastned hath her foot, which standes so hy,[4]
          That it a wonder of the world is song
          In forreine landes, and all which passen by,
      Beholding it from farre, doe thinke it threates the skye.

46   "The *Trojan Brute*[5] did first that citie fownd,
          And Hygate made the meare[6] thereof by west,
          And *Overt* gate by North: that is the bownd[7]
          Toward the land; two rivers bownd the rest.
          So huge a scope at first him seemed best,
          To be the compasse of his kingdomes seat:
          So huge a mind could not in lesser rest,
          Ne in small meares containe his glory great,
      That *Albion*[8] had conquered first by warlike feat."

47   "Ah fairest Lady knight," (said *Paridell*)
          "Pardon I pray my heedlesse oversight,
          Who had forgot, that whylome I hard tell
          From aged *Mnemon*;[9] for my wits beene light.
          Indeed he said (if I remember right,)
          That of the antique *Trojan* stocke, there grew
          Another plant, that raught to wondrous hight,
          And far abroad his mightie braunches threw,
      Into the utmost Angle[10] of the world he knew.

---

[1] *Thamis:* the Thames River, which runs through London.

[2] **throng:** press.

[3] **tempt:** attempt (to sail upon; few English of this period could swim, even in a calm pond).

[4] I.e., the London Bridge, which had tall buildings constructed on it.

[5] *Brute:* Brutus, legendary founder of the British race.

[6] **Hygate:** a village supposed to have been intended by the Brute to be the location of the western gate of London; **meare:** boundary (OED "mere" sb²1a).

[7] **bownd:** boundary.

[8] *Albion:* Britain.

[9] *Mnemon:* "mindful" (Greek).

[10] **Angle:** corner.

48   "For that same *Brute*, whom much he did advaunce[1]
        In all his speach, was *Sylvius* his[2] sonne,
        Whom having slain, through luckles arrowes glaunce
        He fled for feare of that he had misdonne,
        Or els for shame, so fowle reproch to shonne,
        And with him ledd to sea an youthly trayne,[3]
        Where wearie wandring they long time did wonne,[4]
        And many fortunes prov'd in th'*Ocean* mayne,
    And great adventures found, that now were long to sayne.

49   "At last by fatall course[5] they driven were
        Into an Island[6] spatious and brode,
        The furthest North, that did to them appeare:
        Which after rest they seeking farre abrode,
        Found it the fittest soyle for their abode,
        Fruitfull of all thinges fitt for living foode,
        But wholy waste, and void of peoples trode,[7]
        Save an huge nation of the Geaunts broode,
    That fed on living flesh, and dronck mens vitall blood.

50   "Whom he through wearie wars and labours long,
        Subdewd with losse of many *Britons* bold:
        In which the great *Goemagot*[8] of strong
        Corineus, and *Coulin* of *Debon* old
        Were overthrowne, and laide on th'earth full cold,
        Which quaked under their so hideous masse,
        A famous history to bee enrold
        In everlasting moniments of brasse,
    That all the antique Worthies merits far did passe.

51   "His worke great *Troynovant,* his worke is eke
        Faire *Lincolne,*[9] both renowmed far away,
        That who from East to West will endlong seeke,
        Cannot two fairer Cities find this day,
        Except *Cleopolis:*[10] so heard I say

[1] **he:** Mnemon; **advance:** praise.

[2] *Sylvius* **his:** Silvius'.

[3] **trayne:** company.

[4] **wonne:** live.

[5] **fatall course:** fated route.

[6] **Island:** Britain.

[7] **waste:** deserted; **trode:** tread.

[8] *Goemagot:* a giant.

[9] *Lincolne:* the English city.

[10] *Cleopolis:* "City of Fame" (Greek). The Faerie Queen's royal city and Spenser's allegorical analogue for London.

Old *Mnemon*. Therefore Sir,[1] I greet you well
Your countrey kin, and you entyrely pray
Of pardon[2] for the strife, which late befell
Betwixt us both unknowne."[3] So ended *Paridell*.

52   But all the while, that he these speeches spent,
      Upon his lips hong faire Dame *Hellenore,*
      With vigilant regard, and dew attent,[4]
      Fashioning worldes of fancies evermore
      In her fraile witt, that now her quite forlore:[5]
      The whiles unwares away her wondring[6] eye,
      And greedy eares her weake hart from her bore:
      Which he perceiving, ever privily
   In speaking, many false belgardes[7] at her let fly.

53   So long these knightes discoursed diversly,
      Of straunge affaires, and noble hardiment,
      Which they had past with mickle[8] jeopardy,
      That now the humid night was farforth spent,
      And hevenly lampes were halfendeale[9] ybrent:
      Which th'old man seeing wel, who too long thought
      Every discourse and every argument,
      Which by the houres he measured, besought
   Them go to rest. So all unto their bowres[10] were brought.

---

[1] **Sir:** He is addressing Britomart, who has already revealed her sex by doffing her helmet and armor (stanzas 20 and 21). The OED gives one other example of the title's being used unambiguously for a woman ("sir" sb 9), but the force of the title was almost certainly masculine. One addresses a knight as "Sir"; therefore Britomart deserves the title, yet it registers a certain amount of confusion on Paridell's part as to whether he should be condescendingly gallant or genuinely respectful toward his interlocutor—who, lest we forget, began by unseating him from his horse.

[2] I.e., I greet your fellow Britons (or kinfolks) well and entirely beg your pardon.

[3] **unknowne:** i.e., when we were still strangers to each other.

[4] **attent:** attention.

[5] I.e., her intelligence, already weak, now completely forsook her.

[6] **wondring:** with a pun on "wandering."

[7] **belgardes:** flirtatious looks.

[8] **mickle:** much.

[9] **halfendeale:** halfway.

[10] **bowres:** bedrooms.

Canto Ten

Paridell rapeth[1] Hellenore:
Malbecco her poursewes:
Fynds emongst Satyres, whence with him
To turne[2] she doth refuse.

1   The morow next, so soone as *Phœbus*[3] Lamp
     Bewrayed[4] had the world with early light,
     And fresh *Aurora*[5] had the shady damp
     Out of the goodly heven amoved quight,
     Faire *Britomart* and that same Faery knight[6]
     Uprose, forth on their journey for to wend:[7]
     But *Paridell* complaynd, that his late fight
     With *Britomart,* so sore did him offend,[8]
That ryde he could not, till his hurts he did amend.

2   So foorth they far'd, but he behind them stayd,
     Maulgre his host, who grudged[9] grievously,
     To house a guest, that would be needes[10] obayd,
     And of his owne him left not liberty:
     Might wanting measure moveth surquedry.[11]
     Two things he feared, but the third was death;
     That fiers youngmans[12] unruly maystery;
     His[13] money, which he lov'd as living breath;
And his faire wife, whom honest[14] long he kept uneath.

---

[1] **rapeth:** abducts; carries off.

[2] **turne:** return.

[3] *Phœbus:* Apollo, in his role of the sun.

[4] **Bewrayed:** revealed, with a pun on "covered with rays of light."

[5] *Aurora:* goddess of the dawn.

[6] I.e., Satyrane.

[7] **wend:** travel.

[8] **offend:** hurt.

[9] **Maulgre:** despite; **grudged:** griped.

[10] **would be needes:** must necessarily be.

[11] I.e., when not restrained, power leads to presumption (e.g., a guest who is too pampered may presume to seduce the lady of the house).

[12] I.e., Paridell's.

[13] **His:** Malbecco's.

[14] **honest:** chaste.

3   But patience perforce he must abie,[1]
         What fortune and his fate on him will lay,
         Fond is the feare, that findes no remedie;
         Yet warily he watcheth every way,
         By which he feareth evill happen may:
         So th'evill thinkes by watching to prevent;
         Ne doth he suffer her, nor night, nor day,
         Out of his sight her selfe once to absent.
      So doth he punish her and eke himselfe torment.

4   But *Paridell* kept better watch, then hee,
         A fit occasion for his turne[2] to finde:
         False love, why do men say, thou canst not see,
         And in their foolish fancy feigne thee blinde,
         That with thy charmes the sharpest sight doest binde,
         And to thy will abuse? Thou walkest free,
         And seest every secret of the minde;
         Thou seest all, yet none at all sees thee;
      All that is by the working of thy Deitee.[3]

5   So perfect in that art was *Paridell*,
         That he *Malbeccoes* halfen eye did wyle,[4]
         His halfen eye he wiled wondrous well,
         And *Hellenors* both eyes did eke beguyle,
         Both eyes and hart attonce, during the whyle
         That he there sojourned his woundes to heale,
         That *Cupid* selfe it seeing, close did smyle,
         To weet how he her love away did steale,
      And bad,[5] that none their joyous treason should reveale.

6   The learned lover[6] lost no time nor tyde,
         That least avantage mote to him afford,
         Yet bore so faire a sayle, that none espyde

---

[1] **abie:** endure. Imagine a semicolon after "perforce."

[2] **turne:** purpose.

[3] **thy Deitee:** thy divinity; thy god (Cupid or Venus).

[4] **halfen eye:** half his eyesight; his one half-good eye (see ix.5.5); **wyle:** beguile, trick.

[5] **bad:** bade.

[6] **learned lover:** sixteenth-century moral pamphlets were filled with warnings to innocent young women to beware the wiles of men who were experienced in the methods of seduction.

His secret drift, till he her layd abord.[1]
When so in open place, and commune bord,[2]
He fortun'd her to meet, with commune speach
He courted her, yet bayted[3] every word,
That his ungentle hoste n'ote him appeach
Of vile ungentlenesse, or hospitages breach.[4]

7   But when apart[5] (if ever her apart)
       He found, then his false engins fast he plyde,
       And all the sleights[6] unbosomd in his hart;
       He sigh'd, he sobd, he swownd, he perdy dyde,[7]
       And cast himselfe on ground her fast besyde:
       Tho when againe he him bethought[8] to live,
       He wept, and wayld, and false laments belyde,[9]
       Saying, but if[10] she Mercie would him give
       That he mote algates dye, yet did his death forgive.[11]

8   And otherwhyles with amorous delights,
       And pleasing toyes[12] he would her entertaine,
       Now singing sweetly, to surprize her sprights,
       Now making layes[13] of love and lovers paine,
       Bransles, Ballads, virelayes,[14] and verses vaine;
       Oft purposes,[15] oft riddles he devysd,

---

[1] **drift:** purpose (and drifting on the water—and drifting morally); **layd abord:** literally "brought (her) aboard." Men spoke of "boarding" women when making bawdy jokes. The marine imagery in these four lines parodies the more innocent (though painful) imagery in Petrarchan sonnets, in which speakers continually complain about being lost on the stormy seas of love with only the beloved's eyes to guide the boat to port.

[2] **commune bord:** table at which everyone sat to eat together.

[3] **bayted:** bated (moderated—in this case, slyly); baited (i.e., spoke in terms that seemed innocent but were designed to draw her in).

[4] I.e., a breach of hospitality.

[5] **apart:** i.e., away from everyone else.

[6] **sleights:** deceitful strategies.

[7] **he perdy dyde:** he died, by God (or, only slightly less hilariously, "he assuredly died"). This is a Chaucerian bit of humor about the extreme declarations found in the mouths of lovers in the Courtly Love tradition.

[8] **he him bethought:** he reminded himself; he resolved.

[9] **belyde:** faked.

[10] **but if:** unless.

[11] I.e., he would forgive her for causing his death.

[12] **toyes:** foolishness; games.

[13] **layes:** songs.

[14] **Bransles:** songs for dance music; **virelayes:** songs of a particular type developed in France two centuries before, with short lines and simple rhyme schemes.

[15] **purposes:** flirtatious question-and-answer games.

And thousands like, which flowed in his braine,
With which he fed her fancy, and entysd
To take with his new love, and leave her old despysd.

9   And every where he might, and everie while
He did her service dewtifull, and sewd[1]
At hand with humble pride, and pleasing guile,
So closely yet, that none but she it vewd,
Who well perceived all, and all indewd.[2]
Thus finely[3] did he his false nets dispred,
With which he many weake harts had subdewd
Of yore, and many had ylike misled:
What wonder then, if she were likewise carried?

10   No fort so fensible,[4] no wals so strong,
But that continuall battery will rive,
Or daily siege through dispurvayaunce[5] long,
And lacke of reskewes will to parley[6] drive;
And Peece,[7] that unto parley eare will give,
Will shortly yield it selfe, and will be made
The vassall of the victors will bylive:[8]
That stratageme had oftentimes assayd
This crafty Paramoure, and now it plaine displayd.

11   For through his traines[9] he her intrapped hath,
That she her love and hart hath wholy sold
To him, without regard of gaine, or scath,[10]
Or care of credite,[11] or of husband old,
Whom she hath vow'd to dub a fayre Cucquold.[12]
Nought wants but time[13] and place, which shortly shee

---

[1] I.e., he served her dutifully and did homage, but with the double entendre of doing her sexual service. (It is only a double entendre here, given that stanza 11 implies no assignation has yet taken place.)

[2] **indewd:** digested.

[3] **finely:** cunningly.

[4] **fensible:** well-fortified; defensive.

[5] **dispurvayaunce:** destitution; denial or lack of provisions.

[6] **parley:** discuss terms (with the besiegers).

[7] **Peece:** fort.

[8] **bylive:** speedily.

[9] **traines:** entrapments.

[10] **scath:** harm.

[11] **credite:** reputation.

[12] **Cucquold:** cuckold.

[13] **time:** opportunity.

Devized hath, and to her lover told.
It pleased well. So well they both agree;
So readie rype to ill, ill wemens counsels bee.

12   Darke was the Evening, fit for lovers stealth,
         When chaunst *Malbecco* busie be elsewhere,
         She to his closet¹ went, where all his wealth
         Lay hid: thereof she countlesse summes did reare,
         The which she meant away with her to beare;
         The rest she fyr'd for sport, or for despight;
         As *Hellene,* when she saw aloft appeare
         The *Trojane* flames, and reach to hevens hight
Did clap her hands, and joyed at that dolefull sight.

13   This second *Helene,* fayre Dame *Hellenore,*
         The whiles her husband ran with sory haste,
         To quench the flames, which she had tyn'd² before,
         Laught at his foolish labour spent in waste;
         And ran into her lovers armes right fast;
         Where streight embraced, she to him did cry,
         And call alowd for helpe, ere helpe were past,
         For lo that Guest did beare her forcibly,
And meant to ravish her, that rather had to dy.

14   The wretched man hearing her call for ayd,
         And ready seeing him with her to fly,
         In his disquiet mind was much dismayd:
         But when againe he backeward cast his eye,
         And saw the wicked fire so furiously
         Consume his hart,³ and scorch his Idoles face,
         He was therewith distressed diversely,
         Ne wist he how to turne, nor to what place.
Was never wretched man in such a wofull cace.

15   Ay when to him she cryde, to her he turnd,
         And left the fire; love money overcame:
         But when he marked,⁴ how his money burnd,

---

¹ **closet:** private room.
² **tyn'd:** kindled.

³ **hart:** heart—here a metaphor for his money, which is also his idol.
⁴ **marked:** noticed.

He left his wife; money did love disclame:
Both was he loth to loose[1] his loved Dame,
And loth to leave his liefest[2] pelfe behinde,
Yet sith he n'ote save both, he sav'd that same,
Which was the dearest to his dounghill[3] minde,
The God of his desire, the joy of misers blinde.

16   Thus whilest all things in troublous uprore were,
      And all men busie to suppresse the flame,
      The loving couple neede no reskew feare,
      But leasure had, and liberty to frame[4]
      Their purpost flight, free from all mens reclame;[5]
      And Night, the patronesse of love-stealth fayre,
      Gave them safe conduct, till to end they came:
      So beene they gone yfere, a wanton payre
Of lovers loosely knit, where list them to repayre.[6]

17   Soone as the cruell flames yslaked were,
      Malbecco seeing, how his losse did lye,
      Out of the flames, which he had quencht whylere
      Into huge waves of griefe and gealosye
      Full deepe emplonged was, and drowned nye,
      Twixt inward doole and felonous[7] despight;
      He rav'd, he wept, he stampt, he lowd did cry,
      And all the passions, that in man may light,
Did him attonce oppresse, and vex his caytive[8] spright.

18   Long thus he chawd the cud of inward griefe,
      And did consume his gall with anguish sore,
      Still when he mused on his late mischiefe,[9]
      So still the smart thereof increased more,
      And seemd more grievous, then it was before:
      At last when sorrow he saw booted nought,

---

[1] **loose:** lose, with a pun on freeing her to lead a loose life.

[2] **liefest:** dearest.

[3] **dounghill:** dunghill.

[4] **frame:** get on with (OED v2).

[5] **reclame:** recall (calling back to a place); reclamation (calling back to the right conduct; laying claim to again).

[6] I.e., they went together—that wanton pair of loosely (and lewdly) united lovers—wherever they wanted to go.

[7] **doole:** grief; **felonous:** cruel.

[8] **caytive:** vile.

[9] **mischiefe:** misfortune.

Ne griefe might not his love to him restore,
He gan devise, how her he reskew mought,
Ten thousand wayes he cast¹ in his confused thought.

19   At last resolving, like a Pilgrim² pore,
        To search her forth, where so she might be fond,
        And bearing with him treasure in close store,
        The rest he leaves in ground:³ So takes in hond
        To seeke her endlong,⁴ both by sea and lond.
        Long he her sought, he sought her far and nere,
        And every where that he mote understond,
        Of knights and ladies any meetings were,
And of eachone he mett, he tidings did inquere.

20   But all in vaine, his woman was too wise,
        Ever to come into his clouch⁵ againe,
        And hee too simple⁶ ever to surprise
        The jolly⁷ *Paridell,* for all his paine.
        One day, as hee forpassed by⁸ the plaine
        With weary pace, he far away espide
        A couple, seeming well to be his twaine,
        Which hoved⁹ close under a forest side,
As if they lay in wait, or els themselves did hide.

21   Well weened hee, that those the same mote bee,
        And as he better did their shape avize,
        Him seemed more their maner did agree;
        For th'one was armed all in warlike wize,
        Whom, to be *Paridell* he did devize;¹⁰

---

¹ **cast:** considered.

² **Pilgrim:** traveler; one who makes a journey to a shrine or other holy place as an act of devotion.

³ There were no banks; nevertheless, by leaving most of his treasure in the ground, Malbecco proves himself like the third servant in the parable of the talents: entrusted with the safekeeping of one of his master's coins, he proves himself unworthy of his master's trust when he buries the coin in the ground rather than risk investing it (Matt. 25.14–30).

⁴ **endlong:** from end to end (of the country—or, hyperbolically, of the earth).

⁵ **clouch:** clutch; claw.

⁶ **simple:** foolish; not acute.

⁷ **jolly:** sprightly; overweeningly self-confident; lustful.

⁸ **forpassed by:** passed over.

⁹ **hoved:** lingered; hovered.

¹⁰ **devize:** figure.

And th'other al yclad in garments light,
Discolourd[1] like to womanish disguise,
He did resemble[2] to his lady bright,
And ever his faint hart much earned[3] at the sight.

22   And ever faine[4] he towards them would goe,
      But yet durst not for dread approchen nie,
      But stood aloofe, unweeting what to doe,
      Till that prickt forth with loves extremity,[5]
      That is the father of fowle gealosy,
      He closely nearer crept, the truth to weet:
      But, as he nigher drew, he easily
      Might scerne,[6] that it was not his sweetest sweet,
Ne yet her Belamour,[7] the partner of his sheet.

23   But it was scornefull *Braggadochio,*
      That with his servant *Trompart* hoverd there,
      Sith late he fled from his too earnest foe:
      Whom such whenas *Malbecco* spyed clere,
      He turned backe, and would have fled arere;[8]
      Till *Trompart* ronning hastely, him did stay,
      And bad before his soveraine Lord appere:
      That was him loth, yet durst he not gainesay,
And comming him before, low louted on the lay.[9]

24   The Boaster at him sternely bent his browe,
      As if he could have kild him with his looke,
      That to the ground him meekely made to bowe,
      And awfull terror deepe into him strooke,
      That every member of his body quooke.[10]
      Said he, "Thou man of nought, what doest thou here,
      Unfitly furnisht with thy bag and booke,[11]
      Where I expected one with shield and spere,
To prove some deeds of armes upon an equall pere."

---

[1] **Discolourd:** multicolored.

[2] **resemble:** liken.

[3] **earned:** yearned; mourned.

[4] **faine:** desirous.

[5] Cf. Britomart's ranckling wound after she has seen Artegall in the mirror (ii.35–39).

[6] **scerne:** discern.

[7] **Belamour:** beautiful lover.

[8] **arere:** to the rear.

[9] **louted:** bowed; **lay:** lea, ground.

[10] **quooke:** quaked.

[11] Accoutrements of a pilgrim.

25   The wretched man at his imperious speach,
          Was all abasht, and low prostrating, said;
          "Good Sir, let not my rudenes be no breach
          Unto your patience, ne be ill ypaid;[1]
          For I unwares this way by fortune straid,
          A silly[2] Pilgrim driven to distresse,
          That seeke a Lady," There he suddein staid,
          And did the rest with grievous sighes suppresse,
    While teares stood in his eies, few drops of bitternesse.

26   "What Lady, man?" (said *Trompart*) "take good hart,
          And tell thy griefe, if any hidden lye;
          Was never better time to shew thy smart,
          Then now, that noble succor[3] is thee by,
          That is the whole worlds commune remedy."
          That chearful word his weak heart much did cheare,
          And with vaine hope his spirits faint supply,
          That bold he sayd, "O most redoubted Pere,
    Vouchsafe[4] with mild regard a wretches cace to heare."

27   Then sighing sore, "It is not long" (saide hee)
          "Sith I enjoyd the gentlest Dame alive;
          Of whom a knight, no knight at all perdee,
          But shame of all, that doe for honor strive,
          By treacherous deceipt did me deprive;
          Through open outrage he her bore away,
          And with fowle force unto his will did drive,
          Which al good knights, that armes do bear this day,
    Are bownd for to revenge, and punish if they may.

28   "And you most noble Lord, that can and dare
          Redresse the wrong of miserable wight,
          Cannot employ your most victorious speare
          In better quarell, then defence of right,
          And for a Lady gainst a faithlesse knight,
          So shall your glory bee advaunced much,
          And all faire Ladies magnify[5] your might,
          And eke my selfe, albee I simple such,
    Your worthy paine shall wel reward with guerdon[6] rich."

---

[1] **ill ypaid:** displeased.

[2] **silly:** lowly; defenseless; unsophisticated.

[3] **succor:** aid.

[4] **Vouchsafe:** grant.

[5] **magnify:** extol.

[6] **guerdon:** reward.

29   With that out of his bouget[1] forth he drew
     Great store of treasure, therewith him to tempt;
     But he[2] on it lookt scornefully askew,
     As much disdeigning to be so misdempt,[3]
     Or a war-monger to be basely nempt;[4]
     And sayd, "Thy offers base I greatly loth,
     And eke thy words uncourteous and unkempt;[5]
     I tread in dust thee and thy money both,
That, were it not for shame,"[6] So turned from him wroth.

30   But *Trompart,* that his maistres humor knew,
     In lofty looks to hide an humble minde,
     Was inly tickled with that golden vew,
     And in his eare him rownded[7] close behinde:
     Yet stoupt he not, but lay still in the winde,
     Waiting advauntage on the pray to sease;[8]
     Till *Trompart* lowly to the grownd inclinde,
     Besought him his great corage[9] to appease,
And pardon simple man, that rash did him displease.

31   Big looking like a doughty Doucepere,[10]
     At last he thus, "Thou clod of vilest clay,
     I pardon yield, and that with rudenes beare;
     But weete henceforth, that all that golden pray,[11]
     And all that els the vaine world vaunten may,
     I loath as doung, ne deeme my dew reward:
     Fame is my meed, and glory vertuous pray.
     But minds of mortal men are muchell[12] mard,
And mov'd amisse with massy mucks unmeet regard.

---

[1] **bouget:** pouch.

[2] **he:** Braggadocchio.

[3] **misdempt:** misdeemed, misjudged.

[4] **nempt:** named, called.

[5] **unkempt:** rude.

[6] He leaves the rest of the sentence unsaid, implying that he would do worse to the pilgrim if it were not shameful for a knight to attack one of lower degree.

[7] **him rownded:** whispered to him (Braggadocchio).

[8] I.e., like a hawk waiting to kill, he didn't swoop but lay in the wind, waiting for the best time to seize his prey.

[9] **corage:** wrath.

[10] **doughty Doucepere:** valiant knight, one of the twelve peers of France.

[11] **pray:** booty.

[12] **muchell:** much.

32   "And more, I graunt to thy great misery
       Gratious respect,[1] thy wife shall backe be sent,
       And that vile knight, who ever that he bee,
       Which hath thy lady reft, and knighthood shent,[2]
       By *Sanglamort* my sword, whose deadly dent[3]
       The blood hath of so many thousands shedd,
       I sweare, ere long shall dearly it repent;
       Ne he twixt heven and earth shall hide his hedd,
But soone he shalbe fownd, and shortly doen be dedd."

33   The foolish man thereat woxe wondrous blith,[4]
       As if the word so spoken, were halfe donne,
       And humbly thanked him a thousand sith,[5]
       That had from death to life him newly wonne.
       Tho forth the Boaster marching, brave begonne
       His stolen steed[6] to thunder furiously,
       As if he heaven and hell would overonne,
       And all the world confound[7] with cruelty,
That much *Malbecco* joyed in his jollity.[8]

34   Thus long they three together traveiled,
       Through many a wood, and many an uncouth way,
       To seeke his wife, that was far wandered:
       But those two sought nought, but the present pray,
       To weete the treasure, which he did bewray,
       On which their eies and harts were wholly sett,
       With purpose, how they might it best betray;[9]
       For sith the howre, that first he did them lett
The same behold, therwith their keene desires were whett.

35   It fortuned as they together far'd,
       They spide, where *Paridell* came pricking fast
       Upon the plaine, the which him selfe prepar'd
       To giust with that brave straunger knight a cast,[10]

---

[1] **respect:** regard.

[2] **shent:** disgraced.

[3] *Sanglamort:* Bloody Death, the name of his sword; **dent:** dint, blow.

[4] **blith:** blithe.

[5] **sith:** times.

[6] **stolen steed:** see II.iii.4, where Bragadocchio finds and steals Guyon's horse.

[7] **confound:** utterly defeat.

[8] **jollity:** high-hearted confidence.

[9] **betray:** deliver it out of his hands.

[10] **giust:** joust; **cast:** bout.

As on adventure by the way he past:
Alone he rode without his Paragone;[1]
For having filcht her bells,[2] her up he cast
To the wide world, and let her fly alone,
He nould[3] be clogd. So had he served many one.

36   The gentle Lady, loose at randon lefte,[4]
       The greene-wood long did walke, and wander wide
       At wilde adventure, like a forlorne wefte,[5]
       Till on a day the *Satyres* her espide
       Straying alone withouten groome or guide;
       Her up they tooke, and with them home her ledd,
       With them as housewife ever to abide,
       To milk their gotes, and make them cheese and bredd,
And every one as commune good[6] her handeled.

37   That shortly she *Malbecco* has forgott,
       And eke Sir *Paridell,* all were he deare;
       Who from her went to seeke another lott,
       And now by fortune was arrived here,
       Where those two guilers with *Malbecco* were:
       Soone as the oldman saw Sir *Paridell,*
       He fainted, and was almost dead with feare,
       Ne word he had to speake, his griefe to tell,
But to him louted[7] low, and greeted goodly well.

38   And after asked him for *Hellenore,*
       "I take no keepe of her" (sayd *Paridell*)
       "She wonneth in the forrest there before."[8]

---

[1] **Paragone:** consort.

[2] **filcht her bells:** i.e., had sex with her, having thus taken her reputation from her. Filching bells is a metaphor from the sport of hawking, in which a falconer attached bells to a hawk's legs so he could keep track of where the hawk was. Paridell has taken what he wanted from Hellenore and has released her.

[3] **nould:** would not.

[4] **at randon lefte:** left at liberty. This is a hawking phrase to describe prey that does not rise for the hawk's attack.

[5] **At wilde adventure:** at hazard in the wilderness; **wefte:** waif—an abandoned piece of property that may legally be claimed by the finder.

[6] **good:** property.

[7] **louted:** bowed.

[8] **before:** before us; in front of us.

So forth he rode, as his adventure fell;[1]
The whiles the Boaster from his loftie sell[2]
Faynd to alight, something amisse to mend;
But the fresh Swayne would not his leasure dwell,
But went his way; whom when he passed kend,[3]
He up remounted light, and after faind to wend.

39   "Perdy nay" (said *Malbecco*) "shall ye not:
      But let him passe as lightly,[4] as he came:
      For litle good of him is to be got,
      And mickle perill to bee put to shame.
      But let us goe to seeke my dearest Dame,
      Whom he hath left in yonder forest wyld:
      For of her safety in great doubt I ame,
      Least salvage beastes her person have despoyld:
Then all the world is lost, and we in vaine have toyld."

40   They all agree, and forward them addrest:
      "Ah but" (said crafty *Trompart*) "weete ye well,
      That yonder in that wastefull wildernesse
      Huge monsters haunt, and many dangers dwell;
      Dragons, and Minotaures, and feendes of hell,
      And many wilde woodmen,[5] which robbe and rend
      All traveilers; therefore advise ye well,
      Before ye enterprise that way to wend:
One may his journey bring too soone to evill end."

41   *Malbecco* stopt in great astonishment,[6]
      And with pale eyes fast fixed on the rest,
      Their counsell crav'd, in daunger imminent.
      Said *Trompart*, "You that are the most opprest[7]
      With burdein of great treasure, I thinke best
      Here for to stay in safetie behynd;
      My Lord and I will search the wide forest."
      That counsell pleased not *Malbeccoes* mynd;
For he was much afraid, him selfe alone to fynd.

---

[1] **as his adventure fell:** to whatever events chance might bring him.

[2] **sell:** saddle.

[3] I.e., when he knew him to have passed; when he passed out of sight.

[4] **lightly:** easily; quickly; without conscience.

[5] **woodmen:** savages; crazy men.

[6] **astonishment:** stupor of indecision and dismay.

[7] **opprest:** weighed down.

42   "Then is it best" (said he)[1] "that ye doe leave
         Your treasure here in some security,
         Either fast closed in some hollow greave,[2]
         Or buried in the ground from jeopardy,
         Till we returne againe in safety:
         As for us two, least doubt of us ye have,
         Hence farre away we will blyndfolded ly,
         Ne privy[3] bee unto your treasures grave."
       It pleased: so he did. Then they march forward brave.[4]

43   Now when amid the thickest woodes they were,
         They heard a noyse of many bagpipes[5] shrill,
         And shrieking Hububs them approching nere,
         Which all the forest did with horrour fill:
         That dreadfull sound the bosters hart did thrill,[6]
         With such amazment, that in hast he fledd,
         Ne ever looked back for good or ill,
         And after him eke fearefull Trompart spedd;
       The old man could not fly, but fell to ground half dedd.

44   Yet afterwardes close creeping, as he might,
         He in a bush did hyde his fearefull hedd,
         The jolly *Satyres* full of fresh delight,
         Came dauncing forth, and with them nimbly ledd
         Faire *Helenore*, with girlonds all bespredd,
         Whom their May-lady they had newly made:
         She proude of that new honour, which they redd,
         And of their lovely[7] fellowship full glade,
       Daunst lively, and her face did with a Lawrell[8] shade.

45   The silly man that in the thickett lay
         Saw all this goodly sport, and grieved sore,
         Yet durst he not against it doe or say,
         But did his hart with bitter thoughts engore,
         To see th'unkindnes[9] of his *Hellenore*.

---

[1] **he:** Trompart.

[2] **greave:** thicket.

[3] **privy:** in on the secret.

[4] **brave:** bravely; with a splendid show.

[5] **bagpipes:** symbolic of lust, because their shape resembles that of the scrotum and penis.

[6] **thrill:** stab.

[7] **lovely:** loving.

[8] **Lawrell:** laurel wreath, associated with poetry as well as with the satyrs' god, Pan.

[9] **unkindnes:** unnatural behavior inappropriate for a woman and for a human.

All day they daunced with great lusty hedd,
And with their horned feet the greene gras wore,
The whiles their Gotes upon the brouzes¹ fedd,
Till drouping *Phœbus* gan to hyde his golden hedd.

46   Tho up they gan their mery pypes to trusse,
         And all their goodly heardes did gather rownd,
         But every *Satyre* first did give a busse²
         To *Hellenore:* so busses did abound.
         Now gan the humid vapour shed³ the grownd
         With perly deaw, and th'Earthes gloomy shade
         Did dim the brightnesse of the welkin⁴ rownd,
         That every bird and beast awarned made,
   To shrowd themselves, whiles sleepe their sences did invade.

47   Which when *Malbecco* saw, out of his bush
         Upon his hands and feete he crept full light,
         And like a Gote emongst the Gotes did rush,
         That through the helpe of his faire hornes⁵ on hight,
         And misty dampe of misconceyving⁶ night,
         And eke through likenesse of his gotish beard,
         He did the better counterfeite aright:
         So home he marcht emongst the horned heard,
   That none of all the *Satyres* him espyde or heard.

48   At night, when all they went to sleepe, he vewd,
         Whereas his lovely wife emongst them lay,
         Embraced of a *Satyre* rough and rude,
         Who all the night did minde⁷ his joyous play:
         Nine times he heard him come aloft⁸ ere day,
         That all his hart with gealosy did swell;

---

¹ **Gotes:** Spenser seems to be imagining ei-
ther that the satyrs—in addition to being
half man, half goat—also keep goats, or else
that they look like men but ride goats;
brouzes: young shoots.

² **busse:** kiss.

³ **shed:** sprinkle.

⁴ **welkin:** sky.

⁵ **hornes:** a cuckold was described
metaphorically as having horns on his head,
like a goat's horns.

⁶ **misconceyving:** liable to cause miscon-
ceptions.

⁷ **minde:** pay attention to.

⁸ **come aloft:** i.e., mount Hellenore;
achieve orgasm.

But yet that nights ensample did bewray,
That not for nought his wife them loved so well,
When one so oft a night did ring his matins bell.[1]

49   So closely as he could, he to them crept,
When wearie of their sport to sleepe they fell,
And to his wife, that now full soundly slept,
He whispered in her eare, and did her tell,
That it was he, which by her side did dwell,
And therefore prayd her wake, to heare him plaine.
As one out of a dreame not waked well,
She turnd her, and returned backe againe:
Yet her for to awake he did the more constraine.[2]

50   At last with irkesom trouble she abrayd;[3]
And then perceiving, that it was indeed
Her old *Malbecco,* which did her upbrayd,
With loosenesse of her love, and loathly deed,
She was astonisht with exceeding dreed,
And would have wakt the *Satyre* by her syde;
But he her prayd, for mercy, or for meed,
To save his life, ne let him be descryde,
But hearken to his lore,[4] and all his counsell hyde.

51   Tho gan he her perswade, to leave that lewd
And loathsom life, of God and man abhord,
And home returne, where all should be renewd
With perfect peace, and bandes[5] of fresh accord,
And she receivd againe to bed and bord,[6]
As if no trespas ever had beene donne:
But she it all refused at one word,
And by no meanes would to his will be wonne,
But chose emongst the jolly *Satyres* still to wonne.

---

[1] **ring his matins bell:** slang for "achieve orgasm" (literally, "ring the bell to call himself to midnight prayers"). Malbecco realizes that Hellenore has a reason to prefer the satyrs to him: they can have nine orgasms in one night.

[2] **constraine:** exert himself; urge her.

[3] **abrayd:** awoke.

[4] **lore:** sage advice.

[5] **bandes:** unifying bonds.

[6] **bord:** table.

52   He wooed her, till day spring he espyde;
        But all in vaine: and then turnd to the heard,
        Who butted him with hornes on every syde,
        And trode downe in the durt, where his hore beard
        Was fowly dight,[1] and he of death afeard.
        Early before the heavens fairest light
        Out of the ruddy East was fully reard,
        The heardes out of their foldes[2] were loosed quight,
    And he emongst the rest crept forth in sory plight.

53   So soone as he the Prison dore[3] did pas,
        He ran as fast, as both his feet could beare,
        And never looked, who behind him was,
        Ne scarsely who before:[4] like as a Beare
        That creeping close, amongst the hives to reare
        An hony combe, the wakefull dogs espy,
        And him assayling, sore his carkas teare,
        That hardly he with life away does fly,
    Ne stayes, till safe him selfe he see from jeopardy.

54   Ne stayd he, till he came unto the place,
        Where late his treasure he entombed had,
        Where when he found it not (for *Trompart* bace
        Had it purloyned for his maister bad:)[5]
        With extreme fury he became quite mad,[6]
        And ran away, ran with him selfe away:[7]
        That who so straungely had him seene bestadd,[8]
        With upstart haire, and staring eyes dismay,
    From Limbo lake him late escaped sure would say.[9]

55   High over hilles and over dales he fledd,
        As if the wind him on his winges had borne,
        Ne banck nor bush could stay[10] him, when he spedd

[1] **dight:** dirtied.

[2] **foldes:** pens (for the Satyrs' goats).

[3] **Prison dore:** referring perhaps to the gate of the goat pen, but more importantly, referring to the fact that the site of the Satyrs' and Hellenore's revels now seems a prison to him.

[4] **before:** in front.

[5] No, this is not an emoticon.

[6] **mad:** insane.

[7] The repetition emphasizes the two ways in which he is running away.

[8] I.e., whoever had seen him so strangely assailed.

[9] I.e., would surely think he had just escaped from the portion of hell where lost souls reside.

[10] **stay:** stop; impede.

His nimble feet, as treading still on thorne:
Griefe, and despight, and gealosy, and scorne
Did all the way him follow hard behynd,
And he himselfe himselfe loath'd so forlorne,
So shamefully forlorne of womankynd;
That[1] as a Snake, still lurked in his wounded mynd.

56   Still fled he forward, looking backward still,
Ne stayd his flight, nor fearefull agony,
Till that he came unto a rocky hill,
Over the sea, suspended dreadfully,
That living creature it would terrify,
To looke adowne, or upward to the hight:
From thence he threw him selfe dispiteously,[2]
All desperate[3] of his fore-damned spright,
That seemd no help for him was left in living sight.

57   But through long anguish, and selfe-murdring thought
He was so wasted and forpined[4] quight,
That all his substance was consum'd to nought,
And nothing left, but like an aery Spright,
That on the rockes he fell so flit and light,
That he thereby receiv'd no hurt at all,
But chaunced on a craggy cliff to light;
Whence he with crooked clawes[5] so long did crall,
That at the last he found a cave with entrance small.

58   Into the same he creepes, and thenceforth there
Resolv'd to build his balefull mansion,
In drery darkenes, and continuall feare
Of that rocks fall, which ever and anon
Threates with huge ruine him to fall upon,
That he dare never sleepe, but that one eye

---

[1] **That:** i.e., that he was "forlorne of wom-ankynd."

[2] **dispiteously:** without mercy toward himself.

[3] **desperate:** despair is the most deadly of the seven deadly sins, because in order to despair of all hope, one must have separated oneself utterly from God. Malbecco is desperate and therefore damned, yet his desperation makes him not care about being damned.

[4] **forpined:** utterly wasted away.

[5] **clawes:** he is turning into a beast.

Still ope he keepes for that occasion;
Ne ever rests he in tranquillity,
The roring billowes beat his bowre so boystrously.[1]

59   Ne ever is he wont on ought to feed,
        But todes and frogs, his pasture[2] poysonous,
        Which in his cold complexion[3] doe breed
        A filthy blood, or humour rancorous,
        Matter of doubt and dread suspitious,
        That doth with curelesse care consume the hart,
        Corrupts the stomacke with gall vitious,[4]
        Croscuts the liver with internall smart,
And doth transfixe the soule with deathes eternall dart.

60   Yet can he never dye, but dying lives,
        And doth himselfe with sorrow new sustaine,
        That death and life attonce unto him gives.
        And painefull pleasure turnes to pleasing paine.
        There dwels he ever, miserable swaine,
        Hatefull both to him selfe, and every wight;
        Where he through privy griefe, and horrour vaine,
        Is woxen so deform'd that he has quight
Forgot he was a man, and *Gelosy* is hight.[5]

---

[1] Malbecco's physical surroundings are a visual metaphor for his emotional state.

[2] **pasture:** food.

[3] **cold complexion:** character caused by an excess of cold humor.

[4] **vitious:** vicious; foul; harmful.

[5] Malbecco has turned into a reductive emblem of himself.

Canto Eleven

Britomart chaceth Ollyphant,[1]
findes Scudamour[2] *distrest:*
Assayes[3] *the house of Busyrane,*
where loves spoyles are exprest.[4]

1   O Hatefull hellish Snake, what furie furst
       Brought thee from balefull house of *Proserpine,*[5]
       Where in her bosome she thee long had nurst,
       And fostred up with bitter milke of tine,[6]
       Fowle Gealosy, that turnest love divine
       To joylesse dread, and mak'st the loving hart
       With hatefull thoughts to languish and to pine,
       And feed it selfe with selfe-consuming smart?
Of all the passions in the mind thou vilest art.

2   O let him far be banished away,
       And in his stead let Love for ever dwell,
       Sweete Love, that doth his golden wings embay[7]
       In blessed Nectar,[8] and pure Pleasures well,
       Untroubled of vile feare, or bitter fell.[9]
       And ye faire Ladies, that your kingdomes make
       In th'harts of men, them governe wisely well,
       And of faire *Britomart* ensample take,
That was as trew in love, as Turtle to her make.[10]

3   Who with Sir *Satyrane,* as earst ye red,[11]
       Forth ryding from *Malbeccoes* hostlesse[12] hous,
       Far off aspyde a young man, the which fled

---

[1] **Ollyphant:** see vii.48.2.n.

[2] **Scudamour:** see vi.53.2.n.

[3] **Assayes:** assails; puts to the test; examines; tries out; attempts. All of these meanings will become quite important.

[4] **exprest:** portrayed.

[5] *Proserpine:* the queen of hell.

[6] **tine:** affliction.

[7] **embay:** steep.

[8] **Nectar:** the favorite drink of the gods.

[9] **fell:** animosity, resentment.

[10] **Turtle:** turtledove; **make:** mate.

[11] **as earst ye red:** at x.1.

[12] **hostlesse:** inhospitable.

From an huge Geaunt, that with hideous
And hatefull outrage long him chaced thus;
It was that *Ollyphant,* the brother deare
Of that *Argante* vile and vitious,
From whom the *Squyre of Dames* was reft[1] whylere;
This all as bad as she, and worse, if worse ought were.

4   For as the sister did in feminine
And filthy lust exceede all woman kinde,
So he surpassed his sex masculine,
In beastly use all, that I ever finde:
Whom when as *Britomart* beheld behinde
The fearefull boy so greedily[2] poursew,
She was emmoved in her noble minde,
T'employ her puissaunce to his reskew,
And pricked fiercely forward, where she did him vew.

5   Ne was Sir *Satyrane* her far behinde,
But with like fiercenesse did ensew[3] the chace:
Whom when the Gyaunt saw, he soone resinde[4]
His former suit,[5] and from them fled apace;
They after both, and boldly bad him bace,[6]
And each did strive the other to outgoe;
But he them both outran a wondrous space,
For he was long, and swift as any Roe,
And now made better speed, t'escape his feared foe.

6   It was not *Satyrane,* whom he did feare,
But *Britomart* the flowre of chastity;
For he the powre of chaste hands might not beare,
But always did their dread encounter fly:
And now so fast his feet he did apply,
That he has gotten to a forrest neare,
Where he is shrouded in security.
The wood they enter, and search everie where,
They searched diversely,[7] so both divided were.

---

[1] **reft:** taken away. See vii.37–52.

[2] **greedily:** avidly.

[3] **ensew:** pursue.

[4] **resinde:** resigned.

[5] **suit:** pursuit.

[6] **bad him bace:** challenged him, turning the pursuer into the pursued (in the words of a children's game called "prisoner's base").

[7] **diversely:** in different directions (a tactic as necessary for Spenser's narrative as for the plots of old westerns).

7   Fayre *Britomart* so long him followed,
      That she at last came to a fountaine sheare,[1]
      By which there lay a knight all wallowed[2]
      Upon the grassy ground, and by him neare
      His haberjeon, his helmet, and his speare;
      A little off[3] his shield was rudely throwne,
      On which the winged boy in colours cleare
      Depeincted[4] was, full easie to be knowne,
  And he thereby, where ever it in field was showne.[5]

8   His face upon the grownd did groveling ly,
      As if he had beene slombring in the shade,
      That the brave Mayd would not for courtesy,
      Out of his quiet slomber him abrade,
      Nor seeme too suddeinly him to invade:[6]
      Still as she stood, she heard with grievous throb
      Him grone, as if his hart were peeces made,
      And with most painefull pangs to sigh and sob,
  That pitty did the Virgins hart of patience rob.

9   At last forth breaking into bitter plaintes[7]
      He sayd, "O soverayne Lord that sit'st on hye,
      And raignst in blis emongst thy blessed Saintes,
      How suffrest[8] thou such shamefull cruelty,
      So long unwreaked[9] of thine enimy?
      Or hast thou, Lord, of good mens cause no heed?
      Or doth thy justice sleepe, and silent ly?
      What booteth then the good and righteous deed,
  If goodnesse find no grace, nor righteousnes no meed?

10   "If good find grace, and righteousnes reward,
      Why then is *Amoret* in caytive[10] band,
      Sith that more bounteous creature never far'd·

---

[1] **fountaine sheare:** clear spring.

[2] **wallowed:** dirtied by having rolled about on the ground.

[3] **off:** away (from him).

[4] **Depeincted:** painted.

[5] I.e., whenever the knight showed the shield on a field of battle, it was easy to identify both the picture of Cupid and the knight who carried the shield (since Cupid is his heraldic sign).

[6] **invade:** intrude upon.

[7] **plaintes:** complaints.

[8] **suffrest:** allow.

[9] **unwreaked:** unavenged.

[10] **caytive:** captive.

On foot, upon the face of living land?
Or if that hevenly justice may withstand
The wrongfull outrage of unrighteous men,
Why then is *Busirane*[1] with wicked hand
Suffred, these seven monethes day[2] in secret den
My Lady and my love so cruelly to pen?

11   "My Lady and my love is cruelly pend
In dolefull darkenes from the vew of day,
Whilest deadly torments doe her chast brest rend,
And the sharpe steele doth rive her hart in tway,[3]
All for she *Scudamore* will not denay.[4]
Yet thou vile man, vile *Scudamore* art sound,[5]
Ne canst her ayde, ne canst her foe dismay;
Unworthy wretch to tread upon the ground,
For whom so faire a Lady feeles so sore a wound."[6]

12   There an huge heape of singulfes[7] did oppresse
His strugling soule, and swelling throbs empeach[8]
His foltring toung with pangs of drerinesse,
Choking the remnant of his plaintife[9] speach,
As if his dayes were come to their last reach.
Which when she heard, and saw the ghastly fit,
Threatning into his life to make a breach,
Both with great ruth[10] and terrour she was smit,
Fearing least from her cage[11] the wearie soule would flit.

13   Tho stouping downe she him amoved[12] light;
Who therewith somewhat starting, up gan looke,
And seeing him behind a stranger knight,

---

[1] **Busirane:** Busiris was a mythical king of Egypt, Poseidon's son, who killed all visitors to his land.

[2] **seven monethes day:** seven months.

[3] **rive:** rend asunder; **in tway:** in two.

[4] **denay:** deny, forswear; refuse to give him anything.

[5] **thou vile man:** Scudamour berates himself; **sound:** whole, unwounded.

[6] Busirane's wounding Amoret represents more than the harms wreaked by a third party; Scudamour feels responsible because he cannot rescue her, but he also feels responsible because in some sense he himself has caused the wound.

[7] **singulfes:** sobs (a Spenserian neologism).

[8] **empeach:** hinder; accuse of treason.

[9] **plaintife:** plaintive; characteristic of one who pleads his own case.

[10] **ruth:** compassion.

[11] **her:** the soul's; **cage:** i.e., the mortal body.

[12] **amoved:** stirred.

Whereas no living creature he mistooke,[1]
With great indignaunce he that sight forsooke,
And downe againe himselfe disdainefully
Abjecting,[2] th'earth with his faire forhead strooke:
Which the bold Virgin seeing, gan apply
Fit medcine to his griefe, and spake thus courtesly.

14   "Ah gentle knight, whose deepe conceived griefe
        Well seemes t'exceede the powre of patience,
        Yet if that hevenly grace some good reliefe
        You send, submit you to high providence,
        And ever in your noble hart prepense,[3]
        That all the sorrow in the world is lesse,
        Then vertues might, and values confidence,
        For who nill bide[4] the burden of distresse,
Must not here thinke to live: for life is wretchednesse.

15   "Therefore, faire Sir, doe comfort to you take,
        And freely read, what wicked felon so
        Hath outrag'd you, and thrald your gentle make.[5]
        Perhaps this hand may helpe to ease your woe,
        And wreake your sorrow on your cruell foe,
        At least it faire endevour will apply."
        Those feeling words so neare the quicke[6] did goe,
        That up his head he reared easily,[7]
And leaning on his elbowe, these few words lett fly.

16   "What boots it plaine,[8] that cannot be redrest,
        And sow vaine sorrow in a fruitlesse eare,
        Sith powre of hand, nor skill of learned brest,
        Ne worldly price cannot redeeme my deare,
        Out of her thraldome and continuall feare?[9]
        For he the tyrant, which her hath in ward[10]

---

[1] I.e., he mistakes the stranger knight for an apparition.

[2] **Abjecting:** throwing; making abject.

[3] **prepense:** consider.

[4] **nill:** will not; **bide:** endure.

[5] **make:** mate.

[6] **neare the quicke:** near the center of his emotional sensitivity (literally, near the sensitive flesh).

[7] **easily:** quickly.

[8] **plaine:** to complain.

[9] **her thraldome and continuall feare:** Hamilton points out that this line suggests that Amoret's continual fear is, in fact, her imprisonment—i.e., that her misgivings about her and Scudamour's relationship are what hold her thrall (Hamilton, *FQ* III.xi.16.3–5.n.).

[10] **in ward:** under guard.

By strong enchauntments and blacke Magicke leare,[1]
Hath in a dungeon deepe her close embard,[2]
And many dreadfull feends hath pointed[3] to her gard.

17 "There he tormenteth her most terribly,
 And day and night afflicts with mortall paine,
 Because to yield him love she doth deny,
 Once to me yold,[4] not to be yolde againe:
 But yet by torture he would her constraine
 Love to conceive in her disdainfull brest;
 Till so she doe, she must in doole[5] remaine,
 Ne may by living meanes[6] be thence relest:
What boots it then to plaine, that cannot be redrest?"

18 With this sad hersall[7] of his heavy stresse,
 The warlike Damzell was empassiond sore,
 And sayd, "Sir knight, your cause is nothing lesse,
 Then is your sorrow, certes if not more;
 For nothing so much pitty doth implore,[8]
 As gentle Ladyes helplesse misery.
 But yet, if please ye listen to my lore,[9]
 I will with proofe of last extremity,[10]
Deliver her fro thence, or with her for you dy."

19 "Ah gentlest knight alive," (sayd *Scudamore*)
 "What huge heroicke magnanimity[11]
 Dwells in thy bounteous brest? what couldst thou more,
 If shee were thine, and thou as now am I?
 O spare thy happy daies, and them apply
 To better boot,[12] but let me die, that ought;
 More is more losse: one is enough to dy."
 "Life is not lost," (said she) "for which is bought
Endlesse renowm, that more then death is to be sought."

---

[1] **leare:** lore, learning.

[2] **embard:** barred in.

[3] **pointed:** appointed.

[4] **yold:** yielded.

[5] **doole:** distress (mental or physical).

[6] **by living meanes:** by any living person; by anything except death.

[7] **hersall:** rehearsal, recounting.

[8] **implore:** beg.

[9] **lore:** wise advice.

[10] **with proofe of last extremity:** risking my life.

[11] **magnanimity:** lofty courage; loftiness of purpose.

[12] **boot:** advantage.

20   Thus shee at length persuaded him to rise,
       And with her wend, to see what new successe
       Mote him befall upon new enterprise;
       His armes, which he had vowed to disprofesse,[1]
       She gathered up, and did about him dresse,
       And his forwandred[2] steed unto him gott:
       So forth they both yfere make their progresse,[3]
       And march not past the mountenaunce of a shott,[4]
    Till they arriv'd, whereas their purpose they did plott.

21   There they dismounting, drew their weapons bold
       And stoutly[5] came unto the Castle gate;
       Whereas no gate they found, them to withhold,
       Nor ward[6] to wait at morne and evening late,
       But in the Porch, that did them sore amate,[7]
       A flaming fire, ymixt with smouldry smoke,
       And stinking Sulphure, that with griesly[8] hate
       And dreadfull horror did all entraunce choke,
    Enforced them their forward footing to revoke.[9]

22   Greatly thereat was *Britomart* dismayd,
       Ne in that stownd[10] wist, how her selfe to beare;
       For daunger vaine it were, to have assayd[11]
       That cruell element,[12] which all things feare,
       Ne none can suffer to approchen neare:
       And turning backe to *Scudamour,* thus sayd;
       "What monstrous enmity provoke[13] we heare,
       Foolhardy, as the Earthes children,[14] which made
    Batteill against the Gods? so we a God[15] invade.

---

[1] **disprofesse:** renounce.
[2] **forwandred:** strayed.
[3] **progresse:** journey.
[4] **mountenaunce of a shott:** distance of a bow shot.
[5] **stoutly:** bravely.
[6] **ward:** guard.
[7] **amate:** overwhelm; dismay; confound.
[8] **griesly:** grisly, causing horror.
[9] **revoke:** retrace, withdraw.
[10] **stownd:** time of trial; state of stupefaction.
[11] **assayd:** tested; attempted.
[12] **cruell element:** i.e., fire, one of the four elements.
[13] **provoke:** challenge; defy; arouse to anger.
[14] **Earthes children:** the Giants, who revolted unsuccessfully against Zeus.
[15] **a God:** either Mulciber, the god of fire (see 26.5), or Cupid, the cruel god of love.

23   "Daunger without discretion to attempt,
        Inglorious and beastlike is: therefore Sir knight,
        Aread what course of you is safest dempt,[1]
        And how we with our foe may come to fight."
        "This is" (quoth he) "the dolorous despight,
        Which earst to you I playnd:[2] for neither may
        This fire be quencht by any witt or might,
        Ne yet by any meanes remov'd away;
So mighty be th'enchauntments, which the same do stay.[3]

24   "What is there ells, but cease these fruitlesse paines,
        And leave me to my former languishing?
        Faire *Amorett* must dwell in wicked chaines,
        And *Scudamore* here die with sorrowing."
        "Perdy not so;" (said shee) "for shameful thing
        Yt were t'abandon noble chevisaunce,[4]
        For shewe of perill, without venturing:
        Rather let try extremities of chaunce,
Then enterprised praise for dread to disavaunce."[5]

25   Therewith resolv'd to prove her utmost might,
        Her ample shield she threw before her face,
        And her swords point directing forward right,[6]
        Assayld the flame, the which eftesoones gave place,
        And did it selfe divide with equall space,[7]
        That through she passed, as a thonder bolt
        Perceth the yielding ayre, and doth displace
        The soring clouds into sad showres ymolt;[8]
So to her yold the flames, and did their force revolt.[9]

---

[1] **dempt:** deemed.

[2] **playnd:** complained.

[3] **stay:** support.

[4] **chevisaunce:** chivalrous enterprise to effect a remedy; chivalrous enterprise to win booty.

[5] I.e., than let dread make us retreat from a praiseworthy enterprise. (Seeking praise through the glory of enterprise was noble.)

[6] The imagery is both Christian and phallic. Britomart has "put on the whole armor of God" and has taken "the shield of faith, with which [she] can quench all the flaming darts of the evil one" (Eph. 6.11,16). At the same time, with her sword pointing forward, she is sexually penetrating the flames of desire.

[7] I.e., in halves.

[8] **sad:** severe; **ymolt:** melted.

[9] **yold:** yielded; **revolt:** turn back.

26   Whome whenas *Scudamour* saw past the fire,
            Safe and untoucht, he likewise gan assay,
            With greedy will, and envious desire,
            And bad the stubborne flames to yield him way:
            But cruell *Mulciber*[1] would not obay
            His threatfull pride, but did the more augment
            His mighty rage, and with imperious sway
            Him forst (maulgre)[2] his fercenes to relent,
And backe retire, all scorcht and pitifully brent.[3]

27   With huge impatience he inly swelt,[4]
            More for great sorrow, that he could not pas,
            Then for the burning torment, which he felt,
            That with fell woodnes he effierced[5] was,
            And wilfully him throwing on the gras,
            Did beat and bounse his head and brest ful sore;
            The whiles the Championesse now entred has
            The utmost rowme, and past the formest[6] dore,
The utmost rowme, abounding with all precious store.[7]

28   For round about, the walls yclothed were
            With goodly arras[8] of great majesty,
            Woven with gold and silke so close and nere,[9]
            That the rich metall[10] lurked privily,
            As faining to be hidd from envious eye;
            Yet here, and there, and every where unwares[11]
            It shewd it selfe, and shone unwillingly;
            Like to a discolourd[12] Snake, whose hidden snares
Through the greene gras his long bright burnisht back declares.[13]

---

[1] *Mulciber:* Vulcan, the god of fire.

[2] **maulgre:** in spite of himself; in spite of his ferocity.

[3] **brent:** burned. It is worth considering why Scudamour cannot enter when Britomart can.

[4] **swelt:** sweltered; burned; perished with strong emotion.

[5] **woodnes:** madness; fury; **effierced:** made fierce; maddened.

[6] **utmost:** outermost; **formest:** foremost.

[7] **store:** cache of goods; treasure.

[8] **arras:** tapestries.

[9] **nere:** tightly (i.e., tightly woven).

[10] I.e., gold threads.

[11] **unwares:** unexpectedly, catching the viewer unawares.

[12] **discolourd:** multicolored.

[13] **declares:** reveals; represents.

29   And in those Tapets[1] weren fashioned
          Many faire pourtraicts,[2] and many a faire feate,
          And all of love, and al of lusty-hed,
          As seemed by their semblaunt did entreat;[3]
          And eke all *Cupids* warres they did repeate,[4]
          And cruell battailes, which he whilome fought
          Gainst all the Gods, to make his empire great;
          Besides the huge massacres, which he wrought
On mighty kings and kesars, into thraldome brought.[5]

30   Therein was writt,[6] how often thondring *Jove*
          Had felt the point of his hart percing dart,
          And leaving heavens kingdome, here did rove
          In straunge disguize, to slake his scalding smart;[7]
          Now like a Ram, faire *Helle* to pervart,[8]
          Now like a Bull, *Europa* to withdraw:[9]
          Ah, how the fearefull Ladies tender hart
          Did lively seeme to tremble, when she saw
The huge seas under her t'obay her servaunts law.[10]

31   Soone after that into a golden showre[11]
          Him selfe he chaung'd, faire *Danaë* to vew,
          And through the roofe of her strong brasen towre
          Did raine into her lap an hony dew,[12]

---

[1] **Tapets:** tapestries.

[2] **pourtraicts:** portraits; pictures.

[3] **semblaunt:** portrayal; deceitful appearance; **entreat:** treat; entice the viewer.

[4] **repeate:** recount.

[5] Cupid's power has mushroomed far beyond shooting a few arrows that ranckle in a few hearts.

[6] **writt:** depicted.

[7] Jove often took on the disguise of an animal or of something else found on earth, in order to rape, or have affairs with, mortal women. Many of the following stories are taken from Ovid's *Metamorphoses;* some are from other sources, including Ariosto's *Orlando Furioso,* Natalis Comes' commentary, and tapestries that Spenser could have seen.

[8] **pervart:** turn away; pervert morally.

[9] In the guise of a bull, Jove put Europa onto his back and carried her off (*Metamorphoses,* 2.836–75, 6.103–7).

[10] The description of the tapestry has begun to seem like a description of moving persons and things. This technique is common in many epics' extended descriptions of art objects—known as *ekphrasis.* In the *Iliad,* for example, the description of Achilles' shield asks us to see far more detail than could actually be depicted on one shield, along with phenomena that cannot be pictured on any surface: movement, sounds, the passage of time, tactile sensations, and so on (*Iliad,* 18.478–617).

[11] I.e., a shower of gold pieces.

[12] **hony dew:** a deliciously sweet liquid mythically supposed to fall like dew.

The whiles her foolish garde, that litle knew
Of such deceipt, kept th'yron dore fast bard,
And watcht, that none should enter nor issew;
Vaine was the watch, and bootlesse all the ward,
Whenas the God to golden hew[1] him selfe transfard.

32   Then was he turnd into a snowy Swan,
    To win faire *Leda* to his lovely trade:[2]
    O wondrous skill, and sweet wit of the man,[3]
    That her in daffadillies sleeping made,
    From scorching heat her daintie limbes to shade:
    Whiles the proud Bird ruffing[4] his fethers wyde,
    And brushing his faire brest, did her invade;
    Shee slept, yet twixt her eielids closely spyde,
How towards her he rusht, and smiled at his pryde.[5]

33   Then shewd it, how the *Thebane Semelee*
    Deceivd of gealous *Juno,* did require
    To see him in his soverayne majestee,
    Armd with his thunderbolts and lightning fire,
    Whens dearely she with death bought her desire.[6]
    But faire *Alcmena* better match did make,
    Joying his love in likenes more entire;
    Three nights in one, they say, that for her sake
He then did put, her pleasures lenger to partake.[7]

[1] **hew:** form.

[2] **lovely trade:** amorous dealings.

[3] **the man:** the artist who designed the tapestry.

[4] **ruffing:** ruffling.

[5] **pryde:** self-satisfaction; erotic desire. Ovid often depicts the objects of Zeus' rapes as being terrified. Here, the author of Busirane's tapestry pictures Leda as a tease, pretending to sleep while actually welcoming Jove's invasion of her body. Spenser is inviting us to compare this tapestry with the tapestries of Venus and Adonis' story in Malecasta's castle (i.34–38) and to compare the intentions of the owners of the two sets of tapestries, as well as the intentions and characters of the viewers. See also xii.4.2.n.

[6] Jealous of Semele, who was her husband's latest paramour, Juno tricked Semele into asking Jove to come to her in his full glory rather than disguised in mortal shape. Reluctantly—but bound by a previous oath—Jove did so, and the encounter with his lightning majesty killed Semele on the spot (Ovid, *Metamorphoses,* 3.259–315). Compare Jove's reluctance with Scudamour's sense of guilt.

[7] Jove disguised himself as Alcmena's husband in order to have sex with her. In order to prolong the encounter, he made the night three times as long as a normal night (Natalis Comes, *Mythologiae,* 6.1).

34　　Twise was he seene in soaring Eagles shape,
　　　　And with wide winges to beat the buxome[1] ayre,
　　　　Once, when he with *Asterie*[2] did scape,
　　　　Againe, when as the *Trojane* boy[3] so fayre
　　　　He snatcht from *Ida* hill, and with him bare:
　　　　Wondrous delight it was, there to behould,
　　　　How the rude Shepheards after him did stare,
　　　　Trembling through feare, least down he fallen should
　　　And often to him calling, to take surer hould.

35　　In *Satyres* shape *Antiopa* he snatcht:
　　　　And like a fire, when he *Aegin'* assayd:
　　　　A shepeheard, when *Mnemosyne* he catcht:[4]
　　　　And like a Serpent to the *Thracian* mayd.[5]
　　　　Whyles thus on earth great *Jove* these pageaunts playd,
　　　　The winged boy did thrust into his throne,
　　　　And scoffing, thus unto his mother sayd,
　　　　"Lo now the hevens obey to me alone,
　　　And take me for their *Jove*, whiles *Jove* to earth is gone."

36　　And thou, faire *Phœbus*,[6] in thy colours bright
　　　　Wast there enwoven, and the sad distresse,
　　　　In which that boy thee plonged, for despight,
　　　　That thou bewray'dst his mothers wantonnesse,
　　　　When she with *Mars* was meynt in joyfulnesse:[7]
　　　　For thy he thrild thee with a leaden dart,
　　　　To love faire *Daphne*, which thee loved lesse:
　　　　Lesse she thee lov'd, then was thy just desart,
　　　Yet was thy love her death, and her death was thy smart.[8]

---

[1] **buxome:** yielding.

[2] In order to escape from Jove's attack, As-
terie changed into a quail, but then Jove
changed himself into an eagle.

[3] *Trojane* **boy:** Ganymede, who became
the cup-bearer to the gods after Jove ab-
ducted him (*Metamorphoses*, 10.155–61).

[4] For this and the following lines, see *Meta-
morphoses*, 6.110–14.

[5] **the *Thracian* mayd:** Proserpina (Greek
"Persephone").

[6] *Phœbus:* Apollo, the sun god.

[7] **meynt:** mingled in sexual intercourse.
When Apollo told Venus' husband, Vul-
can, that she was being unfaithful to him,
Venus got revenge by using her power to
make Apollo fall painfully in love with
Leucothoë, after which one of Apollo's
discarded women killed Leucothoë (*Meta-
morphoses*, 4.190–255). Apollo later fell in
love with Daphne, who fled from him and
was changed into a laurel tree by a com-
passionate god; Spenser combines the two
episodes.

[8] **smart:** pain.

37   So lovedst thou the lusty *Hyacinct,*[1]
    So lovedst thou the faire *Coronis*[2] deare:
    Yet both are of thy haplesse hand extinct,
    Yet both in flowres doe live; and love thee beare,
    The one a Paunce,[3] the other a sweet breare:
    For griefe whereof, ye mote have lively seene
    The God himselfe rending his golden heare,
    And breaking quite his garlond ever greene,
With other signes of sorrow and impatient teene.[4]

38   Both for those two, and for his owne deare sonne,
    The sonne of *Climene*[5] he did repent,
    Who bold to guide the charet of the Sunne,
    Himselfe in thousand peeces fondly rent,[6]
    And all the world with flashing fire brent:
    So like, that all the walles did seeme to flame.
    Yet cruell *Cupid,* not herewith content,
    Forst him[7] eftsoones to follow other game,
And love a Shephards daughter for his dearest Dame.

39   He loved *Isse* for his dearest Dame,
    And for her sake her cattell fedd a while,
    And for her sake a cowheard vile became,
    The servant of *Admetus* cowheard vile,
    Whiles that from heaven he suffered exile.[8]
    Long were to tell each other lovely fitt,[9]
    Now like a Lyon, hunting after spoile,
    Now like a Stag,[10] now like a faulcon flit:
All which in that faire arras was most lively writ.

---

[1] **lusty:** lively; beautiful; full of sexual appetite; **Hyacinct:** see vi.45.3.n.

[2] *Coronis:* see *Metamorphoses,* 2.542–632.

[3] **Paunce:** pansy, which is purple, like the hyacinth.

[4] **teene:** affliction; sorrow.

[5] **sonne of *Climene*:** Phaethon asked to drive his father's sun chariot for one day. With misgivings, Phoebus allowed it, but Phaethon lost control of the horses and repeatedly bumped into the earth, causing conflagrations everywhere and ultimately killing himself (*Metamorphoses,* 2.19–400).

[6] **fondly rent:** foolishly ripped.

[7] **him:** Phoebus Apollo.

[8] Apollo disguised himself as a shepherd in order to approach Isse; at another time, Jove threw him out of heaven. Spenser combines the two stories.

[9] **fitt:** passion; section of a story told in verse.

[10] **Stag:** although all early editions have "Hag," there is no record of Jove's disguising himself as an old woman, whereas in the same passage upon which Spenser is relying for this list, Natalis Comes describes Jove as taking on the disguise of a stag (Smith, textual note, citing Jortin).

40   Next unto him was *Neptune* pictured,
        In his divine resemblance wondrous lyke:
        His face was rugged, and his hoarie hed
        Dropped with brackish deaw; his threeforkt Pyke
        He stearnly shooke, and therewith fierce did stryke
        The raging billowes, that on every syde
        They trembling stood, and made a long broad dyke,
        That his swift charet might have passage wyde,
    Which foure great *Hippodames* did draw in temewise[1] tyde.

41   His seahorses did seeme to snort amayne,[2]
        And from their nosethrilles[3] blow the brynie streame,
        That made the sparckling waves to smoke agayne,
        And flame with gold, but the white fomy creame,
        Did shine with silver, and shoot forth his beame.
        The God himselfe did pensive seeme and sad,
        And hong adowne his head, as[4] he did dreame:
        For privy love his brest empierced had,
    Ne ought but deare *Bisaltis*[5] ay could make him glad.

42   He loved eke *Iphimedia*[6] deare,
        And *Aeolus*[7] faire daughter *Arne* hight.
        For whom he turnd him selfe into a Steare,
        And fedd on fodder, to beguile her sight.
        Also to win *Deucalions* daughter[8] bright,
        He turnd him selfe into a Dolphin fayre;
        And like a winged horse he tooke his flight,
        To snaky-locke *Medusa*[9] to repayre,
    On whom he got[10] faire *Pegasus,* that flitteth in the ayre.

---

[1] **Hippodames:** hippopotami or seahorses; **in temewise:** as a team.

[2] **amayne:** with all their might (with a pun on "on the main," on the sea).

[3] **nosethrilles:** nostrils.

[4] **as:** as if.

[5] According to Hyginus, it was Bisaltis' daughter, Theophane, to whom Neptune came in the form of a ram (*Fabulae,* 188).

[6] **Iphimedia:** to whom Neptune came in the disguise of a river.

[7] **Aeolus:** the god of the winds.

[8] **Deucalions daughter:** Melantho.

[9] **Medusa:** the most famous of the Gorgons (see ix.22.8.n.). Medusa was a beautiful woman who served Minerva as a vestal virgin. After Neptune raped Medusa in Minerva's temple, Minerva punished the victim by changing Medusa's hair into snakes and giving her the power to turn into stone any men who looked at her. Perseus finally figured out how to cut off Medusa's head without having to look at her, whereupon Minerva put either the head or a representation of it upon her breastplate, to frighten off her enemies.

[10] **got:** begot.

43   Next *Saturne* was, (but who would ever weene,
            That sullein *Saturne* ever weend to love?[1]
            Yet love is sullein, and *Saturnlike* seene,
            As he did for *Erigone*[2] it prove,)
            That to a *Centaure* did him selfe transmove.[3]
            So proov'd it eke that gratious God of wine,[4]
            When for to compasse *Philliras* hard love,
            He turnd himselfe into a fruitfull vine,
      And into her faire bosome made his grapes decline.

44   Long were to tell the amorous assayes,[5]
            And gentle pangues, with which he[6] maked meeke
            The mightie *Mars*,[7] to learne his wanton playes:
            How oft for *Venus*, and how often eek
            For many other Nymphes he[8] sore did shreek,
            With womanish teares, and with unwarlike smarts,
            Privily moystening his horrid[9] cheeke.
            There was he painted full of burning dartes,
      And many wide woundes launched[10] through his inner partes.

45   Ne did he spare (so cruell was the Elfe[11])
            His owne deare mother, (ah why should he so?)
            Ne did he spare sometime to pricke himselfe,
            That he might taste the sweet consuming woe,[12]
            Which he had wrought to many others moe.
            But to declare the mournfull Tragedyes,

---

[1] Saturn was believed the farthest planet, with an inimical astrological influence. As a god, he was sullen and bellicose.

[2] *Erigone:* in Ovid, but either Spenser or his printer seems to have confused her with Philliras, mentioned in line 7.

[3] *Centaure:* half man, half horse, and known for lust; **transmove:** transform.

[4] **God of wine:** Bacchus.

[5] **assayes:** assaults; experiments.

[6] **pangues:** pangs; **he:** Love personified; Cupid (see 29.5, the word "love" repeated three times in stanza 43, and all of stanza 45).

[7] *Mars:* god of war.

[8] **he:** Mars, whose pains are uncharacteristically "unwarlike"(6).

[9] **horrid:** bristly.

[10] **launched:** lanced.

[11] **the Elfe:** Cupid.

[12] The image of Cupid's giving himself a wound in order to feel the sweet pain of love will intensify and darken in the following canto, when we meet Amoret and her torturer.

And spoiles, wherewith he all the ground did strow,
More eath to number, with how many eyes[1]
High heven beholdes sad lovers nightly theeveryes.[2]

46   Kings Queenes, Lords Ladies, Knights and Damsels gent
    Were heap'd together with the vulgar sort,
    And mingled with the raskall rablement,
    Without respect of person or of port,[3]
    To shew Dan[4] *Cupids* powre and great effort:
    And round about a border was entrayld,[5]
    Of broken bowes and arrowes shivered[6] short,
    And a long bloody river through them rayld,[7]
So lively and so like, that living sence it fayld.[8]

47   And at the upper end of that faire rowme,
    There was an Altar built of pretious stone,
    Of passing valew, and of great renowme,[9]
    On which there stood an Image all alone,
    Of massy[10] gold, which with his owne light shone;
    And winges it had with sondry colours dight,
    More sondry colours, then the proud *Pavone*[11]
    Beares in his boasted fan, or *Iris*[12] bright,
When her discolourd[13] bow she spreds through heven bright.

48   Blyndfold he[14] was, and in his cruell fist
    A mortall bow and arrowes keene did hold,
    With which he shot at randon, when him list,
    Some headed with sad[15] lead, some with pure gold;
    (Ah man beware, how thou those dartes behold)
    A wounded Dragon under him did ly,

[1] **eath:** easy; **eyes:** i.e., stars.

[2] **theeveryes:** thieveries—i.e., stealing hearts.

[3] I.e., without distinguishing among types of persons or among social positions.

[4] **Dan:** courtesy title for a male member of a religious order or for a male scholar, knight, poet, or deity.

[5] I.e., around the tapestry was twined a border.

[6] **shivered:** splintered.

[7] **rayld:** flowed.

[8] **like:** lifelike; **fayld:** made to fail (i.e., it tricked the eye).

[9] **renowme:** renown.

[10] **massy:** weighty; solid.

[11] *Pavone:* peacock (Italian).

[12] *Iris:* the rainbow.

[13] **discolourd:** multicolored.

[14] **he:** the gold statue of Cupid, who is conventionally depicted as blindfolded because he does not care whom he shoots; love is random.

[15] **sad:** heavy; causing sorrow.

Whose hideous tayle his lefte foot did enfold,
And with a shaft was shot through either eye,
That no man forth might draw, ne no man remedye.[1]

49   And underneath his feet was written thus,
"Unto the Victor of the Gods this bee:"
And all the people in that ample hous
Did to that image bowe their humble knee,
And oft committed fowle Idolatree,
That wondrous sight faire *Britomart* amazd,
Ne seeing could her wonder satisfie,
But evermore and more upon it gazd,
The whiles the passing brightnes her fraile sences dazd.

50   Tho as she backward[2] cast her busie eye,
To search each secrete of that goodly sted,[3]
Over the dore thus written she did spye
"Bee bold:" she oft and oft it over-red
Yet could not find what sence it figured:
But what so were therein, or writ or ment,
She was no whit thereby discouraged,
From prosecuting of her first intent,
But forward with bold steps into the next roome went.

51   Much fayrer, then the former, was that roome,
And richlier by many partes arayd:
For not with arras made in painefull loome,[4]
But with pure gold it all was overlayd,
Wrought with wilde Antickes,[5] which their follies playd,
In the rich metall, as they living were:
A thousand monstrous formes therein were made,
Such as false love doth oft upon him weare,
For love in thousand monstrous formes doth oft appeare.

---

[1] In a well-known emblem book, the emblem *"Custodienda virgines"* ("Virgins Must Be Protected") depicts a woman with a dragon by her side (Alciati, 22). Here in the House of Busirane, then, Cupid has defeated the dragon that guards chastity.

[2] **backward:** behind the statue of Cupid.

[3] **sted:** place.

[4] I.e., made painstakingly on a loom.

[5] **Antickes:** grotesque figures.

52   And all about, the glistring walles were hong
            With warlike spoiles, and with victorious prayes,[1]
            Of mighty Conquerours and Captaines strong,
            Which were whilome captived in their dayes,
            To cruell love, and wrought their owne decayes:[2]
            Their swerds and speres were broke, and hauberques[3] rent
            And their proud girlonds of tryumphant bayes,
            Troden in dust with fury insolent,
        To shew the victors might and mercilesse intent.

53   The warlike Mayd beholding earnestly
            The goodly ordinaunce[4] of this rich Place,
            Did greatly wonder, ne could satisfy
            Her greedy eyes with gazing a long space,[5]
            But more she mervaild that no footings trace,
            Nor wight appear'd, but wastefull emptinesse,[6]
            And solemne silence over all that place:
            Straunge thing it seem'd, that none was to possesse
        So rich purveyaunce,[7] ne them keepe with carefulnesse.

54   And as she lookt about, she did behold,
            How over that same dore[8] was likewise writ,
            "Be bolde, be bolde," and every where *"Be bold,"*
            That much she muz'd, yet could not construe it[9]
            By any ridling skill, or commune wit.[10]
            At last she spyde at that rowmes upper end,
            Another yron dore, on which was writ,
            "Be not too bold;" whereto though she did bend
        Her earnest minde, yet wist not what it might intend.[11]

---

[1] **prayes:** booty.

[2] **decayes:** downfalls (from pining away or committing suicide in despair).

[3] **hauberques:** tunics of chain mail.

[4] **ordinaunce:** weapons, ammunition, and other martial equipment.

[5] **space:** time.

[6] In contrast to the first room, which held bowing people.

[7] **purveyaunce:** furnishings.

[8] I.e., the inside of the door through which she has now come.

[9] **construe it:** figure it out.

[10] **commune wit:** common sense.

[11] **intend:** mean. The phrases come from the well-known folk tale of Mr. Fox (in later versions called Bluebeard), who forbade his fiancée, Lady Mary, to enter a certain room of his castle. Over the doors was written, "Be bold, be bold, but not too bold, lest that your heart's blood should run cold." When she opened the door, she saw the bones and blood of Mr. Fox's previous wives. If Busirane can persuade Britomart to feel horror at the idea that she could

55   Thus she there wayted untill eventyde,
        Yet living creature none she saw appeare:
        And now sad shadowes gan the world to hyde
        From mortall vew, and wrap in darkenes dreare;
        Yet nould she d'off[1] her weary armes, for feare
        Of secret daunger, ne let sleepe oppresse
        Her heavy eyes with natures burdein deare,
        But drew her selfe aside in sickernesse,[2]
And her welpointed wepons did about her dresse.[3]

---

become a prisoner of love like Amoret, perhaps he will keep her from trying to rescue Amoret.

[1] **nould:** would not; **d'off:** doff, remove.

[2] **sickernesse:** security.

[3] **welpointed:** well appointed; well pointed (sharp); **dresse:** arrange; prepare.

Canto Twelve

The maske[1] of Cupid, and th'enchanted
Chamber are displayd,
Whence Britomart redeemes faire
Amoret, through charmes decayd.[2]

1   Tho when as chearelesse Night ycovered had
      Fayre heaven with an universall clowd,
      That every wight dismayd with darkenes sad,
      In silence and in sleepe themselves did shrowd,
      She heard a shrilling Trompet sound alowd,
      Signe of nigh battaill, or got victory;[3]
      Nought therewith daunted was her courage prowd,
      But rather stird to cruell enmity,
     Expecting ever,[4] when some foe she might descry.

[1] **maske:** a masque was a form of entertainment popular at court and at the houses of the very wealthy, where only invited guests attended. Performed only once, a masque was an emblematic presentation of actors—sometimes drawn from the noble families themselves—dressed to represent virtues, vices, and other abstract concepts. Costumes and sets were usually elaborate, with special effects, e.g., thunder and lightning. Whereas many masques involved songs, dancing, and poetry, the Masque of Cupid in the House of Busirane belongs to a subgenre of the masque, in which the actors passed by in a silent procession. Some masques ended with the audience joining the actors in a dance that symbolized, among other things, the audience's participation in the concepts represented in the masque. Although the Masque of Cupid does not end this way, it is useful to remember the customary symbolism of such dances when we consider Britomart's relationship to the scene that she views. It is also useful to note that masques were often presented at weddings of the aristocracy and that a wedding masque often might include a mock abduction of the bride. Although Spenser waited six years after first publishing the cantos about the Masque of Cupid to develop the idea that the way Amoret got into Busirane's house in the first place was that he abducted her on her wedding day (IV.i.3), and although we need to consider what the Masque of Cupid means to readers before they encounter the account of the abduction in Book Four, we also need to see what happens when we read that later part of the story back into the final canto of Book Three.

[2] I.e., Amoret has wasted away through the power of charms. As in *A Midsummer Night's Dream,* it is important to consider the magic not simply as an external force, but as a representation of what may happen to ordinary people who experience love without being affected by literal magic.

[3] **got victory:** victory that has been achieved.

[4] **Expecting ever:** always on the lookout for.

2	With that, an hideous storme of winde arose,
With dreadfull thunder and lightning atwixt,[1]
And an earthquake, as if it streight would lose
The worlds foundations from his centre fixt;
A direfull stench of smoke and sulphure mixt
Ensewd, whose noyaunce fild the fearefull sted,[2]
From the fourth howre of night untill the sixt;[3]
Yet the bold *Britonesse* was nought ydred,
Though much emmov'd, but stedfast still persevered.

3	All suddeinly a stormy whirlwind blew
Throughout the house, that clapped[4] every dore,
With which that yron wicket[5] open flew,
As it with mighty levers had bene tore:[6]
And forth yssewd, as on the readie[7] flore
Of some Theatre, a grave personage,
That in his hand a braunch of laurell bore,
With comely haveour[8] and count'nance sage,
Yclad in costly garments, fit for tragicke Stage.

4	Proceeding to the midst, he stil did stand,
As if in minde he somewhat[9] had to say,
And to the vulgare[10] beckning with his hand,
In signe of silence, as to heare a play,

[1] **atwixt:** i.e., between the claps of thunder.

[2] **noyaunce:** noxiousness; annoyance; **fearefull:** causing fear; **sted:** place.

[3] I.e., from ten o'clock until midnight.

[4] **clapped:** slammed.

[5] **wicket:** the iron door mentioned at xi.54.7.

[6] Whereas one might compare the special effects of an ordinary masque to magic, here Busirane's magic is being compared to the special-effects machinery of an ordinary masque.

[7] **readie:** prepared for performance.

[8] **haveour:** bearing.

[9] **somewhat:** something.

[10] **vulgare:** lowest of the commoners in the audience; groundlings standing to watch the performance. Here, only Britomart is watching, from her hiding place (27.4–5), so the "grave personage" is beckoning to an imaginary or invisible audience. The question of who constitutes the *allegorical* audience for the entire performance is both crucial and complicated, as is the question of who constitutes its author. Allegorically, possible audiences include Britomart, Scudamour, Amoret, Busirane, Queen Elizabeth, and us. Possible authors include Spenser, Busirane, Amoret, Scudamour, and Britomart (the latter three as unwitting authors of their own anxieties)—as well as Elizabeth, whom Spenser will eventually name as the source of the entire poem (VI.Arg.7). An interpretation of the Masque of Cupid can incorporate most of the possible combinations of these authors and audiences; they are not mutually exclusive.

By lively actions he gan bewray[1]
Some argument of matter passioned;[2]
Which doen, he backe retyred soft away,
And passing by, his name discovered,
Ease, on his robe in golden letters cyphered.[3]

5   The noble Mayd, still standing all this vewd,
    And merveild at his straunge intendiment;[4]
    With that a joyous fellowship[5] issewd
    Of Minstrales,[6] making goodly meriment,
    With wanton Bardes, and Rymers impudent,
    All which together song full chearefully
    A lay of loves delight, with sweet concent:[7]
    After whom marcht a jolly company,
In manner of a maske, enranged[8] orderly.

6   The whiles a most delitious harmony,
    In full straunge notes was sweetly heard to sound,
    That the rare sweetnesse of the melody
    The feeble sences wholy did confound,
    And the frayle soule in deepe delight nigh drownd:
    And when it ceast, shrill trompets lowd did bray,
    That their report[9] did far away rebound,
    And when they ceast, it[10] gan againe to play,
The whiles the maskers marched forth in trim[11] aray.

---

[1] **bewray:** reveal.

[2] **argument:** plot; **passioned:** passionate.

[3] **cyphered:** written in letters.

[4] **intendiment:** intent.

[5] **fellowship:** company.

[6] **Minstrales:** minstrels. They sang, told stories, and performed silly tricks for their patrons, especially at feasts, weddings, and other celebrations.

[7] **concent:** harmony; giving in to love or to sexual overtures.

[8] **enranged:** arranged.

[9] **report:** explosive noise.

[10] **it:** the music described in lines 1 through 5, which causes a pleasantly drugged state of mind.

[11] **trim:** finely and neatly arranged, spruced up.

7   The first was Fansy,[1] like a lovely Boy,
            Of rare aspect, and beautie without peare,[2]
            Matchable ether to that ympe[3] of *Troy,*
            Whom *Jove* did love, and chose his cup to beare,
            Or that same daintie lad,[4] which was so deare
            To great *Alcides,* that when as he[5] dyde,
            He[6] wailed womanlike with many a teare,
            And every wood, and every valley wyde
        He fild with *Hylas* name; the Nymphes eke *"Hylas"* cryde.

8   His garment nether was of silke nor say,[7]
            But paynted plumes, in goodly order dight,
            Like as the sunburnt *Indians* do aray
            Their tawney bodies, in their proudest plight:
            As those same plumes, so seemd he vaine and light,
            That by his gate[8] might easily appeare;
            For still he far'd[9] as dauncing in delight,
            And in his hand a windy fan did beare,
        That in the ydle ayre he mov'd still here and theare.

---

[1] **Fansy:** desire; capricious desire; imagination. The three meanings are bound up with each other. Early modern poets were fascinated with the ability of the lover to create imaginary and therefore misleading versions of the beloved inside the mind. Petrarchan poets ironized their own tendency to prefer their imaginary versions of their mistresses to the actual women whom they loved (see, e.g., Sidney's "This night while sleepe begins with heavy wings," *Astrophil and Stella*). Britomart is trying to understand what it means to be a woman who is at least partly in the position of a traditionally male Petrarchan lover, pursuing an image of her beloved; and both Britomart and Amoret are trying to figure out what it means for a woman to give herself in marriage. Figures in the pageant represent the most delusional and tormenting aspects of Petrarchan love. Busirane wants his viewers to learn from the pageant that they should fear love—or wants Amoret in particular to learn to fear loving Scudamour in particular—yet Busirane's pageant is also *produced* by the fears that already torment Amoret, Britomart, and Scudamour. Some of the same fears surface, albeit more subtly, in Spenser's *Epithalamion,* which celebrates his second marriage and which registers an uneasiness that the groom might hurt the bride physically or psychologically on their wedding night (not an unreasonable anxiety, especially given that women often died in childbirth).

[2] **peare:** peer.

[3] **ether:** either; **ympe:** offspring, here referring to Ganymede. See xi.34.4 and n.

[4] I.e., Hylas.

[5] **he:** Hylas.

[6] **He:** Alcides.

[7] **say:** a finely woven cloth.

[8] **gate:** gait.

[9] **still he far'd:** always he behaved.

9   And him beside marcht amorous *Desyre,*
            Who seemd of ryper yeares, then th'other Swayne,
            Yet was that other swayne this elders syre,[1]
            And gave him being, commune to them twayne:
            His garment was disguysed very vayne,
            And his embrodered Bonet[2] sat awry;
            Twixt both his hands few sparks he close did strayne,[3]
            Which still he blew, and kindled busily,
      That soone they life conceiv'd, and forth in flames did fly.

10   Next after him went *Doubt,* who was yclad
            In a discolour'd cote, of straunge disguyse,
            That at his backe a brode Capuccio[4] had,
            And sleeves dependaunt *Albanese*-wyse:[5]
            He lookt askew with his mistrustfull eyes,
            And nycely trode, as[6] thornes lay in his way
            Or that the flore to shrinke he did avyse
            And on a broken reed he still did stay,[7]
      His feeble steps, which shrunck, when hard thereon he lay.[8]

11   With him went *Daunger,* cloth'd in ragged weed,[9]
            Made of Beares skin, that him more dreadfull made,
            Yet his owne face was dreadfull, ne did need
            Straunge horrour, to deforme his griesly shade;[10]
            A net in th'one hand, and a rusty blade
            In th'other was, this Mischiefe,[11] that mishap;
            With th'one his foes he threatned to invade,
            With th'other he his friends ment to enwrap:
      For whom he could not kill, he practizd[12] to entrap.

---

[1] Showing allegorically that fancy produces desire.

[2] **Bonet:** soft cap for men.

[3] **close did strayne:** closely clasped.

[4] **Capuccio:** a hood or cowl, emblematic of fraud.

[5] *Albanese*-**wyse:** in the Scottish (or Celtic) manner.

[6] **nycely:** carefully; daintily; **as:** as if.

[7] **stay:** prop up, as with a crutch.

[8] **shrunck:** bent or collapsed; **lay:** leaned.

[9] *Daunger:* primarily danger in the modern sense, as indicated by the rest of his portrait, but also the medieval concept of *daunger:* the coyness, hesitation, or ungraciousness exhibited by one who wished to discourage—or appear to discourge—another's advances; **weed:** clothing.

[10] **Straunge:** added from outside himself; **shade:** image.

[11] **Mischiefe:** in the sixteenth century, used more often in a serious sense than to describe adorable infractions.

[12] **practizd:** schemed.

12   Next him was *Feare,* all arm'd from top to toe,
      Yet thought himselfe not safe enough thereby,
      But feard each shadow moving to or froe,[1]
      And his owne armes when glittering he did spy,
      Or clashing heard, he fast away did fly,
      As ashes pale of hew, and winged heeld;[2]
      And evermore on daunger fixt his eye,
      Gainst whom he alwayes bent a brasen shield,
    Which his right hand unarmed fearefully did wield.

13   With him went *Hope* in rancke,[3] a handsome Mayd
      Of chearefull looke and lovely to behold;
      In silken samite[4] she was light arayd,
      And her fayre lockes were woven[5] up in gold;
      She alway smyld, and in her hand did hold
      An holy water Sprinckle, dipt in deowe,[6]
      With which she sprinckled favours manifold,
      On whom she list, and did great liking sheowe,
    Great liking unto many, but true love to feowe.

14   And after them *Dissemblaunce,*[7] and *Suspect*
      Marcht in one rancke, yet an unequall paire:
      For she was gentle, and of milde aspect,
      Courteous to all, and seeming debonaire,[8]
      Goodly adorned, and exceeding faire:
      Yet was that all but paynted, and pourloynd,[9]
      And her bright browes were deckt with borrowed haire:[10]
      Her deeds were forged, and her words false coynd,
    And alwaies in her hand two clewes[11] of silke she twynd.

---

[1] **to or froe:** toward or away from him.

[2] I.e., Fear's appearance is as pale as ashes, and his heels have wings.

[3] **in rancke:** by his side; everyone proceeds in pairs.

[4] **samite:** a heavy, expensive silk fabric, often interwoven with gold and silver threads.

[5] **woven:** braided or twined.

[6] **Sprinckle:** an aspergillum, the brush that is used to sprinkle holy water during the Catholic mass; **deowe:** dew, as if the water came from heaven.

[7] **Dissemblaunce:** dissimulation.

[8] **debonaire:** courteous, affable.

[9] **pourloynd:** purloined, stolen.

[10] In emblem books, sermons, and moral tracts, women's makeup, wigs, and deceptive clothing were often held up as evidence of hypocrisy and of using physical beauty to conceal moral corruption.

[11] **clewes:** balls of thread.

15   But he was fowle, ill favoured, and grim,
      Under his eiebrowes looking still askaunce;[1]
      And ever as *Dissemblaunce* laught on him,
      He lowrd[2] on her with daungerous eyeglaunce;
      Shewing his nature in his countenaunce;
      His rolling eies did never rest in place,
      But walkte each where,[3] for feare of hid mischaunce,
      Holding a lattis[4] still before his face,
    Through which he stil did peep, as forward he did pace.

16   Next[5] him went *Griefe,* and *Fury* matcht yfere;
      Griefe all in sable sorrowfully clad,
      Downe hanging his dull head, with heavy chere,
      Yet inly being more, then seeming sad:
      A paire of Pincers in his hand he had,
      With which he pinched people to the hart,
      That from thenceforth a wretched life they ladd,
      In wilfull languor[6] and consuming smart,
    Dying each day with inward wounds of dolours dart.

17   But *Fury* was full ill[7] appareiled,
      In rags, that naked nigh she did appeare,
      With ghastly looks and dreadfull drerihed;[8]
      For from her backe her garments she did teare,
      And from her head ofte rent her snarled heare:
      In her right hand a firebrand shee did tosse[9]
      About her head, still roming here and there;
      As a dismayed Deare in chace embost,[10]
    Forgetfull of his safety, hath his right way lost.

18   After them went *Displeasure* and *Pleasaunce,*
      He looking lompish[11] and full sullein sad,
      And hanging downe his heavy countenaunce;

[1] **askaunce:** out of the corner of his eye, mistrustfully.

[2] **lowrd:** scowled.

[3] **each where:** everywhere.

[4] **lattis:** lattice, which is also called a "jalousie," a word just then coming into the English language from the Italian *gelosia.* A jealous person might spy through a jalousie.

[5] **Next:** following.

[6] **languor:** languishing.

[7] **ill:** badly.

[8] **drerihed:** dreariness.

[9] **tosse:** brandish.

[10] **embost:** driven to extremity; driven into the woods; foaming at the mouth.

[11] **lompish:** lumpish, dejected.

She chearfull fresh and full of joyaunce glad,
As if no sorrow she ne felt ne dread;
That evill[1] matched paire they seemd to bee:
An angry Waspe th'one in a viall had,
Th'other in hers an hony-lady Bee;
Thus marched these six couples forth in faire degree.

19   After all these there marcht a most faire Dame,
Led of two grysie villeins,[2] th'one *Despight*,
The other cleped *Cruelty* by name:
She dolefull Lady, like a dreary Spright,
Cald by strong charmes out of eternall night,
Had Deathes owne ymage figurd in her face,
Full of sad signes, fearfull to living sight,
Yet in that horror shewd a seemely grace,
And with her feeble feete did move a comely[3] pace.

20   Her brest all naked, as nett[4] yvory,
Without adorne[5] of gold or silver bright,
Wherewith the Craftesman[6] wonts it beautify,
Of her dew honour was despoyled quight,
And a wide wound therein (O ruefull sight)
Entrenched deep with knyfe accursed[7] keene,
Yet freshly bleeding forth her fainting spright,
(The worke of cruell hand) was to be seene,
That dyde in sanguine red her skin all snowy cleene.

21   At that wide orifice her trembling hart
Was drawne forth, and in silver basin layd,
Quite through transfixed[8] with a deadly dart,
And in her blood yet steeming fresh embayd:[9]
And those two villeins, which her steps upstayd,
When her weake feete could scarcely her sustaine,

---

[1] **evill:** badly.

[2] **grysie:** grisly; gray; **villeins:** serfs; base-minded wretches.

[3] **comely:** decent; seemly.

[4] **nett:** pure.

[5] **adorne:** adornment.

[6] **Craftesman:** crafter of jewelry.

[7] **Entrenched:** cut deeply (a Spenserian neologism); **accursed:** by means of magic spells.

[8] **transfixed:** pierced.

[9] **embayd:** steeped.

And fading vitall powres gan to fade,
Her forward still with torture did constraine,
And evermore encreased her consuming paine.[1]

22   Next after her, the winged God him selfe[2]
Came riding on a Lion ravenous,
Taught to obay the menage[3] of that Elfe,
That man and beast with powre imperious
Subdeweth to his kingdome tyrannous:
His blindfold eies he bad a while unbinde,
That his proud spoile of that same dolorous
Faire Dame he might behold in perfect kinde,[4]
Which seene, he much rejoyced in his cruell minde.

23   Of which ful prowd, him selfe up rearing hye,
He looked round about with sterne disdayne;
And did survay his goodly company:
And marshalling the evill ordered trayne,
With that the darts which his right hand did straine,[5]
Full dreadfully he shooke that all did quake,
And clapt on hye his coulourd winges twaine,
That all his many[6] it affraide did make:
Tho blinding him againe, his way he forth did take.

24   Behinde him was *Reproch, Repentaunce, Shame;*
Reproch the first, *Shame* next, *Repent* behinde:
Repentaunce feeble, sorowfull, and lame:
Reproch despightful, carelesse, and unkinde;
Shame most ill favourd, bestiall, and blinde:
Shame lowrd, *Repentaunce* sigh'd, *Reproch* did scould;
Reproch sharpe stings, *Repentaunce* whips entwinde,
Shame burning brond-yrons[7] in her hand did hold:
All three to each unlike, yet all made in one mould.[8]

---

[1] Like Malbecco, Amoret has become a visual emblem of her own state of mind.

[2] I.e., Cupid.

[3] **menage:** manège, the handling and training of horses.

[4] **kinde:** manner, sort.

[5] **With that:** whereupon; **straine:** grip.

[6] **many:** company.

[7] **brond-yrons:** a neologism, perhaps meaning "branding irons," but perhaps, as at VI.viii.10.4, meaning "sword."

[8] The constantly reordered repetition of the three figures' names enacts the bewildering and unrelenting manner in which reproach (and self-reproach), repentance, and shame can assault someone who is in love.

25   And after them a rude confused rout[1]
          Of persons flockt, whose names is hard to read:
          Emongst them was sterne *Strife,* and *Anger* stout,
          Unquiet *Care,* and fond *Unthriftyhead,*
          Lewd *Losse of Time,* and *Sorrow* seeming dead,
          Inconstant *Chaunge,* and false *Disloyalty,*
          Consuming *Riotise,*[2] and guilty *Dread*
          Of heavenly vengeaunce, faint *Infirmity,*
     Vile *Poverty,* and lastly *Death* with infamy.

26   There were full many moe like maladies,
          Whose names and natures I note readen well;
          So many moe, as there be phantasies
          In wavering wemens witt, that none can tell,[3]
          Or paines in love, or punishments in hell;
          All which disguized marcht in masking[4] wise,
          About the chamber by the Damozell,[5]
          And then returned, having marched thrise,
     Into the inner rowme, from whence they first did rise.[6]

27   So soone as they were in, the dore streight way
          Fast locked, driven with that stormy blast,
          Which first it opened; nothing did remayne.
          Then the brave Maid,[7] which al this while was plast,
          In secret shade, and saw both first and last,
          Issewed forth, and went unto the dore,
          To enter in, but fownd it locked fast:
          It vaine she thought with rigorous uprore[8]
     For to efforce, when charmes had closed it afore.

28   Where force might not availe, there sleights and art
          She cast to use, both fitt for hard emprize;[9]
          For thy from that same rowme not to depart
          Till morrow next, shee did her selfe avize,

---

[1] The experience of love has degenerated into utter confusion.

[2] *Riotise:* riotousness.

[3] I.e., too many for anyone to count. Cf. the description of Alma's wavering wit at II.ix.50–52 and of Britomart's constant mind at III.i.19. See Introduction, 5d.

[4] **masking:** masquing, of a masque.

[5] **the Damozell:** either Amoret or Britomart—and the ambiguity is significant.

[6] **rise:** issue.

[7] **the brave Maid:** Britomart.

[8] **rigorous uprore:** vehement turbulence; boisterous shaking.

[9] **emprize:** enterprise, undertaking.

When that same Maske againe should forth arize.
The morrowe next appeard with joyous cheare,
Calling men to their daily exercize,
Then she, as morrow fresh, her selfe did reare
Out of her secret stand,[1] that day for to outweare.

29   All that day she outwore in wandering,
      And gazing on that Chambers ornament,
      Till that againe the second evening
      Her covered with her sable vestiment,
      Wherewith the worlds faire beautie she hath blent:[2]
      Then when the second watch[3] was almost past,
      That brasen[4] dore flew open, and in went
      Bold *Britomart,* as she had late forecast,
Nether of ydle showes, nor of false charmes aghast.

30   So soone as she was entred, rownd about
      Shee cast her eies, to see what was become
      Of all those persons, which she saw without:
      But lo, they streight were vanisht all and some,[5]
      Ne living wight she saw in all that roome,
      Save that same woefull Lady, both whose hands
      Were bounden fast, that did her ill become,
      And her small waste girt rownd with yron bands,
Unto a brasen pillour,[6] by the which she stands.

31   And her before the vile Enchaunter[7] sate,
      Figuring straunge characters of his art,[8]
      With living blood he those characters wrate,

---

[1] **stand:** hiding place; post.

[2] **blent:** obscured—i.e., she has covered her beauty (the world's best) with a black cloak, or she has shut out the beauty of the world (specifically, the room) with a black cloak.

[3] **second watch:** the period between nine o'clock and midnight.

[4] **brasen:** as strong as brass, though made of iron (xi.54.7, xii.3.3—and the pageant exited the same way it entered, according to xii.26.9).

[5] **all and some:** one and all.

[6] Amoret is bound to the phallus that she fears—taking "phallus" to mean both the erect penis and, in the more symbolic sense, the sum total of masculine power, including the power to define the world through words.

[7] **the vile Enchaunter:** Busirane.

[8] Cf. Merlin, who is also an "Enchaunter" and whom Britomart sees "writing straunge characters in the grownd" (iii.17.1, 14.8). Busirane is not to be equated with either Merlin or Spenser, but clearly Spenser uses him to comment upon the relationship between authorship, authority, enchantment, and coercion.

Dreadfully dropping from her[1] dying hart,
Seeming transfixed with a cruell dart,
And all perforce to make her him to love.
Ah who can love the worker of her smart?[2]
A thousand charmes he formerly did prove;
Yet thousand charmes could not her stedfast hart remove.

32   Soone as that virgin knight he saw in place,[3]
His wicked bookes[4] in hast he overthrew,
Not caring his long labours to deface,
And fiercely running to that Lady[5] trew,
A murdrous knife out of his pocket drew,
The which he thought, for villeinous despight,
In her tormented bodie to embrew:[6]
But the stout Damzell to him leaping light,
His cursed hand withheld, and maistered his might.

33   From her, to whom his fury first he ment,[7]
The wicked weapon rashly[8] he did wrest,
And turning to the next[9] his fell intent,
Unwares it strooke into her snowie chest,
That litle drops empurpled her faire brest.
Exceeding wroth therewith the virgin grew,
Albe the wound were nothing deepe imprest,[10]
And fiercely forth her mortall blade she drew,
To give him the reward for such vile outrage dew.

34   So mightily she smote him, that to ground
He fell halfe dead; next stroke him should have slaine,
Had not the Lady, which by him stood bound,

---

[1] **her:** Amoret's.

[2] The answer, of course, is, "Everyone." In using an intentionally cruel and unscrupulous magician to stand in for the unintentionally cruel and conscience-stricken Scudamour, Spenser is examining the blurred line that separates ordinary love from sadomasochism.

[3] **in place:** in the vicinity.

[4] **wicked bookes:** books of spells.

[5] **that Lady:** Amoret.

[6] **embrew:** imbrue, stain with blood; plunge.

[7] I.e., from Amoret, to whom he first directed his fury.

[8] **rashly:** hastily.

[9] **the next:** Britomart.

[10] **nothing deepe imprest:** not at all deeply imprinted. Busirane has not succeeded in writing deeply into Britomart's heart.

Dernly[1] unto her called to abstaine,
From doing him to dy. For else her paine
Should be remedilesse, sith none but hee,
Which wrought it, could the same recure[2] againe.
Therewith she stayd her hand, loth stayd to bee;
For life she him envyde, and long'd revenge to see.

35   And to him said, "Thou wicked man, whose meed
  For so huge mischiefe, and vile villany
  Is death, or if that ought doe death exceed,
  Be sure, that nought may save thee from to dy,
  But if that thou this Dame doe presently
  Restore unto her health,[3] and former state;
  This doe and live, els dye undoubtedly."
  He glad of life, that lookt for[4] death but late,
Did yield him selfe right willing to prolong his date.[5]

36   And rising up, gan streight to overlooke[6]
  Those cursed leaves, his charmes back to reverse;[7]
  Full dreadfull thinges out of that balefull booke
  He red, and measur'd many a sad[8] verse,
  That horrour gan the virgins hart to perse,
  And her faire locks up stared[9] stiffe on end,
  Hearing him those same bloody lynes reherse;[10]
  And all the while he red, she did extend
Her sword high over him, if ought he did offend.[11]

37   Anon she gan perceive the house to quake,
  And all the dores to rattle round about;
  Yet all that did not her dismaied make,

---

[1] **Dernly:** dismally; secretly; earnestly.

[2] **recure:** heal.

[3] Imagine a dash before "whose"(1) and after "exceed"(3): "You wicked man—who deserve death or worse, if there is anything worse—be sure that nothing will save you from death unless you restore this woman to her health."

[4] **lookt for:** expected.

[5] **date:** term of life.

[6] **overlooke:** look over.

[7] **reverse:** thus unwinding a charm that has been wound up, to use the terminology employed by Macbeth's witches (*Macbeth*, 1.3.35).

[8] **measur'd:** read, presumably with grave emphasis upon the meter; **sad:** solemn.

[9] **up stared:** stood up.

[10] **reherse:** go over.

[11] **if ought he did offend:** in case he said anything wrong; whenever he did anything wrong.

Nor slack her threatfull hand for daungers dout,
But still with stedfast eye and courage stout,
Abode to weet, what end[1] would come of all.
At last that mightie chaine, which round about
Her tender waste was wound, adowne gan fall,
And that great brasen pillour broke in peeces small.

38   The cruell steele, which thrild her dying hart,
Fell softly forth, as of his owne accord,
And the wyde wound, which lately did dispart[2]
Her bleeding brest, and riven bowels gor'd,
Was closed up, as it had not beene sor'd,[3]
And every part to safety full sownd,[4]
As[5] she were never hurt, was soone restor'd:
Tho when she felt her selfe to be unbownd,
And perfect hole,[6] prostrate she fell unto the grownd.

39   Before faire *Britomart*, she fell prostrate,
Saying, "Ah noble knight, what worthy meede
Can wretched Lady, quitt[7] from wofull state,
Yield you in lieu of this your gracious deed;[8]
Your vertue selfe her owne reward shall breed,[9]
Even[10] immortall prayse, and glory wyde
Which I your vassall, by your prowesse freed,
Shall through the world make to be notifyde,
And goodly well advaunce that goodly well was tryde."[11]

40   But *Britomart* uprearing her from grownd,
Said, "Gentle Dame, reward enough I weene
For many labours more, then I have found,

---

[1] **Abode:** waited; **end:** result.

[2] **dispart:** divide.

[3] **sor'd:** pained.

[4] **full sownd:** fully healed.

[5] **As:** as if.

[6] Goldberg discusses the odd pun: she is now perfectly whole; or she is now a perfect hole, vaginally at her husband's service (78–9).

[7] **quitt:** released.

[8] **in lieu of:** to equal; as payment for. Amoret is vastly relieved and grateful, but she is also worried: she believes she has been rescued by a male knight, and the time-honored reward for a man who has saved one's virtue is to give it to him. Cf. IV.i.5–8.

[9] I.e., your virtue itself will breed its own reward.

[10] **Even:** that is to say (OED adv 8).

[11] **advaunce:** extol; **that:** that which (Britomart's prowess and virtue); **tryde:** proved through being tested.

This, that in safetie now I have you seene,
And meane[1] of your deliverance have beene:
Henceforth faire Lady comfort to you take,
And put away remembraunce of late teene;
In sted thereof know, that your loving Make,[2]
Hath no lesse griefe endured for your gentle sake."

41   She much was cheard to heare him mentiond,
Whom of all living wightes she loved best.
Then laid the noble Championesse strong hond
Upon th'enchaunter, which had her[3] distrest
So sore, and with foule outrages opprest:
With that great chaine, wherewith not long ygoe
He bound that pitteous Lady prisoner, now relest,[4]
Himselfe she bound, more worthy to be so,
And captive with her led to wretchednesse and wo.

42   Returning back,[5] those goodly rowmes, which erst
She saw so rich and royally arayd,
Now vanisht utterly, and cleane subverst[6]
She found, and all their glory quite decayd,
That sight of such a chaunge her much dismayd.
Thenceforth descending to that perlous Porch,
Those dreadfull flames she also found delayd,[7]
And quenched quite, like a consumed torch,
That erst all entrers[8] wont so cruelly to scorch.

43a   At last she came unto the place, where late
She left Sir *Scudamour* in great distresse,
Twixt dolour and despight halfe desperate,
Of his loves succour, of his owne redresse,[9]
And of the hardie *Britomarts* successe:
There on the cold earth him now thrown she found,

---

[1] **meane:** the means.

[2] **Make:** mate.

[3] **her:** until we reach line 6, this pronoun is nicely ambiguous.

[4] The line has an extra metrical foot—making her release somehow superfluous? Or an overflowing boon?

[5] **Returning back:** i.e., retracing her former path through the house.

[6] **subverst:** razed.

[7] **delayd:** quenched.

[8] **entrers:** incomers.

[9] **redresse:** aid (his to Amoret); reparation (Busirane's to him, after having stolen his bridal property).

> In wilfull[1] anguish, and dead heavinesse,
> And to him cald; whose voices knowen sound
> Soone as he heard, himself he reared light from ground.

44a   There did he see, that[2] most on earth him joyd,
>   His dearest love, the comfort of his dayes,
>   Whose too long absence him had sore annoyd,
>   And wearied his life with dull delayes:
>   Straight he upstarted from the loathed layes,[3]
>   And to her ran with hasty egernesse,
>   Like as a Deare, that greedily embayes[4]
>   In the coole soile,[5] after long thirstinesse,
> Which he in chace endured hath, now nigh breathlesse.

45a   Lightly he clipt[6] her twixt his armes twaine,
>   And streightly[7] did embrace her body bright,
>   Her body, late the prison of sad paine,
>   Now the sweet lodge of love and deare delight:
>   But she faire Lady overcommen quight
>   Of huge affection, did in pleasure melt,[8]
>   And in sweete ravishment[9] pourd out her spright:
>   No word they spake, nor earthly thing they felt,
> But like two senceles stocks[10] in long embracement dwelt.

46a   Had ye them seene, ye would have surely thought,
>   That they had beene that faire *Hermaphrodite*,
>   Which that rich *Romane* of white marble wrought,[11]

---

[1] **wilfull:** the word implies that at some level Scudamour may even be enjoying his own grief by now; at the very least, the word strengthens the idea that he has utterly given in to despair when he should be taking up arms against it.

[2] **that:** that which, i.e., Amoret.

[3] **layes:** ground.

[4] **embayes:** plunges.

[5] **soile:** pool of water.

[6] **clipt:** clasped.

[7] **streightly:** tightly.

[8] The "huge affection" and melting suggest the mutual pleasure of orgasm.

[9] **ravishment:** ecstasy—with the peripheral hint that her being taken away from herself is psychologically dangerous as well as psychologically pleasurable.

[10] **stocks:** sticks of wood.

[11] No particular Roman or statue has been identified, although Romans were fond of putting statues of Priapus—with a gigantically erect penis—in their private gardens and baths. Here, the narrator is comparing Amoret's and Scudamour's close embrace to a statue of an hermaphrodite, a person with genitalia of both sexes. The image comes from a Greek myth in which the nymph Salmacis loved the youth Hermaphroditus

And in his costly Bath causd to bee site:
So seemd those two, as growne together quite,
That *Britomart* halfe envying their blesse,[1]
Was much empassiond in her gentle sprite,
And to her selfe oft wisht like happinesse,
In vaine she wisht, that fate n'ould[2] let her yet possesse.

47a   Thus doe those lovers with sweet countervayle,[3]
Each other of loves bitter fruit despoile.[4]
But now my teme[5] begins to faint and fayle,
All woxen weary of their journall[6] toyle:
Therefore I will their sweatie yokes assoyle,[7]
At this same furrowes[8] end, till a new day:
And ye faire Swayns,[9] after your long turmoyle,
Now cease your worke, and at your pleasure play;
Now cease your worke; to morrow is an holy day.

Finis.

[The 1590 edition, which was published when Spenser had finished only Books One through Three, ends with the above stanzas, 43a–47a. The 1596 edition, which consists of Books One through Six, omits stanzas 43a through 47a above and substitutes the following three stanzas, 43b through 45b, to provide a transition into Book Four.]

---

so fervently that she asked the gods never to separate them—upon which the gods made their two bodies into one (Ovid, *Metamorphoses,* 4.285–388). Another Greek source is Plato's *Symposium,* in which the character Aristophanes says that humans originally had two heads, four arms, four legs, and two sets of genitals. Some had two male sets of genitals, some two female, and some a set of each. But because this anatomy made humans strong enough to challenge the gods, the gods divided each human in two. Ever after, each human searches for his or her half, and upon finding that half, falls in love. The natural inclination to love someone of the same sex or of the opposite sex is determined by the sex with whom one was originally joined in one body (Plato 190b–193e).

[1] **blesse:** bliss.

[2] **n'ould:** would not.

[3] **countervayle:** reciprocation.

[4] **despoile:** plunder.

[5] The georgic metaphor is a common one, comparing the poet's labor to that of a farmer who directs a team of oxen.

[6] **woxen:** grown; **journall:** daily.

[7] **assoyle:** release, with overtones of the meaning "absolve."

[8] The furrows offer a visual analogy for parallel lines of verse.

[9] Amoret and Scudamour suddenly become georgic figures.

1596 Ending

43b More easie issew now, then entrance late
 She found: for now that fained dreadfull flame,[1]
 Which chokt the porch of that enchaunted gate,
 And passage bard to all, that thither came,
 Was vanisht quite, as it were not the same,
 And gave her leave at pleasure[2] forth to passe.
 Th'Enchaunter selfe, which all that fraud did frame,
 To have efforst[3] the love of that faire lasse,
Seeing his worke now wasted deepe engrieved was.

44b But when the victoresse arrived there,
 Where late she left the pensife[4] *Scudamore,*
 With her owne trusty Squire, both full of feare,
 Neither of them she found where she them lore:[5]
 Thereat her noble hart was stonisht sore;
 But most faire *Amoret,* whose gentle spright
 Now gan to feede on hope, which she before
 Conceived had, to see her owne deare knight,
Being thereof beguyld[6] was fild with new affright.

45b But he[7] sad man, when he had long in drede
 Awayted there for *Britomarts* returne,
 Yet saw her not nor signe of her good speed,[8]
 His expectation to despaire did turne,
 Misdeeming[9] sure that her those flames did burne;
 And therefore gan advize with her old Squire,[10]

---

[1] **fained dreadfull flame:** imaginary flame; flame imagined to be dreadful.

[2] **at pleasure:** whenever she wished.

[3] **efforst:** compelled.

[4] **pensife:** apprehensive; sad.

[5] **lore:** left.

[6] **beguyld:** tricked; cheated; enchanted.

[7] **he:** Scudamour.

[8] **speed:** success.

[9] **Misdeeming:** mistakenly believing.

[10] **advize:** consult; **her old Squire:** Glauce.

Who her deare nourslings losse no lesse did mourne,
Thence to depart for further aide t'enquire:
Where let them wend at will, whilest here I doe respire.[1]

---

[1] **respire:** take a breather; rest from exertion. Spenser's deletion of the neater ending of Book Three in favor of an open ending must make us ask about his attitudes toward endings in general, as Goldberg argues (*Endlesse*, passim). Yet the original ending can be seen as less than perfectly neat, given that it makes Amoret's and Scudamour's transition from self-tormenting anxiety to utter happiness uncomfortably abrupt (Stephens, 25–46). At the very least, the deletion of the original ending allows Spenser to develop Britomart's and Amoret's relationship. Britomart saw Malecasta as someone monstrously unlike herself (i.62–3), but Busirane's attempt to get her to avoid Amoret for similar reasons is defeated, and the cantos of Book Four in which Britomart and Amoret support each other are the fruit of that defeat.

THE FAERIE

QVEENE.

Difpofed into twelue bookes,

Fashioning

XII. Morall vertues.

LONDON
Printed for VVilliam Ponfonbie.

1 5 9 6.

Title page to the 1596 edition of *The Faerie Queene* (STC 23082)

TO
THE MOST HIGH,
MIGHTIE
And
MAGNIFICENT
EMPRESSE RENOVV-
MED FOR PIETIE, VER-
TVE, AND ALL GRATIOVS
GOVERNMENT ELIZABETH BY
THE GRACE OF GOD QVEENE
OF ENGLAND FRAVNCE AND
IRELAND AND OF VIRGI-
NIA, DEFENDOVR OF THE
FAITH, &c. HER MOST
HVMBLE SERVAVNT
EDMVND SPENSER
DOTH IN ALL HV-
MILITIE DEDI-
CATE, PRE-
SENT
AND CONSECRATE THESE
HIS LABOVRS TO LIVE
VVITH THE ETERNI-
TIE OF HER
FAME.

THE FOVRTH
BOOKE OF THE
FAERIE QUEENE.
Containing
The Legend of CAMBEL and TELAMOND,[1]
OR
OF FRIENDSHIP.[2]

1   The rugged[3] forhead that with grave foresight
       Welds kingdomes causes, and affaires of state,[4]
       My looser rimes (I wote) doth sharply wite,[5]
       For praising love, as I have done of late,
       And magnifying lovers deare debate;[6]

---

[1] **Cambel:** the name comes from the character Cambal (or Cambalo) in Chaucer's *Squire's Tale;* Spenser recounts, adapts, and extends Chaucer's version (beginning in ii.32); **Telamond:** everywhere else in Book Four, this character is called Triamond. It is useful, however, to know that Spenser was originally considering a name meaning "perfect world" (from the Greek τέλειος and the Latin *mundus;* see Roche 1964, 16–7).

[2] **FRIENDSHIP:** a civic virtue as well as a personal one, friendship was thought of as keeping the body politic united. McCoy observes that friendship was "the virtue the Order of the Garter was supposed to inculcate in its members" (McCoy, 134).

[3] **rugged:** furrowed, as in a frown.

[4] **Welds:** wields; manages. These lines most likely refer to criticism made of the first installment of *The Faerie Queene* by William Cecil, Lord Burghley, who was Queen Elizabeth's Lord High Treasurer and trusted advisor. He was also, as McCabe points out, "one of the most senior members of the Order of the Garter" (208). Burghley would have learned about Spenser's poem

by 1589, when Spenser traveled from Ireland to England and was allowed to read portions of his poem to the Queen at court. The first three books of the poem, published less than a year later, had as an appendix 17 sonnets dedicated to powerful people; the second of these sonnets is addressed, "*To the right honourable the Lo. Burleigh Lo. high Threasurer of England*":

> TO you right noble Lord, whose carefull brest
>   To menage of most grave affaires is bent,
>   And on whose mightie shoulders most doth rest
>   The burdein of this kingdomes governement,
> As the wide compasse of the firmament,
>   On *Atlas* mighty shoulders is upstayd;
>   Unfitly I these ydle rimes present,
>   The labor of lost time, and wit unstayd
> Yet if their deeper sence be inly wayd,
>   And the dim vele, with which from commune vew
>   Their fairer parts are hid, aside be layd,
>   Perhaps not vaine they may appeare to you.
> Such as they be, vouchsafe them to receave,
>   And wipe their faults out of your censure grave.

[5] **looser:** too loose; lightweight or licentious; **wite:** impute blame to; criticize.

[6] **magnifying:** extolling; dilating upon; **deare debate:** loving or flirtatious arguments; emotionally costly arguments.

247

By which fraile youth is oft to follie led,
Through false allurement of that pleasing baite,
That better were in vertues discipled,[1]
Then with vaine poemes weeds[2] to have their fancies fed.

2   Such ones ill judge of love, that cannot love,[3]
Ne in their frosen hearts feele kindly flame:
For thy they ought not thing unknowne reprove,
Ne naturall affection faultlesse blame,[4]
For fault of few that have abusd the same.
For it[5] of honor and all vertue is
The roote, and brings forth glorious flowres of fame,
That crowne true lovers with immortall blis,
The meed of them that love, and do not live amisse.

3   Which who so list looke backe to former ages,
And call to count[6] the things that then were donne,
Shall find, that all the workes of those wise sages,
And brave exploits which great Heroes[7] wonne,
In love were either ended or begunne:
Witnesse the father of Philosophie,[8]
Which to his *Critias*,[9] shaded oft from sunne,
Of love full manie lessons did apply,
The which these Stoicke censours[10] cannot well deny.

---

[1] **discipled:** taught; disciplined. Sidney had praised poetry for teaching morals through its sweet fictions; others criticized poetry for not being direct enough in its moralizing (*Defence,* 100–11). In "The Letter to Raleigh," Spenser declares that his aim with this poem is "to fashion a gentleman or noble person in vertuous and gentle discipline" ("The Letter to Raleigh," p. 451).

[2] **weeds:** clothing; undesirable plants.

[3] I.e., those who cannot love make poor judges of love. As Hamilton points out in his note, the criticism of Burghley is perhaps exaggerated, given his long and apparently strong marriage to Mildred Cecil.

[4] Either "cannot blame natural and [therefore] faultless affection" or "cannot faultlessly blame natural affection."

[5] **it:** love.

[6] **call to count:** bring up for consideration.

[7] Heroes were traditionally thought to be capable of great love, not only of persons, but of the ideals that prompted heroic deeds.

[8] **father of Philosophie:** Socrates.

[9] *Critias:* a mistake for Phaedrus, with whom Socrates discussed the philosophy of love in the shade of a tree (Plato, *Phaedrus,* 230b).

[10] **Stoicke censours:** those who attempt to banish love in themselves and criticize it in others.

4   To such therefore I do not sing at all,[1]
            But to that sacred Saint my soveraigne Queene,
            In whose chast breast all bountie[2] naturall,
            And treasures of true love enlocked beene,
            Bove all her sexe that ever yet was seene;
            To her I sing of love, that loveth best,
            And best is lov'd of all alive I weene:
            To her this song most fitly is addrest,
        The Queene of love, and Prince of peace[3] from heaven blest.

5   Which that she may the better deigne to heare,
            Do thou dred infant, *Venus* dearling dove,[4]
            From her high spirit chase imperious feare,[5]
            And use of awfull[6] Majestie remove:
            In sted thereof with drops of melting love,
            Deawd with ambrosiall kisses, by thee[7] gotten
            From thy sweete smyling mother from above,
            Sprinckle her heart, and haughtie courage[8] soften,
        That she may hearke to love, and reade[9] this lesson often.

[1] With a sweeping gesture, the narrator sets Burghley and other critics aside.

[2] **bountie:** excellence; generosity.

[3] **Queene of love:** this title aligns Elizabeth with Venus; **Prince of peace:** this title aligns Elizabeth with the messiah whose coming is foretold in Isa. 9.6.

[4] I.e., Cupid.

[5] **imperious feare:** majesty that makes those around her afraid; the fear felt by a queen (presumably fear of hearing too much about—or experiencing—love).

[6] **awfull:** awe-inspiring.

[7] **thee:** Cupid.

[8] **her:** Queen Elizabeth's; **haughtie courage:** lofty heart, emotions, or bravery; emotional remoteness.

[9] **reade:** almost every meaning of this word comes into play: is Spenser asking his queen to peruse his poem, learn its lessons, discern its truth, interpret it for those around her, or promulgate the lessons it teaches? If her breast is the source of "all bountie naturall" and yet she teaches or promulgates the lessons that she has learned from Cupid through Spenser's poem, who is ventriloquizing though whom? Furthermore, exactly what is this lesson? Hamilton interprets it as "Cupid's lesson, which is not to fear love," but it is difficult to forget the horrific form that Cupid's lesson took in the final canto of the previous book.

Canto One

Fayre Britomart saves Amoret,
Duessa¹ discord breedes
Twixt Scudamour and Blandamour.²
Their fight and warlike deedes.

1   Of lovers sad calamities of old,
          Full many piteous stories doe remaine,
          But none more piteous ever was ytold,
          Then that of *Amorets* hart-binding chaine,
          And this of *Florimels* unworthie³ paine:
          The deare compassion of whose bitter fit
          My softened heart so sorely doth constraine,⁴
          That I with teares full oft doe pittie it,
      And oftentimes doe wish it never had bene writ.⁵

2   For from the time that *Scudamour* her bought⁶
          In perilous fight, she never joyed day,
          A perilous fight when he with force her brought

---

¹ **Duessa:** a character who does not appear
in Book Three but is important for Books
One, Two, Four, and Five. She first appears
in I.ii.13. Her name means "double being"
(Italian *due* + Latin *esse*); she usually goes
disguised as a beautiful woman (I.ii.35),
though she is actually a bald hag with with-
ered breasts, rotten gums, one foot like an
eagle's claw, the other like a bear's paw, and
a fox's tail covered in dung (I.viii.46–48). At
various points in the poem, she represents
deceit, self-delusion, witchcraft, the Whore
of Babylon in the Book of Revelation, the
Roman Catholic Church, and Mary, Queen
of Scots. In Book One, Duessa seduces
Redcrosse into believing she is a fit com-
panion for him, which enables her to lead
him into various types of error. Redcrosse
finally sees her for what she is (I.viii.46–48),
but in Book Two, Archimago uses her to
trick Guyon into believing temporarily that
she has been raped by Redcrosse
(II.i.8–30).

² **Scudamour:** see III.vi.53 and notes;
Blandamour: the name means "flattering
lover" (Latin *blandus* + *amor*).

³ **unworthie:** undeserved.

⁴ **constraine:** press upon; distress.

⁵ As at III.viii.1 and III.viii.43.8, the narra-
tor's tearful distress over Florimell's tor-
ments is humorously undercut by his relish
in inventing those torments. The poem asks
us to consider what distinguishes this relish
from that of the torturer Busirane (see
III.xii.31.2.n.).

⁶ **her:** Amoret; **bought:** freed by paying a
price; redeemed; purchased. See Canto Ten
for Scudamour's account of his fight for,
and abduction of, the reluctant Amoret.

From twentie Knights, that did him all assay:
Yet fairely[1] well he did them all dismay:
And with great glorie both the shield of love,
And eke the Ladie selfe he brought away,
Whom having wedded as did him behove,[2]
A new unknowen mischiefe did from him remove.

3   For that same vile Enchauntour *Busyran*,
      The very selfe same day that she was wedded,
      Amidst the bridale feast, whilest every man
      Surcharg'd with wine, were heedlesse and ill hedded,
      All bent to mirth before the bride was bedded,[3]
      Brought in that mask of love which late was showen:[4]
      And there the Ladie ill of friends bestedded,[5]
      By way of sport, as oft in maskes is knowen,
Conveyed quite away to living wight unknowen.

4   Seven moneths he so her kept in bitter smart,
      Because his sinfull lust she would not serve,
      Untill such time as noble *Britomart*
      Released her, that else was like to sterve,[6]
      Through cruell knife that her deare heart did kerve.[7]
      And now she is with her upon the way,

---

[1] **fairely:** very; completely.

[2] **behove:** befit, be appropritate for; be useful for.

[3] While the wedding guests were still celebrating, it was the custom for the bride to be ceremoniously conducted to the nuptial chamber, put into her nightgown, and arranged in bed to await the groom—to the accompaniment of prayers or bawdy jokes, as the case might be. The next morning, the bloodied wedding sheets were sometimes displayed from a window to prove that consummation had taken place.

[4] See III.xii.Arg.1.n. for information about the custom of presenting masques at weddings. In terms of a logical, chronological plot, Busirane brings his masque to Amoret and Scudamour's wedding, abducts the bride in earnest rather than in jest, and then forces her to watch repeated performances of his masque while imprisoned in his house. Allegorically, however, one could say that Amoret's anxieties about giving herself in marriage are what remove her psychologically from the wedding celebration and trap her inside her own mind, which compulsively replays horrifying fantasies.

[5] I.e., badly looked after by her friends. This part of Amoret's story is appropriate for the Book of Friendship.

[6] **sterve:** die a lingering death.

[7] **kerve:** cut; slice. For Britomart's rescue of Amoret, see III.xii.

Marching in lovely wise, that[1] could deserve
No spot of blame, though spite did oft assay
To blot her with dishonor of so faire a pray.[2]

5   Yet should it be a pleasant tale, to tell
       The diverse usage and demeanure daint,[3]
       That each to other made, as oft befell.
       For *Amoret* right fearefull was and faint,
       Lest she with blame her honor should attaint,[4]
       That everie word did tremble as she spake,
       And everie looke was coy, and wondrous quaint,[5]
       And everie limbe that touched her did quake:
       Yet could she not but curteous countenance[6] to her make.

6   For well she wist, as true it was indeed,
       That her lives Lord and patrone[7] of her health
       Right well deserved as his duefull[8] meed,
       Her love, her service,[9] and her utmost wealth.
       All is his justly, that all freely dealth:[10]
       Nathlesse her honor dearer then her life,
       She sought to save, as thing reserv'd from stealth;[11]
       Die had she lever with Enchanters knife,
       Then to be false in love, profest a virgine wife.

---

[1] **lovely:** affectionate; **that:** who, i.e., Britomart.

[2] **pray:** booty. Since she looks like a male knight, spiteful people who see her carrying Amoret on her horse spread the rumor that the two of them are engaging in premarital or extramarital sex.

[3] **diverse usage:** different conduct (as becomes evident in 5.4–5 and 7.1–5, this phrase means that Amoret's conduct toward Britomart differed from Britomart's conduct toward Amoret); **demeanure daint:** delightful, careful, or fastidious demeanor.

[4] **attaint:** taint; convict.

[5] **quaint:** prim; ingenious—though one cannot help remembering that for Chaucer, "quainte," meaning "clever," was a homonym for "queinte," meaning "a woman's external genitals" or "cunt" (*The Miller's Tale*, 89–90). Amoret is, after all, "perfect hole" (III.xii.38.9 and note).

[6] **countenance:** expression.

[7] **patrone:** lord; protector.

[8] **duefull:** due, rightful.

[9] **service:** servitude; sexual favors. Cf. III.xii.39.4.n.

[10] **dealth:** deals out, gives. Believing she has been rescued by a man, Amoret has a moral dilemma: the protocols of medieval chivalric romance demand that she reward her rescuer by giving herself to him, yet she is already married—and still a virgin, to boot.

[11] **reserv'd from stealth:** preserved from being stolen.

7 Thereto her feare was made so much the greater
  Through fine abusion[1] of that Briton mayd:
  Who for to hide her fained sex[2] the better,
  And maske[3] her wounded mind, both did and sayd
  Full many things so doubtfull to be wayd,[4]
  That well she[5] wist not what by them to gesse,
  For other whiles to her she purpos[6] made
  Of love, and otherwhiles[7] of lustfulnesse,
That much she[8] feard his mind would grow to some excesse.

8 His will[9] she feard; for him she surely thought
  To be a man, such as indeed he seemed,
  And much the more, by that[10] he lately wrought,
  When her from deadly thraldome he redeemed,
  For which no service[11] she too much esteemed,
  Yet dread of shame, and doubt of fowle dishonor
  Made her not yeeld so much, as due she deemed.
  Yet *Britomart* attended duly on her,
As well became a knight, and did to her all honor.[12]

9 It so befell one evening, that they came
  Unto a Castell, lodged there to bee,
  Where many a knight, and many a lovely Dame
  Was then assembled, deeds of armes to see:
  Amongst all which was none more faire then shee,[13]
  That many of them mov'd to eye her sore.[14]

---

[1] **fine abusion:** clever or subtle deceit, misuse, or shameful treatment.

[2] **fained sex:** pretended sex, with a pun on the sense "sex she wished she could be."

[3] **maske:** disguise or cover, with a pun on "masque," by which she would represent her mind.

[4] **doubtfull to be wayd:** ambiguous; difficult to judge. In order to maintain her cover, Britomart is deliberately flirting.

[5] **she:** Amoret.

[6] **she:** Britomart; **purpos:** conversation.

[7] **other whiles . . . otherwhiles:** at times . . . at other times.

[8] **she:** Amoret.

[9] **will:** sexual desire.

[10] **that:** that which (referring to "his" manly triumph over Busirane).

[11] **service:** helpful deed; sexual favors.

[12] The feminine rhyme asks us to compare "on her" (with its bawdy overtones) to "honor."

[13] **shee:** Amoret (since no one can see Britomart through her armor).

[14] **sore:** sorely, enviously.

The custome of that place was such, that hee
Which had no love nor lemman there in store,[1]
Should either winne him one, or lye without the dore.[2]

10   Amongst the rest there was a jolly knight,
        Who being asked for his love, avow'd
        That fairest *Amoret* was his by right,
        And offred that to justifie alowd.[3]
        The warlike virgine seeing his so prowd
        And boastfull chalenge, wexed inlie wroth,
        But for the present did her anger shrowd;
        And sayd, her love to lose she was full loth,
    But either he should neither of them have, or both.[4]

11   So foorth they went, and both together giusted;[5]
        But that same younker[6] soone was overthrowne,
        And made repent, that he had rashly lusted
        For thing unlawfull, that was not his owne:
        Yet since he seemed valiant, though unknowne,
        She that[7] no lesse was courteous then stout,
        Cast how to salve, that both the custome showne[8]
        Were kept, and yet that Knight not locked out,[9]
    That seem'd full hard t'accord two things so far in dout.

12   The Seneschall[10] was cal'd to deeme the right,
        Whom she requir'd,[11] that first fayre *Amoret*
        Might be to her allow'd, as to a Knight,
        That did her win and free from chalenge set:
        Which straight to her was yeelded without let.[12]

---

[1] **in store:** at hand.

[2] Unlike most other castles in the poem, this one is not given a specific name. David Lee Miller calls it "the Castle of Compulsory Heterosexuality" (forthcoming).

[3] **alowd:** i.e., to proclaim his rights publicly.

[4] An important critical question is whether Britomart wants Amoret, wants only to free Amoret from being claimed by various people as a tournament prize, or wants to free (or claim) herself through Amoret.

[5] **giusted:** jousted.

[6] **younker:** young man of high rank.

[7] **that:** who.

[8] **showne:** made known.

[9] I.e., Britomart tries to figure out how both to observe the custom of the castle and to allow the knight whom she has defeated to come inside.

[10] **Seneschall:** steward; officer of a household appointed to adjudicate domestic disputes and infractions.

[11] I.e., of whom Britomart requested.

[12] **let:** hindrance.

> Then since that strange Knights love from him was quitted,[1]
> She claim'd that to her selfe, as Ladies det,
> He as a Knight might justly be admitted;[2]
> So none should be out shut, sith all of loves were fitted.[3]

13 With that her glistring helmet she unlaced;
    Which doft, her golden lockes, that were up bound
    Still in a knot, unto her heeles downe traced,[4]
    And like a silken veile in compasse[5] round
    About her backe and all her bodie wound:
    Like as the shining skie in summers night,
    What time[6] the dayes with scorching heat abound,
    Is creasted all with lines of firie light,
That it prodigious[7] seemes in common peoples sight.

14 Such when those Knights and Ladies all about
    Beheld her, all were with amazement smit,
    And every one gan grow in secret dout
    Of this and that, according to each wit:
    Some thought that some enchantment faygned it;
    Some, that *Bellona*[8] in that warlike wise
    To them appear'd, with shield and armour fit;
    Some, that it was a maske[9] of strange disguise:
So diversely each one did sundrie doubts devise.

---

[1] **quitted:** gone.

[2] In claiming Amoret, Britomart claims the reward due to a victorious man, but since the acquisition of that reward still leaves her with "no love nor lemman" (9.8), she claims the male knight, as well. She does not intend to make him her love or leman, but she has made use of the onlookers' sense of heterosexual propriety to satisfy her own sense of military propriety (in that she considers the knight valiant enough to be well treated even though he has lost the match).

[3] **fitted:** provided.

[4] **traced:** passed—though this verb most often indicates the braiding of hair rather than the loosening of it. This is the third time that Britomart has unveiled, revealing her sex; see III.i.42–3 and III.ix.20–24.

[5] **in compasse:** encompassing, surrounding.

[6] **What time:** when.

[7] **prodigious:** portentious; ominous.

[8] *Bellona:* the goddess of battle.

[9] **maske:** masque, costumed performance (see III.xii.Arg.1.n.). It is not entirely clear whether this subset of onlookers thinks that the masque consists of a woman dressing in a man's armor or of a man pulling off his armor to reveal himself dressed and wigged as a woman. What is quite clear is that all of the onlookers feel bewildered.

15   But that young Knight, which through her[1] gentle deed
       Was to that goodly fellowship restor'd,
       Ten thousand thankes did yeeld her for her meed,
       And doubly overcommen, her ador'd:[2]
       So did they all their former strife accord;
       And eke fayre *Amoret* now freed from feare,
       More franke affection did to her afford,
       And to her bed, which she was wont forbeare,
Now freely drew, and found right safe assurance theare.[3]

16   Where all that night they of their loves did treat,[4]
       And hard adventures twixt themselves alone,
       That each the other gan with passion great,
       And griefull pittie privately bemone.[5]
       The morow next so soone as *Titan* shone,
       They both uprose, and to their waies[6] them dight:
       Long wandred they, yet never met with none,
       That to their willes[7] could them direct aright,
Or to them tydings tell, that mote their harts delight.

17   Lo thus they rode, till at the last they spide
       Two armed Knights, that toward them did pace,
       And ech of them had ryding by his side
       A Ladie, seeming in so farre a space,[8]

[1] **young Knight:** the one with whom Britomart jousted for Amoret; **her:** Britomart's.

[2] **ador'd:** the word's religious overtones register the inappropriate swiftness of the knight's falling in love, even though Britomart is an appropriately admirable object of love.

[3] In a world without central heating or inexpensive furniture, almost no one slept alone.

[4] **treat:** converse.

[5] **griefull:** sorrowful. The two women are sharing their hard-luck stories about the emotional pain of searching for their two male beloveds, but the location of the conversation—in bed—and the words "passion" and "privately bemone" illogically but powerfully evoke the idea of two women having sex with each other. Spenser is fond of setting up such conditionally erotic passages, but one could say that this is one of the few bed scenes in the poem about which the readers are asked to be happy. (Hellenore is happy with the satyrs, and Malecasta is at first happy to lie with Britomart, but the narrative does not encourage us to celebrate either event.) The mastery that Britomart has wielded over Amoret disappears for this night, and the two women at least temporarily find what they are seeking in each other.

[6] **waies:** the plural may reflect the fact that although they are traveling with each other (as stanza 17 makes clear), their goals differ.

[7] I.e., toward their goals.

[8] I.e., someone who seemed, from that far off, to be a lady (a highborn woman).

But Ladies none they were, albee[1] in face
And outward shew faire semblance they did beare;
For under maske of beautie and good grace,
Vile treason and fowle falshood hidden were,
That mote to none but to the warie wise appeare.

18   The one of them the false *Duessa* hight,
      That now had chang'd her former wonted hew:
      For she could d'on so manie shapes in sight,
      As ever could Cameleon colours new;
      So could she forge all colours, save[2] the trew.
      The other no whit better was then shee,
      But that such as she was, she plaine did shew;[3]
      Yet otherwise much worse, if worse might bee,
And dayly more offensive unto each degree.[4]

19   Her name was *Ate*,[5] mother of debate,
      And all dissention, which doth dayly grow
      Amongst fraile men, that many a publike state
      And many a private oft doth overthrow.
      Her false *Duessa* who full well did know,
      To be most fit to trouble noble knights,
      Which hunt for honor, raised from below,[6]
      Out of the dwellings of the damned sprights,
Where she in darknes wastes her cursed daies and nights.

---

[1] **albee:** albeit.

[2] **save:** except for.

[3] I.e., she was better only in that she revealed honestly how bad she was. She is described in stanza 17 as being "faire" in "outward semblance," but she is often later called a hag (e.g., at i.31.1 and ii.12.5), and at iv.9–10, it is clear that everyone regards her elderly appearance with loathing. The inconsistencies are part and parcel with her nature, which not only is duplicitous, but preys upon people's ability to delude themselves even when confronted with the truth.

[4] **unto each degree:** to people of every social class.

[5] *Ate:* in the *Iliad*, Ate is the eldest daughter of Zeus, thrown by him out of heaven onto the earth. She blinds people's judgment in order to bring them affliction, and she is described as trampling men's skulls (*Iliad*, 19.91–128). In Hesiod's *Theogony*, Ate is the great-granddaughter of Chaos, descended through Night and Strife (*Theogony*, 230). Cf. also Allecto in the *Aeneid* (7.435–55). Spenser identifies Ate's origin as hell and makes her into the personification of Discord, the chief enemy of the virtue of Friendship. Stanzas 19 through 30 digress from the plot to describe her dwelling and habits, in one of Spenser's most evocative renderings of an emblematic architectural space.

[6] I.e., Duessa knew that Ate was best able to trouble knights who hunt for honor, Ate being raised from hell.

20   Hard by[1] the gates of hell her dwelling is,
              There whereas all the plagues and harmes abound,
              Which punish wicked men, that walke amisse:
              It is a darksome delve[2] farre under ground,
              With thornes and barren brakes[3] environd round,
              That none the same may easily out win;
              Yet many waies to enter may be found,
              But none to issue forth when one is in:
          For discord harder is to end then to begin.

21   And all within the riven walls were hung
              With ragged monuments[4] of times forepast,
              All which the sad effects of discord sung:
              There were rent robes, and broken scepters plast,
              Altars defyl'd, and holy things defast,[5]
              Disshivered speares, and shields ytorne in twaine,
              Great cities ransackt, and strong castles rast,[6]
              Nations captived, and huge armies slaine:
          Of all which ruines there some relicks did remaine.[7]

22   There was the signe of antique Babylon,
              Of fatall Thebes, of Rome that raigned long,
              Of sacred Salem, and sad Ilion,[8]

[1] **Hard by:** right by.

[2] **delve:** cave.

[3] **brakes:** bracken, ferns; briars.

[4] **monuments:** souvenirs, reminders; tributes. Here and elsewhere, Spenser is acutely aware of the etymological relationship of the word "monument" (which he often spells "moniment") to the word "admonishment." Monuments serve to remind us of past glories so that we may imitate them—and of past follies so that we may avoid them. Ate's house is thus the result of her power, a museum to that power, and a possible deterrent to that power's success. Yet these twelve stanzas demonstrate that humans are more likely to contribute to Ate's collection than to take lessons from it.

[5] Although this line refers generally to the religious desecrations of all wars, and although Spenser might well be thinking, for example, of the passage in the *Aeneid* in which Priam is murdered in front of an altar (2.547–53), there were also numerous defaced churches to be seen in England after Henry VIII broke with the Pope, dissolved the English monasteries, and ransacked their properties in the late 1530s.

[6] **rast:** razed.

[7] The stanza progresses smoothly from describing a wall hung with trophies of war to describing some of war's aftereffects that could not possibly be contained in one room. It then slips into a description of the actions of the wars themselves. The final line brings us back to mere relics of those wars, but the total effect is of a room that encloses a howling chaos, bringing great stretches of geography and time into the "riven" confines of its walls.

[8] The Jewish scriptures represent Babylon (the capital of Babylonia, in present-day Iraq) as the place to which the Babylonian

For memorie of which on high there hong
The golden Apple, cause of all their wrong,
For which the three faire Goddesses did strive:[1]
There also was the name of *Nimrod*[2] strong,
Of *Alexander,* and his Princes five,[3]
Which shar'd to them the spoiles that he had got alive.

23   And there the relicks of the drunken fray,
The which amongst the *Lapithees* befell,
And of the bloodie feast, which sent away
So many *Centaures* drunken soules to hell,
That under great *Alcides* furie fell:[4]
And of the dreadfull discord, which did drive
The noble *Argonauts*[5] to outrage fell,
That each of life sought others to deprive,
All mindlesse of the Golden fleece, which made them strive.[6]

---

king Nebuchadnezzar II exiled the Jews. Jerusalem (Salem), by contrast, was the Jews' chosen—and lost—home. According to numerous mythologies, Thebes, in ancient Egypt, was "fatall" because its king, Laius, was told by an oracle that he was destined to be killed by his own son, Oedipus. Raised by a shepherd, Oedipus did not know his own parents, and so could not know that a robber he killed was his own father or that the woman whom he then married was his own mother. When he discovered his unwitting errors, Oedipus put out his own eyes. Ilion (Troy) was the site of the Trojan War and supposedly the origin of the British race after the fall of Troy scattered its people (see III.iii.22.6.n. and III.iii.26.2.n.).

[1] See III.ix.34.9.n. for the story of how the Goddess of Discord used a golden apple to start the Trojan War.

[2] **Nimrod:** a giant and king of Babel, believed by Renaissance theologians to be responsible for the building of the Tower of Babel. Because the people's intention in building the tower toward heaven was to make themselves great, God punished and weakened them by dividing humans into various language groups who were unable to

communicate with each other (Gen. 10–1).

[3] For the story of Alexander the Great, see 1 Macc. 1.7–8, according to which the division of Alexander's kingdom brought evils upon the earth.

[4] Like other contemporary mythographers, Spenser combines his account of the battle between the Greek Lapiths and the Centaurs (when the Centaurs attempted to carry off the Lapith women during a wedding feast) with his account of the battle between Hercules (Alcides) and the Centaurs; see Ovid, *Metamorphoses,* 12.210–535 and 536–41.

[5] **Argonauts:** in Greek mythology, when Pelias took the throne that rightfully belonged to Jason, he got Jason out of the way by commanding him to fetch the fabled—and fabulously guarded—golden ram's fleece of Colchis. Jason and volunteers from all over Greece sailed in the ship Argo to Colchis and back, undergoing many trials in order to claim the fleece.

[6] **strive:** work assiduously toward a goal; engage in war. In Book Four, Spenser plays with the relationship between these two meanings.

24   And eke of private persons many moe,
            That were too long a worke to count them all;
            Some of sworne friends, that did their faith forgoe;
            Some of borne brethren, prov'd unnaturall;[1]
            Some of deare lovers, foes perpetuall:
            Witnesse their broken bandes there to be seene,
            Their girlonds rent, their bowres despoyled all;
            The moniments whereof there byding beene,[2]
        As plaine as at the first, when they were fresh and greene.

25   Such was her house within; but all without,
            The barren ground was full of wicked weedes,
            Which she her selfe had sowen all about,
            Now growen great, at first of little seedes,
            The seedes of evill wordes, and factious deedes;
            Which when to ripenesse due they growen arre,
            Bring foorth an infinite increase, that breedes
            Tumultuous trouble and contentious jarre,[3]
        The which most often end in bloudshed and in warre.[4]

26   And those same cursed seedes doe also serve
            To her for bread, and yeeld her living food:[5]
            For life it is to her, when others sterve[6]
            Through mischievous debate, and deadly feood,[7]
            That she may sucke their life, and drinke their blood,
            With which she from her childhood had bene fed.
            For she at first was borne of hellish brood,
            And by infernall furies nourished,
        That by her monstrous shape might easily be red.

27   Her face most fowle and filthy was to see,
            With squinted eyes contrarie wayes intended,[8]
            And loathly mouth, unmeete a mouth to bee,

---

[1] **unnaturall:** in breaking the bonds that are natural among siblings.

[2] **byding beene:** abide.

[3] **jarre:** discord.

[4] Cf. the Garden of Adonis, III.vi. McCabe compares Ate's tumultuous garden with that in which Spenser worked: the garden that was Ireland (McCabe, 77).

[5] Cf. John 6.41–58, in which Jesus tells his listeners to stop disputing among themselves and to believe that he is the bread and blood of life, which makes the eater and drinker immortal.

[6] **sterve:** die.

[7] **feood:** feud.

[8] **intended:** directed.

That nought but gall and venim comprehended,[1]
And wicked wordes that God and man offended:
Her lying tongue was in two parts divided,
And both the parts did speake, and both contended;
And as her tongue, so was her hart discided,
That never thoght one thing, but doubly stil was guided.

28   Als[2] as she double spake, so heard she double,
      With matchlesse[3] eares deformed and distort,
      Fild with false rumors and seditious trouble,
      Bred in assemblies of the vulgar sort,
      That still are led with every light report.[4]
      And as her eares so eke her feet were odde,[5]
      And much unlike, th'one long, the other short,
      And both misplast; that when th'one forward yode,
The other backe retired, and contrarie trode.[6]

29   Likewise unequall were her handes twaine,
      That[7] one did reach, the other pusht away,
      That one did make, the other mard againe,
      And sought to bring all things unto decay;
      Whereby great riches gathered manie a day,
      She in short space did often bring to nought,
      And their possessours often did dismay.
      For all her studie was and all her thought,
How she might overthrow the things that Concord wrought.

30   So much her malice did her might surpas,
      That even th'Almightie selfe she did maligne,
      Because to man so mercifull he was,
      And unto all his creatures so benigne,
      Sith she her selfe was of his grace indigne:[8]

---

[1] **comprehended:** enclosed.

[2] **Als:** also.

[3] **matchlesse:** mismatched.

[4] **light report:** careless or frivolous rumor.

[5] **odde:** unlike each other.

[6] Naturally, one cannot walk this way without splitting oneself apart. Ate's self-contradictory nature, which should render her unable to move, much less able to effect her designs, effects those designs purely by its being: thwarting herself, she is the personification and source of all self-thwarting.

[7] **That:** whatever, that which.

[8] **indigne:** undeserving.

For all this worlds faire workmanship[1] she tride,
Unto his last confusion[2] to bring,
And that great golden chaine[3] quite to divide,
With which it blessed Concord hath together tide.

31   Such was that hag, which with *Duessa* roade,
      And serving her in her malitious use,
      To hurt good knights, was as it were her baude,[4]
      To sell her borrowed beautie to abuse.[5]
      For though like withered tree, that wanteth juyce,
      She old and crooked were, yet now of late,
      As fresh and fragrant as the floure deluce[6]
      She was become, by chaunge of her estate,[7]
And made full goodly joyance[8] to her new found mate.

32   Her mate he was a jollie youthfull knight,
      That bore great sway in armes and chivalrie,
      And was indeed a man of mickle might:
      His name was *Blandamour,* that did descrie[9]
      His fickle mind full of inconstancie.
      And now himselfe he fitted[10] had right well,
      With two companions of like qualitie,
      Faithlesse *Duessa,* and false *Paridell,*
That whether[11] were more false, full hard it is to tell.

---

[1] **this worlds faire workmanship:** both the natural world, as evidence of God's master craft, and the work that human hands produce using God-given talents. In the following canto, Spenser will further develop the idea that Ate wants to destroy human art, which is a repository of the sorts of understanding that could counteract her discordant power. (See ii.33.5.n.)

[2] **his:** its; **confusion:** ruin.

[3] **golden chaine:** see I.ix.1.1. When the gods in the *Iliad* quarrel over which mortals should win the Trojan War, Zeus angrily tells them to stop interfering. To demonstrate his power, he tells them that if they let down a golden chain from heaven and combine their forces to try to pull him down, they will not succeed, but that he could pull up all of them—along with the whole earth and sea—and dangle the whole mass from Mount Olympus (*Iliad,* 8.18–27). The golden chain between heaven and earth was interpreted as representing cosmic concord.

[4] **baude:** bawd, pimp.

[5] **to abuse:** (v.) to defile sexually; (n.) into sexual defilement.

[6] **floure deluce:** fleur-de-lis, a white iris associated with chastity.

[7] I.e., change of her condition, now having a mate.

[8] **joyance:** sexual dalliance.

[9] **that did descrie:** which name revealed.

[10] **fitted:** provided.

[11] **whether:** which.

33 Now when this gallant with his goodly crew,
        From farre espide the famous *Britomart,*
        Like knight adventurous in outward vew,
        With his faire paragon, his conquests part,[1]
        Approching nigh, eftsoones his[2] wanton hart
        Was tickled with delight, and jesting sayd;
        "Lo there Sir *Paridel,* for your desart,
        Good lucke presents you with yond lovely mayd,
    For pitie that ye want a fellow for your ayd."

34 By that the lovely paire drew nigh to hond:
        Whom when as *Paridel* more plaine beheld,
        Albee in heart he like affection fond,
        Yet mindfull how he late by one was feld,
        That did those armes and that same scutchion[3] weld,
        He had small lust to buy his love so deare,
        But answerd, "Sir him wise I never held,
        That having once escaped perill neare,
    Would afterwards afresh the sleeping evill reare.

35 "This knight too late his manhood[4] and his might,
        I did assay, that me right dearely cost,
        Ne list I for revenge provoke new fight,
        Ne for light Ladies love, that soone is lost."
        The hot-spurre[5] youth so scorning to be crost,
        "Take then to you this Dame of mine" (quoth hee)

---

[1] Lines 3 and 4 are absolutely ambiguous as to whether they refer to Blandamour accompanied by Duessa or to Britomart accompanied by Amoret. As a result, the lines must refer to both pairs, inviting us to decide how much Spenser is contrasting Britomart's seeming with that of Blandamour and Duessa and how much he is inviting us to compare them. (Like Duessa and Ate in stanza 17, Britomart appears from far off to be what she is not: in this case, a knight with a woman whom he has won in battle.)

[2] **his:** Blandamour's.

[3] **scutchion:** shield. For the earlier encounter between Paridell and Britomart, see III.ix.14–16.

[4] **manhood:** Paridell saw Britomart take off her armor in Malbecco's house, and we know that he was not blind to the fact that she was a woman, given the narrator's comment that despite Paridell's chagrin at having been felled by a female knight, he began to adore her beauty (III.ix.21–25). What his reference to Britomart's "manhood" means here is a matter for interpretation: does he restore some of his own dignity by remaking his vanquisher into a man; does he mislead Blandamour for some other reason; or does his language reflect his conviction that Britomart, though a woman, is masculine?

[5] **hot-spurre:** impetuous, as being always ready to spur on his horse.

"And I without your perill or your cost,
Will chalenge yond same other for my fee:"[1]
So forth he fiercely prickt, that one him scarce could see.

36	The warlike Britonesse her soone addrest,
And with such uncouth[2] welcome did receave
Her fayned Paramour, her forced guest,
That being forst his saddle soone to leave,
Him selfe he did of his new love deceave:[3]
And made him selfe thensample of his follie.
Which done, she passed forth not taking leave,
And left him now as sad, as whilome jollie,
Well warned to beware with whom he dar'd to dallie.

37	Which when his other companie beheld,
They to his succour ran with readie ayd:
And finding him unable once to weld,[4]
They reared him on horsebacke, and upstayd,[5]
Till on his way they had him forth convayd:
And all the way with wondrous griefe of mynd,
And shame, he shewd him selfe to be dismayd,
More for the love which he had left behynd,
Then that which he had to Sir *Paridel* resynd.[6]

38	Nathlesse he forth did march well as he might,
And made good semblance to his companie,
Dissembling his disease[7] and evill plight;
Till that ere long they chaunced to espie
Two other knights, that towards them did ply[8]
With speedie course, as bent[9] to charge them new.
Whom when as *Blandamour* approching nie,
Perceiv'd to be such as they seemd in vew,
He was full wo, and gan his former griefe renew.

---

[1] I.e., will claim yonder woman for my prize.

[2] **uncouth:** rude.

[3] I.e., he cheats himself out of Amoret—and of Britomart, though he does not know that he is dallying with two women rather than one.

[4] **once to weld:** even to move.

[5] **upstayd:** propped him up.

[6] He is not so utterly benighted as not to recognize Amoret's worth.

[7] **disease:** physical uneasiness, pain.

[8] **ply:** direct their course.

[9] **bent:** aiming.

39 For th'one of them he perfectly descride,
   To be Sir *Scudamour,* by that[1] he bore
   The God of love, with wings displayed wide,[2]
   Whom mortally he[3] hated evermore,
   Both for his worth, that[4] all men did adore,
   And eke because his love he wonne by right:
   Which when he[5] thought, it grieved him full sore,
   That through the bruses of his former fight,
  He now unable was to wreake his old despight.

40 For thy he thus to *Paridel* bespake,
   "Faire Sir, of friendship let me now you pray,
   That as I late adventured for your sake,
   The hurts whereof me now from battell stay,
   Ye will me now with like good turne repay,
   And justifie my cause on yonder knight."
   "Ah Sir" (said *Paridel*) "do not dismay
   Your selfe for this, my selfe will for you fight,
  As ye have done for me: the left hand rubs the right."[6]

41 With that he put his spurres unto his steed,
   With speare in rest, and toward him did fare,
   Like shaft out of a bow preventing speed.[7]
   But *Scudamour* was shortly well aware
   Of his approch, and gan him selfe prepare
   Him to receive with entertainment meete.
   So furiously they met, that either bare[8]
   The other downe under their horses feete,
  That what of them became, themselves did scarsly weete.

---

[1] **by that:** because.

[2] I.e., Cupid is pictured on Scudamour's shield, tunic, and/or pennon, as his coat of arms. Glauce is still with Scudamour, as is made clear by stanzas 50 through 54. She left Busirane's house with him after the two of them gave up hoping that Britomart would emerge with Amoret (III.xii. 44b–45b).

[3] **Whom:** Scudamour, but also in a sense Cupid; **he:** Blandamour.

[4] **that:** whom (referring to Scudamour); which (referring to Scudamour's worth).

[5] **he:** Blandamour.

[6] Paridell is defining their particular form of friendship.

[7] **preventing speed:** surpassing speed itself.

[8] **either bare:** each bore.

42   As when two billowes in the Irish sowndes,[1]
            Forcibly driven with contrarie tydes
            Do meete together, each abacke rebowndes
            With roaring rage; and dashing on all sides,
            That filleth all the sea with fome, divydes
            The doubtfull current into divers[2] wayes:
            So fell those two in spight of both their prydes,
            But *Scudamour* himselfe did soone uprayse,
And mounting light his foe for lying long upbrayes.[3]

43   Who rolled on an heape lay still in swound,
            All carelesse of his taunt and bitter rayle,[4]
            Till that the rest him seeing lie on ground,
            Ran hastily, to weete what did him ayle.
            Where finding that the breath gan him to fayle,
            With busie care they strove him to awake,
            And doft his helmet, and undid his mayle:[5]
            So much they did, that at the last they brake
His slomber, yet so mazed, that he nothing spake.

44   Which when as *Blandamour* beheld, he sayd,
            "False faitour *Scudamour,* that hast by slight[6]
            And foule advantage this good Knight dismayd,
            A Knight much better then thy selfe behight,[7]
            Well falles it thee that I am not in plight[8]
            This day, to wreake the dammage by thee donne:
            Such is thy wont, that still when any Knight
            Is weakned, then thou doest him overronne:
So hast thou to thy selfe false honour often wonne."

45   He little answer'd, but in manly heart
            His mightie indignation did forbeare,[9]
            Which was not yet so secret, but some part

---

[1] **sowndes:** (n.) wide bodies of water that connect still larger bodies of water; (v.) makes noise. As an English official living in occupied Ireland, Spenser would have had ample opportunity to observe opposing waves being driven against each other, literally and figuratively.

[2] **divers:** separate, various.

[3] I.e., and mounting easily, upbraided his foe for lying down so long.

[4] **carelesse of:** oblivious to, unmindful of; **rayle:** railing.

[5] **mayle:** chain mail.

[6] **faitour:** impostor; **slight:** trickery.

[7] **behight:** named, considered, esteemed.

[8] **in plight:** in condition.

[9] **forbeare:** restrain.

Thereof did in his frouning face appeare:
Like as a gloomie cloud, the which doth beare
An hideous storme, is by the Northerne blast
Quite overblowne, yet doth not passe so cleare,
But that it all the skie doth overcast
With darknes dred, and threatens all the world to wast.

46   "Ah gentle knight,"[1] then false *Duessa* sayd,
    "Why do ye strive for Ladies love so sore,
    Whose chiefe desire is love and friendly aid
    Mongst gentle Knights to nourish evermore?
    Ne be ye wroth Sir *Scudamour* therefore,
    That she your love list love another knight,
    Ne do your selfe dislike a whit the more;
    For Love is free, and led with selfe delight,
Ne will enforced be with maisterdome or might."[2]

47   So false *Duessa*, but vile *Ate* thus;
    "Both foolish knights, I can but laugh at both,
    That strive and storme with stirre[3] outrageous,
    For her that each of you alike doth loth,
    And loves another, with whom now she goth
    In lovely wise, and sleepes, and sports, and playes;
    Whilest both you here with many a cursed oth,
    Sweare she is yours, and stirre up bloudie frayes,
To win a willow bough, whilest other weares the bayes."[4]

48   "Vile hag" (sayd *Scudamour*) "why dost thou lye?
    And falsly seekst a vertuous wight to shame?"
    "Fond knight" (sayd she) "the thing that with this eye
    I saw, why should I doubt to tell the same?"
    "Then tell" (quoth *Blandamour*) "and feare no blame,
    Tell what thou saw'st, maulgre who so it heares."
    "I saw" (quoth she) "a stranger knight, whose name
    I wote not well, but in his shield he beares
(That well I wote) the heads of many broken speares.[5]

---

[1] Duessa is speaking to Blandamour.

[2] **maisterdome:** mastery. Cf. III.i.25.7–9, Britomart's version of this aphorism.

[3] **stirre:** commotion.

[4] Willow was the sign of an unhappy lover. In the ancient world, victors in athletics, battles, and poetry contests were crowned with bay laurel leaves.

[5] The knight's shield is studded with the broken-off heads of foes' spears, giving proof of—and forming an emblem of—the knight's prowess in battle.

49   "I saw him have your *Amoret* at will,[1]
        I saw him kisse, I saw him her embrace,
        I saw him sleepe with her all night his fill,
        All manie nights, and manie by in place,[2]
        That present were to testifie the case."
        Which when as *Scudamour* did heare, his heart
        Was thrild with inward griefe, as when in chace
        The Parthian strikes a stag with shivering[3] dart,
    The beast astonisht stands in middest of his smart.

50   So stood Sir *Scudamour*, when this he heard,
        Ne word he had to speake for great dismay,
        But lookt on *Glauce* grim,[4] who woxe afeard
        Of outrage for the words, which she heard say,
        Albee untrue she wist them by assay.[5]
        But *Blandamour*, whenas he did espie
        His chaunge of cheere, that anguish did bewray,[6]
        He woxe full blithe, as he had got thereby,
    And gan thereat to triumph without victorie.

---

[1] Here we begin to suspect we know the identity of this knight.

[2] **in place:** there.

[3] **shivering:** quivering; having the power to split what it hits.

[4] Believing that the knight who rescued Amoret from Busirane's house was male (see III.xi.13–27), Scudamour easily persuaded that the strange knight has taken Amoret for himself rather than returning her to her husband. He knows that Glauce is the strange knight's squire, so because the strange knight is not present, Scudamour directs his anger at Glauce. At the same time, the narrative suggests that he is redirecting some of the anger he feels against himself by projecting his faults onto Glauce. Just as Scudamour stood by while another knight rescued his lady, he believes that Glauce has stood by while the knight has stolen Amoret. The narrative has hinted earlier that jealousy is one of Scudamour's failings: although the canto in which Scud-

amour enters the poem begins by banishing the "Hatefull hellish snake" of jealousy, the stanza that describes the banished jealousy functions as *occultatio*, declaring that something is absent while yet describing it so powerfully that we experience it as a presence (III.xi.1). Spenser does not tell us whether Scudamour believes that the sexual intercourse between Amoret and the strange knight was rape or whether Scudamour is quick to mistrust Amoret as soon as he hears Duessa's tale; however, given the allegorical significance of a virgin's inability to fend off attackers, giving credit even to the idea that Amoret was forcibly raped betrays Scudamour's lack of trust in the strength of Amoret's chastity.

[5] Duessa's words are actually true—though not in the crude sense in which she means them or in which Glauce interprets them.

[6] I.e., when he noticed Scudamour's change of mood, which was revealed by (or which revealed) Scudamour's anguish.

51   "Lo recreant"[1] (sayd he) "the fruitlesse end
        Of thy vaine boast, and spoile of love misgotten,
        Whereby the name of knight-hood thou dost shend,
        And all true lovers with dishonor blotten,
        All things not rooted well, will soone be rotten."
        "Fy fy[2] false knight" (then false *Duessa* cryde)
        "Unworthy life that love with guile hast gotten,
        Be thou, where ever thou do go or ryde,
Loathed of ladies all, and of all knights defyde."

52   But *Scudamour* for passing great despight
        Staid not to answer, scarcely did refraine,
        But that in all those knights and ladies sight,
        He for revenge had guiltlesse *Glauce* slaine:[3]
        But being past, he thus began amaine;[4]
        "False traitour squire, false squire, of falsest knight,
        Why doth mine hand from thine avenge[5] abstaine,
        Whose Lord hath done my love this foule despight?
Why do I not it wreake, on thee now in my might?

53   "Discourteous, disloyall *Britomart*,
        Untrue to God, and unto man unjust,
        What vengeance due can equall[6] thy desart,
        That hast with shamefull spot of sinfull lust
        Defil'd the pledge committed to thy trust?
        Let ugly shame and endlesse infamy
        Colour thy name with foule reproaches rust.[7]
        Yet thou false Squire his fault shalt deare aby,
And with thy punishment his penance shalt supply."

---

54   The aged Dame him seeing so enraged,
    Was dead with feare, nathlesse as neede required,
    His flaming furie sought to have assuaged
    With sober words, that sufferance[1] desired,
    Till time the tryall of her truth expyred:[2]
    And evermore sought *Britomart* to cleare.
    But he the more with furious rage was fyred,
    And thrise his hand to kill her did upreare,
And thrise he drew it backe: so did at last forbeare.[3]

---

[1] **sufferance:** forbearance.

[2] I.e., until the passage of time brings to an end this trial of Britomart's honesty, when evidence of that honesty will appear. Note that Glauce withholds the knowledge that could save her life and ease Scudamour's mind: that the knight who rescued Amoret is female. Whether she suspects he would not believe her or whether she decides he could benefit from remaining in torment a while longer is a matter of interpretation. Cf. Britomart's decision temporarily to keep Amoret in anxiety about her rescuer's sex (stanza 7).

[3] The image recalls the ending of the *Aeneid,* when Aeneas pauses indecisively with his sword hovering over the fallen Turnus, until a fresh surge of burning fury (*furiis accensus*) causes him to plunge the blade into Turnus' breast (*Aeneid,* 12.938–51).

Canto Two

Blandamour winnes false Florimell,
Paridell for her strives,
They are accorded: Agape[1]
doth lengthen her sonnes lives.

1   Firebrand of hell first tynd in Phlegeton,[2]
       By thousand furies, and from thence out throwen
       Into this world, to worke confusion,[3]
       And set it all on fire by force unknowen,
       Is wicked discord,[4] whose small sparkes once blowen
       None but a God or godlike man can slake;[5]
       Such as was *Orpheus,* that when strife was growen
       Amongst those famous ympes[6] of Greece, did take
His silver Harpe in hand, and shortly friends them make.[7]

2   Or such as that celestiall Psalmist was,
       That when the wicked feend[8] his Lord tormented,
       With heavenly notes, that did all other pas,
       The outrage of his furious fit relented.[9]
       Such Musicke is wise words with time concented,[10]
       To moderate stiffe[11] minds, disposd to strive:

[1] **Agape:** charity, the love characteristic of friendship (Greek).

[2] **tynd:** kindled; **Phlegeton:** a river of fire in the underworld.

[3] **confusion:** ruin.

[4] "Discord" is the main grammatical subject of the whole stanza.

[5] **slake:** abate.

[6] **ympes:** youths (the Argonauts; see i.23.7.n.).

[7] The first example of a "God or godlike man" who can quell others' discord is Orpheus, whose skill with the lyre made all of the Greeks stop to listen. The musical concord (i.e., harmony) of his notes dispelled their interpersonal discord. During the Renaissance, Orpheus was held up as the epitome of a skilled and inspired poet.

[8] **wicked feend:** evil spirit—a description of Saul's mental illness.

[9] **relented:** relieved, ameliorated. The second "God or godlike man" is David, whose skill with the lyre eased Saul's mental torment (1 Sam. 16.14–23). David was believed to be the author of 73 of the Psalms, and thus a consummate poet (in addition to being one of the most successful kings of ancient Israel).

[10] I.e., wise words uttered at the right time (literally, at a time with which they are harmonious) are like calming music.

[11] **stiffe:** stubborn.

271

Such as that prudent Romane[1] well invented,
What time his people into partes did rive,
Them reconcyld againe, and to their homes did drive.

3   Such us'd wise *Glauce* to that wrathfull knight,[2]
To calme the tempest of his troubled thought:
Yet *Blandamour* with termes of foule despight,
And *Paridell* her scornd, and set at nought,
As old and crooked and not good for ought.
Both they unwise, and warelesse[3] of the evill,
That by themselves unto themselves is wrought,
Through that false witch, and that foule aged drevill,[4]
The one a feend, the other an incarnate devill.

4   With whom as they thus rode accompanide,
They were encountred of[5] a lustie Knight,
That had a goodly Ladie by his side,
To whom he made great dalliance and delight.
It was to weete the bold Sir *Ferraugh*[6] hight,
He that from *Braggadocchio* whilome reft
The snowy *Florimell*,[7] whose beautie bright
Made him seeme happie for so glorious theft;
Yet was it in due triall but a wandring weft.[8]

---

[1] **prudent Romane:** Menenius Agrippa, whose use of a particularly apt allegorical tale quieted a Roman mob. In the Renaissance, he was held up as the epitome of a wise and skillful orator.

[2] **that wrathfull knight:** Scudamour. Given Glauce's depiction thus far in Books Three and Four as a kindly but largely ineffectual old woman, the discovery that the preceding three examples of consummate poetic artistry are all similes for Glauce is startling. Indeed, literary critics of this passage have tended to discuss Orpheus, David, and Menenius Agrippa in their relation to the poet without ever mentioning Glauce. In a sense, the passage sublimates the rage of old women who are called "old and crooked and not good for ought" into a fantasy in which an old woman at least temporarily assumes the power of a great poet of the ancient world. Male poets of Spenser's day could not, of course, presume upon their own power, so the fantasy is Spenser's to share.

[3] **warelesse:** unaware; unwary.

[4] **false witch:** Duessa; **aged drevill:** Ate; a "drevill" is a drudge, one who works at dirty and menial jobs.

[5] **of:** by.

[6] *Ferraugh:* Ferrau is a knight who pursues the heroine Angelica in Ariosto's *Orlando Furioso* (1.14–21). Spenser may also be thinking of "Ferragh," an Irish battle cry.

[7] At III.viii.15–19, where he was not given a name.

[8] **weft:** waif; stray animal; unclaimed property—with the suggestion that it has little value to make anyone claim it.

5   Which when as *Blandamour,* whose fancie light
       Was alwaies flitting as the wavering wind,
       After each beautie, that appeard in sight,
       Beheld, eftsoones it prickt his wanton mind
       With sting of lust, that reasons eye did blind,
       That to Sir *Paridell* these words he sent;
       "Sir knight why ride ye dumpish[1] thus behind,
       Since so good fortune doth to you present
So fayre a spoyle, to make you joyous meriment?"

6   But *Paridell* that had too late a tryall
       Of the bad issue of his counsell vaine,
       List not to hearke, but made this faire denyall;
       "Last turne was mine, well proved to my paine,
       This now be yours, God send you better gaine."
       Whose scoffed words he[2] taking halfe in scorne,
       Fiercely forth prickt his steed as in disdaine,
       Against that Knight, ere he him well could torne;
By meanes whereof he hath him lightly overborne.

7   Who with the sudden stroke astonisht sore,
       Upon the ground a while in slomber[3] lay;
       The whiles his love away the other bore,
       And shewing her, did *Paridell* upbray;[4]
       "Lo sluggish Knight the victors happie pray:
       So fortune friends the bold:" whom *Paridell*
       Seeing so faire indeede, as he did say,
       His hart with secret envie gan to swell,
And inly grudge at him, that he had sped[5] so well.

8   Nathlesse proud man himselfe the other deemed,
       Having so peerelesse paragon[6] ygot:
       For sure the fayrest *Florimell* him seemed,[7]
       To him was fallen for his happie lot,
       Whose like alive on earth he weened not:
       Therefore he her did court, did serve, did wooe,

---

[1] **dumpish:** slow-witted; spiritless.

[2] **scoffed:** scoffing; **he:** Blandamour.

[3] **in slomber:** unconscious.

[4] **upbray:** upbraid.

[5] **sped:** succeeded.

[6] **paragon:** companion; model of excellence.

[7] **him seemed:** as it seemed to him.

With humblest suit that he imagine mot,[1]
And all things did devise, and all things dooe,
That might her love prepare, and liking win theretoo.

9   She in regard thereof him recompenst
    With golden words, and goodly countenance,
    And such fond favours sparingly dispenst:
    Sometimes him blessing with a light eye-glance,
    And coy lookes tempring with loose dalliance;
    Sometimes estranging him in sterner wise,
    That having cast him in a foolish trance,
    He seemed brought to bed in Paradise,
And prov'd himselfe most foole, in what he seem'd most wise.

10   So great a mistresse of her art she was,
    And perfectly practiz'd in womans craft,
    That though therein himselfe he thought to pas,[2]
    And by his false allurements wylie draft,[3]
    Had thousand women of their love beraft,[4]
    Yet now he was surpriz'd: for that false spright,[5]
    Which that same witch had in this forme engraft,
    Was so expert in every subtile slight,
That it could overreach the wisest earthly wight.

11   Yet he to her did dayly service more,
    And dayly more deceived was thereby;
    Yet *Paridell* him envied therefore,
    As seeming plast in sole felicity:
    So blind is lust, false colours to descry.
    But *Ate* soone discovering his[6] desire,
    And finding now fit opportunity
    To stirre up strife, twixt love and spight and ire,
Did privily put coles unto his secret fire.

12   By sundry meanes thereto she prickt him forth,
    Now with remembrance of those spightfull speaches,
    Now with opinion of his owne more worth,

---

[1] **mot:** might.

[2] **pas:** surpass.

[3] **draft:** attraction; power to draw astray; power of persuading a reluctant person.

[4] **beraft:** bereft.

[5] See III.viii.7–9 for the implanting of a false spright in the False Florimell.

[6] **his:** Paridell's.

Now with recounting of like former breaches
Made in their friendship, as that Hag him teaches:
And ever when his passion is allayd,
She it revives and new occasion reaches:[1]
That on a time as they together way'd,[2]
He made him open chalenge, and thus boldly sayd.

13   "Too boastfull *Blandamour,* too long I beare
The open wrongs, thou doest me day by day;
Well know'st thou, when we friendship first did sweare,
The covenant was, that every spoyle or pray
Should equally be shard betwixt us tway:[3]
Where is my part then of this Ladie bright,
Whom to thy selfe thou takest quite away?
Render therefore therein to me my right,
Or answere for thy wrong, as shall fall out in fight."

14   Exceeding wroth thereat was *Blandamour,*
And gan this bitter answere to him make;
"Too foolish *Paridell,* that fayrest floure
Wouldst gather faine, and yet no paines wouldst take:
But not so easie will I her forsake;
This hand her wonne, this hand shall her defend."
With that they gan their shivering speares to shake,
And deadly points at eithers breast to bend,
Forgetfull each to have bene ever others frend.

15   Their firie Steedes with so untamed forse
Did beare them both to fell avenges end,[4]
That both their speares with pitilesse remorse,[5]
Through shield and mayle, and haberjeon did wend,
And in their flesh a griesly passage rend,
That with the furie of their owne affret,[6]
Each other horse and man to ground did send;
Where lying still a while, both did forget
The perilous present stownd, in which their lives were set.

---

[1] **reaches:** gives.
[2] **way'd:** went on their way.
[3] **tway:** two.

[4] **to fell avenges end:** to the goal of cruel revenge.
[5] **remorse:** cutting force.
[6] **affret:** attack (a Spenserian neologism).

16   As when two warlike Brigandines at sea,
        With murdrous weapons arm'd to cruell fight,
        Doe meete together on the watry lea,[1]
        They stemme[2] ech other with so fell despight,
        That with the shocke of their owne heedlesse might,
        Their wooden ribs are shaken nigh a sonder;
        They which from shore behold the dreadfull sight
        Of flashing fire, and heare the ordenance thonder,
Do greatly stand amaz'd at such unwonted wonder.

17   At length they both upstarted in amaze;
        As men awaked rashly out of dreme,[3]
        And round about themselves a while did gaze,
        Till seeing her, that *Florimell* did seme,
        In doubt to whom she victorie should deeme,[4]
        Therewith their dulled sprights they edgd[5] anew,
        And drawing both their swords with rage extreme,
        Like two mad mastiffes each on other flew,
And shields did share, and mailes did rash, and helmes did hew.[6]

18   So furiously each other did assayle,
        As if their soules they would attonce have rent
        Out of their brests, that streames of bloud did rayle[7]
        Adowne, as if their springs of life were spent;
        That all the ground with purple bloud was sprent,[8]
        And all their armours staynd with bloudie gore,
        Yet scarcely once to breath[9] would they relent,
        So mortall was their malice and so sore,
Become of fayned friendship which they vow'd afore.

---

[1] **lea:** meadow (here Spenser's metaphor for the sea).

[2] **stemme:** ram.

[3] Spenser is fascinated with dreamlike states and with stupefaction; they are topics worth investigating in his poetry.

[4] The lady must decide who has won, so she will know to whom she now belongs.

[5] **edgd:** sharpened (by the sight of her).

[6] **share:** cut into parts; **rash:** slash; smash. The three parallel clauses of this line mirror the confusion of the quick action.

[7] **rayle:** gush.

[8] **sprent:** sprinkled.

[9] **to breath:** to take a breather.

19   And that which is for Ladies most besitting,[1]
      To stint[2] all strife, and foster friendly peace,
      Was from those Dames so farre and so unfitting,[3]
      As that in stead of praying them surcease,[4]
      They did much more their cruelty encrease;
      Bidding them fight for honour of their love,
      And rather die then Ladies cause release.[5]
    With which vaine termes so much they did them move,
That both resolv'd the last extremities to prove.[6]

20   There they I weene would fight untill this day,
      Had not a Squire, even he the Squire of Dames,[7]
      By great adventure travelled that way;
      Who seeing both bent to so bloudy games,
      And both of old well knowing by their names,
      Drew nigh, to weete the cause of their debate:
      And first laide on those Ladies thousand blames,[8]
    That did not seeke t'appease their deadly hate,
But gazed on their harmes, not pittying their estate.

21   And then those Knights he humbly did beseech,
      To stay[9] their hands, till he a while had spoken:
      Who lookt a little up at that his speech,
      Yet would not let their battell so be broken,
      Both greedie fiers on other to be wroken.[10]
      Yet he to them so earnestly did call,
      And them conjur'd by some well knowen token,[11]
    That they at last their wrothfull hands let fall,
Content to heare him speake, and glad to rest withall.

---

[1] **besitting:** befitting.

[2] **stint:** put a stop to.

[3] **unfitting:** foreign to their natures.

[4] **surcease:** stop.

[5] **release:** give up, relinquish.

[6] I.e., to fight to the death.

[7] **even he:** none other than; **Squire of Dames:** first seen at III.vii.37; most recently seen at III.viii.52–ix.6.

[8] The Squire of Dames seems to have learned how to be less than perfectly pleasing to all women.

[9] **stay:** hold, keep still.

[10] **wroken:** wreaked, avenged.

[11] **conjur'd:** constrained by oath; entreated; used magic upon. We are not told what the token is.

22	First he desir'd their cause of strife to see:
	They said, it was for love of *Florimell*.
	"Ah gentle knights" (quoth he) "how may that bee,
	And she so farre astray, as none can tell."
	"Fond Squire," full angry then sayd *Paridell*,
	"Seest not the Ladie there before thy face?"
	He looked backe, and her advizing well,
	Weend as he said, by that her outward grace,
That fayrest *Florimell* was present there in place.

23	Glad man was he to see that joyous sight,
	For none alive but joy'd in *Florimell*,[1]
	And lowly to her lowting[2] thus behight;
	"Fayrest of faire, that fairenesse doest excell,
	This happie day I have to greete you well,
	In which you safe I see, whom thousand late
	Misdoubted[3] lost through mischiefe that befell;
	Long may you live in health and happie state."
She litle answer'd him, but lightly did aggrate.[4]

24	Then turning to those Knights, he gan a new;
	"And you Sir *Blandamour* and *Paridell*,
	That for this Ladie present in your vew,
	Have rays'd this cruell warre and outrage fell,
	Certes me seemes bene not advised well,
	But rather ought in friendship for her sake
	To joyne your force, their forces to repell,
	That seeke perforce her from you both to take,
And of your gotten spoyle their owne triumph to make."

25	Thereat Sir *Blandamour* with countenance sterne,
	All full of wrath, thus fiercely him bespake;
	"A read thou Squire, that I the man may learne,
	That[5] dare fro me thinke *Florimell* to take."

[1] *Florimell:* i.e., the False Florimell, also known as the Snowy Florimell. From here on, Spenser often simply uses "Florimell" to designate the False Florimell, when the context tells us who is meant. If the practice occasionally confuses us, we are experiencing only a small part of the confusion experienced by characters in the poem.

[2] **lowting:** bowing.

[3] **Misdoubted:** feared.

[4] **lightly did aggrate:** carelessly thanked him.

[5] **That:** who.

"Not one" (quoth he) "but many doe partake
Herein, as thus. It lately so befell,[1]
That *Satyran* a girdle did uptake,[2]
Well knowne to appertaine to *Florimell,*
Which for her sake he wore, as him beseemed well.

26   "But when as she her selfe was lost and gone,
Full many knights, that loved her like deare,
Thereat did greatly grudge, that he alone
That lost faire Ladies ornament should weare,
And gan therefore close[3] spight to him to beare:
Which he to shun, and stop vile envies sting,
Hath lately caus'd to be proclaim'd each where
A solemne feast, with publike turneying,[4]
To which all knights with them their Ladies are to bring.

27   "And of them all she that is fayrest found,
Shall have that golden girdle for reward,
And of those Knights who is most stout on ground,
Shall to that fairest Ladie be prefard.[5]
Since therefore she her selfe[6] is now your ward,
To you that ornament of hers pertaines,
Against all those, that chalenge it to gard,
And save her honour with your ventrous[7] paines;
That shall you win more glory, then ye here find gaines."

28   When they the reason of his words had hard,
They gan abate the rancour of their rage,
And with their honours and their loves regard,

---

[1] **befell:** chanced, happened.

[2] After the real Florimell lost her sash while fleeing the hyena, Satyrane found it and used it to tie up the hyena (III.vii.31, 36). The hyena dragged it back to the witch (III.viii.2). Hamilton speculates that Satyrane must be wearing not the original sash, but its *eidolon*—its demonic shadow—just as the False Florimell is the demonic shadow of Florimell. Yet this sash refuses to let itself be worn by the False Florimell, justly indicating her lack of virtue and Amoret's virtue (see v.2–6, 16–20; iv.15 indicates that it is the same girdle), so perhaps its reappearance is one of Spenser's inconsistencies rather than consciously arranged on his part.

[3] **close:** secret, disguised.

[4] **turneying:** jousting in a tournament.

[5] I.e., will be recommended to the lady who has been judged most beautiful (with the idea that the two of them will become a couple).

[6] **she her selfe:** the False Florimell.

[7] **ventrous:** adventurous, willing to risk hazards.

The furious flames of malice to asswage.
Tho each to other did his faith engage,
Like faithfull friends thenceforth to joyne in one
With all their force, and battell strong to wage
Gainst all those knights, as their professed fone,
That chaleng'd ought in *Florimell,* save they alone.[1]

29   So well accorded forth they rode together
        In friendly sort, that lasted but a while;
        And of all old dislikes they made faire weather,[2]
        Yet all was forg'd and spred with golden foyle,
        That under it hidde hate and hollow guyle.
        Ne certes can that friendship long endure,
        How ever gay and goodly be the style,[3]
        That doth ill cause or evill end enure:[4]
For vertue is the band, that bindeth harts most sure.

30   Thus as they marched all in close disguise,
        Of fayned love, they chaunst to overtake
        Two knights, that lincked rode in lovely[5] wise,
        As if they secret counsels did partake;
        And each not farre behinde him had his make,[6]
        To weete, two Ladies of most goodly hew,
        That twixt themselves did gentle purpose[7] make,
        Unmindfull both of that discordfull crew,
The which with speedie pace did after them pursew.

31   Who as they now approched nigh at hand,
        Deeming them doughtie as they did appeare,
        They sent that Squire afore, to understand,
        What mote they be: who viewing them more neare
        Returned readie newes, that those same weare
        Two of the prowest[8] Knights in Faery lond;

---

[1] I.e., against all knights who fought to gain
Florimell, except for the two of them.

[2] I.e., they now made light of—or
smoothed over—all of their previous en-
mity toward each other.

[3] **style:** manner.

[4] **enure:** enact, bring about.

[5] **lovely:** loving.

[6] **make:** mate.

[7] **purpose:** conversation.

[8] **prowest:** most worthy, most valiant.

And those two Ladies their two lovers deare,
Couragious *Cambell,* and stout *Triamond,*
With *Canacee* and *Cambine*[1] linckt in lovely bond.

32   Whylome as antique stories tellen us,[2]
Those two were foes the fellonest[3] on ground,
And battell made the dreddest daungerous,
That ever shrilling trumpet did resound;
Though now their acts be no where to be found,
As that renowmed Poet them compyled,
With warlike numbers[4] and Heroicke sound,
Dan *Chaucer,* well of English undefyled,[5]
On Fames eternall beadroll[6] worthie to be fyled.

33   But wicked Time that all good thoughts doth waste,
And workes of noblest wits to nought out weare,
That famous moniment hath quite defaste,
And robd the world of threasure endlesse deare,
The which mote have enriched all us heare.[7]

---

[1] **Cambell:** see note to Book Four title; **Tri-amond:** the name means "third world"; also see note to Book Four title; **Canacee:** the name of Cambalo's sister in Chaucer's *Squire's Tale;* **Cambine:** from the Italian *cambiare,* meaning "to exchange" or "to change," or from the English "combine."

[2] The "antique stories" are one story, Chaucer's *Squire's Tale,* which Chaucer never completed. Spenser takes up Chaucer's tale to finish it. Chaucer's own sources included Ovid's *Heroides* 11.

[3] **Those two:** Cambell and Triamond; **fellonest:** fiercest.

[4] **numbers:** poetic meter.

[5] **Dan:** courtesy title for a male member of a religious order or for a male scholar, knight, poet, or deity; Spenser uses the title only for deities, except when applying it to Chaucer; **English undefyled:** Spenser imitated many of Chaucer's medieval spellings and usages, at least partly from the belief that Chaucer's English was more pure and less corrupted by French and Italian additions than that of the late sixteenth century.

It is instructive to compare Spenser's remarks throughout *A View of the Present State of Ireland* about the ways that English settlers in Ireland allowed themselves to be corrupted by the acquisition of Irish manners and speech.

[6] **beadroll:** catalogue; list of persons to be prayed for.

[7] Spenser believes that Chaucer wrote an ending to *The Squire's Tale* that was then lost sometime before the sixteenth century, rather than that he never finished it in the first place (quite possibly because he wanted to imply that the other pilgrims couldn't bear to listen to any more of the Squire's prolixity). It is useful to compare Spenser's encomium to Chaucer with the earlier description of Ate's museum of relics (i.21–26; see also i.21.2.n. and i.30.6.n.). Taken together, the two passages imply that great poetry such as Chaucer's is a "moniment" to the past and a crucial repository of human knowledge, the loss of which is both the result and the cause of much human discord. Our unwariness toward Ate—whose treason and falsehood "mote

O cursed Eld the cankerworme of writs,[1]
How may these rimes, so rude as doth appeare,
Hope to endure, sith workes of heavenly wits
Are quite devourd, and brought to nought by little bits?

34   Then pardon, O most sacred happie spirit,[2]
That I thy labours lost may thus revive,
And steale from thee the meede of thy due merit,
That none durst ever whilest thou wast alive,
And being dead in vaine yet many strive:[3]
Ne dare I like,[4] but through infusion sweete
Of thine owne spirit, which doth in me survive,
I follow here the footing of thy feete,[5]
That with thy meaning so I may the rather meete.[6]

35   *Cambelloes* sister was fayre *Canacee,*
That was the learnedst Ladie in her dayes,
Well seene in everie science that mote bee,[7]
And every secret worke of natures wayes,
In wittie riddles, and in wise soothsayes,
In power of herbes, and tunes of beasts and burds;
And, that[8] augmented all her other prayse,
She modest was in all her deedes and words,
And wondrous chast of life, yet lov'd of Knights and Lords.[9]

---

to none but to the warie wise appeare"
(i.17.9)—proceeds from our having obliter-
ated not only our political history, but also
our literary history. This entire discussion is
a redevelopment and extension of the ideas
broached in the descriptions of Time and
immortality in the Garden of Adonis
(III.vi).

[1] **Eld:** age; **writs:** writings.

[2] **happie:** blessed; Spenser addresses the
spirit of Chaucer.

[3] I.e., and you being dead, many still strive
in vain.

[4] **Ne dare I like:** nor would I dare to do
the same (as those who have already vainly
tried to imitate you).

[5] **feete:** with a pun on the metrical feet of
poetry.

[6] **That:** in order that; **meete:** agree; find.

[7] I.e., well taught in every possible branch
of learning.

[8] **that:** something which.

[9] With this stanza, Spenser picks up where
The Squire's Tale leaves off. In that tale, King
Cambuscan of Tartary receives gifts from
the King of Arabia, including a magic ring
that enables Cambuscan's daughter,
Canacee, to understand the language of
birds. A bleeding female falcon tells
Canacee about having been wooed by a
male falcon who then abandoned her to her
self-mutilating grief. Full of sympathy,
Canacee nurses the female falcon back to
health. The Squire who is narrating prom-
ises to describe how the falcon regained her
mate and how Cambalo fought with two

36   Full many Lords, and many Knights her loved,
        Yet she to none of them her liking lent,
        Ne ever was with fond affection moved,
        But rul'd her thoughts with goodly governement,[1]
        For dread of blame and honours blemishment;
        And eke unto her lookes a law she made,
        That none of them once out of order went,
        But like to warie Centonels well stayd,
    Still watcht on every side, of secret foes affrayd.[2]

37   So much the more as she refusd to love,
        So much the more she loved was and sought,
        That oftentimes unquiet strife did move
        Amongst her lovers, and great quarrels wrought,
        That oft for her in bloudie armes they fought.
        Which whenas *Cambell,* that was stout and wise,
        Perceiv'd would breede great mischiefe, he bethought
        How to prevent the perill that mote rise,
    And turne both him and her to honour in this wise.

38   One day, when all that troupe of warlike wooers
        Assembled were, to weet whose she should bee,
        All mightie men and dreadfull derring dooers,[3]
        (The harder it to make them well agree)
        Amongst them all this end[4] he did decree;
        That of them all, which love to her did make,[5]
        They by consent should chose the stoutest three,
        That with himselfe should combat for her sake,
    And of them all the victour should his sister take.[6]

---

brothers for Canacee in order to win her—but there the tale breaks off.

[1] Elizabethans generally considered good rule, rather than democracy or individual freedoms, to be the primary source of civic concord. Good rule included that of God over humanity, of a monarch over the nation, of men over women, and of each person over his or her unruly impulses.

[2] I.e., she guarded her glances, making sure not to let them stray flirtatiously. She is the chaste opposite of Malecasta, whose "wanton eyes, ill signes of womanhed, / Did roll too highly, and too often glaunce, / Without regard of grace, or comely amenaunce" (III.i.41.7–9).

[3] **dreadfull derring dooers:** awe-inspiring in their commission of daring deeds.

[4] **end:** goal.

[5] Making love was wooing a woman, not necessarily having sex with her; the term did not have unchaste overtones.

[6] Whereas Chaucer follows his sources in having Cambalo fight to win Canacee for himself—thus implying that the brother and sister have an incestuous love for each

39   Bold was the chalenge, as himselfe was bold,
           And courage full of haughtie hardiment,[1]
           Approved oft in perils manifold,
           Which he atchiev'd to his great ornament:[2]
           But yet his sisters skill unto him lent
           Most confidence and hope of happie speed,[3]
           Conceived by a ring, which she him sent,
           That mongst the manie vertues, which we reed,
       Had power to staunch[4] al wounds, that mortally did bleed.

40   Well was that rings great vertue knowen to all,
           That dread thereof, and his[5] redoubted might
           Did all that youthly rout so much appall,[6]
           That none of them durst undertake the fight;
           More wise they weend to make of love delight,
           Then life to hazard for faire Ladies looke,
           And yet uncertaine by such outward sight,
           Though for her sake they all that perill tooke,
       Whether she would them love, or in her liking brooke.[7]

41   Amongst those knights there were three brethren bold,
           Three bolder brethren never were yborne,
           Borne of one mother in one happie mold,
           Borne at one burden[8] in one happie morne,
           Thrise happie mother, and thrise happie morne,
           That bore three such, three such not to be fond;[9]
           Her name was *Agape* whose children werne
           All three as one, the first hight *Priamond*,
       The second *Dyamond*, the youngest *Triamond*.[10]

---

other—Spenser has Cambello fight to
choose the most valiant opponent to wed
Canacee, thus emphasizing the brother and
sister's chaste friendship.

[1] **hardiment:** hardihood.

[2] **ornament:** good reputation, credit.

[3] **speed:** success.

[4] **staunch:** stanch, stop the flow of blood
from.

[5] **his:** Cambello's.

[6] **appall:** intimidate.

[7] I.e., they were wary of risking their lives
for a fair lady, given that they couldn't tell
simply by looking at her whether she would
love the victor or be constant in her prefer-
ence.

[8] **burden:** that which is borne in the
womb, a child—or in this case, triplets.

[9] **fond:** found.

[10] I.e., first, second, and third world (Latin).

42   Stout *Priamond,* but not so strong to strike,
       Strong *Diamond,* but not so stout a knight,
       But *Triamond* was stout and strong alike:
       On horsebacke used *Triamond* to fight,
       And *Priamond* on foote had more delight,
       But horse and foote knew *Diamond* to wield:
       With curtaxe[1] used *Diamond* to smite,
       And *Triamond* to handle speare and shield,
    But speare and curtaxe both usd *Priamond* in field.

43   These three did love each other dearely well,
       And with so firme affection were allyde,
       As if but one soule in them all did dwell,
       Which did her powre into three parts divyde;
       Like three faire branches budding farre and wide,
       That from one roote deriv'd their vitall sap:
       And like that roote that doth her life divide,
       Their mother was, and had full blessed hap,
    These three so noble babes to bring forth at one clap.[2]

44   Their mother was a Fay, and had the skill[3]
       Of secret things, and all the powres of nature,
       Which she by art could use unto her will,
       And to her service bind each living creature,
       Through secret understanding of their feature.[4]
       Thereto she was right faire, when so her face
       She list discover, and of goodly stature;
       But she as Fayes are wont, in privie place
    Did spend her dayes, and lov'd in forests wyld to space.

45   There on a day a noble youthly knight
       Seeking adventures in the salvage wood,
       Did by great fortune get of her the sight;
       As she sate carelesse by a cristall flood,[5]

---

[1] **curtaxe:** a short battle-ax. Note the triplets in the verse form and in the repeated naming of the brothers. Cf. the tripled description of Reproch, Repentaunce, and Shame at III.xii.24.

[2] **at one clap:** in one event, at once.

[3] **Fay:** fairy—not a diminutive being, but a supernatural creature, outwardly resembling a human being, living in a world that overlaps that of mortals; **skill:** knowledge.

[4] **feature:** nature; form.

[5] **carelesse:** free of care; unwary; **flood:** stream or river.

Combing her golden lockes, as seemd her good:
And unawares upon her laying hold,
That strove in vaine him long to have withstood,
Oppressed[1] her, and there (as it is told)
Got[2] these three lovely babes, that prov'd three champions bold.

46   Which she with her long fostred in that wood,
        Till that to ripenesse of mans state they grew:
        Then shewing forth signes of their fathers blood,
        They loved armes, and knighthood did ensew,[3]
        Seeking adventures, where they anie knew.
        Which when their mother saw, she gan to dout
        Their safetie, least by searching daungers new,
        And rash provoking perils all about,
        Their days mote be abridged through their corage stout.

47   Therefore desirous th'end of all their dayes
        To know, and them t'enlarge with long extent,[4]
        By wondrous skill, and many hidden wayes,
        To the three fatall sisters[5] house she went.
        Farre under ground from tract of living went,[6]
        Downe in the bottome of the deepe *Abysse*,[7]
        Where *Demogorgon*[8] in dull darknesse pent,
        Farre from the view of Gods and heavens blis,
        The hideous *Chaos* keepes,[9] their dreadfull dwelling is.

48   There she them found, all sitting round about
        The direfull distaffe[10] standing in the mid,
        And with unwearied fingers drawing out

---

[1] **Oppressed:** raped.

[2] **Got:** begot.

[3] **ensew:** pursue.

[4] I.e., wanting to know how they will die
and wanting to lengthen their lives greatly.

[5] **three fatall sisters:** the three Fates—
Clotho, Lachesis, and Atropos—who at
each baby's birth determine the events in
that child's life by spinning out a length of
thread and then determine the length of the
child's life by cutting the thread. In Greek
mythology, not even the gods could change
what the Fates decreed.

[6] **tract:** track, path; **went:** creature.

[7] *Abysse:* bowels of the earth; infernal pit.

[8] *Demogorgon:* a god of the underworld.

[9] As Fowler points out, either Demogor-
gon, pent in darkness, keeps Chaos, or
Chaos keeps Demogorgon pent in darkness
(Fowler 1989, 46).

[10] **distaffe:** a cleft staff that holds flax,
wool, or tow so that it can be drawn out
and spun into thread by hand.

The lines of life, from living knowledge hid.
Sad *Clotho* held the rocke, the whiles the thrid[1]
By griesly *Lachesis* was spun with paine,[2]
That cruell *Atropos* eftsoones undid,
With cursed knife cutting the twist[3] in twaine:
Most wretched men, whose dayes depend on thrids so vaine.

49 She them saluting, there by them sate still,
 Beholding how the thrids of life they span:[4]
 And when at last she had beheld her fill,
 Trembling in heart, and looking pale and wan,
 Her cause of comming she to tell began.
 To whom fierce *Atropos,* "Bold Fay, that durst[5]
 Come see the secret of the life of man,
 Well worthie thou to be of *Jove* accurst,
And eke thy childrens thrids to be a sunder burst."

50 Whereat she sore affrayd,[6] yet her besought
 To graunt her boone,[7] and rigour to abate,
 That she might see her childrens thrids forth brought,
 And know the measure of their utmost date,[8]
 To them ordained by eternall fate.
 Which *Clotho* graunting, shewed her the same:
 That when she saw, it did her much amate,[9]
 To see their thrids so thin, as spiders frame,[10]
And eke so short, that seemd their ends out shortly came.

51 She then began them humbly to intreate,
 To draw them longer out, and better twine,
 That so their lives might be prolonged late.
 But *Lachesis* thereat gan to repine,
 And sayd, "Fond dame that deem'st of things divine
 As of humane, that they may altred bee,

[1] **Sad:** solemn; **rocke:** distaff; **thrid:** thread.

[2] **paine:** care.

[3] **twist:** fiber twisted into thread.

[4] **span:** spun.

[5] **Bold:** the word is not a compliment here; when applied to a woman, it usually means "presumptuous" or "immodest"; **durst:** dares.

[6] **affrayd:** feared.

[7] **boone:** entreaty.

[8] I.e., know the time remaining until their deaths.

[9] **amate:** dismay.

[10] **frame:** construction (i.e., a web).

And chaung'd at pleasure for those impes[1] of thine.
     Not so; for what the Fates do once decree,
Not all the gods can chaunge, nor *Jove* him self can free."

52   "Then since" (quoth she) "the terme of each mans life
     For nought may lessened nor enlarged bee,
     Graunt this, that when ye shred with fatall knife
     His line, which is the eldest of the three,
     Which is of them the shortest, as I see,
     Eftsoones his life may passe into the next;
     And when the next shall likewise ended bee,
     That both their lives may likewise be annext
Unto the third, that his may so be trebly wext."[2]

53   They graunted it; and then that carefull[3] Fay
     Departed thence with full contented mynd;
     And comming home, in warlike fresh aray
     Them found all three according to their kynd:[4]
     But unto them what destinie was assynd,
     Or how their lives were eekt,[5] she did not tell;
     But evermore, when she fit time could fynd,
     She warned them to tend their safeties well,
And love each other deare, what ever them befell.

54   So did they surely during all their dayes,
     And never discord did amongst them fall;
     Which much augmented all their other praise.
     And now t'increase affection naturall,
     In love of *Canacee* they joyned all:[6]
     Upon which ground this same great battell grew,
     Great matter growing of beginning small;
     The which for length I will not here pursew,
But rather will reserve it for a Canto new.

---

[1] **impes:** children.

[2] **wext:** grown, increased. Spenser may be thinking of Feronia, in the *Aeneid,* who gives her son, Erulus, three lives so that he must be killed three times in order to die permanently (*Aeneid,* 8.563–67).

[3] **carefull:** burdened with cares.

[4] I.e., each provided with weapons and gear befitting his talents (see 42.7–9).

[5] **eekt:** eked out, lengthened.

[6] They can love the same woman without destroying their love for each other.

Canto Three

*The battell twixt three brethren with
Cambell for Canacee:
Cambina with true friendships bond
doth their long strife agree.*[1]

1   O why doe wretched men so much desire,
      To draw their dayes unto the utmost date,[2]
      And doe not rather wish them soone expire,
      Knowing the miserie of their estate,[3]
      And thousand perills which them still awate,
      Tossing them like a boate amid the mayne,
      That every houre they knocke at deathes gate?[4]
      And he that happie seemes and least in payne,
Yet is as nigh his end, as he that most doth playne.

2   Therefore this Fay I hold but fond and vaine,
      The which in seeking for her children three
      Long life, thereby did more prolong their paine.
      Yet whilest they lived none did ever see
      More happie creatures, then they seem'd to bee,
      Nor more ennobled for their courtesie,
      That made them dearely lov'd of each degree;[5]
      Ne more renowmed for their chevalrie,
That made them dreaded much of all men farre and nie.

3   These three that hardie chalenge tooke in hand,
      For *Canacee* with *Cambell* for to fight:
      The day was set, that all might understand,
      And pledges pawnd the same to keepe a right,[6]
      That day, the dreddest day that living wight

---

[1] **agree:** bring to agreement; settle.

[2] I.e., to extend their lives as long as possible.

[3] **estate:** situation (as human beings).

[4] Cf. Despaire's question at I.ix.46.1–2, 47.7–8.

[5] **of each degree:** by people of every social level.

[6] I.e., they threw gloves or other tokens on the ground as symbolic promises that they would engage in battle; these pledges were called "gages" and were regarded as challenges to the opponent.

Did ever see upon this world to shine,
So soone as heavens window shewed light,
These warlike Champions all in armour shine,[1]
Assembled were in field, the chalenge to define.[2]

4   The field with listes[3] was all about enclos'd,
          To barre the prease[4] of people farre away;
          And at th'one side six judges were dispos'd,[5]
          To view and deeme the deedes of armes that day;
          And on the other side in fresh aray,
          Fayre *Canacee* upon a stately stage
          Was set, to see the fortune of that fray,
          And to be seene, as his most worthie wage,[6]
       That could her purchase with his lives adventur'd gage.[7]

5   Then entred *Cambell* first into the list,[8]
          With stately steps, and fearelesse countenance,
          As if the conquest his he surely wist.
          Soone after did the brethren three advance,
          In brave aray and goodly amenance,[9]
          With scutchins gilt[10] and banners broad displayd:
          And marching thrise in warlike ordinance,
          Thrise lowted[11] lowly to the noble Mayd,
       The whiles shril trompets and loud clarions[12] sweetly playd.

6   Which doen the doughty chalenger came forth,
          All arm'd to point his chalenge to abet:[13]
          Gainst whom Sir *Priamond* with equall worth,
          And equall armes himselfe did forward set.
          A trompet blew; they both together met,
          With dreadfull force, and furious intent,

---

[1] **shine:** shining.

[2] **define:** decide.

[3] **listes:** railings or fences placed about a field to be used for a tournament or for duels.

[4] **prease:** press, crowd.

[5] **dispos'd:** arranged, situated.

[6] **wage:** prize.

[7] **gage:** see stanza 3.4.n. above. Cambello is offering his own life as a gage.

[8] **into the list:** into the enclosure.

[9] **amenance:** noble bearing.

[10] **gilt:** gilded with gold leaf or gold paint.

[11] **lowted:** bowed.

[12] **clarions:** trumpets with narrow tubes, used in war and in tournaments.

[13] **to point:** thoroughly; **abet:** maintain.

> Carelesse of perill in their fiers affret,[1]
> As if that life to losse they had forelent,[2]
> And cared not to spare, that should be shortly spent.

7   Right practicke[3] was Sir *Priamond* in fight,
>   And throughly skild in use of shield and speare;
>   Ne lesse approved was *Cambelloes* might,
>   Ne lesse his skill in weapons did appeare,
>   That hard it was to weene which harder[4] were.
>   Full many mightie strokes on either side
>   Were sent, that seemed death in them to beare,
>   But they were both so watchfull and well eyde,
> That they avoyded were, and vainely by did slyde.

8   Yet one of many was so strongly bent
>   By *Priamond,* that with unluckie glaunce
>   Through *Cambels* shoulder it unwarely[5] went,
>   That forced him his shield to disadvaunce:[6]
>   Much was he grieved with that gracelesse[7] chaunce,
>   Yet from the wound no drop of bloud there fell,
>   But wondrous paine, that did the more enhaunce
>   His haughtie courage to advengement[8] fell:
> Smart daunts not mighty harts, but makes them more to swell.

9   With that his poynant speare he fierce aventred,[9]
>   With doubled force close underneath his shield,
>   That through the mayles into his[10] thigh it entred,
>   And there arresting, readie way did yield,
>   For bloud to gush forth on the grassie field;
>   That he for paine himselfe n'ote[11] right upreare,

---

[1] **affret:** attack.

[2] **forelent:** given up in advance.

[3] **practicke:** practiced, skilled.

[4] **harder:** hardier.

[5] **unwarely:** unexpectedly, because he was unwary.

[6] **disadvaunce:** draw back; lower.

[7] **gracelesse:** unfortunate.

[8] **advengement:** revenge.

[9] **poynant:** piercing (literally poignant); **aventred:** set in its rest, in preparation for striking (or, given the next line, perhaps "thrust").

[10] **his:** Priamond's.

[11] **n'ote:** ne wote, knew not how to.

But too and fro in great amazement reel'd,
    Like an old Oke whose pith and sap is seare,[1]
At puffe of every storme doth stagger[2] here and theare.

10   Whom so dismayd when *Cambell* had espide,
            Againe he drove at him with double might,
            That nought mote stay the steele, till in his side
            The mortall point most cruelly empight:[3]
            Where fast infixed, whilest he sought by slight
            It forth to wrest, the staffe a sunder brake,
            And left the head behind: with which despight
            He all enrag'd, his shivering speare did shake,
And charging him a fresh thus felly him bespake.

11   "Lo faitour[4] there thy meede unto thee take,
            The meede of thy mischalenge and abet:[5]
            Not for thine owne, but for thy sisters sake,
            Have I thus long thy life unto thee let:
            But to forbeare doth not forgive the det."
            The wicked weapon heard his wrathfull vow,
            And passing forth with furious affret,
            Pierst through his bever[6] quite into his brow,
That with the force it backward forced him to bow.

12   Therewith a sunder in the midst it brast,
            And in his hand nought but the troncheon[7] left,
            The other halfe behind yet sticking fast,
            Out of his headpeece *Cambell* fiercely reft,[8]
            And with such furie backe at him it heft,[9]
            That making way unto his dearest life,
            His weasand pipe it through his gorget[10] cleft:
            Thence streames of purple bloud issuing rife,
Let forth his wearie ghost and made an end of strife.

---

[1] **seare:** dried up.

[2] **stagger:** sway unsteadily.

[3] **empight:** planted itself.

[4] **faitour:** villain.

[5] I.e., the reward for your pursuing a wrongful challenge. Priamond's words seem unnecessarily angry, given that he and Cambello both entered the lists voluntarily over a formal challenge, rather than in the field of battle.

[6] **bever:** helmet visor.

[7] **troncheon:** the spear fragment still in Priamond's hand.

[8] **reft:** ripped.

[9] **heft:** heaved.

[10] **weasand pipe:** windpipe; **gorget:** armor over the throat.

13   His wearie ghost assoyld from fleshly band,[1]
        Did not as others wont, directly fly
        Unto her rest in Plutoes griesly land,[2]
        Ne into ayre did vanish presently,[3]
        Ne chaunged was into a starre in sky:
        But through traduction was eftsoones derived,[4]
        Like as his mother prayd the Destinie,
        Into his other brethren, that survived,
   In whom he liv'd a new, of former life deprived.

14   Whom when on ground his brother next beheld,
        Though sad and sorie for so heavy sight,
        Yet leave[5] unto his sorrow did not yeeld,
        But rather stird to vengeance and despight,
        Through secret feeling of his generous spright,
        Rusht fiercely forth, the battell to renew,
        As in reversion[6] of his brothers right;
        And chalenging the Virgin as his dew.[7]
   His foe was soone addrest: the trompets freshly blew.

15   With that they both together fiercely met,
        As if that each ment other to devoure;
        And with their axes both so sorely bet,[8]
        That neither plate nor mayle,[9] whereas their powre
        They felt, could once sustaine the hideous stowre,
        But rived were like rotten wood a sunder,
        Whilest through their rifts the ruddie bloud did showre
        And fire did flash, like lightning after thunder,
   That fild the lookers on attonce with ruth and wonder.[10]

---

[1] **assoyld:** set free; acquitted; absolved; **band:** bond.

[2] I.e., it did not go directly to hell.

[3] **presently:** immediately.

[4] **traduction:** transmission or transmigration of the soul; **derived:** transferred.

[5] **leave:** permission for it to express itself.

[6] **reversion:** a legal term designating someone's right to take over an office after the previous officeholder has died.

[7] **dew:** due.

[8] **bet:** beat.

[9] **mayle:** chain mail.

[10] **ruth and wonder:** as Hamilton points out in his note, these are the emotions traditionally thought to be aroused by viewing a tragic play.

16   As when two Tygers prickt with hungers rage,
    Have by good fortune found some beasts fresh spoyle,
    On which they weene their famine to asswage,
    And gaine a feastfull guerdon[1]of their toyle,
    Both falling out doe stirre up strifefull broyle,
    And cruell battell twixt themselves doe make,
    Whiles neither lets the other touch the soyle,[2]
    But either sdeignes with other to partake:[3]
So cruelly these Knights strove for that Ladies sake.

17   Full many strokes, that mortally were ment,
    The whiles were enterchaunged twixt them two;
    Yet they were all with so good wariment[4]
    Or warded, or avoyded and let goe,
    That still the life stood fearelesse of her foe:[5]
    Till *Diamond* disdeigning long delay
    Of doubtfull fortune wavering to and fro,
    Resolv'd to end it one or other way;
And heav'd his murdrous axe at him with mighty sway.[6]

18   The dreadfull stroke in case[7] it had arrived,
    Where it was ment, (so deadly it was ment)
    The soule had sure out of his bodie rived,
    And stinted all the strife incontinent.[8]
    But *Cambels* fate that fortune did prevent:[9]
    For seeing it at hand, he swarv'd asyde,
    And so gave way unto his fell intent:
    Who missing of the marke which he had eyde,
Was with the force nigh feld whilst his right foot did slyde.

19   As when a Vulture greedie of his pray,
    Through hunger long, that hart to him doth lend,
    Strikes at an Heron with all his bodies sway,
    That from his force seemes nought may it defend;

---

[1] **guerdon:** reward, recompense.

[2] **the soyle:** where the spoil lies.

[3] I.e., each disdains to fight another, or each disdains to go after different prey.

[4] **wariment:** wariness.

[5] **her foe:** death.

[6] **sway:** power, force.

[7] **in case:** if, in the event that.

[8] I.e., immediately ceased all the strife, or ceased all the intemperate strife.

[9] **prevent:** anticipate (literally come before).

The warie fowle that spies him toward bend
His dreadfull souse, avoydes it shunning light,[1]
And maketh him his wing in vaine to spend;
That with the weight of his owne weeldlesse[2] might,
He falleth nigh to ground, and scarse recovereth flight.

20　　Which faire adventure[3] when *Cambello* spide,
Full lightly, ere himselfe he could recover,[4]
From daungers dread to ward his naked side,[5]
He can[6] let drive at him with all his power,
And with his axe him smote in evill hower,
That from his shoulders quite his head he reft:
The headlesse tronke, as heedlesse of that stower,[7]
Stood still a while, and his fast footing kept,
Till feeling life to fayle, it fell, and deadly slept.

21　　They which that piteous spectacle beheld,
Were much amaz'd the headlesse tronke to see
Stand up so long, and weapon vaine to weld,[8]
Unweeting of the Fates divine decree,
For lifes succession in those brethren three.
For notwithstanding that one soule was reft,
Yet, had the bodie not dismembred bee,
It would have lived, and revived eft;[9]
But finding no fit seat, the lifelesse corse it left.

22　　It left; but that same soule,[10] which therein dwelt,
Streight entring into *Triamond,* him fild
With double life, and griefe, which when he felt,
As one whose inner parts had bene ythrild
With point of steele, that close his hartbloud spild,
He lightly lept out of his place of rest,

---

[1] **souse:** swoop; **light:** nimbly.

[2] **weeldlesse:** unwieldy.

[3] **adventure:** chance, opportunity.

[4] **recower:** recover (OED "recour" v. trans.).

[5] **ward:** guard; **naked side:** the right side, not covered by the shield.

[6] **can:** gan, did.

[7] **stower:** commotion; stress.

[8] **weld:** wield.

[9] **eft:** afterwards; again.

[10] **It:** Priamond's soul, which had entered into Diamond; **that same soule:** Diamond's own soul.

    And rushing forth into the emptie field,
     Against *Cambello* fiercely him addrest;
   Who him affronting soone to fight was readie prest.[1]

23 Well mote ye wonder how that noble Knight,
    After he had so often wounded beene,
    Could stand on foot, now to renew the fight.
    But had ye then him forth advauncing seene,
    Some newborne wight ye would him surely weene:
    So fresh he seemed and so fierce in sight;
    Like as a Snake, whom wearie winters teene,
   Hath worne to nought, now feeling sommers might,
  Casts off his ragged skin and freshly doth him dight.

24 All was through vertue of the ring he wore,
    The which not onely did not from him let
    One drop of bloud to fall, but did restore
    His weakned powers, and dulled spirits whet,
    Through working of the stone therein yset.
    Else how could one of equall might with most,[2]
    Against so many no lesse mightie met,
   Once thinke to match three such on equall cost,[3]
  Three such as able were to match a puissant host.

25 Yet nought thereof was *Triamond* adredde,[4]
    Ne desperate[5] of glorious victorie,
    But sharpely him assayld, and sore bestedde,
    With heapes of strokes, which he at him let flie,
    As thicke as hayle forth poured from the skie:
    He stroke, he soust, he foynd,[6] he hewd, he lasht,
    And did his yron brond[7] so fast applie,
    That from the same the fierie sparkles flasht,
  As fast as water-sprinkles gainst a rocke are dasht.

---

[1] **affronting:** confronting; **prest:** prepared.

[2] I.e., of average might.

[3] **on equall cost:** on even terms; on an even playing field (literally coast).

[4] **adredde:** made to dread.

[5] **desperate:** despairing.

[6] **soust:** swooped; pounced; **foynd:** thrust; lunged.

[7] **brond:** brand, sword.

26 Much was *Cambello* daunted with his blowes:
      So thicke they fell, and forcibly were sent,
      That he was forst from daunger of the throwes[1]
      Backe to retire, and somewhat to relent,
      Till th'heat of his fierce furie he had spent:
      Which when for want of breath gan to abate,
      He then afresh with new encouragement
      Did him assayle, and mightily amate,
As fast as forward erst, now backward to retrate.

27 Like as the tide that comes fro th'Ocean mayne,
      Flowes up the Shenan[2] with contrarie forse,
      And overruling him in his owne rayne,[3]
      Drives backe the current of his kindly course,
      And makes it seeme to have some other sourse:
      But when the floud is spent, then backe againe
      His borrowed waters forst to redisbourse,[4]
      He sends the sea his owne with double gaine,
And tribute eke withall, as to his Soveraine.[5]

28 Thus did the battell varie to and fro,
      With diverse fortune doubtfull to be deemed:
      Now this the better had, now had his fo;
      Then he halfe vanquisht, then the other seemed,
      Yet victors both them selves alwayes esteemed.
      And all the while the disentrayled[6] blood
      Adowne their sides like litle rivers stremed,
      That with the wasting of his vitall flood,
Sir *Triamond* at last full faint and feeble stood.

29 But *Cambell* still more strong and greater grew,
      Ne felt his blood to wast, ne powres emperisht,[7]
      Through that rings vertue, that with vigour new,

---

[1] **throwes:** blows.

[2] **the Shenan:** the Sionainn (also known as Shannon), Ireland's largest tidal river, about 30 miles north of Spenser's Kilcolman Castle. As Clerk of the Council, Spenser would often have been in Limerick, which is right on the Sionainn.

[3] **rayne:** realm.

[4] **redisbourse:** repay (i.e., empty again out to sea).

[5] **tribute:** tax paid to a lord or monarch. Note the pun on "tributary." Cf. VI.Pr. 7.4–5, in which Spenser describes himself as a river receiving water from, and repaying water to, the Ocean, Queen Elizabeth.

[6] **disentrayled:** produced from the entrails.

[7] **emperisht:** enfeebled.

Still when as he enfeebled was, him cherisht,
And all his wounds, and all his bruses guarisht,[1]
Like as a withered tree through husbands[2] toyle
Is often seene full freshly to have florisht,
And fruitfull apples to have borne awhile,
As fresh as when it first was planted in the soyle.

30 Through which advantage, in his strength he rose,
And smote the other with so wondrous might,
That through the seame, which did his hauberk close,
Into his throate and life it pierced quight,
That downe he fell as dead in all mens sight:
Yet dead he was not, yet he sure did die,
As all men do, that lose the living spright:
So did one soule out of his bodie flie
Unto her native home from mortall miserie.

31 But nathelesse whilst all the lookers on
Him dead behight,[3] as he to all appeard,
All unawares he started up anon,
As one that had out of a dreame bene reard,
And fresh assayld his foe, who halfe affeard
Of th'uncouth sight, as he some ghost had seene,
Stood still amaz'd, holding his idle sweard;
Till having often by him stricken beene,
He forced was to strike, and save him selfe from teene.

32 Yet from thenceforth more warily he fought,
As one in feare the Stygian gods t'offend,
Ne followd on so fast, but rather sought
Him selfe to save, and daunger to defend,[4]
Then life and labour both in vaine to spend.
Which *Triamond* perceiving, weened sure
He gan to faint, toward the battels end,
And that he should not long on foote endure,
A signe which did to him the victorie assure.

---

[1] **guarisht:** healed.
[2] **husbands:** farmer's.
[3] **behight:** considered.
[4] **defend:** defend against, fend off.

33 Whereof full blith, eftsoones his mightie hand
  He heav'd on high, in mind with that same blow
  To make an end of all that did withstand:
  Which *Cambell* seeing come, was nothing slow
  Him selfe to save from that so deadly throw;[1]
  And at that instant reaching forth his sweard
  Close underneath his shield, that scarce did show,
  Stroke him, as he his hand to strike upreard,
In th'arm-pit full, that through both sides the wound appeard.

34 Yet still that direfull stroke kept on his way,
  And falling heavie on *Cambelloes* crest,
  Strooke him so hugely, that in swowne he lay,
  And in his head an hideous wound imprest:[2]
  And sure had it not happily found rest
  Upon the brim of his brode plated shield,
  It would have cleft his braine downe to his brest.
  So both at once fell dead upon the field,
And each to other seemd the victorie to yield.

35 Which when as all the lookers on beheld,
  They weened sure the warre was at an end,
  And Judges rose, and Marshals of the field
  Broke up the listes, their armes away to rend;
  And *Canacee* gan wayle her dearest frend.
  All suddenly they both upstarted light,
  The one out of the swownd, which him did blend,[3]
  The other breathing now another spright,[4]
And fiercely each assayling, gan afresh to fight.

36 Long while they then continued in that wize,
  As if but then the battell had begonne:
  Strokes, wounds, wards,[5] weapons, all they did despise,
  Ne either car'd to ward, or perill shonne,
  Desirous both to have the battell donne;
  Ne either cared life to save or spill,

---

[1] **throw:** strike.

[2] **imprest:** imprinted.

[3] **blend:** blind.

[4] Having lost Diamond's spirit, he now proceeds to use his own.

[5] **wards:** defensive postures; defenses.

Ne which of them did winne, ne which were wonne.
So wearie both of fighting had their fill,
That life it selfe seemd loathsome, and long safetie ill.

37   Whilst thus the case in doubtfull ballance hong,
        Unsure to whether[1] side it would incline,
        And all mens eyes and hearts, which there among
        Stood gazing, filled were with rufull tine,
        And secret feare, to see their fatall fine,[2]
        All suddenly they heard a troublous noyes,
        That seemd some perilous tumult to desine,[3]
        Confusd[4] with womens cries, and shouts of boyes,
    Such as the troubled Theaters oftimes annoyes.

38   Thereat the Champions both stood still a space,
        To weeten what that sudden clamour ment;
        Lo where they spyde with speedie whirling pace,
        One in a charet of straunge furniment,[5]
        Towards them driving like a storme out sent.
        The charet decked was in wondrous wize,
        With gold and many a gorgeous ornament,
        After the Persian Monarks antique guize,
    Such as the maker selfe could best by art devize.

39   And drawne it was (that wonder is to tell)[6]
        Of two grim lyons, taken from the wood,
        In which their powre all others did excell;
        Now made forget their former cruell mood,
        T'obey their riders hest,[7] as seemed good.
        And therein sate a Ladie passing faire
        And bright, that seemed borne of Angels brood,
        And with her beautie bountie did compare,[8]
    Whether[9] of them in her should have the greater share.

---

[1] **whether:** which.

[2] **fine:** finish.

[3] **desine:** indicate. (OED "design" v. I.1. trans. Not in the OED as a variant spelling, but the seven times Spenser uses this word conform with this definition.)

[4] **Confusd:** mingled.

[5] **charet:** chariot; **furniment:** fittings.

[6] **that wonder is to tell:** a standard formula.

[7] **hest:** command.

[8] **bountie:** goodness, virtue; **compare:** compete.

[9] **Whether:** which.

40   Thereto she learned was in Magicke leare,[1]
       And all the artes, that subtill wits discover,
       Having therein bene trained many a yeare,
       And well instructed by the Fay her mother,
       That in the same she farre exceld all other.
       Who understanding by her mightie art,
       Of th'evill plight, in which her dearest brother
       Now stood, came forth in hast to take his part,
   And pacifie the strife, which causd so deadly smart.

41   And as she passed through th'unruly preace[2]
       Of people, thronging thicke her to behold,
       Her angrie teame breaking their bonds of peace,
       Great heapes of them, like sheepe in narrow fold,
       For hast did over-runne, in dust enrould,[3]
       That thorough rude confusion of the rout,
       Some fearing shriekt, some being harmed hould,[4]
       Some laught for sport, some did for wonder shout,
   And some that would seeme wise, their wonder turnd to dout.

42   In her right hand a rod of peace shee bore,
       About the which two Serpents weren wound,
       Entrayled mutually in lovely lore,[5]
       And by the tailes together firmely bound,
       And both were with one olive garland crownd,
       Like to the rod which *Maias* sonne[6] doth wield,
       Wherewith the hellish fiends he doth confound.
       And in her other hand a cup she hild,
   The which was with Nepenthe[7] to the brim upfild.

---

[1] **leare:** lore.

[2] **preace:** crowd.

[3] Like most relatively wealthy Elizabethans, Spenser may not have seen any contradiction in bringing Concord to his country—and to Ireland—over the trampled bodies of ordinary people. Like Sidney, Shakespeare, and many others, he seems more often to have thought of the lower classes of people as mobs or potential criminals than as citizens with personal aspirations.

[4] **hould:** howled.

[5] **Entrayled:** entwined; **lovely lore:** loving fashion; loving instruction. Canacee holds a *caduceus*, a staff twined with two snakes (or two representations of snakes), such as was supposedly carried by the god Mercury and in ancient Greece and Rome by heralds. Mercury was often described as having the power to cause people to sleep and to cause the fiends of the underworld to obey him.

[6] *Maias* **sonne:** Mercury.

[7] **Nepenthe:** a mythological drug supposed to eradicate grief.

43   Nepenthe is a drinck of soverayne grace,
          Devized by the Gods, for to asswage
          Harts grief, and bitter gall away to chace,
          Which stirs up anguish and contentious rage:
          In stead thereof sweet peace and quiet age[1]
          It doth establish in the troubled mynd.
          Few men, but such as sober are and sage,
          Are by the Gods to drinck thereof assynd;
     But such as drinck, eternall happinesse do fynd.

44   Such famous men, such worthies of the earth,
          As *Jove* will have advaunced to the skie,
          And there made gods, though borne of mortall berth,[2]
          For their high merits and great dignitie,[3]
          Are wont, before they may to heaven flie,
          To drincke hereof, whereby all cares forepast
          Are washt away quite from their memorie.
          So did those olde Heroes hereof taste,
     Before that they in blisse amongst the Gods were plaste.

45   Much more of price and of more gratious powre[4]
          Is this, then that same water of Ardenne,
          The which *Rinaldo* drunck in happie howre,[5]
          Described by that famous Tuscane penne:
          For that had might to change the hearts of men
          Fro love to hate, a change of evill choise:
          But this doth hatred make in love to brenne,[6]
          And heavy heart with comfort doth rejoyce.
     Who would not to this vertue rather yeeld his voice?

46   At last arriving by the listes side,
          Shee with her rod did softly smite the raile,
          Which straight flew ope, and gave her way to ride.
          Eftsoones out of her Coch she gan availe,[7]

---

[1] **quiet age:** quietage, quietude, calm.

[2] **berth:** birth.

[3] **dignitie:** worth.

[4] **price:** value; **gratious powre:** power to bestow grace.

[5] Either the fountain of hate from which Ranaldo drank in Boiardo's *Orlando Innamorato* (1.3.34–36) or the fountains of love and hate from which Rinaldo drank in Ariosto's *Orlando Furioso* (1.78–79).

[6] **brenne:** burn.

[7] **Coch:** coach; **availe:** descend.

And pacing fairely forth, did bid all haile,
First to her brother, whom she loved deare,
That so to see him made her heart to quaile:
And next to *Cambell,* whose sad ruefull cheare
Made her to change her hew, and hidden love t'appeare.

47   They lightly her requit[1] (for small delight
       They had as then her long to entertaine,)
       And eft them turned both againe to fight,
       Which when she saw, downe on the bloudy plaine
       Her selfe she threw, and teares gan shed amaine;[2]
       Amongst her teares immixing prayers meeke,
       And with her prayers reasons to restraine,
       From blouddy strife, and blessed peace to seeke,
By all that unto them was deare, did them beseeke.[3]

48   But when as all might nought with them prevaile,
       Shee smote them lightly with her powrefull wand.
       Then suddenly as if their hearts did faile,
       Their wrathfull blades downe fell out of their hand,
       And they like men astonisht still did stand.
       Thus whilest their minds were doubtfully distraught,[4]
       And mighty spirites bound with mightier band,
       Her golden cup to them for drinke she raught,[5]
Whereof full glad for thirst, ech drunk an harty draught.

49   Of which so soone as they once tasted had,
       Wonder it is that sudden change to see:
       Instead of strokes, each other kissed glad,
       And lovely haulst[6] from feare of treason free,
       And plighted hands for ever friends to be.[7]
       When all men saw this sudden change of things,

---

[1] **requit:** greeted in return.

[2] **amaine:** vehemently.

[3] **beseeke:** beseech.

[4] **distraught:** distracted.

[5] **raught:** reached, handed.

[6] **lovely haulst:** lovingly embraced.

[7] Cavanagh interprets this new friendship between Canacee's brother and her future husband in terms of Levi-Strauss' investigations into the reasons for prohibitions against incest: once Cambello gives up his vaguely incestuous protection of his sister, he forms a sociopolitical bond with another man (Cavanagh 79).

So mortall foes so friendly to agree,
For passing joy, which so great marvaile brings,
They all gan shout aloud, that all the heaven rings.

50   All which, when gentle *Canacee* beheld,
        In hast she from her lofty chaire descended,
        To weet what sudden tidings was befeld:
        Where when she saw that cruell war so ended,
        And deadly foes so faithfully affrended,[1]
        In lovely wise she gan that Lady greet,
        Which had so great dismay so well amended,
        And entertaining her with curt'sies[2] meet,
    Profest to her true friendship and affection sweet.

51   Thus when they all accorded goodly were,
        The trumpets sounded, and they all arose,
        Thence to depart with glee and gladsome chere.[3]
        Those warlike champions both together chose,
        Homeward to march, themselves there to repose,
        And wise *Cambina* taking by her side
        Faire *Canacee,* as fresh as morning rose,
        Unto her Coch remounting, home did ride,
    Admir'd[4] of all the people, and much glorifide.

52   Where making joyous feast theire daies they spent
        In perfect love, devoide of hatefull strife,
        Allide with bands of mutuall couplement;[5]
        For *Triamond* had *Canacee* to wife,
        With whom he ledd a long and happie life;
        And *Cambel* tooke *Cambina* to his fere,[6]
        The which as life were each to other liefe.
        So all alike did love, and loved were,
    That since their days such lovers were not found elswere.[7]

---

[1] **affrended:** changed into friends; reconciled.

[2] **curt'sies:** courtesies.

[3] **glee:** joy; entertainment; music; **chere:** gaiety; mirth; mood.

[4] **Admir'd:** marveled at.

[5] **couplement:** pairings.

[6] **fere:** mate.

[7] **elswere:** elsewhere.

Canto Four

Satyrane makes a Turneyment
For love of Florimell:
Britomart winnes the prize from all,
And Artegall doth quell.

1   It often fals, (as here it earst befell)
          That mortall foes doe turne to faithfull frends,
          And friends profest[1] are chaungd to foemen fell:
          The cause of both, of both their minds depends,
          And th'end of both likewise of both their ends.[2]
          For enmitie, that of no ill proceeds,
          But of occasion, with th'occasion ends;
          And friendship, which a faint affection breeds
      Without regard of good, dyes like ill grounded seeds.

2   That well (me seemes) appeares, by that[3] of late
          Twixt *Cambell* and Sir *Triamond* befell,
          As els by this, that now a new debate
          Stird up twixt *Scudamour*[4] and *Paridell,*
          The which by course befals me here to tell:
          Who having those two other Knights espide
          Marching afore, as ye remember well,
          Sent forth their Squire[5] to have them both descride,
      And eke those masked Ladies riding them beside.[6]

3   Who backe returning, told as he had seene,
          That they were doughtie knights of dreaded name;
          And those two Ladies, their two loves unseene;

---

[1] **profest:** declared; pretended.

[2] **end:** result; **ends:** goals, intentions.

[3] **that:** that which.

[4] *Scudamour:* an error for Blandamour. Although Blandamour and Paridell do not begin a "new debate" until v.24, Scudamour cannot logically be present when Britomart displays Amoret at v.13, since at v.28–34 we learn that Scudamour was elsewhere, still firmly believing that Britomart was a male knight who abducted Amoret.

[5] **their Squire:** the Squire of Dames.

[6] The narrative now picks up where it left off at ii.31.

And therefore wisht them without blot or blame,
To let them passe at will, for dread of shame.
But *Blandamour* full of vainglorious spright,
And rather stird by his discordfull Dame,[1]
Upon them gladly would have prov'd his might,
But that he yet was sore of his late lucklesse fight.[2]

4   Yet nigh approching, he them fowle bespake,
Disgracing[3] them, him selfe thereby to grace,
As was his wont, so weening way to make
To Ladies love, where so he came in place,[4]
And with lewd termes their lovers to deface.[5]
Whose sharpe provokement them incenst so sore,
That both were bent t'avenge his usage base,
And gan their shields addresse them selves afore:
For evill deedes may better then bad words be bore.[6]

5   But faire *Cambina* with perswasions myld,
Did mitigate the fiercenesse of their mode,[7]
That for the present they were reconcyld,
And gan to treate[8] of deeds of armes abrode,
And strange adventures, all the way they rode:
Amongst the which they told, as then befell,
Of that great turney, which was blazed brode,[9]
For that rich girdle of faire *Florimell*,
The prize of her, which did in beautie most excell.

6   To which folke-mote[10] they all with one consent,
Sith each of them his Ladie had him by,
Whose beautie each of them thought excellent,[11]
Agreed to travell, and their fortunes try.[12]

---

[1] **discordfull Dame:** Ate.

[2] I.e., his fight with Paridell (ii.11–20).

[3] **Disgracing:** insulting.

[4] **in place:** there.

[5] **deface:** defame.

[6] **bore:** borne.

[7] **mode:** mood.

[8] **treate:** talk.

[9] **blazed:** blazoned, proclaimed; **brode:** widely.

[10] **folke-mote:** in *A View of the Present State of Ireland,* Spenser describes folk-motes as gathering places bounded by earthen walls, where the native Irish held public discussions to settle disputes—and to raise mischief against the English (Spenser, *View,* 77). Here, the folke-mote is a place where knights go to settle their disputes militarily.

[11] **excellent:** best.

[12] I.e., each knight will fight to prove his lady the most beautiful.

So as they passed forth, they did espy
One in bright armes, with ready speare in rest,
That toward them his course seem'd to apply,
Gainst whom Sir *Paridell* himselfe addrest,
Him weening, ere he nigh approcht to have represt.

7   Which th'other seeing, gan his course relent,[1]
And vaunted[2] speare eftsoones to disadvaunce,
As if he naught but peace and pleasure ment,
Now falne into their fellowship by chance,
Whereat they shewed curteous countenaunce.
So as he rode with them accompanide,
His roving eie did on the Lady glaunce,
Which *Blandamour* had riding by his side:
Whom sure he weend, that he somwhere tofore[3] had eide.

8   It was to weete that snowy *Florimell,*
Which *Ferrau* late from *Braggadochio* wonne,[4]
Whom he now seeing, her remembred well,[5]
How having reft her from the witches sonne,
He soone her lost: wherefore he now begunne
To challenge[6] her anew, as his owne prize,
Whom formerly he had in battell wonne,
And proffer made by force her to reprize,[7]
Which scornefull offer, *Blandamour* gan soone despize.

9   And said, "Sir Knight, sith ye this Lady clame,
Whom he that hath, were loth to lose so light,
(For so to lose a Lady, were great shame)
Yee shall her winne, as I have done in fight:
And lo shee shall be placed here in sight
Together with this Hag beside her set,
That who so winnes her, may her have by right:
But he shall have the Hag that is ybet,[8]
And with her alwaies ride, till he another get."

---

[1] **relent:** slacken.

[2] **vaunted:** displayed proudly.

[3] **tofore:** before.

[4] At III.viii.15–19.

[5] We now see that Braggadocchio is the newcomer in "bright armes" whose "vaunted" spear quickly came down when he was intimidated by Paridell (stanzas 6 and 7).

[6] **challenge:** make a challenge for; claim.

[7] **proffer:** offer; attempt; **reprize:** reclaim.

[8] **ybet:** beaten.

10   That offer pleased all the company,
     So *Florimell* with *Ate* forth was brought,
     At which they all gan laugh full merrily:[1]
     But *Braggadochio* said, he never thought
     For such an Hag, that seemed worse then nought,
     His person to emperill so in fight.
     But if to match that Lady they had sought
     Another like, that were like faire and bright,
His life he then would spend to justifie his right.[2]

11   At which his vaine excuse they all gan smile,
     As scorning his unmanly cowardize:
     And *Florimell* him fowly gan revile,
     That for her sake refus'd to enterprize
     The battell, offred in so knightly wize.
     And *Ate* eke provokt him privily,
     With love of her, and shame of such mesprize.[3]
     But naught he car'd for friend or enemy,
For in base mind nor friendship dwels nor enmity.

12   But *Cambell* thus did shut up all in jest,
     "Brave Knights and Ladies, certes ye doe wrong
     To stirre up strife, when most us needeth rest,
     That we may us reserve both fresh and strong,
     Against the Turneiment which is not long.[4]
     When who so list to fight, may fight his fill,
     Till then your challenges ye may prolong;[5]
     And then it shall be tried, if ye will,
Whether[6] shall have the Hag, or hold the Lady still."

---

[1] Plays, poems, and romance narratives written during the sixteenth century are almost unanimous in considering elderly women fair game for scornful humor and for disgust, unless they are speaking of actual women who are patrons or potential patrons. Cf. i.17–19 and notes.

[2] I.e., Braggadocchio is unwilling to risk fighting when he has a chance of losing and being stuck with Ate, but he offers to participate in the tournament if, instead of the Snowy Florimell and Ate, the prizes offered to the winner and loser will both be as beautiful as the Snowy Florimell. It would be unheard of to reward the victor and loser equally, so Braggadocchio is risking nothing in making this proposal.

[3] **mesprize**: contempt; slander.

[4] **Against**: in preparation for; **long**: far off (in time).

[5] **prolong**: postpone.

[6] **Whether**: which one.

13   They all agreed, so turning all to game,
      And pleasaunt bord,[1] they past forth on their way,
      And all that while, where so they rode or came,
      That masked Mock-knight[2] was their sport and play.
      Till that at length upon th'appointed day,
      Unto the place of turneyment they came;
      Where they before them found in fresh aray
      Manie a brave knight, and manie a daintie dame
    Assembled, for to get the honour of that game.

14   There this faire crewe arriving, did divide
      Them selves asunder: *Blandamour* with those
      Of his, on th'one; the rest on th'other side.[3]
      But boastfull *Braggadocchio* rather chose,
      For glorie vaine their fellowship to lose,
      That men on him the more might gaze alone.[4]
      The rest them selves in troupes did else dispose,
      Like as it seemed best to every one;
    The knights in couples marcht, with ladies linckt attone.

15   Then first of all forth came Sir *Satyrane*,
      Bearing that precious relicke in an arke
      Of gold, that bad eyes might it not prophane:[5]
      Which drawing softly forth out of the darke,
      He open shewd, that all men it mote marke.
      A gorgeous girdle, curiously embost
      With pearle and precious stone, worth many a marke;[6]
      Yet did the workmanship farre passe the cost:
    It was the same, which lately *Florimel* had lost.

---

[1] **bord:** bourd, joking.

[2] **masked Mock-knight:** Braggadocchio, who was masquerading as a knight when in fact he is a coward.

[3] Just before the tournament, on one side are the false friends: Blandamour, the Snowy Florimell, Paridell, Ate, Duessa, and possibly the Squire of Dames. On the other side are the true friends: Cambello, Cambina, Triamond, and Canacee. Braggadocchio, who is capable neither of friendship nor of enmity (stanza 11.8–9), is on neither side. During the tournament itself, however, all of the above fight against Satyrane and several other Knights of Maidenhead (for which military order, see III.viii.47.7.n.). Thus the forces of false and true friendship battle the forces of chastity.

[4] **alone:** if he is alone.

[5] Cf. the Ark of the Covenant of the ancient Hebrews, which, once placed in the Temple, could not be seen by any but the high priest.

[6] **marke:** a unit of currency.

16   That same aloft he hong in open vew,
           To be the prize of beautie and of might;
           The which eftsoones discovered, to it drew
           The eyes of all, allur'd with close delight,
           And hearts quite robbed[1] with so glorious sight,
           That all men threw out vowes and wishes vaine.
           Thrise happie Ladie, and thrise happie knight,
           Them seemd that could so goodly riches gaine,
       So worthie of the perill, worthy of the paine.

17   Then tooke the bold Sir *Satyrane* in hand
           An huge great speare,[2] such as he wont to wield,
           And vauncing forth from all the other band
           Of knights, addrest his maiden-headed shield,[3]
           Shewing him selfe all ready for the field.
           Gainst whom there singled from the other side
           A Painim[4] knight, that well in armes was skild,
           And had in many a battell oft bene tride,
       Hight *Bruncheval*[5] the bold, who fiersly forth did ride.

18   So furiously they both together met,
           That neither could the others force sustaine;
           As two fierce Buls,[6] that strive the rule to get
           Of all the heard, meete with so hideous maine,[7]
           That both rebutted, tumble on the plaine:
           So these two champions to the ground were feld,
           Where in a maze they both did long remaine,
           And in their hands their idle troncheons[8] held,
       Which neither able were to wag, or once to weld.[9]

---

[1] **robbed:** ravished.

[2] **An huge great speare:** the phallic comedy is complicated, given that here and in Britomart's entire story, Spenser uses large spears to emblematize the defense of chastity.

[3] **maiden-headed shield:** at III.vii.30.6, Satyrane's shield displays a satyr's head, but here he represents the Knights of Maidenhead (see III.viii.47.7.n.).

[4] **Painim:** pagan.

[5] *Bruncheval:* his name can be interpreted "Brown Knight," "Brown Horse," "Dark Knight," or "Dark Horse" (French).

[6] Note the animal imagery used to describe masculinity throughout this episode.

[7] **maine:** force.

[8] **troncheons:** broken spear shafts.

[9] **wag:** brandish; **weld:** wield.

19   Which when the noble *Ferramont*[1] espide,
          He pricked forth in ayd of *Satyran;*
          And him against Sir *Blandamour* did ride
          With all the strength and stifnesse[2] that he can.
          But the more strong and stiffely that he ran,
          So much more sorely to the ground he fell,
          That on an heape were tumbled horse and man.
          Unto whose rescue forth rode *Paridell;*
      But him likewise with that same speare he[3] eke did quell.

20   Which *Braggadocchio* seeing, had no will
          To hasten greatly to his parties ayd,
          Albee his turne were next; but stood there still,
          As one that seemed doubtfull or dismayd.[4]
          But *Triamond* halfe wroth to see him staid,[5]
          Sternly stept forth, and raught away his speare,
          With which so sore he *Ferramont* assaid,[6]
          That horse and man to ground he quite did beare,
      That neither could in hast themselves againe upreare.

21   Which to avenge, Sir *Devon*[7] him did dight,
          But with no better fortune then the rest:
          For him likewise he quickly downe did smight,
          And after him Sir *Douglas* him addrest,
          And after him Sir *Paliumord* forth prest,
          But none of them against his strokes could stand,
          But all the more,[8] the more his praise increst.
          For either they were left uppon the land,
      Or went away sore wounded of his haplesse[9] hand.

---

[1] **Ferramont:** the name means either "Iron Mount" or "Iron Tools" (Latin). He fights for the Knights of Maidenhead.

[2] **stifnesse:** firmness; strength. Given that he fights against the Knights of Maidenhead, his stiffness suggests the hardness of an erection.

[3] **he:** Satyrane.

[4] **dismayd:** Spenser's favorite pun is especially intriguing here, given that Brag-gadocchio's opponents are supposed to be defending virginity.

[5] **staid:** stayed, motionless.

[6] **assaid:** assailed.

[7] Sirs Devon, Douglas, and Palimord fight for the Knights of Maidenhead.

[8] **all the more:** the more of them there were.

[9] **of:** by; **haplesse:** causing mishap.

22   And now by this, Sir *Satyrane* abraid,[1]
          Out of the swowne, in which too long he lay;
          And looking round about, like one dismaid,
          When as he saw the mercilesse affray,
          Which doughty *Triamond* had wrought that day,
          Unto the noble Knights of Maidenhead,
          His mighty heart did almost rend in tway,[2]
          For very gall, that rather wholly dead
   Himselfe he wisht have beene, then in so bad a stead.

23   Eftsoones he gan to gather up around
          His weapons, which lay scattered all abrode,
          And as it fell, his steed he ready found.
          On whom remounting, fiercely forth he rode,
          Like sparke of fire that from the andvile glode,[3]
          There where he saw the valiant *Triamond*
          Chasing, and laying on them heavy lode,
          That none his force were able to withstond,
   So dreadfull were his strokes, so deadly was his hond.

24   With that at him his beamlike speare he aimed,
          And thereto all his power and might applide:
          The wicked steele for mischiefe first ordained,
          And having now misfortune got for guide,
          Staid not, till it arrived in his[4] side,
          And therein made a very griesly wound,
          That streames of bloud his armour all bedide.[5]
          Much was he daunted with that direfull stound,
   That scarse he him upheld from falling in a sound.[6]

25   Yet as he might, himselfe he soft[7] withdrew
          Out of the field, that none perceiv'd it plaine,
          Then gan the part[8] of Chalengers anew
          To range the field, and victorlike to raine,
          That none against them battell durst maintaine.

---

[1] **by this:** by this time; **abraid:** started up; burst into motion.

[2] **in tway:** in two.

[3] **andvile:** anvil; **glode:** glided.

[4] **his:** Triamond's.

[5] **bedide:** dyed.

[6] **sound:** swoon.

[7] **soft:** unobtrusively (literally quietly).

[8] **part:** faction.

By that the gloomy evening on them fell,
That forced them from fighting to refraine,
And trumpets sound to cease did them compell,
So *Satyrane* that day was judg'd to beare the bell.[1]

26   The morrow next the Turney gan anew,
        And with the first the hardy *Satyrane*
        Appear'd in place, with all his noble crew,
        On th'other side, full many a warlike swaine,
        Assembled were, that glorious prize to gaine.
        But mongst them all, was not Sir *Triamond,*
        Unable he new battell to darraine,[2]
        Through grievaunce of his late received wound,
    That doubly did him grieve, when so himselfe he found.

27   Which *Cambell* seeing, though he could not salve,[3]
        Ne done undoe, yet for to salve[4] his name,
        And purchase honour in his friends behalve,[5]
        This goodly counterfesaunce he did frame.[6]
        The shield and armes well knowne to be the same,
        Which *Triamond* had worne, unwares to wight,
        And to his friend unwist, for doubt of blame,
        If he misdid, he on himselfe did dight,[7]
    That none could him discerne, and so went forth to fight.

28   There *Satyrane* Lord of the field he found,
        Triumphing in great joy and jolity;
        Gainst whom none able was to stand on ground;
        That much he gan his glorie to envy,
        And cast t'avenge his friends indignity.
        A mightie speare eftsoones at him he bent;

---

[1] **beare the bell:** win the day's competition (from the bell worn by the wether that leads a flock of sheep).

[2] **darraine:** prepare for.

[3] **salve:** remedy.

[4] **salve:** preserve.

[5] **behalve:** behalf.

[6] **counterfesaunce:** deception; **frame:** devise.

[7] Cambello puts on Triamond's arms in order to frighten their foes into thinking Triamond is still fighting. He does not tell Triamond in advance, in case the plan does not turn out well. Given that Triamond will be blamed if Cambello does not fight well, Cambello's aversion to telling Triamond of his plan seems flawed.

Who seeing him come on so furiously,
    Met him mid-way with equall hardiment,
That forcibly to ground they both together went.

29   They up againe them selves can[1] lightly reare,
    And to their tryed swords them selves betake;
    With which they wrought such wondrous marvels there,
    That all the rest it did amazed make,
    Ne any dar'd their perill to partake;[2]
    Now cuffling[3] close, now chacing to and fro,
    Now hurtling round advantage for to take:
    As two wild Boares together grapling go,
Chaufing and foming choler[4] each against his fo.

30   So as they courst, and turneyd here and theare,
    It chaunst Sir *Satyrane* his steed at last,
    Whether through foundring or through sodein feare
    To stumble, that his rider nigh he cast;
    Which vauntage *Cambell* did pursue so fast,
    That ere him selfe he had recovered well,
    So sore he sowst him on the compast creast,[5]
    That forced him to leave his loftie sell,
And rudely tumbling downe under his horse feete fell.

31   Lightly *Cambello* leapt downe from his steed,
    For to have rent his shield and armes away,
    That whylome wont to be the victors meed;[6]
    When all unwares he felt an hideous sway
    Of many swords, that lode on him did lay.
    An hundred knights had him enclosed round,
    To rescue *Satyrane* out of his pray;[7]
    All which at once huge strokes on him did pound,
In hope to take him prisoner, where he stood on ground.

---

[1] **can:** gan, did.

[2] **partake:** share.

[3] **cuffling:** scuffling (?). The OED is doubtful of the definition and gives only this example.

[4] **Chaufing:** chafing; fuming; **foming choler:** foaming bile; foaming with anger.

[5] **compast creast:** round helmet.

[6] It was standard practice to take the armor and weapons from one's slain foe as trophies.

[7] **out of his pray:** from being Cambello's prey.

32   He with their multitude was nought dismayd,
    But with stout courage turnd upon them all,
    And with his brondiron[1] round about him layd;
    Of which he dealt large almes,[2] as did befall:
    Like as a Lion that by chaunce doth fall
    Into the hunters toile,[3] doth rage and rore,
    In royall heart disdaining to be thrall.
    But all in vaine: for what might one do more?
They have him taken captive, though it grieve him sore.

33   Whereof when newes to *Triamond* was brought,
    There as he lay, his wound he soone forgot,
    And starting up, streight for his armour sought:
    In vaine he sought; for there he found it not;
    Cambello it away before had got:
    Cambelloes armes therefore he on him threw,[4]
    And lightly issewd forth to take his lot.
    There he in troupe[5] found all that warlike crew,
Leading his friend away, full sorie to his vew.

34   Into the thickest of that knightly preasse
    He thrust, and smote downe all that was betweene,
    Caried with fervent zeale, ne did he ceasse,
    Till that he came, where he had *Cambell* seene,
    Like captive thral two other Knights atweene,[6]
    There he amongst them cruell havocke makes;
    That they which lead him, soone enforced beene
    To let him loose, to save their proper stakes,[7]
Who being freed, from one a weapon fiercely takes.

35   With that he drives at them with dreadfull might,
    Both in remembrance of his friends late harme,
    And in revengement of his owne despight,
    So both together give a new allarme,[8]

---

[1] **brondiron:** sword.

[2] I.e., with which he generously distributed blows (as one would generously distribute money for charity).

[3] **toile:** net; trap.

[4] Hamilton comments that "in an exemplum of erotic friendship, they fight in one another's arms" (Hamilton, iv.27.7–8.n.).

[5] **in troupe:** in a group; in large numbers; in battle array.

[6] **atweene:** between.

[7] **their proper stakes:** their own chances of living.

[8] **allarme:** unexpected attack; call to arms.

As if but now the battell wexed warme.
As when two greedy Wolves doe breake by force
Into an heard, farre from the husband farme,[1]
They spoile and ravine without all[2] remorse,
So did these two through all the field their foes enforce.[3]

36   Fiercely they followd on their bolde emprize,
Till trumpets sound did warne them all to rest;
Then all with one consent did yeeld the prize
To *Triamond* and *Cambell* as the best.
But *Triamond* to *Cambell* it relest.
And *Cambell* it to *Triamond* transferd;
Each labouring t'advance the others gest,
And make his praise before his owne preferd:
So that the doome was to another day differd.[4]

37   The last day came, when all those knightes againe
Assembled were their deedes of armes to shew.
Full many deedes that day were shewed plaine:
But *Satyrane* bove all the other crew,
His wondrous worth declared[5] in all mens view.
For from the first he to the last endured,
And though some while[6] Fortune from him withdrew,
Yet evermore his honour he recured,[7]
And with unwearied powre his party still assured.

38   Ne was there Knight that ever thought of armes,
But that his utmost prowesse there made knowen,
That by their many wounds, and carelesse harmes,[8]
By shivered speares, and swords all under strowen,[9]
By scattered shields was easie to be showen.
There might ye see loose steeds at randon ronne,

---

[1] **husband farme:** farmer's house; tilled
land.

[2] **without all:** completely without.

[3] **enforce:** drive.

[4] **doome:** decision about who has won;
differd: deferred (with a possible pun on
"differed").

[5] **declared:** demonstrated.

[6] **some while:** at times.

[7] **recured:** restored.

[8] **carelesse harmes:** injuries that they ig-
nored.

[9] **strowen:** strewn.

Whose luckelesse riders late were overthrowen;
And squiers make hast to helpe their Lords fordonne,[1]
But still the Knights of Maidenhead the better wonne.

39   Till that there entred on the other side,[2]
   A straunger knight, from whence no man could reed,
   In quyent disguise, full hard to be describe.[3]
   For all his armour was like salvage weed,[4]
   With woody mosse bedight, and all his steed
   With oaken leaves attrapt,[5] that seemed fit
   For salvage wight, and thereto well agreed
   His word,[6] which on his ragged shield was writ,
   Salvagesse sans finesse, shewing secret wit.[7]

40   He at his first incomming, charg'd his spere
   At him, that first appeared in his sight:
   That was to weet, the stout Sir *Sangliere,*[8]
   Who well was knowen to be a valiant Knight,
   Approved oft in many a perlous fight.
   Him at the first encounter downe he smote,

---

[1] **fordonne:** utterly done in; exhausted; overthrown.

[2] **on the other side:** on the side against the Knights of Maidenhead.

[3] **quyent:** strange; ingenious; **describe:** described; figured out.

[4] As Hamilton points out, Elizabethan tournaments often featured someone dressed up as a wild man. In general, Elizabethans were fascinated with so-called "wild" peoples, such as Africans and Native Americans, who helped Europeans define their own noble civility in contrast to what they thought of as the bestial or fiendish qualities of the non-Christian and less technologically developed cultures. At the same time, however, Europeans believed that "wild" peoples showed them what their own Celtic ancestors were like. Another interpretation that they made of such peoples—apparently contradictory, but freely mingled with the above interpretations—was that those peoples represented a prelapsarian innocence, before the corrupting effects of civilization.

[5] **attrapt:** decked out.

[6] **word:** motto.

[7] *Salvagesse sans finesse:* savagery without refinement; **secret wit:** secret meaning of the motto, but also the humor of having a wild man sport a French motto. From the time of the Norman Conquest until the time of Chaucer, French had been the language of the English court and aristocracy—the language of power, education, and refinement.

[8] *Sangliere:* the name means "wild boar" (French).

And overbore beyond his crouper[1] quight,
And after him another Knight, that hote[2]
Sir *Brianor*, so sore, that none him life behote.[3]

41   Then ere his hand he reard,[4] he overthrew
         Seven Knights one after other as they came:
         And when his speare was brust,[5] his sword he drew,
         The instrument of wrath, and with the same
         Far'd[6] like a lyon in his bloodie game,
         Hewing, and slashing shields, and helmets bright,
         And beating downe, what ever nigh him came,
         That every one gan shun his dreadfull sight,
No lesse then death it selfe, in daungerous affright.

42   Much wondred all men, what, or whence he came,
         That did amongst the troupes so tyrannize;
         And each of other gan inquire his name.
         But when they could not learne it by no wize,[7]
         Most answerable[8] to his wyld disguize
         It seemed, him to terme the salvage knight.
         But certes his right name was otherwize,
         Though knowne to few, that *Arthegall*[9] he hight,
The doughtiest knight that liv'd that day, and most of might.

43   Thus was Sir *Satyrane* with all his band
         By his sole manhood and atchievement stout
         Dismayd, that none of them in field durst stand,
         But beaten were, and chased all about.
         So he[10] continued all that day throughout,
         Till evening, that the Sunne gan downward bend.[11]

---

[1] **overbore:** note the pun on "boar"; **crouper:** crupper, the horse's rump or the strap that loops from the saddle under the horse's tail.

[2] **hote:** hight, was named.

[3] ***Brianor:*** the name suggests "bruin," meaning "bear"; it also may derive from Irish Gaelic names; **behote:** promised, assured.

[4] I.e., before raising his sword.

[5] **brust:** burst, shattered.

[6] **Far'd:** conducted himself; raged.

[7] **wize:** means.

[8] **answerable:** corresponding, fitting.

[9] For the name, see III.ii.8.9.n.

[10] **he:** Artegall.

[11] Hamilton notes that the masculine power of the sun (associated with the god Phoebus Apollo) is about to be displaced by the feminine power of the moon (associated with the goddess Diana, also known as Phoebe).

Then rushed forth out of the thickest rout
A stranger knight, that did his glorie shend:
So nought may be esteemed happie till the end.

44 He at his entrance charg'd his powrefull speare
At *Artegall*, in middest of his pryde,
And therewith smote him on his Umbriere[1]
So sore, that tombling backe, he downe did slyde
Over his horses taile above a stryde;[2]
Whence litle lust he had to rise againe.
Which *Cambell* seeing, much the same envyde,
And ran at him with all his might and maine;
But shortly was likewise seene lying on the plaine.

45 Whereat full inly wroth was *Triamond,*
And cast t'avenge the shame doen to his freend:
But by his friend himselfe eke soone he fond,
In no lesse neede of helpe, then him he weend.
All which when *Blandamour* from end to end
Beheld, he woxe therewith displeased sore,
And thought in mind it shortly to amend:
His speare he feutred,[3] and at him it bore;
But with no better fortune, then the rest afore.

46 Full many others at him likewise ran:
But all of them likewise dismounted were,
Ne certes wonder; for no powre of man
Could bide the force of that enchaunted speare,
The which this famous *Britomart* did beare;[4]
With which she wondrous deeds of arms atchieved,
And overthrew, what ever came her neare,
That all those stranger knights full sore agrieved,
And that late weaker band of chalengers relieved.

---

[1] **Umbriere:** visor of a helmet.

[2] **above a stryde:** more than the length of a stride behind his horse.

[3] **feutred:** set in its rest, ready for action.

[4] In other words, Spenser has been teasing us with all of the male pronouns above. For her spear's enchantment, see III.iii.60.

47   Like as in sommers day when raging heat
         Doth burne the earth,[1] and boyled rivers drie,
         That all brute beasts forst to refraine fro meat,[2]
         Doe hunt for shade, where shrowded they may lie,
         And missing it, faine from themselves to flie;
         All travellers tormented are with paine:
         A watry cloud doth overcast the skie,
         And poureth forth a sudden shoure of raine,
    That all the wretched world recomforteth againe.

48   So did the warlike *Britomart* restore
         The prize, to knights of Maydenhead that day,
         Which else was like to have bene lost, and bore
         The prayse of prowesse from them all away.
         Then shrilling trompets loudly gan to bray,
         And bad them leave their labours and long toyle,
         To joyous feast and other gentle play,
         Where beauties prize[3] shold win that pretious spoyle:
    Where I with sound of trompe will also rest a whyle.

---

[1] As Artegall raged among the knights while the sun shone.

[2] **meat:** food.

[3] **beauties prize:** the woman chosen as most beautiful.

Canto Five

The Ladies for the girdle strive
of famous Florimell:
Scudamour comming to Cares house,
doth sleepe from him expell.

1   It hath bene through all ages ever seene,
        That with the praise of armes and chevalrie,
        The prize of beautie still hath joyned beene;
        And that for reasons speciall privitie:[1]
        For either doth on other much relie.
        For he me seemes most fit the faire to serve,
        That can her best defend from villenie;
        And she most fit his service doth deserve,
    That fairest is and from her faith will never swerve.

2   So fitly now here commeth next in place,
        After the proofe of prowesse ended well,
        The controverse[2] of beauties soveraine grace;
        In which to her that doth the most excell,
        Shall fall the girdle of faire *Florimell:*
        That many wish to win for glorie vaine,
        And not for vertuous use, which some doe tell
        That glorious belt did in it selfe containe,
    Which Ladies ought to love, and seeke for to obtaine.

3   That girdle gave the vertue of chast love,
        And wivehood true, to all that did it beare;[3]
        But whosoever contrarie doth prove,
        Might not the same about her middle weare,
        But it would loose, or else a sunder teare.
        Whilome it was (as Faeries wont report)

---

[1] **for reasons speciall privitie:** because of special secrets that Reason knows about.

[2] **controverse:** controversy.

[3] Cf. the girdles that excite desire in Homer's *Iliad* (14.214–21) and in Tasso's *Gerusalemme Liberata* (16.24–25), along with the girdle that restrains desire in Boccaccio's *Genealogiae* (1976, 3.22 and 4.47).

321

Dame *Venus* girdle, by her steemed[1] deare,
    What time she usd to live in wively sort;
But layd aside, when so she usd her looser sport.[2]

4   Her husband *Vulcan* whylome for her sake,
    When first he loved her with heart entire,
    This pretious ornament they say[3] did make,
    And wrought in *Lemno* with unquenched fire:
    And afterwards did for her loves first hire,[4]
    Give it to her, for ever to remaine,
    Therewith to bind lascivious desire,
    And loose affections streightly to restraine;
Which vertue it for ever after did retaine.

5   The same one day, when she her selfe disposd
    To visite her beloved Paramoure,
    The God of warre,[5] she from her middle loosd,
    And left behind her in her secret bowre,
    On *Acidalian* mount,[6] where many an howre
    She with the pleasant *Graces* wont to play.
    There *Florimell* in her first ages flowre
    Was fostered by those *Graces,* (as they say)
And brought with her from thence that goodly belt away.

6   That goodly belt was *Cestus*[7] hight by name,
    And as her life by her esteemed deare.
    No wonder then, if that to winne the same
    So many Ladies sought, as shall appeare;
    For pearelesse she was thought, that did it beare.
    And now by this their feast all being ended,
    The judges which thereto selected were,
    Into the Martian field adowne descended,
To deeme this doutfull case, for which they all contended.

---

[1] **steemed:** esteemed.

[2] **looser sport:** sexual dalliance.

[3] **they say:** Spenser seems to have made up the story himself, however.

[4] **hire:** reward; payment.

[5] **God of warre:** Mars.

[6] *Acidalian* **mount:** featured in VI.x as a site for pastoral song and dance.

[7] **Cestus:** girdle, belt—especially the one worn by Venus (Latin).

7　　But first was question made, which of those Knights
　　　　That lately turneyd, had the wager wonne:
　　　　There was it judged by those worthie wights,
　　　　That *Satyrane* the first day best had donne:
　　　　For he last ended, having first begonne.
　　　　The second was to *Triamond* behight,[1]
　　　　For that he sav'd the victour from fordonne:[2]
　　　　For *Cambell* victour was in all mens sight,
　　Till by mishap he in his foemens hand did light.

8　　The third dayes prize unto that straunger Knight,
　　　　Whom all men term'd Knight of the Hebene speare,[3]
　　　　To *Britomart* was given by good right;
　　　　For that with puissant stroke she downe did beare
　　　　The *Salvage* Knight, that victour was whileare,
　　　　And all the rest, which had the best afore,
　　　　And to the last unconquer'd did appeare;
　　　　For last is deemed best. To her therefore
　　The fayrest Ladie was adjudgd for Paramore.[4]

9　　But thereat greatly grudged[5] *Arthegall,*
　　　　And much repynd, that both of victors meede,
　　　　And eke of honour she did him forestall.
　　　　Yet mote he not withstand, what was decreede;
　　　　But inly thought of that despightfull deede
　　　　Fit time t'awaite avenged for to bee.
　　　　This being ended thus, and all agreed,
　　　　Then next ensew'd the Paragon to see
　　Of beauties praise,[6] and yeeld the fayrest her due fee.

10　　Then first *Cambello* brought unto their view
　　　　His faire *Cambina*, covered with a veale;[7]
　　　　Which being once withdrawne, most perfect hew

---

[1] **behight:** designated.

[2] **from fordonne:** from being done in.

[3] **Knight of the Hebene speare:** this title for Britomart indicates that her spear is made of ebony, but the title also evokes Hebe, the goddess of youthly beauty and fertility, as well as Cupid, who carries a "Heben bowe" (I.Pr.3.5), and Prince Arthur, who carries a "speare of heben wood" (I.vii.37.2).

[4] I.e., she will be given the fairest lady as her lover.

[5] **grudged:** complained.

[6] I.e., the next event of the day was to see who would be praised as the Paragon of beauty.

[7] **veale:** veil.

And passing beautie did eftsoones reveale,
That able was weake harts away to steale.
Next did Sir *Triamond* unto their sight
The face of his deare *Canacee* unheale;[1]
Whose beauties beame eftsoones did shine so bright,
That daz'd the eyes of all, as with exceeding light.

11   And after her did *Paridell* produce
His false *Duessa*, that she might be seene,
Who with her forged beautie did seduce
The hearts of some, that fairest her did weene;
As diverse wits affected divers[2] beene.
Then did Sir *Ferramont* unto them shew
His *Lucida*,[3] that was full faire and sheene,
And after these an hundred Ladies moe
Appear'd in place, the which each other did outgoe.

12   All which who so dare thinke for to enchace,[4]
Him needeth sure a golden pen I weene,
To tell the feature of each goodly face.
For since the day that they created beene,
So many heavenly faces were not seene
Assembled in one place: ne he that thought
For *Chian* folke[5] to pourtraict beauties Queene,
By view of all the fairest to him brought,[6]
So many faire did see, as here he might have sought.

13   At last the most redoubted *Britonesse*,
Her lovely *Amoret* did open shew;
Whose face discovered, plainely did expresse
The heavenly pourtraict of bright Angels hew.
Well weened all, which her that time did vew,

---

[1] **unheale:** uncover for display.

[2] **divers:** diversely.

[3] ***Lucida:*** from the Latin *lucere*, "to shine."

[4] **enchace:** portray in words (literally, to put a jewel in its setting or to engrave metal with designs).

[5] ***Chian* folke:** people from the Greek island of Chios.

[6] Zeuxis, a Greek painter in the early fourth century BC, used five women as models for his painting of Helen of Troy, choosing each model's best features. However, Spenser may be confusing Zeuxis with Apelles, a Greek painter from slightly later in the fourth century BC, who was famous for his painting of Venus rising from the sea. It is not known for certain whether either painter was born on Chios.

That she should surely beare the bell away,[1]
Till *Blandamour*, who thought he had the trew
And very *Florimell*, did her display:
The sight of whom once seene did all the rest dismay.

14   For all afore that seemed fayre and bright,
      Now base and contemptible did appeare,
      Compar'd to her, that shone as Phebes[2] light,
      Amongst the lesser starres in evening cleare.
      All that her saw with wonder ravisht weare,
      And weend no mortall creature she should bee,[3]
      But some celestiall shape, that flesh did beare:
      Yet all were glad there *Florimell* to see;
Yet thought that *Florimell* was not so faire as shee.

15   As guilefull Goldsmith that by secret skill,
      With golden foyle doth finely over spred
      Some baser metall, which commend he will
      Unto the vulgar for good gold insted,
      He much more goodly glosse thereon doth shed,
      To hide his falshood, then if it were trew:
      So hard, this Idole was to be ared,
      That *Florimell* her selfe in all mens vew
She seem'd to passe: so forged things do fairest shew.

16   Then was that golden belt by doome[4] of all
      Graunted to her, as to the fayrest Dame.
      Which being brought, about her middle small
      They thought to gird, as best it her became;
      But by no meanes they could it thereto frame.
      For ever as they fastned it, it loos'd
      And fell away, as feeling secret blame.
      Full oft about her wast[5] she it enclos'd;
And it as oft was from about her wast disclos'd.[6]

---

[1] I.e., win the contest. The addition of the word "away" to the phrase used in iv.25.9 may represent a common confusion between the image of a bell-wether and the image of a gold or silver bell presented as a prize (OED "bell" sb¹ III.7.a).

[2] **Phebes:** the chaste goddess of the moon is Phoebe, also called Artemis (Diana).

[3] As indeed she is not, being an illusion wrapped around an evil spirit.

[4] **doome:** judgment.

[5] **wast:** waist.

[6] **disclos'd:** unfastened.

17   That all men wondred at the uncouth sight,
       And each one thought, as to their fancies came.[1]
       But she her selfe did thinke it doen for spight,
       And touched was with secret wrath and shame
       Therewith, as thing deviz'd her to defame.
       Then many other Ladies likewise tride,
       About their tender loynes to knit[2] the same;
       But it would not on none of them abide,
But when they thought it fast,[3] eftsoones it was untide.

18   Which when that scornefull *Squire of Dames* did vew,
       He lowdly gan to laugh, and thus to jest;
       "Alas for pittie that so faire a crew,
       As like can not be seene from East to West,
       Cannot find one this girdle to invest.[4]
       Fie on the man, that did it first invent,
       To shame us all with this, *Ungirt unblest.*[5]
       Let never Ladie to his love assent,
That hath this day so many so unmanly shent."

19   Thereat all Knights gan laugh, and Ladies lowre:
       Till that at last the gentle *Amoret*
       Likewise assayd, to prove that girdles powre;
       And having it about her middle set,
       Did find it fit, withouten breach or let.[6]
       Whereat the rest gan greatly to envie:
       But *Florimell* exceedingly did fret,
       And snatching from her hand halfe angrily
The belt againe, about her bodie gan it tie.

20   Yet nathemore[7] would it her bodie fit;
       Yet nathelesse to her, as her dew right,
       It yeelded was by them, that judged it:
       And she her selfe adjudged to the Knight,
       That bore the Hebene speare, as wonne in fight.

---

[1] I.e., viewers interpreted the strange sight according to whatever came into their imaginations.

[2] **knit:** fasten or knot together.

[3] **fast:** secure.

[4] **invest:** put on.

[5] This was a proverb.

[6] **breach:** gap; **let:** hindrance.

[7] **nathemore:** none the more (i.e., despite all of her efforts it would not).

But *Britomart* would not thereto assent,
Ne her owne *Amoret* forgoe so light
For that strange Dame, whose beauties wonderment
She lesse esteem'd, then th'others vertuous government.[1]

21   Whom when the rest did see her to refuse,
       They were full glad, in hope themselves to get her:
       Yet at her choice they all did greatly muse.
       But after that the Judges did arret[2] her
       Unto the second best, that lov'd her better;
       That was the *Salvage* Knight: but he was gone
       In great displeasure, that he could not get her.
       Then was she judged *Triamond* his one;
But *Triamond* lov'd *Canacee,* and other none.[3]

22   Tho unto *Satyran* she was adjudged,
       Who was right glad to gaine so goodly meed:
       But *Blandamour* thereat full greatly grudged,
       And litle prays'd his labours evill speed,[4]
       That for to winne the saddle, lost the steed.[5]
       Ne lesse thereat did *Paridell* complaine,
       And thought t'appeale from that, which was decreed,
       To single combat with Sir *Satyrane.*
Thereto him *Ate* stird, new discord to maintaine.

23   And eke with these, full many other Knights
       She through her wicked working did incense,
       Her to demaund, and chalenge[6] as their rights,
       Deserved for their perils recompense.

---

[1] Given that Britomart has previously revealed herself at crucial moments in the poem, we might expect her to doff her helmet here in order to show the onlookers that her sex makes her an inappropriate paramour for the Snowy Florimell. Instead, the narrator simply tells us that Britomart turns down the prize on behalf of her loyalty to "her owne *Amoret.*" The poem is asking us to contrast her and Amoret's relationship with what will be the False Florimell's relationship to any of the knights who have jousted for her, including some of the poem's heroes.

[2] **arret:** consign; entrust.

[3] It is proving difficult to dispose of the fairest lady of the land.

[4] **evill speed:** poor success.

[5] This proverbial saying refers here to the fact that after Blandamour finally bestirred himself to fight Ferrau for the Snowy Florimell at ii.7 (instead of following his previous habit of having Paridell fight for him), he loses her at this tournament.

[6] **chalenge:** claim.

Amongst the rest with boastfull vaine pretense[1]
Stept *Braggadochio* forth, and as his thrall
Her claym'd, by him in battell wonne long sens:
Whereto her selfe he did to witnesse call;
Who being askt, accordingly confessed all.

24   Thereat exceeding wroth was *Satyran;*
    And wroth with *Satyran* was *Blandamour;*
    And wroth with *Blandamour* was *Erivan;*
    And at them both Sir *Paridell* did loure.
    So all together stird up strifull stoure,
    And readie were new battell to darraine.
    Each one profest to be her paramoure,
    And vow'd with speare and shield it to maintaine;
Ne Judges powre, ne reasons rule mote them restraine.

25   Which troublous stirre when *Satyrane* aviz'd,
    He gan to cast how to appease the same,
    And to accord them all, this meanes deviz'd:
    First in the midst to set that fayrest Dame,
    To whom each one his chalenge should disclame,
    And he himselfe his right would eke releasse:
    Then looke to whom she voluntarie came,[2]
    He should without disturbance her possesse:
Sweete is the love that comes alone[3] with willingnesse.

26   They all agreed, and then that snowy Mayd
    Was in the middest plast among them all;
    All on her gazing wisht, and vowd, and prayd,
    And to the Queene of beautie[4] close did call,
    That she unto their portion might befall.
    Then when she long had lookt upon each one,
    As though she wished to have pleasd them all,
    At last to *Braggadochio* selfe alone
She came of her accord, in spight of all his fone.[5]

---

[1] **pretense:** spurious claim.

[2] I.e., each knight who currently claims the Snowy Florimell will renounce his claim, as will Satyrane. They will then set her in their midst and see toward whom she walks. The scenario is like that of parents competing for a toddler's love by seeing toward whom she or he toddles.

[3] **alone:** of its own accord.

[4] **Queene of beautie:** Venus.

[5] **fone:** foes.

27 Which when they all beheld they chaft and rag'd,
   And woxe nigh mad for very harts despight,
   That from revenge their willes they scarse asswag'd:
   Some thought from him her to have reft by might;
   Some proffer made with him for her to fight.
   But he nought car'd for all that they could say:
   For he their words as wind esteemed light.
   Yet not fit place he thought it there to stay,
But secretly from thence that night her bore away.

28 They which remaynd, so soone as they perceiv'd,
   That she was gone, departed thence with speed,
   And follow'd them, in mind her to have reav'd[1]
   From wight unworthie of so noble meed.
   In which poursuit how each one did succeede,
   Shall else[2] be told in order, as it fell.
   But now of *Britomart* it here doth neede,
   The hard adventures and strange haps to tell;
Since with the rest she went not after *Florimell*.[3]

29 For soone as she them saw to discord set,
   Her list no longer in that place abide;
   But taking with her lovely *Amoret*,
   Upon her first adventure forth did ride,
   To seeke her lov'd,[4] making blind love her guide.
   Unluckie Mayd to seeke her enemie,
   Unluckie Mayd to seeke him farre and wide,
   Whom, when he was unto her selfe most nie,
She through his late disguizement could him not descrie.

30 So much the more her griefe, the more her toyle:
   Yet neither toyle nor griefe she once did spare,
   In seeking him, that should her paine assoyle;
   Whereto great comfort in her sad misfare[5]
   Was *Amoret*, companion of her care:
   Who likewise sought her lover long miswent,[6]

---

[1] **reav'd:** carried away; robbed.

[2] **else:** elsewhere. See ix.20–36.

[3] Cf. III.i.18–19, in which Britomart does not follow the men in chasing the true Florimell.

[4] **lov'd:** beloved, i.e., Artegall.

[5] **misfare:** misfortune.

[6] **miswent:** gone astray.

The gentle *Scudamour,* whose hart whileare
That stryfull[1] hag with gealous discontent
Had fild, that he to fell reveng was fully bent.[2]

31   Bent to revenge on blamelesse *Britomart*
    The crime, which cursed *Ate* kindled earst,
    The which like thornes did pricke his gealous hart,
    And through his soule like poysned arrow perst,
    That by no reason it might be reverst,[3]
    For ought that *Glauce* could or doe or say.
    For aye the more that she the same reherst,[4]
    The more it gauld, and griev'd him night and day,
That nought but dire revenge his anger mote defray.

32   So as they travelled, the drouping[5] night
    Covered with cloudie storme and bitter showre,
    That dreadfull seem'd to every living wight,
    Upon them fell, before her timely howre;
    That forced them to seeke some covert bowre,
    Where they might hide their heads in quiet rest,
    And shrowd their persons from that stormie stowre.
    Not farre away, not meete for any guest
They spide a little cottage, like some poore mans nest.

33   Under a steepe hilles side it placed was,
    There where the mouldred[6] earth had cav'd the banke;
    And fast beside a little brooke did pas
    Of muddie water, that like puddle stanke,
    By which few crooked sallowes[7] grew in ranke:
    Whereto approaching nigh, they heard the sound
    Of many yron hammers beating ranke,[8]
    And answering their wearie turnes[9] around,
That seemed some blacksmith dwelt in that desert ground.

---

[1] **stryfull:** strife-causing.

[2] Ate provoked Scudamour's jealousy at i.47–54.

[3] **reverst:** pulled out.

[4] **reherst:** told.

[5] **drouping:** drooping; the word conveys the image of low-hanging clouds as well as that of dropping rain.

[6] **mouldred:** decayed; crumbled.

[7] **sallowes:** a type of willow associated with lovers.

[8] **ranke:** strongly; violently.

[9] I.e., echoing wearily.

34   There entring in, they found the goodman[1] selfe,
       Full busily unto his worke ybent;
       Who was to weet a wretched wearish elfe,[2]
       With hollow eyes and rawbone cheekes forspent,[3]
       As if he had in prison long bene pent:
       Full blacke and griesly did his face appeare,
       Besmeard with smoke that nigh his eye-sight blent;[4]
       With rugged beard, and hoarie shagged heare,
    The which he never wont to combe, or comely sheare.

35   Rude was his garment, and to rags all rent,
       Ne better had he, ne for better cared:
       With blistred hands emongst the cinders brent,
       And fingers filthie, with long nayles unpared,
       Right fit to rend the food, on which he fared.
       His name was *Care;* a blacksmith by his trade,
       That neither day nor night, from working spared,
       But to small purpose yron wedges made;
    Those be unquiet thoughts, that carefull minds invade.

36   In which his worke he had six servants prest,[5]
       About the Andvile standing evermore,
       With huge great hammers, that did never rest
       From heaping stroakes, which thereon soused sore:
       All six strong groomes, but one then other more;
       For by degrees they all were disagreed;[6]
       So likewise did the hammers which they bore,
       Like belles in greatnesse orderly succeed,
    That he which was the last, the first did farre exceede.[7]

---

[1] **goodman:** a courtesy title for any man under the rank of gentleman, sometimes used ironically (OED 3b).

[2] **wearish:** wizened (with a pun on "weary"); **elfe:** Spenser sometimes uses this word to designate the natives of Faerie Land, but at other times, as here, he uses its more common definition: a malignant imp.

[3] **forspent:** wasted away.

[4] **blent:** blinded.

[5] **prest:** enlisted; forced into service; at hand.

[6] I.e., each differed from the next a fixed amount, and all differed from each other.

Nelson points out that the image comes from Pythagoras' discovery that six different weights of a blacksmith's hammer produced six tones that could be harmonized (Nelson, 250). Steadman observes that in Care's house, the Pythagorean harmony becomes discord (Steadman, 157, as noted in Hamilton). In other words, these six blacksmiths' hammers are tuned to a discordant scale.

[7] I.e., the largest hammer and the servant who wielded it were considerably larger than the smallest hammer and its wielder.

37   He like a monstrous Gyant seem'd in sight,
       Farre passing *Bronteus,* or *Pyracmon*[1] great,
       The which in *Lipari*[2] doe day and night
       Frame thunderbolts for *Joves* avengefull threate.
       So dreadfully he did the andvile beat,
       That seem'd to dust he shortly would it drive:
       So huge his hammer and so fierce his heat,
       That seem'd a rocke of Diamond it could rive,
    And rend a sunder quite, if he thereto list strive.

38   Sir *Scudamour* there entring, much admired[3]
       The manner of their worke and wearie paine;
       And having long beheld, at last enquired
       The cause and end thereof: but all in vaine;
       For they for nought would from their worke refraine,
       Ne let his speeches come unto their eare.
       And eke the breathfull bellowes blew amaine,
       Like to the Northren winde, that none could heare:
    Those *Pensifenesse* did move; and *Sighes* the bellows weare.

39   Which when that warriour saw, he said no more,
       But in his armour layd him downe to rest:[4]
       To rest he layd him downe upon the flore,
       (Whylome for ventrous Knights the bedding best)
       And thought his wearie limbs to have redrest.[5]
       And that old aged Dame, his faithfull Squire,
       Her feeble joynts layd eke a downe to rest;
       That needed much her weake age to desire,[6]
    After so long a travell,[7] which them both did tire.

40   There lay Sir *Scudamour* long while expecting,
       When gentle sleepe his heavie eyes would close;
       Oft chaunging sides, and oft new place electing,

---

[1] **Bronteus, or Pyracmon:** two of the Cyclops in Vulcan's smithy in Virgil's *Aeneid* (8.416–53), where they and one other worker divide the work equally and strike their hammers in a measured cadence.

[2] **Lipari:** the location of Vulcan's smithy, according to some sources.

[3] **admired:** marveled at.

[4] Compare Britomart's doffing her armor before resting in Malecasta's house, signifying that she has let down her guard (III.i.58).

[5] **redrest:** relieved; restored.

[6] I.e., rest being much needed by her advanced age, she desired it; or her advanced age, needing much rest, asked for it.

[7] **travell:** travel; travail.

Where better seem'd he mote himselfe repose;
And oft in wrath he thence againe uprose;
And oft in wrath he layd him downe againe.
But wheresoever he did himselfe dispose,
He by no meanes could wished ease obtaine:
So every place seem'd painefull, and ech changing vaine.

41   And evermore, when he to sleepe did thinke,
The hammers sound his senses did molest;
And evermore, when he began to winke,[1]
The bellowes noyse disturb'd his quiet rest,
Ne suffred sleepe to settle in his brest.
And all the night the dogs did barke and howle
About the house, at sent of stranger guest:
And now the crowing Cocke, and now the Owle
Lowde shriking him afflicted to the very sowle.[2]

42   And if by fortune any litle nap
Upon his heavie eye-lids chaunst to fall,
Eftsoones one of those villeins him did rap
Upon his headpeece with his yron mall;[3]
That he was soone awaked therewithall,
And lightly started up as one affrayd;
Or as if one him suddenly did call.
So oftentimes he out of sleepe abrayd,
And then lay musing long, on that him ill apayd.[4]

43   So long he muzed, and so long he lay,
That at the last his wearie sprite opprest
With fleshly weaknesse, which no creature may
Long time resist, gave place to kindly rest,
That all his senses did full soone arrest:
Yet in his soundest sleepe, his dayly feare
His ydle braine gan busily molest,[5]
And made him dreame those two disloyall were:
The things that day most minds,[6] at night doe most appeare.

---

[1] **winke:** nod off, close his eyes.

[2] **sowle:** soul.

[3] **mall:** maul, a heavy, long-handled hammer.

[4] **that him ill apayd:** that which ill pleased or ill rewarded him.

[5] I.e., his daytime fear—that Amoret and Britomart were lovers—began to molest his sleeping brain.

[6] I.e., the things that one attends to most during the day (literally, that day attends to most).

44   With that, the wicked carle the maister Smith
          A paire of redwhot yron tongs did take
          Out of the burning cinders, and therewith
          Under his side him nipt, that forst to wake,
          He felt his hart for very paine to quake,
          And started up avenged for to be
          On him, the which his quiet slomber brake:
          Yet looking round about him none could see;
        Yet did the smart remaine, though he himselfe did flee.[1]

45   In such disquiet and hartfretting payne,[2]
          He all that night, that too long night did passe.
          And now the day out of the Ocean mayne
          Began to peepe above this earthly masse,
          With pearly dew sprinkling the morning grasse:
          Then up he rose like heavie lumpe of lead,
          That in his face, as in a looking glasse,
          The signes of anguish one mote plainely read,
        And ghesse the man to be dismayd with gealous dread.

46   Unto his lofty steede he clombe[3] anone,
          And forth upon his former voiage fared,
          And with him eke that aged Squire attone;
          Who whatsoever perill was prepared,
          Both equall paines and equall perill shared:
          The end whereof and daungerous event[4]
          Shall for another canticle[5] be spared.
          But here my wearie teeme nigh over spent
        Shall breath it selfe awhile, after so long a went.[6]

---

[1] I.e., the pain of the blacksmith's pinches remains although the blacksmith, himself, flees—but the phrase also means that the smart remains although Scudamour flees from himself. Cf. Redcrosse "Still flying from his thoughts and gealous feare" (I.ii.12).

[2] **hartfretting payne:** pain that gnaws, corrodes, or consumes the heart.

[3] **clombe:** climbed.

[4] **event:** outcome.

[5] **canticle:** canto (literally, little song).

[6] **went:** journey.

Canto Six

Both Scudamour and Arthegall
Doe fight with Britomart,
He sees her face; doth fall in love,
and soone from her depart.[1]

1   What equall torment to the griefe of mind,
        And pyning anguish hid in gentle hart,
        That inly feeds it selfe with thoughts unkind,
        And nourisheth her owne consuming smart?
        What medicine can any Leaches[2] art
        Yeeld such a sore, that doth her grievance hide,
        And will to none her maladie impart?
        Such was the wound that *Scudamour* did gride;[3]
    For which *Dan Phebus*[4] selfe cannot a salve provide.

2   Who having left that restlesse house of *Care*,
        The next day, as he on his way did ride,
        Full of melancholie and sad misfare,[5]
        Through misconceipt;[6] all unawares espide
        An armed Knight under a forrest side,
        Sitting in shade beside his grazing steede;
        Who soone as them[7] approaching he descride,
        Gan towards them to pricke with eger speede,
    That seem'd he was full bent to some mischievous deede.

---

[1] Eggert observes of this comic argument that the male hero's response to marriage in Book Four is "either to flee it . . . or to contemplate it only from several heavily mediated removes" (Eggert, 35–6).

[2] **Leaches:** physician's.

[3] **gride:** pierce with an intense, rasping pain.

[4] ***Dan Phebus:*** Phoebus Apollo, god of healing and sunshine as well as of plagues, politics, music, poetry, and oracles.

[5] **misfare:** misfortune—though its placement in his mind suggests the noun "misfaring," meaning "transgression."

[6] **misconceipt:** misconception—i.e., his belief that Britomart is male.

[7] **them:** Glauce is still traveling with Scudamour. (Both in *The Faerie Queene* and in everyday sixteenth-century writings such as private letters, aristocrats are often described as entering or leaving a room, traveling to or from a place, without any mention of the servants who accompany them.)

3   Which *Scudamour* perceiving, forth issewed
To have rencountred him in equall race;[1]
But soone as th'other nigh approaching, vewed
The armes he bore, his speare he gan abase,
And voide[2] his course: at which so suddain case
He wondred much. But th'other thus can[3] say;
"Ah gentle *Scudamour,* unto your grace
I me submit, and you of pardon pray,
That almost had against you trespassed this day."

4   Whereto thus *Scudamour,* "Small harme it were
For any knight, upon a ventrous knight
Without displeasance[4] for to prove his spere.
But reade you Sir, sith ye my name have hight,
What is your owne, that I mote you requite."[5]
"Certes" (sayd he) "ye mote as now excuse
Me from discovering you my name aright:
For time yet serves that I the same refuse,[6]
But call ye me the *Salvage Knight,* as others use."

5   "Then this, Sir *Salvage Knight*" (quoth he) "areede;
Or doe you here within this forrest wonne,
That seemeth well to answere to your weede?[7]
Or have ye it for some occasion donne?
That rather seemes, sith knowen armes ye shonne."[8]
"This other day" (sayd he) "a stranger knight

---

[1] **rencountred:** met in battle; **race:** act of riding rapidly on horseback in a tournament or single combat.

[2] **voide:** turn aside to avoid.

[3] **can:** gan, did.

[4] **displeasance:** cause of displeasure; according to the chivalric code, two knights could fight each other unprovoked, so long as both were willing.

[5] **requite:** return the favor (by calling you by your name).

[6] I.e., it is presently still useful for me to refuse to tell you my name.

[7] **weede:** clothing.

[8] I.e., "Tell me, do you live in this forest, as your wild clothing would seem to indicate, or have you come to the forest for some particular reason? It would seem the latter, since you are not carrying arms that identify you as a particular knight." Scudamour is confused because, on the one hand, a woodsman normally would not carry the arms of a knight, but on the other hand, a knight would normally carry a shield or wear a tunic with a specific, recognizable coat of arms instead of the strange motto "*Salvagesse sans finesse*" (iv.39).

> Shame and dishonour hath unto me donne;
> On whom I waite to wreake that foule despight,
> When ever he this way shall passe by day or night."[1]

6   "Shame be his meede" (quoth he) "that meaneth shame.[2]
> But what is he, by whom ye shamed were?"
> "A stranger knight," sayd he, "unknowne by name,
> But knowne by fame, and by an Hebene speare,
> With which he all that met him, downe did beare.
> He in an open Turney lately held,
> Fro me the honour of that game did reare;[3]
> And having me all wearie earst, downe feld,
> The fayrest Ladie reft, and ever since withheld."

7   When *Scudamour* heard mention of that speare,
> He wist right well, that it was *Britomart,*
> The which from him his fairest love did beare.
> Tho gan he swell in every inner part,
> For fell despight, and gnaw his gealous hart,
> That thus he sharply sayd; "Now by my head,[4]
> Yet is not this the first unknightly part,
> Which that same knight, whom by his launce I read,
> Hath doen to noble knights, that many makes him dread.[5]

8   "For lately he my love hath fro me reft,
> And eke defiled with foule villanie
> The sacred pledge, which in his faith was left,
> In shame of knighthood and fidelitie;
> The which ere long full deare he shall abie.
> And if to that avenge by you decreed[6]
> This hand may helpe, or succour ought supplie,
> It shall not fayle, when so ye shall it need."
> So both to wreake their wrathes on *Britomart* agreed.

[1] In Book Five, Artegall will represent the virtue of justice in ways that modern readers tend to find problematic. Hamilton remarks of Artegall's plans here in Book Four, "Nursing a grudge and plotting revenge show Artegall's virtue of justice at its most primitive level."

[2] **meaneth:** intends. This line is a translation of the French motto of the English Knights of the Garter: *Honi soit qui mal y pense.*

[3] **reare:** take away (the only example of this usage in the OED).

[4] **by my head:** a traditional oath.

[5] I.e., that makes many dread him.

[6] **avenge:** revenge; **decreed:** pronounced; determined.

9   Whiles thus they communed,[1] lo farre away
         A Knight soft[2] ryding towards them they spyde,
         Attyr'd in forraine armes and straunge aray:
         Whom when they nigh approcht, they plaine descryde
         To be the same, for whom they did abyde.[3]
         Sayd then Sir *Scudamour*, "Sir *Salvage* knight
         Let me this crave, sith first I was defyde,
         That first I may that wrong to him requite:
       And if I hap to fayle, you shall recure my right."

10   Which being yeelded, he his threatfull speare
         Gan fewter, and against her[4] fiercely ran.
         Who soone as she him saw approaching neare
         With so fell rage, her selfe she lightly gan
         To dight, to welcome him, well as she can:
         But entertaind him in so rude a wise,
         That to the ground she smote both horse and man;
         Whence neither greatly hasted to arise,
       But on their common harmes together did devise.[5]

11   But *Artegall* beholding his mischaunce,
         New matter added to his former fire;
         And eft[6] aventring his steeleheaded launce,
         Against her rode, full of despiteous ire,
         That nought but spoyle and vengeance did require.[7]
         But to himselfe his felonous[8] intent
         Returning, disappointed his desire,
         Whiles unawares his saddle he forwent,[9]
       And found himselfe on ground in great amazement.

12   Lightly he started up out of that stound,
         And snatching forth his direfull deadly blade,
         Did leape to her, as doth an eger hound
         Thrust to an Hynd[10] within some covert glade,

---

[1] The phrase emphasizes that they have formed a friendship (based on their mutual grievances).

[2] **soft:** easily; at a calm pace.

[3] **abyde:** wait.

[4] **fewter:** set in its rest, ready for action; **her:** the pronoun reminds us of all that Artegall and Scudamour do not know.

[5] **devise:** consult; deliberate.

[6] **eft:** likewise, in return.

[7] **require:** seek.

[8] **felonous:** violent; wicked.

[9] **forwent:** left; forfeited.

[10] **Hynd:** female deer.

Whom without perill he cannot invade.[1]
With such fell greedines he her assayled,
That though she mounted were, yet he her made
To give him ground, (so much his force prevayled)
And shun his mightie strokes, gainst which no armes avayled.

13   So as they coursed here and there, it chaunst
      That in her wheeling round, behind her crest
      So sorely he her strooke, that thence it glaunst
      Adowne her backe, the which it fairely blest[2]
      From foule mischance; ne did it ever rest,
      Till on her horses hinder parts it fell;
      Where byting deepe, so deadly it imprest,
      That quite it chynd his backe[3] behind the sell,
And to alight on foote her algates did compell.

14   Like as the lightning brond from riven skie,
      Throwne out by angry *Jove* in his vengeance,
      With dreadfull force falles on some steeple hie;
      Which battring, downe it on the church doth glance,
      And teares it all with terrible mischance.
      Yet she no whit dismayd, her steed forsooke,
      And casting from her that enchaunted lance,
      Unto her sword and shield her soone betooke;
And therewithall at him right furiously she strooke.

15   So furiously she strooke in her first heat,
      Whiles with long fight on foot he breathlesse was,
      That she him forced backward to retreat,
      And yeeld unto her weapon way to pas:
      Whose raging rigour neither steele nor bras
      Could stay, but to the tender flesh it went,
      And pour'd the purple bloud forth on the gras;
      That all his mayle[4] yriv'd, and plates yrent,
Shew'd all his bodie bare unto the cruell dent.[5]

---

[1] The imagery of sexual aggression in the advances that Scudamour and Artegall have made with their spear and lance becomes more frantic in these lines.

[2] **fairely blest:** kept entirely safe.

[3] **chynd his backe:** split his back (with a pun on two meanings of "chine": "split" and "backbone").

[4] **mayle:** chain mail, but with a pun on "male."

[5] **dent:** blow.

16   At length when as he saw her hastie heat
          Abate, and panting breath begin to fayle,
          He through long sufferance[1] growing now more great,
          Rose in his strength, and gan her fresh assayle,
          Heaping huge strokes, as thicke as showre of hayle,
          And lashing dreadfully at every part,
          As if he thought her soule to disentrayle.[2]
          Ah cruell hand, and thrise more cruell hart,
That workst such wrecke[3] on her, to whom thou dearest art.

17   What yron courage ever could endure,
          To worke such outrage on so faire a creature?
          And in his madnesse thinke with hands impure
          To spoyle so goodly workmanship of nature,
          The maker selfe resembling in her feature?[4]
          Certes some hellish furie, or some feend
          This mischiefe framd, for their first loves defeature,[5]
          To bath their hands in bloud of dearest freend,
Thereby to make their loves beginning, their lives end.

18   Thus long they trac'd,[6] and traverst to and fro,
          Sometimes pursewing, and sometimes pursewed,
          Still as advantage they espyde thereto:
          But toward th'end Sir *Arthegall* renewed
          His strength still more, but she still more decrewed.[7]
          At last his lucklesse hand he heav'd on hie,
          Having his forces all in one accrewed,[8]
          And therewith stroke at her so hideouslie,
That seemed nought but death mote be her destinie.

19   The wicked stroke upon her helmet chaunst,
          And with the force, which in it selfe it bore,
          Her ventayle shard[9] away, and thence forth glaunst

---

[1] **sufferance:** respite, time out.

[2] **disentrayle:** draw out of the entrails or inward parts.

[3] **wrecke:** injury; vengeance; outrage.

[4] Note the repetition of the *a-* and *b-* rhymes.

[5] **defeature:** defeat; disfigurement.

[6] **trac'd:** pursued, with a pun on the meaning "danced."

[7] **decrewed:** decreased (cf. "accrued").

[8] **accrewed:** accrued, augmented.

[9] **ventayle:** moveable front of the helmet, either distinct from the visor or including it (depending on whether Spenser is thinking of early or late Medieval or Renaissance versions); **shard:** cut.

A downe in vaine, ne harm'd her any more.
With that her angels face, unseene afore,
Like to the ruddie morne appeard in sight,
Deawed with silver drops, through sweating sore,[1]
But somewhat redder, then beseem'd aright,
Through toylesome heate and labour of her weary fight.

20   And round about the same, her yellow heare
       Having through stirring loosd their wonted band,
       Like to a golden border did appeare,
       Framed in goldsmithes forge with cunning hand:
       Yet goldsmithes cunning could not understand
       To frame such subtile[2] wire, so shinie cleare.
       For it did glister[3] like the golden sand,
       The which *Pactolus* with his waters shere,[4]
    Throwes forth upon the rivage[5] round about him nere.

21   And as his hand he up againe did reare,
       Thinking to worke on her his utmost wracke,[6]
       His powrelesse arme benumbd with secret feare
       From his revengefull purpose shronke abacke,
       And cruell sword out of his fingers slacke
       Fell downe to ground, as if the steele had sence,
       And felt some ruth, or sence his hand did lacke,
       Or both of them did thinke, obedience
    To doe to so divine a beauties excellence.[7]

22   And he himselfe long gazing thereupon,
       At last fell humbly downe upon his knee,
       And of his wonder made religion,
       Weening some heavenly goddesse he did see,
       Or else unweeting, what it else might bee;
       And pardon her besought his errour frayle,

---

[1] **sore:** severely.

[2] **subtile:** fine.

[3] **glister:** shine.

[4] *Pactolus:* a river in Lydia, supposed to have golden sand; **shere:** clear.

[5] **rivage:** banks.

[6] **wracke:** violence.

[7] In Tasso's *Gerusalemme Liberata,* Tancred is smitten with Clorinda's beauty when her helmet comes off (3.21–22).

That had done outrage in so high degree:
Whilest trembling horrour[1] did his sense assayle,
And made ech member[2] quake, and manly hart to quayle.

23   Nathelesse she full of wrath for that late[3] stroke,
            All that long while upheld her wrathfull hand,
            With fell intent, on him to bene ywroke,[4]
            And looking sterne, still over him did stand,
            Threatning to strike, unlesse he would withstand:[5]
            And bad him rise, or surely he should die.
            But die or live for nought he would upstand
            But her of pardon prayd more earnestlie,
    Or wreake on him her will for so great injurie.

24   Which when as *Scudamour,* who now abrayd,
            Beheld, whereas he stood not farre aside,
            He was therewith right wondrously dismayd,
            And drawing nigh, when as he plaine descride
            That peerelesse paterne of Dame natures pride,
            And heavenly image of perfection,
            He blest himselfe, as one sore terrifide,
            And turning his feare to faint devotion,
    Did worship her as some celestiall vision.

25   But *Glauce,* seeing all that chaunced there,
            Well weeting how their errour to assoyle,
            Full glad of so good end, to them drew nere,
            And her salewd with seemely belaccoyle,[6]
            Joyous to see her safe after long toyle.
            Then her besought, as she to her was deare,
            To graunt unto those warriours truce a whyle;
            Which yeelded, they their bevers[7] up did reare,
    And shew'd themselves to her, such as indeed they were.

---

[1] **horrour:** shuddering (from Latin).

[2] **member:** limb, with a double entendre on the male member, the penis.

[3] **late:** recent.

[4] **ywroke:** avenged.

[5] **withstand:** defend himself.

[6] **salewd:** saluted; **belaccoyle:** welcome, kindly greeting.

[7] **bevers:** lower portions of the face-guards of helmets, with or without separate visors.

26   When *Britomart* with sharpe avizefull[1] eye
         Beheld the lovely face of *Artegall,*
         Tempred with sternesse and stout majestie,
         She gan eftsoones it to her mind to call,
         To be the same which in her fathers hall
         Long since in that enchaunted glasse she saw.[2]
         Therewith her wrathfull courage gan appall,[3]
         And haughtie spirits meekely to adaw,[4]
    That her enhaunced[5] hand she downe can soft withdraw.

27   Yet she it forst to have againe upheld,
         As fayning choler,[6] which was turn'd to cold:
         But ever when his visage she beheld,
         Her hand fell downe, and would no longer hold
         The wrathfull weapon gainst his countnance bold:
         But when in vaine to fight she oft assayd,
         She arm'd her tongue, and thought at him to scold;
         Nathlesse her tongue not to her will obayd,
    But brought forth speeches myld, when she would have missayd.[7]

28   But *Scudamour* now woxen inly glad,
         That all his gealous feare he false had found,
         And how that Hag[8] his love abused had
         With breach of faith and loyaltie unsound,
         The which long time his grieved hart did wound,
         He thus bespake; "Certes Sir *Artegall,*
         I joy to see you lout so low on ground,
         And now become to live a Ladies thrall,
    That whylome in your minde wont to despise them all."

29   Soone as she heard the name of *Artegall,*
         Her hart did leape, and all her hart-strings tremble,
         For sudden joy, and secret feare withall,
         And all her vitall powres with motion nimble,
         To succour it,[9] themselves gan there assemble,

---

[1] **avizefull:** considering.
[2] See III.ii.22–26.
[3] **appall:** fail in strength.
[4] **adaw:** be subdued; be daunted; be over-awed.
[5] **enhaunced:** raised.

[6] **choler:** anger (literally bile, one of the four humors, associated with heat and thought to cause irascibility).
[7] **missayd:** spoken harshly.
[8] **Hag:** Ate; see i.47–54.
[9] **it:** her heart.

That by the swift recourse of flushing blood
Right plaine appeard, though she it would dissemble,
And fayned still her former angry mood,
Thinking to hide the depth by troubling of the flood.[1]

30   When *Glauce* thus gan wisely all upknit;[2]
"Ye gentle Knights, whom fortune here hath brought,
To be spectators of this uncouth fit,
Which secret fate hath in this Ladie wrought,
Against the course of kind,[3] ne mervaile nought,
Ne thenceforth feare the thing that hethertoo
Hath troubled both your mindes with idle thought,
Fearing least she your loves away should woo,
Feared in vaine, sith meanes ye see there wants thereto.[4]

31   "And you Sir *Artegall,* the salvage knight,
Henceforth may not disdaine, that womans hand
Hath conquered you anew in second fight:
For whylome they have conquerd sea and land,[5]
And heaven it selfe, that nought may them withstand,
Ne henceforth be rebellious unto love,
That is the crowne of knighthood, and the band
Of noble minds derived from above,
Which being knit with vertue, never will remove.

32   "And you faire Ladie knight, my dearest Dame,
Relent the rigour of your wrathfull will,
Whose fire were better turn'd to other flame;

[1] I.e., thinking to conceal the depth of the water (her powerful emotions) by stirring up the surface (her demeanor) so that it is no longer transparent.

[2] **all upknit:** explain or summarize everything; bring everyone together.

[3] Now that Britomart's destined husband is aware that Britomart is female, Glauce seems to be apologizing for Britomart's unladylike aggression by assuring the two men that this aggression was merely a "fit"—a sudden, transitory, and uncharacteristic activity. Alternatively, Glauce could be interpreted as saying that the men shouldn't feel bad about having been conquered by a woman since it was fate that, using the person of Britomart, wrought this ultimately beneficial marvel. Either way, Glauce is placating the egos of men who have been comically inept at penetrating Britomart's body with their erect weapons.

[4] "Don't worry; she doesn't have a penis, so another woman couldn't possibly find her interesting."

[5] With this argument about female conquerors, Glauce becomes less placating to the men, while at the same time, Spenser becomes more complimentary to his queen.

And wiping out remembrance of all ill,
Graunt him your grace, but so that he fulfill
The penance, which ye shall to him empart:
For lovers heaven must passe by sorrowes hell."
Thereat full inly blushed *Britomart*;
But *Artegall* close smyling joy'd in secret hart.

33　　Yet durst he not make love[1] so suddenly,
Ne thinke th'affection of her hart to draw
From one to other so quite contrary:
Besides her modest countenance he saw
So goodly grave, and full of princely aw,
That it his ranging fancie did refraine,
And looser thoughts to lawfull bounds withdraw;
Whereby the passion grew more fierce and faine,
Like to a stubborne steede whom strong hand would restraine.[2]

34　　But *Scudamour* whose hart twixt doubtfull feare
And feeble hope hung all this while suspence,[3]
Desiring of his *Amoret* to heare
Some gladfull newes and sure intelligence,[4]
Her thus bespake; "But Sir[5] without offence
Mote I request you tydings of my love,
My *Amoret*, sith you her freed fro thence,
Where she captived long, great woes did prove;
That where ye left, I may her seeke, as doth behove."

35　　To whom thus *Britomart*, "Certes Sir knight,
What is of her become, or whether[6] reft,
I can not unto you aread a right.
For from that time I from enchaunters theft
Her freed, in which ye her all hopelesse left,
I her preserv'd from perill and from feare,

---

[1] **make love:** woo her (without connotations of sexual intercourse).

[2] This image is influenced by the *Phaedrus*, in which Plato compares the soul to a charioteer (reason) who must try to coordinate a team of two mismatched horses: a noble one (spirit) and an unruly one (appetite). A man in love must learn to curb the impulses of the unruly horse and force it to treat the beloved with reverence (*Phaedrus*, 246–56).

[3] **suspence:** suspended; in suspense.

[4] **intelligence:** news, report.

[5] **Sir:** the title was occasionally applied to women, but Spenser never uses it for any woman who is not a knight.

[6] **whether:** where.

And evermore from villenie her kept:
Ne ever was there wight to me more deare
Then she, ne unto whom I more true love did beare.[1]

36   "Till on a day as through a desert wyld
We travelled, both wearie of the way
We did alight, and sate in shadow myld;
Where fearelesse I to sleepe me downe did lay.
But when as I did out of sleepe abray,
I found her not, where I her left whyleare,
But thought she wandred was, or gone astray.
I cal'd her loud, I sought her farre and neare;
But no where could her find, nor tydings of her heare."

37   When *Scudamour* those heavie tydings heard,
His hart was thrild with point of deadly feare;
Ne in his face or bloud or life appeard,
But senselesse stood, like to a mazed steare,[2]
That yet of mortall stroke the stound doth beare.
Till *Glauce* thus; "Faire Sir, be nought dismayd
With needelesse dread, till certaintie ye heare:
For yet she may be safe though somewhat strayd;
Its best to hope the best, though of the worst affrayd."

38   Nathlesse he hardly of her chearefull speech
Did comfort take, or in his troubled sight
Shew'd change of better cheare: so sore a breach
That sudden newes had made into his spright;
Till *Britomart* him fairely thus behight;[3]
"Great cause of sorrow certes Sir ye have:
But comfort take: for by this heavens light
I vow, you dead or living not to leave,
Till I her find, and wreake on him that her did reave."[4]

---

[1] In the chronology of the plot, Britomart is separated from Amoret before Britomart and Artegall reveal themselves to each other. In the order of the narrative, however, we read about Britomart's and Artegall's union before reading about Britomart and Amoret's separation, as though the narrative pressure of the heterosexual union effectively forces the female friendship apart. Britomart's declaration of love for Amoret is crucially in the past tense.

[2] **mazed steare:** stupefied steer (a powerful animal rendered powerless).

[3] **behight:** held out hope.

[4] **reave:** steal away.

39   Therewith he rested, and well pleased was.
        So peace being confirm'd amongst them all,
        They tooke their steeds, and forward thence did pas
        Unto some resting place, which mote befall,[1]
        All being guided by Sir *Artegall.*
        Where goodly solace[2] was unto them made,
        And dayly feasting both in bowre and hall,
        Untill that they their wounds well healed had,
   And wearie limmes recur'd after late usage bad.

40   In all which time, Sir *Artegall* made way
        Unto the love of noble *Britomart,*
        And with meeke service and much suit did lay
        Continuall siege unto her gentle hart,
        Which being whylome launcht[3] with lovely dart,
        More eath was new impression to receive,
        How ever she her paynd with womanish art
        To hide her wound, that none might it perceive:
   Vaine is the art that seekes it selfe for to deceive.

41   So well he woo'd her, and so well he wrought[4] her,
        With faire entreatie and sweet blandishment,
        That at the length unto a bay[5] he brought her,
        So as she to his speeches was content
        To lend an eare, and softly to relent.
        At last through many vowes which forth he pour'd,

---

[1] This is one of the few places where Spenser mentions a rest stop at a castle without describing and allegorizing the castle.

[2] **solace:** entertainment; comfort.

[3] **launcht:** lanced, pierced. At III.ii.26–27, the narrator describes Britomart as having been wounded by Cupid's dart, which leaves her "sad, solemne, sowre, and full of fancies fraile." At III.ii.39, Britomart describes herself as having swallowed a baited hook that has caused a festering, running sore in her entrails. Now that she has met Artegall, the narrator rewrites that earlier wounding as a lancing—i.e., caused either by a warrior's lance or by a medical lancet. The word thus makes way for the idea that Britomart's pain has been an unavoidable byproduct of an essentially beneficial process: the lancet's releasing of infected matter from an abscess. That which caused her infection now cures it.

[4] **wrought:** prepared, fashioned; worked upon; persuaded; made war upon.

[5] **unto a bay:** to the point at which a hunted animal has no choice but to turn and face its pursuer.

And many othes, she yeelded her consent
To be his love, and take him for her Lord,[1]
Till they with mariage meet might finish that accord.

42   Tho when they had long time there taken rest,
      Sir *Artegall,* who all this while was bound
      Upon an hard adventure yet in quest,[2]
      Fit time for him thence to depart it found,
      To follow that, which he did long propound;
      And unto her his congee[3] came to take.
      But her therewith full sore displeasd he found,
      And loth to leave her late betrothed make,[4]
Her dearest love full loth so shortly to forsake.

43   Yet he with strong perswasions her asswaged,
      And wonne her will to suffer him depart;
      For which his faith with her he fast engaged,
      And thousand vowes from bottome of his hart,
      That all so soone as he by wit or art
      Could that atchieve, whereto he did aspire,
      He unto her would speedily revert:
      No longer space thereto he did desire,
But till the horned moone three courses did expire.

44   With which she for the present was appeased,
      And yeelded leave,[5] how ever malcontent
      She inly were, and in her mind displeased.
      So early in the morrow next he went
      Forth on his way, to which he was ybent.
      Ne wight him to attend, or way to guide,
      As whylome was the custome ancient
      Mongst Knights, when on adventures they did ride,
Save that she algates him a while accompanide.

---

[1] A knight takes a man of higher status as his lord in order to serve him militarily, but here, Britomart gives up knighthood in order to take Artegall as her lord in marriage. This marriage was the object of her knightly quest all along, yet that quest only partly summarizes her experience of knighthood.

[2] **yet in quest:** still uncompleted.

[3] **congee:** farewell.

[4] **make:** mate.

[5] **leave:** permission to leave.

45 And by the way she sundry purpose[1] found
  Of this or that, the time for to delay,
  And of the perils whereto he was bound,
  The feare whereof seem'd much her to affray:
  But all she did was but to weare out day.
  Full oftentimes she leave of him did take;
  And eft againe deviz'd some what to say,
  Which she forgot, whereby excuse to make:[2]
So loth she was his companie for to forsake.

46 At last when all her speeches she had spent,
  And new occasion fayld her more to find,
  She left him to his fortunes government,
  And backe returned with right heavie mind,
  To *Scudamour,* who she had left behind,
  With whom she went to seeke faire *Amoret,*
  Her second care, though in another kind;
  For vertues onely sake, which doth beget
True love and faithfull friendship, she by her did set.[3]

47 Backe to that desert[4] forrest they retyred,
  Where sorie *Britomart* had lost her late;
  There they her sought, and every where inquired,
  Where they might tydings get of her estate;
  Yet found they none. But by what haplesse fate,
  Or hard misfortune she was thence convayd,
  And stolne away from her beloved mate,
  Were long to tell; therefore I here will stay[5]
Untill another tyde,[6] that I it finish may.

---

[1] **sundry purpose:** various topics of conversation.

[2] I.e., as a way of keeping him a bit longer, she told him she had something to say that had slipped her mind.

[3] I.e., virtue, which begets true love and faithful friendship, makes Britomart care for Amoret. In what sense this true love and faithful friendship are "another kind" from the true love she feels for Artegall is a matter for interpretation.

[4] **desert:** deserted; wild.

[5] **stay:** stop.

[6] **tyde:** time; occasion.

Canto Seven

Amoret rapt[1] by greedie lust
Belphebe saves from dread,
The Squire her loves, and being blam'd
his dayes in dole[2] doth lead.

1   Great God of love,[3] that with thy cruell dart
      Doest conquer greatest conquerors on ground,
      And setst thy kingdome in the captive harts
      Of Kings and Keasars, to thy service bound,
      What glorie, or what guerdon hast thou found
      In feeble Ladies tyranning[4] so sore;
      And adding anguish to the bitter wound,
      With which their lives thou lanchedst[5] long afore,
By heaping stormes of trouble on them daily more?

2   So whylome didst thou to faire *Florimell;*
      And so and so[6] to noble *Britomart:*
      So doest thou now to her, of whom I tell,
      The lovely *Amoret,* whose gentle hart
      Thou martyrest with sorow and with smart,
      In salvage forrests, and in deserts wide,
      With Beares and Tygers taking heavie part,
      Withouten comfort, and withouten guide,
That pittie is to heare the perils, which she tride.[7]

3   So soone as she with that brave Britonesse
      Had left that Turneyment for beauties prise,
      They travel'd long, that now for wearinesse,
      Both of the way, and warlike exercise,
      Both through a forest ryding did devise
      T'alight, and rest their wearie limbs awhile.

---

[1] **rapt:** violently seized and carried away.

[2] **dole:** grief.

[3] I.e., Cupid.

[4] **tyranning:** tyrannizing.

[5] **lanchedst:** lanced, pierced.

[6] **so and so:** likewise and likewise again.

[7] **tride:** experienced; suffered.

> There heavie sleepe the eye-lids did surprise
> Of *Britomart* after long tedious toyle,
> That did her passed paines in quiet rest assoyle.[1]

4   The whiles faire *Amoret,* of nought affeard,
      Walkt through the wood, for pleasure, or for need;[2]
      When suddenly behind her backe she heard
      One rushing forth out of the thickest weed,[3]
      That ere she backe could turne to taken heed,
      Had unawares her snatched up from ground.
      Feebly she shriekt, but so feebly indeed,
      That *Britomart* heard not the shrilling sound,
    There where through weary travel she lay sleeping sound.

5   It was to weet a wilde and salvage man,[4]
      Yet was no man, but onely like in shape,
      And eke in stature higher by a span,[5]
      All overgrowne with haire, that could awhape[6]
      An hardy hart, and his wide mouth did gape
      With huge great teeth, like to a tusked Bore:[7]
      For he liv'd all on ravin[8] and on rape
      Of men and beasts; and fed on fleshly gore,
    The signe whereof yet stain'd his bloudy lips afore.

6   His neather lip was not like man nor beast,
      But like a wide deepe poke, downe hanging low,[9]
      In which he wont the relickes of his feast,
      And cruell spoyle, which he had spard, to stow:
      And over it his huge great nose did grow,

---

[1] The narrator is backtracking to fill in the details of the experience that Britomart summarized at vi.35–36.

[2] **for need:** to empty her bladder—or out of an unconscious desire to be raped (see Silberman 1995, 118; and Cavanagh, 145). In either case, in allegorical terms, her being alone in the woods indicates that she has let down her guard of chastity. As Cavanagh points out, however, the passage also asks us to evaluate what it is that makes Britomart fall asleep when she should be watching over Amoret (145).

[3] **weed:** underbrush.

[4] **salvage man:** identified by the Argument as Lust.

[5] **span:** the distance from thumbtip to fingertip of a fully spread hand.

[6] **awhape:** amaze; stupefy with fear.

[7] Cf. the boar beneath Venus' Mount in the Garden of Adonis (III.vi.48).

[8] **ravin:** plunder; prey.

[9] His form is that of the male genitals; the "poke" is the scrotum.

Full dreadfully empurpled all with bloud;[1]
And downe both sides two wide long eares did glow,
And raught downe to his waste, when up he stood,
More great then th'eares of Elephants by *Indus* flood.[2]

7   His wast was with a wreath of yvie greene
Engirt about, ne other garment wore:[3]
For all his haire was like a garment seene;
And in his hand a tall young oake he bore,[4]
Whose knottie snags were sharpned all afore,
And beath'd in fire for steele to be in sted.[5]
But whence he was, or of what wombe ybore,
Of beasts, or of the earth, I have not red:
But certes was with milke of Wolves and Tygres fed.

8   This ugly creature in his armes her snatcht,
And through the forrest bore her quite away,
With briers and bushes all to rent[6] and scratcht;
Ne care he had, ne pittie of the pray,
Which many a knight had sought so many a day.
He stayed not, but in his armes her bearing
Ran, till he came to th'end of all his way,
Unto his cave farre from all peoples hearing,
And there he threw her in, nought feeling, ne nought fearing.[7]

9   For she deare Ladie all the way was dead,
Whilest he in armes her bore; but when she felt
Her selfe downe soust,[8] she waked out of dread
Streight into griefe, that her deare hart nigh swelt,[9]

---

[1] His nose is like an erect penis.

[2] **Indus flood:** the waters of the Indus River, which flows through Pakistan.

[3] A man sporting long hair and ivy signifies lust.

[4] Oaks were emblematic of Druidism, an ancient Celtic religion that Spenser's contemporaries associated with magic and torture.

[5] I.e., heated in fire (to harden it) so it could serve in the place of steel.

[6] **all to rent:** thoroughly torn.

[7] Until the first line of stanza 9, the grammar of this line is ambiguous as to whether it is Lust or Amoret who neither feels nor fears.

[8] **soust:** thumped; fallen.

[9] **swelt:** swooned; perished—but with inevitable reference to an alternative meaning that is quite antithetical to the narrator's insistence upon Amoret's virtue: the verb could mean that her dear heart "burned with fever." Cf. the passage in which Redcrosse succumbs to Duessa's insidious charms and gives himself over to volup-

And eft gan into tender teares to melt.
Then when she lookt about, and nothing found
But darknesse and dread horrour, where she dwelt,
She almost fell againe into a swound,
Ne wist whether above she were, or under ground.

10   With that she heard some one close by her side
        Sighing and sobbing sore, as if the paine
        Her tender hart in peeces would divide:
        Which she long listning, softly askt againe[1]
        What mister wight it was that so did plaine?[2]
        To whom thus aunswer'd was: "Ah wretched wight
        That seekes to know anothers griefe in vaine,
        Unweeting of thine owne like haplesse plight:
Selfe to forget to mind another, is oversight."

11   "Aye me" (said she) "where am I, or with whom?
        Emong the living, or emong the dead?
        What shall of me unhappy maid become?[3]
        Shall death be th'end, or ought else worse, aread."
        "Unhappy mayd" (then answerd she) "whose dread
        Untride, is lesse then when thou shalt it try:
        Death is to him, that wretched life doth lead,
        Both grace and gaine;[4] but he in hell doth lie,
That lives a loathed life, and wishing cannot die.

12   "This dismall day hath thee a caytive made,
        And vassall to the vilest wretch alive,
        Whose cursed usage and ungodly trade[5]
        The heavens abhorre, and into darkenesse drive.

---

tuousness, "Till crudled cold his corage gan
assayle, / And chearefull blood in fayntnes
chill did melt, / Which like a fever fit
through all his body swelt" (I.vii.6).

[1] **againe:** in response.

[2] **mister:** type of. After Amoret temporar-
ily loses her sense of feeling and then all of
her other senses (stanza 8.9–9.1), she also
temporarily loses her name: for eight stan-
zas, she and the invisible woman beside her
in the dark are designated only by inter-
changeable pronouns. One could argue that

they regain their names (in 18.9 and 19.1)
through their mutual expressions of grief,
by reading themselves in each other. (See
Stephens, *Limits*, 41–5.)

[3] I.e., "What shall become of me, an un-
happy maid?"

[4] I.e., to him who leads a wretched life,
death is a grace and a gain.

[5] **usage:** habits; **trade:** practice—though
with a gesture toward sex for hire, the trade
in human flesh.

For on the spoile of women he doth live,
Whose bodies chast, when ever in his powre
He may them catch, unable to gainestrive,[1]
He with his shamefull lust doth first deflowre,[2]
And afterwards themselves doth cruelly devoure.

13   "Now twenty daies, by which the sonnes of men
Divide their works, have past through heven sheene,
Since I was brought into this dolefull den;
During which space these sory eies have seen
Seaven women by him slaine, and eaten clene.
And now no more for him but I alone,
And this old woman here remaining beene;
Till thou cam'st hither to augment our mone,[3]
And of us three to morrow he will sure eate one."

14   "Ah dreadfull tidings which thou doest declare,"
(Quoth she) "of all that ever hath bene knowen:
Full many great calamities and rare
This feeble brest endured hath, but none
Equall to this, where ever I have gone.
But what are you, whom like unlucky lot
Hath linckt with me in the same chaine attone?"
"To tell" (quoth she) "that which ye see, needs not;
A wofull wretched maid, of God and man forgot.

15   "But what I was, it irkes me to reherse;[4]
Daughter unto a Lord of high degree;
That joyd in happy peace, till fates perverse
With guilefull love did secretly agree,
To overthrow my state and dignitie.
It was my lot to love a gentle swaine,
Yet was he but a Squire of low degree;
Yet was he meet, unlesse mine eye did faine,
By any Ladies side for Leman[5] to have laine.

---

[1] **gainestrive:** resist.

[2] **deflowre:** deprive of virginity by rape. Cf. Belphoebe's flower of chastity (III.v.51–54). Cf. also another of the poem's embodiments of unrestrained sexuality: Cupid, who wreaks havoc in court, city, and country (III.vi.13–15).

[3] **mone:** moan; sorrow.

[4] **reherse:** relate.

[5] **Leman:** lover, paramour.

16   "But for his meannesse and disparagement,[1]
        My Sire, who me too dearely well did love,
        Unto my choise by no meanes would assent,
        But often did my folly fowle[2] reprove.
        Yet nothing could my fixed mind remove,
        But whether willed or nilled[3] friend or foe,
        I me resolv'd the utmost end to prove,[4]
        And rather then my love abandon so,
   Both sire, and friends, and all for ever to forgo.

17   "Thenceforth I sought by secret meanes to worke
        Time to my will,[5] and from his wrathfull sight
        To hide th'intent, which in my heart did lurke,
        Till I thereto had all things ready dight.
        So on a day unweeting unto wight,
        I with that Squire agreede away to flit,
        And in a privy place, betwixt us hight,
        Within a grove appointed him to meete;
   To which I boldly came upon my feeble feete.

18   "But ah unhappy houre me thither brought:
        For in that place where I him thought to find,
        There was I found, contrary to my thought,
        Of this accursed Carle[6] of hellish kind,
        The shame of men, and plague of womankind,[7]
        Who trussing[8] me, as Eagle doth his pray,
        Me hether brought with him, as swift as wind,
        Where yet untouched till this present day,
   I rest his wretched thrall, the sad *AEmylia.*"

---

[1] **meannesse:** low rank; **disparagement:** the loss in status that she would incur from marrying him.

[2] **fowle:** unfavorably; unfairly; harshly; grievously.

[3] **willed or nilled:** agreeing or disagreeing.

[4] I.e., to attain the ultimate goal (of marrying—or sleeping with—her beloved).

[5] **will:** inclination; intent; pleasure; sexual desire; willfulness. There is a submerged pun on "will" as a slang term for the male or female sexual organs (not in the OED, but see Booth, 466–67, for ample evidence from contemporary texts).

[6] **Carle:** base fellow.

[7] The strongly implied moral of her narrative is that she unwittingly found "in that place" exactly what she had set out to find—though Spenser's representation of her is not confined to this moral.

[8] **trussing:** a term from the sport of falconry, describing a falcon seizing its prey with its talons.

19   "Ah sad *AEmylia*" (then sayd *Amoret*,)
    "Thy ruefull plight I pitty as mine owne.
    But read to me, by what devise or wit,
    Hast thou in all this time, from him unknowne
    Thine honor sav'd, though into thraldome throwne."
    "Through helpe" (quoth she) "of this old woman here
    I have so done, as she to me hath showne.
    For ever when he burnt in lustfull fire,
She in my stead supplide his bestiall desire."

20   Thus of their evils as they did discourse,
    And each did other much bewaile and mone;
    Loe where the villaine selfe,[1] their sorrowes sourse,
    Came to the cave, and rolling thence the stone,
    Which wont to stop the mouth thereof, that none
    Might issue forth, came rudely rushing in,
    And spredding over all the flore alone,
    Gan dight him selfe unto his wonted sinne;[2]
Which ended, then his bloudy banket[3] should beginne.

21   Which when as fearefull *Amoret* perceived,
    She staid not the utmost end[4] thereof to try,
    But like a ghastly Gelt,[5] whose wits are reaved,
    Ran forth in hast with hideous outcry,
    For horrour of his shamefull villany.
    But after her full lightly he uprose,
    And her pursu'd as fast as she did flie:
    Full fast she flies, and farre afore him goes,
Ne feeles the thorns and thickets pricke her tender toes.

22   Nor hedge, nor ditch, nor hill, nor dale she staies,[6]
    But overleapes them all, like Robucke light,
    And through the thickest makes her nighest waies;
    And evermore when with regardfull sight
    She looking backe, espies that griesly wight

---

[1] **selfe:** himself.

[2] Hamilton comments that "his act here suggests masturbation."

[3] **banket:** banquet.

[4] **end:** Hamilton notes that in its allusion to Lust's nose, the phrase "the utmost end" is the first of several bawdy jokes in this stanza.

[5] **ghastly Gelt:** horror-struck lunatic (from the Irish *geilt*).

[6] **staies:** stops for.

Approching nigh, she gins to mend her pace,
And makes her feare a spur to hast her flight:
More swift then *Myrrh'* or *Daphne*[1] in her race,
Or any of the Thracian Nimphes[2] in salvage chase.

23   Long so she fled, and so he follow'd long;
Ne living aide for her on earth appeares,
But if[3] the heavens helpe to redresse her wrong,
Moved with pity of her plenteous teares.
It fortuned *Belphebe* with her peares[4]
The woody Nimphs, and with that lovely boy,[5]
Was hunting then the Libbards[6] and the Beares,
In these wild woods, as was her wonted joy,
To banish sloth, that oft doth noble mindes annoy.

24   It so befell, as oft it fals[7] in chace,
That each of them from other sundred were,
And that same gentle Squire arriv'd in place,
Where this same cursed caytive did appeare,
Pursuing that faire Lady full of feare,
And now he her quite overtaken had;
And now he her away with him did beare
Under his arme, as seeming wondrous glad,
That by his grenning laughter mote farre off be rad.[8]

25   Which drery sight the gentle Squire espying,
Doth hast to crosse him by the nearest way,
Led with that wofull Ladies piteous crying,
And him assailes with all the might he may,
Yet will not he[9] the lovely spoile downe lay,

---

[1] For Myrrha and Daphne, see III.vii.26.1 and 4, notes. When Myrrha's father discovered he had slept with his own daughter, he attempted to stab her, but she fled to Saba, in ancient southwestern Arabia (Ovid, *Metamorphoses,* 10.471–80).

[2] **Thracian Nimphes:** the Maenads, Greek women whose inebriated and frenetic worship of Bacchus drove them to hack Orpheus into pieces when he refused to marry any of them after his beloved Euridice had died (Ovid, *Metamorphoses,* 11.1–66). Spenser may also have been thinking of the Thracian Amazons in Virgil's *Aeneid,* 11.659–63.

[3] **But if:** unless.

[4] **peares:** peers, companions.

[5] **that lovely boy:** Timias.

[6] **Libbards:** leopards.

[7] **fals:** happens; chances.

[8] **grenning:** grinning; **rad:** read, perceived.

[9] **he:** Lust.

> But with his craggy club in his right hand,
> Defends him selfe, and saves his gotten pray.
> Yet had it bene right hard him to withstand,
> But that he was full light and nimble on the land.[1]

26   Thereto the villaine used craft in fight;
>   For ever when the Squire his javelin shooke,
>   He held the Lady forth before him right,
>   And with her body, as a buckler,[2] broke
>   The puissance of his intended stroke.
>   And if it chaunst, (as needs it must in fight)
>   Whilest he on him was greedy to be wroke,[3]
>   That any little blow on her did light,
> Then would he laugh aloud, and gather great delight.

27   Which subtill sleight did him[4] encumber much,
>   And made him oft, when he would strike, forbeare;
>   For hardly could he come the carle to touch,
>   But that he her must hurt, or hazard neare:
>   Yet he his hand so carefully did beare,
>   That at the last he did himselfe attaine,[5]
>   And therein left the pike head of his speare.
>   A streame of coleblacke bloud[6] thence gusht amaine,
> That all her silken garments did with bloud bestaine.

---

[1] "Yet" in line 8 is more logical if we assign the pronouns in lines 8 and 9 thus: "Lust defended himself with his club, but it would have been difficult for Lust to withstand Timias, except that Lust was nimble on his feet." The first line of stanza 26, however, suggests that we should reverse that pronoun assignment: "Lust defended himself with his club, and it would have been difficult for Timias to withstand him, except that Timias was nimble on his feet—because of which, Lust used craft" (to substitute for agility). By interpreting "But that" as meaning "Because," Hamilton assigns the two pronouns to the same combatant, without specifying which one (Hamilton vii.25.9.n.). No matter what interpretation we give, the pronoun ambiguity is surely the point: Timias is temporarily difficult to distinguish from Lust.

[2] **buckler:** small shield used to parry an opponent's thrust.

[3] **wroke:** revenged.

[4] **him:** Timias, who is having trouble striking Lust for fear of inadvertently hurting Amoret, whom Lust has cleverly held in front of himself—but see note to 25.9.

[5] The ambiguity of pronouns reaches its apex in this line, conveying the psychological and moral complexity of Timias' position: he is fighting against a passion that is also resident in himself. In one sense of the line, Timias finally owns himself only when he stabs Lust.

[6] It is difficult to tell here whether Lust or Æmylia is wounded, although stanza 35 will provide an answer. Throughout the poem, Spenser uses "coleblacke" only to convey the idea of moral or spiritual corruption;

28   With that he threw her rudely on the flore,[1]
      And laying both his hands upon his glave,[2]
      With dreadfull strokes let drive at him so sore,
      That forst him flie abacke, himselfe to save:
      Yet he therewith so felly[3] still did rave,
      That scarse the Squire his hand could once upreare,
      But for advantage ground unto him gave,
      Tracing and traversing,[4] now here, now there;
For bootlesse thing it was to think such blowes to beare.

29   Whilest thus in battell they embusied were,
      Belphebe raunging in that forrest wide,
      The hideous noise of their huge strokes did heare,
      And drew thereto, making her eare her guide.
      Whom when that theefe approching nigh espide,
      With bow in hand, and arrowes ready bent,
      He by his former combate would not bide,[5]
      But fled away with ghastly dreriment,
Well knowing her to be his deaths sole instrument.

30   Whom seeing flie, she speedily poursewed
      With winged feete, as nimble as the winde,
      And ever in her bow she ready shewed,
      The arrow, to his deadly marke desynde.[6]
      As when *Latonaes* daughter cruell kynde,
      In vengement of her mothers great disgrace,
      With fell despight her cruell arrowes tynde
      Gainst wofull *Niobes* unhappy race,
That all the gods did mone her miserable case.[7]

---

see I.i.24.9, I.iv.44.2, I.v.20.8, I.xi.44.8, and II.vii.3.8, as well as the black blood at I.xi.22.4 and V.xi.14.6.

[1] **flore:** ground.

[2] **glave:** glaive, a term used at different periods to describe three distinct weapons: lance, bill, and broadsword. Here it apparently refers to Lust's club, unless he has a second weapon at hand. If the latter, Spenser's customary archaism makes it impossible to know to which type of weapon he refers.

[3] **felly:** cruelly.

[4] **Tracing and traversing:** pursuing and turning aside.

[5] I.e., when Lust saw Belphoebe approaching with her bow in her hand and her arrows aimed, Lust would not stay by Timias.

[6] I.e., the arrow, meant for its deadly (or imminently dead) target.

[7] Niobe told her Theban friends that she was more worthy to be worshipped than the goddess Latona, given that Latona had only two children to her fourteen. Enraged at hearing of this boast, Latona told her two children, Phoebus and Diana, to kill Niobe's

31 So well she sped her and so far she ventred,
    That ere unto his hellish den he raught,
    Even as he ready was there to have entred,
    She sent an arrow forth with mighty draught,[1]
    That in the very dore him overcaught,
    And in his nape arriving, through it thrild
    His greedy throte, therewith in two distraught,[2]
    That all his vitall spirites thereby spild,
And all his hairy brest with gory bloud was fild.[3]

32 Whom when on ground she groveling saw to rowle,
    She ran in hast his life to have bereft:
    But ere she could him reach, the sinfull sowle
    Having his carrion corse quite sencelesse left,
    Was fled to hell, surcharg'd with spoile and theft.
    Yet over him she there long gazing stood,
    And oft admir'd[4] his monstrous shape, and oft
    His mighty limbs, whilest all with filthy bloud
The place there overflowne, seemd like a sodaine flood.

33 Thenceforth[5] she past into his dreadfull den,
    Where nought but darkesome drerinesse she found,
    Ne creature saw, but hearkned now and then
    Some litle whispering, and soft groning sound.
    With that she askt, what ghosts there under ground
    Lay hid in horrour of eternall night?
    And bad them, if so be they were not bound,
    To come and shew themselves before the light,
Now freed from feare and danger of that dismall wight.

34 Then forth the sad *AEmylia* issewed,
    Yet trembling every joynt through former feare;
    And after her the Hag, there with her mewed,[6]

---

fourteen children with arrows. Niobe turned to stone and wept unceasingly forever after (Ovid, *Metamorphoses*, 6.165–312).

[1] **draught:** pulling of the bowstring.

[2] **distraught:** split asunder.

[3] **fild:** defiled.

[4] **admir'd:** wondered or marveled at—though the modern sense of gazing with

pleasure and esteem had just begun to enter the language in Spenser's time, and generations of British schoolboys have enjoyed applying that sense here.

[5] **Thenceforth:** from there forward.

[6] **mewed:** caged.

A foule and lothsome creature did appeare;
A leman fit for such a lover deare.
That mov'd *Belphebe* her no lesse to hate,
Then for to rue the others heavy cheare;[1]
Of whom she gan enquire of her estate.
Who all to her at large,[2] as hapned, did relate.

35   Thence she them brought toward the place, where late
       She left the gentle Squire with *Amoret:*[3]
       There she him found by that new lovely mate,[4]
       Who lay the whiles in swoune, full sadly set,
       From her faire eyes wiping the deawy wet,
       Which softly stild, and kissing them atweene,[5]
       And handling soft the hurts, which she did get.
       For of that Carle she sorely bruz'd had beene,
Als of his owne rash hand one wound was to be seene.[6]

36   Which when she[7] saw, with sodaine glauncing eye,
       Her noble heart with sight thereof was fild
       With deepe disdaine, and great indignity,
       That in her wrath she thought them both[8] have thrild,
       With that selfe arrow, which the Carle had kild:
       Yet held her wrathfull hand from vengeance sore,
       But drawing nigh, ere he her well beheld;
       "Is this the faith," she said, and said no more,
But turnd her face, and fled away for evermore.[9]

---

[1] In the light of day, the old woman who saved Æmylia from being raped has now been transformed into a "hag," a term of disgust.

[2] **at large:** at length.

[3] *Amoret:* Belphoebe's twin sister, lest we forget.

[4] **mate:** paramour.

[5] **stild:** trickled down; **atweene:** i.e., between wiping her eyes and caring for her wounds.

[6] Timias inadvertently wounded Amoret when Lust was using her as a human shield. In an allegory, however, supposedly nothing happens entirely by accident, so a second interpretation would be that despite Timias' originally noble intentions, his lust has led him to penetrate Amoret sexually. We must keep both of these situations simultaneously in mind—that the wounding was accidental and unavoidable, and that it resulted from Timias' lust—if we are to understand the following stanzas.

[7] **she:** Belphoebe.

[8] **both:** the fact that Belphoebe's wrath is directed not only at Timias but also at Amoret indicates that she believes Amoret's deflowering to have been consensual.

[9] Innumerable readers have noticed the evidence that this episode allegorizes a specific historical incident: in 1592, Sir Walter Raleigh impregnated Elizabeth Throckmorton, one of Queen Elizabeth's maids of

37   He seeing her depart, arose up light,
          Right sore agrieved at her sharpe reproofe,
          And follow'd fast: but when he came in sight,
          He durst not nigh approch, but kept aloofe,
          For dread of her displeasures utmost proofe.[1]
          And evermore, when he did grace entreat,
          And framed speaches fit for his behoofe,[2]
          Her mortall arrowes, she at him did threat,
And forst him backe with fowle dishonor to retreat.

38   At last when long he follow'd had in vaine,
          Yet found no ease of griefe, nor hope of grace,[3]
          Unto those woods he turned backe againe,
          Full of sad anguish, and in heavy case:
          And finding there fit solitary place
          For wofull wight, chose out a gloomy glade,
          Where hardly eye mote see bright heavens face,
          For mossy trees, which covered all with shade
And sad melancholy: there he his cabin[4] made.

39   His wonted warlike weapons all he broke,
          And threw away, with vow to use no more,
          Ne thenceforth ever strike in battell stroke,
          Ne ever word to speake to woman more;

---

honor, and then secretly married her. Queen Elizabeth had been mostly successful in keeping a tight rein on her maids of honor, who were supposed to be just that: honorable virgins. To deflower an aristocratic woman before marriage was to deprive her family and the Queen of a valuable political and financial playing piece. Indeed, all aristocrats, but especially those close to the crown, were wise to obtain the monarch's tacit or explicit permission before marrying, an expectation that had developed over the centuries as a way of preventing aristocratic families from forming political alliances that could challenge the throne—and of giving the monarch temporary control over the estates of those aristocrats who were official Wards of the Court because they had inherited their estates while still under the age of 21.

Unlike her predecessors, however, Elizabeth had exercised her control over both male and female courtiers chiefly by denying their requests to marry. The handsome Raleigh had been one of the Queen's favorites, but (or therefore) his betrayal of her trust infuriated her, and she banished him from court for five years. During his friend's period of banishment, Spenser finished Books Four through Six of *The Faerie Queene,* including this episode, which portrays Belphoebe as sexually jealous and quick to pronounce judgment on Timias.

[1] **proofe:** effect.

[2] **behoofe:** benefit.

[3] **grace:** favor or mercy (from Belphoebe).

[4] **cabin:** hut; dwelling of a hermit; cell in a convent or prison; den of a wild beast.

But in that wildernesse, of men forlore,
And of the wicked world forgotten quight,
His hard mishap in dolor to deplore,
And wast his wretched daies in wofull plight;
So on him selfe to wreake his follies[1] owne despight.

40 And eke his garment, to be thereto meet,
  He wilfully did cut and shape anew;
  And his faire lockes, that wont with ointment sweet
  To be embaulm'd,[2] and sweat out dainty dew,
  He let to grow and griesly to concrew,[3]
  Uncomb'd, uncurl'd, and carelesly unshed;[4]
  That in short time his face they overgrew,
  And over all his shoulders did dispred,
That who he whilome was, uneath was to be red.[5]

41 There he continued in this carefull[6] plight,
  Wretchedly wearing out his youthly yeares,
  Through wilfull penury[7] consumed quight,
  That like a pined[8] ghost he soone appeares.
  For other food then that wilde forrest beares,
  Ne other drinke there did he ever tast,
  Then running water, tempred with his teares,
  The more his weakened body so to wast:
That out of all mens knowledge he was worne at last.

42 For on a day, by fortune as it fell,
  His owne deare Lord Prince *Arthure* came that way,
  Seeking adventures, where he mote heare tell;[9]
  And as he through the wandring wood did stray,
  Having espide this Cabin far away,
  He to it drew, to weet who there did wonne;

[1] **follies:** foolishness'; madness'; wickedness'; lewdness'.

[2] **embaulm'd:** balmed, anointed.

[3] **concrew:** become matted.

[4] **unshed:** not parted.

[5] Spenser objected to the Irish habit of wearing long hair that covered the face, making identification of malefactors difficult (*View,* 53). McCabe argues that Belphoebe's anger "transforms the civil English squire into a 'wild' Irishman" and observes that when Elizabeth sent Raleigh to Ireland in 1589, his position was seen by some as advancement, by others as punishment (McCabe, 18).

[6] **carefull:** burdened with cares.

[7] **penury:** starvation.

[8] **pined:** wasted away with suffering.

[9] I.e., wherever he heard of them.

Weening therein some holy Hermit lay,
  That did resort[1] of sinfull people shonne;
Or else some woodman shrowded there from scorching sunne.

43   Arriving there, he found this wretched man,
        Spending his daies in dolour and despaire,
        And through long fasting woxen pale and wan,
        All overgrowen with rude and rugged haire;
        That albeit his owne deare Squire he were,
        Yet he him knew not, ne aviz'd at all,
        But like strange wight, whom he had seene no where,
        Saluting[2] him, gan into speach to fall,
  And pitty much his plight, that liv'd like outcast thrall.

44   But to his speach he aunswered no whit,
        But stood still mute, as if he had beene dum,
        Ne signe of sence did shew, ne common wit,
        As one with griefe and anguishe overcum,
        And unto every thing did aunswere mum:[3]
        And ever when the Prince unto him spake,
        He louted lowly, as did him becum,
        And humble homage did unto him make,
  Midst sorrow shewing joyous semblance for his sake.

45   At which his uncouth guise and usage quaint[4]
        The Prince did wonder much, yet could not ghesse
        The cause of that his sorrowfull constraint;
        Yet weend by secret signes of manlinesse,
        Which close appeard in that rude brutishnesse,
        That he whilome some gentle swaine had beene,
        Traind up in feats of armes and knightlinesse;
        Which he observ'd, by that he him had seene
  To weld his naked sword, and try the edges keene.[5]

46   And eke by that he saw on every tree,
        How he the name of one engraven had,
        Which likly was his liefest love to be,
        For whom he now so sorely was bestad;

---

[1] **resort:** habitual locations.
[2] **Saluting:** greeting.
[3] **mum:** not a word.

[4] **usage quaint:** strange behavior.
[5] Timias has been contemplating suicide.

Which was by him "*BELPHEBE*" rightly rad.
Yet who was that *Belphebe*, he ne wist;
Yet saw he often how he wexed glad,
When he it heard, and how the ground he kist,
Wherein it written was, and how himselfe he blist:[1]

47   Tho when he long had marked his demeanor,
    And saw that all he said and did, was vaine,
    Ne ought mote make him change his wonted tenor,
    Ne ought mote ease or mitigate his paine,
    He left him there in languor to remaine,
    Till time for him should remedy provide,
    And him restore to former grace againe.
    Which for it is too long here to abide,
I will deferre the end untill another tide.[2]

---

[1] **blist:** blessed (by crossing himself); blasted (with presumably silent curses).   [2] **tide:** opportunity; time.

Canto Eight

The gentle Squire recovers grace,
Sclaunder her guests doth staine:
Corflambo chaseth Placidas,[1]
And is by Arthure slaine.

1   Well said the wiseman,[2] now prov'd true by this,
        Which to this gentle Squire did happen late,
        That the displeasure of the mighty[3] is
        Then death it selfe more dread and desperate.
        For naught the same may calme ne mitigate,
        Till time the tempest doe thereof delay[4]
        With sufferaunce[5] soft, which rigour can abate,
        And have the sterne remembrance wypt away
    Of bitter thoughts, which deepe therein infixed lay.

2   Like as it fell to this unhappy boy,[6]
        Whose tender heart the faire *Belphebe* had,
        With one sterne looke so daunted, that no joy
        In all his life, which afterwards he lad,
        He ever tasted, but with penaunce sad
        And pensive sorrow pind and wore away,
        Ne ever laught, ne once shew'd countenance glad;
        But alwaies wept and wailed night and day,
    As blasted bloosme[7] through heat doth languish and decay;

3   Till on a day,[8] as in his wonted wise
        His doole he made, there chaunst a turtle Dove[9]
        To come, where he his dolors did devise,
        That likewise late had lost her dearest love,
    Which losse her made like passion also prove.

---

[1] **Corflambo:** heart (Latin *cor*) + flaming torch (French *flambeau*); **Placidas:** quiet, gentle (Latin).

[2] **wiseman:** Solomon (in Prov. 16.14).

[3] **mighty:** a term most often used of rulers.

[4] **delay:** temper.

[5] **sufferaunce:** uncomplaining endurance.

[6] **unhappy boy:** Timias.

[7] **bloosme:** bloom.

[8] **on a day:** one day.

[9] Symbolizing true love.

Who seeing his sad plight, her tender heart
With deare compassion deeply did emmove,
That she gan mone his undeserved smart,
And with her dolefull accent beare with him a part.[1]

4   Shee sitting by him as on ground he lay,
    Her mournefull notes full piteously did frame,
    And thereof made a lamentable lay,[2]
    So sensibly compyld,[3] that in the same
    Him seemed oft he heard his owne right name.
    With that he forth would poure so plenteous teares,
    And beat his breast unworthy of such blame,
    And knocke his head, and rend his rugged[4] heares,
That could have perst the hearts of Tigres and of Beares.

5   Thus long this gentle bird to him did use,
    Withouten dread of perill to repaire
    Unto his wonne, and with her mournefull muse
    Him to recomfort in his greatest care,
    That much did ease his mourning and misfare:
    And every day for guerdon of her song,
    He part of his small feast to her would share;
    That at the last of all his woe and wrong
Companion she became, and so continued long.

6   Upon a day as she him sate beside,
    By chance he certaine miniments[5] forth drew,
    Which yet with him as relickes did abide
    Of all the bounty, which *Belphebe* threw
    On him, whilst goodly grace she did him shew:
    Amongst the rest a jewell rich he found,
    That was a Ruby[6] of right perfect hew,
    Shap'd like a heart, yet bleeding of the wound,
And with a litle golden chaine about it bound.

---

[1] **accent:** sound; **a part:** a harmonizing musical part.

[2] **lamentable lay:** lamenting song.

[3] **sensibly compyld:** sensitively composed.

[4] **rugged:** ragged.

[5] **miniments:** proofs of Belphoebe's past kindness shown to him and of his former (or present) rights to that kindness; literally documents, such as title deeds or charters, which provide evidence of certain rights or privileges.

[6] Thought to affect the wearer's erotic passions.

7   The same he tooke, and with a riband[1] new,
     In which his Ladies colours[2] were, did bind
     About the turtles[3] necke, that with the vew
     Did greatly solace his engrieved mind.[4]
     All unawares[5] the bird, when she did find
     Her selfe so deckt, her nimble wings displaid,
     And flew away, as lightly as the wind:
     Which sodaine accident[6] him much dismaid,
And looking after long, did marke[7] which way she straid.

8   But when as long he looked had in vaine,
     Yet saw her forward still to make her flight,
     His weary eie returnd to him againe,
     Full of discomfort and disquiet plight,
     That both his juell he had lost so light,
     And eke his deare companion of his care.
     But that sweet bird departing, flew forth right
     Through the wide region of the wastfull[8] aire,
Untill she came where wonned his *Belphebe* faire.

9   There found she her (as then it did betide)[9]
     Sitting in covert shade of arbors sweet,
     After late weary toile, which she had tride[10]
     In salvage chase, to rest as seem'd her meet.
     There she alighting, fell before her feet,
     And gan to her her mournfull plaint to make,
     As was her wont, thinking to let her weet
     The great tormenting griefe, that for her sake
Her gentle Squire through her displeasure did pertake.[11]

10   She her beholding with attentive eye,
     At length did marke[12] about her purple brest
     That precious juell, which she formerly

---

[1] **riband:** ribbon.

[2] **colours:** of her insignia or device.

[3] **turtles:** turtle dove's.

[4] As well as enjoying books of printed emblems, sixteenth-century aristocrats enjoyed constructing living emblems or finding emblems in the world around them.

[5] **unawares:** unknown to Timias; before he knew it. (Stanzas 8 and 9 indicate that the bird is aware.)

[6] **accident:** occurrence; chance occurrence.

[7] **marke:** take note of.

[8] **wastfull:** empty; desolate.

[9] **betide:** happen.

[10] **tride:** undergone.

[11] **pertake:** partake.

[12] **marke:** notice.

Had knowne right well with colourd ribbands drest:
Therewith she rose in hast, and her addrest
With ready hand it to have reft away.
But the swift bird obayd not her behest,[1]
But swarv'd aside, and there againe did stay;
She follow'd her, and thought againe it to assay.

11   And ever when she nigh approcht, the Dove
Would flit a litle forward, and then stay,
Till she drew neare, and then againe remove;
So tempting her still to pursue the pray,
And still from her escaping soft away:
Till that at length into that forrest wide,
She drew her far, and led with slow delay.[2]
In th'end she her unto that place did guide,
Whereas that wofull man in languor did abide.

12   Eftsoones she flew unto his fearelesse hand,
And there a piteous ditty new deviz'd,
As if she would have made him understand,
His sorrowes cause to be of her despis'd.
Whom when she saw in wretched weedes disguiz'd,
With heary glib[3] deform'd, and meiger face,
Like ghost late risen from his grave agryz'd,[4]
She knew him not, but pittied much his case,
And wisht it were in her[5] to doe him any grace.

13   He her beholding, at her feet downe fell,
And kist the ground on which her sole did tread,
And washt the same with water,[6] which did well
From his moist eies, and like two streames procead,
Yet spake no word, whereby she might aread
What mister wight he was, or what he ment,

---

[1] **behest:** command.

[2] Cf. the doves in the stories of Noah's flood (Gen. 8), Jesus' baptism (Matt. 3.16–7), and Aeneas' search for the golden bough that will enable him to visit his dead father in the underworld (Virgil, *Aeneid,* 6.183–204). Note that the dove is performing for Timias the same reconciling role that Spenser is attempting to perform for Raleigh.

[3] **glib:** heavy, matted mass of hair worn over the eyes by the Irish; see vii.42.3.n. Unrequited lovers were stereotyped as ceasing to care for their appearance, wearing half-fastened clothing and untrimmed hair, but not as actually wearing glibs.

[4] **agryz'd:** shuddering; horrified.

[5] **in her:** in her power.

[6] **water:** the Queen's nickname for Sir Walter Raleigh was "Water."

But as one daunted with her presence dread,[1]
Onely few ruefull lookes unto her sent,
As messengers of his true meaning and intent.

14　Yet nathemore his meaning she ared,
　　But wondred much at his so selcouth[2] case,
　　And by his persons secret seemlyhed[3]
　　Well weend, that he had beene some man of place,[4]
　　Before misfortune did his hew deface:
　　That being mov'd with ruth she thus bespake.
　　"Ah wofull man, what heavens hard disgrace,
　　Or wrath of cruell wight on thee ywrake?[5]
Or selfe disliked life[6] doth thee thus wretched make?

15　"If heaven, then none may it redresse or blame,
　　Sith to his[7] powre we all are subject borne:
　　If wrathfull wight, then fowle rebuke and shame
　　Be theirs, that have so cruell thee forlorne;[8]
　　But if through inward griefe or wilfull scorne
　　Of life it be, then better doe advise.[9]
　　For he whose daies in wilfull woe are worne,
　　The grace of his Creator doth despise,
That will not use his gifts for thanklesse nigardise."[10]

16　When so he heard her say, eftsoones he brake
　　His sodaine[11] silence, which he long had pent,
　　And sighing inly deepe, her thus bespake;
　　"Then have they all[12] themselves against me bent:
　　For heaven, first author of my languishment,
　　Envying my too great felicity,
　　Did closely with a cruell one consent,
　　To cloud my daies in dolefull misery,
And make me loath this life, still longing for to die.

---

[1] **dread:** dreaded; awe-inspiring.

[2] **selcouth:** seldom known; strange.

[3] **secret seemlyhed:** disguised handsomeness, decency, or appropriateness.

[4] **of place:** of a high social rank.

[5] **ywrake:** wreaked.

[6] **selfe disliked life:** a life that dislikes itself.

[7] **his:** its (i.e., heaven's); his (i.e., God's).

[8] **forlorne:** abandoned.

[9] I.e., then think better of it.

[10] **nigardise:** niggardliness, stinginess.

[11] **sodaine:** too hastily begun.

[12] **they all:** all three of the reasons for his woe, as outlined by Belphoebe in stanzas 14 and 15.

17   "Ne any but your selfe, ô dearest dred,[1]
         Hath done this wrong, to wreake on worthlesse wight
         Your high displesure, through misdeeming[2] bred:
         That when your pleasure is to deeme aright,[3]
         Ye may redresse, and me restore to light."
      Which sory words her mightie hart did mate[4]
         With mild[5] regard, to see his ruefull plight,
         That her inburning wrath she gan abate,
And him receiv'd againe to former favours state.

18   In which he long time afterwards did lead
         An happie life with grace and good accord,
         Fearlesse of fortunes chaunge or envies dread,
         And eke all mindlesse of his owne deare Lord
         The noble Prince, who never heard one word
         Of tydings, what did unto him betide,
         Or what good fortune did to him afford,
         But through the endlesse world did wander wide,
Him seeking evermore, yet no where him descride.[6]

19   Till on a day as through that wood he[7] rode,
         He chaunst to come where those two Ladies late,
         Æmylia and *Amoret* abode,
         Both in full sad and sorrowfull estate;
         The one right feeble through the evill rate[8]
         Of food, which in her duresse she had found:
         The other almost dead and desperate
         Through her late hurts, and through that haplesse wound,
With which the Squire in her defence her sore astound.[9]

---

[1] **dearest dred:** the speaker addresses the Queen with these words in I.Pr.4.9.

[2] **misdeeming:** misunderstanding—or, less diplomatically, lack of perception. Kaplan argues that this word aligns the Queen with Lord Burghley and others who misread Spenser's poetry because they "ill judge of love" (Pr.2.1; Kaplan, 44). These same people have "frosen hearts" (Pr.2.2).

[3] I.e., whenever it pleases you to judge (me) correctly.

[4] **mate:** join; checkmate; subdue; abash. I.e., his words do this to her heart.

[5] **mild:** gentle; gracious (but with a hint of the meaning "not exuberant").

[6] We do not see Timias and Arthur together again until VI.v.11.

[7] **he:** Arthur.

[8] **evill rate:** poor amount or quality.

[9] **astound:** stunned; amazed (by accidentally striking her).

20   Whom when the Prince beheld, he gan to rew
         The evill case in which those Ladies lay;
         But most was moved at the piteous vew
         Of *Amoret*, so neare unto decay,
         That her great daunger did him much dismay.
         Eftsoones that pretious liquour[1] forth he drew,
         Which he in store about him kept alway,
         And with few drops thereof did softly dew
      Her wounds, that unto strength restor'd her soone anew.

21   Tho when they both recovered were right well,
         He gan of them inquire, what evill guide
         Them thether brought, and how their harmes befell.
         To whom they told all, that did them betide,
         And how from thraldome vile they were untide
         Of that same wicked Carle, by Virgins hond;[2]
         Whose bloudie corse they shew'd him there beside,
         And eke his cave, in which they both were bond:
      At which he wondred much, when all those signes he fond.

22   And evermore he greatly did desire
         To know, what Virgin did them thence unbind;
         And oft of them did earnestly inquire,
         Where was her won, and how he mote her find.
         But when as nought according to his mind
         He could outlearne,[3] he them from ground did reare:
         No service lothsome to a gentle kind;
         And on his warlike beast them both did beare,
      Himselfe by them on foot, to succour them from feare.

23   So when that forrest they had passed well,
         A litle cotage farre away they spide,
         To which they drew, ere night upon them fell;
         And entring in, found none therein abide,
         But one old woman sitting there beside,

---

[1] **liquour:** a not necessarily alcoholic, not necessarily potable liquid; Arthur carries a liquor that magically heals all wounds; see I.ix.19.

[2] I.e., how they were untied, by the hand of a Virgin, from the vile imprisonment imposed by that previously mentioned wicked churl.

[3] **outlearne:** find out.

Upon the ground in ragged rude attyre,
With filthy lockes about her scattered wide,
Gnawing her nayles for felnesse and for yre,
And there out sucking venime to her parts entyre.[1]

24   A foule and loathly creature sure[2] in sight,
And in conditions to be loath'd no lesse:
For she was stuft with rancour and despight
Up to the throat, that oft with bitternesse
It forth would breake, and gush in great excesse,
Pouring out streames of poyson and of gall
Gainst all, that truth or vertue doe professe,
Whom she with leasings[3] lewdly did miscall,
And wickedly backbite: Her name men *Sclaunder*[4] call.

25   Her nature is all goodnesse to abuse,
And causelesse[5] crimes continually to frame,
With which she guiltlesse persons may accuse,
And steale away the crowne of their good name;
Ne ever Knight so bold, ne ever Dame
So chast and loyall liv'd, but she would strive
With forged cause them falsely to defame;
Ne ever thing so well was doen alive,
But she with blame would blot, and of due praise deprive.[6]

26   Her words were not, as common words are ment,
T'expresse the meaning of the inward mind,
But noysome[7] breath, and poysnous spirit sent
From inward parts, with cancred malice lind,

---

[1] **parts entyre:** inward parts (OED adj. 11). She sucks venom from herself and back into herself.

[2] **sure:** surely.

[3] **leasings:** lies.

[4] *Sclaunder:* the spelling links the word with "scandal," which, as Kaplan points out, may be true even while being malicious (13).

[5] **causelesse:** having no basis in fact; unexplained (OED "cause" v[1]4).

[6] Kaplan argues that by inventing the character of Sclaunder, Spenser is addressing not only the slanders about Raleigh and, in other contexts, about his own choice of love as a poetic theme, but also the common accusation that poets themselves were slanderers (29). Slander was a highly charged topic in Elizabethan society, where one's good name was one's most important possession, where the courts considered a bad reputation partial evidence of wrongdoing, and where slander was believed to be a source of civil disorder (Kaplan, 19, 26, 20).

[7] **noysome:** stinking; noxious.

And breathed forth with blast of bitter wind;
Which passing through the eares, would pierce the hart,
And wound the soule it selfe with griefe unkind:
For like the stings of Aspes, that kill with smart,
Her spightfull words did pricke, and wound the inner part.

27   Such was that Hag, unmeet to host such guests,
      Whom greatest Princes court would welcome fayne,
      But neede, that answers not to all requests,
      Bad them not looke for better entertayne;[1]
      And eke that age despysed nicenesse[2] vaine,
      Enur'd to hardnesse and to homely[3] fare,
      Which them to warlike discipline did trayne,
      And manly limbs endur'd with litle care
Against all hard mishaps and fortunelesse misfare.

28   Then all that evening welcommed with cold,
      And chearelesse hunger, they together spent;
      Yet found no fault, but that the Hag did scold
      And rayle at them with grudgefull discontent,
      For lodging there without her owne consent:[4]
      Yet they endured all with patience milde,
      And unto rest themselves all onely[5] lent,
      Regardlesse of that queane[6] so base and vilde,
To be unjustly blamd, and bitterly revilde.

29   Here well I weene, when as these rimes be red
      With misregard, that some rash witted wight,
      Whose looser[7] thought will lightly be misled,
      These gentle Ladies will misdeeme too light,
      For thus conversing with this noble Knight;[8]
      Sith now of dayes such temperance is rare

---

[1] **entertayne:** treatment; reception.

[2] **age:** historical period; **nicenesse:** luxury; delicacy; fastidiousness.

[3] **homely:** homelike; simple.

[4] About travelers' rights to lodging, see III.viii.52.5.n.

[5] **onely:** i.e., only rest, since they could get no hospitality.

[6] **queane:** badly behaved woman.

[7] **looser:** too loose; lewd.

[8] **conversing:** associating; having sex with. The narrator intends the first, whereas the misreader believes the second. Misreading now becomes the prime example of slander, injurious not only to the poet's characters but to the poet, who is himself misdeemed a scandalmonger (Kaplan, 38).

And hard to finde, that heat of youthfull spright
For ought will from his greedie pleasure spare,
More hard for hungry steed t'abstaine from pleasant lare.[1]

30   But antique age[2] yet in the infancie
      Of time, did live then like an innocent,
      In simple truth and blamelesse chastitie,
      Ne then of guile had made experiment,
      But voide of vile and treacherous intent,
      Held vertue for it selfe in soveraine[3] awe:
      Then loyall love had royall regiment,[4]
      And each unto his lust[5] did make a lawe,
      From all forbidden things his liking to withdraw.

31   The Lyon there did with the Lambe consort,[6]
      And eke the Dove sate by the Faulcons side,
      Ne each of other feared fraud or tort,[7]
      But did in safe securitie abide,
      Withouten perill of the stronger pride:
      But when the world woxe old, it woxe warre old[8]

---

[1] **lare:** pasture.

[2] **antique age:** stanzas 30 through 32 transform the early Middle Ages (the setting for this poem) into a Golden Age like that described by Greek and Roman writers, a period sometimes set in the future but usually set in the misty past when the world was supposedly a better place. See, e.g., Hesiod, *Works and Days,* 109–20; Virgil, *Eclogue* 4; Ovid, *Metamorphoses,* 1.89–112, Tasso, *Aminta,* 1 Chorus; and Guarini, *Il Pastor Fido* 4 Chorus. The degeneration of the world was an important theme for Spenser, who mentioned it at least once in each book of *The Faerie Queene;* cf. I.xii.14.8–9, II.vii.16–17, III.i.13, V.Pr. and passim, VI.xii.40–41, and Cantos of Mutabilitie passim.

[3] **soveraine:** due to a ruler; supremely beneficial.

[4] **regiment:** rule; self-control.

[5] **lust:** desire or pleasure of any sort, but Spenser is also addressing a Renaissance debate over whether a perfect world would include marriage laws and restrictions and whether it would privilege pleasure. Cf. Chrysogone's conceiving without pleasure and giving birth without pain (III.vi.27).

[6] A much-repeated fantasy about the Golden Age, adapted from Isa. 11.6.

[7] **tort:** injustice.

[8] **warre old:** a false etymology for "world," suggested by the Old English "worold." Like many Renaissance scholars, Spenser experimented with the idea that words were inherently related to truths, rather than arbitrary signifiers. One could therefore use etymologies not only to prove something about a word's historical meaning, but also to prove philosophical and other theorems. His and other scholars' etymologies were often erroneous, but they can give us insight into Renaissance beliefs and needs.

(Whereof it hight) and having shortly tride
The traines of wit, in wickednesse woxe bold,
And dared of all sinnes the secrets to unfold.

32   Then beautie, which was made to represent
The great Creatours owne resemblance bright,
Unto abuse of lawlesse lust was lent,
And made the baite of bestiall delight:
Then faire grew foule, and foule grew faire in sight,
And that which wont to vanquish God and man,
Was made the vassall of the victors might;
Then did her glorious flowre wex dead and wan,
Despisd and troden downe of all that overran.

33   And now it is so utterly decayd,
That any bud thereof doth scarse remaine,
But if[1] few plants preserv'd through heavenly ayd,
In Princes Court doe hap to sprout againe,
Dew'd with her drops of bountie Soveraine,
Which from that goodly glorious flowre proceed,
Sprung of the auncient stocke of Princes straine,
Now th'onely remnant of that royall breed,
Whose noble kind at first was sure[2] of heavenly seed.

34   Tho soone as day discovered heavens face
To sinfull men with darknes overdight,[3]
This gentle crew gan from their eye-lids chace
The drowzie humour[4] of the dampish night,
And did themselves unto their journey dight.
So forth they yode, and forward softly paced,
That them to view had bene an uncouth sight;
How all the way the Prince on footpace traced,[5]
The Ladies both on horse, together fast embraced.

35   Soone as they thence departed were afore,
That shamefull Hag, the slaunder of her sexe,
Them follow'd fast, and them reviled sore,

---

[1] **But if:** unless.
[2] **sure:** surely.
[3] **overdight:** covered overhead.

[4] **humour:** state of mind (with a pun on "moisture").
[5] **on footpace traced:** traveled at a walking pace.

Him calling theefe, them whores; that much did vexe
His noble hart; thereto she did annexe[1]
False crimes and facts,[2] such as they never ment,
That those two Ladies much asham'd did wexe:
The more did she pursue her lewd intent,
And rayl'd[3] and rag'd, till she had all her poyson spent.

36   At last when they were passed out of sight,
       Yet she did not her spightfull speach forbeare,
       But after them did barke, and still backbite,
       Though there were none her hatefull words to heare:
       Like as a curre doth felly bite and teare
       The stone, which passed straunger at him threw;
       So she them seeing past the reach of eare,
       Against the stones and trees did rayle anew,
Till she had duld the sting, which in her tongs end grew.

37   They passing forth kept on their readie way,
       With easie steps so soft as foot could stryde,
       Both for great feeblesse, which did oft assay[4]
       Faire *Amoret,* that scarcely she could ryde,
       And eke through heavie armes, which sore annoyd
       The Prince on foot,[5] not wonted so to fare;
       Whose steadie hand was faine his steede to guyde,
       And all the way from trotting hard to spare,[6]
So was his toyle the more, the more that was his care.

38   At length they spide, where towards them with speed
       A Squire came gallopping, as he would flie,
       Bearing a litle Dwarfe before his steed,
       That all the way full loud for aide did crie,
       That seem'd his shrikes would rend the brasen[7] skie:
       Whom after did a mightie man pursew,

---

[1] **annexe:** add on.

[2] **facts:** evil deeds.

[3] **rayl'd:** reviled.

[4] **feeblesse:** feebleness; **assay:** put to the test.

[5] A medieval outfit of chain mail, helmet, shield, belt, sword, and spear could easily weigh eighty pounds, and the metal was sweltering in summer, freezing in winter.

[6] **spare:** refrain, spare himself and the horse.

[7] **brasen:** brassy (in color, shine, or apparent hardness).

Ryding upon a Dromedare[1] on hie,
Of stature huge, and horrible of hew,[2]
That would have maz'd a man his dreadfull face to vew.

39   For from his fearefull eyes two fierie beames,
    More sharpe then points of needles did proceede,
    Shooting forth farre away two flaming streames,
    Full of sad powre, that poysonous bale[3] did breede
    To all, that on him lookt without good heed,
    And secretly his enemies did slay:
    Like as the Basiliske[4] of serpents seede,
    From powrefull eyes close venim doth convay
Into the lookers hart, and killeth farre away.

40   He all the way did rage at that same Squire,
    And after him full many threatnings threw,
    With curses vaine in his avengefull ire:
    But none of them (so fast away he flew)
    Him overtooke, before he came in vew.[5]
    Where when he saw the Prince in armour bright,
    He cald to him aloud, his case to rew,
    And rescue him through succour of his might,
From that his cruell foe, that him pursewd in sight.

41   Eftsoones the Prince tooke downe those Ladies twaine
    From loftie steede, and mounting in their stead
    Came to that Squire, yet trembling every vaine:[6]
    Of whom he gan enquire his cause of dread;
    Who as he gan the same to him aread,
    Loe hard behind his backe his foe was prest,

---

[1] **Dromedare:** dromedary, the one-humped domesticated camel, known for its speed.

[2] Although at first this line seems to refer to the camel, the subsequent lines indicate that it refers to the rider. The camel, however, would also be horrible or at least ugly to English audiences, partly because it was so foreign and partly because it was associated with Muslims, whom Europeans had for centuries seen as the archenemy.

[3] **sad:** grave; **bale:** evil; a consuming fire. Renaissance optics held that eyes emitted rays; this camel-rider's eyes emit rays of fire.

[4] **Basiliske:** a legendary dragon-like serpent with a lethal gaze.

[5] The squire runs faster than the speed of sound.

[6] I.e., to the squire, who was still trembling in every vein.

With dreadfull weapon aymed at his head,
That unto death had doen him unredrest,[1]
Had not the noble Prince his readie stroke represt.

42   Who thrusting boldly twixt him and the blow,
     The burden of the deadly brunt[2] did beare
     Upon his shield, which lightly he did throw
     Over his head, before the harme came neare.
     Nathlesse it fell with so despiteous dreare[3]
     And heavie sway, that hard unto his crowne
     The shield it drove, and did the covering reare,[4]
     Therewith both Squire and dwarfe did tomble downe
Unto the earth, and lay long while in senselesse swowne.

43   Whereat the Prince full wrath, his strong right hand
     In full avengement heaved up on hie,
     And stroke the Pagan with his steely brand[5]
     So sore, that to his saddle bow[6] thereby
     He bowed low, and so a while did lie:
     And sure had not his massie yron mace[7]
     Betwixt him and his hurt bene happily,
     It would have cleft him to the girding place,[8]
Yet as it was, it did astonish[9] him long space.

---

[1] I.e., who would have killed him without hope of his being saved.

[2] **brunt:** blow; physical shock.

[3] **despiteous dreare:** contemptuous, malevolent, or violent direness.

[4] **reare:** raise. Like Atlante in Ariosto's *Orlando Furioso* (2.55–6, 8.11, 22.84–6), Arthur normally keeps his shield covered with a veil, since it strikes viewers blind and causes the sun and moon to feel sick in comparison to its brightness. Arthur uses the shield only when the odds are hugely in his opponent's favor from the start, as when the opponent is a monster or an entire army (I.vii.33–34). Made of one perfect diamond, the shield has the magic power to cause all disguised or hypocritical opponents to turn into dust (I.vii.35). Here, the "covering" comes at least partly off, yet it causes no harm to Arthur's opponent. The "covering" may be interpreted as the shield itself, which covers the Squire and dwarf until knocked aside. Alternatively, the passage may be interpreted as meaning that only the Squire and dwarf see the uncovered part of the shield, which causes them to swoon in temporary blindness.

[5] **brand:** sword.

[6] **saddle bow:** the arched front and back portions of a saddle, curving to fit the horse's back.

[7] **massie:** weighty; **mace:** heavy club, usually metal, usually with a spiked head.

[8] **girding place:** waist (about which belts are girded).

[9] **astonish:** stupefy.

44   But when he to himselfe returnd againe,
           All full of rage he gan to curse and sweare,
           And vow by *Mahoune*[1] that he should be slaine.
           With that his murdrous mace he up did reare,
           That seemed nought the souse thereof could beare,
           And therewith smote at him with all his might.
           But ere that it to him approched neare,
           The royall child[2] with readie quicke foresight,
       Did shun the proofe thereof and it avoyded light.

45   But ere his hand he could recure againe,
           To ward his bodie from the balefull stound,
           He smote at him with all his might and maine,
           So furiously, that ere he wist, he found

---

[1] **Mahoune:** the camel-rider's invocation of Mohammed, the highest prophet of Islam, identifies the rider as a Muslim. Since long before the bloodbath of the Crusades, Western Europeans had nursed the misconception that Muslims worshipped Mohammed or that Mohammed was the Muslim god, though in fact Muslims did not even consider Mohammed divine. In turn, Muslims thought of Europeans as worshipping multiple gods, out of a misconception about the unified being of the Father, Son, and Holy Spirit (though of course Europeans did consider Jesus divine). Another Western European misconception centered upon the word "pagan," which was defined by most scholars as designating those who did not worship the one true God, i.e., heathens. Thus theologians usually did not call Jews pagans. Nonetheless, they freely applied the term to Muslims, as Spenser does in stanza 43 above. Many of Spenser's contemporaries would have been astonished to learn that Muslims worshipped the same god as Jews and Christians, venerated Abraham, Mary, and Jesus, and considered the Jewish and Christian scriptures part of "The Book" of God (albeit flawed by human transmission). Yet Islam had seriously encroached upon the Middle East, North Africa, and Europe during the Middle Ages, spreading much faster than had Christianity in earlier centuries and meeting less resistance, partly because the policies of the Islamic conquerors toward those who did not convert were, for the most part, far more lenient than those of Christian conquerors (who tended to massacre entire villages first and ask questions later, and who treated many nonorthodox sects of Christians with more severity than did the Muslim invaders). For each side, then, the other became almost synonymous with evil. Yet Tasso and Ariosto both featured several Muslim characters in their epics, often making them complex and sympathetic characters. Spenser's Muslim characters are usually nefarious, although he follows one standard literary formula in converting the Muslim woman into a member of Western European society. (For a discussion of such characters, see Kahf, 55–110.) Ironically, the European code of chivalry had originally come from Arab commanders such as Salah al-Din, whose chivalric manners on and off the battlefield had so impressed the Crusaders that they had composed many stories and poems of which "Saladin" was the dashing hero.

[2] **royall child:** royal offspring, i.e., Arthur.

His head before him tombling on the ground.
The whiles his babling tongue did yet blaspheme
And curse his God, that did him so confound;[1]
The whiles his life ran foorth in bloudie streame,
His soule descended downe into the Stygian reame.[2]

46   Which when that Squire beheld, he woxe full glad
     To see his foe breath out his spright in vaine:
     But that same dwarfe right sorie seem'd and sad,
     And howld aloud to see his Lord there slaine,
     And rent his haire and scratcht his face for paine.
     Then gan the Prince at leasure to inquire
     Of all the accident,[3] there hapned plaine,
     And what he was, whose eyes did flame with fire;
All which was thus to him declared by that Squire.

47   "This mightie man" (quoth he) "whom you have slaine,
     Of an huge Geauntesse[4] whylome was bred;
     And by his strength rule to himselfe did gaine
     Of many Nations into thraldome led,
     And mightie kingdomes of his force adred;
     Whom yet he conquer'd not by bloudie fight,
     Ne hostes of men with banners brode dispred,
     But by the powre of his infectious sight,
With which he killed all, that came within his might.

48   "Ne was he ever vanquished afore,
     But ever vanquisht all, with whom he fought;
     Ne was there man so strong, but he downe bore,
     Ne woman yet so faire, but he her brought
     Unto his bay,[5] and captived her thought.
     For most of strength and beautie his desire
     Was spoyle to make,[6] and wast them unto nought,
     By casting secret flakes[7] of lustfull fire
From his false eyes, into their harts and parts entire.

---

[1] **confound:** destroy; send to hell.

[2] **Stygian reame:** realm of the Greek underworld (bordered by the river Styx, adjectivally "Stygian") or, by analogy, of hell.

[3] **accident:** event.

[4] **Geauntesse:** giantess.

[5] **bay:** the point at which a hunted animal has no choice but to turn and face its pursuer.

[6] I.e., his desire chiefly made strength and beauty into his booty.

[7] **flakes:** sparks.

49   "Therefore *Corflambo*[1] was he cald aright,
      Though namelesse there his bodie now doth lie,
      Yet hath he left one daughter that is hight
      The faire *Pœana*,[2] who seemes outwardly
      So faire, as ever yet saw living eie:
      And were her vertue like her beautie bright,
      She were as faire as any under skie.
      But ah she given is to vaine delight,
And eke too loose of life, and eke of love too light.

50   "So as it fell there was a gentle Squire,
      That lov'd a Ladie of high parentage,
      But for[3] his meane degree might not aspire
      To match so high, her friends with counsell sage,
      Dissuaded her from such a disparage.[4]
      But she, whose hart to love was wholly lent,
      Out of his hands could not redeeme her gage,[5]
      But firmely following her first intent,
Resolv'd with him to wend, gainst all her friends consent.

51   "So twixt themselves they pointed[6] time and place,
      To which when he according did repaire,[7]
      An hard mishap and disaventrous case[8]
      Him chaunst; in stead of his *AEmylia* faire
      This Gyants sonne, that lies there on the laire[9]
      An headlesse heape, him unawares there caught,
      And all dismayd through mercilesse despaire,[10]
      Him wretched thrall unto his dongeon brought,
Where he remaines, of all unsuccour'd and unsought.

---

[1] *Corflambo*: see Arg.3.n. for the etymology.

[2] *Pœana*: punishment (Latin).

[3] **for**: because.

[4] **disparage**: marriage to one of inferior rank; the disgrace resulting from such a marriage.

[5] I.e., could not back out of the commitment; regarding gages as challenges, see iii.3.4.n.

[6] **pointed**: appointed.

[7] **according**: accordingly; **repaire**: go; retreat.

[8] **disaventrous case**: unfortunate situation.

[9] **laire**: pasture.

[10] **mercilesse despaire**: the despair of the damned. Despair was the deadliest of the Seven Deadly Sins, because it meant that one had utterly given up hope of God's help and was therefore completely separated from God. One who despaired, then, was beyond mercy.

52   "This Gyants daughter came upon a day[1]
         Unto the prison in her joyous glee,[2]
         To view the thrals, which there in bondage lay:
         Amongst the rest she chaunced there to see
         This lovely swaine the Squire of low degree;
         To whom she did her liking lightly cast,
         And wooed him her paramour to bee:
         From day to day she woo'd and prayd him fast,[3]
And for his love him promist libertie at last.

53   "He though affide[4] unto a former love,
         To whom his faith he firmely ment to hold,
         Yet seeing not how thence he mote remove,[5]
         But by that meanes, which fortune did unfold,
         Her graunted love, but with affection cold
         To win her grace his libertie to get.
         Yet she him still detaines in captive hold,
         Fearing least if she should him freely set,[6]
He would her shortly leave, and former love forget.

54   "Yet so much favour she to him hath hight,[7]
         Above the rest, that he sometimes may space[8]
         And walke about her gardens of delight,[9]
         Having a keeper still with him in place,
         Which keeper is this Dwarfe, her dearling base,[10]
         To whom the keyes of every prison dore
         By her committed be, of speciall grace,
         And at his will may whom he list restore,[11]
And whom he list reserve,[12] to be afflicted more.

---

[1] **Gyants daughter:** Pœana; **upon a day:** one day.

[2] **glee:** joy.

[3] **fast:** earnestly; so as to bind him to her (thus to offset the liberty from prison that she offers him).

[4] **affide:** affianced, betrothed.

[5] **remove:** leave.

[6] **freely set:** set free.

[7] **hight:** pledged.

[8] **space:** ramble.

[9] **gardens of delight:** the phrase suggests that she allows him to explore sexually as well as horticulturally.

[10] **dearling base:** base-born or basely minded darling.

[11] **restore:** i.e., to liberty.

[12] **reserve:** keep (pent up).

55   "Whereof when tydings came unto mine eare,
        Full inly sorie for[1] the fervent zeale,
        Which I to him as to my soule did beare;
        I thether went where I did long conceale
        My selfe, till that the Dwarfe did me reveale,
        And told his Dame, her Squire of low degree
        Did secretly out of her prison steale;
        For me he did mistake[2] that Squire to bee;
For never two so like did living creature see.

56   "Then was I taken and before her brought,
        Who through the likenesse of my outward hew,
        Being likewise beguiled[3] in her thought,
        Gan blame me much for being so untrew,
        To seeke by flight her fellowship t'eschew,
        That lov'd me deare, as dearest thing alive.
        Thence she commaunded me to prison new;[4]
        Whereof I glad did not gainesay nor strive,
But suffred that same Dwarfe me to her dongeon drive.

57   "There did I finde mine onely faithfull frend
        In heavy plight and sad perplexitie;
        Whereof I sorie, yet my selfe did bend,
        Him to recomfort with my companie.
        But him the more agreev'd I found thereby:
        For all his joy, he said, in that distresse
        Was mine and his *Æmylias* libertie.
        Æmylia well he lov'd, as I mote ghesse;
Yet greater love to me then her he did professe.

58   "But I with better reason him aviz'd,
        And shew'd him how through error and mis-thought[5]
        Of our like persons eath[6] to be disguiz'd,
        Or his exchange, or freedome might be wrought.
        Whereto full loth was he, ne would for ought
        Consent, that I who stood all feareless free,

___

[1] **for:** because of.
[2] **mistake:** mistakenly suppose.
[3] **beguiled:** deluded.
[4] **new:** anew.

[5] **mis-thought:** i.e., others' erroneous belief that he is his friend.
[6] **eath:** easy.

Should wilfully be into thraldome brought,
Till fortune did perforce it so decree.
Yet overrul'd at last, he did to me agree.

59   "The morrow next about the wonted howre,
The Dwarfe cald at the doore of *Amyas*,[1]
To come forthwith unto his Ladies bowre.
In steed of whom forth came I *Placidas*,[2]
And undiscerned, forth with him did pas.
There with great joyance and with gladsome glee,[3]
Of faire *Pœana* I received was,
And oft imbrast, as if that I were hee,
And with kind words accoyd,[4] vowing great love to mee.

60   "Which I, that was not bent to former love,
As was my friend, that had her long refusd,
Did well accept, as well it did behove,
And to the present neede it[5] wisely usd.
My former hardnesse[6] first I faire excusd;
And after promist large amends to make.
With such smooth termes her error I abusd,
To my friends good, more then for mine owne sake,
For whose sole libertie I love and life did stake.

61   "Thenceforth I found more favour at her hand,
That to her Dwarfe, which had me in his charge,
She bad to lighten my too heavie band,[7]
And graunt more scope to me to walke at large.
So on a day as by the flowrie marge[8]
Of a fresh streame I with that Elfe did play,
Finding no meanes how I might us enlarge,[9]
But if[10] that Dwarfe I could with me convay,
I lightly snatcht him up, and with me bore away.

---

[1] *Amyas:* friend (from *ami*, French).

[2] *Placidas:* see Arg.3.n. for etymology.

[3] **glee:** entertainment; happiness.

[4] **accoyd:** soothed, placated (after having suffered imprisonment).

[5] **it:** her love; the whole situation.

[6] **hardnesse:** standoffishness.

[7] **band:** chain, shackles, fetters; custody.

[8] **marge:** margin, bank.

[9] **enlarge:** set free.

[10] **But if:** unless.

62   "Thereat he shriekt aloud, that with his cry
            The Tyrant selfe came forth with yelling bray,
            And me pursew'd; but nathemore would I
            Forgoe the purchase of my gotten pray,
            But have perforce him hether brought away."
        Thus as they talked, loe where nigh at hand
        Those Ladies two yet[1] doubtfull through dismay
        In presence came, desirous t'understand
Tydings of all, which there had hapned on the land.

63   Where soone as sad *Æmylia* did espie
            Her captive lovers friend, young *Placidas;*
            All mindlesse of her wonted modestie,
            She to him ran, and him with streight embras[2]
            Enfolding said, "And lives yet *Amyas?*"
        "He lives" (quoth he) "and his *Æmylia* loves."
        "Then lesse" (said she) "by all the woe I pas,
        With which my weaker patience fortune proves.[3]
But what mishap thus long him fro my selfe removes?"

64   Then gan he all this storie to renew,[4]
            And tell the course of his captivitie;
            That her deare hart full deepely made to rew,
            And sigh full sore, to heare the miserie,
            In which so long he mercilesse[5] did lie.
        Then after many teares and sorrowes spent,
        She deare besought the Prince[6] of remedie:
        Who thereto did with readie will consent,
And well perform'd, as shall appeare by his event.[7]

<hr>

[1] **yet:** still.

[2] **embras:** embrace.

[3] I.e., then I attach less importance to all the woes I endure, with which Fortune tests my too-weak patience.

[4] **renew:** retell.

[5] **mercilesse:** with no hope of mercy.

[6] **Prince:** Arthur.

[7] **event:** by his resulting action; by what happens to him.

Canto Nine

The Squire of low degree releast
Pœana¹ takes to wife:
Britomart fightes with many Knights,
Prince Arthur stints their strife.

1   Hard is the doubt, and difficult to deeme,
         When all three kinds of love together meet,
         And doe dispart² the hart with powre extreme,
         Whether shall weigh the balance downe; to weet³
         The deare affection unto kindred sweet,
         Or raging fire of love to woman kind,
         Or zeale of friends combynd with vertues meet.
         But of them all the band of vertuous mind⁴
      Me seemes the gentle hart should most assured bind.

2   For naturall affection⁵ soone doth cesse,
         And quenched is with *Cupids* greater flame:
         But faithfull friendship doth them both suppresse,
         And them with maystring discipline doth tame,
         Through thoughts aspyring to eternall fame.
         For as the soule doth rule the earthly masse,
         And all the service of the bodie frame,
         So love of soule doth love of bodie passe,
      No lesse then perfect gold surmounts the meanest brasse.

3   All which who list by tryall to assay,
         Shall in this storie find approved⁶ plaine;
         In which these Squires true friendship more did sway,

---

¹ The squire of low degree loves, and in-
tends to marry, Æmylia, but the only mar-
riage mentioned in the canto is the one
between Placidas and Pœana. Hamilton
suggests that Spenser may intend this Argu-
ment's pairing of the squire of low degree
with Pœana as a witty comment on Pœana's
inability to tell the difference between the
two men.

² **dispart:** divide.

³ **Whether:** which (of the three types of
love); **to weet:** to wit; that is.

⁴ I.e., the bond of friendship.

⁵ **naturall affection:** inborn affection for
one's kindred.

⁶ **approved:** proved.

Then either care of parents could refraine,
Or love of fairest Ladie could constraine.
For though *Pæana* were as faire as morne,
Yet did this trustie Squire[1] with proud disdaine
For his friends sake her offred favours scorne,
And she her selfe her syre, of whom she was yborne.

4   Now after that Prince *Arthur* graunted had,
To yeeld strong succour to that gentle swayne,
Who now long time had lyen in prison sad,
He gan advise how best he mote darrayne
That enterprize, for greatest glories gayne.
That headlesse tyrants tronke he reard from ground,
And having ympt[2] the head to it agayne,
Upon his usuall beast[3] it firmely bound,
And made it so to ride, as it alive was found.

5   Then did he take that chaced Squire, and layd
Before the ryder, as[4] he captive were,
And made his Dwarfe, though with unwilling ayd,
To guide the beast, that did his maister beare,
Till to his castle they approched neare.
Whom when the watch, that kept continuall ward
Saw comming home; all voide of doubtfull feare,
He running downe, the gate to him unbard;
Whom straight the Prince ensuing,[5] in together far'd.

6   There he did find in her delitious boure
The faire *Pæana* playing on a Rote,[6]
Complayning of her cruell Paramoure,
And singing all her sorrow to the note,
As she had learned readily by rote.
That with the sweetnesse of her rare delight,
The Prince halfe rapt, began on her to dote:
Till better him bethinking of the right,[7]
He her unwares attacht,[8] and captive held by might.

---

[1] **this trustie Squire:** the phrase could refer either to Amyas or Placidas.

[2] **ympt:** grafted (as one grafts a slip of one plant onto a branch of another).

[3] I.e., the dromedary camel.

[4] **as:** as though.

[5] **ensuing:** following.

[6] **Rote:** a medieval musical instrument, probably related to the violin or lute.

[7] **the right:** what was right.

[8] **attacht:** seized; arrested.

7   Whence being forth produc'd, when she perceived
        Her owne deare sire, she cald to him for aide.
        But when of him no aunswere she received,
        But saw him sencelesse by the Squire upstaide,[1]
        She weened well, that then she was betraide:
        Then gan she loudly cry, and weepe, and waile,
        And that same Squire of treason to upbraide.
        But all in vaine, her plaints might not prevaile,[2]
Ne none there was to reskue her, ne none to baile.[3]

8   Then tooke he that same Dwarfe, and him compeld
        To open unto him the prison dore,
        And forth to bring those thrals, which there he held.
        Thence forth were brought to him above a score[4]
        Of Knights and Squires to him unknowne afore:
        All which he did from bitter bondage free,
        And unto former liberty restore.
        Amongst the rest, that Squire of low degree[5]
Came forth full weake and wan, not like him selfe to bee.

9   Whom soone as faire *AEmylia* beheld,
        And *Placidas,* they both unto him ran,
        And him embracing fast betwixt them held,
        Striving to comfort him all that they can,
        And kissing oft his visage pale and wan.
        That faire *Pœana* them beholding both,
        Gan both envy, and bitterly to ban;[6]
        Through jealous passion weeping inly wroth,
To see the sight perforce, that both her eyes were loth.

10   But when a while they had together beene,
        And diversly conferred of their case,
        She, though full oft she both of them had seene
        A sunder, yet not ever in one place,
        Began to doubt, when she them saw embrace,
        Which was the captive Squire she lov'd so deare,

---

[1] **upstaide:** propped up.

[2] **prevaile:** succeed; profit her.

[3] **baile:** post bail.

[4] **a score:** twenty.

[5] I.e., Amyas.

[6] **ban:** curse.

Deceived through great likenesse of their face,
For they so like in person did appeare,
That she uneath discerned, whether whether weare.[1]

11   And eke the Prince, when as he them avized,
      Their like resemblaunce much admired[2] there,
      And mazd how nature had so well disguized[3]
      Her worke, and counterfet her selfe so nere,
      As if that by one patterne seene somewhere,
      She had them made a paragone[4] to be,
      Or whether it through skill, or errour were.
      Thus gazing long, at them much wondred he,
    So did the other knights and Squires, which him did see.

12   Then gan they ransacke that same Castle strong,
      In which he found great store of hoorded threasure,[5]
      The which that tyrant gathered had by wrong
      And tortious[6] powre, without respect or measure.
      Upon all which the Briton Prince made seasure,[7]
      And afterwards continu'd there a while,
      To rest him selfe, and solace in soft pleasure
      Those weaker Ladies after weary toile;
    To whom he did divide part of his purchast[8] spoile.

13   And for more joy, that captive Lady faire
      The faire *Pœana* he enlarged[9] free;
      And by the rest did set in sumptuous chaire,
      To feast and frollicke; nathemore would she
      Shew gladsome countenaunce nor pleasaunt glee:
      But grieved was for losse both of her sire,
      And eke of Lordship, with both land and fee:[10]
      But most she touched was with griefe entire,[11]
    For losse of her new love, the hope of her desire.

---

[1] I.e., she could hardly tell which was which.

[2] I.e., when he noticed their marked resemblance, he greatly wondered.

[3] **mazd:** was bewildered about; was amazed at; **disguized:** decked out, though with overtones of trickery (cf. "counterfet" in line 4).

[4] **paragone:** match.

[5] **hoorded threasure:** hoarded treasure.

[6] **tortious:** legally wrongful.

[7] **seasure:** seizure.

[8] **purchast:** acquired by effort; in other contexts, the word could mean "acquired by money."

[9] **enlarged:** let loose.

[10] **fee:** legal possessions.

[11] **entire:** utter; sincere; inner.

14   But her the Prince through his well wonted grace,
       To better termes of myldnesse did entreat,
       From that fowle rudenesse,[1] which did her deface;
       And that same bitter corsive,[2] which did eat
       Her tender heart, and made refraine from meat,
       He with good thewes[3] and speaches well applyde,
       Did mollifie, and calme her raging heat.
       For though she were most faire, and goodly dyde,[4]
    Yet she it all did mar with cruelty and pride.

15   And for to shut up all in friendly love,
       Sith love was first the ground[5] of all her griefe,
       That trusty Squire he wisely well did move
       Not to despise that dame, which lov'd him liefe,
       Till he had made of her some better priefe,
       But to accept her to[6] his wedded wife.
       Thereto he offred for to make him chiefe
       Of all her land and lordship during life:
    He yeelded, and her tooke; so stinted all their strife.

16   From that day forth in peace and joyous blis,
       They liv'd together long without debate,[7]
       Ne private jarre,[8] ne spite of enemis
       Could shake the safe assuraunce of their state.
       And she whom Nature did so faire create,
       That she mote match the fairest of her daies,[9]
       Yet with lewd loves and lust intemperate
       Had it defaste; thenceforth reformd her waies,
    That all men much admyrde her change, and spake her praise.

---

[1] This is one of those phrases that make one wonder whether an Elizabethan audience would have responded entirely differently from a modern one (the latter being likely to protest that a young woman whose father has just been murdered may be excused for being cool toward the murderer and his friends) or whether the author is asking us to be uncomfortable.

[2] **corsive:** corrosive.

[3] **thewes:** behavior, manners.

[4] **dyde:** colored, complected. The phrase may mean that she has pink cheeks, or it may emphasize that she is not a dark-complected Muslim.

[5] **ground:** basis; source.

[6] **to:** as.

[7] **debate:** argument.

[8] **jarre:** discord.

[9] I.e., so that she could compare with the fairest women of her day.

17   Thus when the Prince had perfectly compylde[1]
        These paires of friends in peace and setled rest,
        Him selfe, whose minde did travell as with chylde,
        Of his old love,[2] conceav'd in secret brest,
        Resolved to pursue his former quest;
        And taking leave of all, with him did beare
        Faire *Amoret,* whom Fortune by bequest
        Had left in his protection whileare,
    Exchanged out of one into an other feare.[3]

18   Feare of her safety did her not constraine,
        For well she wist now in a mighty hond,
        Her person late in perill, did remaine,
        Who able was all daungers to withstond.[4]
        But now in feare of shame she more did stond,
        Seeing her selfe all soly succourlesse,
        Left in the victors powre, like vassall bond;
        Whose will her weakenesse could no way represse,
    In case his burning lust should breake into excesse.

19   But cause of feare sure had she none at all
        Of him, who goodly learned had of yore[5]
        The course of loose affection to forstall,
        And lawlesse lust to rule with reasons lore;
        That all the while he by his side her bore,
        She was as safe as in a Sanctuary;
        Thus many miles they two together wore,[6]
        To seeke their loves dispersed diversly,
    Yet neither shewed to other their hearts privity.[7]

[1] **compylde:** composed; sorted out; collected together.

[2] **travell:** travail, labor; **with chylde, / Of his old love:** pregnant with his longtime beloved (Gloriana, the Faerie Queen, whom he has seen only in an erotic dream, described at I.ix.13–14).

[3] For Amoret's initial fear of Britomart, see i.5–8.

[4] I.e., she knew well that she, who had lately been in peril, now remained in a mighty hand (a synecdoche for "abide with a mighty man") who was able to withstand all dangers.

[5] **of yore:** a long time before.

[6] **wore:** passed over gradually.

[7] From here on in the poem, Amoret remains silent and invisible. Cf. Amoret and Britomart's exchange of confidences at i.15–16.

20   At length they came, whereas a troupe of Knights
      They saw together skirmishing, as seemed:
      Sixe they were all, all full of fell despight,
      But foure of them the battell best beseemed,[1]
      That which of them was best, mote not be deemed.
      Those foure were they, from whom false *Florimell*
      By *Braggadochio* lately was redeemed.
      To weet, sterne *Druon*, and lewd *Claribell*,[2]
Love-lavish *Blandamour*, and lustfull *Paridell*.

21   *Druons* delight was all in single life,
      And unto Ladies love would lend no leasure:
      The more was *Claribell* enraged rife
      With fervent flames, and loved out of measure:[3]
      So eke lov'd *Blandamour*, but yet at pleasure
      Would change his liking, and new Lemans prove:
      But *Paridell* of love did make no threasure,[4]
      But lusted after all, that him did move.
So diversly these foure disposed were to love.

22   But those two other which beside them stoode,
      Were *Britomart*, and gentle *Scudamour*,
      Who all the while beheld their wrathfull moode,
      And wondred at their impacable[5] stoure,
      Whose like they never saw till that same houre:
      So dreadfull strokes each did at other drive,
      And laid on load with all their might and powre,
      As if that every dint the ghost[6] would rive
Out of their wretched corses, and their lives deprive.

23   As when *Dan AEolus*[7] in great displeasure,
      For losse of his deare love by *Neptune* hent,[8]
      Sends forth the winds out of his hidden threasure,

---

[1] I.e., four of them were most fit for battle.

[2] **Druon:** cruel (from Latin *durus,* hard) or oak (from Greek δρῦς); **Claribell:** famous in war (Latin *clarus* + *bellum*).

[3] **out of measure:** immoderately.

[4] **threasure:** treasure.

[5] **impacable:** implacable.

[6] **ghost:** soul.

[7] **AEolus:** a god who keeps the four winds pent up in his cave some of the time, letting them out when it pleases him.

[8] **hent:** taken; seized. For a summary of the story of Neptune's love for Æolus's daughter, Arne, see III.xi.42.

Upon the sea to wreake his fell intent;
They breaking forth with rude unruliment,[1]
From all foure parts of heaven doe rage full sore,
And tosse the deepes, and teare the firmament,[2]
And all the world confound with wide uprore,
As if in stead thereof they *Chaos* would restore.[3]

24 Cause of their discord, and so fell debate,
  Was for the love of that same snowy maid,[4]
  Whome they had lost in Turneyment of late,
  And seeking long, to weet which way she straid
  Met here together, where through lewd upbraide
  Of *Ate* and *Duessa* they fell out,
  And each one taking part in others aide,
  This cruell conflict raised thereabout,
Whose dangerous successe depended yet[5] in dout.

25 For sometimes *Paridell* and *Blandamour*
  The better had, and bet[6] the others backe,
  Eftsoones the others did the field recoure,[7]
  And on their foes did worke full cruell wracke:
  Yet neither would their fiendlike fury slacke,
  But evermore their malice did augment;
  Till that uneath they forced were for lacke
  Of breath, their raging rigour to relent,
And rest themselves for to recover spirits spent.

26 There gan they change their sides, and new parts take;
  For *Paridell* did take to *Druons* side,
  For old despight, which now forth newly brake
  Gainst *Blandamour*, whom alwaies he envide:

---

[1] **unruliment:** unruliness.

[2] **firmament:** sky.

[3] The ordered earth supposedly came out of Chaos, a pit of disordered matter and energy. Cf. III.vi.36.

[4] **snowy maid:** the Snowy Florimell.

[5] **successe:** outcome; **depended:** hung; **yet:** still. This word is temporarily confusing, suggesting that we have returned to the present time—when Arthur and Amoret are first seeing the six fighting knights from a distance—after a brief digression in stanza 24 has told us how the fight originally began. However, given that Scudamour and Britomart join the other four knights in stanza 28, it becomes clear that stanzas 25 through 31 continue the digression begun in stanza 24. We catch up with the present in stanza 32.

[6] **bet:** beat.

[7] **recoure:** recover.

And *Blandamour* to *Claribell* relide.[1]
So all afresh gan former fight renew.
As when two Barkes, this[2] caried with the tide,
That with the wind, contrary courses sew,[3]
If wind and tide doe change, their courses change anew.

27 Thenceforth they much more furiously gan fare,
    As if but then the battell had begonne,
    Ne helmets bright, ne hawberks strong did spare,
    That through the clifts the vermeil bloud out sponne,[4]
    And all adowne their riven sides did ronne.
    Such mortall malice, wonder was to see
    In friends profest, and so great outrage donne:
    But sooth is said, and tride in each degree,
Faint friends when they fall out, most cruell fomen[5] bee.

28 Thus they long while continued in fight,
    Till *Scudamour,* and that same Briton maide,
    By fortune in that place did chance to light:
    Whom soone as they with wrathfull eie bewraide,[6]
    They gan remember of the fowle upbraide,
    The which that Britonesse had to them donne,
    In that late Turney for the snowy maide;
    Where she had them both shamefully fordonne,
And eke the famous prize of beauty from them wonne.

29 Eftsoones all burning with a fresh desire
    Of fell revenge, in their malicious mood
    They from them selves gan turne their furious ire,
    And cruell blades yet steeming with whot bloud,
    Against those two let drive, as they were wood:[7]
    Who[8] wondring much at that so sodaine fit,

---

[1] **relide:** rallied.

[2] **Barkes:** small ships; **this . . . That:** this one . . . That one.

[3] **contrary:** opposing; **sew:** pursue.

[4] I.e., through the clefts (in their armor), the vermilion blood spurted out.

[5] **fomen:** foes.

[6] **bewraide:** discovered.

[7] **wood:** crazy. The dizzily shifting alliances and animosities make this episode like one of the more wonderfully absurd passages in *Alice's Adventures in Wonderland* or *Through the Looking-Glass.*

[8] **Who:** Scudamour and Britomart.

> Yet nought dismayd, them stoutly well withstood;
> Ne yeelded foote, ne once abacke did flit,[1]
> But being doubly smitten likewise doubly smit.

30   The warlike Dame was on her part assaid,
         Of[2] *Claribell* and *Blandamour* attone;
         And *Paridell* and *Druon* fiercely laid
         At *Scudamour,* both his professed fone.[3]
         Foure charged[4] two, and two surcharged one;
         Yet did those two them selves so bravely beare,
         That the other litle gained by the lone,[5]
         But with their owne repayed duely weare,
     And usury[6] withall: such gaine was gotten deare.

31   Full oftentimes did *Britomart* assay
         To speake to them, and some emparlance move;[7]
         But they for nought their cruell hands would stay,
         Ne lend an eare to ought, that might behove,
         As when an eager mastiffe once doth prove
         The tast of bloud of some engored beast,
         No words may rate,[8] nor rigour him remove
         From greedy hold of that his blouddy feast:
     So litle did they hearken to her sweet beheast.

32   Whom when the Briton Prince a farre beheld
         With ods of so unequall match opprest,
         His mighty heart with indignation sweld,

---

[1] **flit:** swerved; gave ground.

[2] **Of:** by.

[3] **fone:** foes.

[4] Note the financial puns here and in the rest of the stanza.

[5] **lone:** loan.

[6] **usury:** interest. Still not understanding the needs of their own developing investment economy, Western Europeans decried all interest as usury, i.e., exorbitant interest. They longed for a past (largely fictional) in which loans were made from friend to friend without any demand for interest. That the sixteenth-century money-lenders in Europe were often Jews, who were not allowed to own significant amounts of land and therefore had to amass property in other ways, added to the general prejudice against interest. These issues are relevant to a book in which the generous bonds of true friendship are aggressively contrasted with the supposedly uncivil habits of the Irish and the Muslims at the same time that present-day England is contrasted unfavorably with a more civil and less legally bound past.

[7] I.e., and to propose some negotiation.

[8] **rate:** chide.

And inward grudge fild his heroicke brest:
Eftsoones him selfe he to their aide addrest,
And thrusting fierce into the thickest preace,
Divided them, how ever loth to rest,
And would them faine from battell to surceasse,
With gentle words perswading them to friendly peace.

33   But they[1] so farre from peace or patience were,
        That all at once at him gan fiercely flie,
        And lay on load, as they him downe would beare;
        Like to a storme, which hovers under skie
        Long here and there, and round about doth stie,[2]
        At length breakes downe in raine, and haile, and sleet,
        First from one coast, till nought thereof be drie;
        And then another, till that likewise fleet;[3]
And so from side to side till all the world it weet.[4]

34   But now their forces greatly were decayd,
        The Prince yet being fresh untoucht afore;
        Who them with speaches milde gan first disswade
        From such foule outrage, and them long forbore:
        Till seeing them through suffrance hartned more,[5]
        Him selfe he bent their furies to abate,
        And layd at them so sharpely and so sore,
        That shortly them compelled to retrate,
And being brought in daunger, to relent too late.

35   But now his courage being throughly fired,
        He ment to make them know their follies prise,[6]
        Had not those two him instantly desired[7]

---

[1] **they:** Britomart's and Scudamour's virtues have not led us to believe that they could be included in this pronoun. Stanza 35 suggests that when Britomart and Scudamour ask Arthur to pardon the combatants, Arthur gives in because the request is made by the only two who abstained from unprovoked violence; however, stanza 35 is not entirely without ambiguity on that point.

[2] **stie:** rise.

[3] **fleet:** floods (literally "floats").

[4] **weet:** wets.

[5] I.e., until he saw that his patience was only encouraging them to keep on the offensive; until he saw that his talk had only allowed them time to recover strength to fight.

[6] **prise:** price; reward (prize).

[7] **those two:** Scudamour and Britomart; **instantly desired:** urgently requested.

T'asswage his wrath, and pardon their mesprise.[1]
    At whose request he gan him selfe advise
    To stay his hand, and of a truce to treat
    In milder tearmes, as list them to devise:
    Mongst which the cause of their so cruell heat
He did them aske, who all that passed gan repeat;[2]

36   And told at large how that same errant Knight,
        To weet faire *Britomart,* them late had foyled
        In open turney, and by wrongfull fight
        Both of their publicke praise had them despoyled,
        And also of their private loves beguyled,
        Of two full hard to read the harder theft.[3]
        But she that wrongfull challenge soone assoyled,
        And shew'd that she had not that Lady[4] reft,
(As they supposd) but her had to her liking left.

37   To whom the Prince thus goodly well replied;
        "Certes sir Knight,[5] ye seemen much to blame,
        To rip up wrong, that battell once hath tried;[6]
        Wherein the honor both of Armes ye shame,
        And eke the love of Ladies foule defame;
        To whom the world this franchise[7] ever yeelded,
        That of their loves choise they might freedom clame,[8]
        And in that right should by all knights be shielded:
Gainst which me seemes this war ye wrongfully have wielded."

---

[1] **their:** presumably the other four, excluding Scudamour and Britomart, though there is a slight ambiguity; **mesprise:** mistake; offense; contempt; failure to recognize someone's worth.

[2] I.e., they began to relate everything that had happened.

[3] I.e., it was difficult to say which was worse, her having stolen their public praise or her having stolen their private loves.

[4] **that Lady:** the Snowy Florimell.

[5] **sir Knight:** some scholars consider this an error for "sir Knights."

[6] I.e., you are to blame for raking up an unjust quarrel, given that you have proven yourself in battle. According to chivalric ideals, a knight was not supposed to fight civilians who were not trained in arms, except to defend himself or someone else whom the civilians had attacked. The ideal had been widely flouted.

[7] **franchise:** freedom; privilege.

[8] When Britomart sees six knights outside Malecasta's castle trying to force Redcrosse to declare his love for their lady, Britomart scolds them by declaring that love may not be compelled (III.i.25).

38   "And yet" (quoth she) "a greater wrong remaines:
            For I thereby my former love have lost,
            Whom seeking ever since with endlesse paines,
            Hath me much sorrow and much travell[1] cost;
            Aye me to see that gentle maide so tost."[2]
            But *Scudamour* then sighing deepe, thus saide,
            "Certes her losse ought me to sorrow most,
            Whose right she is, where ever she be straide,
        Through many perils wonne, and many fortunes waide.[3]

39   "For from the first that I her love profest,
            Unto this houre, this present lucklesse howre,
            I never joyed happinesse nor rest,
            But thus turmoild from one to other stowre,
            I wast my life, and doe my daies devowre
            In wretched anguishe and incessant woe,
            Passing the measure of my feeble powre,
            That living thus, a wretch I and loving so,
        I neither can my love, ne yet my life forgo."[4]

40   Then good sir *Claribell* him thus bespake,
            "Now were it not sir *Scudamour* to you,
            Dislikefull paine, so sad a taske to take,
            Mote we entreat you, sith this gentle crew
            Is now so well accorded all anew;
            That as we ride together on our way,

[1] **travell:** travail, labor.

[2] At vi.36, Britomart describes looking for Amoret soon after losing her; at vi.38, she promises Scudamour to help him search for Amoret; and at vi.47, the two of them undertake that search.

[3] **waide:** weighed.

[4] Britomart declares her own pain but begins by mentioning a "wrong" that could apply either to her or to Amoret and ends by lamenting Amoret's ill treatment; whereas Scudamour begins by mentioning his "right" in Amoret and, from then on, emphasizes his woes rather than hers. From his first appearance in the poem, he has been prone to self-pity. One might expect Arthur to call Amoret forward here, so as to restore both Britomart and Scudamour to happiness, but he does not. Yet three stanzas into the following canto, Scudamour speaks of Amoret as though she is present. Upton speculates that Spenser meant to insert here, with a few changes, the five stanzas with which he ended the 1590 version of Book Three (Greenlaw, *Variorum,* 213). More recent scholars—e.g., Goldberg and Stephens—often take such lacunae as they come, analyzing them as registering ideas (intentional or otherwise on the part of the poet) about incompletion, loss of selfhood, superfluity, or absence.

Ye will recount to us in order dew
All that adventure, which ye did assay
For that faire Ladies love: past perils well apay."[1]

41   So gan the rest him likewise to require,[2]
      But *Britomart* did him importune hard,
      To take on him that paine: whose great desire
      He glad to satisfie, him selfe prepar'd
      To tell through what misfortune he had far'd,
      In that atchievement, as to him befell.
      And all those daungers unto them declar'd,
      Which sith they cannot in this Canto well
Comprised be, I will them in another tell.

---

[1] **apay:** i.e., once they have passed, perils please and/or profit us (because we enjoy hearing stories of triumph over peril and/or because we learn from hearing such stories).

[2] **require:** request.

Canto Ten

Scudamour doth his conquest tell,
Of vertuous Amoret:
Great Venus Temple is describ'd,
And lovers life forth set.

1 "True he it said, what ever man it sayd,
  That love with gall and hony doth abound,[1]
  But if the one be with the other wayd,
  For every dram[2] of hony therein found,
  A pound of gall doth over it redound.
  That I too true by triall have approved:
  For since the day that first with deadly wound
  My heart was launcht,[3] and learned to have loved,
I never joyed howre, but still with care was moved.

2 "And yet such grace is given them[4] from above,
  That all the cares and evill which they meet,
  May nought at all their setled mindes remove,
  But seeme gainst common sence to them most sweet;
  As bosting in their martyrdome unmeet.[5]
  So all that ever yet I have endured,
  I count as naught, and tread downe under feet,
  Since of my love at length I rest assured,
That to disloyalty she will not be allured.[6]

---

[1] Scudamour is speaking.

[2] **dram:** one-sixteenth ounce in avoirdupois weight; one-eighth ounce in apothecaries' weight (used for medicines, and in some forms sugars were considered medicinal). A pound was twelve ounces.

[3] **launcht:** lanced. (See vi.40.5.n.)

[4] **them:** lovers; suitors.

[5] I.e., as though they were proud of their inappropriate martyrdom (inappropriate either because a man should not martyr himself abjectly to a woman or because no one should martyr him- or herself for a secular cause).

[6] Not even by torture, as in the House of Busirane.

3   "Long were to tell the travell[1] and long toile,
             Through which this shield of love I late have wonne,
             And purchased this peerelesse beauties spoile,[2]
             That[3] harder may be ended, then begonne.
             But since ye so desire, your will be donne.
             Then hearke ye gentle knights and Ladies free,[4]
             My hard mishaps, that ye may learne to shonne;
             For though sweet love to conquer glorious bee,
     Yet is the paine thereof much greater then the fee.[5]

4   "What time the fame of this renowmed prise[6]
             Flew first abroad, and all mens eares possest,
             I having armes then taken,[7] gan avise
             To winne me honour by some noble gest,
             And purchase me some place amongst the best.[8]
             I boldly thought (so young mens thoughts are bold)
             That this same brave emprize for me did rest,
             And that both shield and she whom I behold,
     Might be my lucky lot; sith all by lot we hold.

5   "So on that hard adventure forth I went,
             And to the place of perill shortly came.
             That was a temple faire and auncient,
             Which of great mother *Venus* bare the name,
             And farre renowmed through exceeding fame;
             Much more then that, which was in *Paphos* built,
             Or that in *Cyprus*,[9] both long since this same,
             Though all the pillours of the one were guilt,[10]
     And all the others pavement were with yvory spilt.[11]

---

[1] **travell:** toil; labor in childbirth; journeying.

[2] **spoile:** a word usually used to describe goods or women seized in battle. Scudamour seems to be referring to a now-present Amoret. (See ix.39.9.n.)

[3] **That:** his narration of his experience; his experience.

[4] **free:** of high birth; not captive.

[5] **fee:** reward. He seems to be forgetting that he has just declared that his possession of Amoret has made the toil seem insignificant. Frustrated Petrarchan lovers are, of course, typified by swings in mood, but

given that this particular lover now has his prize, his pessimism is odd.

[6] I.e., Amoret.

[7] I.e., having taken the vows of a knight, swearing to be loyal to his lord and to aid the defenseless.

[8] These were the admirable goals of every knight; it was not considered unseemly to declare one's intention to acquire fame.

[9] *Paphos . . . Cyprus:* locations of two famous ancient temples to Venus.

[10] **guilt:** gilt, gilded with gold.

[11] **spilt:** overlaid or covered, in this case perhaps with ivory mosaic (OED "spill" v. 12.a).

6 "And it was seated in an Island strong,
　　Abounding all with delices[1] most rare,
　　And wall'd by nature gainst invaders wrong,
　　That none mote have accesse, nor inward fare,
　　But by one way, that passage did prepare.
　　It was a bridge ybuilt in goodly wize,
　　With curious Corbes and pendants[2] graven faire,
　　And arched all with porches, did arize
On stately pillours, fram'd after the Doricke guize.[3]

7 "And for defence thereof, on th'other end
　　There reared was a castle faire and strong,
　　That warded[4] all which in or out did wend,
　　And flancked both the bridges sides along,
　　Gainst all that would it faine to force or wrong.
　　And therein wonned twenty valiant Knights;
　　All twenty tride in warres experience long;
　　Whose office was, against all manner wights
By all meanes to maintaine, that castels ancient rights.

8 "Before that Castle was an open plaine,
　　And in the midst thereof a piller placed;
　　On which this shield, of many sought in vaine,
　　The shield of Love, whose guerdon me hath graced,
　　Was hangd on high with golden ribbands laced;
　　And in the marble stone was written this,
　　With golden letters goodly well enchaced,
　　Blessed the man that well can use his blis:
Whose ever be the shield, faire Amoret be his.

9 "Which when I red, my heart did inly earne,[5]
　　And pant with hope of that adventures hap:[6]
　　Ne stayed further newes thereof to learne,

---

[1] **delices:** voluptuous delights; delicacies.

[2] **curious Corbes:** intricately wrought corbels, projections of stone, brick, or wood jutting out from a wall in order to support other architectural elements; **pendants:** stone or wooden decorative knobs hanging from stems; posts set close against the wall, resting on the corbels or supporting them.

[3] **Doricke guize:** in the manner of Doric architecture, the simplest, strongest, and most massive of the four ancient Greek styles (which also included Ionic, Æolian, and Corinthian). In the late sixteenth century, interest in copying Greek style was beginning to develop in England, following the earlier Italian interest.

[4] **warded:** guarded.

[5] **earne:** yearn.

[6] **hap:** good fortune.

But with my speare upon the shield did rap,[1]
That all the castle ringed with the clap.
Streight forth issewd a Knight all arm'd to proofe,[2]
And bravely mounted to his most mishap:[3]
Who staying nought to question from aloofe,
Ran fierce at me, that fire glaunst from his horses hoofe.

10   "Whom boldly I encountred (as I could)[4]
And by good fortune shortly him unseated.
Eftsoones out sprung two more of equall mould;[5]
But I them both with equall hap defeated:
So all the twenty I likewise entreated,[6]
And left them groning there upon the plaine.
Then preacing[7] to the pillour I repeated
The read[8] thereof for guerdon of my paine,
And taking downe the shield, with me did it retaine.

11   "So forth without impediment[9] I past,
Till to the Bridges utter[10] gate I came:
The which I found sure lockt and chained fast.
I knockt, but no man aunswred me by name;
I cald, but no man answerd to my clame.[11]
Yet I persever'd still to knocke and call,
Till at the last I spide within the same,
Where one stood peeping through a crevis[12] small,
To whom I cald aloud, halfe angry therewithall.

---

[1] Upton explains that it was a custom in some tournaments—or at least in literary descriptions of tournaments—to hang up a shield for each knight to rap as a symbolic demonstration of his issuing a challenge (Greenlaw, *Variorum*, 220).

[2] **to proofe:** to the point of being impenetrable.

[3] I.e., mounted well enough to withstand the greatest misfortune.

[4] I.e., as well as I could.

[5] **mould:** stature; quality.

[6] **entreated:** treated.

[7] **preacing:** pressing.

[8] **read:** inscription.

[9] **without impediment:** in the approved marriage ceremony, at one point the priest was required to ask the congregation whether anyone present knew of any impediment to the couple's becoming lawfully married.

[10] **utter:** outermost.

[11] **clame:** shout (OED "claim" sb. 4); claim.

[12] **crevis:** crevice.

12   "That was to weet the Porter of the place,
         Unto whose trust the charge thereof was lent:
         His name was *Doubt,* that had a double face,
         Th'one forward looking, th'other backeward bent,
         Therein resembling *Janus*[1] auncient,
         Which hath in charge the ingate of the yeare:
         And evermore his eyes about him went,
         As if some proved perill he did feare,
Or did misdoubt some ill, whose cause did not appeare.

13   "On th'one side he, on th'other sate *Delay,*
         Behinde the gate, that none her might espy;
         Whose manner was all passengers[2] to stay,
         And entertaine with her occasions[3] sly,
         Through which some lost great hope unheedily,[4]
         Which never they recover might againe;
         And others quite excluded forth,[5] did ly
         Long languishing there in unpittied paine,
And seeking often entraunce, afterwards in vaine.

14   "Me when as he had privily[6] espide,
         Bearing the shield which I had conquerd late,
         He kend[7] it streight, and to me opened wide.
         So in I past, and streight he closd the gate.
         But being in, *Delay* in close awaite[8]
         Caught hold on me, and thought my steps to stay,
         Feigning full many a fond excuse to prate,[9]
         And time to steale, the threasure of mans day,
Whose smallest minute[10] lost, no riches render may.

15   "But by no meanes my way I would forslow,[11]
         For ought that ever she could doe or say,
         But from my lofty steede dismounting low,

---

[1] *Janus:* Roman god of gateways and be-
ginnings; he had two faces, looking in op-
posite directions. Cf. "January."

[2] **passengers:** passers-by.

[3] **occasions:** pretexts.

[4] **unheedily:** heedlessly; unheeding.

[5] **forth:** from going onward.

[6] **privily:** stealthily.

[7] **kend:** recognized.

[8] **awaite:** ambush.

[9] **prate:** prattle.

[10] The OED gives the earliest use of the
word "second" to record a unit of time as
1588, so minutes were still widely thought
of as the smallest units of time in 1596.

[11] **forslow:** slacken.

Past forth on foote, beholding all the way
The goodly workes, and stones of rich assay,[1]
Cast into sundry shapes by wondrous skill,
That like on earth no where I recken may:
And underneath, the river rolling still
With murmure soft, that seem'd to serve the workmans will.

16   "Thence forth[2] I passed to the second gate,
The *Gate of good desert,* whose goodly pride
And costly frame, were long here to relate.
The same to all stoode alwaies open wide:
But in the Porch did evermore abide
An hideous[3] Giant, dreadfull to behold,
That stopt the entraunce with his spacious stride,[4]
And with the terrour of his countenance bold
Full many did affray, that else faine enter would.

17   "His name was *Daunger*[5] dreaded over all,
Who day and night did watch and duely ward,
From fearefull cowards, entrance to forstall,
And faint-heart-fooles, whom shew of perill hard
Could terrifie from Fortunes faire adward:[6]
For oftentimes faint hearts at first espiall[7]
Of his grim face, were from approaching scard;
Unworthy they of grace, whom one deniall
Excludes from fairest hope, withouten further triall.

18   "Yet many doughty warriours, often tride
In greater perils to be stout and bold,
Durst not the sternnesse of his looke abide,
But soone as they his countenance did behold,
Began to faint, and feele their corage cold.
Againe some other, that in hard assaies
Were cowards knowne, and litle count did hold,[8]
Either through gifts, or guile, or such like waies,
Crept in by stouping low, or stealing of the kaies.[9]

---

[1] **assay:** tested worth.

[2] **Thence forth:** from that place.

[3] **hideous:** frightful; monstrously large.

[4] **spacious stride:** wide straddling stance.

[5] ***Daunger:*** a standoffish attitude or behav- ior from one being wooed, often a compo- nent of especially teasing or cruel flirtation.

[6] **adward:** award.

[7] **espiall:** glimpse.

[8] I.e., had low reputations.

[9] **kaies:** keys.

19   "But I though meanest[1] man of many moe,
       Yet much disdaining unto him to lout,
       Or creepe betweene his legs, so in to goe,
       Resolv'd him to assault with manhood stout,
       And either beat him in, or drive him out.
       Eftsoones advauncing that enchaunted shield,
       With all my might I gan to lay about:
       Which when he saw, the glaive[2] which he did wield
    He gan forthwith t'avale,[3] and way unto me yield.

20   "So as I entred, I did backeward looke,
       For feare of harme, that might lie hidden there;
       And loe his hindparts, whereof heed I tooke,
       Much more deformed fearefull ugly were,
       Then all his former parts did earst appere.
       For hatred, murther, treason, and despight,
       With many moe lay in ambushment there,[4]
       Awayting to entrap the warelesse wight,
    Which did not them prevent with vigilant foresight.

21   "Thus having past all perill, I was come
       Within the compasse of that Islands space;
       The which did seeme unto my simple doome,[5]
       The onely pleasant and delightfull place,
       That ever troden was of footings trace.
       For all that nature by her mother wit[6]
       Could frame[7] in earth, and forme of substance base,
       Was there, and all that nature did omit,
    Art playing second natures part,[8] supplyed it.

---

[1] 1609 edition; the 1596 edition has "near-est." The handwritten words are easy to confuse, but it is worth considering the possibility that instead of denigrating himself, Scudamour is saying that even though he was closest to the intimidating giant, he did not bow.

[2] **glaive:** a term used at different periods to describe three distinct weapons: lance, bill, and broadsword. Given his deliberate archaism, Spenser could mean any of the three.

[3] **avale:** lower.

[4] Presumably they have been hiding behind the giant; the alternative of their actually being part of his "hindparts" is mind-boggling, but just possible.

[5] **doome:** judgment.

[6] **mother wit:** inherent powers.

[7] **frame:** construct.

[8] Spenser's friend Sidney argued that whereas nature created only a brass world, poets used fiction to create a golden one (Sidney, *Defence*, 100).

22   "No tree, that is of count, in greenewood growes,[1]
         From lowest Juniper to Ceder tall,
         No flowre in field, that daintie odour throwes,
         And deckes his branch with blossomes over all,
         But there was planted, or grew naturall:
         Nor sense of man so coy and curious nice,[2]
         But there mote find to please it selfe withall;
         Nor hart could wish for any queint device,[3]
      But there it present was, and did fraile sense entice.

23   "In such luxurious plentie of all pleasure,
         It seem'd a second paradise to ghesse,[4]
         So lavishly enricht with natures threasure,
         That if the happie soules, which doe possesse
         Th'Elysian fields,[5] and live in lasting blesse,
         Should happen this with living eye to see,
         They soone would loath their lesser happinesse,
         And wish to life return'd againe to bee,
      That in this joyous place they mote have joyance[6] free.

24   "Fresh shadowes, fit to shroud from sunny ray;
         Faire lawnds,[7] to take the sunne in season dew;
         Sweet springs, in which a thousand Nymphs did play;
         Soft rombling[8] brookes, that gentle slomber drew;
         High reared mounts, the lands about to vew;
         Low looking dales, disloignd[9] from common gaze;
         Delightfull bowres, to solace lovers trew;
         False Labyrinthes,[10] fond runners eyes to daze;
      All which by nature made did nature selfe amaze.[11]

---

[1] **of count:** of importance; **in greenewood growes:** in greenwood groves; that grows in any greenwood.

[2] **coy:** reserved; **curious nice:** fastidious about details; wonderfully fastidious.

[3] **queint device:** ingeniously wrought design or art object.

[4] **to ghesse:** as one might guess (reiterates and intensifies "seem'd").

[5] **Th'Elysian fields:** Elysium—in Greek mythology, the home of fortunate people after death.

[6] **joyance:** pleasure.

[7] **lawnds:** glades, open spaces among woods.

[8] **rombling:** rumbling, murmuring.

[9] **disloignd:** remote.

[10] **Labyrinthes:** hedge mazes often constructed in Elizabethan gardens.

[11] Cf. the trees in the Garden of Adonis that are wild but train themselves into an arbor atop Venus' Mount (III.vi.44).

25   "And all without were walkes and alleyes[1] dight,
      With divers trees, enrang'd in even rankes;
      And here and there were pleasant arbors pight,[2]
      And shadie seates, and sundry flowring bankes,
      To sit and rest the walkers wearie shankes,
      And therein thousand payres of lovers walkt,
      Praysing their god, and yeelding him great thankes,
      Ne ever ought but of their true loves talkt,
Ne ever for rebuke or blame of any balkt.[3]

26   "All these together by themselves did sport
      Their spotlesse pleasures, and sweet loves content.
      But farre away from these, another sort[4]
      Of lovers lincked in true harts consent;
      Which loved not as these, for like intent,
      But on chast vertue grounded their desire,
      Farre from all fraud, or fayned blandishment;
      Which in their spirits kindling zealous fire,
Brave thoughts and noble deedes did evermore aspire.

27   "Such were great *Hercules,* and *Hyllus*[5] deare;
      Trew *Jonathan,* and *David*[6] trustie tryde;
      Stout *Theseus,* and *Pirithous* his feare;[7]
      Pylades and *Orestes*[8] by his syde;
      Myld *Titus* and *Gesippus* without pryde;[9]
      Damon and *Pythias* whom death could not sever:[10]

---

[1] **alleyes:** walks or long greens bordered by trees, hedges, or beds of flowers.

[2] **pight:** placed; set up.

[3] **balkt:** quit conversing; i.e., they didn't have to worry about rumors or slander.

[4] **sort:** group.

[5] **Hyllus:** Hyllus was Hercules' son; Spenser likely means "Hylas," a boy whom Hercules loved. (See III.xii.7.5–9.)

[6] For David, see ii.2.1–4 and notes. Jonathan was Saul's son; he loved David as though David were himself, and he saved David from being murdered by Saul (1 Sam. 18–20).

[7] **feare:** fere, companion. Theseus helped Pirithous fight against the Centaurs; later he helped him abduct Proserpina from Hades.

[8] Pylades was Orestes' friend who fought beside him on numerous occasions and risked death for his sake.

[9] When Gesippus found out that his bride-to-be was the beloved of his friend Titus, he offered to give her to him. At a later time, Titus offered to serve a sentence of death pronounced upon Gesippus.

[10] While Damon and Pythias were visiting Syracuse, Damon was arrested and condemned to death by the tyrant Dionysius. Pythias offered himself as a hostage while Damon went home to settle his affairs; when Damon returned, he and Pythias each demanded to be the one executed. Dionysius was so impressed with their friendship that he pardoned Damon.

All these and all that ever had bene tyde,
In bands of friendship there did live for ever,
Whose lives although decay'd, yet loves decayed never.

28   "Which when as I, that never tasted blis,
Nor happie howre, beheld with gazefull eye,
I thought there was none other heaven then this;
And gan their endlesse happinesse envye,
That being free from feare and gealosye,
Might frankely there their loves desire possesse;
Whilest I through paines and perlous jeopardie,
Was forst to seeke my lifes deare patronesse:
Much dearer[1] be the things, which come through hard distresse.

29   "Yet all those sights, and all that else I saw,
Might not my steps withhold, but that forthright[2]
Unto that purposd place I did me draw,
Where as my love was lodged day and night:
The temple of great *Venus*, that is hight
The Queene of beautie, and of love the mother,
There worshipped of every living wight;
Whose goodly workmanship farre past all other
That ever were on earth, all were they set together.

30   "Not that same famous Temple of *Diane*,[3]
Whose hight all *Ephesus* did oversee,
And which all *Asia* sought with vowes prophane,
One of the worlds seven wonders sayd to bee,
Might match with this by many a degree:
Nor that, which that wise King of *Jurie*[4] framed,
With endlesse cost, to be th'Almighties see;[5]
Nor all that else through all the world is named
To all the heathen Gods, might like to this be clamed.

---

[1] **dearer:** more valuable; more valued.

[2] **forthright:** directly.

[3] **Temple of *Diane*:** the widely famed Temple of Artemis, or Diana, built in Ephesus (in what is now Turkey) in the sixth century BC and rebuilt in 356 BC after it burned.

[4] ***Jurie*:** Jewry, i.e., King Solomon; see 1 Kings 6–7 for the building of the Temple of Jerusalem.

[5] **see:** seat; dwelling (as a particular city or jurisdiction is said to be a bishop's see).

31   "I much admyring that so goodly frame,
         Unto the porch approcht, which open stood;
         But therein sate an amiable Dame,
         That seem'd to be of very sober mood,
         And in her semblant shewed great womanhood:
         Strange was her tyre; for on her head a crowne
         She wore much like unto a Danisk¹ hood,
         Poudred² with pearle and stone, and all her gowne
      Enwoven was with gold, that raught full low a downe.

32   "On either side of her, two young men stood,
         Both strongly arm'd, as fearing one another;
         Yet were they brethren both of halfe the blood,
         Begotten by two fathers of one mother,
         Though of contrarie natures each to other:
         The one of them hight *Love*, the other *Hate*,
         Hate was the elder, *Love* the younger brother;
         Yet was the younger stronger in his state
      Then th'elder, and him maystred still in all debate.

33   "Nathlesse that Dame so well them tempred both,
         That she them forced hand to joyne in hand,
         Albe that *Hatred* was thereto full loth,
         And turn'd his face away, as he did stand,
         Unwilling to behold that lovely band.³
         Yet she was of such grace and vertuous might,
         That her commaundment he could not withstand,
         But bit his lip for felonous⁴ despight,
      And gnasht his yron tuskes at that displeasing sight.⁵

34   "*Concord* she cleeped was in common reed,
         Mother of blessed *Peace*, and *Friendship* trew;
         They both her twins, both borne of heavenly seed,
         And she her selfe likewise divinely grew;
         The which right well her workes divine did shew:

---

¹ **Danisk:** Danish.
² **Poudred:** powdered.
³ **lovely band:** loving bond.
⁴ **felonous:** fierce.

⁵ Lotspeich writes, "Lady Concord is a mythical expression of the Neo-Platonic doctrine of the cosmic love which holds in harmony the four elements and all the conflicting forces of the world" (Greenlaw, *Variorum*, 226).

For strength, and wealth,[1] and happinesse she lends,
  And strife, and warre, and anger does subdew:
  Of litle much, of foes she maketh frends,
And to afflicted minds sweet rest and quiet sends.

35   "By her the heaven is in his course contained,
      And all the world in state unmoved stands,
      As their Almightie maker first ordained,
      And bound them with inviolable bands;[2]
      Else would the waters overflow the lands,
      And fire devoure the ayre, and hell them quight,[3]
      But that she holds them with her blessed hands.
      She is the nourse of pleasure and delight,
  And unto *Venus* grace the gate doth open right.[4]

36   "By her I entring halfe dismayed was,
      But she in gentle wise me entertayned,[5]
      And twixt her selfe and *Love* did let me pas;
      But *Hatred* would my entrance have restrayned,
      And with his club me threatned to have brayned,
      Had not the Ladie with her powrefull speach
      Him from his wicked will uneath refrayned;
      And th'other eke his malice did empeach,[6]
  Till I was throughly past the perill of his reach.

37   "Into the inmost Temple thus I came,
      Which fuming all with frankensence[7] I found,
      And odours rising from the altars flame.
      Upon an hundred marble pillors round
      The roofe up high was reared from the ground,
      All deckt with crownes, and chaynes, and girlands gay,
      And thousand pretious gifts worth many a pound,
      The which sad lovers for their vowes did pay;[8]
  And all the ground was strow'd with flowres, as fresh as May.

---

[1] **wealth:** well-being.

[2] Cf. V.Pr., where the narrator laments the degeneration of the world and the changing of the planets' courses.

[3] **quight:** requite; completely.

[4] I.e., and helps us gain access to love (which is the happiness offered by Venus).

[5] **entertayned:** received.

[6] **empeach:** hinder.

[7] **frankensence:** an aromatic tree gum burned as incense.

[8] I.e., which they brought to the temple for offerings; **sad:** unhappy; serious (about their love).

38 "An hundred Altars round about were set,
  All flaming with their sacrifices fire,
  That with the steme thereof the Temple swet,[1]
  Which rould in clouds to heaven did aspire,
  And in them bore true lovers vowes entire:
  And eke an hundred brasen caudrons bright,
  To bath in joy and amorous desire,
  Every of which was to a damzell hight;[2]
 For all the Priests were damzels, in soft linnen dight.

39 "Right in the midst the Goddesse selfe did stand
  Upon an altar of some costly masse,
  Whose substance was uneath to understand:
  For neither pretious stone, nor durefull[3] brasse,
  Nor shining gold, nor mouldring[4] clay it was;
  But much more rare and pretious to esteeme,[5]
  Pure in aspect, and like to christall glasse,
  Yet glasse was not, if one did rightly deeme,
 But being faire and brickle,[6] likest glasse did seeme.

40 "But it[7] in shape and beautie did excell
  All other Idoles, which the heathen adore,
  Farre passing that, which by surpassing skill
  Phidias did make in *Paphos*[8] Isle of yore,
  With which that wretched Greeke, that life forlore
  Did fall in love: yet this much fairer shined,
  But covered with a slender[9] veile afore;
  And both her feete and legs together twyned
 Were with a snake, whose head and tail were fast combyned.

---

[1] **steme:** steam; **swet:** sweated.

[2] **hight:** designated.

[3] **durefull:** enduring.

[4] **mouldring:** decaying; crumbling.

[5] **to esteeme:** to be valued.

[6] **brickle:** brittle. Berger points out the instability of the altar, despite its mass: "The 'masse' which really stands under the idol . . . is the oceanic world of cosmic violence and fecundity presented in the next canto as the setting for the Marriage of Rivers" (Berger, 199).

[7] **it:** the statue of Venus.

[8] As Hillard argues in the *Variorum*, Spenser may be confusing Phidias of Paphos with Praxiteles of Cnidus, about whom Pliny writes that he was the first sculptor to make a statue of Venus without drapery. Upon seeing the statue, supposedly a young man fell in love with it (*Variorum,* 231; Pliny, *Natural History,* 36.5.21).

[9] **slender:** thin; long and narrow.

41   "The cause why she was covered with a vele,
            Was hard to know, for that her Priests the same
            From peoples knowledge labour'd to concele.
        But sooth it was not sure[1] for womanish shame,
        Nor any blemish, which the worke mote blame;[2]
        But for, they say, she hath both kinds[3] in one,
        Both male and female, both under one name:
        She syre and mother is her selfe alone,
    Begets and eke conceives, ne needeth other none.

42   "And all about her necke and shoulders flew
            A flocke of litle loves, and sports, and joyes,[4]
            With nimble wings of gold and purple hew;
        Whose shapes seem'd not like to terrestriall boyes,
        But like to Angels playing heavenly toyes;[5]
        The whilest their eldest brother was away,
        Cupid their eldest brother; he enjoyes
        The wide kingdome of love with Lordly sway,
    And to his law compels all creatures to obay.

43   "And all about her altar scattered lay
            Great sorts of lovers piteously complayning,[6]
            Some of their losse, some of their loves delay,
        Some of their pride, some paragons disdayning,[7]
        Some fearing fraud, some fraudulently fayning,
        As every one had cause of good or ill.
        Amongst the rest some one through loves constrayning,
        Tormented sore, could not containe it still,
    But thus brake forth, that all the temple it did fill.

44   "'Great *Venus*, Queene of beautie and of grace,[8]
            The joy of Gods and men, that under skie
            Doest fayrest shine, and most adorne thy place,

---

[1] **not sure:** surely not.

[2] I.e., which might lessen the perfection of the statue.

[3] **kinds:** sexes.

[4] **loves, and sports, and joyes:** putti, winged babies embodying amorous enjoyments. As Berger notes, the love in this canto does not include the presence of human babies (Berger, 199).

[5] **toyes:** frivolous games or tunes.

[6] **sorts:** groups; **complayning:** uttering Petrarchan plaints about the woes of being in love.

[7] I.e., some complained about their disdainful beloveds.

[8] Stanzas 44 through 47 are elegantly translated from Lucretius' invocation to Venus at the beginning of *De Rerum Natura* (Greenlaw, *Variorum,* 234).

That with thy smyling looke doest pacifie
The raging seas, and makst the stormes to flie;
Thee goddesse, thee the winds, the clouds doe feare,
And when thou spredst thy mantle[1] forth on hie,
The waters play and pleasant lands appeare,
And heavens laugh, and all the world shews joyous cheare.

45   "'Then doth the dædale[2] earth throw forth to thee
Out of her fruitfull lap aboundant flowres,
And then all living wights, soone as they see
The spring breake forth out of his lusty bowres,
They all doe learne to play the Paramours;
First doe the merry birds, thy prety pages
Privily pricked[3] with thy lustfull powres,
Chirpe loud to thee out of their leavy[4] cages,
And thee their mother call to coole their kindly rages.[5]

46   "'Then doe the salvage beasts begin to play
Their pleasant friskes,[6] and loath their wonted food;
The Lyons rore, the Tygres loudly bray,
The raging Buls rebellow through the wood,
And breaking forth, dare tempt[7] the deepest flood,
To come where thou doest draw them with desire:
So all things else,[8] that nourish vitall blood,
Soone as with fury thou doest them inspire,
In generation[9] seeke to quench their inward fire.

47   "'So all the world by thee at first was made,
And dayly yet thou doest the same repayre:
Ne ought on earth that merry is and glad,
Ne ought on earth that lovely is and fayre,
But thou the same for pleasure didst prepayre.[10]
Thou art the root of all that joyous is,

---

[1] **mantle:** cloak.

[2] **dædale:** consummately artistic; skillfully inventive; variously adorned.

[3] **pricked:** spurred.

[4] **leavy:** leafy.

[5] **rages:** vehement urges or passions.

[6] **friskes:** frisking, games.

[7] **tempt:** risk.

[8] **all things else:** all other things.

[9] **generation:** propagation.

[10] Berger comments that these lovers "isolate love as a game from love as a function, love as a state of mind and a way of life from love as a natural process" (198).

Great God of men and women, queene of th'ayre,
Mother of laughter, and welspring of blisse,
O graunt that of my love at last I may not misse.'

48   "So did he say: but I with murmure[1] soft,
      That none might heare the sorrow of my hart,
      Yet inly groning deepe and sighing oft,
      Besought her to graunt ease unto my smart,
      And to my wound her gratious help impart.
      Whilest thus I spake, behold with happy eye
      I spyde, where at the Idoles feet apart[2]
      A bevie of fayre damzels close[3] did lye,
Wayting when as the Antheme should be sung on hye.

49   "The first of them did seeme of ryper yeares,
      And graver countenance then all the rest;
      Yet all the rest were eke her equall peares,
      Yet unto her obayed all the best.
      Her name was *Womanhood,* that she exprest
      By her sad semblant and demeanure wyse:
      For stedfast still her eyes did fixed rest,
      Ne rov'd at randon after gazers guyse,
Whose luring baytes oftimes doe heedlesse harts entyse.[4]

50   "And next to her sate goodly *Shamefastnesse,*
      Ne ever durst her eyes from ground upreare,
      Ne ever once did looke up from her desse,[5]
      As if some blame of evill she did feare,
      That in her cheekes made roses oft appeare:
      And her against[6] sweet *Cherefulnesse* was placed,
      Whose eyes like twinkling stars in evening cleare,
      Were deckt with smyles, that all sad humors chaced,
And darted forth delights, the which her goodly graced.

---

[1] **murmure:** complaint.

[2] **apart:** separated from the rest of the room (perhaps by being hidden by the idol's skirts); near but slightly separated from the idol.

[3] **close:** covered; together.

[4] For women's wandering eyes, see III.i.41.8.n.

[5] **desse:** dais.

[6] **against:** facing; on the opposite side. Despite the term "a round" in 52.1, it is not clear whether the women are in a circle, a line, or some other formation.

51 "And next to her sate sober *Modestie,*
　　　Holding her hand upon her gentle hart;
　　　And her against sate comely *Curtesie,*
　　　That unto every person knew her part;[1]
　　　And her before was seated overthwart[2]
　　　Soft *Silence,* and submisse *Obedience,*
　　　Both linckt together never to dispart,[3]
　　　Both gifts of God not gotten but from thence,
　　Both girlonds of his Saints against their foes offence.[4]

52　　"Thus sate they all a round[5] in seemely rate:
　　　And in the midst of them a goodly mayd,
　　　Even in the lap of *Womanhood* there sate,
　　　The which was all in lilly white arayd,
　　　With silver streames[6] amongst the linnen stray'd;
　　　Like to the Morne, when first her shyning face
　　　Hath to the gloomy world it selfe bewray'd,
　　　That same was fayrest *Amoret* in place,
　　Shyning with beauties light, and heavenly vertues grace.

53　　"Whom soone as I beheld, my hart gan throb,
　　　And wade in doubt, what best were to be donne:
　　　For sacrilege me seem'd the Church to rob,[7]
　　　And folly seem'd to leave the thing undonne,
　　　Which with so strong attempt I had begonne.
　　　Tho shaking off all doubt and shamefast feare,
　　　Which Ladies love I heard had never wonne
　　　Mongst men of worth, I to her stepped neare,
　　And by the lilly hand her labour'd up to reare.

54　　"Thereat that formost matrone me did blame,
　　　And sharpe rebuke, for being over bold;
　　　Saying it was to Knight unseemely shame,

---

[1] I.e., knew how to behave appropriately toward every person.

[2] **overthwart:** obliquely; opposite.

[3] **dispart:** part, separate.

[4] The reader must decide whether all of these characteristics of womanhood are idealized only by Scudamour or also by the poem. Cf. the characteristics of ideal womanhood mentioned in Spenser's marriage poem *Epithalamion*—especially in stanzas 9, 11, and 13.

[5] **a round:** in a circle; around about.

[6] **silver streames:** i.e., silvery threads.

[7] He would be robbing the temple of one of its vestal virgins.

Upon a recluse Virgin to lay hold,
That unto *Venus* services was sold.[1]
To whom I thus, 'Nay but it fitteth best,
For *Cupids* man with *Venus* mayd to hold,
For ill your goddesse services are drest[2]
By virgins, and her sacrifices let to rest.'[3]

55   "With that my shield I forth to her did show,
Which all that while I closely had conceld;
On which when *Cupid* with his killing bow
And cruell shafts emblazond she beheld,
At sight thereof she was with terror queld,
And said no more: but I which all that while
The pledge of faith, her hand engaged held,[4]
Like warie Hynd within the weedie soyle,[5]
For no intreatie would forgoe so glorious spoyle.

56   "And evermore upon the Goddesse face
Mine eye was fixt, for feare of her offence,[6]
Whom when I saw with amiable grace
To laugh at me, and favour my pretence,[7]
I was emboldned with more confidence,
And nought for nicenesse nor for envy sparing,
In presence of them all forth led her thence,
All looking on, and like astonisht staring,
Yet to lay hand on her, not one of all them daring.

57   "She often prayd,[8] and often me besought,
Sometime with tender teares to let her goe,
Sometime with witching[9] smyles: but yet for nought,
That ever she to me could say or doe,

---

[1] **sold:** dedicated.

[2] **drest:** managed; ordered.

[3] **let to rest:** allowed to cease. Scudamour argues that Venus' temple should not be served by vestal *virgins* since virgins cannot perform the rites of love.

[4] During an Anglican marriage, the groom took the bride by the right hand; see Spenser, *Epithalamion,* stanza 13.

[5] **Hynd:** female deer; **soyle:** a stretch of water used as a refuge by hunted animals.

[6] **offence:** being offended.

[7] Either he imagines that the statue comes alive, or else it does so.

[8] **prayd:** begged me; made prayers to the goddess.

[9] **witching:** bewitching.

Could she her wished freedome fro me wooe;
But forth I led her through the Temple gate,
By which I hardly[1] past with much adoe:
But that same Ladie which me friended late
In entrance, did me also friend in my retrate.

58   "No lesse did *Daunger* threaten me with dread,
When as he saw me, maugre all his powre,
That glorious spoyle of beautie with me lead,
Then *Cerberus,* when *Orpheus* did recoure
His Leman from the Stygian Princes boure.[2]
But evermore my shield did me defend,
Against the storme of every dreadfull stoure:
Thus safely with my love I thence did wend."
So ended he his tale, where I this Canto end.

---

[1] **hardly:** would hardly have.

[2] After his beloved wife, Eurydice, died, Orpheus journeyed into Hades to attempt to recover her and was threatened by Cerberus, the many-headed dog who was stationed at the mouth of Hades to keep dead souls from leaving and live persons from entering. Orpheus recovered Eurydice after pleasing Pluto with his music, so poets used him as a type of the spectacularly gifted poet. Yet Pluto gave up Eurydice only on the condition that Orpheus would not look back at her as they left Hades. When Orpheus could not restrain himself and glanced back at her, she vanished and was lost to him forever. In other contexts, then, poets used Orpheus as an example of a man who tragically lacked erotic self-control.

Canto Eleven

Marinells former wound is heald,
he comes to Proteus hall,
Where Thames doth the Medway wedd,
and feasts the Sea-gods all.

1   But ah for pittie that I have thus long
     Left a fayre Ladie languishing in payne:
     Now well away,[1] that I have doen such wrong,
     To let faire *Florimell* in bands remayne,
     In bands of love, and in sad thraldomes chayne;
     From which unlesse some heavenly powre her free
     By miracle, not yet appearing playne,
     She lenger yet is like captiv'd to bee:
     That even to thinke thereof, it inly pitties mee.[2]

2   Here neede you to remember, how erewhile
     Unlovely *Proteus*, missing[3] to his mind
     That Virgins love to win by wit or wile,
     Her threw into a dongeon deepe and blind,[4]
     And there in chaynes her cruelly did bind,
     In hope thereby her to his bent to draw:
     For when as neither gifts nor graces kind
     Her constant mind could move at all he saw,
     He thought her to compell by crueltie and awe.

3   Deepe in the bottome of an huge great rocke
     The dongeon was, in which her bound he left,
     That neither yron barres, nor brasen locke

---

[1] **well away:** an exclamation of lament: "alas!"

[2] With this stanza, the narrator picks up a thread he let drop fourteen cantos ago, when we last saw the true Florimell (III.viii.43). At that point, the narrator lamented the necessity of his leaving Florimell imprisoned in a cave hemmed in by the sea, in imminent danger of being raped, but he promised to make her famous by way of compensation. Fourteen cantos later, he now shows signs of recalling that promise—though he considerately lets us know that only a miracle will prevent his writing a few other things first.

[3] **missing:** failing.

[4] **blind:** completely dark.

Did neede to gard from force, or secret theft
Of all her lovers, which would her have reft.
For wall'd it was with waves, which rag'd and ror'd
As they the cliffe in peeces would have cleft;
Besides ten thousand monsters foule abhor'd
Did waite about it, gaping griesly all begor'd.[1]

4   And in the midst thereof did horror dwell,
      And darkenesse dredd, that never viewed day,
      Like to the balefull house of lowest hell,
      In which old *Styx*[2] her aged bones alway,
      Old *Styx* the Grandame of the Gods, doth lay.
    There did this lucklesse mayd seven months abide,
      Ne ever evening saw, ne mornings ray,
      Ne ever from the day the night describe,
But thought it all one night, that did no houres divide.

5   And all this was for love of *Marinell,*
      Who her despysd (ah who would her despyse?)
      And wemens love did from his hart expell,
      And all those joyes that weake mankind entyse.[3]
      Nathlesse his pride full dearely he did pryse;
    For of a womans hand it was ywroke,[4]
      That of the wound he yet in languor lyes,
      Ne can be cured of that cruell stroke
Which *Britomart* him gave, when he did her provoke.[5]

6   Yet farre and neare the Nymph his mother sought,[6]
      And many salves did to his sore applie,
      And many herbes did use. But when as nought
      She saw could ease his rankling[7] maladie,

---

[1] **begor'd:** smeared with gore (from their previous victims).

[2] *Styx:* a personification of the River Styx in Hades.

[3] Marinell's reasons for avoiding women are explained at III.iv.20–26; Florimell searches for him and hears a false report of his being slain at III.v.8–10.

[4] **ywroke:** wreaked.

[5] Britomart wounds Marinell at III.iv.12–18 (chronologically after his mother warns him against women, but narratively before we are given that information); his mother takes him to Liagore's bower to be nursed at III.iv.29–44.

[6] Mentally place commas around "his mother," which is in apposition to "the Nymph"; she is not searching for some other nymph, but for cures.

[7] **rankling:** festering.

At last to *Tryphon* she for helpe did hie,[1]
(This *Tryphon* is the seagods surgeon[2] hight)
Whom she besought to find some remedie:
And for his paines a whistle him behight[3]
That of a fishes shell was wrought with rare delight.

7   So well that Leach[4] did hearke to her request,
And did so well employ his carefull paine,
That in short space his hurts he had redrest,
And him restor'd to healthfull state againe:
In which he long time after did remaine
There with the Nymph his mother, like her thrall;
Who sore against his will did him retaine,
For feare of perill, which to him mote fall,
Through his too ventrous prowesse proved over all.

8   It fortun'd then, a solemne feast was there
To all the Sea-gods and their fruitfull seede,
In honour of the spousalls, which then were
Betwixt the *Medway* and the *Thames* agreed.[5]

---

[1] As told at III.iv.43.

[2] **surgeon:** physician (whose practice is not confined to surgery in the modern sense).

[3] **behight:** promised.

[4] **Leach:** physician.

[5] The remainder of the canto is devoted to the marriage ceremony of these two rivers, and especially to the cataloguing of other rivers who attend. The Thames (pronounced "Tims") and the Medway issue into the North Sea right next to each other, mingling their waters. Approximately ten statute miles up the Medway lies the city of Rochester, where Spenser lived from 1579 to 1580 as secretary to the Bishop of Rochester; and Spenser would also have associated the Medway with the Sidney family's estate of Penshurst, which lies further up the Medway. In writing this canto about a marriage of rivers, Spenser was following the example of several other poets, including Leland (*Cygnea Cantio)* and Camden (*De Connubio Tamae et Isis,* now surviving only in fragments). Indeed, Spenser himself had earlier written *Epithalamion Thamesis,* a poem about the marriage of the Thames. Although that poem was not published and does not survive, Spenser describes it in a letter to Gabriel Harvey in 1580 as "setting forth the marriage of the Thames : I shewe his first beginning, and offspring, and all the Countrey, that he passeth thorough, and also describe all the Rivers throughout Englande, whyche came to this Wedding, and their righte names, and right passage, &c. A worke beleeve me, of much labour . . ." (Smith, 612). As Osgood points out in the *Variorum,* however, Spenser cannot simply have transferred that earlier poem to this canto, given that this canto draws heavily from Camden's *Britannia,* which was not published until 1596; and given that the canto also draws heavily from knowledge Spenser gained of the Irish rivers during his years living there, which began in 1580 (Greenlaw, 241). The structure of the canto is intricate, with careful groupings of sea

Long had the *Thames* (as we in records reed)
Before that day her wooed to his bed;[1]
But the proud Nymph would for no worldly meed,
Nor no entreatie to his love be led;
Till now at last relenting, she to him was wed.

9   So both agreed, that this their bridale feast
    Should for the Gods in *Proteus* house be made;
    To which they all repayr'd, both most and least,[2]
    Aswell which in the mightie Ocean trade,[3]
    As that in rivers swim, or brookes doe wade.
    All which not if an hundred tongues to tell,
    And hundred mouthes, and voice of brasse I had,
    And endlesse memorie, that mote excell,
In order as they came, could I recount them well.

10   Helpe therefore, O thou sacred imp of *Jove*,
    The noursling of Dame *Memorie* his deare,[4]
    To whom those rolles, layd up in heaven above,
    And records of antiquitie appeare,
    To which no wit of man may comen neare;
    Helpe me to tell the names of all those floods,[5]

---

gods, river gods, and rivers according to geography, genealogy, and etymology; yet the canto cannot be explained by pattern alone. It is no accident that Spenser wrote this canto in a century when cartography and books of national history flourished, the same century in which John Stow made his name by describing the important buildings, works, and history of every ward in London (Stow, *Survey*, 1598). All of these works helped construct England as a nation. More ambiguously, Spenser did some of the same for Ireland, even though in 1596 he advocated using dire means to subdue the Irish who resisted English rule (Spenser, *View*, e.g., 99–101). Fowler comments, "The choice of the Thames emphasizes both the edge and the interior of the island, and thus England's relation to other nations, as well as the arrangement of its internal regions. . . . In Spenser's time, English military power was overwhelmingly water-based . . ." (Fowler, 2003, 196).

[1] **bed:** note the pun.

[2] **repayr'd:** went; **most and least:** highest and lowest in social status. Note that although the feast is held in Proteus' house, he is absent, being otherwise occupied in his dungeon. Fowler comments that this canto is built on a "doubled architectural space (hall and cave) and [a] doubled ceremony (marriage and rape)" (Fowler, 2003, 193).

[3] **trade:** go.

[4] The narrator is asking for inspiration from either Clio, the muse of history, or Calliope, the muse of epic poetry; all of the nine muses were daughters of Jove and Mnemosyne, the goddess of memory. Cf. I.Pr.2 and I.xi.5.

[5] **floods:** bodies of water.

And all those Nymphes, which then assembled were
To that great banquet of the watry Gods,
And all their sundry kinds, and all their hid abodes.

11   First came great *Neptune* with his threeforkt mace,
        That rules the Seas, and makes them rise or fall;
        His dewy lockes did drop with brine apace,
        Under his Diademe imperiall:
        And by his side his Queene with coronall,[1]
        Faire *Amphitrite,*[2] most divinely faire,
        Whose yvorie shoulders weren covered all,
        As with a robe, with her owne silver haire,
And deckt with pearles, which th'Indian seas for her prepaire.

12   These marched farre afore the other crew;
        And all the way before them as they went,
        Triton[3] his trompet shrill before them blew,
        For goodly triumph[4] and great jollyment,
        That made the rockes to roare, as[5] they were rent.
        And after them the royall issue came,[6]
        Which of them sprung by lineall descent:
        First the Sea-gods, which to themselves doe clame
The powre to rule the billowes, and the waves to tame.

13   *Phorcys,* the father of that fatall brood,
        By whom those old Heroes wonne such fame;[7]
        And *Glaucus,*[8] that wise southsayes understood;
        And tragicke *Inoes* sonne,[9] the which became

---

[1] **coronall:** crown or coronet.

[2] *Amphitrite:* Neptune's wife, the daughter of Nereus.

[3] *Triton:* half man, half fish. As Neptune's son, he has the responsibility of blowing a trumpet to command the movement of the waves, as a herald would blow a trumpet to command a crowd to part for an important procession or to fall silent for an announcement.

[4] **triumph:** Goldberg comments that this word designates the specific form of this entertainment: a "triumph" celebrated conquest and possession, whether of a territory, a country, or a bride (Goldberg, 140).

[5] **as:** as if.

[6] I.e., Neptune and Amphitrite's offspring.

[7] Phorcys was the father of many monsters, including the Graeae (old women from the moment of birth), the Gorgons (including Medusa), the Chimaera (who breathed fire), and the dragon that guarded the Garden of the Hesperides. Heroes such as Perseus and Hercules acquired fame by vanquishing these monsters.

[8] *Glaucus:* a prophet.

[9] *Inoes* **sonne:** maddened by grief at seeing her husband kill her other son, Ino picked up her son Melicerta and jumped off a cliff

A God of seas through his mad mothers blame,
Now hight *Palemon*, and is saylers frend;
Great *Brontes*, and *Astræus*, that did shame
Himselfe with incest of his kin unkend;[1]
And huge *Orion*, that doth tempests still portend.[2]

14   The rich *Cteatus*, and *Eurytus* long;[3]
Neleus and *Pelias* lovely brethren both;
Mightie *Chrysaor*, and *Caïcus* strong;
Eurypulus, that calmes the waters wroth;
And faire *Euphœmus*, that upon them goth
As on the ground, without dismay or dread:
Fierce *Eryx*, and *Alebius* that know'th
The waters depth, and doth their bottome tread;
And sad *Asopus*, comely with his hoarie head.

15   There also some most famous founders were
Of puissant Nations, which the world possest;[4]
Yet sonnes of *Neptune*, now assembled here:
Ancient *Ogyges*, even th'auncientest,
And *Inachus* renowmd above the rest;
Phœnix, and *Aon*, and *Pelasgus* old,
Great *Belus*, *Phœax*, and *Agenor* best;
And mightie *Albion*, father of the bold
And warlike people, which the *Britaine* Islands hold.[5]

16   For *Albion* the sonne of *Neptune* was,
Who for the proofe of his great puissance,
Out of his *Albion* did on dry-foot pas
Into old *Gall*, that now is cleeped *France*,[6]

---

into the sea. Taking pity on the two of them, the gods changed them into immortals and gave them new names.

[1] Brontes was one of the Cyclops; Astræus committed incest with his sister.

[2] The rising of the constellation Orion was said to bring rain.

[3] Most of the adjectives given to the gods in this stanza play on the etymology of their names.

[4] Spenser depends chiefly on Natalis Comes for his information about the founders of nations (*Mythologiae*, 2.8).

[5] Stanza 15 names the founders of Thebes, Argos, Phoenicia, Aonia, the Pelasgian inhabitants of early Greece, Babylon, Phaeacia, Carthage, and Britain, in that order. This and the geographical notes to the rest of this canto are greatly indebted to the researches of Osgood, Roche, and Hamilton.

[6] The British Isles were thought to have been connected to the Continent at that time.

To fight with *Hercules*, that did advance
To vanquish all the world with matchlesse might,
And there his mortall part by great mischance
Was slaine: but that which is th'immortall spright
Lives still: and to this feast with *Neptunes* seed was dight.

17   But what doe I their names seeke to reherse,[1]
       Which all the world have with their issue[2] fild?
       How can they all in this so narrow verse
       Contayned be, and in small compasse hild?
       Let them record them, that are better skild,
       And know the moniments of passed times:
       Onely what needeth, shall be here fulfild,
       T'expresse some part of that great equipage,[3]
Which from great *Neptune* do derive their parentage.

18   Next came the aged *Ocean*, and his Dame,
       Old *Tethys*, th'oldest two of all the rest,
       For all the rest of[4] those two parents came,
       Which afterward both sea and land possest:
       Of all which *Nereus* th'eldest, and the best,
       Did first proceed, then which none more upright,
       Ne more sincere in word and deed profest;
       Most voide of guile, most free from fowle despight,
Doing him selfe, and teaching others to doe right.

19   Thereto he was expert in prophecies,
       And could the ledden[5] of the Gods unfold,
       Through which, when *Paris* brought his famous prise
       The faire Tindarid lasse,[6] he him fortold,
       That her all *Greece* with many a champion bold
       Should fetch againe, and finally destroy
       Proud *Priams* towne.[7] So wise is *Nereus* old,
       And so well skild; nathlesse he takes great joy
Oft-times amongst the wanton Nymphs to sport and toy.[8]

---

[1] **reherse:** recount.

[2] **issue:** offspring.

[3] **equipage:** retinue, following.

[4] **of:** from.

[5] **ledden:** language; speech.

[6] **Tindarid lasse:** Helen, daughter of Tyndareus (see III.ix.34.9.n.).

[7] **Priams towne:** Troy, the town of King Priam.

[8] **toy:** play.

20   And after him the famous rivers came,
      Which doe the earth enrich and beautifie:
      The fertile Nile, which creatures new doth frame;[1]
      Long Rhodanus,[2] whose sourse springs from the skie;
      Faire Ister, flowing from the mountaines hie;
      Divine Scamander,[3] purpled yet with blood
      Of Greekes and Trojans, which therein did die;
      Pactolus[4] glistring with his golden flood,
    And Tygris[5] fierce, whose streames of none may be withstood.

21   Great Ganges, and immortall Euphrates,[6]
      Deepe Indus, and Mæander intricate,[7]
      Slow Peneus, and tempestuous Phasides,[8]
      Swift Rhene, and Alpheus still immaculate:[9]
      Ooraxes, feared for great *Cyrus* fate;[10]
      Tybris,[11] renowmed for the Romaines fame,
      Rich Oranochy,[12] though but knowen late;
      And that huge River, which doth beare his name
    Of warlike Amazons, which doe possesse the same.

22   Joy on those warlike women, which so long
      Can from all men so rich a kingdome hold;
      And shame on you, ô men, which boast your strong
      And valiant hearts, in thoughts lesse hard and bold,

[1] For the Nile's ability to cause spontaneous generation, see III.vi.8.5.n.

[2] **Rhodanus:** the Rhone, which, like the Ister, flows from high in the Alps.

[3] **Scamander:** a river that flowed through ancient Troy.

[4] **Pactolus:** a Lydian river with a bed of golden sand.

[5] **Tygris:** a river in Mesopotamia, named "tiger" for its fierce current.

[6] **Ganges . . . Euphrates:** rivers in India and Syria.

[7] **Indus:** a river on what was then the west border of India; **Mæander:** a winding river in Ionia.

[8] **Peneus:** a Greek river; **Phasides:** the Phasis, a river in Colchis, on the Black Sea.

[9] **Rhene:** the Rhine, in Germany; **Alpheus:** said to flow from the Peloponnesus through the sea to Sicily, magically keeping its own waters separated from the ocean.

[10] **Ooraxes:** the River Araxes, between the Caspian and Black Seas; **Cyrus:** founder of Persia, who died in battle after crossing the Araxes.

[11] **Tybris:** the River Tiber, which runs past Rome.

[12] **Oranochy:** the Orinoco, a river in Venezuela discovered (in European terms) by Raleigh and thought by him to be the route to El Dorado, a city of gold that turned out to be mythical.

Yet quaile in conquest of that land of gold.[1]
But this to you, ô Britons, most pertaines,
To whom the right hereof it selfe hath sold;
The which for sparing litle cost or paines,
Loose so immortall glory, and so endlesse gaines.

23   Then was there heard a most celestiall sound,
          Of dainty musicke, which did next ensew
          Before the spouse: that was *Arion*[2] crownd;
          Who playing on his harpe, unto him drew
          The eares and hearts of all that goodly crew,
          That even yet the Dolphin, which him bore
          Through the Agæan[3] seas from Pirates vew,
          Stood still by him astonisht at his lore,
And all the raging seas for joy forgot to rore.

24   So went he playing on the watery plaine.
          Soone after whom the lovely Bridegroome came,
          The noble Thamis, with all his goodly traine,
          But him before there went, as best became,
          His auncient parents, namely th'auncient Thame.[4]
          But much more aged was his wife then he,
          The Ouze, whom men doe Isis rightly name;
          Full weake and crooked creature seemed shee,
And almost blind through eld, that scarce her way could see.

25   Therefore on either side she was sustained
          Of two smal grooms, which by their names were hight
          The *Churne,* and *Charwell,*[5] two small streames, which pained
          Them selves her footing to direct aright,

---

[1] **that land of gold:** Guiana, in northern South America, which Raleigh explored and which he believed to be just north of a realm of Amazons. In his *Discovery of Guiana,* Raleigh balanced, as Spenser does here, between praising Elizabeth for her ability to command great armies and urging her to use those armies to put the Amazons under the rightful rule of men by having them perform a figural rape upon the country (see Montrose, 78).

[2] *Arion:* a poet and musician of Lesbos who was thrown into the sea by pirates but saved from drowning by dolphins, whom he had enchanted with his music.

[3] **Agæan:** Ægæan.

[4] Holinshed notes that the Rivers Thame and Isis join to become the Thamesis or Thames (1.79).

[5] *Churne,* **and** *Charwell:* tributaries to the Isis.

Which fayled oft through faint and feeble plight:
But *Thame* was stronger, and of better stay;[1]
Yet seem'd full aged by his outward sight,
With head all hoary, and his beard all gray,
Deawed with silver drops, that trickled downe alway.

26   And eke he somewhat seem'd to stoupe afore
        With bowed backe, by reason of the lode,
        And auncient heavy burden, which he bore
        Of that faire City,[2] wherein make abode
        So many learned impes, that shoote abrode,[3]
        And with their braunches spred all Britany,[4]
        No lesse then do her elder sisters[5] broode.
        Joy to you both, ye double noursery,
Of Arts, but Oxford thine doth *Thame* most glorify.

27   But he their sonne[6] full fresh and jolly was,
        All decked in a robe of watchet[7] hew,
        On which the waves, glittering like Christall glas,
        So cunningly enwoven were, that few
        Could weenen, whether they were false or trew.
        And on his head like to a Coronet
        He wore, that seemed strange to common vew,
        In which were many towres and castels set,
That it encompast round as with a golden fret.[8]

28   Like as the mother of the Gods, they say,
        In her great iron charet wonts to ride,
        When to *Joves* pallace she doth take her way;

---

[1] The Isis was actually a more major river, but Spenser wishes to privilege London's river, the Thames, which takes more of its name from the Thame than from the Isis (Greenlaw, 252).

[2] **that faire City:** Oxford, which was actually on the Isis rather than on the Thame.

[3] As an imped, or grafted, branch shoots out new twigs.

[4] **Britany:** Britain (rather than Bretagne, in France).

[5] Spenser's contemporaries at Oxford and Cambridge argued heatedly about which

university was older; Spenser awards the prize to Cambridge, his *alma mater.*

[6] **their sonne:** the Thames.

[7] **watchet:** light blue.

[8] **fret:** ornamental, interlaced work, such as a gold net worn over the hair and adorned with jewels. Another definition is recorded in the language only 30 years later than *The Faerie Queene* and therefore may already have been in use: an ornamental border of intersecting lines (OED sb[1] 3). Hamilton speculates that the image may refer to London's streets that border the Thames.

Old *Cybele*,[1] arayd with pompous pride,
Wearing a Diademe embattild wide
With hundred turrets, like a Turribant.[2]
With such an one was Thamis beautifide;
That was to weet the famous Troynovant,[3]
In which her kingdomes throne is chiefly resiant.[4]

29   And round about him[5] many a pretty Page
Attended duely, ready to obay;
All little Rivers, which owe vassallage
To him, as to their Lord, and tribute pay:
The chaulky Kenet, and the Thetis gray,
The morish[6] Cole, and the soft sliding Breane,
The wanton Lee, that oft doth loose his way,
And the still Darent, in whose waters cleane
Ten thousand fishes play, and decke his pleasant streame.

30   Then came his neighbour flouds, which nigh him dwell,
And water all the English soile throughout;
They all on him this day attended well;
And with meet service waited him about;
Ne none disdained low to him to lout:
No not the stately[7] Severne grudg'd at all,
Ne storming[8] Humber, though he looked stout;
But both him honor'd as their principall,
And let their swelling waters low before him fall.

---

[1] **Cybele:** a Phrygian goddess who became associated with the Greek Rhea; she was mother of the gods and the goddess of civilization.

[2] **Turribant:** turban.

[3] **Troynovant:** New Troy, a popular description of London. (For the connection between Troy and England, see III.iii.22.6.n., III.iii.26.2.n., and III.ix.34–46). Fowler points out that the name also derives "from the British tribe 'Trinobantes,' who are found on many early maps to occupy the land north and west of the Thames estuary. In the annals of Tacitus (14.29–38), their revolt for freedom from the Roman empire is described. Thus 'Troynouant' calls up both imperialist and anti-imperialist histories" (Fowler, 2003, 199).

[4] **her:** Cybele's; **resiant:** resident.

[5] **him:** the Thames, to which the following six rivers are tributaries.

[6] **morish:** marshy, swampy.

[7] **stately:** because its name means "sovereign."

[8] **storming:** because its name derives from the Greek word for storm.

31   There was the speedy Tamar, which devides
        The Cornish and the Devonish confines;[1]
        Through both whose borders swiftly downe it glides,
        And meeting Plim,[2] to Plimmouth thence declines:
        And Dart, nigh chockt with sands of tinny mines.
        But Avon marched in more stately path,
        Proud of his Adamants,[3] with which he shines
        And glisters wide, as als' of wondrous Bath,[4]
And Bristow[5] faire, which on his waves he builded hath.

32   And there came Stoure with terrible aspect,
        Bearing his sixe deformed heads on hye,[6]
        That doth his course through Blandford plains direct,
        And washeth Winborne meades[7] in season drye.
        Next him went Wylibourne[8] with passage slye,
        That of his wylinesse his name doth take,[9]
        And of him selfe doth name the shire thereby:
        And Mole, that like a nousling[10] Mole doth make
His way still under ground, till Thamis he overtake.

33   Then came the Rother, decked all with woods
        Like a wood God, and flowing fast to Rhy:[11]
        And Sture, that parteth with his pleasant floods
        The Easterne Saxons from the Southerne ny,[12]
        And Clare, and Harwitch[13] both doth beautify:

---

[1] Cornwall and Devon were shires in southwest England, though the Celtic inhabitants of Cornwall still did not think of themselves as English.

[2] Actually, it doesn't.

[3] **Adamants:** not real diamonds in this case, but the so-called "Bristol diamonds," of quartz.

[4] **Bath:** a spa founded by the Roman occupiers of Britain.

[5] **Bristow:** Bristol.

[6] The Stoure has six sources. It is terrible because of its name: as one of Spenser's favorite non-proper nouns, it means tumult, time of stress, or battle.

[7] **meades:** meadows.

[8] **Wylibourne:** the modern Wylye.

[9] This etymology is Spenser's invention.

[10] **nousling:** nuzzling, nosing.

[11] **Rhy:** Rye, in Sussex.

[12] The River Stour separates the county of Essex from that of Suffolk. The names' etymological connections to the words "east" and "south" do not derive from the counties' relationship to each other; indeed, Essex is south of Suffolk. Suffolk, or "South-Folk," was so named because in the early Middle Ages it was in the southern portion of the Angle kingdom of East Anglia. Essex, whose name means "East Saxons," was on the eastern part of a Saxon kingdom, much larger than the present county.

[13] **Clare, and Harwitch:** towns beside the Stour.

Him follow'd Yar,[1] soft washing Norwitch wall,
And with him brought a present joyfully
Of his owne fish unto their festivall,
Whose like none else could shew, the which they Ruffins[2] call.

34   Next these the plenteous Ouse[3] came far from land,
By many a city, and by many a towne,
And many rivers taking under hand
Into his waters, as he passeth downe,
The Cle, the Were, the Grant, the Sture, the Rowne.[4]
Thence doth by Huntingdon and Cambridge flit,
My mother Cambridge, whom as with a Crowne
He doth adorne, and is adorn'd of it
With many a gentle Muse, and many a learned wit.

35   And after him the fatall Welland went,
That if old sawes prove true (which God forbid)
Shall drowne all Holland with his excrement,
And shall see Stamford, though now homely hid,
Then shine in learning, more then ever did
Cambridge or Oxford, Englands goodly beames.[5]
And next to him the *Nene*[6] downe softly slid;
And bounteous Trent, that in him selfe enseames[7]
Both thirty sorts of fish, and thirty sundry streames.[8]

---

[1] **Yar:** the River Yare, in Norfolk. A yare or yair is an enclosure extending into a river, for catching fish.

[2] **Ruffins:** ruffs, prickly freshwater fish (*Acerina cernua*) of the perch family.

[3] **Next:** next to; immediately after; **Ouse:** the Great Ouse, which flows from the East Midlands north into the Wash, an inlet of the North Sea.

[4] The Grant is the Cam, which flows by Cambridge University and is a tributary to the Great Ouse. Huntingdon is not on the Cam, but on the Great Ouse, so line 6 must refer to the entire river system.

[5] The *Variorum* and Roche mention various possible sources for this "old saw"—actually two prophecies—that the River Welland would someday flood the part of Norfolk called Holland and that the University of Stamford would someday surpass Cambridge and Oxford.

[6] *Nene:* another river that flows into the Wash.

[7] **enseames:** brings together; introduces to each other.

[8] Holinshed describes the Trent as teeming with salmon, sturgeon, and other fish, and he mentions its many tributaries (1.162), but Spenser gets the idea of thirty species and thirty tributaries from the river's name, which means "thirty" in French.

36   Next these came Tyne, along whose stony bancke
       That Romaine Monarch built a brasen wall,[1]
       Which mote the feebled Britons strongly flancke
       Against the Picts, that swarmed over all,
       Which yet thereof Gualsever they doe call:
       And Twede[2] the limit betwixt Logris land
       And Albany: And Eden[3] though but small,
       Yet often stainde with bloud of many a band
    Of Scots and English both, that tyned[4] on his strand.

37   Then came those sixe sad brethren, like forlorne,
       That whilome were (as antique fathers tell)
       Sixe valiant Knights, of one faire Nymphe yborne,
       Which did in noble deedes of armes excell,
       And wonned there, where now Yorke people dwell;
       Still Ure, swift Werfe, and Oze the most of might,[5]
       High Swale, unquiet Nide, and troublous Skell;[6]
       All whom a Scythian king, that Humber hight,
    Slew cruelly, and in the river drowned quight.[7]

38   But past not long, ere *Brutus*[8] warlicke sonne
       Locrinus them aveng'd, and the same date,[9]
       Which the proud Humber unto them had donne,

[1] **Romaine Monarch:** in CE 208, Emperor Lucius Septimius Severus directed the building of the Picts Wall (called "Gaul Sever" by the Romans) from coast to coast, approximately a hundred miles south of Hadrian's wall, to keep out the Picts. In Book Two, however, Spenser credits this feat to Constantine II, who was emperor in the fourth century (II.x.62–63); **brasen:** in this context, the word simply means "firm and strong," not actually made of brass.

[2] **Twede:** a river that forms the border between England (Logris Land) and Scotland (Albany).

[3] **Eden:** a river in Westmorland, alongside which the Scots and the English had fought.

[4] **tyned:** perished; were defeated.

[5] **Still Ure, swift Werfe:** tributaries to the Ouse in North Yorkshire (not to be confused with the Great Ouse discussed in 34.1.n.).

[6] These three rivers are also tributaries to the Ouse; their epithets match the etymologies of their names.

[7] The Ouse flows into the Humber, which empties into the sea. The story of the Scythian king is apparently Spenser's invention, inspired by his interest in tracing both the English and the Irish back to the Scythian "barbarians" of northern Europe (as he mentions in *View*, 37–38; for a discussion of the Scythian connection, see Shuger, "Irishmen," 495–501).

[8] ***Brutus:*** legendary founder of the British race.

[9] **date:** limit to the length of a life.

By equall dome[1] repayd on his owne pate:
For in the selfe same river, where he late
Had drenched them, he drowned him againe;
And nam'd the river of his wretched fate;
Whose bad condition yet it doth retaine,
Oft tossed with his stormes, which therein still remaine.

39   These after, came the stony shallow Lone,[2]
      That to old Loncaster his name doth lend;
      And following Dee, which Britons long ygone
      Did call divine, that doth by Chester tend;[3]
      And Conway[4] which out of his streame doth send
      Plenty of pearles to decke his dames withall,
      And Lindus[5] that his pikes doth most commend,
      Of which the auncient Lincolne men doe call,
      All these together marched toward *Proteus* hall.

40   Ne thence the Irishe Rivers absent were,
      Sith no lesse famous then the rest they bee,[6]
      And joyne in neighbourhood of kingdome nere,
      Why should they not likewise in love agree,
      And joy likewise this solemne day to see?
      They saw it all, and present were in place;
      Though I them all according their degree,
      Cannot recount, nor tell their hidden race,
      Nor read the salvage cuntreis,[7] thorough which they pace.

41   There was the Liffy[8] rolling downe the lea,
      The sandy Slane, the stony Aubrian,[9]
      The spacious Shenan[10] spreading like a sea,

---

[1] **dome:** judgment.

[2] **Lone:** the River Lune, which empties into the Irish Sea at Lancaster, on the northwest coast of England.

[3] **divine:** because "Dee" was supposed to have come from the Latin "diva," the river was said to have the power of divination (predicting the future); **tend:** direct its course.

[4] **Conway:** a river in North Wales.

[5] **Lindus:** now known as the Witham; it flows through Lincoln and was said to have given that city its name.

[6] To a primarily English readership, this would not have been a foregone conclusion.

[7] **cuntreis:** countries, here meaning counties or regions of Ireland.

[8] **Liffy:** a river that flows through the plains of Kildare.

[9] **Slane:** a river whose bed is notably sandy for much of its length; it empties into the sea below Wexford; **Aubrian:** no one has identified this river, despite much speculation.

[10] **Shenan:** the River Sionainn or Shannon, in Limerick, whose estuary is approximately fifty miles long.

The pleasant Boyne, the fishy fruitfull Ban,[1]
Swift Awniduff, which of the English man
Is cal'de Blacke water, and the Liffar deep,[2]
Sad Trowis,[3] that once his people overran,
Strong *Allo*[4] tombling from Slewlogher steep,
And *Mulla*[5] mine, whose waves I whilom taught to weep.

42   And there the three renowmed brethren[6] were,
      Which that great Gyant *Blomius* begot,[7]
      Of the faire Nimph *Rheusa*[8] wandring there.
      One day, as she to shunne the season whot,
      Under Slewbloome in shady grove was got,
      This Gyant found her, and by force deflowr'd,
      Whereof conceiving, she in time forth brought
      These three faire sons, which being thence forth powrd
In three great rivers ran, and many countreis scowrd.

[1] **Boyne:** a river that flows from Kildare to Drogheda; it was noted for its passage through beautiful countryside; **Ban:** a river in Wexford.

[2] **Awniduff . . . Blacke water:** Joyce explains that this is not Blackwater in Munster, near Spenser's estate, but the northern Blackwater, which flows between Counties Armagh and Derry (Greenlaw, 266); **Liffar:** the River Foyle at Lifford in Donegal. McCabe discusses the extent to which English colonials rewrote Ireland's history by reassigning place names: "The 'Irish' rivers can join in the celebrations only when they, like the people living along their banks, become 'English'" (McCabe, 202).

[3] **Trowis:** the Drowes, flowing from Lough Melvin into Donegal Bay. Joyce believes that Spenser thought the name came from the Irish *truaghas,* meaning "sadness" (Greenlaw, 268).

[4] *Allo:* the Blackwater in Munster, near Spenser's estate.

[5] *Mulla:* the River Awbeg, which bordered Spenser's estate on the west and south; it is a tributary to the Munster Blackwater. For additional lines about the Mulla, see Spenser's *Colin Clouts Come Home Againe,* lines 56 through 155. Spenser may have "taught" the Mulla "to weep" by constructing a small waterfall, but by the time he wrote Book Four, he had lived at Kilcolman long enough to associate the estate not only with beauty but also with sadness; his hopes for preferment at court in England had waned, and he did not believe that Elizabeth's policies in Ireland would lead to the unification of Britain. (See, e.g., Hadfield 2004, 140–41; and Rambuss 2001, 30–32.)

[6] **three renowmed brethren:** these three rivers, which Spenser's contemporaries usually called the Three Sisters, are described in stanza 43.

[7] *Blomius:* a personification of the Slieve Bloom Mountains. Spenser invented this story of the rivers' origination in these mountains (and in the Devil's Bit Mountains, which Spenser probably considered part of the same range).

[8] *Rheusa:* meaning "to flow" (Greek).

43   The first, the gentle Shure[1] that making way
           By sweet Clonmell, adornes rich Waterford;[2]
           The next, the stubborne Newre,[3] whose waters gray
           By faire Kilkenny and Rosseponte boord,[4]
           The third, the goodly Barow,[5] which doth hoord
           Great heapes of Salmons in his deepe bosome:
           All which long sundred, doe at last accord
           To joyne in one, ere to the sea they come,
    So flowing all from one, all one at last become.

44   There also was the wide embayed Mayre,[6]
           The pleasaunt Bandon[7] crownd with many a wood,
           The spreading Lee,[8] that like an Island fayre
           Encloseth Corke with his devided flood;
           And balefull Oure,[9] late staind with English blood:
           With many more, whose names no tongue can tell.
           All which that day in order seemly good
           Did on the Thamis attend, and waited well
    To doe their duefull service, as to them befell.

45   Then came the Bride, the lovely *Medua*[10] came,
           Clad in a vesture of unknowen geare,[11]
           And uncouth fashion, yet her well became;
           That seem'd like silver, sprinckled here and theare
           With glittering spangs,[12] that did like starres appeare,

---

[1] **Shure:** the River Suir, flowing southward from Tipperary into Waterford.

[2] **Clonmell:** this town is "sweet" because its name includes the Latin word for honey: *mel;* **Waterford:** a city on Waterford Harbor, where the Three Sisters empty into St. George's Channel.

[3] **Newre:** the River Nore, flowing southward through County Kilkenny.

[4] **Kilkenny and Rosseponte:** towns, the latter now New Ross, in County Wexford; **boord:** border on.

[5] **Barow:** the second longest river in Ireland, still noted for its salmon. It flows from Counties Laois and Kildare southward.

[6] **embayed:** incorporating bays; **Mayre:** the River Kenmare in southwest County Kerry.

[7] **Bandon:** flows eastward through County Cork, emptying into the Celtic Sea at Kinsale.

[8] **Lee:** flows eastward through County Cork, dividing into many branches to encircle the smaller city of Cork in Spenser's time before emptying into Cork Harbour.

[9] **Oure:** Joyce identifies this as the River Avonberg in the County Wicklow. The Avonberg flows through a glen where the man whom Spenser served as secretary in Ireland, Lord Grey de Wilton, lost 800 men to an ambush by Irish rebels in 1580 (Greenlaw, 271).

[10] *Medua:* the Medway.

[11] **geare:** material.

[12] **spangs:** spangles.

And wav'd upon, like water Chamelot,[1]
To hide the metall, which yet every where
Bewrayd it selfe,[2] to let men plainely wot,
It was no mortall worke, that seem'd and yet was not.

46   Her goodly lockes adowne her backe did flow
    Unto her waste, with flowres bescattered,
    The which ambrosiall odours forth did throw
    To all about, and all her shoulders spred
    As a new spring; and likewise on her hed
    A Chapelet[3] of sundry flowers she wore,
    From under which the deawy humour[4] shed,
Did tricle downe her haire, like to the hore[5]
Congealed litle drops, which doe the morne adore.

47   On her two pretty handmaides did attend,
    One cald the *Theise,* the other cald the *Crane;*[6]
    Which on her waited, things amisse to mend,
    And both behind upheld her spredding traine;
    Under the which, her feet appeared plaine,
    Her silver feet, faire washt against this day:
    And her before there paced Pages twaine,
    Both clad in colours like, and like array,
The *Doune* and eke the *Frith,* both which prepard her way.[7]

48   And after these the Sea Nymphs marched all,
    All goodly damzels, deckt with long greene haire,
    Whom of their sire *Nereides*[8] men call,

---

[1] **water Chamelot:** watered camlet, an expensive fabric with a moiré weave, which tricks the eye into seeing wavy movement in the threads (originally made in the east of silk and camel hair, later of silk and wool or other materials).

[2] The hiding and self-betrayal are not necessarily allegorically sinister. Aristocrats of the sixteenth century loved being fooled in clever ways during court entertainments, as for example by disguises; and in order to acquire the *sprezzatura* lauded by Castiglione, one built the self by concealing the self: a courtier pretended that a difficult skill acquired through hard practice had instead come naturally and easily (Castiglione, *Courtier,* 45–9).

[3] **Chapelet:** wreath for the head.

[4] **humour:** moisture, in this case either dew or nectar from the flowers or river water from Medway herself.

[5] **hore:** hoarfrost.

[6] *Theise . . . Crane:* tributaries to the Medway.

[7] *Doune . . . Frith:* it is unclear which streams Spenser means.

[8] *Nereides:* Nereus and Doris' fifty daughters, who are beneficent sea nymphs. Among them is Thetis, the mother of

All which the Oceans daughter to him bare
The gray eyde *Doris:* all which fifty are;
All which she there on her attending had.
Swift *Proto,* milde *Eucrate, Thetis* faire,
Soft *Spio,* sweete *Eudore, Sao* sad,
Light *Doto,* wanton *Glauce,* and *Galene* glad.

49   White hand *Eunica,* proud *Dynamene,*
    Joyous *Thalia,* goodly *Amphitrite,*
    Lovely *Pasithee,* kinde *Eulimene,*
    Light foote *Cymothoe,* and sweete *Melite,*
    Fairest *Pherusa, Phao* lilly white,
    Wondred[1] *Agave, Poris,* and *Nesæa,*
    With *Erato* that doth in love delite,
    And *Panopæ,* and wise *Protomedæa,*
And snowy neckd *Doris,* and milkewhite *Galathæa.*

50   Speedy *Hippothoe,* and chaste *Actea,*
    Large *Lisianassa,* and *Pronæa* sage,
    Euagore, and light *Pontoporea,*
    And she, that with her least word can asswage
    The surging seas, when they do sorest rage,
    Cymodoce, and stout *Autonoe,*
    And *Neso,* and *Eione* well in age,
    And seeming still to smile, *Glauconome,*
And she that hight of many heastes[2] *Polynome.*

51   Fresh *Alimeda,* deckt with girlond greene;
    Hyponeo, with salt bedewed wrests:[3]
    Laomedia, like the christall sheene;
    Liagore, much praisd for wise behests;
    And *Psamathe,* for her brode snowy brests;
    Cymo, Eupompe, and *Themiste* just;

Achilles. Although Homer names fifty Nereids (*Iliad,* 18.39–49), Spenser's list more closely matches the list in Hesiod (*Theogony,* 240–64). Spenser invents the names Phao and Poris (to replace Hesiod's Protho and Cymatolege). Some of the Nereids' epithets come from Homer and Hesiod, whereas Spenser invented others; many of them are derived etymologically from the names.

[1] **Wondred:** wonderful.

[2] **heastes:** names.

[3] **wrests:** wrists.

And she that vertue loves and vice detests
Euarna, and *Menippe* true in trust,
And *Nemertea* learned well to rule her lust.

52   All these the daughters of old *Nereus* were,
        Which have the sea in charge to them assinde,
        To rule his tides, and surges to uprere,
        To bring forth stormes, or fast them to upbinde,
        And sailers save from wreckes of wrathfull winde.
        And yet besides three thousand more there were
        Of th'Oceans seede, but *Joves* and *Phœbus* kinde;
        The which in floods and fountaines doe appere,
And all mankinde do nourish with their waters clere.

53   The which, more eath it were for mortall wight,
        To tell[1] the sands, or count the starres on hye,
        Or ought more hard, then thinke to reckon right.
        But well I wote, that these which I descry,[2]
        Were present at this great solemnity:
        And there amongst the rest, the mother was
        Of luckelesse *Marinell Cymodoce,*[3]
        Which, for my Muse her selfe now tyred has,
Unto an other Canto I will overpas.

---

[1] **tell:** count.

[2] **descry:** reveal; perceive.

[3] *Cymodoce:* called Cymoent at III.iv.19.

Canto Twelve

Marin for love of Florimell,
In languor wastes his life:
The Nymph his mother getteth her,
And gives to him for wife.

1   O what an endlesse worke have I in hand,
　　To count the seas abundant progeny,
　　Whose fruitfull seede farre passeth those in land,
　　And also those which wonne in th'azure sky?
　　For much more eath[1] to tell the starres on hy,
　　Albe they endlesse seeme in estimation,
　　Then to recount the Seas posterity:
　　So fertile be the flouds in generation,
So huge their numbers, and so numberlesse their nation.

2   Therefore the antique wisards[2] well invented,
　　That *Venus* of the fomy sea was bred;[3]
　　For that the seas by her are most augmented.
　　Witnesse th'exceeding fry, which there are fed,
　　And wondrous sholes, which may of none be red.
　　Then blame me not, if I have err'd in count
　　Of Gods, of Nymphs, of rivers yet unred:
　　For though their numbers do much more surmount,
Yet all those same were there, which erst I did recount.

3   All those were there, and many other more,
　　Whose names and nations[4] were too long to tell,
　　That *Proteus* house they fild even to the dore;

---

[1] **eath:** easy.

[2] **antique wisards:** sages of ancient times.

[3] Hesiod writes that Kronos was the son of Gaea and Uranus (Earth and Heaven). Because Uranus loathed all of his children, Gaea urged them to take revenge on him, upon which advice Kronos took a scythe, cut off his father's genitals, and threw them into the sea. A white foam frothed around them, and from it the goddess Aphrodite (whom the Romans identified with Venus) stepped onto the island of Cytherea (*Theogony*, 130–201).

[4] **nations:** classes, kinds, or races. (Spenser could also conceivably have been thinking of the fact that Irish clans were called nations.)

Yet were they all in order, as befell,
According their degrees disposed well.
Amongst the rest, was faire *Cymodoce,*
The mother of unlucky *Marinell,*
Who thither with her came, to learne and see
The manner of the Gods when they at banquet be.

4   But for[1] he was halfe mortall, being bred
Of mortall sire, though of immortall wombe,
He might not with immortall food be fed,
Ne with th'eternall Gods to bancket[2] come;
But walkt abrode, and round about did rome,
To view the building of that uncouth place,
That seem'd unlike unto his earthly home:
Where, as he to and fro by chaunce did trace,
There unto him betid a disaventrous case.[3]

5   Under the hanging of an hideous clieffe,
He heard the lamentable voice of one,
That piteously complaind her carefull grieffe,
Which never she before disclosd to none,
But to her selfe her sorrow did bemone.
So feelingly her case she did complaine,
That ruth it moved in the rocky stone,
And made it seeme to feele her grievous paine,
And oft to grone with billowes beating from the maine.

6   "Though vaine I see my sorrowes to unfold,
And count my cares, when none is nigh to heare,
Yet hoping griefe may lessen being told,[4]
I will them tell though unto no man neare:
For heaven that unto all lends equall eare,
Is farre from hearing of my heavy plight;

[1] **for:** because.

[2] **bancket:** banquet.

[3] **betid:** betided, befell; **disaventrous case:** unlucky event, though Silberman observes that it could also mean "not accidental" in not being "adventurous" (OED 1; Silberman, 139). Alpers argues that Marinell's walking away from the marriage celebration enables the poem to demonstrate a "contrast between the enclosed world of the water deities and the fuller range of human experience" (122).

[4] I.e., yet hoping that telling about the grief may lessen it.

And lowest hell, to which I lie most neare,
    Cares not what evils hap to wretched wight;
And greedy seas doe in the spoile of life delight.

7   "Yet loe the seas I see by often beating,
            Doe pearce the rockes, and hardest marble weares;
            But his hard rocky hart for no entreating
            Will yeeld, but when my piteous plaints he heares,
            Is hardned more with my aboundant teares.
            Yet though he never list to me relent,
            But let me waste in woe my wretched yeares,
            Yet will I never of my love repent,
    But joy that for his sake I suffer prisonment.

8   "And when my weary ghost with griefe outworne,
            By timely death shall winne her wished rest,
            Let then this plaint unto his eares be borne,
            That blame it is to him, that armes profest,
            To let her die, whom he might have redrest."
            There did she pause, inforced to give place,
            Unto the passion, that her heart opprest,
            And after she had wept and wail'd a space,
    She gan afresh thus to renew her wretched case.

9   "Ye Gods of seas, if any Gods at all
            Have care of right, or ruth of wretches wrong,
            By one or other way me woefull thrall,
            Deliver hence out of this dungeon strong,
            In which I daily dying am too long.
            And if ye deeme me death for loving one,
            That loves not me, then doe it not prolong,
            But let me die and end my daies attone,[1]
    And let him live unlov'd, or love him selfe alone.

10   "But if that life ye unto me decree,
            Then let mee live, as lovers ought to do,
            And of my lifes deare love beloved be:
            And if he shall through pride your doome[2] undo,

---

[1] **attone:** at once (rather than in this pro-   [2] **doome:** judgment.
tracted manner).

Do you by duresse him compell thereto,
And in this prison put him here with me:
One prison fittest is to hold us two:
So had I rather to be thrall, then free;
Such thraldome or such freedome let it surely be.

11   "But ô vaine judgement, and conditions vaine,
          The which the prisoner points unto the free,[1]
          The whiles I him condemne, and deeme his paine,
          He where he list goes loose,[2] and laughes at me.
          So ever loose, so ever happy be.
          But where so loose or happy that thou art,
          Know *Marinell* that all this is for thee."
          With that she wept and wail'd, as if her hart
Would quite have burst through great abundance of her smart.

12   All which complaint when *Marinell* had heard,
          And understood the cause of all her care
          To come of him, for using[3] her so hard,
          His stubborne heart, that never felt misfare
          Was toucht with soft remorse and pitty rare;
          That even for griefe of minde he oft did grone,
          And inly wish, that in his powre it weare
          Her to redresse: but since he meanes found none
He could no more but her great misery bemone.

13   Thus whilst his stony heart with tender ruth
          Was toucht, and mighty courage mollifide,[4]
          Dame *Venus* sonne that tameth stubborne youth
          With iron bit, and maketh him abide,
          Till like a victor on his backe he ride,
          Into his mouth his maystring[5] bridle threw,
          That made him stoupe, till he did him bestride:
          Then gan he make him tread his steps anew,
And learne to love, by learning lovers paines to rew.

---

[1] I.e., it is useless for the prisoner to appoint judgment and conditions for the free person.

[2] **loose:** free, unfettered—but also suggesting that he is too free in his laughter.

[3] **of:** from; **using:** treating.

[4] **mollifide:** softened.

[5] **maystring:** mastering.

14 Now gan he in his grieved minde devise,
  How from that dungeon he might her enlarge;
  Some while he thought, by faire and humble wise
  To *Proteus* selfe to sue[1] for her discharge:
  But then he fear'd his mothers former charge
  Gainst womens love, long given him in vaine.
  Then gan he thinke, perforce with sword and targe[2]
  Her forth to fetch, and *Proteus* to constraine:
But soone he gan such folly to forthinke again.

15 Then did he cast to steale her thence away,
  And with him beare, where none of her might know.
  But all in vaine: for why[3] he found no way
  To enter in, or issue forth below:
  For all about that rocke the sea did flow.
  And though unto his will she given were,[4]
  Yet without ship or bote her thence to row,
  He wist not how her thence away to bere;
And daunger well he wist long to continue there.

16 At last when as no meanes he could invent,
  Backe to him selfe, he gan returne the blame,
  That was the author of her punishment;
  And with vile curses, and reprochfull shame
  To damne him selfe by every evill name;
  And deeme unworthy or of love or life,
  That had despisde so chast and faire a dame,
  Which him had sought through trouble and long strife;
Yet had refusde a God[5] that her had sought to wife.

17 In this sad plight he walked here and there,
  And romed round about the rocke in vaine,
  As he had lost him selfe, he wist not where;
  Oft listening if he mote her heare againe;
  And still bemoning her unworthy[6] paine.
  Like as an Hynde[7] whose calfe is falne unwares

---

[1] **sue:** ask.
[2] **targe:** lightweight shield.
[3] **for why:** because.
[4] I.e., even if she agreed to do what he asked.

[5] **a God:** Proteus.
[6] **unworthy:** undeserved.
[7] **Hynde:** female deer.

> Into some pit, where she him heares complaine,
> An hundred times about the pit side fares,
> Right sorrowfully mourning her bereaved cares.[1]

18   And now by this the feast was throughly ended,
> And every one gan homeward to resort.
> Which seeing, *Marinell* was sore offended,[2]
> That his departure thence should be so short,[3]
> And leave his love in that sea-walled fort.
> Yet durst he not his mother disobay,
> But her attending in full seemly sort,
> Did march amongst the many all the way:
> And all the way did inly mourne, like one astray.

19   Being returned to his mothers bowre,
> In solitary silence far from wight,
> He gan record[4] the lamentable stowre,
> In which his wretched love lay day and night,
> For his deare sake, that[5] ill deserv'd that plight:
> The thought whereof empierst his hart so deepe,
> That of no worldly thing he tooke delight;
> Ne dayly food did take, ne nightly sleepe,
> But pyn'd, and mourn'd, and languisht, and alone did weepe.

20   That in short space his wonted chearefull hew
> Gan fade, and lively spirits deaded quight:
> His cheeke bones raw, and eie-pits hollow grew,
> And brawney armes had lost their knowen might,
> That nothing like himselfe he seem'd in sight.
> Ere long so weake of limbe, and sicke of[6] love
> He woxe, that lenger he note[7] stand upright,
> But to his bed was brought, and layd above,
> Like ruefull ghost, unable once to stirre or move.

---

[1] **her bereaved cares:** the loss of the fawn, which has been the focus of her cares.

[2] **offended:** displeased.

[3] **short:** happening shortly.

[4] **record:** go over in his mind; meditate on.

[5] **that:** who (referring to "his wretched love," i.e., Florimell).

[6] **of:** from, though with a play on "tired of love."

[7] **note:** could not.

21 Which when his mother saw, she in her mind
       Was troubled sore, ne wist well what to weene,
       Ne could by search nor any meanes out find
       The secret cause and nature of his teene,
       Whereby she might apply some medicine;
       But weeping day and night, did him attend,
       And mourn'd to see her losse before her eyne,
       Which griev'd her more, that she it could not mend:
    To see an helpelesse evill,[1] double griefe doth lend.

22 Nought could she read the roote of his disease,
       Ne weene what mister maladie it is,
       Whereby to seeke some meanes it to appease.[2]
       Most did she thinke, but most she thought amis,
       That that same former fatall wound of his
       Whyleare by *Tryphon* was not throughly healed,
       But closely rankled under th'orifis:[3]
       Least did she thinke, that which he most concealed,
    That love it was, which in his hart lay unrevealed.

23 Therefore to *Tryphon* she againe doth hast,
       And him doth chyde as false and fraudulent,
       That fayld the trust, which she in him had plast,
       To cure her sonne, as he his faith had lent:
       Who now was falne into new languishment
       Of his old hurt, which was not throughly cured.
       So backe he came unto her patient,[4]
       Where searching every part, her well assured,
    That it was no old sore, which his new paine procured.

24 But that it was some other maladie,
       Or griefe unknowne, which he could not discerne:
       So left he her withouten remedie.
       Then gan her heart to faint, and quake, and earne,[5]
       And inly troubled was, the truth to learne.
       Unto himselfe she came, and him besought,

---

[1] **helpelesse evill:** a misfortune or trouble that cannot be alleviated.

[2] **appease:** ameliorate.

[3] **th'orifis:** i.e., the scar where the orifice of the wound had been.

[4] I.e., to her patient (Marinell, who is under her care) or to her, patient (i.e., patiently).

[5] **earne:** yearn.

Now with faire speches, now with threatnings sterne,
If ought lay hidden in his grieved thought,
It to reveale: who still her answered, there was nought.

25   Nathlesse she rested not so satisfide,
      But leaving watry gods, as booting nought,[1]
      Unto the shinie heaven in haste she hide,[2]
      And thence *Apollo* King of Leaches[3] brought.
      Apollo came; who soone as he had sought
      Through his disease, did by and by out find,
      That he did languish of some inward thought,
      The which afflicted his engrieved mind;
    Which love he red to be, that leads each living kind.

26   Which when he had unto his mother told,
      She gan thereat to fret, and greatly grieve.
      And comming to her sonne, gan first to scold,
      And chyde at him, that made her misbelieve:
      But afterwards she gan him soft to shrieve,[4]
      And wooe with faire intreatie, to disclose,
      Which of the Nymphes his heart so sore did mieve.[5]
      For sure she weend it was some one of those,
    Which he had lately seene, that for his love he chose.

27   Now lesse she feared that same fatall read,[6]
      That warned him of womens love beware:
      Which being ment of mortall creatures sead,
      For love of Nymphes she thought she need not care,
      But promist him, what ever wight she weare,
      That she her love, to him would shortly gaine:
      So he her told: but soone as she did heare
      That *Florimell* it was, which wrought his paine,
    She gan a fresh to chafe, and grieve in every vaine.

[1] Her sudden dismissal of the efficacy of all "watry gods" makes complete sense psychologically but carries a certain amount of humor for the reader, who has just finished an entire canto devoted to the praises of watery gods.

[2] **hide:** hied, hastened.

[3] **Leaches:** physicians. Cf. vi.1.9 and note.

[4] **shrieve:** question; ask him to confess.

[5] **mieve:** move.

[6] **read:** prophecy (see III.iv.25–27). The prophecy told him to beware women, not to beware women's love. Cymodoce still does not understand that Marinell has already suffered—and recovered from—the fulfillment of the prophecy, in being wounded by Britomart (III.iv.12–18).

28 Yet since she saw the streight extremitie,
In which his life unluckily was layd,
It was no time to scan[1] the prophecie,
Whether old *Proteus* true or false had sayd,
That his decay should happen by a mayd.
It's late in death of daunger to advize,
Or love forbid him, that is life denayd:
But rather gan in troubled mind devize,
How she that Ladies libertie might enterprize.

29 To *Proteus* selfe to sew[2] she thought it vaine,
Who was the root and worker of her woe:
Nor unto any meaner[3] to complaine,
But unto great king *Neptune* selfe did goe,
And on her knee before him falling lowe,
Made humble suit unto his Majestie,
To graunt to her, her sonnes life, which his foe
A cruell Tyrant had presumpteouslie
By wicked doome condemn'd, a wretched death to die.

30 To whom God *Neptune* softly smyling, thus;
"Daughter me seemes of double wrong ye plaine,
Gainst one that hath both wronged you, and us:[4]
For death t'adward[5] I ween'd did appertaine
To none, but to the seas sole Soveraine.
Read therefore who it is, which this hath wrought,
And for what cause; the truth discover plaine.
For never wight so evill did or thought,
But would some rightfull cause pretend, though rightly nought."

31 To whom she answerd, "Then it is by name
Proteus, that hath ordayn'd my sonne to die;
For that a waift,[6] the which by fortune came
Upon your seas, he claym'd as propertie:
And yet nor his, nor his in equitie,

---

[1] **scan:** estimate the correctness or value of.

[2] **sew:** apply; ask.

[3] **meaner:** less powerful or important.

[4] **us:** the royal pronoun, applying only to himself.

[5] **adward:** award, sentence.

[6] **waift:** waif; legally, unclaimed property that should have reverted to the crown; something wafted over water.

But yours the waift by high prerogative.
Therefore I humbly crave your Majestie,
It to replevie, and my sonne reprive:[1]
So shall you by one gift save all us three alive."

32   He graunted it: and streight his warrant made,
Under the Sea-gods seale autenticall,[2]
Commaunding *Proteus* straight t'enlarge the mayd,
Which wandring on his[3] seas imperiall,
He lately tooke, and sithence kept as thrall.
Which she receiving with meete thankefulnesse,
Departed straight to *Proteus* therewithall:
Who reading it with inward loathfulnesse,[4]
Was grieved to restore the pledge, he did possesse.

33   Yet durst he not the warrant to withstand,
But unto her delivered *Florimell.*
Whom she receiving by the lilly hand,
Admyr'd her beautie much, as she mote well:
For she all living creatures did excell;
And was right joyous, that she gotten had
So faire a wife for her sonne *Marinell.*
So home with her she streight the virgin lad,
And shewed her to him, then being sore bestad.

34   Who soone as he beheld that angels face,
Adorn'd with all divine perfection,
His cheared heart eftsoones away gan chace
Sad death, revived with her sweet inspection,[5]
And feeble spirit inly felt refection;[6]
As withered weed through cruell winters tine,
That feeles the warmth of sunny beames reflection,
Liftes up his head, that did before decline
And gins to spread his leafe before the faire sunshine.[7]

---

[1] **replevie:** repleve, to post bail for some-one in prison or restore goods to a person on condition that he or she will undergo a trial to determine whether the goods may be permanently retained; **reprive:** reprieve; rescue from death (OED 4).

[2] **autenticall:** legally authentic.

[3] **his:** Neptune's.

[4] **loathfulnesse:** deep reluctance.

[5] **her sweet inspection:** her sweet regard of him; his sweet regard of her.

[6] **refection:** refreshment.

[7] The woman with the flower name has spent time in the sea, and now the man with the marine name is rejuvenated like a flower.

35 Right so himselfe did *Marinell* upreare,
   When he in place his dearest love did spy;
   And though his limbs could not his bodie beare,
   Ne former strength returne so suddenly,
   Yet chearefull signes he shewed outwardly.
   Ne lesse was she in secret hart affected,
   But that she masked it with modestie,
   For feare she should of lightnesse be detected:[1]
  Which to another place I leave to be perfected.[2]

---

[1] **detected:** accused.

[2] Alpers observes that although Book Four ends happily, its ending is about the incipient stages of Florimell and Marinell's union, rather than about the completion of that union (Alpers, 109). Although Book Four ends somewhat more abruptly than do the other books, none of the books concludes with a resolution. See Introduction, 5g, and see Goldberg, *Endlesse Worke,* passim.

THE LETTER TO RALEIGH

A
Letter of the Authors expounding his
whole intention in the course of this worke: which
for that it giueth great light to the Reader, for
the better vnderstanding is hereunto
annexed.

To the Right noble, and Valorous, Sir Walter Raleigh knight, Lo. Wardein of the Stanneryes, and her Maiesties liefetenaunt of the County of Cornewayll.[1]

Sir knowing how doubtfully all Allegories may be construed, and this booke of mine, which I have entituled the Faery Queene, being a continued Allegory, or darke conceit, I have thought good aswell for avoyding of gealous opinions and misconstructions, as also for your better light in reading thereof, (being so by you commanded,) to discover unto you the general intention and meaning, which in the whole course thereof I have fashioned, without expressing of any particular purposes or by accidents therein occasioned. The generall end therefore of all the booke is to fashion a gentleman or noble person in vertuous and gentle discipline:[2] Which for that I conceived shoulde be most plausible[3] and pleasing, being coloured with an historicall fiction, the which the most part of men delight to read, rather for variety of matter, then for profite of the ensample: I chose the historye of king Arthure, as most fitte for the excellency of his person, being made famous by many mens former workes, and also furthest from the daunger of envy, and suspition of present time. In which I have followed all the antique Poets historicall, first Homere, who in the Persons of Agamemnon and Ulysses hath ensampled a good governour and a vertuous man, the one in his Ilias, the other in his Odysseis: then Virgil, whose like intention was to doe in the person of Aeneas: after him Ariosto comprised them

---

[1] Appended to the 1590 edition of *The Faerie Queene*, Spenser's "Letter to Raleigh," also called "A Letter of the Authors," has been read as a preface, detailing both the larger plot and the poetics underlying the poem. It was not included in the 1596 edition, and so only discusses the first three books directly.

[2] **discipline:** learning, training, orderly conduct, the system by which a church exercises control over its members.

[3] **plausible:** deserving applause, acceptable.

both in his Orlando:[1] and lately Tasso dissevered them againe, and formed both parts in two persons, namely that part which they in Philosophy call Ethice, or vertues of a private man, coloured in his Rinaldo: The other named Politice in his Godfredo.[2] By ensample of which excellente Poets, I labour to pourtraict in Arthure, before he was king, the image of a brave knight, perfected in the twelve private morall vertues, as Aristotle hath devised,[3] the which is the purpose of these first twelve bookes: which if I finde to be well accepted, I may be perhaps encoraged, to frame the other part of polliticke vertues in his person, after that hee came to be king.[4] To some I know this Methode will seeme displeasaunt, which had rather have good discipline delivered plainly in way of precepts, or sermoned at large, as they use, then thus clowdily enwrapped in Allegoricall devises. But such, me seeme, should be satisfide with the use of these dayes seeing all things accounted by their showes, and nothing esteemed of, that is not delightfull and pleasing to commune sence. For this cause is Xenophon preferred before Plato, for that the one in the exquisite depth of his judgement, formed a Commune welth such as it should be, but the other in the person of Cyrus and the Persians fashioned a government such as might best be: So much more profitable and gratious is doctrine by ensample, then by rule.[5] So have I laboured to doe in the person of Arthure: whome I conceive after his long education by Timon, to whom he was by Merlin delivered to be brought up, so soone as he was borne of the Lady Igrayne, to have seene in a dream or vision the Faery Queen, with whose excellent beauty ravished, he awaking resolved to seeke her out, and so being by Merlin armed, and by Timon throughly instructed, he went to seeke her forth in Faerye land. In that Faery Queene I meane glory in my generall intention, but in my particular I conceive the most excellent and glorious person of our soveraine the Queene, and her kingdome in Faery land. And yet in some places els, I doe otherwise shadow her. For considering she beareth two persons, the one of a most royall Queene or Empresse, the other of a most vertuous and beautifull Lady, this latter part in some places I doe expresse in Belphoebe, fashioning her name according to your owne excellent conceipt of Cynthia, (Phoebe and Cynthia being both names of Diana).[6] So in the person of

[1] Lodovico Ariosto, Italian author of *Orlando Furioso* (1532).

[2] Torquato Tasso, Italian author of *Rinaldo* (1562) and *Gerusalemme Liberata* (1581), in which the hero Godfredo embodies public or political virtues.

[3] Aristotle does not name twelve particular moral virtues in the *Nicomachaean Ethics*. There are, however, several Medieval and Renaissance commentaries on Aristotle from which twelve could be construed.

[4] Spenser indicates that he planned twelve books for *The Faerie Queene* and would willingly write twenty-four, the former matching Virgil, the latter Homer.

[5] Spenser says that Xenophon's *Cyropaedia*, celebrated for teaching by example, is commonly preferred to Plato's *Republic*, which taught by precepts.

[6] Belphoebe appears in Books Two, Three, and Four. Cynthia refers to Raleigh's poem of that name, which also celebrated Elizabeth. Spenser suggests that Gloriana, the Faerie Queen, represents Elizabeth's public role as monarch, while Belphoebe personifies her private, virginal life.

Prince Arthure I sette forth magnificence in particular, which vertue for that (according to Aristotle and the rest) it is the perfection of all the rest, and conteineth in it them all, therefore in the whole course I mention the deedes of Arthure applyable to that vertue, which I write of in that booke. But of the xii. other vertues, I make xii. other knights the patrones, for the more variety of the history: Of which these three bookes contayn three. The first of the knight of the Redcrosse, in whome I expresse Holynes: The seconde of Sir Guyon, in whome I sette forth Temperaunce: The third of Britomartis a Lady knight, in whome I picture Chastity. But because the beginning of the whole worke seemeth abrupte and as depending upon other antecedents, it needs that ye know the occasion of these three knights severall adventures. For the Methode of a Poet historical is not such, as of an Historiographer. For an Historiographer discourseth of affayres orderly as they were donne, accounting as well the times as the actions, but a Poet thrusteth into the middest,[1] even where it most concerneth him, and there recoursing to the thinges forepaste, and divining of thinges to come, maketh a pleasing Analysis of all. The beginning therefore of my history, if it were to be told by an Historiographer should be the twelfth booke, which is the last, where I devise that the Faery Queene kept her Annuall feaste xii. dayes, uppon which xii. severall dayes, the occasions of the xii. severall adventures hapned, which being undertaken by xii. severall knights, are in these xii. books severally handled and discoursed. The first was this. In the beginning of the feast, there presented him selfe a tall clownishe[2] younge man, who falling before the Queen of Faries desired a boone (as the manner then was) which during that feast she might not refuse: which was that hee might have the atchievement of any adventure, which during that feaste should happen, that being graunted, he rested him on the floore, unfitte through his rusticity for a better place. Soone after entred a faire Ladye in mourning weedes, riding on a white Asse, with a dwarfe behind her leading a warlike steed, that bore the Armes of a knight, and his speare in the dwarfes hand. Shee falling before the Queene of Faeries, complayned that her father and mother an ancient King and Queene, had bene by an huge dragon many years shut up in a brasen[3] Castle, who thence suffred them not to yssew: and therefore besought the Faery Queene to assygne her some one of her knights to take on him that exployt. Presently that clownish person upstarting, desired that adventure: whereat the Queene much wondering, and the Lady much gainesaying, yet he earnestly importuned his desire. In the end the Lady told him that unlesse that armour which she brought, would serve him (that is the armour of a Christian man specified by Saint Paul v. Ephes.[4]) that he could not succeed in that enterprise, which being forthwith put upon him with dewe furnitures[5] thereunto, he seemed

---

[1] See Horace, *Ars Poetica*, 146–52.

[2] **clownishe:** rustic.

[3] **brasen:** strong like brass.

[4] See Eph. 6.11–17.

[5] **dewe furnitures:** proper equipment.

the goodliest man in al that company, and was well liked of the Lady. And efte-soones[1] taking on him knighthood, and mounting on that straunge Courser, he went forth with her on that adventure: where beginneth the first booke, vz.

A gentle knight was pricking on the playne. &c.

The second day ther came in a Palmer bearing an Infant with bloody hands, whose Parents he complained to have bene slayn by an Enchaunteresse called Acra-sia: and therfore craved of the Faery Queene, to appoint him some knight, to per-forme that adventure, which being assigned to Sir Guyon, he presently went forth with that same Palmer: which is the beginning of the second booke and the whole subject thereof.[2] The third day there came in, a Groome who complained before the Faery Queene, that a vile Enchaunter called Busirane had in hand a most faire Lady called Amoretta, whom he kept in most grievous torment, because she would not yield him the pleasure of her body. Whereupon Sir Scudamour the lover of that Lady presently tooke on him that adventure. But being unable to performe it by reason of the hard Enchauntments, after long sorrow, in the end met with Brito-martis, who succoured him, and reskewed his love.

But by occasion hereof, many other adventures are intermedled, but rather as Ac-cidents, then intendments.[3] As the love of Britomart, the overthrow of Marinell, the misery of Florimell, the vertuousnes of Belphoebe, the lasciviousnes of Hellenora, and many the like.[4]

Thus much Sir, I have briefly overronne to direct your understanding to the wel-head of the History, that from thence gathering the whole intention of the conceit, ye may as in a handfull gripe al the discourse, which otherwise may happily[5] seeme tedious and confused. So humbly craving the continuaunce of your honorable favour towards me, and th'eternall establishment of your happines, I humbly take leave.

23. January. 1589.[6]

Yours most humbly affectionate.
Ed. Spenser.

---

[1] **eftesoones:** immediately.

[2] This description is at variance with the beginning of Book Two at several points— e.g., the Palmer is already with Guyon when they encounter the bloody baby in Canto One.

[3] **intendments:** matters of central import.

[4] This description seems to make Scud-amour the hero, rather than Britomart.

[5] **happily:** by chance.

[6] In the new calendar, 1590.

The Life of Edmund Spenser

Spenser (c. 1552–1599) was from a merchant family, possibly involved in the cloth trade and probably living in London. Although he may have been related to the noble family of Spencers, Spenser was not a gentleman. He was fortunate to attend the Merchant Taylors' School, an academy founded by the tailors' guild, and was registered there as a "poor scholar." The school, however, was excellent; in his eight years there, Spenser received a humanist education that was rich in classical scholarship and languages. In 1569 he entered Pembroke Hall, Cambridge. Again he was a scholarship student, called a sizar, earning room and board by performing servants' duties. In the same year that he arrived at Cambridge, Spenser was first published: several of his translations from Italian and French appeared in the Protestant miscellany *A Theatre for Worldlings.* Spenser completed a Bachelor of Arts degree in 1573, and then, in 1576, a Master of Arts (finishing 66th out of a class of 70). Spenser then began a career as secretary to high-ranking men, a position of some importance involving a broad array of duties that included much traveling and writing. Intermittent records show him serving as an emissary for the earl of Leicester, and in 1578 he was secretary to John Young, Bishop of Rochester. In 1579 he married Maccabaeus Chylde; we know little about the couple's family life other than the fact that they had two children. In 1580 he was appointed secretary to Lord Grey de Wilton, the new Lord Deputy of Ireland, and traveled there with him. Spenser's career as a secretary and subsequent work as a civil servant in Ireland no doubt took up much of his time. But he was simultaneously establishing a second career as a poet. Probably while working for Leicester, Spenser met Philip Sidney and entered into his sophisticated literary circle. In 1579 Spenser published *The Shepheardes Calender,* his innovative and enormously influential collection of pastorals. It revealed Spenser not only as one of England's most skilled poets, but as a deeply interested and progressive Protestant thinker. He also cultivated his university friendship with the humanist scholar Gabriel Harvey, which in 1580 led to the publication of several of their letters. The Harvey letters mention several lost works, and suggest that by 1580 Spenser had begun working on *The Faerie Queene.*

Meanwhile, in Ireland with Lord Grey, Spenser participated in the complicated and exceedingly violent project of English colonialism. Grey was sent to govern a country that was struggling broadly against English domination, and he adopted a strategy of overwhelming force, including the notorious slaughter of 600 military prisoners at Smerwick, and policies aimed at subduing the population through famine. To what extent Spenser participated in Grey's governance, and to what extent he merely accompanied him and performed secretarial duties, is unclear. But it is clear that Spenser profited personally from empire building. Although Grey was recalled to England in 1582, Spenser made Ireland his permanent home, first in the New Abbey estate, and in 1589 in the three thousand acres of the Kilcolman estate. Throughout the 1580s, Spenser received a number of governmental appointments and established himself in Ireland as a well-off planter and gentleman. His complex relationship to Ireland is largely understood through *A View of the Present State of Ireland,* a prose dialogue that forthrightly defends Grey's violent tactics and advocates deeply repressive measures against the Irish. It has called forth both defenses of the poet and declarations of his complicity in the outrages of colonialism. The subtleties of *A View* cast a similarly complicated light on *The Faerie Queene,* which was written in Ireland, and reflects its beautiful and pitifully war-torn landscape.

In Ireland Spenser became friends with the explorer, author, and courtier Sir Walter Raleigh, who in 1589 traveled with him to England. Probably with the sponsorship of Raleigh, Spenser presented the first three books of *The Faerie Queene* to Elizabeth, who, by Spenser's report, was well pleased. Spenser secured the printer William Ponsonby in London, and Books One through Three of *The Faerie Queene* were published in 1590. The poem was a clear effort to win court favor, with a dedication to Elizabeth and as many as seventeen dedicatory sonnets to the major figures in court. As a reward, Spenser was granted a pension of £50 a year for life. Such a position in the patronage system of the day was not unusual, as poetry was commonly used as a means of preferment in court—for noblemen such as Sidney and Raleigh, it was one more personal accomplishment; for those like Spenser who were not noble, it was a way to win social and economic advantages. Spenser, however, maintained skepticism toward court life. In his pastoral "Colin Clouts Come Home Againe," which tells of his and Raleigh's journey to court, Colin declares that

> it is no sort of life,
> For shepheard fit to lead in that same place,
> Where each one seeks with malice and with strife,
> To thrust downe other into foule disgrace,
> Himselfe to raise.   (688–92)

Spenser returned to Ireland, where he lived, worked, and wrote throughout the 1590s. He published several important poems under the title of *Complaints* in 1591. In 1594 he married Elizabeth Boyle, resulting in at least one child, and in the following year he published *Amoretti* and *Epithalamion*, which celebrate their love and marriage. Throughout these years he continued work on *The Faerie Queene*, and in 1596 published the second edition. This extended the poem to six books; its final form was reached in the posthumous 1609 edition, with the inclusion of the fragment of a seventh book, *The Mutabilitie Cantos*. In 1596 he also published *Fowre Hymnes* and *Prothalamion*.

Spenser may have traveled to London to oversee the second printing of *The Faerie Queene*. If so, he returned to an Ireland wracked by rebellion. In 1598 the Tyrone Rebellion reached Munster, and Spenser and his family fled Kilcolman just before the estate was sacked and burned. Spenser carried letters from the President of Munster to the Privy Council in England, describing the military crisis. On January 13, 1599, while still in England, Spenser died. His life ended under the shadow cast by the destruction of his home and the scattering of his interests in Ireland, which Ben Jonson described, possibly hyperbolically, as dying "for lack of bread." Spenser's hearse was reportedly attended by poets, who threw their verses and pens into his tomb as he was buried in Poets' Corner at Westminster Abbey.

Textual Notes

The text of Book Three in this volume is based upon the 1590 edition of *The Faerie Queene* (STC 23081), though the University of Oregon graciously allowed the downloading of their Renascence Online text of the Grosart edition (based on the 1596 edition) as a point of departure. The text in this volume was edited from a reproduction of the original in the British Library by way of microfilm (UMI, Early English Books, 1475–1640) and Early English Books Online (eebo.chadwyck.com). It has been checked against the *Faults Escaped* printed at the end of the 1590 edition (*F.E.*) and against the 1596 edition (STC 23082) and the 1609 edition (STC 23083). The text of the 1596 ending to Book Three and the text of Book Four in this volume are based upon the 1596 edition of *The Faerie Queene* (again with the assistance of Renascence Online). These were edited from a reproduction of the original in the Huntington Library by way of UMI microfilm and Early English Books Online. They have been checked against the 1609 edition. For both books, quotation marks have been added; *i, j, u, v,* the long *s,* and *vv* have been modernized; the erratically-used spaces before punctuation marks have been deleted; and abbreviations, ampersands, and diphthongs have been spelled out. Departures from the 1590 edition in Book Three or from the 1596 edition in Book Four have been made only with the aim of clarifying the text for modern readers. The table below lists substantive variants from each of the copy texts, variants of punctuation (except for inverted typefaces), significant variants of the spellings of proper nouns, and any other variants that might influence interpretation. In addition, the table lists instances in which this edition differs from the text edited by Hamilton, Yamashita, and Suzuki. For a complete list of all variants in these editions, see Hamilton.

III.Pr. *Praxiteles*] 1596, 1609; *Praxitcles* 1590.

III.i.Arg.3 *Malecastaes*] *F.E.; Materastaes* 1590, 1596, 1609.

III.i.6.5 But] 1596, 1609; Rut 1590.

III.i.7.6 thee] 1596, 1609; the 1590.

III.i.12.9 ryde.] 1596, 1609; ryde, 1590.

III.i.29.9 fight.] 1596, 1609; fight, 1590.

III.i.30.6 mard] *F.E.;* shard 1590, 1596, 1609.

III.i.44.5 brethen] 1590; brethren P.V. in 1590.

III.i.47.1 wight,] 1609; wight. 1590, 1596.

III.i.49.8 deeds] 1590; deeds, P.V. in 1590.

III.i.53.2 griefe,] 1596, 1609; griefe. 1590.

III.i.60.8 wary] 1609; weary 1590, 1596.

III.i.61.6 spake,] 1596, 1609; spake. 1590.

III.i.67.9 went.] 1596, 1609; went 1590.

III.ii.3.6 too] 1596, 1609; to 1590.

III.ii.6.8 thread;] 1596, 1609; thread, 1590.

III.ii.8.5 I to prove,] 1596, 1609; to prove, I 1590, Hamilton.

III.ii.30.5 dight] 1596, 1609; dight, 1590.

III.ii.33.9 debarre;] 1609; debarre. 1590; debarre, 1596, Hamilton.

III.ii.36.1 others] 1596, 1609; other 1590, Hamilton.

III.ii.41.2 Nor] F.E.; Not 1590, 1596, 1609.

III.ii.50.1 off] 1596, 1609; of 1590.

III.ii.50.2 Them] F.E., 1596, 1609; Then 1590.

III.iii.1.8 Dame,] 1596, 1609; Dame. 1590.

III.iii.2.9 moniments.] 1596, 1609; moniments 1590.

III.iii.39.9 guifts] 1596, 1609; guists 1590.

III.iii.43.9 from off the earth] F.E.; from th'earth 1590, 1596, 1609.

III.iii.50.9 Hee] F.E., 1609; Shee 1590, 1596.

III.iii.53.3 teach] 1596, 1609; teach. 1590.

III.iii.55.1 sway,] 1596, 1609; sway 1590.

III.iii.60.9 fit.] 1609; fit 1590, 1596.

III.iv.4.9 meed.] 1596, 1609; meed 1590.

III.iv.5.8 she] 1596, 1609; he 1590.

III.iv.6.9 to the] 1596, 1609; tot he 1590.

III.iv.15.6 speare] 1609; speares 1590, 1596, Hamilton.

III.iv.20.9 sonne.] 1596, 1609; sonne 1590.

III.iv.27.6 fleshly] 1596, 1609; fleshy 1590.

III.iv.28.1 this that] 1596, 1609; this thar 1590.

III.iv 30.4 gamesome] 1609; gameson 1590, 1596.

III.iv.30.6 swownd] 1590; swowne 1596, 1609, Hamilton.

III.iv.41.7 there] 1609; their 1590, 1596.

III.iv.48.1 off] 1596; of 1590, 1609.

III.iv.53.4 dismayd;] 1596, 1609; dismayd, 1590.

III.iv.60.4 bright,] 1609; bright? 1590, 1596.

III.iv.60.9 rowme] 1596, 1609; ro wme 1590.

III.v.6.9 where?] 1609; where. 1590, 1596.

III.v.14.2 beast,] 1609; beast; 1590, 1596.

III.v.16.9 despight.] 1596, 1609; despight 1590.

III.v.17.3 wade] F.E., 1596, 1609; made 1590.

III.v.19.5 no] 1596, 1609; now 1590.

III.v.20.2 will;] 1596, 1609; will, 1590.

III.v.21.9 bloud] 1596, 1609; flood 1590.

III.v.30.7 better] 1596, 1609; bitter 1590.

III.v.33.2 peeces] 1596, 1609; peeees 1590.

III.v.40.4 loves sweet] 1596, 1609; sweet loves 1590, Hamilton.

III.v.40.9 living] 1596, 1609; liking 1590.

III.v.41.2 rest.] 1609; rest, 1590, 1596; rest; Hamilton.

III.v.41.4 drest;] 1596, 1609; drest, 1590.

III.v.46.5 restore:] 1590, 1596, 1609; restore? Smith, Hamilton.

III.v.52.6 admyre:] 1609; admyre 1590, 1596.

III.v.53.9 weare] 1596, 1609; were 1590.

III.v.55.9 complement.] 1596, 1609; complement; 1590.

III.vi.3.9 was] 1596, 1609; were 1590.

III.vi.4.4 *Belphœbe*] 1609; *Belphœbe* 1590, 1596.

III.vi.17.6 off] 1596, 1609; of 1590.

III.vi.21.5 apayd,] 1590; apayd. 1596, 1609, Hamilton.

III.vi.26.4 fugitive.] 1590; fugitive, both farre and nere. 1596, 1609; Hamilton.

III.vi.28.3 *Phœbe*] 1609; *Phœbe* 1590, 1596.

III.vi.29.5 *Gnidus*] 1596, 1609; Gnidas 1590.

III.vi.45.3 $^1/_2$ ____] 1590, 1596; And dearest love, 1609, Hamilton. (This line is not in 1590 or 1596.)

III.vi.45.4 *Narcisse*] 1596, 1609; *Marcisse* 1590.

III.vi.52.9 launched] 1596; launch 1590; launced 1609.

III.vii.Arg.4 *Gyaunts*] 1596, 1609; *Gynunt* 1590.

III.vii.1.8 she did] 1596, 1609; he did 1590.

III.vii.1.9 escapt] 1596, 1609; eseapt 1590.

III.vii.15.8 mind;] 1596, 1609; mind, 1590.

III.vii.17.7 conquered] 1596, 1609; conpuered 1590.

III.vii.23.4 he] 1596, 1609; she 1590.

III.vii.36.3 beast,] 1596; beast. 1590; Beast 1609.

III.vii 39.9 tare.] 1596, 1609; tare 1590.

III.vii.42.6 hee] F.E., 1596, 1609; she 1590. (F.E. "500" refers to the wrong page.)

III.vii.42.6 stund] F.E., 1596, 1609; stuned 1590. (F.E. "500" refers to the wrong page.)

III.vii.43.8 nere] F.E., 1596, 1609; were 1590. (F.E. "ibid." refers to the wrong page.)

III.vii.49.4 devoure] 1596, 1609; devoure: 1590.

III.vii.50.2 thurst] 1596, 1609; thrust 1590, Hamilton.

III.vii.52.4 is] 1596, 1609; it 1590.

III.vii.53.3 ta'ne?] 1596, 1609; ta'ne, 1590; ta'ne. Hamilton.

III.vii.53.5 amis.] 1596, 1609; amis, 1590.

III.vii.55.4 Three] 1596, 1609; Thre 1590.

III.vii.58.3 a do] 1596; adoe 1590; a-do 1609.

III.vii.61.5 backe] 1596, 1609; bace 1590.

III.viii.18.5 said,] 1596, 1609; said 1590.

III.viii.23.1 perceiv'd] 1596, 1609; peceiv'd 1590.

III.viii.24.5 befell.] 1596, 1609; befell, 1590.

III.viii.25.9 rudenes] 1596, 1609; rudenes 1590.

III.viii.30.3 frowy] 1590, 1596; frory 1609, Hamilton.

III.viii.31.9 so] 1596, 1609; fo 1590.

III.viii.37.9 hight] 1596, 1609; high 1590.

III.viii.46.9 unworthy] 1596, 1609; unworthy' 1590, Hamilton.

III.viii.50.1 *Paridell*] 1596, 1609; *Pavidell* 1590.

III.viii.50.6 succeed] 1596, 1609; succed 1590.

III.ix.2.4 attone] 1596, 1609; attonce 1590.

III.ix.5.2 supply,] 1590; supply; 1596, 1609, Hamilton.

III.ix.7.3 misdonne] 1596, 1609; dis-donne 1590.

III.ix.9.7 hayno us] 1596, 1609; haynous 1590.

III.ix.16.9 throw.] 1596, 1609; throw 1590.

III.ix.18.7 call.] 1596, 1609; call, 1590.

III.ix.20.1 rest,] 1609; rest; 1590, 1596.

III.ix.27.5 that] 1596, 1609; with 1590.

III.ix.45.3 neck] 1596, 1609; necks 1590.

III.ix.47.3 hard] 1590; heard 1596, 1609, Hamilton.

III.ix.48.9 sayne.] 1596, 1609; sayne 1590.

III.x.Arg.2 *Malbecco*] 1596, 1609; *Malbceco* 1590.

III.x.10.4 drive;] 1596, 1609; drive, 1590.

III.x.11.7 told.] 1596, 1609; told, 1590.

III.x.13.3 before,] 1596, 1609; before. 1590.

III.x.14.8 place;] 1596, 1609; place, 1590.

III.x.17.6 despight;] 1596, 1609; de-spight, 1590.

III.x.32.1 more] 1596, 1609; mote 1590.

III.x.40.3 wastefull] 1596, 1609; faith-full 1590.

III.x.45.8 fedd,] 1609; fedd. 1590, 1596.

III.x.46.4 abound.] 1596, 1609; abound, 1590.

III.x.46.5 grownd] 1596, 1609; grownd. 1590.

III.x.51.9 wonne.] 1596, 1609; wonne 1590.

III.xi.Arg.4 exprest.] 1596, 1609; *exprest,* 1590.

III.xi.2.3 golden] 1609; golding 1590, 1596.

III.xi.7.6 off] 1596, 1609; of 1590.

III.xi.9.6 hast thou,] 1609; hast, thou 1590, 1596.

III.xi.14.3 grace some] 1596, 1609; gracesome 1590.

III.xi.19.7 dy.] 1596, 1609; dy, 1590.

III.xi.23.3 dempt,] 1596, 1609; dempt. 1590.

III.xi.27.7 entred] 1596, 1609; decked 1590, Hamilton.

III.xi.31.3 And] 1596, 1609; Ant 1590.

III.xi.33.7 entire;] 1596, 1609; entire, 1590.

III.xi.36.7 thee] 1596, 1609; the 1590.

III.xi.39.6 each] 1596, 1609; his 1590, Hamilton.

III.xi.39.8 Stag] Smith (citing Jortin); Hag 1590, 1596, 1609.

III.xi.43.4 prove,)] Smith; prove. 1590; prove.) 1596, 1609, Hamilton.

III.xi.50.2 sted,] 1609; sted 1590, 1596.

III.xi.50.4 over-red] 1590; over-red,] 1596, 1609, Hamilton.

III.xii.7.8 wood] 1596, 1609; word 1590.

III.xii.9.3 other] 1609; others 1590, 1596.

III.xii.11.4 shade;] 1596, 1609; shade, 1590.

III.xii.12.3 to] 1596, 1609; too 1590.

III.xii.18.7 had,] Hamilton; had 1590, 1596; had: 1609.

III.xii.18.8 Bee;] 1596, 1609; Bee, 1590.

III.xii.18.9 degree.] 1596, 1609; degree 1590.

III.xii.21.8 still] 1596, 1609; skill 1590.

III.xii.23.5 right hand] *F.E.*, 1609; right 1590, 1596. (*F.E.* "502" refers to the wrong page.)

III.xii.28.1 there] 1609; their 1590, 1596.

III.xii.34.4 her] 1609; him 1590, 1596.

III.xii.38.9 grownd.] 1596; grownd, 1590; ground: 1609.

III.xii.39.4 deed;] 1590; deed? 1596, 1609, Hamilton.

III.xii.40.6 Lady] 1596, 1609; Lad 1590.

III.xii.42.2 She] *F.E.*, 1596, 1609; He 1590.

III.xii.42.4 She] *F.E.*, 1596, 1609; He 1590.

III.xii.42.5 her] *F.E.*, 1596, 1609; him 1590.

IV.i.7.9 excesse.] 1609; excesse 1596.

IV.i.20.3 amisse:] 1609; amisse, 1596.

IV.i.38.5 ply] 1609; ply. 1596.

IV.i.46.1 knight,] 1609; knight 1596.

IV.i.51.5 rotten.] 1609; rotten, 1596.

IV.ii.6.8 torne;] 1609; torne 1596.

IV.ii.13.2 by day;] 1609; by day, 1596.

IV.ii.22.2 *Florimell.*] 1609; *Florimell,* 1596.

IV.ii.22.4 tell.] 1609; tell, 1596.

IV.ii.23.8 state.] 1609; state, 1596.

IV.ii.44.4 creature,] 1609; creature: 1596.

IV.ii.46.9 stout.] 1609; stout 1596.

IV.ii.50.9 came.] 1609; came 1596.

IV.ii.51.5 Fond dame] Smith; fond dame 1596; Fond Dame 1609.

IV.iii.Arg.2 *Canacee:*] Smith; *Canacee* 1596; *Canacee.* 1609.

IV.iii.6.3 worth,] 1609; worth: 1596.

IV.iii.7.4 skill] 1609; sill 1596.

IV.iii.8.4 disadvaunce:] 1609; disadvaunce, 1596.

IV.iii.9.6 n'ote] 1609; not 1596, Hamilton.

IV.iii.26.1 blowes:] 1609; blowes, 1596.

IV.iii.50.3 To] 1609; Too 1596.

IV.iv.1.4 depends,] Smith; depends. 1596; depends; 1609.

IV.iv.9.5 sight] 1609; sight. 1596.

IV.iv.10.5 worse] 1609; worst 1596.

IV.iv.21.5 *Paliumord*] 1596; *Palimord* 1609, Hamilton.

IV.iv.22.4 affray,] 1609; affray. 1596.

IV.iv.23.5 glode,] 1609; glode. 1596.

IV.iv.24.4 guide,] 1609; guide. 1596.

IV.iv.24.5 side,] 1609; side. 1596.

IV.iv.27.3 behalve,] 1609; behalve. 1596.

IV.iv.27.8 misdid,] Smith; misdid: 1596; misdid; 1609.

IV.iv.27.9 fight.] 1609; fight 1596.

IV.iv.34.6 makes;] 1609; makes. 1596.

IV.v.25.1 aviz'd,] 1609; aviz'd: 1596.

IV.v.25.5 one] 1609; once 1596.

IV.v.31.3 his] 1609; her 1596.

IV.v.38.8 heare:] 1609; heare, 1596.

IV.vi.28.6 He] 1609; Her 1596.

IV.vi.31.5 withstand.] 1609; withstand 1596.

IV.vi.46.4 mind,] 1609; mind. 1596.

IV.vii.25.1 Which] 1609; With 1596.

IV.vii.34.1 sad] 1609; said 1596.

IV.vii.36.8 faith,] 1609; faith 1596.

IV.viii.2.9 decay;] 1609; decay 1596.

IV.viii.30.4 then] 1609; them 1596.

IV.viii.38.2 flie,] Hamilton; flie 1596;
flie; 1609.

IV.ix.Arg.3 Knights,] 1609; Knights
1596.

IV.ix.1.8 vertuous] 1609; vertues
1596.

IV.ix.3.7 trustie Squire] 1609; Trustie
squire 1596.

IV.ix.9.6 *Pæana*] 1596, 1609; *Pæana*
Hamilton.

IV.ix.13.2 *Pæana*] 1596, 1609; *Pæana*
Hamilton.

IV.ix.17.5 quest] Smith; guest 1596,
1609.

IV.ix.18.8 represse,] 1609; represse.
1596.

IV.ix.24.4 straid] 1596, 1609; straid,
Smith, Hamilton.

IV.ix.26.1 There] 1609; Their 1596.

IV.ix.30.8 repayed] 1609; repayred
1596.

IV.ix.35.9 repeat;] 1609; repeat. 1596;
repeat, Hamilton.

IV.x.7.9 ancient] 1609; ancients 1596.

IV.x.19.1 meanest] 1609; nearest
1596.

IV.x.25.1 alleyes] 1609; all eyes 1596.

IV.x.27.1 *Hyllus*] 1596; *Hylus* 1609;
Hylas Smith, Hamilton.

IV.x.36.3 *Love*] 1609; love 1596.

IV.x.37.9 May] 1609; may 1596.

IV.x.58.1 *Daunger*] Smith; daunger
1596, 1609, Hamilton.

IV.xi.23.7 Agæan] 1596, 1609;
Ægæan Smith, Hamilton.

IV.xi.24.4 became,] 1609; became;
1596.

IV.xi.34.5 Grant] Smith; Guant 1596,
1609.

IV.xi.35.7 *Nene*] 1596, 1609; Nene
Smith, Hamilton.

IV.xi.40.5 see?] 1609; see. 1596.

IV.xi.41.8 *Allo*] 1596, 1609; Allo
Smith, Hamilton.

IV.xi.41.9 *Mulla*] 1596, 1609; Mulla
Smith, Hamilton.

IV.xi.48.8 *Eudore*] Smith; *Endore*
1596, 1609.

IV.xi.52.4 upbinde,] 1609; upbinde.
1596.

IV.xii.5.4 none,] 1609; none. 1596.

IV.xii.5.5 bemone.] 1609; bemone,
1596.

IV.xii.18.3 seeing, *Marinell*] 1609; see-
ing *Marinell,* 1596.

IV.xii.21.1. th'earnest] 1590; th'heed-
full 1596.

IV.xii.23.6. *Hydraes*] 1596; *Hydres* 1590.

IV.xii.32.4. That] 1590; Thou 1596.

IV.xii.39.8. upstaring] 1590; upstart-
ing 1596.

IV.xii.48.7. of this] 1596; oft his
1590.

IV.xii.51.1. Therewith] 1590; Thereto
1596.

IV.xii.61.8. fearefully] 1590; tenderly
1596.

IV.xii.75.5. Lady'] 1590; Ladie 1596.

IV.xii.81.4. that] 1590; the 1596.

IV.xii.83.7. spoyle] 1590; spoyld 1596.

GLOSSARY

abie: *See* aby(e).

abraid, abrayd, abray: Startle awake; burst into motion. All three forms serve as both present and past tenses.

abroad, abrode: Outside; far and wide; openly.

aby(e): Endure; pay the penalty; abide.

address(e): Direct, turn.

admire, admyre: Marvel at.

advise: Consider; consult each other about; remind.

affray: Frighten.

affret: Attack.

agrise; agrize: Shudder; be horrified; horrify.

albe, allbee, all be: Although; even if.

algates: Always; by any means; at any rate; altogether; nevertheless.

als: Also.

amaine, amayne: Mightily, vigorously.

amate: Overwhelm; dismay; confound.

ap(p)all: Trans. v.: make pale or feeble with pity; check; quell; intimidate; intrans. v.: become pale or dim; lose heart; fail in strength.

apply: Direct, steer; prepare; employ; follow.

approve: Prove; demonstrate; test.

aread, ared, areed: *See* read.

assay: V.: assail; put to the test; examine; try out; attempt; n.: tested worth; attempt; test.

assoyle: Set free; acquit; absolve; purge.

attonce: At once.

attone: In concord; together.

avise: *See* advise.

ay: Always, forever; ever.

band: Bond.

bay: The point at which a hunted animal has no choice but to turn and face its pursuer.

be-: A prefix that may either intensify a verb or make an intransitive verb transitive.

beheast; behest: Command; promise.

behight: Name; consider, esteem; promise; hold out hope; grant; command.

behove: Befit, be appropriate for; be useful for.

beldame: Elderly woman, literally "grandmother."

bend: Aim.

beseeme: Suit, be appropriate for; look well on.

bestad(d), bestedde: Past part.: beset; assailed from all sides; pres. tense: assist.

bewray: Betray, reveal (what was hidden).

boot(e): Avail; profit.

bountie, bounty: Goodness, virtue.

brasen: Brass; firm and strong.

brave: Resplendent.

brenne, brent: Burn, burnt.

buxome: Favorable; welcoming; yielding.

can: Gan, did; know; is or are able.

careful: Sorrowing; burdened with cares.

cast: Aim, direct; resolve; plan; attempt; consider.

caytive: Captive; vile; wretched (to call someone a "slave" or "caytive" was a serious insult—unless, of course, that someone was literally and unfairly imprisoned).

certes: Certainly.

charet: Chariot.

choler: Anger (literally bile, one of the four humors, associated with heat and thought to cause irascibility).

clep, cleep: Call.

close: Adj.: secret; private; near; adv.: secretly; privately; close by.

corage, courage: The heart as the source of emotion and thought; spirit; sexual vigor.

corse: Body; corpse.

couch: N.: bed; v.: crouch; lower (a weapon) to the position for attack.

courage: *See* corage.

courtesie, courtesy, curtesie: Not only courtesy in the modern sense, but the whole panoply of good manners, talents, and virtues to which any knight, lord, or lady serving at court was supposed to aspire. The lower classes were not usually considered capable of true courtesy, although humanists gestured toward the idea that education was as important as lineage in determining noble virtue.

crest: Helmet; crest on a helmet.

crew: Group; bunch; gang; mob.

dainty: Delightful; precious; choice; fastidious; careful.

Dan: Courtesy title for a male member of a religious order or for a male scholar, knight, poet, or deity; Spenser uses the title only for deities, except when applying it to Chaucer.

darraine, darrayne: Prepare for battle; set up a battle formation; marshal forces; maintain a battle challenge.

date: Term; term of life; time of death.

deare: Adj.: precious; severe; earnest; beloved; adv.: with great cost; severely; earnestly; lovingly.

decay: Destroy; waste away; weaken; die.

deem(e): Form an opinion, consider; ajudge; pass judgment; sentence or condemn; decree; think (of someone or something); expect, hope; surmise; proclaim.

degree: Social rank; level; amount.

desert: Deserted place; wilderness.

despight: Contempt.

dight: Appoint, ordain; place; put in order, make ready; dress, don armor. Past participle has the same form.

discolour(e)d: Multicolored.

discover: Disclose.

disdaine: N.: contempt; indignation; v.: contemn; feel indignation toward.

dismaid: Having lost all moral courage; defeated; appalled; discouraged; made badly. Often also a pun on "made no longer a maid," i.e., deflowered.

dole, doole: Grief; lamentation.

dolor, dolour: Grief.

doubt, dout: N.: fear; suspicion; wonder; v.: fear; suspect; wonder.

doughtie, doughty: Valiant.

drerihed(d): Dreariness.

earst: Previously.

eft: A second time; again; back; moreover; likewise.

eftsoones: Afterwards; soon afterwards.

eke: Also.

elfe: Inhabitant of Faerie Land (whether good or evil); malignant imp.

embay: Steep; soak; bathe; plunge.

emprize: Enterprise.

endyte, endite: Indite, compose in words; dictate.

engin(e): Machination; plot; wicked tool.

ensample: Example.

envie, envy: V.: deny; begrudge, malevolently withhold; admire (with overtones of feeling mortified at being less admirable oneself); n.: malevolent grudging; admiration (with overtones of mortification at one's own inferiority).

ere: Before; ever.

erst: *See* earst.

estate: State, condition, fortune.

faine, fayne: V.: desire, wish; feign; adv.: gladly; adj.: desirous.

fay: Fairy (not a diminutive being, but a supernatural creature, outwardly resembling a human, living in a world that resembles and overlaps that of mortals).

fell: Adj.: cruel, dire; n.: animosity, resentment. (From the Latin *fello,* felon).

flood: Body of water.

fond: Adj.: foolish; v.: found.

for thy: Therefore; because.

fordonne: Destroyed; exhausted; made powerless.

forlore: Abandoned.

froward: Adverse; inimical; uncooperative, untoward; counter to what is reasonable or desirable.

gan, gin: Began, begin.

gentle: Of gentle birth (by the late sixteenth century an indeterminate category including some commoners who owned land and were considered by their neighbors to be persons of good breeding, but also including all people with titles); having the virtues appropriate to one of gentle birth.

gest: Exploit; romance tale; demeanor.

ghost: Soul; spirit.

girdle: Sash (not an undergarment).

giust: Joust.

grace: Favor; kindness; mercy.

griesly: Grisly, causing horror.

grudge: Complain.

guerdon: Reward, recompense.

haberjeon: Habergeron, chainmail tunic (sometimes sleeveless).

hardiment: Hardihood; strength.

hauberk, hauberque, hawberk: Chain-mail tunic.

hew: N.: form, appearance; condition; color; v.: cut down.

hight: Call, name; pledge.

his: His; its.

humour: Moisture; state of mind; one of four chief fluids of the body, which were believed to determine each person's physical and mental constitution by their balance or imbalance: blood, phlegm, choler or yellow bile, and melancholy or black bile—causing sanguine, phlegmatic, choleric, and melancholy temperaments.

imp: Offspring, son or daughter; scion; grafted shoot.

in place: There; here.

issue: Offspring.

jolly: Sprightly; gallant; brave; splendid; pleasant; handsome; lustful; overweeningly self-confident.

kind, kynd: Type; nature.

kindly, kyndly: According to type; according to nature, innate.

late: Adj.: old; advanced; tardy; recent; adv.: tardily; recently.

launch: Lance; pierce.

least: Lest.

leman: Beloved; lover, paramour; mistress.

lever: *Comparative of* lief.

lewd: Ignorant; evil; unchaste.

lief(e): V.: rather, prefer; wish; like; adj.: dear.

lightly: Nimbly; easily; quickly; carelessly.

list: Intrans. v.: be inclined to, wish to do; trans. v.: please (someone or oneself).

loose: Adj.: wanton; intemperate; frivolous; v.: loosen; solve; lose.

loure, lowre: Scowl.

lout, lowt: Bow.

lust: Pleasure; liking; inclination; desire; sexual appetite; immoderate sexual desire; vigor.

lusty: Lively; beautiful; full of sexual appetite; vigorous; arrogant.

magnify: Extol.

maide, mayd: Virgin; unmarried woman (presumed virginal).

maile, mayle: Chain mail.

maine, mayne: Sea; force.

make: N.: mate; v.: most of the modern meanings of the word.

maugre, maulgre: Despite; "a curse upon!"

mean(e): Adj.: inferior; base; low; middling; n.: middle; common ground; v.: intend.

meat: Food.

meed(e): Reward; gain; repayment.

meet(e): Adj.: fit, appropriate; v.: be in agreement; blend.

mesprise: Mistake; offense; contempt; failure to recognize someone's worth; slander.

mickle: Much.

mischance: Ill success; bad luck.

misfare: Misfortune; misfaring: transgression.

mishap: Misfortune.

mister: Sort, kind, type (of).

moniment: Monument, memorial; evidence; mark.

mote: Might.

ne: Nor.

ne . . . ne: Neither . . . nor.

nice: Fastidious; choosy.

niceness: Luxury; delicacy.

nie, nigh: Near; nearly.

nor . . . nor: Neither . . . nor.

or . . . or: Either . . . or.

ought: Aught, anything; at all.

paine, payne: Labor, trouble; hurt.

paramour: Lover, sexual partner.

pas, passe: Surpass.

passing: Surpassing; surpassingly.

paynim: Pagan; non-Christian (therefore designating not only pagans but also Muslims and sometimes Jews).

perdy, perdee, perdie: Mild oath, literally "by God" (French *par dieu*).

perforce: Of necessity; by force.

pight: Placed; set up.

place, in: There; here.

plaine: Complain.

plaint: Complaint.

plight: Condition, state.

port: Carriage (of oneself); demeanor.

pray: N.: prey; booty; v.: pray, prey upon.

preace, preas(s)e, press: Crowd, throng.

prick: Spur on one's horse, ride swiftly; puncture.

privy: Secret; private; in on a secret.

prove: Test by experience; bring about an effect.

puissance: Might, power; potency.

purpose: Conversation; intent.

raught: Reached.

read: Read; discern, see; understand; interpret; predict; prophesy; guess; believe; name; identify; declare; teach; advise; decree.

recoure: Recover.

recure: Recover; restore; ameliorate; heal.

redresse: Reparation; remedy; aid; relief; restoration.

reft: Bereft; stolen; ripped; split.

relent: Yield, slacken.

repair: Go to a place, to stay there for a while.

ribbands: Ribbons.

rive: Cleave.

rude: Rustic, crude, uncivilized; turbulent, disorderly.

ruth: Compassion; remorse.

salvage: Savage, wild.

satyr: Half-man, half-goat. Known for lechery. The god of satyrs is Pan, who plays a flute.

scu(t)chi(o)n: Shield.

sell: Seat; saddle.

semblance: Deceitful appearance; show; resemblance; demeanor; appearance.

semblaunt: Appearance; demeanor; deceitful appearance; likeness.

sew: Pursue; follow; attend upon; take as a guide; court; apply to for favor.

shade: Shadow; unsubstantial image; spirit; reflection.

shadow: *See* shade.

sheene: Bright; beautiful.

shend (*past tense* shent): Disgrace.

shivered: Shattered.

shivering: Quivering; capable of splitting something (said of a spear or dart).

silly: Helpless; innocent.

sith: Since (the time that); given that.

sithens: *See* sith.

sleight, slight: Cunning trick.

smart: Pain.

sore: Adj.: painful, severe; adv.: painfully, severely.

souse, sowse: Swoop (like a falcon hunting); pounce.

speed: N.: success; v.: succeed.

spill: Spoil; destroy.

spoil(e), spoyle: V.: despoil, plunder; ravage; deprive, rob; n.: booty, trophy.

spright: Spirit.

stay: V.: pause; hinder; stop; prop up; n.: stamina; prop.

stead: Place; situation.

still: Always, constantly.

stint: Intrans. v.: cease; trans. v.: put a stop to.

stound, stownd: Time of trial; attack; state of stupefaction.

stout: Proud; brave; hardy.

stowre, stower: Tumult; time of stress; combat.

strand, strond: Shore.

streight: Adv.: straightway; closely; adj.: close; narrow; strict.

Stygian: Of the river Styx, in the Greek underworld; hellish.

succour, succor: Aid; shelter.

suffer: Allow.

surquedry: Arrogance.

sway: Power, force.

swain: Young man; farm laborer; suitor.

swownd: Swoon.

teen(e): *See* tine.

then: Than.

thence: From there.

thereto: Moreover; also.

therewithall: In addition to that; besides.

tho: Then.

thral(l): Prisoner; imprisonment.

thrill: Pierce.

tidings: News.

tind, tynd: Ignite (related to "tinder").

tine, tyne: N.: affliction, trouble, sorrow; v.: lose (something); be defeated; waste; forget; destroy; perish.

to weet: That is. *See also* weet.

toy: N.: game; foolishness; v.: play.

trace: V.: track; tread; walk; pursue; travel; dance; n.: path.

traine, trayne: N.: entrapment; v.: coach.

traveile, travell: Toil; labor in childbirth; journey.

treat: Talk; parley.

uncouth: Unknown; unusual; rude.

uneath, uneth: Adv.: scarcely, with difficulty; adj.: difficult.

upstaide: Propped up.

vaine, vayne: Empty, useless, in vain.

villein, villaine, villayn: Originally a serf; by the sixteenth century, it was nearly impossible to tell whether the speaker meant "serf" or "base-minded wretch," given that the two social categories were both cause for contempt.

want: Lack.

wanton: Undisciplined, wild; frisky; full of life; unchaste; extravagant; frivolous.

weede: Clothing; undesirable plant.

weene: Believe; expect.

weet: Know; discover. *See also* to weet.

wend: Travel.

wex(e): Wax, grow.

whileare, whilere, whyleare: Erewhile, previously; lately.

whilom(e), whylom(e): While; previously; at some time, once.

wight: Person.

wist: Know; knew.

withal, withall: In addition, moreover.

won: Was wont, was accustomed.

wonne: N.: dwelling place; v.: dwell, abide.

wont: N.: habit; adj.: accustomed; adv.: usually.

wonted: Usual, habitual.

wox(e): Past tense of wax or wex.

wracke: Wreck; ruin; violence.

y: Often begins past-tense verbs, e.g., "ymett" for "met."

yclep: *See* clep.

yfere: Companionably; together.

yode: Went.

INDEX OF CHARACTERS

Appearances of, and some references to, major characters in Books Three and Four are listed. In parentheses are appearances in other books. This index is indebted to Shohachi Fukuda's "The Characters of *The Faerie Queene*" in Hamilton.

WORKS CITED

Because the Introduction and footnotes for this volume are designed primarily to motivate readers to form their own interpretations, some strong works of Spenserian literary criticism focusing on Books Three and Four have not been cited and therefore do not appear below. The works cited below are all recommended reading, but the scholar can find a great deal of additional useful material by searching the MLA Bibliography Online and Early English Books Online, available through most university library Web sites.

Adelman, Janet. "Re: Question about Fetal Nourishment." E-mail to the editor. February 1, 2006.

Alciati, Andreas Alciatus. *The Latin Emblems.* Vol. 1 of *Index Emblematicus.* 1531. Edited by Peter M. Daly and Virginia W. Callahan. 2 vols. Toronto: University of Toronto Press, 1985.

Alpers, Paul. *The Poetry of* The Faerie Queene. Princeton: Princeton University Press, 1967. Reprinted, Columbia: University of Missouri Press, 1982.

Anderson, Judith H. "'In Liuing Colours and Right Hew': The Queen of Spenser's Central Books." In *Poetic Traditions of the English Renaissance.* Edited by Maynard Mack and George de Forest Lord. New Haven: Yale University Press, 1982, 47–66.

Ariosto, Ludovico. *Orlando Furioso.* Edited by Marcello Turchi and Edoardo Sanguineti. Italy: Garzanti, 1982.

Baker, David J. *Between Nations: Shakespeare, Spenser, Marvell, and the Question of Britain.* Stanford: Stanford University Press, 1997.

Berger, Harry, Jr. "Two Spenserian Retrospects: The Antique Temple of Venus and the Primitive Marriage of Rivers." *Revisionary Play: Studies in the Spenserian Dynamics.* Berkeley: University of California Press, 1988.

Berry, Craig. "'Sundrie Doubts': Vulnerable Understanding and Dubious Origins in Spenser's Continuation of the Squire's Tale." In *Refiguring Chaucer in the Renaissance.* Edited by Theresa M. Krier. Gainesville: University Press of Florida, 1998, 106–27.

Boccaccio, Giovanni. *Genealogiae.* 1494. The Renaissance and the Gods Series. New York: Garland Publishing, 1976.

Boiardo, Matteo Maria. *Orlando Innamorato.* Translated and edited by Charles Stanley Ross and Anne Finnigan. Berkeley: University of California Press, 1989.

Booth, Stephen, ed. *Shakespeare's Sonnets.* By William Shakespeare. New Haven: Yale University Press, 1977.

Bray, Alan. "Homosexuality and the Signs of Male Friendship in Elizabethan England." In *Queering the Renaissance*. Edited by Jonathan Goldberg. Q Series. Durham: Duke University Press, 1994, 40–61.

Camden, William. *De Connubio Tamae et Isis.* Excerpted in *Britannia*. London: R. Newbery, 1586.

Castiglione, Baldassare. *The Book of the Courtier.* Translated by Sir Thomas Hoby, 1561. Introduced by J. H. Whitfield. London: J. M. Dent and Sons, 1975. Translation of *Il Libro del Cortegiano,* 1528.

Cavanagh, Sheila T. *Wanton Eyes and Chaste Desires: Female Sexuality in* The Faerie Queene. Bloomington: Indiana University Press, 1994.

Chaucer, Geoffrey. *The Works of Geoffrey Chaucer.* 2nd ed. Edited by F[red] N[orris] Robinson. Boston: Houghton Mifflin, 1961.

Collier, J[ohn] Payne, ed. *The Works of Edmund Spenser.* By Edmund Spenser. 5 vols. London: Bell and Daldy, 1862.

Comes, Natalis. *Mythologiae sive Explicationum Fabularum.* Venice, 1568.

Eggert, Katherine. *Showing Like a Queen: Female Authority and Literary Experiment in Spenser, Shakespeare, and Milton.* Philadelphia: University of Pennsylvania Press, 2000.

Fowler, Alastair. "Six Knights at Castle Joyous." *Studies in Philology* 56 (1959): 583–99.

———. "Spenser and War." In *War, Literature and the Arts in Sixteenth-Century Europe.* Edited by J. R. Mulryne and Margaret Shewring. London: St. Martin's Press, 1989, 147–64.

Fowler, Elizabeth. *Literary Character: The Human Figure in Early English Writing.* Ithaca: Cornell University Press, 2003.

Fraunce, Abraham. *The Lamentations of Amyntas.* 1587. In *Thomas Watson's Latin Amyntas.* Edited by Franklin M. Dickey. Chicago: University of Chicago Press, 1967, 1–99.

Geoffrey of Monmouth. *British History.* C. 1135. In *Six Old English Chronicles.* Edited by J[ohn] A[llen] Giles. London: G. Bell, 1891, 89–292.

Goldberg, Jonathan. *Endlesse Worke: Spenser and the Structures of Discourse.* Baltimore: Johns Hopkins University Press, 1981.

Greenlaw, Edwin, et al., eds. *The Works of Edmund Spenser: A Variorum Edition.* By Edmund Spenser. 11 vols. Baltimore: Johns Hopkins University Press, 1932–1957.

Grosart, Alexander Balloch, ed. *The Complete Works in Verse and Prose of Edmund Spenser.* By Edmund Spenser. 9 vols. London: Spenser Society, 1882–1884. *Renascence Editions: An Online Repository of Works Printed in English Between the Years 1477 and 1799.* Published by Risa Stephanie Bear. 1992–2005. May 30, 2006. http://darkwing.uoregon.edu/~rbear/ren.htm.

Gross, Kenneth. "Re: commune food." E-mail to the editor. February 2, 2006.

Guarini, Battista. *The Faithful Shepherd: A Translation of Battista Guarini's* Il Pastor Fido. Translated by Thomas Sheridan et al. Newark: University of Delaware Press, 1989.

Hadfield, Andrew. "*The Faerie Queene,* Books IV–VII." In *The Cambridge Companion to Spenser.* Edited by Hadfield. Cambridge: Cambridge University Press, 2001, 124–42.

———. *Shakespeare, Spenser and the Matter of Britain.* Early Modern Literature in History Series. Houndmills, England: Palgrave Macmillan, 2004.

Hamilton, A[lbert] C., Hiroshi Yamashita, and Toshiyuki Suzuki, eds. *The Faerie Queene.* By Edmund Spenser. Harlow, England: Longman, 2001.

Hardyng, John. *The Chronicle of John Hardyng.* 1543. Edited by Henry Ellis. London, F. C. and J. Rivington, 1812. Facsimile New York: AMS Press, 1974.

Harington, Sir John, trans. *Orlando Furioso.* By Ludovico Ariosto. 1591. Edited by Robert McNulty. Oxford: Clarendon Press, 1972.

Helgerson, Richard. *Forms of Nationhood: The Elizabethan Writing of England.* Chicago: University of Chicago Press, 1992.

Hesiod. *Theogony and Works and Days.* Translated by M[artin] L[itchfield] West. World's Classics Series. Oxford: Oxford University Press, 1990.

Holinshed, Raphael. *Chronicles of England, Scotland, and Ireland.* 1577, revised 1587. Edited by Henry Ellis et al. 6 vols. London: J. Johnson, 1807–1808.

Hough, Graham. *A Preface to* The Faerie Queene. New York: Norton, 1963.

Hyginus. *Fabulae.* Edited by Peter K. Marshall. Bibliotheca scriptorum Graecorum et Romanorum Teubneriana. Monachii: in aedibus K.G. Saur, 2002.

Jortin, John. *Remarks on Spenser's Poems.* London: J. Whiston, 1734. Facsimile New York: Garland, 1970.

Kahf, Mohja. *Western Representations of the Muslim Woman: From Termagant to Odalisque.* Austin: University of Texas Press, 1999.

Kaplan, M. Lindsay. *The Culture of Slander in Early Modern England.* Cambridge Studies in Renaissance Literature and Culture 19. Cambridge: Cambridge University Press, 1997.

Leland, John. *Kykneion Asma / Cygnea Cantio.* London: R. Wolfe, 1545.

Lucretius Carus, Titus. *On the Nature of Things / De Rerum Natura.* Edited and translated by Anthony M. Esolen. Baltimore: Johns Hopkins University Press, 1995.

Malory, Sir Thomas. *Le Morte D'Arthur.* London: J. M. Dent, 1906.

McCabe, Richard A. *Spenser's Monstrous Regiment: Elizabethan Ireland and the Poetics of Difference.* Oxford: Oxford University Press, 2002.

McCoy, Richard C. *The Rites of Knighthood: The Literature and Politics of Elizabethan Chivalry*. Berkeley: University of California Press, 1989.

Miller, David Lee. "Re: Footnotes." E-mail to the editor. March 6, 2006.

———. "Gender, Justice, and the Gods in *The Faerie Queene*, Book 5." In *Reading Renaissance Ethics*. Edited by Marshall Grossman. New York: Routledge, 2007.

Montrose, Louis Adrian. "*A Midsummer Night's Dream* and the Shaping Fantasies of Elizabethan Culture: Gender, Power, Form." In *Rewriting the Renaissance: The Discourses of Sexual Difference in Early Modern Europe*. Edited by Margaret W. Ferguson et al. Women in Culture and Society Series. Chicago: University of Chicago Press, 1986, 65–87.

Mueller, Martin, et al. *Wordhoard: An Application for the Close Reading and Scholarly Analysis of Deeply Tagged Literary Texts*. Version 1.1. 2006. Northwestern University. http://wordhoard.northwestern.edu.

Nelson, William. *The Poetry of Edmund Spenser: A Study*. New York: Columbia University Press, 1963.

Osgood, Charles Grosvenor, ed. *A Concordance to the Poems of Edmund Spenser*. 2 vols. Philadelphia: Carnegie Institution of Washington, 1915.

Ovid. *Metamorphoses*. 3rd ed. 2 vols. Translated by Frank Justus Miller. Loeb Classical Series. Cambridge, MA: Harvard University Press, 1977.

Oxford English Dictionary. 2nd ed. 1991.

Paradise, Jean, Maron L. Wasman, et al., eds. *Great Soviet Encyclopedia*. 3rd ed. Vol. 22. New York: Macmillan, 1979. Translation of *Bol'shaia Sovetskaia Entsiklopediia*. Edited by Prokhorov, A. M., et al. 3rd ed. Vol. 22. Moscow: Sovetskaia Engsiklopediia Publishing House, 1945.

Parker, Patricia. *Literary Fat Ladies: Rhetoric, Gender, Property*. London: Methuen, 1987.

Plato. *The Dialogues of Plato*. Translated by B[enjamin] Jowett. 4th ed. 4 vols. Oxford: Oxford University Press, 1953.

Pliny, the Elder. *Natural History*. Translated by H. Rackham et al. Cambridge, MA: Harvard University Press, 1938–1963.

Quitslund, Jon A. *Spenser's Supreme Fiction: Platonic Natural Philosophy and* The Faerie Queene. Toronto: University of Toronto Press, 2001.

Raleigh, Sir Walter. *The Discoverie of the Large, Rich and Bewtiful Empire of Guiana*. London: Robert Robinson, 1596.

Rambuss, Richard. "Spenser's Life and Career." In *The Cambridge Companion to Spenser*. Edited by Andrew Hadfield. Cambridge: Cambridge University Press, 2001, 13–36.

———. *Spenser's Secret Career*. Cambridge Studies in Renaissance Literature and Culture 3. Cambridge: Cambridge University Press, 1993.

Roche, Thomas P. *The Kindly Flame*. Princeton: Princeton University Press, 1964.

Roche, Thomas P., and C. Patrick O'Donnell, Jr., eds. *Edmund Spenser:The Faerie Queene*. By Edmund Spenser. The English Poets Series. New Haven: Yale University Press, 1978.

Shuger, Debora. "Irishmen, Aristocrats, and Other White Barbarians." *Renaissance Quarterly* 50.2 (1997): 494–525.

Sidney, Sir Philip. *An Apology for Poetry or The Defence of Poesy*. Edited by Geoffrey Shepherd. Edinburgh: Nelson, 1967.

———. *Astrophil and Stella*. In *The Poems of Sir Philip Sidney*. Edited by William A. Ringler, Jr. Oxford: Clarendon Press, 1971.

Silberman, Lauren. *Transforming Desire: Erotic Knowledge in Books III and IV of* The Faerie Queene. Berkeley: University of California Press, 1995.

Sircy, Jonathan. "All Bondage is *Not* Created Equally: The Sadistic Institution and Masochistic Contract in *The Faerie Queene*." Paper presented at the Spenser's Civilizations Conference. Toronto: University of Toronto, May 19 2006.

Smith, J. C., and E. de Selincourt, eds. *Spenser: Poetical Works*. By Edmund Spenser. Oxford Standard Authors Series. London: Oxford University Press, 1912. Oxford: Oxford University Press, 1979.

Spenser, Edmund. For editions of the poetical works, see Collier, Greenlaw, Grosart, Hamilton, Mueller, Roche, and Smith.

———. *A View of the Present State of Ireland*. Edited by W. L. Renwick. Oxford: Clarendon Press, 1970.

Stallybrass, Peter. "Patriarchal Territories: The Body Enclosed." In *Rewriting the Renaissance:The Discourses of Sexual Difference in Early Modern Europe*. Edited by Margaret W. Ferguson et al. Women in Culture and Society Series. Chicago: University of Chicago Press, 1986, 123–42.

Steadman, John M. *Nature into Myth: Medieval and Renaissance Moral Symbols*. Pittsburgh: Duquesne University Press, 1979.

Stephens, Dorothy. *The Limits of Eroticism in Post-Petrarchan Narrative: Conditional Pleasure from Spenser to Marvell*. Cambridge Studies in Renaissance Literature and Culture 29. Cambridge: Cambridge University Press, 1998.

Stow, John. *Stow's Survey of London*. Introduced by H. B. Wheatley. London: J. M. Dent and Sons, 1980.

Tasso, Torquato. *Gerusalemme Liberata*. Ferrara: Appresso gli heredi di Francesco de Rossi, 1581.

———. "O bella età de l'oro." *Aminta*. 1581. Edited by B. T. Sozzi. Padua: Liviana Editrice, 1957. Chorus to Act I. Translated by Samuel Daniel as "O Happie Golden Age." *Works*. 1601. In *Three Renaissance Pastorals:Tasso, Guarini, Daniel*.

Medieval and Renaissance Texts and Studies 102. Edited by Elizabeth Story Donno. Binghamton, 1993. Appendix 2, 257–8.

Traub, Valerie. "The (In)Significance of 'Lesbian' Desire in Early Modern England." In *Queering the Renaissance.* Edited by Jonathan Goldberg. Q Series. Durham: Duke University Press, 1994, 62–83.

Virgil. *Eclogues.* In *The Singer of the* Eclogues: *A Study of Virgilian Pastoral.* Translated and introduced by Paul Alpers. Berkeley: University of California Press, 1979, 9–63.

———. *Aeneid.* Translated by Robert Fitzgerald. 1983. Reprinted, New York: Vintage, 1984.

Watkins, John. *The Specter of Dido: Spenser and Virgilian Epic.* New Haven: Yale University Press, 1995.

Wordsworth, Dorothy. *Journals of Dorothy Wordsworth: The Alfoxden Journal, 1798, the Grasmere Journals, 1800–1803.* 2nd ed. Edited by Mary Moorman and Mary Trevelyan. Oxford: Oxford University Press, 1991.

Zurcher, Andrew. "Re: Opposite of hyperbole." E-mail to the editor. January 10, 2006.